The
New International
Lesson Annual

2015–2016

September–August

Abingdon Press
Nashville

The New International Lesson Annual 2015–2016

Copyright © 2015 by Abingdon Press

All rights reserved.
No part of this work may be reproduced or transmitted in any form or by any means, electronic or mechanical, including photocopying and recording, or by any information storage or retrieval system, except as may be expressly permitted by the 1976 Copyright Act or in writing from the publisher. Requests for permission should be addressed in writing to Permissions, The United Methodist Publishing House, 2222 Rosa L. Parks Boulevard, P.O. Box 280988, Nashville, TN, 37228-0988, or e-mailed to permissions@umpublishing.org.

ISBN 978-1-4267-7481-2

ISSN 1084-872X

15 16 17 18 19 20 21 22 23 24—10 9 8 7 6 5 4 3 2 1

MANUFACTURED IN THE UNITED STATES OF AMERICA

PREFACE

Welcome to the global community of Bible students and teachers who study resources based on the work of the Committee on the Uniform Series, known by many as the International Lesson Series! *The New International Lesson Annual* is designed for teachers who seek a solid biblical basis for each session and a step-by-step teaching plan that will help them lead their classes. *The New International Lesson Annual* can be used with any student curriculum based on the International Lesson Series. In many classes, both the students and teacher rely on *The New International Lesson Annual* as their companion to the Bible.

Over the four quarters of the 2015–2016 Sunday school year we will explore the themes of *community, tradition, faith,* and *creation.* We begin in the fall with "The Christian Community Comes Alive," an extensive study of Acts. During the winter quarter, we examine religious traditions spanning both testaments from Genesis to Revelation in "Sacred Gifts and Holy Gatherings." "The Gift of Faith," our course for the spring, investigates examples of faith as recorded in Mark and Luke. We conclude in the summer quarter by looking ahead "Toward a New Creation," which delves into Genesis, selected psalms, Zephaniah, and Romans.

The New International Lesson Annual provides numerous features that are especially valuable for busy teachers who want to provide in-depth Bible study experiences for their students. Each lesson includes the following sections:

Previewing the Lesson highlights the background and lesson Scriptures, focus of the lesson, three goals for the learners, and supplies you will need to teach.

Reading the Scripture includes the Scripture lesson printed in both the New Revised Standard Version and the Common English Version. By printing these two translations in parallel columns, you can easily compare them for detailed study. If your own Bible is another version, you will then have three translations to explore as you prepare each lesson.

Understanding the Scripture closely analyzes the background Scripture by looking at each verse. Here you will find help in understanding concepts, ideas, places, and people pertinent to each week's lesson. You may also find explanations of Greek or Hebrew words that are helpful for understanding the text.

Interpreting the Scripture looks specifically at the lesson Scripture, delves into its meaning, and relates it to contemporary life.

Sharing the Scripture provides you with a detailed teaching plan. Written by your editor, who is a very experienced educator, this section is divided into two major sections: *Preparing to Teach* and *Leading the Class.*

In the *Preparing to Teach* section you will find a devotional reading and probing questions for your own spiritual enrichment, as well as ideas to help you prepare for the session.

The *Leading the Class* portion begins with Gather to Learn activities designed to welcome the students and draw them into the lesson. Here, the students' stories and experiences or other contemporary stories are highlighted as preparation for the Bible story. The next three headings under *Leading the Class* are the three Goals for the Learners that were introduced in the Previewing the Lesson portion. The first goal always focuses on the Bible story itself. The second goal relates the Bible story to the lives of the learners. The third goal encourages the students to take action on what they have learned. These goals are foundational for each session, but they are by no means exhaustive, since we trust that students will leave the sessions with many ideas to reinforce and expand their knowledge, beliefs, and actions as Christian disciples. To that end, you will find diverse activities to appeal to a wide variety of learning styles. These activities suggest listening, reading, writing, speaking, singing, drawing, conducting research, interacting with others, meditating, and pursuing other possibilities. The lesson ends with Continue the Journey, where you will find closing activities, preparation for the following week, and ideas to help students commit themselves to action during the week so that they can put into practice what they have learned.

In addition to these weekly features, each quarter begins with the following helps:

- **Introduction to the Quarter** offers you a quick survey of each lesson to be studied during the quarter. You will find the title, background Scripture, date, and a brief summary of each week's basic thrust. This feature is on the first page of each quarter.
- **Meet Our Writer**, which follows the quarterly introduction, provides biographical information about each writer, including education, pastoral and/or academic teaching experience, previous publications, and family information.
- **The Big Picture**, written by the same writer who authored the quarter's lessons, is designed to give you a broader scope of the materials to be covered than is possible in each weekly lesson. You will find this background article immediately following the writer's biography.
- **Close-up** furnishes additional information, such as a time line, chart, overview, short article, map, or list that you may choose to use for a specific week or anytime during the quarter, perhaps even repeatedly.
- **Faith in Action** describes ideas related to the broad sweep of the quarter that the students can use individually or as a class to act on what they have been studying. These ideas are usually intended for use beyond the classroom.
- **Pronunciation Guide**, a familiar feature that our readers requested, has been moved from the Previewing the Scripture portion of each lesson to a single page before Lesson 1 in each quarter, thereby gathering all words for which pronunciation is provided in one convenient location.

Finally, two annual features are included:

- **List of Background Scriptures** is offered especially for those of you who keep back copies of *The New International Lesson Annual*. This feature, found immediately after the Contents, will enable you to locate Bible background passages used during the current year and refer to them in the future.

- **Teacher enrichment article**, which follows the List of Background Scriptures, is intended to be useful throughout the year. We hope you will read it immediately and refer to it often. This year's article, "Traditions of the Community," draws on the themes for the fall and winter quarters to explore how the church celebrates its special days and seasons.

We are always open to your suggestions! Some of our features were specifically added because you, our readers, asked for them. We want *The New International Lesson Annual* to be the first resource you consult when planning your lesson. Please send your questions, comments, and suggestions to me. I invite you to include your e-mail address and/or phone number. I will respond as soon as your message reaches my home office in Maryland.

> Dr. Nan Duerling
> Abingdon Press
> 2222 Rosa L. Parks Blvd.
> Nashville, TN 37228

All who use *The New International Lesson Annual* are blessed by the collective community of readers. We pray that you and your study partners will be transformed by the Word of God and the power of the Holy Spirit so as to be conformed to the image of our Lord and Savior Jesus Christ.

> Nan Duerling, Ph.D.
> Editor, *The New International Lesson Annual*

CONTENTS

First Quarter: The Christian Community Comes Alive
September 6, 2015–November 29, 2015

UNIT 1: SEEDS OF NEW GROWTH
(September 6–September 27)

UNIT 2: GIVING BOLD TESTIMONY
(October 4–October 25)

Second Quarter: Sacred Gifts and Holy Gatherings
December 6, 2015–February 28, 2016

UNIT 1: WHAT WE BRING TO GOD
(December 6–December 27)

UNIT 2: FOUR WEDDINGS AND A FUNERAL
(January 3–January 31)

UNIT 3: HOLY DAYS
(February 7–February 28)

Third Quarter: The Gift of Faith
March 6–May 29

UNIT 1: TESTS OF FAITH
(March 6–March 27)

UNIT 2: RESTORATIVE FAITH
(April 3–April 24)

UNIT 3: FULLNESS OF FAITH
(May 1–May 29)

Fourth Quarter: Toward a New Creation
June 5, 2016–August 28, 2016

UNIT 1: JUDGMENT AND SALVATION
(June 5–June 19)

UNIT 2: A WORLD GONE WRONG
(June 26–July 24)

UNIT 3: LIFE ON GOD'S TERMS
(July 31–August 28)

LIST OF BACKGROUND SCRIPTURES, 2015–2016

Old Testament

Genesis 1:1–2:3	June 5, 12, 19	Numbers 28:26-31	February 14
Genesis 28–30	January 3	Numbers 29:7-11	February 21
Exodus 12:1-14	February 7	Numbers 29:12-40	February 28
Exodus 13:11-16	December 20	Deuteronomy 5:12-15	December 6
Exodus 16:23	December 6	Deuteronomy 16:13-17	February 28
Exodus 20:8-11	December 6	Deuteronomy 22:6-7	December 13
Exodus 31:12-18	December 6	Psalm 8	June 26
Leviticus 12	December 20	Psalm 104	July 3
Leviticus 16	February 21	Psalm 136:1-9, 26	July 10
Leviticus 22:17-33	December 13	Psalm 148	July 17
Leviticus 23:3-8	December 6	Song of Solomon	January 10
Leviticus 23:9-14, 31-32	December 13	Isaiah 1:10-20	December 13
Leviticus 23:15-22	February 14	Hosea 1–3	January 17
Leviticus 23:26-32	February 21	Micah 6:6-8	December 13
Leviticus 23:33-43	February 28	Zephaniah 1:2–2:4	June 5
Numbers 3:5-13	December 20	Zephaniah 3:1-8	June 12
Numbers 28:16-25	February 7	Zephaniah 3:9-20	June 19

New Testament

Matthew 12:1-14	December 6	Acts 8:9-25	October 4
Matthew 23:1-12	December 27	Acts 9:19b-31	October 11
Mark 9:14-29	March 6	Acts 10:1-44	October 18
Mark 10:13-16	May 22	Acts 11:1-18	October 25
Mark 10:17-31	March 13	Acts 12:1-24	November 1
Mark 12:38-44	December 27	Acts 13:42	December 6
Mark 14:12-26	February 7	Acts 15:1-35	November 8
Mark 14:26-31, 66-72	March 20	Acts 16:1-15	November 15
Mark 16:1-8	March 27	Acts 17:1-32	November 22
Luke 2:21-39	December 20	Acts 18	November 29
Luke 7:1-10	April 3	Romans 1:18-32	June 26
Luke 7:36-50	April 10	Romans 2:14-29	July 3
Luke 8:26-39	April 17	Romans 3:9-20	July 10
Luke 15:11-32	April 24	Romans 3:21-31	July 17
Luke 17:1-10	May 1	Romans 5:1-11	July 24
Luke 17:11-19	May 8	Romans 6	July 31
Luke 18:9-14	May 15	Romans 8:28-39	August 7
Luke 18:15-17	May 22	Romans 9:6-29	August 14
Luke 19:1-10	May 29	Romans 11:11-36	August 21
John 2:1-12	January 24	Romans 12:1-2 December 13; August 28	
John 10:1-11	January 10	Romans 13:8-14	August 28
John 11:1-44	January 31	1 Corinthians 10:14-22	December 13
Acts 2:1-36	February 14	1 Corinthians 15:20-29	February 28
Acts 4:1-31	September 6	Hebrews 7:26-28	February 21
Acts 4:32–5:11	September 13	Hebrews 9:24	February 21
Acts 5:12-42	September 20	Hebrews 10:4-18	February 21
Acts 7:1-55	September 27	Revelation 14:1-5	February 28

Teacher Enrichment: Traditions of the Community

Community, the theme for the fall quarter, and *tradition*, the theme for the winter quarter, intertwine as we consider how the community of faith draws on its traditions to celebrate holy days. Jewish wedding and funeral traditions are highlighted during the winter study, as are the sacred observances of Passover, Feast of Weeks, Day of Atonement, and Feast of Booths. The formation of the Christian community is spotlighted in Acts during the fall. In this article we will explore how major Christian holy days and seasons are celebrated within the church community.

Since the church year, also known as the liturgical year, begins on the first Sunday of Advent, our review of special celebrations will also begin with Advent. The word "Advent" means "coming" or "arrival." During this season, the church prepares to receive Jesus the Christ, recalling how he came in the flesh as a baby in Bethlehem and looking ahead to prepare for his coming again in glory. All of the church's actions during this season help us to be alert and ready.

Many churches set up an Advent wreath on the first Sunday of Advent, which is the Sunday that falls closest to November 30. The wreath always takes the shape of a circle and is made of evergreen branches to signify life without end. Four candles are placed within the wreath to be lit on each of the four Sundays of the season. Before lighting the candle for the current week, the ones for the prior week(s) are lit. Generally a short reading is used as the candles are being lit. Often this reading and candle-lighting is led by a layperson, sometimes families. For many years, three of the candles were purple—the color of penitence and royalty—while the fourth was pink. The pink candle was lit on the third Sunday, known as Gaudette Sunday, from the Latin, which means "rejoice." At that point Advent was more than half completed. Some churches use only purple candles. In more recent years, an increasing number of churches use four blue candles, symbolizing both hope and the association of blue with the Virgin Mary in artistic depictions of her.

Another Advent tradition practiced in many churches is the decorating of a Chrismon Tree. First used in 1957 in Ascension Lutheran Church of Danville, Virginia, Chrismons are decorations that depict well-known theological symbols associated with Jesus, such as a cross, crown, fish, or staff. With dominant colors of white and gold, Chrismons are often made of Styrofoam, fabric, or felt and decorated with ribbons, beads, or glitter. Groups or individuals within the church fashion these decorations and hang them on a tree during Advent, perhaps with the help of children. Information is often provided about the symbols, usually in a bulletin insert.

During Advent (or Christmas), churches can celebrate with a service of lessons and carols. Advent Scripture lessons, which recall prophecies of a king who will come to establish a reign of peace, are read by individual readers and interspersed with carols appropriate for the season sung by the congregation.

One tradition that can move the church community from the four-week season of Advent to the two-week season of Christmas to the Day of Epiphany is the use of a nativity scene. During Advent an empty manger may be set up in the sanctuary to help create a mood of expectancy as the congregation awaits the arrival of the Christ Child. The holy family, animals, shepherds, and angels are added for the service on Christmas Eve or Christmas Day. The magi may be added on Epiphany, January 6 (or the Sunday closest to it). Some churches enlist members of the congregation to create a living nativity on the church lawn. Costumed players and live animals in a crèche on the church property can create excitement in the neighborhood. Even those who do not attend a church may be drawn to drive or walk by to experience this tableau.

Although many Protestant churches do not hold services on Christmas Day, sanctuaries are usually packed on Christmas Eve. Some congregations hold a service early in the evening to accommodate families. Later in the evening there may be one more service, often featuring the lighting of candles to signify the coming of the light of Christ into the world.

When the first cycle of the Christian year ends—Advent-Christmas-Epiphany—we spend up to eight weeks in what is known as "ordinary time," that is, time when there are no specific holy celebrations. On Ash Wednesday the second cycle of the life of Jesus begins with Lent, followed by the season of Easter, which ends on Pentecost Sunday.

Many churches hold services on Ash Wednesday to commemorate the start of the forty-day season of Lent. If you count the actual days from Ash Wednesday to Easter Sunday, you will find that they number forty-six. The reason for this apparent discrepancy is that Sundays, the Day of the Lord, are not included in the count. The decision to observe forty days comes from numerous references in the Bible to "forty," especially the forty days Jesus spent in the wilderness when he was tempted by the devil. Ash Wednesday services begin a period of penitence and reflection. During the Ash Wednesday service in many churches, the pastor uses ashes to make the sign of the cross on each congregant's forehead. This action symbolically reminds us of our mortality. Frequently, palm branches from the preceding year's celebration of Jesus' entry into Jerusalem are burned and their ashes are used, thereby creating a link between the beginning of Lent and the events of Holy Week.

During the season of Lent, faith communities often gather for Bible study or midweek services to strengthen their faith and grow together. Churches also encourage members to make a commitment to take action that will draw each individual closer to God. For some, that will mean giving up certain meals or beloved foods. For others, the "action" will be to refrain from an activity, such as watching television or spending leisure time on the computer. The emphasis, however, is not so much on "giving up" or "refraining" but on using whatever time would have been spent, for example, in preparing and eating a meal, to draw nearer to God by praying, meditating, writing in a spiritual journal, or walking while focused on God. Some congregations link these activities to raising money for a particular mission or ministry. For example, a family that chooses to fast for X meals per week would estimate the amount of money they saved by not eating and put that money in a jar that would then be given to a designated project, such as a food pantry.

As Lent draws to a close, Christians observe numerous traditions during Holy Week. Jesus' procession into Jerusalem is often reenacted by children waving palm branches as they march into the sanctuary at the beginning of the Palm Sunday service. Palm branches may be distributed to all members of the congregations. Sometimes, instead of handing out branches, each person is given a palm that is shaped like a cross.

On Holy Thursday congregations gather to commemorate the Last Supper. Communion is served and sometimes members participate in a seder-like meal, thus recalling Passover. As this service concludes, some churches observe a tradition of stripping the altar. Everything is removed from the altar or at least covered. A wooden cross may be set up to replace a gold cross. The symbolism reflects the bleakness of Good Friday. And so the sanctuary is now prepared for the congregation to return tomorrow.

Many different traditions surround the somber commemoration of Jesus' death on the cross. In some neighborhoods churches of all denominations unite to do a crosswalk. Participants walk from one church in the community to another, along a designated route. At each stop, mirroring the Seven Stations of the Cross so familiar in the Roman Catholic tradition, Scripture is read, a hymn is sung, and the walkers continue to the next church. Usually several different people carry a wooden cross from one church to the next. A crosswalk not only provides a rich spiritual experience for participants but also serves as a witness to the community as those who pass by the procession can clearly see the purpose of this walk being led by cross-bearers.

Another long-standing Good Friday tradition is that of a series of sermons based on Jesus' seven last words on the cross. These services, which may be ecumenical and include pastors from different traditions, are scheduled between noon and three o'clock, the hours that Jesus suffered on the cross.

On the evening of Good Friday, congregations gather to commemorate Jesus' death with a Tenebrae service. "Tenebrae" is the Latin word for "shadows." You might think of this service as the reverse of a Christmas Eve candlelight service. Instead of the sanctuary being lit with candles, candles placed on or near the altar are extinguished as one by one different people read portions of Scripture associated with Jesus' death. After each reading, one candle is snuffed out until only the Christ candle remains lit. A final lector reads, perhaps the first part of Psalm 22 or a Gospel quotation signaling the end of Jesus' life, and that light is either extinguished or carried out, leaving the congregation in darkness. The congregation departs in silence without a final hymn or benediction. Churches that do a Tenebrae service may begin their first Easter service with just enough light for people to enter safely. With the proclamation that "Christ is risen" the sanctuary is then filled with light.

Passion plays bring to life the physical, emotional, and spiritual suffering that Jesus endured from the Last Supper on Thursday night through his death on Good Friday. The earliest known written passion play was performed in England during the ninth century. Scholars believe that such plays had existed long before this time and were performed in the streets to enable mostly illiterate viewers to see and hear the story of events that they could not read. Although now performed for mostly literate populations, this tradition continues as some churches present such plays. The most famous of these is performed every ten years in Oberammergau, Germany, where townspeople reenact Jesus' passion as their ancestors have since 1634.

A very different way of commemorating Jesus' death is with hot cross buns, which are traditionally eaten on Good Friday. These may be baked in advance and even sold to raise funds for a church project. Hot cross buns are sweet breads flavored with fruit and spices. The white icing on the top forms a cross to remind those who eat the buns of Jesus' suffering.

Saturday evening marks the first service of Easter in some churches, particularly in the Roman Catholic, Anglican (Episcopal), Lutheran, and Orthodox faith communities. Known as Easter Vigil, this service includes four parts that begin with the bringing of light into the sanctuary, followed by lengthy Scripture readings that cover the scope of salvation history. Next, candidates for baptism or confirmation are presented and welcomed. Finally, Holy Communion (Mass) is celebrated.

In other Christian traditions, the first Easter service takes place at sunrise with services held in individual congregations or as an ecumenical service for the entire community. Breakfast is often served after these services to allow people time to fellowship together.

Services later on Sunday morning usually find sanctuaries adorned with flowers, often Easter lilies, and bright white and gold paraments. Special music and large crowds accentuate the primary importance of Jesus' resurrection. Members of the congregation may be dressed in new clothing, symbolizing that they have put on Christ. Most congregations are prepared to welcome visitors on Easter, since this is the most important day on the Christian calendar.

Easter Day is actually the beginning of a seven-week season of the church year. The week following the seventh week is Pentecost, the day on which the divine promise of the coming of the Holy Spirit was fulfilled. The paraments on the altar, pulpit, and lectern change from white to red, the color of fire, to spotlight the work of the Holy Spirit. Moreover, it was on this day that the believers, who numbered 120 (Acts 1:15), were huddled together when the Spirit fell upon them and they began to speak in languages they had never studied. By the time the day was over, about three thousand people who had heard the testimonies of God's deeds and Peter's powerful sermon had sought baptism (2:41). Consequently, Pentecost is often referred to as the birthday of the church. To celebrate this day, some churches have a birthday party, complete with a cake and red balloons. This day ends the second great cycle in the life of Christ: Lent-Easter-Pentecost.

FIRST QUARTER
The Christian Community
Comes Alive

SEPTEMBER 6, 2015–NOVEMBER 29, 2015

During the fall quarter we will explore the formation and growth of the Christian community as Luke tells the story of the church in The Acts of the Apostles. Seeds are planted at Pentecost and take root as the apostles give bold testimony. The movement spreads out, just as Jesus had commanded in Acts 1:8. Although the first people to claim the name of Jesus are Jews, Gentiles soon become part of the church as well. Obstacles need to be overcome in order for Jews and Gentiles to accept each other and worship together.

The four lessons of Unit 1, "Seeds of New Growth," begin in Acts 4:1-31 on September 6 with "Praying for One Another," the story of Peter and John being upheld in prayer by the church as they witnessed boldly before the Jewish council, which had forbidden them to teach about Jesus. "Sharing All Things," the lesson for September 13, explores Acts 4:32–5:11 to see how the early church lived in community. On September 20, we turn to Acts 5:12-42 to hear the apostles boldly "Witnessing to the Truth." Acts 7:1-55 is the background Scripture on September 27 for Stephen's speech before the Jewish council, "Remembering God's Faithfulness."

On October 4, the first session for Unit 2, "Giving Bold Testimony," reports that Peter told Simon, who practiced magic, that "The Spirit Is Not for Sale," as recorded in Acts 8:9-25. "Saul Earns Credibility," the lesson for October 11 from Acts 9:19b-31, looks at Saul's acceptance among Christians and his zeal in preaching Christ. "Peter Takes a Risk" by going to the home of a Gentile to witness, as described in Acts 10:1-44 on October 18. The story of Peter and Cornelius continues on October 25 as we hear Peter explain to the church in Jerusalem in Acts 11:1-18 that he acted the way he did with the Gentiles because he was "Trusting the Spirit."

The final unit, "Spreading the Gospel," opens on November 1 with the story of how "God Rescues Peter" from prison, as told in Acts 12:1-24. Paul and Barnabas address the Jewish council with their argument that "God Makes No Distinction," as recounted in Acts 15:1-35 on November 8. The background Scripture for November 15 from Acts 16:1-15 follows Paul and his team as they spread the good news "From Derbe to Philippi." On November 22, Acts 17:1-32 describes how Paul moves on to "Thessalonica, Beroea, and Athens," where some but not all listeners accept his message. On November 29, "Teaching God's Word," the final lesson of this quarter, focuses on Paul's zeal for proclaiming the gospel to the Gentiles as reported in Acts 18.

Meet Our Writer

DR. O. WESLEY ALLEN JR.

O. Wesley Allen Jr. is the professor of homiletics and worship at Lexington Theological Seminary (LTS).

Dr. Allen, an ordained United Methodist elder, has served as pastor of churches in Alabama, Connecticut, and Georgia; in campus ministry posts in Georgia and Indiana; and as a professor in New Jersey and Kentucky. At LTS he teaches a wide range of introductory and advanced courses in preaching and worship.

Wes received his B.A. with a double major in religion and ancient languages from Birmingham-Southern College, his M.Div. from Yale Divinity School, and his Ph.D. in New Testament (with minors in preaching and Hebrew Scriptures) from the Graduate School of Arts and Sciences at Emory University.

In the arena of New Testament, Allen specializes in the Synoptic Gospels and Acts. In this arena he has written *The Death of Herod: The Narrative and Theological Function of Retribution in Luke–Acts*; a textbook, *Reading the Synoptic Gospels: Basic Methods for Interpreting Matthew, Mark and Luke*; and a preaching commentary, *Matthew*.

In the arena of preaching and worship, Dr. Allen has special interest in rethinking the role of preaching and liturgy week in and week out in community in a shifting, postmodern world. In the arena of preaching he has published a collection of story-sermons, *Good News from Tinyville: Stories of Hope and Heart*; a postmodern theology of preaching, *The Homiletic of All Believers: A Conversational Approach*; a lectionary resource, *Preaching and Reading the Lectionary: A Three-Dimensional Approach to the Liturgical Year*; and a textbook on sermonic structure, *Determining the Form*.

In addition to these works, Dr. Allen has edited or coedited a number of works, including an eight-volume preaching textbook series titled Elements of Preaching; *The Renewed Homiletic*; and *Under the Oak Tree: The Church as Community of Conversation in a Conflicted and Pluralistic World*.

Wes is married to Bonnie L. Cook, who is the executive director of the Kentucky Psychiatric Medical Association and the Arkansas Psychiatric Society. Wes and Bonnie have a daughter, Maggie Cook-Allen, who is in high school in a math, science, and technology magnet program.

THE BIG PICTURE: LUKE–ACTS

Background

The readings for this quarter are all drawn from The Acts of the Apostles, specifically from chapters 4–18. Before exploring particular passages of this New Testament work, it will be helpful to step back and take a look at the narrative as a whole.

By whole narrative, we actually mean both the Gospel of Luke and The Acts of the Apostles, and not Acts alone. Luke's writing is a single narrative written across two volumes (see Acts 1:1-2), to which scholars often refer as "Luke–Acts" for shorthand.

Although due to convention scholars continue to call the author of this work "Luke," we do not know who actually wrote Luke and Acts. Nowhere in the writings themselves is the author named; the tradition of Luke the Physician writing them is highly unlikely. This does not mean that we know nothing about the author, however. The style and grammar of the two volumes is some of the best in the New Testament, indicating that the author was well educated, which also fits with the possibility of a patron (Theophilus) financially supporting the writing project (Luke 1:3; Acts 1:1). Moreover, the author's perspective on the early church is one of looking back from some distance—there is no indication that he knew any of the characters about whom he writes. They are heroes of the past, and the author likely writes about them from the late first century. Add to his facility with Greek and his perspective on the church the fact that the author has a strong working knowledge of the Septuagint (that is, the Hebrew Bible translated into Greek) and we can conjecture that "Luke" was a third-generation Christian, a Gentile raised in the church (or converted at a very young age).

With this view of the author in hand we can also draw some conclusions about his intended audience. He writes not so much to outsiders either to convert them to the Way or to defend the church to the world, but to the church itself to confirm the readers and help them grow in their faith. In his prologue to the Gospel, Luke says to his patron, Theophilus (which is a Greek name that translates as "God-lover"), that he writes "so that you may know the truth concerning the things about which you have been instructed" (Luke 1:4). Theophilus as the representative reader already knows the story Luke is about to tell. The reader, however, does *not* know it the way Luke is going to tell it. The readers' faith is more strongly established by reading or hearing a new take on the story that has been shaped to meet their particular needs and concerns.

This means that while Acts is often referred to as a church history, it is not history in the sense that we think of history. While Luke probably does share qualities with ancient Greco-Roman historiographers in his approach to writing

Acts, he is not concerned with establishing dates and details that confirm a historical perspective on a specific era of the church's evolution. The author has written a theological story for the community of believers, not a historical treatise for historians. Simply put, Acts is more of a story-sermon than it is an objective history.

Structure of Luke–Acts

Two Volumes, One Narrative. Luke opens his two-volume work by referring to his writing as an "orderly account" (Luke 1:1, 3). His theology, therefore, unfolds as the plot unfolds. Proper interpretation of any individual passage in Luke–Acts, therefore, requires the reader to take note of the context of the passage—what leads up to it and what follows from it.

The most obvious structural element of the work is the two–volume structure itself. The division between the two volumes is a chronological one. The first volume focuses on the story of Jesus (Acts 1:1), and the second volume picks up from there and tells the story of the early church that claims Jesus to be the Messiah. The hinge between the two volumes is the story of the ascension, which is narrated in both but told differently depending on whether it concludes or begins the volume (Luke 24:50-53; Acts 1:3-11). Luke's use of this story as the hinge is perfect in both literary and theological terms: The departure of Jesus draws to an end his story and makes possible the story of the church.

Geographical Structure. In addition to this breaking of the two volumes at a critical chronological point, Luke also employs a geographical device for ordering his two-volume narrative. The geographic center of the narrative is Jerusalem. The importance of Jerusalem is foreshadowed in three important scenes in the first half of the Gospel: The twelve-year-old Jesus is teaching in the Jerusalem Temple (Luke 2:41-50); the just-baptized Jesus is tempted by Satan on the pinnacle of the Temple in Jerusalem (4:9-13); and the transfigured Jesus is talking with Moses and Elijah about his "departure" in Jerusalem (9:31). In the next section of the Gospel, then, the narrative focuses on Jesus moving toward Jerusalem (in 9:51, Jesus "set his face toward Jerusalem") with the whole of 9:51–19:48 serving as a travel narrative headed toward, and finally entering, the city. Throughout the journey, the author reminds the readers of the looming destination (9:53; 13:22, 33; 17:11; 18:31; 19:11, 28). The remaining four chapters of the Gospel are then all set in Jerusalem.

Acts, picking up where Luke ends, starts in Jerusalem. Indeed, as Jesus ascends he instructs his disciples not to leave Jerusalem, because it is there that they will receive the promise of the Father (Acts 1:4). But then in 1:8 Jesus goes on to say that after they have received the Holy Spirit, they are to be his witnesses "in Jerusalem, in all Judea and Samaria, and to the ends of the earth." This notice serves not only to lift up the importance of Jerusalem as the location of the parent-church, if you will, but lays out the broad plot structure for Luke's second volume. The apostles establish the church in Jerusalem (Acts 1–7). Due to persecution, the church's witness then spreads throughout Judea and Samaria (see Acts 8:1). And each of Paul's missionaries travels (beginning in chapter 13) takes him farther and farther from Jerusalem out into the regions of Asia Minor and Greece until he is finally arrested in Jerusalem (chapters 21–23) and slowly taken to Rome, the end of the world, where the story concludes (28:14-31).

This geographical structure means that for Luke the setting of a particular scene is not simply a superfluous element. It is a theological element of the story. Readers must attend to geographical notices in Acts to see how the gospel is spreading from Jerusalem, the center of Luke's world, to Rome, the end of the world.

Acts of Peter and Paul. A final structural element of Acts involves the main characters. In truth the title "The Acts of the Apostles" is a misnomer. There are many apostles the reader never hears about at all. And while there are various leaders of the church who play key roles in this or that scene throughout the narrative, the overarching story focuses primarily on Peter in the first half (chapters 1–12) and on Paul in the second (chapters 13–28).

Luke's interest in Peter and Paul is not biographical in the way that we think of biography in the modern world. Note how little the author tells us about details of Peter's or Paul's background, experience outside the church, or personhood that would be of interest to readers of a biography.

Moreover, the author gives us no insight into the unique theology of Peter over against Paul or vice versa or the two of them over against other preachers and church leaders for that matter. Indeed, when we compare the theology of Paul as presented in Acts with the theology of Paul as put forth in the apostle's letters, the connections are few and far between (making it all but certain that Luke is not familiar with Paul's letters, which would have been written in the mid-first century). Instead, Peter and Paul are representative of *Luke's* theology. While Luke must certainly offer some biographical data that is historically correct (for instance, concerning some elements of Paul's travels), Luke mainly uses the two heroes of the early church as literary characters that help convey the message(s) he intends for his particular readers.

Theological Themes

Main Characters. To contradict a bit what we just claimed, Peter and Paul are actually not the main characters of Luke's second volume. They do get the most explicit attention by the author but two characters behind the scenes serve as the "real" main characters.

The first is God, or specifically the presence of God symbolized by the activity of the Holy Spirit. The Holy Spirit is a main character in Luke's narrative from the beginning (for example, in the Gospel narrative before Jesus even begins his ministry, see Luke 1:17, 35, 41, 67; 2:25-27; 3:16; 4:1). Yet one gets the sense that at Pentecost (Acts 2:1-4) the prominence of the Holy Spirit (as a character in the story) increases. Instead of popping up here or there, inspiring this or that person, in Acts the Holy Spirit seems to be omnipresent, guiding and influencing everything that happens.

Indeed, throughout Acts, it is clear that God is behind all that occurs. It is not that God is a puppeteer and the ancient Roman Empire is God's stage. Yet God gives meaning and direction to the flow of the whole history. More specifically, God guides the movement and growth of the church. The church, then, is the second main character of the story of Acts. The church is God's partner, God's servant, with various groups and individuals—especially Peter and Paul—representing the church at different times in the story.

Thus, to interpret almost any passage in Acts fully, readers must ask what God and the church are doing in the scene, whether the two are mentioned explicitly or not. Otherwise, we miss nuances Luke intends to convey.

God's Consistency. Because God is the main character of Luke's narrative (because for Luke, God is the main character of history), one of Luke's goals is to show that God is consistent as God throughout history. In other words, Luke wants to demonstrate that God's activity in the church is in continuity with God's activity in Israel's story and in Jesus' story.

This continuity is a problem for Luke in relation to both Jews and Gentiles. If God has promised Israel that they are God's people, why is there the need for the church in first place and why are Gentiles included in the church without requiring circumcision in the second place?

In relation to the first part of the concern, scholars have long debated what Luke's view of the Jews actually is. The author seems to contradict himself. The "people" (usually used of Israel throughout Luke–Acts) are clearly God's favored ones. God is in covenant with them and has promised them salvation through a messiah. But once Christ has ascended and the church is growing, "the Jews" are the ones who resist the gospel (for example, Acts 9:22-23; 12:3; 14:2, 19; 17:5; 18:5-6, 12). On the other hand, plenty of Jews accept the gospel and become part of the messianic community. If this is not confusing enough, consider two side by side references to "the Jews." In 13:43 Luke says that "many Jews" follow Paul and Barnabas but in his next breath in verse 45 he says that "the Jews" saw the crowds following Paul, and they became jealous and argued against what Paul said. Which is it? It is likely the case that at times Luke is using the term "the Jews" as a label for the group of leaders of a local synagogue and at other times he is speaking more broadly of Jews as an ethnic, religious identity. What is absolutely clear is that Luke in no way ever presents God as turning away from the Jews. When Paul travels to a new town, he first goes to the synagogue and only when rejected turns to Gentiles (for example, 13:46; 18:6), even though God chooses him to carry the gospel to the Gentiles from the very beginning (9:15). Even at the end of Paul's career, in the very last chapter of the book, Luke presents Paul as proclaiming Jesus as the Christ to Jews (28:17-24).

But if God has not turned away from the divine promise that the Jews are to be God's people, what is to be made of Gentiles who are uncircumcised in the church? Early in his first volume, Luke already indicates that extending divine grace to the Gentiles (in the second volume) is *part* of the promise to Israel (see Luke 2:29-32). God therefore fulfills this promise by sending the church to the Gentiles.

Luke makes clear that neither Peter nor Paul initiate the move to include Gentiles in the church. This movement is completely God's doing. God announces that Paul will bring God's name before Gentiles when he is first converted (Acts 9:15). God instructs Cornelius to seek out Peter, instructs Peter to go to Cornelius, and gives the Holy Spirit to the Gentiles before Peter can even finish his sermon (chapter 10).

In sum, Luke presents God as consistent in divine action toward Israel in that God's love and salvation are universal, extended to any and all who would receive them.

Salvation. Luke is unique among the Gospel writers in his view of salvation. For most of the New Testament, in fact, the central event and revelation of God's salvation is the cross. But in Luke–Acts, Jesus' death does not bring salvation; it is simply the necessary death of a martyr. Instead, the resurrection is God's primary saving act in the Christ event, and the proclamation of this event extends God's salvation to all. This pattern of Jesus being martyred at the hands of the Jewish authorities, raised by God, and witnessed by the apostles is the core of evangelistic proclamation in Acts (see 2:22-24, 32; 3:14-15; 4:10; 5:29-32; 10:39-42; 13:26-33).

For Luke, the salvation offered through Christ's resurrection is experienced by inclusion in the church. In other words, there is no salvation apart from the messianic community. It is not that Luke asserts that joining the community is a requirement for salvation. Instead it is that by being included in the church one experiences salvation.

This correlation between community and salvation may be hard for modern people of faith to accept because individualism is such a strong part of our Western worldview. This was not the case in Luke's day. Individual identity was inseparable from communal connections. Thus when hearers receive the good news of the Messiah being raised from the dead for the forgiveness of their sins, they repent; are baptized; *and* dedicate themselves to the apostles' teaching, fellowship, the breaking of bread, communal prayer/worship, and sharing of possessions (for example, 2:42, 46, 47; 20:7, 11; 4:31-35).

CLOSE-UP: HIGHLIGHTS OF PAUL'S SECOND MISSIONARY JOURNEY, A.D. 49–52

Passage in Acts (Lesson date)	Cities	Events
15:40–16:1 (November 15)	**Antioch (in Syria)** to Cilicia (15:41) to Derbe (16:1) to **Lystra** (16:1)	Paul and Barnabas had parted ways. Barnabas and his cousin John Mark set out for Cyprus. Paul and Silas headed through Syria. Paul selected Timothy and then, because his mother was a Jewish-Christian and Paul wanted Jews to accept his companion, he had Timothy circumcised.
16:6-8 (November 15)	**Lystra** to Phrygia to Galatia to Mysia to **Troas**	Holy Spirit did not allow Paul to witness in Asia (16:6). Spirit did not allow Paul to go to Bithynia in northwest Asia Minor (16:7). Paul has a vision at Troas (16:9) of a call from man in Macedonia, and he followed that call.
16:11-12 (November 15)	**Troas** to Samothrace to Neapolis to **Philippi (in Macedonia)**	Lydia converted at Philippi (16:13-15). At risk to herself and household, she provides hospitality for Paul and his companions (16:15). Paul and Silas in prison at Philippi (16:24) because they cast a demon out of a slave girl. Her owners were furious because she could no longer make money as a fortune-teller (16:16-23). An earthquake strikes, but instead of fleeing, Paul stays and his jailer is converted.
16:40–17:1 (November 22)	**Philippi** to Amphipolis to Apollonia to **Thessalonica**	Paul taught in the synagogue at Thessalonica and some Jews and Greeks were converted (17:4). Some jealous Jews created a mob scene. When the mob was unable to find Paul and Silas, they attacked the home of Jason, who had hosted the missionaries (17:5-9).

17:10 (November 22)	**Thessalonica** to **Beroea**	Believers in Thessalonica had sent Paul and Silas off during the night of the melee at Jason's home (17:10). Paul went to the synagogue and found a receptive audience among the Beroeans, who searched the Scriptures to see if Paul's message accorded with them. Many became believers (17:11-12). Some Jews from Thessalonica arrived and incited the crowds (17:13).
17:14-15 (November 22)	**Beroea** to **Athens**	Believers in Beroea took Paul as far as Athens to escape the mob. Silas and Timothy remained behind, though they were to be reunited as quickly as possible (17:14-15). Paul preached at Areopagus (17:22-31). Some listeners became believers (17:32-34).
18:1 (November 29)	**Athens** to **Corinth**	Paul met Priscilla and Aquila and stayed with them (18:1-3). Paul was not well received at the synagogue, so he left, saying he would now go to Gentiles (18:4-6). He went next door, where people came to hear him and believed. He stayed in Corinth for 18 months (18:7-11). Some angry Jews brought Paul before a magistrate, who refused to rule on the matter (18:12-17).
18:18-19 (November 29)	**Corinth** to Cenchreae to **Ephesus**	Paul preached at Ephesus (18:19) but declined their invitation to stay.
18:21-22 (November 29)	**Ephesus** to Caesarea (by boat) to Jerusalem to **Antioch**	Paul greeted the church in Jerusalem and then went to Antioch until about A.D. 54 when he departed on his third journey.

FAITH IN ACTION: MAKING A BOLD WITNESS

During the fall we are studying The Acts of the Apostles to discern how "The Christian Community Comes Alive." In these lessons we see bold faith in action as people take risks and suffer consequences for spreading the news of Jesus Christ. Here are several ideas for you to share verbally and/or in writing with the students at whatever times during the quarter you find appropriate. Encourage the adults to act on these suggestions.

1. Review Acts 4:32–5:11, discussed in the lesson for September 13. Brainstorm ways that members of your congregation might be able to discreetly help one another financially, perhaps through a pastor's discretionary fund, a food pantry or clothes closet, or group that will help with home maintenance or personal assistance. If no mechanism for assistance is in place, what can this study group do to model the care for members described in Acts 4?

2. Recall from the lesson for September 27 that Stephen spoke boldly to the Jewish leadership about God's faithfulness and, as a result, was stoned to death. Where do you need to speak truth to power today? What needs to be said—and to whom? What action will you take?

3. Look again at Acts 9:19b-31, the Scripture for the lesson on October 11. Christians initially received this newly transformed Saul/Paul, the former Christian persecutor who now proclaimed that Jesus was the Son of God, with great skepticism. How can you help someone who has turned his or her life around be accepted into the community of faith, just as Barnabas helped Saul?

4. Reread Acts 10:1-44 and 11:1-18, the Scriptures for October 18 and 25, respectively. The observant Jew Peter took a huge risk by going to the home of the Gentile soldier Cornelius. In doing so, he learned that God shows no partiality. Do you feel that God favors one group over another? If so, what help do you need from God to open your heart to all who are created in God's image?

5. Remember the story of Peter's rescue from prison as told in Acts 12:1-24, our study on November 1. Pray for those who are persecuted or otherwise in difficult circumstances. Trust that God will answer your prayers.

6. Review Acts 15:1-35, the basis for the session on November 8, in which a serious matter of conflict was resolved. Consider conflicts currently facing the church. Try to study at least one issue from several perspectives. What can you do to help your church find a resolution?

7. Read again Acts 18, the background Scripture for November 29, to see how Paul made the transition from one occupation (tentmaker) to another (evangelist and preacher). Consider whether God might be calling you to a new vocation, perhaps one related to ministry. Explore this call and take steps to act on it, if you feel so led.

PRONUNCIATION GUIDE

Achaia (uh kay' yuh)
Achan (ay' kan)
Amphipolis (am fip' uh lis)
Ananias (an uh ni' uhs)
Antioch (an tee' ok)
Apollonia (ap uh loh' nee uh)
apologia (ap uh loh jee' uh)
Aquila (ak' wi luh)
Areopagus (air ee op' uh guhs)
Barnabas (bahr' nuh buhs)
Beroea (bi ree' uh)
Bithynia (bi thin' ee uh)
Caesarea (ses uh ree' uh)
Cenchreae (sen' kree uh)
Chaldean (kal dee' uhn)
Cilicia (suh lish' ee uh)
Crispus (kris' puhs)
dei (die)
Derbe (duhr' bee)
Diaspora (di as' puh ruh)
Epicurean (ep uh kyoo ree' uhn)
epiphany (i pif' uh nee)
eschatological (es kat uh loj' i kuhl)
Galatia (guh lay' shuh)
Gallio (gal' ee oh)
Gamaliel (guh may' lee uhl)
Haran (hair' uhn)
Herod Agrippa (her' uhd uh grip' uh)

Herod Antipas (her' uhd an' tee puhs)
Iconium (i koh' nee uhm)
laos (lah os')
Levite (lee' vite)
Lystra (lis' truh)
Macedonia (mas uh doh' nee uh)
Mesopotamia (mes uh puh tay' mee uh)
Mysia (mis' ee uh)
Neapolis (nee ap' uh lis)
Philippi (fi lip' i) or (fil' i pi)
Phoenicia (fi nish' uh)
Phrygia (frij' ee uh)
Pontus (pon' tuhs)
Prisca (pris' kuh)
Samothrace (sam' uh thrays)
Sanhedrin (san hee' druhn)
Sapphira (suh fi' ruh)
Sidon (si' duhn)
Stoic (stoh' ik)
tetrarch (tet' rahrk)
Thessalonica (thes uh luh ni' kuh)
Theudas (thoo' duhs)
Thyatira (thi uh ti' ruh)
Titius Justus (tish ee uhs juhs' tuhs)
Torah (toh' ruh)
Troas (troh' az)
Tyre (tire)
Via Egnatia (vee uh eg nah' tee uh)

UNIT 1: SEEDS OF NEW GROWTH
PRAYING FOR ONE ANOTHER

PREVIEWING THE LESSON

Lesson Scripture: Acts 4:23-31
Background Scripture: Acts 4:1-31
Key Verse: Acts 4:31

Focus of the Lesson:
At critical times in their lives, people search for strength to weather the storm. Where do they find the necessary strength? The followers of Christ raised their voices together to God in prayer and were filled with strength from the Holy Spirit to speak God's word with boldness.

Goals for the Learners:
(1) to examine the apostles' prayer for strength to speak with boldness and continue Jesus' ministry while under political duress.
(2) to share insights into prayer as a means through which Christians can remain strong voices for change and effective ministries today.
(3) to ask God in bold prayers to empower their mission and ministry.

Supplies:
Bibles, newsprint and marker, paper and pencils, hymnals

READING THE SCRIPTURE

NRSV
Lesson Scripture: Acts 4:23-31

[23]After they [Peter and John] were released, they went to their friends and reported what the chief priests and the elders had said to them. [24]When they heard it, they raised their voices together to God and said, "Sovereign Lord, who made the

CEB
Lesson Scripture: Acts 4:23-31

[23]After their release, Peter and John returned to the brothers and sisters and reported everything the chief priests and elders had said. [24]They listened, then lifted their voices in unison to God, "Master, you are the one who created the heaven, the earth, the

heaven and the earth, the sea, and everything in them, [25]it is you who said by the Holy Spirit through our ancestor David, your servant: 'Why did the Gentiles rage, and the peoples imagine vain things? [26]The kings of the earth took their stand, and the rulers have gathered together against the Lord and against his Messiah.' [27]For in this city, in fact, both Herod and Pontius Pilate, with the Gentiles and the peoples of Israel, gathered together against your holy servant Jesus, whom you anointed, [28]to do whatever your hand and your plan had predestined to take place. [29]And now, Lord, look at their threats, and grant to your servants to speak your word with all boldness, [30]while you stretch out your hand to heal, and signs and wonders are performed through the name of your holy servant Jesus." **[31]When they had prayed, the place in which they were gathered together was shaken; and they were all filled with the Holy Spirit and spoke the word of God with boldness.**

sea, and everything in them. [25]You are the one who spoke by the Holy Spirit through our ancestor David, your servant:

Why did the Gentiles rage,
  and the peoples plot in vain?
[26]The kings of the earth took their stand
  and the rulers gathered together as one
  against the Lord and against his Christ.

[27]Indeed, both Herod and Pontius Pilate, with Gentiles and Israelites, did gather in this city against your holy servant Jesus, whom you anointed. [28]They did what your power and plan had already determined would happen. [29]Now, Lord, take note of their threats and enable your servants to speak your word with complete confidence. [30]Stretch out your hand to bring healing and enable signs and wonders to be performed through the name of Jesus, your holy servant." **[31]After they prayed, the place where they were gathered was shaken. They were all filled with the Holy Spirit and began speaking God's word with confidence.**

UNDERSTANDING THE SCRIPTURE

Acts 4:1-22. The scene in which the apostles (or the church; see below on 4:23) pray for boldness comes on the heels of Peter and John being tried by the Jewish council. The two apostles had healed a lame man in the Temple; and then when a crowd gathered, they used the occasion to proclaim Jesus as the crucified and risen Christ (Acts 3). The Temple guard and the Sadducees (who are characterized in the New Testament as not believing in the resurrection; for example, see Luke 20:27) arrest them for proclaiming the resurrection (Acts 4:1-4). The council hopes to silence the apostles,

but not only do they proclaim the resurrection in the midst of the questioning they also refuse to be silent after they have left (4:5-22). It is this detention, trial, and act of faith and bravery from which Peter and John (simply referred to as "they") come to their "friends" in 4:23.

Acts 4:23. Peter and John come from their trial and report the warning given them by the council. It is unclear to whom they come. Although the NRSV says "their friends" and the CEB "the brothers and sisters," the Greek simply reads, "they came to their own." This could mean Peter and John have returned either to the other apostles or to the Jerusalem church more broadly. Given that the next scene (starting in verse 32) is about the wider community of believers, it is likely the author is indicating the church in verse 23.

Acts 4:24. The church's response to the warning given by the council is to pray. But it is more than that. The council has exerted power in arresting and threatening the apostles if they continue preaching the resurrection. In turn, the church addresses God in terms of God's much greater power—the power to create the universe. Such a naming of God immediately puts the council's threat in perspective.

Acts 4:25-28. After addressing God as the powerful Creator, the church quotes Psalm 2:1-2 in its prayer. Psalm 2 was already interpreted by the early church as relating to Christ based on verse 7, so it is natural that the author would use other parts of the psalm also to interpret the story of Christ. Being Hebrew poetry, the psalm was written using the common technique of parallelism. Similar to the way English poetry might follow a certain meter and rhyming scheme, Hebrew poets would often write lines in pairs where the second line basically repeated the first line using synonymous terms. Thus "people imagine vain things" repeats "Gentiles [or nations] rage" and "rulers have gathered together" repeats "kings of the earth took their stand." But Luke reads the lines as prophesying the rejection of Jesus so that Herod = king, Pilate = ruler, nations (in the psalm) = Gentiles, and peoples = Israel (compare Jesus' trial scene in Luke 22:66–23:25). This sort of reading of the Old Testament

in the early church is not surprising. The rationale for the reading is explicitly provided in verse 28: The reason Scripture accords with what happened to Jesus is that Jesus' persecution was all part of the all-powerful Creator's plan. Luke here is not claiming that God willed Jesus to be executed, but instead that it was necessary. Over and over again the small, unassuming Greek word *dei*, which can simply be translated as "must," is used in Luke–Acts to name the cross as a necessary part of God's plan. But unlike other New Testament authors who assert the cross as the locus of salvation, Luke emphasizes the resurrection as the moment that Christ saves. This is why throughout sermons in Acts, preachers say, "*you* (that is, Jerusalem) killed him, *God* raised him, and *we* are witnesses" (see 3:14-15). So "predestined" in verse 28 does not mean God willed the cross, but that it was necessary for God to achieve what God did will: salvation through the resurrection.

Acts 4:29-30. It may seem odd that the church is concerned with a correlation between Psalm 2:1-2 and Christ's crucifixion in this prayer. Peter and John (and thus the church as a whole) have been threatened to be silent about the resurrection or else. Why pray about the crucifixion as a necessary part of God's plan for salvation? The reason is that as Christ was threatened and suffered, so will the church be threatened and suffer. God's will being at work in Jesus' crucifixion (and resurrection) is a model for the church. It is on the basis of knowing that God was working toward God's plan even in Christ's trials that the church can imagine God at work through its own struggles. It is on the basis of this theological connection that the church can (and should!) ask for boldness in its struggles to proclaim Christ, even when they are rejected as Christ was rejected. In a sense, the request for boldness is really less about the apostles and the church's ability and more about God's power. The prayer ends by asking that God give them boldness *while* God heals and performs signs and wonders. This ending echoes the healing of the lame man in the Temple (3:1-10). Peter makes very clear after the healing that he did not make the lame man walk by his own power, but that God did the wondrous work (3:12 and following). Similarly, the prayer makes clear that any boldness the church might hope for is not its own doing, but a gift of God's power.

Acts 4:31. Luke in no way leaves the reader to guess whether God hears and answers the church's prayer. The power of God named in the prayer and requested by those praying is manifested in the conclusion to the story through the physical symbol of the shaking of the place where the church was gathered. The language and imagery is intentionally reminiscent of Pentecost (2:1-4): A physical epiphany accompanies the gift of the Holy Spirit so that the recipients might speak the word of God in a new way. In spite of very real threats and struggles ahead, the church receives God's Spirit and is thus emboldened to speak God's word.

INTERPRETING THE SCRIPTURE

Christ as Our Model

The apostles have been called to the carpet by the religious leaders and recognize the serious threat represented by the warning they have received. It is a very real threat, not only to Peter and John but also to the church as a whole. The council acts as a supreme court of sorts for the Jewish people in Jerusalem, and if they were to condemn these Jewish-Christians, they will likely suffer the same fate Jesus did.

When Peter and John gather during this stressful time with "their own," the church prays and in doing so lifts up Christ as their model. They do not, in the prayer, ask WWJD (What would Jesus do?). Instead, they recall WHTJ (what happened to Jesus). In other words, they remembered that Jesus' suffering was part of God's plan (Acts 4:25-28).

The reason they recite this understanding of the Christ event as part of their prayer is not to give them an example of what they should do but to help them interpret what was happening to them. The early church struggled with the question of why they suffered through persecution if God had called them into being. If they truly were of God, then who could be against them?

In this prayer, such questions are answered by saying, "As Christ went, so goes the church." If Christ suffered, why should we not expect to suffer as well? As opposed to being a sign that the church might not be under God's providential care, the persecution against Peter and John is a sign that the church is very much about God's business, and those who benefit from the status quo find God's good news (of which the Greek root is "new") threatening.

Of course, in our culture we do not share the same kind of risk of political duress the early church had for its dedication to Jesus as the Messiah (and that some expressions of the Christian faith find in other parts of the world still today). Nonetheless, when we live out our resurrection faith publicly and share it in the world, we can expect to face some level of rejection. The rejection might range from innocent misunderstanding to intentional resistance. The message of resurrection is a challenge to the powers of death in the world. So when Christians attempt to stand boldly and connect with the gospel in relation to healing the lame, empowering the poor, giving voice to the silenced, and setting free the oppressed, it is always a radical stance that political powers and privileged individuals will attempt to thwart. But we are in good company: We stand with the early church and pray, WHTJ.

Boldness, Not Escape

In the midst of our struggles we naturally (and faithfully) turn to God in prayer. But what is it we hope for in our praying?

After Peter and John are persecuted in the Temple and report their persecution to the church, it is instructive to notice what they do *not* pray for. They do not petition God to remove the threat of persecution, to bring retribution on the persecutors, or to "fix" or change the situation in any fashion.

Instead, they pray, "And now, Lord, look at their threats, and grant to your servants to speak your word with all boldness, while you stretch out your hand to heal, and signs and wonders are performed through the name of your holy servant Jesus" (4:29-30). They ask only one thing: that God

give them boldness to continue the task God has called them to do, even though that very task is at risk of being squashed by the powers that be.

So often we pray and even worship in ways that are escapist. We come to church to get away from the trials of family, work, politics, economic struggles, violence, oppression, and so on. We bow our heads in silence, we sing beautiful songs of praise, we share announcement after announcement, partially in hope of drowning out the sounds of pain, conflict, depression, illness, hatred, and death "out there." But if the prayer of the church in Acts 4 should be in some way the prayer of the church today, we should not look to God or worship for such escape.

The church in Acts 4 asks God not for relief from the situation, but strength to face it. We should not expect God to rescue us from reality in all its ugliness but to embolden us in dealing with the ugliness of reality. Philips Brooks, in his sermon "Going Up to Jerusalem," said it well:

O, do not pray for easy lives. Pray to be stronger men! Do not pray for tasks equal to your powers. Pray for powers equal to your tasks! Then the doing of your work shall be no miracle. But you shall be a miracle. Every day you shall wonder at yourself, at the richness of life which has come to you by the grace of God.

God's Response to Prayer

After Peter, John, and their own friends conclude their prayer, the narrator says, "When they had prayed, the place in which they were gathered together was shaken; and they were all filled with the Holy Spirit and spoke the word of God with boldness" (4:31, key verse). Echoing the scene at Pentecost (2:1-4), this description of God's response to the prayer serves as a reminder that while Pentecost might have been a one-time event, God's giving of the Spirit to the church is a recurring gift.

We may question whether this is really so. After all, when was the last time we experienced God's presence in terms of the rushing of violent winds inside the church, or tongues of fire descending on everyone in the pews, or the church having a small, localized earthquake? But Luke simply uses these sorts of descriptions of physical manifestations of the Spirit to make sure the reader does not forget what the Spirit brings to the church. Just before Jesus ascended, he said to the disciples, "You will receive *power* when the Holy Spirit has come upon you; and you will be my witnesses" (1:8, emphasis added). The extraordinary physical signs in Acts are a narrative reminder that the gift of the Holy Spirit is the gift of power.

In other words, the gift of the Spirit is the gift of boldness to witness to the risen Christ in the midst of all that would attempt to assert the power of death over us. Every time the church stands up for the marginalized over against those who stand on their backs in society, there is a rush of wind. Every time the church proclaims hope in God's reign over against the despair we see on the news, there are tongues of flame. Every time some Christian— rightfully scared that doing what the faith requires will bring rejection and resistance from those who hold to the self-serving values of the world— does what the faith calls for anyway, the ground shakes violently.

But as the passage reminds us, we do not do any of these sorts of acts of faith by our own accord. Any boldness we have is a gift from the all-powerful One who created the universe. Only through God will we be empowered to speak truth to power. Only through the gift of the Holy Spirit can we speak and claim an Easter message in a Good Friday world.

SHARING THE SCRIPTURE

PREPARING TO TEACH

Preparing Our Hearts

Ponder this week's devotional reading from Matthew 6:9-15, which are the familiar words of the Lord's Prayer. How do the petitions of this prayer compare with the kinds of petitions you often raise in your own prayers? Do you come boldly before the throne of grace, believing that God will hear and answer? If not, what holds you back?

Pray that you and the students will be open to praying as Jesus prayed.

Preparing Our Minds

Study the background Scripture from Acts 4:1-31 and the lesson Scripture from Acts 4:23-31.

Consider this question as you prepare the lesson: *Where do people find the necessary strength to weather the storms of life?*

Write on newsprint:
- ❏ information for next week's lesson, found under Continue the Journey.
- ❏ activities for further spiritual growth in Continue the Journey.

Review the Introduction, The Big Picture, Close-up, and Faith in Action, which all precede the first lesson of this quarter. Consider how you might use any of this material in today's lesson.

Prepare to retell the events of Acts 4:1-22.

LEADING THE CLASS

(1) Gather to Learn

❖ Welcome the class members and guests.

❖ Pray that those who have come today will be open to new growth in their faith.

❖ Set the stage for this quarter's study, "The Christian Community Comes Alive," by reading or retelling The Big Picture: Luke–Acts. If time allows you to use only a portion of this article today, plan to work the rest of the information into a future session.

❖ Read aloud today's focus statement: **At critical times in their lives, people search for strength to weather the storm. Where do they find the necessary strength? The followers of Christ raised their voices together to God in prayer and were filled with strength from the Holy Spirit to speak God's word with boldness.**

(2) Goal 1: Examine the Apostles' Prayer for Strength to Speak With Boldness and Continue Jesus' Ministry While Under Political Duress

❖ Retell Acts 4:1-22 so that students will have a context for today's lesson.

❖ Select a volunteer to read Acts 4:23-31 and then ask:

1. **What do you learn from this prayer concerning the believers' understanding of God?**

2. **How does the quotation from Psalm 2:1-2 in verses 25-26 help believers to interpret their circumstances?** (See Acts 4:25-28 in Understanding the Scripture.)

3. **On what grounds do the believers pray with boldness even though they are under great duress?** (See Acts 4:29-30 in Understanding the Scripture.)

4. **What happens as a result of the prayers of the church?** (See Acts 4:31 in Understanding the Scripture and "God's Response to Prayer" in Interpreting the Scripture.)

5. **What lessons can the church of today learn from this prayer of the early church?**

(3) Goal 2: Share Insights Into Prayer as a Means Through Which Christians Can Remain Strong Voices for Change and Effective Ministries Today

❖ Ask: **Where have you seen the power of prayer change circumstances, both in the lives of individuals and on a broader scale?**

❖ Form small groups and encourage each one to identify situations in their own communities where prayers are needed to bring about change. Suggest that they think of instances of oppression or injustice. Encourage the groups to talk about the kinds of changes that are needed and how the church can play a role in bringing about such change. Give each group a sheet of newsprint and a marker to record ideas.

❖ Call the groups together and ask a spokesperson from each group to report on their insights and ideas.

❖ Read this information concerning a call for prayer from Archbishop Demetrios of America, issued in July

2014 on behalf of Christians suffering in the Middle East: **Archbishop Demetrios reminds us that Christians caught in the crossfire of violence in Israel and Syria face severe persecution and death. Although many would respond to such brutal treatment and genocide with violence, Christian communities in these hot spots have consistently shown unconditional love for their neighbors. Archbishop Demetrios urges believers to stand together with those who are suffering. "Together," he writes, "we must intensify our prayers, asking for an end to the bloodshed and for the prevalence of God's peace in the tormented lands of the Middle East."**

❖ Respond to this request by encouraging the adults to offer sentence prayers on behalf of those in the Middle East, as well as in other situations you have identified.

(4) Goal 3: Ask God in Bold Prayers to Empower the Learners' Mission and Ministry

❖ Read the words of Phillip Brooks's sermon under "Boldness, Not Escape" in Interpreting the Scripture.

❖ Distribute paper and pencils. Invite participants to write (or silently offer) a prayer to God concerning a difficult situation or a decision that they are facing. What do they need from God to empower them to be bold in order to overcome whatever challenges they face? Provide quiet time for the adults to reflect.

(5) Continue the Journey

❖ Break the silence by praying that as the learners depart, they will continue to call upon the Holy Spirit so as to pray boldly for one another.

❖ Post information for next week's session on newsprint for the students to copy:
- **Title: Sharing All Things**
- **Background Scripture: Acts 4:32–5:11**
- **Lesson Scripture: Acts 4:34–5:10**
- **Focus of the Lesson: Although there are exceptions, most people are glad to share what they have with those in need. What is it that enables people to give up what is theirs for the good of someone else? The early followers of Jesus shared everything with one another, and, although some acted deceitfully and were punished as a result, there was not a needy person among them.**

❖ Post the following information on newsprint and provide paper and pencils for the students to copy it. Challenge the adults to grow spiritually by completing one or more of these activities related to this week's session.

(1) **Make a list of issues that your congregation and/or denomination is facing. Pray each day that through the Holy Spirit leaders and members alike will discern how to address these issues.**

(2) **Identify places in the world where Christians are being persecuted. Learn what you can about how these groups are being oppressed, by whom, and what they are doing to hold fast to their faith. Intercede for these brothers and sisters in**

prayer. **Take whatever other action you can to assist these people.**

(3) **Pray that you will witness boldly for Christ whenever you see an opportunity to do so.**

❖ Sing or read aloud "It's Me, It's Me, O Lord (Standing in the Need of Prayer)."

❖ Conclude today's session by leading the class in this benediction, which is adapted from Acts 9:20, the key verse for October 11: **Let us go forth to boldly proclaim that Jesus is the Son of God. Amen.**

UNIT 1: SEEDS OF NEW GROWTH
SHARING ALL THINGS

PREVIEWING THE LESSON

Lesson Scripture: Acts 4:34–5:10
Background Scripture: Acts 4:32–5:11
Key Verse: Acts 4:34

Focus of the Lesson:
Although there are exceptions, most people are glad to share what they have with those in need. What is it that enables people to give up what is theirs for the good of someone else? The early followers of Jesus shared everything with one another, and, although some acted deceitfully and were punished as a result, there was not a needy person among them.

Goals for the Learners:
(1) to understand the sacrifices and rewards that come from the early Christians' willingness to share possessions with others.
(2) to examine one's motivation for making sacrificial offerings that benefit the larger community.
(3) to encourage others to contribute to a community project.

Supplies:
Bibles, newsprint and marker, paper and pencils, hymnals

READING THE SCRIPTURE

NRSV
Lesson Scripture: Acts 4:34–5:10

³⁴There was not a needy person among them, for as many as owned lands or houses sold them and brought the proceeds of what was sold. ³⁵They laid it at the apostles' feet, and it was distributed to each as any had need. ³⁶There was a Levite, a native of Cyprus, Joseph, to whom the apostles gave the name Barnabas

CEB
Lesson Scripture: Acts 4:34–5:10

³⁴There were no needy persons among them. Those who owned properties or houses would sell them, bring the proceeds from the sales, ³⁵and place them in the care and under the authority of the apostles. Then it was distributed to anyone who was in need.

³⁶Joseph, whom the apostles

(which means "son of encourage-ment"). [37]He sold a field that belonged to him, then brought the money, and laid it at the apostles' feet.

[5:1]But a man named Ananias, with the consent of his wife Sapphira, sold a piece of property; [2]with his wife's knowledge, he kept back some of the proceeds, and brought only a part and laid it at the apostles' feet. [3]"Ananias," Peter asked, "why has Satan filled your heart to lie to the Holy Spirit and to keep back part of the proceeds of the land? [4]While it remained unsold, did it not remain your own? And after it was sold, were not the proceeds at your disposal? How is it that you have contrived this deed in your heart? You did not lie to us but to God!" [5]Now when Ananias heard these words, he fell down and died. And great fear seized all who heard of it. [6]The young men came and wrapped up his body, then carried him out and buried him. [7]After an interval of about three hours his wife came in, not knowing what had happened. [8]Peter said to her, "Tell me whether you and your husband sold the land for such and such a price." And she said, "Yes, that was the price." [9]Then Peter said to her, "How is it that you have agreed together to put the Spirit of the Lord to the test? Look, the feet of those who have buried your husband are at the door, and they will carry you out." [10]Immediately she fell down at his feet and died. When the young men came in they found her dead, so they carried her out and buried her beside her husband.

nicknamed Barnabas (that is, "one who encourages"), was a Levite from Cyprus. [37]He owned a field, sold it, brought the money, and placed it in the care and under the authority of the apostles.

[5:1]However, a man named Ananias, along with his wife Sapphira, sold a piece of property. [2]With his wife's knowledge, he withheld some of the proceeds from the sale. He brought the rest and placed it in the care and under the authority of the apostles. [3]Peter asked, "Ananias, how is it that Satan has influenced you to lie to the Holy Spirit by withholding some of the proceeds from the sale of your land? [4]Wasn't that property yours to keep? After you sold it, wasn't the money yours to do with whatever you wanted? What made you think of such a thing? You haven't lied to other people but to God!" [5]When Ananias heard these words, he dropped dead. Everyone who heard this conversa-tion was terrified. [6]Some young men stood up, wrapped up his body, car-ried him out, and buried him.

[7]About three hours later, his wife entered, but she didn't know what had happened to her husband. [8]Peter asked her, "Tell me, did you and your husband receive this price for the field?"

She responded, "Yes, that's the amount."

[9]He replied, "How could you scheme with each other to challenge the Lord's Spirit? Look! The feet of those who buried your husband are at the door. They will carry you out too." [10]At that very moment, she dropped dead at his feet. When the young men entered and found her dead, they car-ried her out and buried her with her husband.

UNDERSTANDING THE SCRIPTURE

Acts 4:32-33. In the previous scene in Acts (4:23-31), the church prays for boldness after being threatened and ordered to cease proclaiming the resurrection of Jesus Christ. In turn, the church receives the gift of the Holy Spirit, symbolically manifested in an earthquake. Verses 32-33 transition from that scene to this week's lesson. Verse 33 shows the reader that the apostles were indeed emboldened by the Holy Spirit to continue proclaiming the resurrection; and verse 32 shows that the gift of the Holy Spirit has united the Jerusalem church as a whole, even to the point of sharing their possessions. This is not a new way of being church for Acts, but a reassertion of the very way the church was constituted after the Spirit was given at Pentecost (2:43-47).

Acts 4:34-35. Verses 34-35 unpack the sharing of possessions mentioned in verse 32 by describing the process by which this takes place: Whoever owned property sold it and laid the proceeds at the apostles' feet to be used so that no one in the church might be in need. The metaphor of laying something at another's feet implies the recognition of their authority—in other words, the proceeds are given to the apostles to be used for the needy in the community of faith as they saw fit.

Luke adapts the ethical principle that no one in the church should be needy from Deuteronomy 15:1-8, where Moses offers commandments about relieving debt and sharing possessions in the Promised Land. It is important to note at the beginning of this discussion, however, that the narrator is intentionally exaggerating the generosity in the Jerusalem church to present the church as an ideal expression of Jesus' commands in Luke 12:33 and 18:22. Otherwise, we would not have the story of Ananias and Sapphira.

Acts 4:36-37. Everyone in Acts may not share all of their possessions (for different reasons), but some do. Barnabas is offered as a positive example of the principle of giving all he has for the common good and the process of placing the proceeds from what he sells at the feet of the apostles. Because the value of his example is so self-evident, the author gives it only the briefest of descriptions compared with what follows in the text.

In truth, Luke spends as much energy introducing Barnabas to the reader in general—his ancestry as a Levite, the region from which he comes, and the meaning of his name—as he does describing his generosity. This is important for Luke because this is Barnabas's first appearance in Acts. He will show up again in chapters 11–15 as a mentor and missionary partner of Paul.

Moreover, Luke is incorrect in translating "Barnabas" to mean "son of encouragement." The name literally means "son of Nebo." But while the etymology may be wrong, the characterization is spot on: In both his generosity in this scene and his legitimizing of Paul's ministry later, Barnabas exemplifies the ethic of Christian encouragement of brothers and sisters in the faith.

Acts 5:1-6. Juxtaposed to Barnabas, Ananias and Sapphira serve as a negative example of the ethical principle of caring for the needy.

The scene is clearly intended to evoke shock. Divine retribution comes swiftly and harshly upon Ananias and Sapphira in the form of immediate death. But Luke likely never meant for his readers to take this story literally as history so much as offering a theological truth with emotional impact.

This interpretation can be seen in the fact that Luke's story is inspired by a story that would have been known to his original readers, that of Achan in Joshua 7. In giving the Israelites success over their enemies in battle, God commands the soldiers not to keep any of the booty from conquered cities for themselves. But Achan keeps and hides some riches he found in battle. In order to keep God's wrath from coming on the whole of the people, Achan's sin is revealed, and he is stoned to death. Luke takes the dynamics and core structure of this story and reshapes them for his theological purposes and his context of the church. Ananias and Sapphira try to hide possessions they have kept for themselves and are struck down in order to maintain unity in the church.

The initial actions of the couple parallel those of Barnabas—they sell property and lay proceeds from the sale at the feet of the apostles. They, however, lie about the proceeds, claiming that they have given all when they gave only a portion. Although Luke has described the practice of selling property and giving the proceeds to the church as the way of the church, in 5:4 Peter clarifies for the reader that such action was voluntary, not a requirement of membership in the community.

Ananias then is punished not for keeping some of the proceeds but for his deceit before Peter. It should also be noted that Peter does not punish Ananias; God does. Ananias's sin is against the Holy Spirit and thus God executes judgment.

Acts 5:7-10. When Sapphira appears before Peter, ignorant of her husband's punishment, Peter asks her if the proceeds (still lying at his feet) are the full sum of the sale. This may seem like a twisted trick to play on her, but it is not. In an ancient patriarchal context, usually the wife would simply be punished along with the husband for his crime. Here she is actually given a chance to save herself apart from the actions of Ananias.

But she has been complicit with the deceit from the beginning (see 5:1-2) and maintains the lie even now. Thus she also receives the same judgment her husband received. The metaphor of submitting to the authority of the Holy Spirit manifested in the leadership of the apostles by laying gifts of charity at their feet is now ironically literalized when her body falls at Peter's feet.

Acts 5:11. This concluding verse repeats the fear named in verse 5. We should be careful not to assume the fear is that of being killed so much as it is fear of the manifestation of the awesome power of God. After Jesus performed miracles, the response of the onlookers was often fear.

INTERPRETING THE SCRIPTURE

Generosity: A Mark of the Church

This passage is not concerned with charity directed toward the poor and marginalized in general. Luke is certainly concerned with this issue elsewhere.

In the Gospel of Luke, passage after passage emphasizes God's care for the poor and, conversely, divine judgment on the rich (for example, Luke 1:46-55; 4:16-21; 6:20-26; 14:12-24). In this week's passage, however, Luke is concerned with the issue of alleviating need *within the church*. When the author names the practice of sharing possessions in the church, he says, "There was not a needy person *among them*" (Acts 4:34, emphasis added; compare Deuteronomy 15:4). The image is not of a Roman Empire or even a Jerusalem that was free of poverty, but of a church that was free of need.

Acts 4:34 echoes the description of the church newly formed after Pentecost in 2:44-45: "All who believed were together and *had all things in common*; they would sell their possessions and goods and distribute the proceeds to all, as any had need" (emphasis added). In other words, sharing possessions to alleviate need was not a characteristic added to church life after the fact, even just a little time after the fact. For Luke, this practice was part and parcel of being church from the very beginning.

We should be careful not to translate this emphasis on sharing possessions within the church as any sort of call to isolationism within the church or as a defense for an attitude of "us, first; others second." Luke's dual emphasis on caring for the needy in the church and caring for the needy outside the church calls for a "both/and" ethic of generosity as opposed to an "either/or" or even a hierarchical approach to caring for those inside the church first and those outside the church second. To care for those outside the church, the church *must* be caring for those inside the community of faith.

Indeed, what is clear is that for Luke it is a violation of the very definition of what it means to be church if there are people who are in economic need within the community of faith. One of the many (but still essential) marks of the church is generosity within the community. If someone in the church is in need, the church is not being church.

This is quite a challenge to today's church (as it always has been; for example, see 1 Corinthians 11:17-22 and James 2:1-7) in which people of different socioeconomic statuses worship together. Calling ourselves sisters and brothers in the church is not to be sentimentalized. As siblings in Christ, we are charged with the care of our family. If we do not take care of one another, why would any outsider consider the gospel that we claim to have appeal?

We must recognize that our situation, however, is more complex than that pictured by Acts. We might be tempted to say our economic situation is more complex and thus it is harder or impractical for modern people to sell property and share those possessions within the church. But in truth this was the case in ancient times as much as now. The complexity instead is that in Luke's picture he is dealing only with the first church in Jerusalem. Today, the body of Christ is spread around the globe, includes hundreds of denominations, and has millions of members. How are we, all of us, to make sure there is no sister or brother who is needy in this worldwide communion of saints?

Generosity: A Gift of the Spirit

In our passage for this week, we are given to radically different examples of responses to the call of the church to sell our possessions, hold our goods in common, and ensure that none among us are needy. Barnabas responds positively and faithfully (4:36-37). Ananias and Sapphira respond negatively and deceitfully (5:1-10). Why do different Christians respond so differently?

In giving us a translation of Barnabas's name as meaning "son of encouragement" (4:36), Luke provides an answer. There is simply something about the character or personality of some people that makes them more generous than others. Barnabas gives all because he is a generous sort of person, and by extension Ananias and Sapphira hold back possessions because they are not. We certainly recognize these different personality types (and a spectrum of generosity in-between) in our own contemporary experience.

Luke also implies, however, that individual character is only a partial answer to why some in the church are generous and some are not. The church was originally formed as sharing possessions in common after Pentecost, when the Holy Spirit has been given to and gives birth to the church (2:37-47). Luke places this story after a second "Pentecost" of sorts when the church prays for boldness and is given the Holy Spirit again with the

sign of an earthquake (4:31). Moreover, Peter makes clear that Ananias and Sapphira's sin against the church is actually a sin against the Holy Spirit (5:3, 9). All of this is to say that generosity is as much a gift of the Holy Spirit given to the church as it is a quality of individual character. In sum, generosity and making sure no one in the community is needy is for Acts as powerful a sign of the Holy Spirit as tongues of fire, rushing winds, and earthquakes.

Generosity: More Than Giving From Excess

There is a reason we rarely hear this passage read during the annual financial stewardship drive. The way it pictures appropriate giving in the church is radical. Acts is not concerned with simply dropping a few extra bucks in the offering plate. It is concerned with more than fulfilling a pledge and even more than tithing. Barnabas does not give 10 percent. He gives 100 percent.

Given the ideal picture of the church in 4:34 and the exaggerated nature of 4:34–5:10 as a whole, we need not take this passage as a literal call to sell our homes, live in Christian communes, and share all in common. But neither should we diminish the fact that the passage calls us to something more radical than that with which we are comfortable. Barnabas serves as a model and Ananias and Sapphira as a warning that we need to rethink generosity as more than simply giving out of our excess.

The reason Barnabas and those like him could give to the church so that no one in the community would be needy is that the flip side of this meant that the church would meet all their needs as well. In today's world, we must, as much as possible, be generous in a way that we can still care for our own needs.

Yet this text calls us to a level of generosity that is a giving of ourselves, not just a portion of our abundance that we hardly notice we gave away. It calls us to think about the difference between what we desire and what we need. We often confuse the two and thus convince ourselves that we need to hold on to more than we do. When we are willing to consider our generosity by comparing what we desire with what others in the church need, Acts calls us to ask of ourselves, "Am I a daughter/son of encouragement, or am I a child of Ananias and Sapphira?"

SHARING THE SCRIPTURE

PREPARING TO TEACH

Preparing Our Hearts

Ponder this week's devotional reading from Isaiah 1:15-18. This passage comes within the context of prophecy concerning the futility of making sacrificial offerings when injustice abounds. What do the people need to do to be right before God? What words of judgment and hope do you hear in verse 18? What is God saying to you through this passage?

Pray that you and the students will seek justice and care for those who are vulnerable.

Preparing Our Minds

Study the background Scripture from Acts 4:32–5:11 and the lesson Scripture from Acts 4:34–5:10.

Consider this question as you prepare the lesson: *What enables people to give up what is theirs for the good of someone else?*

Write on newsprint:

❏ information for next week's lesson, found under Continue the Journey.

❏ activities for further spiritual growth in Continue the Journey.

Review the Introduction, The Big Picture, Close-up, and Faith in Action, which all precede the first lesson of this quarter. Consider how you might use any of this material in today's lesson.

LEADING THE CLASS

(1) Gather to Learn

❖ Welcome the class members and guests.

❖ Pray that those who have come today will consider how they might share with those in need.

❖ **Option:** Continue introducing the lessons for the fall quarter by finishing The Big Picture: Luke–Acts if you were unable to do so last week.

❖ Post a sheet of newsprint and list answers to this question: **How does our congregation share food, clothing, shelter, and other essentials with those in need?** Think of programs within the church that may help both members and non-members. Consider ecumenical or community programs to which your church contributes volunteers, goods, or money. Also add programs that individual church members may participate in to help those in need.

(Leave the paper posted for use later in the session.)

❖ Read aloud today's focus statement: **Although there are exceptions, most people are glad to share what they have with those in need. What is it that enables people to give up what is theirs for the good of someone else? The early followers of Jesus shared everything with one another, and, although some acted deceitfully and were punished as a result, there was not a needy person among them.**

(2) Goal 1: Understand the Sacrifices and Rewards that Come From the Early Christians' Willingness to Share Possessions With Others

❖ Introduce today's passage by reading Acts 4:32-33, which transitions from last week's lesson to this week's.

❖ Choose one volunteer to read Acts 4:34-37 and another to read Acts 5:1-10.

❖ Discuss these questions:

1. **What does Luke tell us about Barnabas?** (See Acts 4:36-37 in Understanding the Scripture.)
2. **Why are Ananias and Sapphira struck down?** (See Acts 5:1-6, 7-10 in Understanding the Scripture.)
3. **What role does the Holy Spirit play in this passage?** (See "Generosity: A Gift of the Spirit" in Interpreting the Scripture.)
4. **What lessons does this story offer to today's church?** (See "Generosity: More Than Giving from Excess" in Interpreting the Scripture.)
5. **How might you as an individual and as part of the community of faith practice these lessons?**

(3) Goal 2: Examine One's Motivation for Making Sacrificial Offerings that Benefit the Larger Community

❖ Distribute pencil and papers. Tell the group that you will read the following list of reasons that some people may cite for giving sacrificially. The adults are to write down any reasons that describe their own motivations. Urge them to be honest, since they will not be asked to reveal specifics about themselves.

1. **Help people meet their basic needs.**
2. **Get a good tax write-off.**
3. **Improve the community.**
4. **Assist students in getting an education.**
5. **Support the arts.**
6. **Show others how generous I am.**
7. **Support my church as a way to show love and gratitude to Jesus.**
8. **Give back to an organization that has helped me.**

❖ Ask: **Which of these reasons, along with any others that you can think of, would be appropriate reasons for a Christian to give? Why? Which of these reasons, along with others, would be inappropriate? Why?**

❖ Conclude by reading "Generosity: A Mark of the Church" from Interpreting the Scripture. Read again this sentence: **"If someone in the church is in need, the church is not being church."** Ask: **How might the motivations for believers' giving change if they more clearly understood that God is the owner (Psalm 24:1) and they are stewards who are responsible for taking care of God's household?**

(4) Goal 3: Encourage Others to Contribute to a Community Project

❖ Refer to the list of ideas generated during the Gather to Learn segment. Take time to ensure that everyone knows about each of the programs listed. Encourage people who volunteer for any of these programs to give information about the project and tell how it impacts both those in need and those who volunteer.

❖ Enlist additional volunteers by asking those who may be interested to raise their hands so that you can write their names next to the appropriate programs. If possible, link a prospective volunteer with one who is currently active. Encourage volunteers to take steps to become involved.

(5) Continue the Journey

❖ Pray that as the learners depart, they will be aware of people in need and reach out to them.

❖ Post information for next week's session on newsprint for the students to copy:

- **Title: Witnessing to the Truth**
- **Background Scripture: Acts 5:12-42**
- **Lesson Scripture: Acts 5:27-29, 33-42**
- **Focus of the Lesson: Sometimes people are so dedicated to a cause that they will go to any lengths, even enduring pain and suffering, to achieve their goals. What is the source of their commitment? As the apostles continued to teach about Jesus as the Messiah and to help many people become** believers, they knew, even though the authorities tried to stop them, that they were obeying God's calling rather than any human authority.

❖ Post the following information on newsprint and provide paper and pencils for the students to copy it. Challenge the adults to grow spiritually by completing one or more of these activities related to this week's session.

(1) **Place a coin bank on the table where you eat. Make a pledge to put a certain amount of money in the bank for at least one meal. Encourage everyone in the household to also make a pledge. After a specified time, give this money to a program that benefits people who are in need.**

(2) **Hold a yard sale. Plan in advance to donate a certain amount or percentage of sales to a church-sponsored program that assists people in need.**

(3) **Take a homeless person to lunch. If you live in an urban area, you may be accustomed to being asked for money. Instead of handing out cash, take someone in need to lunch at a nearby eatery. Fellowship with this person over a simple meal and listen to his or her story.**

❖ Sing or read aloud "Where Cross the Crowded Ways of Life."

❖ Conclude today's session by leading the class in this benediction, which is adapted from Acts 9:20, the key verse for October 11: **Let us go forth to boldly proclaim that Jesus is the Son of God. Amen.**

UNIT 1: SEEDS OF NEW GROWTH
WITNESSING TO THE TRUTH

PREVIEWING THE LESSON

Lesson Scripture: Acts 5:27-29, 33-42
Background Scripture: Acts 5:12-42
Key Verse: Acts 5:29

Focus of the Lesson:
Sometimes people are so dedicated to a cause that they will go to any lengths, even enduring pain and suffering, to achieve their goals. What is the source of their commitment? As the apostles continued to teach about Jesus as the Messiah and to help many people become believers, they knew, even though the authorities tried to stop them, that they were obeying God's calling rather than any human authority.

Goals for the Learners:
(1) to study the apostles' proclamation of Jesus as the Messiah, despite being ordered not to do so by the Sanhedrin.
(2) to compare their commitments to witnessing to that of the apostles.
(3) to identify and overcome barriers to evangelism efforts within and beyond the church community.

Supplies:
Bibles, newsprint and marker, paper and pencils, hymnals

READING THE SCRIPTURE

NRSV
Lesson Scripture: Acts 5:27-29, 33-42

27When they [the Temple police] had brought them [Peter and the other apostles], they had them stand before the council. The high priest questioned them, 28saying, "We gave you strict orders not to teach in this name, yet here you have filled Jerusalem with

CEB
Lesson Scripture: Acts 5:27-29, 33-42

27The apostles were brought before the council where the high priest confronted them: 28"In no uncertain terms, we demanded that you not teach in this name. And look at you! You have filled Jerusalem with your teaching. And you are determined your teaching and you are determined to bring this man's blood on us." **²⁹But Peter and the apostles answered, "We must obey God rather than any human authority."**

³³When they heard this, they were enraged and wanted to kill them. ³⁴But a Pharisee in the council named Gamaliel, a teacher of the law, respected by all the people, stood up and ordered the men to be put outside for a short time. ³⁵Then he said to them, "Fellow Israelites, consider carefully what you propose to do to these men. ³⁶For some time ago Theudas rose up, claiming to be somebody, and a number of men, about four hundred, joined him; but he was killed, and all who followed him were dispersed and disappeared. ³⁷After him Judas the Galilean rose up at the time of the census and got people to follow him; he also perished, and all who followed him were scattered. ³⁸So in the present case, I tell you, keep away from these men and let them alone; because if this plan or this undertaking is of human origin, it will fail; ³⁹but if it is of God, you will not be able to overthrow them— in that case you may even be found fighting against God!"

They were convinced by him, ⁴⁰and when they had called in the apostles, they had them flogged. Then they ordered them not to speak in the name of Jesus, and let them go. ⁴¹As they left the council, they rejoiced that they were considered worthy to suffer dishonor for the sake of the name. ⁴²And every day in the temple and at home they did not cease to teach and proclaim Jesus as the Messiah.

to hold us responsible for this man's death."

²⁹Peter and the apostles replied, "We must obey God rather than humans!"

³³When the council members heard this, they became furious and wanted to kill the apostles. ³⁴One council member, a Pharisee and teacher of the Law named Gamaliel, well-respected by all the people, stood up and ordered that the men be taken outside for a few moments. ³⁵He said, "Fellow Israelites, consider carefully what you intend to do to these people. ³⁶Some time ago, Theudas appeared, claiming to be somebody, and some four hundred men joined him. After he was killed, all of his followers scattered, and nothing came of that. ³⁷Afterward, at the time of the census, Judas the Galilean appeared and got some people to follow him in a revolt. He was killed too, and all his followers scattered far and wide. ³⁸Here's my recommendation in this case: Distance yourselves from these men. Let them go! If their plan or activity is of human origin, it will end in ruin. ³⁹If it originates with God, you won't be able to stop them. Instead, you would actually find yourselves fighting God!" The council was convinced by his reasoning. ⁴⁰After calling the apostles back, they had them beaten. They ordered them not to speak in the name of Jesus, then let them go. ⁴¹The apostles left the council rejoicing because they had been regarded as worthy to suffer disgrace for the sake of the name. ⁴²Every day they continued to teach and proclaim the good news that Jesus is the Christ, both in the temple and in houses.

UNDERSTANDING THE SCRIPTURE

Introduction. Acts 5:12-42 resembles the pattern of 4:1-31—the apostles' ministry in the Temple results in their arrest; the religious leaders confront and threaten the apostles; the apostles reject the authority of the leaders; and the apostles proclaim the gospel. The story here, however, is not simply a rerun of the earlier story. New elements are added that advance Luke's narrative and theology.

Acts 5:12-16. This summary of the success of the apostles' public ministry shows that they manifest the boldness for which they prayed and received in 4:23-31 (see the lesson for September 6). The note in 5:13—that not all the believers would join the apostles in the Temple—shows that Luke has a realistic view of the church. Boldness and passion in ministry are held by some but not by all.

Acts 5:17-26. As in 4:1-3, the apostles are arrested and held in custody overnight, awaiting a hearing the next day. In this scene, however, God frees the apostles. Such miraculous escape from prison is a common motif in Acts (compare 12:1-11; 16:16-34). God does not free them to escape persecution, but to return to their public ministry in the Temple as an even stronger witness to the gospel when they are discovered and rearrested.

Acts 5:27-29. The hearing opens with the high priest announcing the charges against the defendants (5:27-28): They have disobeyed the prohibition the council gave them (in 4:17-21) to discontinue teaching in "this name" (note how the high priest avoids even mentioning Jesus' name). This accusation does two important things. First, it confirms the boldness and success of the apostles' ministry

in that Jerusalem has been filled with their teaching. Second, it names a primary motivation for the leaders' opposition to the apostles in Luke's narrative: The apostles blame those leaders for Jesus' death (for example, see 5:30).

With the accusation announced, the apostles make their defense. They do not, however, claim to be innocent. Their response has two parts. First, in verse 29, they reject the authority of the council and claim explicitly to be acting on God's authority, repeating the assertion they made in 4:19. This is the central theological claim of the scene, and one that echoes throughout Acts in different ways every time the church is persecuted.

Acts 5:30-32. The second part of the apostles' response is a restatement of the core message of the church. Preaching follows a standard form in most of Acts: You crucified him, God raised him, and we are witnesses (compare 3:13-15).

Acts 5:33-40. Following the accusation and "defense," the council deliberates the case. Since they serve as both prosecution and judge (and the apostles responded to the accusation by rejecting their authority and offering a counter-accusation that the leaders killed Jesus), it is no wonder that their immediate reaction is one of outrage and a desire to declare a death sentence (5:33).

Gamaliel, however, steps up to offer a word of caution (5:33-39a). A Pharisaic member of the council known as the Sanhedrin, Gamaliel is later referenced as a teacher of Paul (22:3), whose first appearance in the Acts narrative is as a persecutor of the church (7:58–8:3). This characterization warns us not to consider Gamaliel's prudence as evidence that he recognizes God at work in the church.

Gamaliel offers a comparison of the movement in Jesus' name to movements centered on the messianic pretenders, Theudas and Judas the Galilean. While these were historical figures, a comparison with references to them made by the first-century Jewish historian Josephus (*Antiquities* 20.97-98 and *The Jewish War* 2.117-18; 7:252-53) shows that Luke may have had some facts about them incorrect. For example, Judas likely preceded Theudas by a few decades; and Theudas's revolt was in the mid-40s of the first century, some ten years after this incident in the council supposedly occurred. Historical errors aside, the analogy Luke presents Gamaliel as employing is clear. As with these other two movements, if the church is not of God, it will fail. If it is of God, the council will be opposing God by opposing the apostles.

What should not be missed is that Gamaliel clearly assumes the movement in Jesus' name is *not* of God. The implication, then, is that the council need not execute the apostles because the movement will die on its own. Ironically, Gamaliel's speech and the council's decision not to execute the apostles confirm that the movement is of God and give witness to the truth of the apostles' claim in verse 29.

Acts 5:41-42. The irony of the scene continues with the closing lines. Instead of bemoaning their arrest, hearing, flogging, and further prohibition, the apostles leave rejoicing (5:41). They do not celebrate that they survived the persecution but that they were persecuted in the first place, that is, that they were worthy to suffer for Jesus' name. The confidence Luke expresses in God's providential direction guiding the church and its ministry in no way translates into a view of protectionism on God's part. Luke is a realist. Persecution at the hands of the powers that be is evidence that the church is doing God's will. If those Luke considered responsible for killing Jesus ignored the church, it would be a sign indicating the opposite. Thus their ministry is sparked on to continued boldness (5:42).

Note how the scene ends: with the narrator declaring that the apostles ceaselessly proclaim Jesus as the Christ. In Greek the very last word of the scene is "Jesus." This is an intentional placement given that the dispute of the case all along has been about the apostles teaching in his name (see 5:28, 40). While on the surface level the scene is about the boldness and obedience of the apostles as heroes of the faith over against the council, underneath it is through and through about Jesus as the leader and savior of the people over against human authorities. The church is simply an instrument of Jesus' ministry in the world.

INTERPRETING THE SCRIPTURE

Jesus as a Threat

When we interpret Luke's portrayal of the Sanhedrin, we must be careful to avoid falling into the unconscious pitfall of anti-Semitism that has characterized much of the interpretation of the persecution of Jesus and the early

Christians throughout the history of the church. Luke does not present the council as a group of Jews persecuting non-Jews. The council of Jewish leaders is exercising their authority over Jews (the apostles). As Luke makes clear, the earliest Christians who proclaimed Jesus to be the crucified and risen Christ did not abandon their Judaism. They (like Jesus) still viewed themselves as Jews, still worshiped in the Temple, and still gathered with the synagogue. So the conflict in this scene is not Jew versus Christian.

It is a conflict over power and influence. The apostles' healing and teaching in the name of Jesus is gathering a community of Jews under Jesus' authority instead of under the Jewish leaders' authority. The apostles constantly reminding the people that the religious and political power structures in Jerusalem killed Jesus (through the Roman means of crucifixion) takes more power away from these Jewish leaders.

Paradoxically, then, proclaiming Jesus as the crucified and risen Lord is itself the primary barrier to proclaiming Jesus as the crucified and risen Lord. This is so because the good news of God's liberating love made manifest in the good news of Jesus Christ is always a threat to the power structures in society. Near the beginning of Luke–Acts, Mary announces in the Magnificat that lifting up the lowly entails bringing down the powerful from their thrones (Luke 1:51-53). In the Sermon on the Plain, Jesus not only blesses the poor, hungry, and weeping but also curses the rich, filled, and laughing (Luke 6:20-26).

Those who carry such a message of salvation to the world in the name of Jesus Christ should expect resistance, even persecution. Either end of the response spectrum—throngs of people accepting our message or masses of people ignoring us—shows that we are not speaking the full gospel with boldness, that we are not, as they say, comforting the afflicted *and* afflicting the comfortable in Jesus' name.

The Church's Leader

As previously stated, when studying The Acts of the Apostles, it is important to remember that it is the second volume of Luke's narrative (often referred to in scholarly shorthand as Luke–Acts). The story of Acts is a continuation of the story of the Gospel of Luke. In other words, the church's story is the second half of the story of Jesus. Thus, while in one sense Acts focuses on the faith, teaching, and works of the apostles (especially Peter and Paul), it is at a deeper level still about the works of Jesus as the risen Christ. Every time the Spirit-filled apostles (or those they appoint) preach the gospel, baptize someone into the faith, or perform a miracle, it is Jesus Christ at work.

In today's scene Luke makes explicit the fact that the apostles recognize that this is the case. As has been the case already in Acts (3:12-16; 4:7-12) the apostles claim not to be acting on their own initiative. Their ministry is authorized by Jesus. Indeed, we can go a step further and say that for Luke, their ministry is Jesus' ministry.

This is why Luke emphasizes the issue of the apostles teaching *in Jesus' name* (Acts 5:28, 40, 41; for other such references in Luke–Acts leading up to this scene, see also Luke 9:48, 49; 10:17; 13:35; 21:8, 12, 17; 24:47; Acts 2:21, 38; 3:6, 16; 4:7, 10, 17, 18, 30). In the ancient world, a servant or messenger had no authority to act on his own. A servant carrying a message from his master could not embellish or interpret the message but only repeat it. The messenger spoke in the master's name. Such is the view Luke has of the apostles' ministry in Acts. They speak and act not of their own accord but in Jesus' name, that is, as subordinate emissaries of Jesus.

Luke's view of the church in this sense is idealistic, and he knows this. Clearly, the early church took initiative as it found its voice and mission in the early post-Easter period. Luke does not present God as a puppeteer controlling everything that happens in the world or even in the life of the church. The ideal of the church's ministry being Jesus' ministry is one Luke offers as a theological model for his readers more than a historical record of the early years of the church.

We would do well to measure the church's life today by this theological standard. Are our beliefs, words, and actions an extension of the ministry of Jesus Christ, or are they really assertions of our self-preservation, our status, our values declared in Jesus' name? Is it significantly easier to look at Christians on the other side of the conservative-progressive divide or in other denominations with different doctrinal and ethical commitments, and point out the ways their proclamation and practices do not accord with the good news of Jesus Christ than it is to see the flaws in our own thinking, speech, and behavior? But we, like those with whom we disagree (well, like everyone) are flawed and sinful creatures. Thus we cannot trust our own judgment of ourselves.

As with Luke's ideal that the apostles were simply continuing Jesus' ministry in new circumstances, so must we constantly strive to align ourselves and our ministries to continue Christ's saving work in our circumstances. Acts portrays different offices and leaders in the church (for example, the twelve apostles, the seven assistants to the apostles [6:1-17], James as leader of the Jerusalem church [12:17], and Barnabas and Paul as missionaries [13:2-3]). But the author of Luke–Acts would agree with the author of Colossians that the only head of the church is Christ (Colossians 1:18). We may fail, but in anything and everything we do as the church we strive to perpetuate Jesus' ministry in the world, speaking and doing only that which we as Jesus' messengers are instructed to do.

The Church's Commitment

Luke presents the apostles in Acts 5:12-42 as never stopping to weigh the cost of their commitment to the gospel of Jesus Christ. They have simply been commissioned by Christ to be his witnesses in Jerusalem, Judea, Samaria, and to the ends of the earth (1:8); and like any servant-messenger of the ancient world, they do not question their orders. Their obedience to the authority of their master is absolute (5:29).

Luke, however, presents others in the church as holding a lower level of commitment. In 5:13, the narrator tells us that "none of the rest dared join" the apostles teaching in the Temple. To judge these early Christians too harshly for their fear would be to minimize the reality of the persecution they faced. Luke includes this notice not to condemn these members of the church but to lift up by way of contrast the faith and commitment of the apostles.

We are likely more often than not more like those afraid to represent Christ in troubling arenas than we are like the apostles. This is exactly why Luke offers the apostles to his readers as ideals. They are the models of evangelism toward which we strive, even if we never reach the goal fully.

SHARING THE SCRIPTURE

PREPARING TO TEACH

Preparing Our Hearts

Ponder this week's devotional reading from Revelation 22:1-7. As you read this passage, what can you see, hear, taste, touch, or feel? What would you expect life to be like near this "river of the water of life" (22:1)? Give thanks for this vision of life in the kingdom of God.

Pray that you and the students will believe the trustworthy and true words of the Lord.

Preparing Our Minds

Study the background Scripture from Acts 5:12-42 and the lesson Scripture from Acts 5:27-29, 33-42.

Consider this question as you prepare the lesson: *What is the source of the commitment of people who are so dedicated to a cause that they will go to any lengths, even enduring pain and suffering, to achieve their goals?*

Write on newsprint:

❏ information for next week's lesson, found under Continue the Journey.
❏ activities for further spiritual growth in Continue the Journey.

Review the Introduction, The Big Picture, Close-up, and Faith in Action, which all precede the first lesson of this quarter. Consider how you might use any of this material in today's lesson.

Use information from Understanding the Scripture (Introduction through Acts 5:17-26) to create a brief lecture to introduce today's Scripture lesson.

Prepare a written list of missionaries who work in hostile environments. Include names and contact information. Enlist help from your pastor or chairperson of your congregation's mission committee, or check your denomination's mission website. For example, United Methodist missionaries may be found here: www.umcmission.org/Explore-Our-Work/Missionaries-in-Service.

LEADING THE CLASS

(1) Gather to Learn

❖ Welcome the class members and guests.

❖ Pray that those who have come today will be willing to witness on behalf of Christ, no matter what the cost.

❖ Post the written list of missionaries you have created, or distribute copies of a list you have photocopied. Explain that you have listed missionaries who work in environments that are hostile to the Christian message, perhaps due to the politics of the area or a lack of religious freedom. Note that although the circumstances may be quite different, these missionaries are as dedicated to Christ and his church as the first apostles were. Provide a few moments of silence for class members to pray silently for at least one of the missionaries on the list.

❖ Read aloud today's focus statement: **Sometimes people are so dedicated to a cause that they will go to any lengths, even enduring pain and suffering, to achieve their goals. What is the source of their commitment? As the apostles continued to teach about Jesus as the Messiah and to help many people become believers, they knew, even though the authorities tried to stop them, that they were obeying God's calling rather than any human authority.**

(2) Goal 1: Study the Apostles' Proclamation of Jesus as the Messiah, Despite Being Ordered Not to Do So by the Sanhedrin

❖ Present the introductory lecture that you have prepared to set the stage for today's Scripture lesson. Pay special attention to what the apostles said and did that caused the Jewish authorities to persecute them.

❖ Select two volunteers, one to read Acts 5:27-29 and another to read verses 33-42.

❖ Discuss these questions:

1. **Why did the Jewish leadership perceive teaching about Jesus to be such a threat?** (See "Jesus as a Threat" in Interpreting the Scripture.)
2. **When the high priest questioned the apostles as to why they continued to preach Jesus even after they had been ordered not to, Peter replied that they must obey God, not human authority. Although the council would have agreed in principle with Peter's statement, what kinds of red flags**

does Peter's insistence that he obey God raise for the Jewish leadership?
3. **How would you answer our writer's question: "Are our beliefs, words, and actions an extension of the ministry of Jesus, or are they really assertions of our self-preservation, our status, our values declared in Jesus' name?"** (See "The Church's Leader" in Interpreting the Scripture.)
4. **How might the apostles have answered this same question?**

(3) Goal 2: Compare the Learners' Commitments to Witnessing to That of the Apostles

❖ Read "The Church's Commitment" in Interpreting the Scripture. Note that even though all believers did not witness with the boldness of the apostles, people supported the apostles by holding them "in high esteem" (Acts 5:13).

❖ Ask: **Based on today's passage from Acts, how would you describe the commitment of Peter and the other apostles?**

❖ Distribute paper and pencils. Invite the learners to write words or phrases to describe their own commitment to witnessing for Christ. You may wish to read these sample descriptors: *bold, timid, willing to speak truth to power, able to stand my ground, ready to back down at the first sign of a challenge.*

❖ Discuss these questions:

1. **What lessons can you learn from the apostles?**
2. **What changes will you try to make in order to be a bolder, more effective witness?**

(4) Goal 3: Identify and Overcome Barriers to Evangelism Efforts Within and Without the Church Community

❖ Form small groups and give each one a sheet of newsprint and marker. Ask each group to answer this question: **What obstacles do believers today face as they attempt to witness on behalf of Jesus?** Suggest that the groups think about obstacles encountered in countries where freedom of religion exists, as well as those places where one's religious beliefs are narrowly circumscribed.

❖ Call time and ask each group now to discuss ways that at least two of the obstacles can be overcome.

❖ Call time again and invite representatives from each group to report on their ideas.

❖ Ask: **How can we as a congregation use these ideas to help our members witness more boldly for Christ?**

(5) Continue the Journey

❖ Pray that as the learners depart, they will feel empowered by the apostles' story to witness boldly for Christ.

❖ Post information for next week's session on newsprint for the students to copy:

- **Title: Remembering God's Faithfulness**
- **Background Scripture: Acts 7:1-55**
- **Lesson Scripture: Acts 7:2-4, 8-10, 17, 33-34, 44-47, 53**
- **Focus of the Lesson: People will defend against all criticism of their beliefs, even if their defense is life-threatening. How do people stand up to such perilous criticism?**

When Stephen spoke to his accusers in the council, he summarized the history of God's faithfulness to the Israelites and then challenged the council members for not keeping the law themselves.

❖ Post the following information on newsprint and provide paper and pencils for the students to copy it. Challenge the adults to grow spiritually by completing one or more of these activities related to this week's session.

(1) **Look at the hymn "Stand Up, Stand Up for Jesus." Write another verse to this hymn using ideas from today's Bible passage to urge people to be bold witnesses for Christ. Sing or say this verse each day this week.**

(2) **Write a note to a missionary identified in the "Gather to Learn" portion. Encourage this person to remain bold and faithful while witnessing for Christ.**

(3) **Read about Christian witnesses who were persecuted for their faith. What traits and commitments do these people exhibit? Which of these traits and commitments do you share?**

❖ Sing or read aloud "God of Love and God of Power."

❖ Conclude today's session by leading the class in this benediction, which is adapted from Acts 9:20, the key verse for October 11: **Let us go forth to boldly proclaim that Jesus is the Son of God. Amen.**

UNIT 1: SEEDS OF NEW GROWTH

REMEMBERING GOD'S FAITHFULNESS

PREVIEWING THE LESSON

Lesson Scripture: Acts 7:2-4, 8-10, 17, 33-34, 44-47, 53
Background Scripture: Acts 7:1-55
Key Verse: Acts 7:55

Focus of the Lesson:
People will defend against all criticism of their beliefs, even if their defense is life-threatening. How do people stand up to such perilous criticism? When Stephen spoke to his accusers in the council, he summarized the history of God's faithfulness to the Israelites and then challenged the council members for not keeping the law themselves.

Goals for the Learners:
(1) to hear Stephen's proclamation before the council in which he reminded those present of God's faithfulness through the ages and their disregard of God's law.
(2) to reflect on their willingness to stand firm on their beliefs in the midst of life's threatening circumstances.
(3) to commit to stand for beliefs about God in all circumstances.

Supplies:
Bibles, newsprint and marker, paper and pencils, hymnals

READING THE SCRIPTURE

NRSV
Lesson Scripture: Acts 7:2-4, 8-10, 17, 33-34, 44-47, 53, 55 (key verse)

²And Stephen replied:

"Brothers and fathers, listen to me. The God of glory appeared to our ancestor Abraham when he was in Mesopotamia, before he lived in

CEB
Lesson Scripture: Acts 7:2-4, 8-10, 17, 33-34, 44-47, 53, 55 (key verse)

²Stephen responded, "Brothers and fathers, listen to me. Our glorious God appeared to our ancestor Abraham while he was still in Mesopotamia, before he settled in Haran. ³God

Haran, [3]and said to him, 'Leave your country and your relatives and go to the land that I will show you.' [4]Then he left the country of the Chaldeans and settled in Haran. After his father died, God had him move from there to this country in which you are now living. . . .[8]Then he gave him the covenant of circumcision. And so Abraham became the father of Isaac and circumcised him on the eighth day; and Isaac became the father of Jacob, and Jacob of the twelve patriarchs.

[9]"The patriarchs, jealous of Joseph, sold him into Egypt; but God was with him, [10]and rescued him from all his afflictions, and enabled him to win favor and to show wisdom when he stood before Pharaoh, king of Egypt, who appointed him ruler over Egypt and over all his household.

[17]"But as the time drew near for the fulfillment of the promise that God had made to Abraham, our people in Egypt increased and multiplied."

[33]Then the Lord said to him [Moses], 'Take off the sandals from your feet, for the place where you are standing is holy ground. [34]I have surely seen the mistreatment of my people who are in Egypt and have heard their groaning, and I have come down to rescue them. Come now, I will send you to Egypt.'

[44]"Our ancestors had the tent of testimony in the wilderness, as God directed when he spoke to Moses, ordering him to make it according to the pattern he had seen. [45]Our ancestors in turn brought it in with Joshua when they dispossessed the nations that God drove out before our ancestors. And it was there until the time of David, [46]who found favor with God and asked that he might find a dwelling place for the house of Jacob. [47]But it was Solomon who built a house for him.

told him, 'Leave your homeland and kin, and go to the land that I will show you.' [4]So Abraham left the land of the Chaldeans and settled in Haran. After Abraham's father died, God had him resettle in this land where you now live. . . .[8]God gave him the covenant confirmed through circumcision. Accordingly, eight days after Isaac's birth, Abraham circumcised him. Isaac did the same with Jacob, and Jacob with the twelve patriarchs.

[9]"Because the patriarchs were jealous of Joseph, they sold him into slavery in Egypt. God was with him, however, [10]and rescued him from all his troubles. The grace and wisdom he gave Joseph were recognized by Pharaoh, king of Egypt, who appointed him ruler over Egypt and over his whole palace.

[17]"When it was time for God to keep the promise he made to Abraham, the number of our people in Egypt had greatly expanded.

[33][Speaking to Moses] The Lord continued, *'Remove the sandals from your feet, for the place where you are standing is holy ground. [34]I have clearly seen the oppression my people have experienced in Egypt, and I have heard their groaning. I have come down to rescue them. Come! I am sending you to Egypt.'*

[44]"The tent of testimony was with our ancestors in the wilderness. Moses built it just as he had been instructed by the one who spoke to him and according to the pattern he had seen. [45]In time, when they had received the tent, our ancestors carried it with them when, under Joshua's leadership, they took possession of the land from the nations whom God expelled. This tent remained in the land until the time of David. [46]God approved of David, who asked that he might provide a dwelling place for the God of

53You are the ones that received the law as ordained by angels, and yet you have not kept it."

55But filled with the Holy Spirit, he [Stephen] gazed into heaven and saw the glory of God and Jesus standing at the right hand of God.

Jacob. 47But it was Solomon who actually built a house for God.

53You received the Law given by angels, but you haven't kept it."

55But Stephen, enabled by the Holy Spirit, stared into heaven and saw God's majesty and Jesus standing at God's right side.

UNDERSTANDING THE SCRIPTURE

Introduction. Stephen's speech is a response to accusations made against him by those he bested in a religious debate with fellow Jews in the synagogue (6:8-15). The false charges were that he blasphemed and claimed Jesus would destroy the Temple and alter the Mosaic law (6:11, 13-14). The charge concerning the Temple is especially striking, given that by the time Luke wrote Acts, the Temple had been destroyed by the Romans in A.D. 70. As a result of the charges, Stephen is brought to trial before the Sanhedrin, the same council that tried Peter and the apostles in chapters 4 and 5. This time, however, the one on trial is not released with a warning; he is stoned and becomes the first Christian martyr.

Stephen does not explicitly defend himself. Instead, in a very complex recitation of God's history with Israel, he sets the current moment of the church as the culmination of God's actions in history and turns the charges back on those who reject Jesus. In the course of doing this, he also subtly refutes the accusations made against him.

Acts 7:1-8. Stephen's account of God's history with Israel naturally begins with Abraham. Abraham, as one who trusted in God's promise of land and descendants, stands

as a model over against Stephen's accusers who do not recognize God as fulfilling promises God has made in Jesus as the Messiah. The account of Abraham's history ends with circumcision as the sign of the covenant between God and Abraham. The note serves two purposes in the speech: First, it shows that Stephen is still invested in the customs passed on by Moses (6:14) and second, it sets up the counter-accusation by Stephen when he calls his Temple audience "uncircumcised" (7:51).

Acts 7:9-16. Having placed Abraham in the Promised Land as a resident alien, Stephen next gets Israel into Egypt with the story of Joseph being sold into slavery but rising to a position of prominence and power. Stephen claims the biblical story as his own (as opposed to rejecting his heritage in the way in which he is accused), by speaking of those in the past as *"our* ancestors" (7:11, 12, 15, 19, 38, 39, 44, 45, emphasis added).

Acts 7:17-43. The longest section of the speech deals with the story of Moses, the Exodus, and the giving of the law. This length is appropriate given that this story is the paradigmatic moment of Israel's salvation history and that Stephen has specifically been accused of speaking blasphemy against Moses.

Stephen opens the story of Moses by describing the advent of God fulfilling God's promise to Abraham (7:17). The long-delayed, yet fulfilled, promise is a key theological emphasis of the speech.

The recitation of the story proceeds in the following order: Moses was saved from childhood death (7:17-22); Moses was rejected by Israelites and fled Egypt (7:23-29, compare verse 35); God called Moses to return to Egypt as an instrument through which God would liberate the Israelites, lead the Israelites into the wilderness, and give them the law at Sinai (7:30-38); the Israelites rejected Moses again, they worshiped an idol, and God turned them over to their worship (7:39-43). A key line in this recitation is verse 37 where Moses said to the Israelites that God will *raise* up a prophet as God *raised* Moses up (a quotation from Deuteronomy 18:15; this line was quoted earlier by Peter in 3:22). In the context of Deuteronomy, this promise clearly refers to Joshua who leads Israel after Moses' death. (Joshua appears in the speech in Acts 7:45.) But in the context of Acts and Luke's post-resurrection theology, the language of being "raised" shows that Luke understands this as a long-awaited, now-fulfilled promise referring to Jesus as a prophet like Moses. (For places where Luke refers to Jesus as a prophet, see Luke 4:24; 7:16, 39; 13:33; 24:19).

Acts 7:44-50. The last segment of Stephen's historical recitation jumps over generations of Israel to focus on the Temple. Stephen does not disregard the Temple but knows and respects its history. Having honored Israel's history from Abraham through Moses to the Temple in which he stands, Stephen has implicitly defended himself against the false charges made against him. But the last piece of historical remembrance sets up another move in Stephen's speech.

He concludes his section on the Temple by quoting Scripture (Isaiah 66:1-2), asserting that God does not dwell in the Temple (7:48-50) as a way of making the point that those who have authority over the Temple do not have authority over God. The implication is that the Sanhedrin does have not the authority to determine whether the messianic movement is "of God" (see 5:38-39) and thus does not have the authority to judge Stephen.

Acts 7:51-55. Stephen ends his speech by turning from implied defense to explicit prosecution. In verse 51 he calls the leaders "stiff-necked," language God used to describe the Israelites when speaking of their rejection to Moses (Exodus 32:9; 33:3, 5). By calling them "uncircumcised" Stephen asserts they have not maintained the covenant God made with Abraham (7:8). He is not the one to turn away from Moses; they are.

Stephen identifies the accusers and the council (notice the shift in verses 51 and 52 from *our* ancestors to *your* ancestors, emphasis added) with those who rejected Moses and persecuted the prophets. And in exactly the same vein, they betrayed and murdered Jesus, the prophet raised up like Moses.

Stephen so successfully makes his defense *and* counter-accusation that the gathering turns on him and stones him (7:54–8:1). Their power of death, however, does not compare to God's power of life, as demonstrated in Stephen's vision. (Compare the reference to God *appearing* to Abraham at the beginning of Stephen's speech in verse 2 and final proclamation of the glory of the resurrected and ascended Christ in verses 7:55-56.) For the reader, this tense ending—a violent death mixed with promise—signals that the persecution that follows Stephen's stoning will not have the last word on what God wants for and from the church.

INTERPRETING THE SCRIPTURE

The Who of Defense

In ancient Greek, when people defended themselves in court, their defense speech was called an *apologia*. In theology, when someone defends the faith, it is called "apologetics." In Stephen's speech, these two types of defense merge into one.

The reader knows Stephen to be innocent. The accusers know he is innocent. The council must determine whether he is innocent or guilty. But Stephen does not argue for his innocence. He does not swear that he has never claimed the Temple will be destroyed by Jesus. He does not call witnesses to attest to his faithfulness in upholding the law (6:11, 13-14). Instead, he defends God.

Stephen recognizes that what is really at issue is the integrity of the gospel, not his own fate. The question he answers in his defense is this: How can the God of Moses and the law and the Temple also be the God of Jesus and the church? In other words, Stephen argues before the Sanhedrin that the Christian gospel is a continuation, not a contradiction, of the foundational stories of Israel.

In today's world, in our pluralistic society with its separation of church and state, it is rare that Christians are persecuted in any serious way (although persecution of Christians and other faiths certainly continues to occur in other parts of the world). Yet we still meet challenges to our faith on a regular basis. As people who recognize our finite knowledge and sinfulness and who believe in the continued guidance of the Holy Spirit, we must always be open to such challenges helping us grow in our theology. This or that particular belief might well need to be rethought.

Yet we need to always be ready to offer a defense for God even while being open to changing elements of our faith. There is a radical difference between an individual being challenged to modify this or that belief or practice and the God of Abraham, Joseph, Moses, Jesus, and Stephen being attacked. Often when people make a challenge against our faith in a way that may feel personally insulting to us, they are actually challenging the character of God and/or the gospel of Jesus Christ.

The How of Defense

The way Stephen defends God is simply to tell the story of God's engagement with Israel, specifically with the historical figures with whom his listeners identify. This story shaped their identities—and Stephen's identity—as children of God. This story of God's engagement with Israel throughout the nation's history showed the character of God as "for us." This recited story, embedded where it is in Luke's narrative, demonstrates that the God active and revealed in the stories of Abraham, Joseph, Moses, and the prophets is also the God who is active and made known in Jesus Christ.

The way Stephen tells the story and the way he leads his listeners to identify with the biblical figures whom God engaged also reveals the character of his accusers. With faith that his true fate did not rest with the council, Stephen spoke truth to power. He allowed the story that he shared with his accusers to accuse them of the very unfaithfulness with which they charged him.

In our society, with religious freedom as a strong principle that binds us together, we should never try to force our faith on anyone. On the other hand, we should never back down from naming our faith and trust in God. Too often, we flinch when situations arise in which we should share our faith but do not do so out of concern not to offend others. Our defense need not be one of argumentation, but of storytelling. We simply need to share the stories of Israel and of Christ and the early church and leave the rest to God.

Of course, we should not be so naive as to pretend Stephen did not put his own spin on those ancient stories he recited. Any telling of a story is an interpretation of the story. The same is true of our storytelling. When we offer the faith, we cannot help offering *our* faith. But that is how *we* defend God. We tell the stories of the faith subjectively as our stories so that others might claim them as their own stories. We do so boldly because those stories have given meaning to our lives, and we offer them to others in case they might also find meaning in them. What

better defense of God is there than this sort of gentle evangelism?

The Commitment of the Defender

Luke presents the apostles and those they chose as assistants (6:1-7) as heroes of the first generation of the church. When the apostles were on trial, they were obedient to their calling to proclaim the gospel of Jesus as the Christ, rather than to the religious leaders who ordered them to be silent (chapters 4–5). Stephen, likewise, refused to back down when backed into a corner by those making false accusations. Luke does not present these heroes as unique in their faithfulness but intends them as models for the readers to follow. Their commitment is presented as characteristic of Christian commitment, not simply as characteristic of their individual personalities.

The character of Stephen's commitment is that in speaking truth to power, in telling the story of Israel in a way that commends Jesus as the Christ and convicts his audience as being unfaithful, he is showing his willingness to take a risk. Stephen could have easily denied the charges, recanted belief in Jesus, and been released. He probably even could have won his case on the basis of lack of real evidence and proved his accusers wrong. But instead he was willing to risk his life for Christ. As one who knew the fate of prophets of the past (7:35, 39, 52), Stephen knew how the leaders could respond to his *apologia*. As one who worshiped the crucified Christ, he knew his witness could mean his death (see Luke 9:23).

In our society today, there is little risk in being a member of the body of Christ. No one hauls us into court when we claim publicly to be Christians. No one throws stones at us as we gather on Sunday morning for worship. Oh, but there is significant risk to proclaiming and living out the depths of the gospel in ways that challenge the status quo. There is risk to telling God's story in a manner that reveals the ways of the world as the ways of death. There is risk in speaking truth to power and revealing the hypocrisy that under-girds the power holders of the world. To refuse to domesticate or compart-mentalize the gospel in our lives and strive faithfully to speak and act as followers of Christ is to put ourselves in harm's way on a daily basis. If our faith requires no serious risks, if it is routine and comfortable, we must ask ourselves whether ours is the faith of Stephen. Because the gospel is worth our commitment, we are empowered by the Holy Spirit to be committed to it. And in turn, we will catch visions of the power, glory, and grace of Jesus Christ that we would not see without such risk-taking.

SHARING THE SCRIPTURE

PREPARING TO TEACH

Preparing Our Hearts

Ponder this week's devotional reading from 1 Corinthians 1:1-9. What do you learn from this passage about Paul and those to whom he writes? What does Paul tell you about God? How does all this information help you to remember God's faithfulness?

Pray that you and the students will give thanks for the ways in which you have seen God at work in other people.

Preparing Our Minds

Study the background Scripture from Acts 7:1-55 and the lesson Scripture from Acts 7:2-4, 8-10, 17, 33-34, 44-47, 53 and 55 (key verse).

Consider this question as you prepare the lesson: *How do people stand up to criticism of their beliefs, even if by taking a stand they put their lives in jeopardy?*

Write on newsprint:

❏ information for next week's lesson, found under Continue the Journey.

❏ activities for further spiritual growth in Continue the Journey.

Review the Introduction, The Big Picture, Close-up, and Faith in Action, which all precede the first lesson of this quarter. Consider how you might use any of this material in today's lesson.

Prepare a brief lecture on all of Acts 7 by using information from throughout the Understanding the Scripture portion.

LEADING THE CLASS

(1) Gather to Learn

❖ Welcome the class members and guests.

❖ Pray that those who have come today will consider God's faithfulness to them and their faithfulness to God.

❖ Invite participants to talk with a partner or small group about examples of God's faithfulness in their own lives. Encourage them to recount perilous situations they have encountered in which speaking out for God meant putting themselves, their jobs, or their reputations at risk.

❖ Bring everyone together and read aloud today's focus statement: **People will defend against all criticism of their beliefs, even if their defense is life-threatening. How do people stand up to such perilous criticism? When Stephen spoke to his accusers in the council, he summarized the history of God's faithfulness to the Israelites and then challenged the council members for not keeping the law themselves.**

(2) Goal 1: Hear Stephen's Proclamation Before the Council in Which He Reminded Those Present of God's Faithfulness Through the Ages and Their Disregard of God's Law

❖ Solicit seven readers for Acts 7:2-4, 8-10, 17, 33-34, 44-47, 53, 55.

❖ Point out that highlights were excerpted from Stephen's speech, but the speech in its entirety clearly traces Israel's history and how God has worked with and through various ancestors. To "connect the dots" present a brief lecture that deals with most of the people mentioned in chapter 7.

❖ Look more carefully at how Stephen tells the story by reading "The How of Defense" in Interpreting the Scripture and asking: **Had you been present at Stephen's trial, on a scale of 1 to 10 how would you rate the way that he went about defending the faith? Explain why you chose this number.**

❖ **Option:** Discuss ways in which this story could be filmed. Who would play the role of Stephen? Who would play the roles of the high priest and other religious leaders? What kind of

music would accompany this film? What special effects would you use?

(3) Goal 2: Reflect on the Learners' Willingness to Stand Firm on Their Beliefs in the Midst of Life's Threatening Circumstances

❖ Read these two scenarios, stopping after each one to discuss the questions below. Perhaps someone in the group has experienced another situation requiring a firm stand that he or she would be willing to comment on.

Scenario 1: You have a good job that pays well at a highly respected company. You discover actions that according to your Christian beliefs are unethical. You want to blow the whistle but you have a spouse and family who depend on your income. Without your income there is a high probability that you will lose your home and be unable to pay for other essentials. What action can you take to stand firm on your beliefs even in this midst of this very risky situation?

Scenario 2: You are at a social gathering when a friend starts on a rant about how more Christians ought to believe the Bible and practice the faith as he (she) does. Several others quickly agree. Although you would not say that his (her) viewpoints are absolutely wrong, you recognize that other believers, including yourself, do not share these views. How do you go about standing up for another perspective?

❖ Provide quiet time after the discussion. Ask the adults to reflect on their own willingness to stand up for their beliefs.

(4) Goal 3: Commit to Stand for Beliefs About God in All Circumstances

❖ Read or retell "The Commitment of the Defender" in Interpreting the Scripture.

❖ Distribute hymnals. Note that in some denominations (for example, The United Methodist Church) members sing their faith. Suggest that the adults page through the book, looking at hymns that deal with strength in tribulation or witnessing or discipleship. Invite each person to select one hymn that speaks to him or her about a firm commitment in Christ.

❖ Gather everyone together and hear the names of the hymns that have been chosen. Perhaps the recommender would like to read one verse or phrase. If several people choose the same hymn, if possible in your space, sing a verse or two.

❖ Conclude by reading these words from an anonymous old hymn and asking the class members to echo what you read as a sign of their own commitment to stand for God. Pause at the punctuation marks so the group can repeat the words.

I have decided to follow Jesus . . . no turning back.
Though none go with me, still I will follow . . . no turning back.

(5) Continue the Journey

❖ Pray that as the learners depart, they will remember God's faithfulness in their own lives and share that good news with others.

❖ Post information for next week's session on newsprint for the students to copy:

■ **Title: The Spirit Is Not for Sale**

■ **Background Scripture: Acts 8:9-25**
■ **Lesson Scripture: Acts 8:9-24**
■ **Focus of the Lesson: People gather in small and large crowds to listen to inspiring speakers. What gives speakers such power? Peter claims such spiritual power is God's gift and cannot be purchased.**

❖ Post the following information on newsprint and provide paper and pencils for the students to copy it. Challenge the adults to grow spiritually by completing one or more of these activities related to this week's session.

(1) **Recall that Stephen reviewed the highlights of Israel's history with God, not to defend himself but to show who God is. If you were called on to present the highlights of Christian history, what would you say? Who would be included in your list of "giants of the faith"? What significant events in church history would you want to lift up?**

(2) **Compare the story of the martyrdom of Stephen in Acts 7:1–8:1a with the story of Jesus' crucifixion in any or all of the Gospels. What similarities do you see?**

(3) **Make a list of three to five bold claims that you could make about God's faithfulness to the church through the ages and to you personally.**

❖ Sing or read aloud "I Want Jesus to Walk with Me."

❖ Conclude today's session by leading the class in this benediction, which is adapted from Acts 9:20, the key verse for October 11: **Let us go forth to boldly proclaim that Jesus is the Son of God. Amen.**

UNIT 2: GIVING BOLD TESTIMONY
THE SPIRIT IS NOT FOR SALE

PREVIEWING THE LESSON

Lesson Scripture: Acts 8:9-24
Background Scripture: Acts 8:9-25
Key Verse: Acts 8:22

Focus of the Lesson:
People gather in small and large crowds to listen to inspiring speakers. What gives speakers such power? Peter claims such spiritual power is God's gift and cannot be purchased.

Goals for the Learners:
(1) to investigate Simon's encounters with Philip, Peter, and John.
(2) to affirm that the Holy Spirit is a gift from God.
(3) to witness to others concerning the power of the Holy Spirit.

Supplies:
Bibles, newsprint and marker, paper and pencils, hymnals

READING THE SCRIPTURE

NRSV

Lesson Scripture: Acts 8:9-24

⁹Now a certain man named Simon had previously practiced magic in the city and amazed the people of Samaria, saying that he was someone great. ¹⁰All of them, from the least to the greatest, listened to him eagerly, saying, "This man is the power of God that is called Great." ¹¹And they listened eagerly to him because for a long time he had amazed them with his magic. ¹²But when they believed

CEB

Lesson Scripture: Acts 8:9-24

⁹Before Philip's arrival, a certain man named Simon had practiced sorcery in that city and baffled the people of Samaria. He claimed to be a great person. ¹⁰Everyone, from the least to the greatest, gave him their undivided attention and referred to him as "the power of God called Great." ¹¹He had their attention because he had baffled them with sorcery for a long time. ¹²After they came to believe

Philip, who was proclaiming the good news about the kingdom of God and the name of Jesus Christ, they were baptized, both men and women. [13]Even Simon himself believed. After being baptized, he stayed constantly with Philip and was amazed when he saw the signs and great miracles that took place.

[14]Now when the apostles at Jerusalem heard that Samaria had accepted the word of God, they sent Peter and John to them. [15]The two went down and prayed for them that they might receive the Holy Spirit [16](for as yet the Spirit had not come upon any of them; they had only been baptized in the name of the Lord Jesus). [17]Then Peter and John laid their hands on them, and they received the Holy Spirit. [18]Now when Simon saw that the Spirit was given through the laying on of the apostles' hands, he offered them money, [19]saying, "Give me also this power so that anyone on whom I lay my hands may receive the Holy Spirit." [20]But Peter said to him, "May your silver perish with you, because you thought you could obtain God's gift with money! [21]You have no part or share in this, for your heart is not right before God. **[22]Repent therefore of this wickedness of yours, and pray to the Lord that, if possible, the intent of your heart may be forgiven you.** [23]For I see that you are in the gall of bitterness and the chains of wickedness." [24]Simon answered, "Pray for me to the Lord, that nothing of what you have said may happen to me."

Philip, who preached the good news about God's kingdom and the name of Jesus Christ, both men and women were baptized. [13]Even Simon himself came to believe and was baptized. Afterward, he became one of Philip's supporters. As he saw firsthand the signs and great miracles that were happening, he was astonished.

[14]When word reached the apostles in Jerusalem that Samaria had accepted God's word, they commissioned Peter and John to go to Samaria. [15]Peter and John went down to Samaria where they prayed that the new believers would receive the Holy Spirit. ([16]This was because the Holy Spirit had not yet fallen on any of them; they had only been baptized in the name of the Lord Jesus.) [17]So Peter and John laid their hands on them, and they received the Holy Spirit.

[18]When Simon perceived that the Spirit was given through the laying on of the apostles' hands, he offered them money. [19]He said, "Give me this authority too so that anyone on whom I lay my hands will receive the Holy Spirit."

[20]Peter responded, "May your money be condemned to hell along with you because you believed you could buy God's gift with money! [21]You can have no part or share in God's word because your heart isn't right with God. **[22]Therefore, change your heart and life! Turn from your wickedness! Plead with the Lord in the hope that your wicked intent can be forgiven,** [23]for I see that your bitterness has poisoned you and evil has you in chains."

[24]Simon replied, "All of you, please, plead to the Lord for me so that nothing of what you have said will happen to me!"

UNDERSTANDING THE SCRIPTURE

Introduction. In the previous lesson, we examined Stephen's speech, which resulted in his martyrdom (see Acts 6:8–7:60). As Luke portrays it, his stoning set off a persecution that resulted in many Christians leaving Jerusalem. Ironically, this persecution then led not to the demise of the church but to the spreading of the witness concerning Jesus Christ beyond the borders of Jerusalem, just as Jesus had wanted (see 1:8).

The first such witness that Luke tells about is Philip. He heads to Samaria, which stands between Judea, the region surrounding Jerusalem, to the south and Galilee to the north. It is important to remember that for Luke, this geographical location is symbolic of the fact that Samaritans stand between Jews and Gentiles. Like Jews, Samaritans traced their heritage to Abraham and considered the first five books of the Bible to be their Scripture. Unlike the Jews, they did not consider the rest of historical, prophetic, or poetic Hebrew writings to be Scripture; did not consider oral teaching of the rabbis to be authoritative; and did not worship in Jerusalem. This in-between status of the Samaritans makes this area the perfect setting for the first expansion of the Christian witness beyond Judea before bringing the gospel to the Gentiles in chapter 10.

Preceding our lesson, Luke tells us that Philip was successful in his ministry in Samaria. His preaching received a positive response, and he performed "signs" (a word for a powerful act) of exorcisms and healings (8:4-8). The passage as a whole, then, alternates between describing the successful ministry of the church in Samaria and the interaction of Simon the Magician with that ministry.

Acts 8:9-11. The CEB's translation of Simon practicing "sorcery" may be misleading to contemporary readers. We must be careful not to think of ancient "magicians" through modern lenses. Simon is described using the same terminology for the magi in Matthew 2:1-12. Magicians were astrologers and healers. We can think of them in terms of analogies with medieval alchemists or medicine men and women in some traditional cultures. They were not grifters or illusionists, but instead they believed in magic and were valued resources in communities for helping people deal with physical, psychological, relational, and economic troubles.

In the ancient world, people believed supernatural powers were all around them in the universe. Although somewhat of an oversimplification, a description that is often used to distinguish religion and magic in the ancient Mediterranean world is that whereas in religion people *prayed* to higher powers asking for aid, in magic people attempted to *manipulate* those powers to do their bidding. A Jew worshiping in the Temple beseeches Yahweh to heal his daughter, while a magician carves the name of Yahweh on a tablet (along with other mystical names and odd words, similar to "abracadabra") to draw on Yahweh's power to heal the girl.

Luke wants his readers to be clear that Simon was indeed a powerful magician (he is twice referred to using the term "great," in verses 9 and 10), and was valued by the people of Samaria for the work he had done among them.

Acts 8:12-13. Having presented Philip's ministry (8:4-8) and Simon's magic (8:9-11) in parallel fashion, Luke now shows that a competition of sorts was at play between the two. Of course, Philip wins. The Samaritans may be amazed at the miracles both perform, but they are baptized into the faith Philip represents. If their baptisms were not a big enough sign of his victory over Simon, the fact that Simon himself becomes a believer, is baptized, follows Philip around, and is amazed at Philip's "great powers" (the literal translation of the Greek translated as "great miracles" in the NRSV) makes clear the superiority of Christianity over magic (8:13).

Acts 8:14-17. While Philip is successful in converting Samaritans and baptizing them into the church, his ministry is limited. He is powerful, but his power and work are secondary to that of the apostles. In ways that may not fit completely with modern theology, Luke presents the apostles (at this early stage in church history) as being the sole figures who can pass on the Holy Spirit to the baptized. Thus for the new converts to reap the full gift of God's grace offered through Jesus Christ and entrance into the church, Peter and John are sent by the Jerusalem church to lay hands on the converts (an action that could have easily been mistaken for magic in the ancient world).

Acts 8:18-24. Simon's attention shifts from Philip and the signs of power he did to the apostles and their greater power of passing on the Spirit through the laying on of hands (see 1:8 for the way Luke equates the gift of the Spirit with power). Simon, the magician, wants to acquire this power from the apostles. But Luke, through Peter's strong rebuke of Simon (8:20-21), makes clear that while the apostles pass on the Holy Spirit through the laying on of hands, they do not possess nor manipulate God's power. Indeed, the reverse is true: Instead of manipulating the power of the Holy Spirit (in the fashion of magic), they are vessels of the Spirit, manipulated by God. The Spirit is a gift (not a purchase) from God that can only be used in service to God. God gives the power of the Spirit when, how, and to whom God pleases (compare John 3:6-8).

It is important to note that Peter rebukes Simon but does not cast him out of the church or strike him down (as was the case with Ananias and Sapphira in 5:1-11). Instead, after chastising him, Peter simply calls Simon to repent and ask that God make his heart right with God (8:22-23). And Simon does just that (8:24).

Acts 8:25. Luke concludes the scene with a transitional summary that returns the apostles to their headquarters in Jerusalem. On the way back they continue the ministry Philip started throughout Samaria.

INTERPRETING THE SCRIPTURE

Good Intentions Pave the Road to . . .

Interpreters have often been too hard on Simon. We criticize him for trying to buy the ability to wield the Holy Spirit for his own purposes and bend the Spirit to his will. But actually this is not what is in the text. Luke gives no indication that Simon wants to purchase the apostles' power for the wrong reasons. Before he seeks to buy the apostles' power, he has converted to the Christian faith, been baptized, and committed himself to following Philip (8:13).

It is natural that a magician by trade would want to possess the apostles' power to serve and heal his clients better. Indeed, now that he is in the church, there is no reason to assume that he wants the power for any other reason than to serve God and the church as the apostles do.

Yet Luke presents Peter as criticizing Simon in strong terms, claiming his heart is not right before God and calling his request to buy the power an act of wickedness (8:21-22). Luke scrutinizes not Simon's intent, but his means. Even though he has converted to Christianity and been baptized, he still thinks and acts like a magician; he still thinks divine power is something to be manipulated—in this case, something he can obtain through purchase and then control and use.

Simon may have been wicked in his desire to gain God's power through improper means, but his desire to serve God and God's power is seen in his response to Peter. He takes Peter's reprimand to heart, repents, and asks that Peter pray for him. This is a complete turnaround from the

Simon introduced to the reader in 8:9-11. The attempt to *manipulate* divine power has given way to *beseeching* divine power. Indeed, the one whom people called the "power of God that is called Great" (8:10) in the end does not even trust in himself to beg God for forgiveness.

And the Oscar Goes to . . .

Our discussion has primarily focused on Simon—on his intent and actions. He is the most vivid character in Acts 8:9-24 and the one with whom the readers are invited to identify as we reflect on our own desire for power. He is not, however, the main character of the story. But neither is Philip or the apostles, for that matter. The main actor in this scene is really the Holy Spirit.

Luke's theology of the Holy Spirit is complicated, but it is central to his narrative. It could be said that as the first volume of Luke–Acts proclaims the gospel of Jesus Christ, the second volume proclaims the gospel of the Holy Spirit (the Holy Spirit is mentioned about seventy times in Acts). Over and over throughout the narrative, the Spirit makes this happen, comes upon someone in that manner, and leads the community in such and such a direction.

The Holy Spirit is active in Luke's narrative long before Pentecost. The Holy Spirit is mentioned frequently in the Gospel of Luke and is portrayed as active in inspiring prophetic speech and action (for example, Luke 1:41-42; 2:25-32) and coming upon Jesus in his baptism (Luke 3:21-22). There is, however, a shift in the Spirit's activity at Pentecost: The Spirit is given and gives rise to the church. Once Jesus had ascended into heaven (a symbol of God's transcendence) and was no longer present with his followers, the Holy Spirit takes his place as the presence of God among God's people (a symbol of God's immanence). The Spirit comes upon the apostles with a sound like a rushing wind (2:1-4) and then is offered to those who respond positively to Peter's sermon through repentance and baptism (2:37-39).

The way in which baptism is associated with the gift of the Holy Spirit has been debated throughout church history and continues to be interpreted differently across denominational lines. Does "baptism of the Spirit" occur simultaneously with water baptism? Is reception of the Spirit a prerequisite for baptism? Does the gift of the Spirit come sometime after baptism as a separate event? Even though different passages in Acts are often cited in these debates, Luke does not present a clear picture of how the two are related. These are not his questions. He simply affirms that the two are unequivocally related.

On the other hand, all who receive the Holy Spirit in Acts do not receive the same gifts of the Spirit. While Paul makes this claim using the imagery of the church as the body of Christ (1 Corinthians 12 and Romans 12:4-8), in Acts it is pictured through the different roles members of the church play in the narrative. Philip presumably received the Spirit in relation to his baptism. He can preach and baptize, but he is unable to offer to others the Holy Spirit. At this point in the narrative, that is the role of the apostles (Acts 8:14-17).

No church policies were established to set up this division of labor.

The Holy Spirit chooses how God uses us. This is the paradoxical nature of a divine gift—God's presence is a free gift of grace that we can neither earn nor manipulate. We experience this presence as offering salvation, providential care, and revelation. The Spirit guides, comforts, and gives us meaning, but also stakes a claim on us, instead of us staking a claim on the Spirit. We do not use the Spirit; the Spirit uses us. And God decides how we are best suited to be used. Like Simon, we do not get to nominate ourselves for apostleship. The Spirit comes to us, comes upon us, and graciously makes us into what God desires of us.

And You Will Be My Witness From . . .

In Acts 1:8, the resurrected Jesus makes a promise and gives a command to his followers: "But you will receive power when the Holy Spirit has come upon you; and you will be my witnesses in Jerusalem, in all Judea and Samaria, and to the ends of the earth." The gift of the Holy Spirit will lead to the evangelistic spread of the gospel throughout the world. Indeed, Luke uses the geographical references in this verse as a programmatic statement of the outline of Acts. The gospel spreads across Jerusalem and Judea following Pentecost; it spreads to Samaria as a result of the persecution in Jerusalem headed up by Saul (Paul), and it spreads throughout the empire and eventually to Rome (which was considered symbolically in the ancient Mediterranean world to be "the ends of the earth") through the ministry of Paul.

Acts presents Philip as carrying the gospel to Samaria not because he "has a heart" for ministry among the Samaritans. He leaves Jerusalem because of necessity. Just as we do not control the will or working of the Holy Spirit in order to wield God's power as we might, we also cannot always control the circumstances in which we find ourselves as Christians. If we had our druthers, we might live somewhere else, work somewhere else, maybe even worship somewhere else. But regardless of where we find ourselves, like Philip we are to serve God wherever we are. As a symbol of God's loving and demanding presence, the Holy Spirit is everywhere. So anywhere we are is the perfect place to share the Spirit with whatever gifts God has given us.

SHARING THE SCRIPTURE

PREPARING TO TEACH

Preparing Our Hearts

Ponder this week's devotional reading from Hebrews 13:5-10. Although many people think that money buys them power and prestige, how does the writer of Hebrews view "the love of money" (13:5; compare 1 Timothy 6:10)? What promises do you hear in this passage? What words of assurance do you find here?

Pray that you and the students will live as faithful believers.

Preparing Our Minds

Study the background Scripture from Acts 8:9-25 and the lesson Scripture from Acts 8:9-24.

Consider this question as you prepare the lesson: *What gives speakers the power to inspire crowds?*

Write on newsprint:

❑ information for next week's lesson, found under Continue the Journey.

❑ activities for further spiritual growth in Continue the Journey.

Review the Introduction, The Big Picture, Close-up, and Faith in Action, which all precede the first lesson of this quarter. Consider how you might use any of this material in today's lesson.

LEADING THE CLASS

(1) Gather to Learn

❖ Welcome the class members and guests.

❖ Pray that those who have come today will recognize the source of true spiritual power.

❖ Call on several volunteers to recount how they felt when they heard an inspiring speaker. For our purposes the topic of the speech and the speaker's field of expertise are unimportant. Encourage the volunteers to discuss whatever traits the speaker exhibited that prompted them to feel inspired or motivated to act.

❖ Read aloud today's focus statement: **People gather in small and large crowds to listen to inspiring speakers. What gives speakers such power? Peter claims such spiritual power is God's gift and cannot be purchased.**

(2) Goal 1: Investigate Simon's Encounters with Philip, Peter, and John

❖ Read the Introduction in Understanding the Scripture to create a context for today's lesson.

❖ Solicit two volunteers, one to read Acts 8:9-13 and the other to read verses 14-24.

❖ Discuss these questions:

1. **In his story, what points does Luke make about Simon?** (See "Good Intentions Pave the Road to . . ." in Interpreting the Scripture.)

2. **Suppose you had seen Simon in action and had, like others, affirmed that he was "Great" (8:10). What would have been your reaction when you realized that he believed, was baptized, and stayed with Philip?**

3. **What role(s) does the Holy Spirit play in the life of the church?** (See "And the Oscar Goes to . . ." in Interpreting the Scripture.)

4. **According to verse 12, Philip had proclaimed the good news and people believed, but it was not until Peter and John arrived that new believers could receive the Holy Spirit. Why?** (See Acts 8:14-17 in Understanding the Scripture.)

5. **How did Simon misunderstand the way in which the Spirit operates?** (See the first paragraph of Acts 8:18-24 in Understanding the Scripture.)

6. **How does Simon respond after Peter rebukes him?** (See the second paragraph of Acts 8:18-24 in Understanding the Scripture.)

(3) Goal 2: Affirm That the Holy Spirit Is a Gift From God

❖ Read the final paragraph of "And the Oscar Goes to . . ." in Interpreting the Scripture. Point out that Simon's error was that he thought he could purchase power that only God can bestow as a gift.

❖ Form four small groups and assign each group to these chapters in Acts: 1–7, 8–14, 15–21, 22–28. Give each group a sheet of newsprint and marker. Tell them to page through their assigned chapters and make brief notes on how they see the Spirit at work. (To cover the entire book in a short time, each person in the group may be asked to look at just two or three chapters.)

❖ Reconvene and ask each group to give examples of what they have found. Note again the Spirit is freely given and distributed as God chooses. The Spirit can neither be bought nor controlled.

❖ Provide quiet time for the students to reflect on and give thanks for the gift and work of the Spirit in their own lives and in the life of the church.

(4) Goal 3: Witness to Others Concerning the Power of the Holy Spirit

❖ Ask: **Why are some believers hesitant about telling others the good news?** (Recognize that you may get a wide variety of answers such as shyness, unwillingness to discuss one's faith, feeling that one's knowledge is inadequate, discomfort about expressing one's belief or telling how God has been at work in one's life.)

❖ Point out that some stumbling blocks can be overcome with practice. Distribute paper and pencils and ask participants to write a few phrases about how God has been at work in their lives and/or several beliefs that they hold about God.

❖ Roleplay a conversation between two people, one who is a believer and one who is seeking to know more but is not yet willing to make a commitment. Allow those who feel more comfortable using their notes, rather than speaking extemporaneously, to do so. Remind the adults that the best way to give their witness is to act naturally and speak from their hearts. Call on several pairs to do this roleplay.

❖ Conclude by challenging the adults to look for opportunities to witness this week. Suggest that they choose someone who seems to be receptive and is interested in knowing more about God. Also suggest that the students try to draw connections between a need that the listener has and a similar situation in which God worked in their own lives. For example, someone dealing with a difficult illness or loss may be open to hearing *briefly* about how God has helped a class member in a similar situation. Although this is not the time for a heady theological discussion or proof-texting, it is an appropriate time to tell a story of God's mighty acts in one's own life.

(5) Continue the Journey

❖ Pray that as the learners depart, they will recognize that the Holy Spirit is a gift from God that cannot be purchased or manipulated.

❖ Post information for next week's session on newsprint for the students to copy:

- **Title: Saul Earns Credibility**
- **Background Scripture: Acts 9:19b-31**
- **Lesson Scripture: Acts 9:19b-31**
- **Focus of the Lesson: Effective advocates boldly tell others about their deepest convictions. What impact**

does a strong and bold testimony have on the lives of others? The Scripture claims that Saul's bold preaching of the gospel was powerful, amazed the people, gave peace to many churches, and caused an increase in the number of followers.

❖ Post the following information on newsprint and provide paper and pencils for the students to copy it. Challenge the adults to grow spiritually by completing one or more of these activities related to this week's session.

(1) **Page through Acts in search of speeches concerning the good news of Jesus Christ made to groups. Here are some samples: Acts 2:14-36; 3:11-26; 7:1– 8:1; 10:34-43; 17:22-31. How do you see the Spirit at work in the proclamation of the gospel?**

(2) **Listen carefully to the preacher in your congregation this week. How do you experience the power of the Spirit through his or her message?**

(3) **Seek opportunities to share the good news of Jesus with others this week. Allow the Holy Spirit to work through you.**

❖ Sing or read aloud "Surely the Presence of the Lord."

❖ Conclude today's session by leading the class in this benediction, which is adapted from Acts 9:20, the key verse for October 11: **Let us go forth to boldly proclaim that Jesus is the Son of God. Amen.**

UNIT 2: GIVING BOLD TESTIMONY
SAUL EARNS CREDIBILITY

PREVIEWING THE LESSON

Lesson Scripture: Acts 9:19b-31
Background Scripture: Acts 9:19b-31
Key Verse: Acts 9:20

Focus of the Lesson:
Effective advocates boldly tell others about their deepest convictions. What impact does a strong and bold testimony have on the lives of others? The Scripture claims that Saul's bold preaching of the gospel was powerful, amazed the people, gave peace to many churches, and caused an increase in the number of followers.

Goals for the Learners:
(1) to recount Saul's acceptance as a Christian and his zeal in preaching about Jesus.
(2) to believe that they can change in Jesus Christ and then, through their bold witness, help others to change.
(3) to invite others to come to Jesus and join the community of faith by sharing their personal testimony of Jesus' saving grace.

Supplies:
Bibles, newsprint and marker, paper and pencils, hymnals, optional map

---

READING THE SCRIPTURE

NRSV

Lesson Scripture: Acts 9:19b-31

¹⁹For several days he was with the disciples in Damascus, ²⁰and immediately he began to proclaim Jesus in the synagogues, saying, "He is the Son of God." ²¹All who heard him were amazed and said, "Is not this the man who made havoc in Jerusalem among those who invoked this name? And has he not come here

CEB

Lesson Scripture: Acts 9:19b-31

¹⁹He stayed with the disciples in Damascus for several days. ²⁰Right away, he began to preach about Jesus in the synagogues. "He is God's Son, he declared.

²¹Everyone who heard him was baffled. They questioned each other, "Isn't he the one who was wreaking havoc among those in Jerusalem who

for the purpose of bringing them bound before the chief priests?" ²²Saul became increasingly more powerful and confounded the Jews who lived in Damascus by proving that Jesus was the Messiah.

²³After some time had passed, the Jews plotted to kill him, ²⁴but their plot became known to Saul. They were watching the gates day and night so that they might kill him; ²⁵but his disciples took him by night and let him down through an opening in the wall, lowering him in a basket.

²⁶When he had come to Jerusalem, he attempted to join the disciples; and they were all afraid of him, for they did not believe that he was a disciple. ²⁷But Barnabas took him, brought him to the apostles, and described for them how on the road he had seen the Lord, who had spoken to him, and how in Damascus he had spoken boldly in the name of Jesus. ²⁸So he went in and out among them in Jerusalem, speaking boldly in the name of the Lord. ²⁹He spoke and argued with the Hellenists; but they were attempting to kill him. ³⁰When the believers learned of it, they brought him down to Caesarea and sent him off to Tarsus.

³¹Meanwhile the church throughout Judea, Galilee, and Samaria had peace and was built up. Living in the fear of the Lord and in the comfort of the Holy Spirit, it increased in numbers.

called on this name? Hadn't he come here to take those same people as prisoners to the chief priests?"

²²But Saul grew stronger and stronger. He confused the Jews who lived in Damascus by proving that Jesus is the Christ.

²³After this had gone on for some time, the Jews hatched a plot to kill Saul. ²⁴However, he found out about their scheme. They were keeping watch at the city gates around the clock so they could assassinate him. ²⁵But his disciples took him by night and lowered him in a basket through an opening in the city wall.

²⁶When Saul arrived in Jerusalem, he tried to join the disciples, but they were all afraid of him. They didn't believe he was really a disciple. ²⁷Then Barnabas brought Saul to the apostles and told them the story about how Saul saw the Lord on the way and that the Lord had spoken to Saul. He also told them about the confidence with which Saul had preached in the name of Jesus in Damascus. ²⁸After this, Saul moved freely among the disciples in Jerusalem and was speaking with confidence in the name of the Lord. ²⁹He got into debates with the Greek-speaking Jews as well, but they tried to kill him. ³⁰When the family of believers learned about this, they escorted him down to Caesarea and sent him off to Tarsus.

³¹Then the church throughout Judea, Galilee, and Samaria enjoyed a time of peace. God strengthened the church, and its life was marked by reverence for the Lord. Encouraged by the Holy Spirit, the church continued to grow in numbers.

UNDERSTANDING THE SCRIPTURE

Introduction. Readers of Acts first meet Saul in the story of Stephen's stoning (7:58), which led to Saul becoming a major figure in the initial persecution of the church in Jerusalem (8:1-3). So committed to this attack on the messianic community is Saul that he initiates expanding it beyond Jerusalem to Damascus, a town about 135 miles as the crow flies northeast in Syria (9:1-2).

On his way to Damascus, however, Saul encounters an appearance of the risen Jesus, which leaves him temporarily blind (9:3-8). According to verse 9, after three days without his sight and without food or drink, the Lord sends a local Christian, Ananias, to heal Saul. Upon regaining his sight, he is immediately baptized even before receiving food to regain his strength (9:9-19a).

Acts 9:19b-22. Luke tells us that Saul only spends a few days with the church in Damascus before he begins proclaiming the gospel in the synagogues there. In the span of these few verses, Luke shows in several ways how powerful a speaker Saul is, foreshadowing the incredible ministry that will be the primary focus of the second half of Acts.

First, Saul's message is unique. He proclaims Jesus to be the Son of God (9:20). While this christological title is used several times in the Gospel of Luke, this is its only occurrence in Acts.

Second, a theme that is repeated throughout chapter 9 is that Saul is well known as a persecutor of the church (9:13-15, 21, 26). The fact that someone so opposed to anyone invoking Jesus' name was now proclaiming him to be the Son of God had considerable impact.

Third, the narrator tells us that Saul "proved" that Jesus was the Messiah (9:22). The language of proof here means less that he convinced those with whom he was debating and more that he bested them in argument. (Luke calls those with whom Saul argues "the Jews." The author, of course, knows that Saul is a Jew, as were all the earliest Christians including those in Damascus, and that Saul did not argue with all the Jews. Whenever Luke uses "the Jews" in a derogatory sense, he is speaking of Jewish leadership or of Jews opposed to the church. So we, as modern readers, must always be careful not to read anti-Semitism into the ancient texts of the New Testament.)

Acts 9:23-25. When Ananias is sent to lay hands on Saul to heal him after he has been blinded, he resists because he fears Saul the persecutor. As the Lord assures Ananias that he has chosen Saul as an instrument to proclaim the gospel to the Gentiles, kings, and Jews, he also tells him that Saul will suffer for the sake of his name (9:16). That suffering begins quickly.

Like the apostles earlier in Acts, opposition to Saul arises specifically because he is successful and persuasive on behalf of the gospel. "After some time" (an intentionally ambiguous designation in verse 23) of his ministry in Damascus, those Saul bested in debate about Jesus (presumably repeatedly) seek to kill him. Because they watch the gates of the city, his only option for escape is to be lowered through a window in the city wall by his disciples. (To compare Paul's version of the incident that is similar but not exactly parallel to this scene in Acts, see 2 Corinthians 11:32-33.)

Acts 9:26-28. Saul escapes to Jerusalem. Even though he has been gone for "some time," he is well known for his violent persecution of those who invoke Jesus' name. It is no wonder then that the Jerusalem church doubts the sincerity of his desire to join them and wonders whether he is trying to infiltrate the community of faith in order to discover who were disciples and have them arrested.

But then Barnabas enters the scene. He was first introduced to readers in 4:32-37 as an example of one who faithfully sold property and laid the proceeds at the apostles' feet so that they might distribute them to any who had need (see Understanding the Scripture for the lesson on September 13). In that scene, Luke incorrectly claims that the origin of the name Barnabas is "son of encouragement." It is actually "son of Nebo," but in this scene we see that Luke was absolutely correct in labeling Barnabas a son of encouragement. Luke does not tell us how Barnabas knew Saul's story or knew it to be true. He simply shows us Barnabas's character in the way he acts to reconcile the persecutor with the persecuted. This foreshadows the way Barnabas will partner in mission with Paul in chapters 11–15.

Acts 9:29-30. Even though Barnabas paved the way for Saul to be accepted by the Jerusalem church, those outside the church become a threat to him just as they had in Damascus. The "Hellenists" with whom Saul debated were non-Christian, Greek-speaking Jews (that is, Jews from the Diaspora) in Jerusalem as opposed to the Greek-speaking Jews inside the church called Hellenists in 6:1. Again it is disciples who help Saul escape, sending him to Tarsus, through Syria into Cilicia.

Luke has constructed the entire story of Saul in chapter 9 using a heavy irony of reversals. Saul goes looking for disciples in Damascus and is blinded. When he regains his sight, he is baptized. The once-persecutor of those who invoke Jesus' name becomes a great proclaimer of Jesus as the Messiah. And three times those whom he persecuted (Ananias, his disciples in Damascus, and the believers in Jerusalem) save his life when he is persecuted.

Acts 9:31. Luke concludes this section of his narrative in a favorite fashion. After dealing with struggles and persecution faced by the messianic community, the narrator describes the success of the church in terms of increased numbers in the church (for example, 6:1, 7; 12:24). Luke states that the church was experiencing peace. Implied in this notice is that Paul had significant power as a persecutor and now that he had become a preacher, there was much less oppression of the church (at least for a while).

INTERPRETING THE SCRIPTURE

From Persecutor to Person of Faith

Luke considers Saul's Damascus road experience to be so significant that he tells it three times in The Acts of the Apostles (9:1-19a; 22:3-16; 26:9-18). It is through direct intervention by the risen Jesus ("the Lord") that

Saul is transformed from one who despised and attacked Christians to being a Christian himself. The story of this turnaround, with all its dramatic elements, is a powerful witness that Saul is able to offer as a testimony to the truth of the good news of Jesus Christ.

The miraculous epiphany Saul experiences, however, is only part of the story of his transformation. After Saul encounters Jesus, he encounters the embrace of the church. A partnership between divine intervention and human confirmation and support helps Saul become not only a disciple of Christ but also an apostle to the Gentiles. Saul's first positive encounter with the messianic community comes in the form of the reluctant but obedient Ananias who heals him (9:10-18a). Ananias's ministry to Saul results in his baptism into the church and spending time with the disciples in Damascus (9:18b-19a, 23a). These very disciples whom Saul had come to persecute not only embrace him and save his life but are called "his [Saul's] disciples" by the time he leaves Damascus (9:25). Finally, when Saul is forced to flee the city he had volunteered to persecute and return to Jerusalem where he began his career as a persecutor, Barnabas helps him become part of the church there (9:27). Of course, the Jerusalem church (like Ananias before it) was reluctant to embrace Saul at first due to his well-earned reputation as a henchman for the religious-political authorities attacking Christians (9:13-14, 21, 26). Nevertheless, they did embrace him.

Luke's inclusion of this element of the story makes a strong theological claim concerning the nature of salvation: One is a person of faith not only through a personal relationship with Christ but also through a personal relationship with a community of faith. And it is by being rooted in this community of faith that one is able to go out and boldly offer witness to the faith in the world. Only after spending time with the disciples in Damascus does Saul begin to proclaim Jesus as the Son of God in the Damascus synagogues (9:19b-20). Only after Barnabas convinces the Jerusalem church to accept Saul and he is able to "go in and out among them" does he preach and debate in Jerusalem (9:27-28).

From Persecutor to Preacher

Scholars like to debate details, and biblical scholars have long debated whether the form of Saul's Damascus road experience is that of an ancient "conversion" story or of a "call" story. Regardless of the answer in technical rhetorical categories, the theological answer to the question is yes. Saul's blinding, epiphany, healing, and baptism are both a conversion to the Christian faith and a calling to Christian ministry.

He is not converted from being a Jew to being a Christian. Saul remains a practicing and devout Jew his entire life—for example, his final arrest occurs when he is worshiping in the Jerusalem Temple (21:17-36). His conversion is from non-Christian to Jewish-Christian, from persecutor of the church to a member of the church.

This conversion, however, also signals a vocational transformation for him. Saul becomes no back-pew sitter, who quietly attends worship on the Lord's Day and goes about his business the rest of the week just like everyone else. He transforms from one whose career was to persecute Jesus (9:4-5) to one whose mission is to proclaim Jesus as the Messiah (9:15, 20-22, 28-29) so that others (especially Gentiles; see 9:15) might, like him, be baptized and enter into the messianic community.

Literature often speeds up the natural course of events for dramatic effect. This is the case in Acts 9 where Saul shifts from persecutor to one who is baptized into the church to an apostle who leads and speaks on behalf of the church. This sort of compression of Saul's calling as a missionary of the early church into his initial conversion makes it immediately clear to the reader that Saul's ministry will be one of profound influence.

This initial characterization of Saul's ministry in chapter 9 unfolds in dramatic ways throughout the second half of Acts, taking the man and his message on multiple journeys in which he preaches in synagogues and to Gentiles and establishes churches across the Roman Empire until he finally lands in Rome itself (chapters 13–28). In Acts 1:8 the risen Jesus tells his followers, "But you will receive power when the Holy Spirit has come upon you; and you will be my witnesses in Jerusalem, in all Judea and Samaria, and to the ends of the earth." No one in the narrative fulfills this prophecy as boldly as does Saul.

From Persecutor to Persecuted

Luke's use of compressed time also highlights the fact that Saul's newfound calling lands him in the precarious position, from the very moment his life of faith as a Christian begins, of becoming the target of the very kind of persecution of which he formerly was a chief agent. His

life is first threatened in Damascus (9:23-24) and then again in Jerusalem (9:29). These are only the beginnings of persecution Saul will face: Beatings, arrest, and imprisonment by both Jewish and Roman powers will be repeated throughout the second half of Acts.

This pattern of suffering is predicted before Saul is even baptized. The Lord reveals to Ananias that Saul must suffer for Jesus' name (9:16). This theme of persecution shows that Luke's compressed narrative in chapter 9 should not be misread as some sort of idealist view of the early church. Saul's transformation is told in light speed to show his power as a minister in service to Christ, but this is no pie-in-the-sky view of Saul's success. It is his very power as a witness to Jesus as the Son of God that attracts real attention by those holding religious and political power in the culture. The liberating gospel of Jesus as the Son of God threatens the forced allegiance to the emperor, understood to be the son of a god and to the emperor's representatives.

It is no surprise that Saul's ministry receives a response of swift persecution. When the church is weak, isolationist, and ineffective in its witness, the world need not respond. The gospel is by its very definition a challenge to the status quo. Christ turns the world on its head, healing the sick, strengthening the weak, rescuing the lost, and freeing the oppressed (see Luke 4:17-21). A hard truth of the world is that most expressions of power are built by some standing— emotionally, physically, economically, even violently—on the backs (or necks) of others. When the church simply tries to meet the spiritual needs of its members as an insider group, these expressions of power are not challenged. But Saul immediately takes the gospel into the public sphere and does so with great credibility. Forcing debate, he makes the powers that be take the gospel seriously.

SHARING THE SCRIPTURE

PREPARING TO TEACH

Preparing Our Hearts

Ponder this week's devotional reading from Psalm 18:20-30 in which the writer gives thanks for the military triumph of a king. More specifically, as the introduction notes, David sang this song in gratitude for God's deliverance of him from his enemies, including King Saul. How does God deal with those who live with integrity according to the way of the Lord? What does the psalmist say about God?

Pray that you and the students will give thanks and praise to God.

Preparing Our Minds

Study the background Scripture and the lesson Scripture, both of which are from Acts 9:19b-31.

Consider this question as you prepare the lesson: *What impact does a strong and bold testimony have on the lives of others?*

Write on newsprint:
❏ information for next week's lesson, found under Continue the Journey.
❏ activities for further spiritual growth in Continue the Journey.

Review the Introduction, The Big Picture, Close-up, and Faith in Action, which all precede the first lesson of this quarter. Consider how you might use any of this material in today's lesson.

LEADING THE CLASS

(1) Gather to Learn

❖ Welcome the class members and guests.

❖ Pray that those who have come today will strive to make a credible witness for Christ.

❖ Define credibility as *"a power that inspires belief; trustworthiness."* Brainstorm answers to this question and write them on newsprint, which you will refer to again later: **What traits indicate that a person has a high level of credibility?** (Here are some possible answers: honesty, dependability, possessing credentials earned through education and/or experience, competence, ability to inspire others, effectiveness in doing whatever needs to be done, willingness to be accountable.)

❖ Read aloud today's focus statement: **Effective advocates boldly tell others about their deepest convictions. What impact does a strong and bold testimony have on the lives of others? The Scripture claims that Saul's bold preaching of the gospel was powerful, amazed the people, gave peace to many churches, and caused an increase in the number of followers.**

(2) Goal 1: Recount Saul's Acceptance as a Christian and His Zeal in Preaching About Jesus

❖ Lay the foundation for today's lesson by reading or retelling the Introduction in Understanding the Scripture.

❖ Choose a volunteer to read Acts 9:19b-31. Before the passage is read, assign four groups of people to listen to the story from the perspective of (a) the disciples in Damascus; (b) non-Christian Jews; (c) disciples in Jerusalem; (d) the Hellenists (Greek-speaking Jews).

❖ Discuss these questions. Encourage members of the various groups to give their perspectives as appropriate.

1. **What happened to cause Saul to move from a passionate persecutor to a member of the household of faith?** (See "From Persecutor to Person of Faith" in Interpreting the Scripture.)

2. **What prompted this persecutor turned member to stand up and preach on behalf of Christ?** (See "From Persecutor to Preacher" in Interpreting the Scripture.)

3. **What pushed those who did not agree with Saul to want to kill him?** (See "From Persecutor to Persecuted" in Interpreting the Scripture.)

4. **How did the stages of spiritual growth that Saul went through help him to establish credibility with others as a follower of Christ?**

❖ **Option:** Identify on a map the places where Saul went before, during, and shortly after this week's passage. Trace a line beginning with Tarsus, moving to Jerusalem, continuing on to Damascus, then to Caesarea, and back to Tarsus.

(3) Goal 2: Believe That the Learners Can Change in Jesus Christ and Then, Through Their Bold Witness, Help Others to Change

❖ Read this story about Lew Wallace, a Civil War general and the author of *Ben Hur.* **Prompted by a discussion on a train during which agnostic Colonel Robert G. Ingersoll quizzed Lew Wallace about Christianity, Wallace realized how little he knew about Christianity. A skeptic, Wallace decided to do an in-depth study in order to discredit Christianity. While writing the second chapter of a book in which he argued against Christianity, Wallace reportedly fell to his knees and cried out, "My Lord and my God." He came to believe in God and in the divinity of Christ. Not only did he come to Christ but he also wrote** *Ben Hur,* **an extremely popular book (1880) and later a movie. Who knows how many people came to Christ because Lew Wallace went in search of God and shared what he learned with others.**

❖ Invite class members to share stories of conversations, books, music, or other media that have prompted spiritual changes in their own lives. Encourage them to tell how they used their newly discovered beliefs and relationship with Jesus to help others find Christ or to grow in their discipleship.

(4) Goal 3: Invite Others to Come to Jesus and Join the Community of Faith by Sharing Personal Testimony of Jesus' Saving Grace

❖ Recall that in the last session students practiced bearing witness to Jesus by doing some roleplaying. Ask: **What experiences did you have this week in witnessing on behalf of Jesus? How difficult—or natural— was this for you? How did the person with whom you were speaking respond?**

❖ Challenge the class members to

take their witnessing a step further in the coming week by inviting those with whom they speak to attend Sunday school and/or worship with them next Sunday.

❖ Talk with the adults about how they might welcome any first-time visitors. Encourage them to be warm and friendly, but not to put pressure on the newcomers to answer questions or make commitments they are not ready to make. If you do not have extra Bibles on hand, ask several students to bring ones from home that guests could borrow during class.

(5) Continue the Journey

❖ Pray that as the learners depart, they will imitate Saul in being a credible witness for Christ.

❖ Post information for next week's session on newsprint for the students to copy:

- **Title: Peter Takes a Risk**
- **Background Scripture: Acts 10:1-44**
- **Lesson Scripture: Acts 10:24-38**
- **Focus of the Lesson: It is very natural for humans to show partiality to some and not to others. What are some possibilities when a person risks being open and welcoming to all? Peter's recognition that God shows no partiality allowed him to tell the good news to the Gentiles.**

❖ Post the following information on newsprint and provide paper and pencils for the students to copy it. Challenge the adults to grow spiritually by completing one or more of these activities related to this week's session.

(1) **Try to rate your own level of credibility as a Christian witness. Does your walk with Christ match your talk about Christ? If not, what changes do you need to make in your behavior?**

(2) **Practice hospitality by welcoming a newcomer to the faith. If this person is new to your congregation, help him or her to meet other people, learn about opportunities for ministry, and become comfortable in the church.**

(3) **Commit yourself financially to assist a missionary who is working in an unwelcoming environment. Recognize that in such an environment there may be those of other faiths or no faith who want to harm this witness for God. Pray daily that this person may have strength and boldness to fulfill God's calling in this place.**

❖ Sing or read aloud "Help Us Accept Each Other."

❖ Conclude today's session by leading the class in this benediction, which is adapted from Acts 9:20, the key verse for today: **Let us go forth to boldly proclaim that Jesus is the Son of God. Amen.**

UNIT 2: GIVING BOLD TESTIMONY
PETER TAKES A RISK

PREVIEWING THE LESSON

Lesson Scripture: Acts 10:24-38
Background Scripture: Acts 10:1-44
Key Verses: Acts 10:34-35

Focus of the Lesson:
It is very natural for humans to show partiality to some and not to others. What are some possibilities when a person risks being open and welcoming to all? Peter's recognition that God shows no partiality allowed him to tell the good news to the Gentiles.

Goals for the Learners:
(1) to recognize Peter's willingness to tell the good news of Jesus Christ to Cornelius, a Gentile.
(2) to appreciate how believers risk possible scorn when they step outside of accepted boundaries to make a bold witness for Jesus.
(3) to identify, support, and give voice to risk-takers for Christ in the local and world community.

Supplies:
Bibles, newsprint and marker, paper and pencils, hymnals

READING THE SCRIPTURE

NRSV
Lesson Scripture: Acts 10:24-38

²⁴The following day they came to Caesarea. Cornelius was expecting them and had called together his relatives and close friends. ²⁵On Peter's arrival Cornelius met him, and falling at his feet, worshiped him. ²⁶But Peter made him get up, saying, "Stand up; I am only a mortal." ²⁷And as he talked with him, he went in and found that many had assembled; ²⁸and he said to

CEB
Lesson Scripture: Acts 10:24-38

²⁴They arrived in Caesarea the following day. Anticipating their arrival, Cornelius had gathered his relatives and close friends. ²⁵As Peter entered the house, Cornelius met him and fell at his feet in order to honor him. ²⁶But Peter lifted him up, saying, "Get up! Like you, I'm just a human." ²⁷As they continued to talk, Peter went inside and found a large gathering of people.

them, "You yourselves know that it is unlawful for a Jew to associate with or to visit a Gentile; but God has shown me that I should not call anyone profane or unclean. ²⁹So when I was sent for, I came without objection. Now may I ask why you sent for me?"

³⁰Cornelius replied, "Four days ago at this very hour, at three o'clock, I was praying in my house when suddenly a man in dazzling clothes stood before me. ³¹He said, 'Cornelius, your prayer has been heard and your alms have been remembered before God. ³²Send therefore to Joppa and ask for Simon, who is called Peter; he is staying in the home of Simon, a tanner, by the sea.' ³³Therefore I sent for you immediately, and you have been kind enough to come. So now all of us are here in the presence of God to listen to all that the Lord has commanded you to say."

³⁴Then Peter began to speak to them: **"I truly understand that God shows no partiality, ³⁵but in every nation anyone who fears him and does what is right is acceptable to him.** ³⁶You know the message he sent to the people of Israel, preaching peace by Jesus Christ—he is Lord of all. ³⁷That message spread throughout Judea, beginning in Galilee after the baptism that John announced: ³⁸how God anointed Jesus of Nazareth with the Holy Spirit and with power; how he went about doing good and healing all who were oppressed by the devil, for God was with him.

²⁸He said to them, "You all realize that it is forbidden for a Jew to associate or visit with outsiders. However, God has shown me that I should never call a person impure or unclean. ²⁹For this reason, when you sent for me, I came without objection. I want to know, then, why you sent for me."

³⁰Cornelius answered, "Four days ago at this same time, three o'clock in the afternoon, I was praying at home. Suddenly a man in radiant clothing stood before me. ³¹He said, 'Cornelius, God has heard your prayers, and your compassionate acts are like a memorial offering to him. ³²Therefore, send someone to Joppa and summon Simon, who is known as Peter. He is a guest in the home of Simon the tanner, located near the seacoast.' ³³I sent for you right away, and you were kind enough to come. Now, here we are, gathered in the presence of God to listen to everything the Lord has directed you to say."

³⁴Peter said, **"I really am learning that God doesn't show partiality to one group of people over another. ³⁵Rather, in every nation, whoever worships him and does what is right is acceptable to him.** ³⁶This is the message of peace he sent to the Israelites by proclaiming the good news through Jesus Christ: He is Lord of all! ³⁷You know what happened throughout Judea, beginning in Galilee after the baptism John preached. ³⁸You know about Jesus of Nazareth, whom God anointed with the Holy Spirit and endowed with power. Jesus traveled around doing good and healing everyone oppressed by the devil because God was with him.

UNDERSTANDING THE SCRIPTURE

Introduction. Acts 10:1–11:18 is an extended narrative concerned with the conversion of the first Gentiles. This is a key set of passages for the whole of Luke–Acts and for Luke's theology. One of Luke's key concerns is to show how the inclusion of Gentiles in the church fulfills God's will and promise to Israel and is not something new that makes God seem inconsistent.

Acts 10:1-8. The narrative opens in Caesarea (a port city in Galilee to be distinguished from Caesarea Philippi further north outside of Palestine) with Cornelius, a charitable centurion who fears God, receiving a vision to send for Peter in Joppa (10:1-8). It is intriguing to note that the angel does not tell Cornelius *why* he is to send for Peter; yet the centurion does so obediently.

Acts 10:9-23. The next day, while in Joppa (around thirty miles south of Caesarea, also on the coast of the Mediterranean Sea), Peter also received a vision from the Lord that declared all animals clean (10:9-16). Such a proclamation was contrary to Jewish law and practice (see Leviticus 11:1-47 and Deuteronomy 14:3-20). As the apostle was trying to make sense of the vision, the messengers from Cornelius arrived and escorted him to Caesarea (10:17-23).

Acts 10:24-26. Since Cornelius was instructed to send for Peter through a divine revelation, he assumes Peter is divine. But Peter immediately disabuses Cornelius of this idea. Readers of Acts remember this issue occurring in chapter 3 where Peter and John healed a lame man and he and the crowd treat Peter like gods (3:12), although Peter denies it and uses the opportunity to preach Christ. While the same pattern is found in our lesson, it is more striking to see a Roman soldier acting this way toward an apostle than it was to see the crowd in the Temple doing so.

Acts 10:27-28. Peter enters Cornelius's house and Luke presents him as naming for the reader the problem at the center of the scene: A Jew was not to enter the house of a Gentile. In truth, this likely happened much more often than the Bible presents, but what is at stake is clear enough: the unique identity of Israel as the people of God. But Peter dismisses this problem with the briefest of references to his earlier vision: "God has shown me that I should not call anyone profane or unclean" (10:28). A modern reader of Acts might be puzzled at this. Peter's dream was about animals, with the instruction to kill and eat. But ancient dream interpretation assumed that dreams were rarely about what they seemed to be about. There was the assumption that dream imagery was usually symbolic of something else. So whereas Peter was initially puzzled about what the vision meant (10:17), now that he has arrived in Cornelius's house through divine guidance, the meaning and significance of the dream are revealed.

Acts 10:29-33. Even though the reader just read the narrative account of Cornelius's vision, Luke shapes the scene so that Cornelius recounts it for Peter. One clear emphasis of this repetition is to make absolutely clear to the reader that Cornelius in no way acted on his own initiative. He did exactly as he was instructed by an angel of God.

Acts 10:34-35. Peter also acted in obedience to divine instruction (10:19-21) as opposed to taking any initiative on his own. The fact that the Spirit gave him a vision overturning his understanding of who is clean and unclean and told him to go with Cornelius's messengers without hesitation shows that God, and not Peter, is responsible for the first Gentiles accepting the good news of Jesus Christ. That is why Peter declares that God shows no partiality in terms of ethnicity. This is a new pronouncement and essential to the early church's inclusion of the Gentiles, but Peter does not create the new pronouncement through his own means; he simply reports what he sees. By appearing to Cornelius and to Peter and bringing them together, and later by giving the Gentiles the Holy Spirit *before* they are baptized with water (10:44-47), God breaks down all boundaries between Jew and Gentile. Both are invited into Christ's fold as children of God.

It would be difficult to exaggerate the radical nature of this shift. Too often modern Christians have portrayed ancient Jewish adherence to kosher and Sabbath laws in terms of strict legalism. This is a terrible misrepresentation. Obedience in following dietary codes, Sabbath practices, and purity boundaries was a sign of the unique relationship God offered to the people of Israel. They were means of grace that set them apart from others, much as Christians

understand baptism to do for us. For God to say Christ has died and risen and is Lord of all, and therefore all are welcome in the church, is an eschatological shift in the ages. History begins anew with the Christ event.

We should, however, punctuate this claim with a caveat that the removal of a boundary does not mean the church is to have no boundaries. All are invited is not the same thing as "anything goes." Faith and ethical action are requirements for entrance into the church, for both Gentile and Jew.

Acts 10:36-43. Upon making the new pronouncement, Peter returns to the traditional proclamation (compare the portions of earlier sermons in Acts 2:22-32; 3:17-26; 5:30-32). In the introduction to the sermon, he tells the beginning of the story of Jesus, that is, his baptism and his works by the Holy Spirit (a foreshadowing of the gift of the Spirit and the baptism to occur in verses 44-47). He goes on to narrate the death and resurrection of Jesus, mentioning the apostles as witnesses in accordance with the prophets (10:39-43).

Acts 10:44. The gift of Holy Spirit in Acts usually follows proclamation and comes in relation to baptism and the laying on of hands of the apostles (for example, see 2:37-41; 8:14-17). In a striking fashion, God gives the Spirit to those listening to Peter while he was still speaking, signaling that it is God and not Peter who brings the Gentiles into the messianic community.

INTERPRETING THE SCRIPTURE

Witness: Seeing Something Happen

In the four Gospels, Peter is sometimes characterized as confused and

filled with misunderstanding. But that is not the case in Acts. In this post-resurrection narrative, Peter understands the good news of Jesus

Christ and proclaims it to the world, starting at Pentecost. He is the head of the church for the first half of the story (chapters 1–11) and a model for readers.

Peter, in Acts, is the epitome of theological understanding, and yet in 10:17 he is "puzzled." He is puzzled because the divine revelation he received came in the form of a dream, and dreams in the ancient world were assumed to be filled with obscure symbols that required unraveling. He was puzzled because the dream seemed to go counter to everything he knew and understood theologically.

Whereas at times confusion in the Gospels is meant to show that Peter does not yet have the faith he needs to have, "puzzlement" here means something else altogether. The Greek word Luke uses for being puzzled shows up two other times in Acts. First, Luke says that the crowds gathered in Jerusalem from all over the Roman Empire are puzzled (or "perplexed") when they hear the apostles speaking in their own languages (2:12). Second, Luke uses the word to describe the response of the religious leaders in the Temple when they discover that the Lord had rescued the apostles from prison (5:24). Those two incidents, along with 10:17, show that being puzzled is the correct response when one has witnessed something extraordinary, something that God has done.

Our whole lesson is predicated on the fact that Peter is a witness to something that would have been as unimaginable as someone who speaks only one language being heard speaking a language he never learned, or as unexplainable as the prison door being locked and guarded but the prison cell miraculously empty. The tearing down of the boundary between Jew and Gentile is just as much a divine act as these other instances. Peter does not go to Joppa to meet with Cornelius out of the goodness of his heart; he does not go because he has a passion for ministry with the "Other." He goes because he witnessed something amazing.

Witness: Testifying to What Happened

When you witness something amazing, you are empowered to give an amazing testimony. Luke makes it clear that none of what happens in this scene is Peter's doing. God gives both Cornelius and Peter visions telling them what to do. God even sends the Spirit upon the Gentiles before Peter finishes his sermon (10:44)! Peter has initiated nothing.

But neither has Peter resisted God's will. Even while perplexed at the vision he receives, he goes without hesitation with Cornelius's messengers to a town where he knows no one. He goes to the house of a Gentile even though he is a Jew. He goes to the house of a Roman centurion with significant power. The scenario is fraught with danger, but Peter goes—not at his own initiative but in trusting obedience to the God who revealed something amazing and perplexing to him.

He goes to share what he has seen. After all, this has been his calling since the beginning of Acts (see 1:8). As one who witnessed the resurrection, he was instructed to give witness to those who would hear him tell of Jesus throughout the world. And now as one who witnessed a new revelation that Jesus as Lord *of all* means all are welcomed by the Lord, he gives a new witness to a new audience.

Peter as a witness is no stranger to the risks that come with the job. He has been arrested, threatened, and beaten, but this is a new risk. Peter cannot know what Cornelius wants from him. He cannot know whether he is friend or foe. He cannot know whether those who hear him will accept or reject the testimony he brings. But he certainly knows what it means for a Jew to be summoned by a Roman centurion. But he goes anyway, because the opportunity to give testimony to what one has witnessed from God is worth the risk.

He does indeed give bold and new testimony to this new Gentile audience. He begins by affirming them. This would have been standard procedure in ancient rhetorical practice. Speak well of your audience in order to mold them into sympathetic hearers. But Peter does not do this in a typical manner. He does not praise them. He does not speak of his own personal view to them. He tells them how the God of Israel views them (10:28, 34). God does not see them as second-class, as unclean, as Gentiles. God judges them just as God judges the Jews—on the basis of their faith ("fear of God") and their treatment of others ("does what is right," 10:35). In other words, all are judged on the basis of the greatest commandments: love of God and love of neighbor (see Luke 10:25-28). This is a radical witness for a Jew to offer to a gathering of Gentiles: You and I stand on the same ground before God. And he goes on to make clear that that ground has been cleared by Jesus of Nazareth, who was baptized by John, did wondrous acts of compassion through the Holy Spirit, was crucified, and raised from the dead. For the first time in history, Gentiles are told that what

the Messiah of Israel did, he did for them as well for Jews.

Witness: Going Out to Spread the Word

Peter not only risks rejection, persecution, and even death by one who represented Roman mighty military power but he also risks scorn from his brothers and sisters in the church. He is not a good church politician in this scene. He failed to consult with other church leaders before preaching to these Gentiles in Joppa. Just because it is the right thing to do, just because the Spirit told him to do it, does not mean others in the church will like it (see next week's lesson).

To be a witness in Acts is to be on the move into new territories and to speak to new people. A witness cannot stay at home and still be a witness. A witness must go *out* and testify before "others" who are not like him or her.

Luke tells Peter's story not as a biographical tale lifting up his unique qualities as a preacher and risk-taker. He tells Peter's story as an example for the church. Christ's grace knows no boundaries, and neither should the church of Jesus Christ. If the church is to continue being a faithful witness to God's good news, we must cross boundaries into new territories, reaching out to those who have scorned us. We must risk rejection and oppression; otherwise the church becomes a country club with a chaplain. Instead of looking to those "like us," the church must assume that God wants those radically different from us in the church with us. Who are the unclean Gentiles to whom the Lord calls us to offer the gospel? Who are "they" that should be part of "us" in Christ?

SHARING THE SCRIPTURE

PREPARING TO TEACH

Preparing Our Hearts

Ponder this week's devotional reading from Romans 8:31-39. In what situations do you need to hear that God is for you? Who else needs to hear this good news? What effect does the news that there is nothing that can separate you from God's love have on your faith?

Pray that you and the students will believe that you are so secure in God's love that you can take risks to help others come to know Jesus.

Preparing Our Minds

Study the background Scripture from Acts 10:1-44 and the lesson Scripture from Acts 10:24-38.

Consider this question as you prepare the lesson: *What are some possibilities when we risk being open and welcoming to all?*

Write on newsprint:

❏ information for next week's lesson, found under Continue the Journey.

❏ activities for further spiritual growth in Continue the Journey.

Review the Introduction, The Big Picture, Close-up, and Faith in Action, which all precede the first lesson of this quarter. Consider how you might use any of this material in today's lesson.

Prepare a brief lecture to help participants understand the background of today's Scripture lesson. Material from Introduction through Acts 10:9-23 in Understanding the Scripture will be useful to you.

LEADING THE CLASS

(1) Gather to Learn

❖ Welcome the class members and guests.

❖ Pray that those who have come today will be ready to welcome all people.

❖ Discuss these questions:

1. **Do you see our congregation as one that welcomes all people? If not, who is excluded—and why?** (While your church will not ban people outright, things within the church could be sending signals that all are not welcome. Think, for example, about how accessible the building, classrooms, and sanctuary are to someone who has mobility challenges. How easy would a person who has difficulty reading find your bulletin to follow? Are receivers for a hearing system, or a sign language interpreter, available for those who have hearing challenges? Is safe childcare in a clean environment available during worship and Sunday school? Do teens have a dedicated room for study and fellowship?)

2. **What steps could we take to become a more hospitable church?**

❖ Read aloud today's focus statement: **It is very natural for humans to show partiality to some and not to others. What are some possibilities when a person risks being open and welcoming to all? Peter's recognition that God shows no partiality allowed him to tell the good news to the Gentiles.**

(2) Goal 1: Recognize Peter's Willingness to Tell the Good News of Jesus Christ to Cornelius, a Gentile

❖ Present the lecture you have prepared to provide background for today's Scripture lesson.

❖ Choose two volunteers, one to read Acts 10:24-33 and the other to read verses 34-38. Ask:

1. **What were some of the risks Peter was taking even to walk into Cornelius's home?** (See "Witness: Testifying to What Happened" in Interpreting the Scripture.)

2. **Considering the fact that Cornelius had invited many others to hear Peter, what do you think he was expecting? What risks was Cornelius, a devout God-fearer, taking in inviting all these people?**

3. **What has Peter learned about Jesus that will help him to strengthen his relationship with the Messiah and with other people?**

(3) Goal 2: Appreciate How Believers Risk Possible Scorn When They Step Outside of Accepted Boundaries to Make a Bold Witness for Jesus

❖ Form two groups and give newsprint and a marker to each group.

Group 1: Brainstorm answers to this question: **What are the characteristics of a person who makes a bold witness for Jesus, no matter what the risks?** List ideas on newsprint. Here are some possibilities: a strong relationship with Jesus, trust that one need not be afraid because Jesus is always present, willingness to rely on the Holy Spirit, honesty, inner motivation to speak with a particular person, abiding concern for the welfare of the person being addressed.

Group 2: Brainstorm answers to this question: **What risks might a believer be called to take in order to make a bold witness for Christ?** Here are possibilities: loss of friends who do not share the same viewpoint, loss of one's own humility in trying to emphasize the rightness of a particular view, censure by the community or in the workplace.

❖ Call the groups together and ask each one to report. Ask: **How can you strengthen your own relationship with Jesus so as to feel that you are willing to take greater risks to spread the good news?**

(4) Goal 3: Identify, Support, and Give Voice to Risk-takers for Christ in the Local and World Community

❖ Ask these questions:

1. **Who is working within our community to make Christ better known to others?** (Consider, for example, a community resident who is trying to open a soup kitchen or homeless shelter in a local church. Or someone who is reaching out in Jesus' name to help those who are immigrants.)

2. **What kinds of risks is this person taking in order to serve God?** (Think about a possible loss of reputation, alienation from the rest of the community, a boycott of the risk-taker's business.)

3. **What can we as a church school class do to support this person who is taking risks not only**

to speak the gospel but also to bring about change that will let others know that God loves and cares about them?

❖ Challenge the adults to stand up for Jesus by standing up for this person (or group) who is trying, against all odds, to speak for those who need to hear the good news and see it become a reality in their lives.

(5) Continue the Journey

❖ Pray that as the learners depart, they will feel a renewed sense of courage and feel empowered to act on behalf of those who are excluded.

❖ Post information for next week's session on newsprint for the students to copy:

- Title: Trusting the Spirit
- Background Scripture: Acts 11:1-18
- Lesson Scripture: Acts 11:1-18
- Focus of the Lesson: When people's actions are contrary to community norms, they will be required to explain the reasons for their actions. How can they justify what they have done? Peter's report of how the Holy Spirit had converted the Gentiles gave rise to the Jerusalem church's endorsement of his actions.

❖ Post the following information on newsprint and provide paper and pencils for the students to copy it.

Challenge the adults to grow spiritually by completing one or more of these activities related to this week's session.

(1) Encourage other church members to work with you to identify and remove barriers that prevent all people from feeling welcome in your church. The information discussed in Gather to Learn can be a good starting point. Figure out how you will correct whatever problems you identify.

(2) Take a risk by making a bold witness this week either to someone who is not currently part of the church in order to invite this person in, or to challenge those within the congregation to do a better job of reaching out to include others.

(3) Volunteer for an ecumenical community ministry that helps the poor. Get to know those in need, as well as members of other faith communities. Recognize that God shows no partiality.

❖ Sing or read aloud "In Christ There Is No East or West."

❖ Conclude today's session by leading the class in this benediction, which is adapted from Acts 9:20, the key verse for October 11: **Let us go forth to boldly proclaim that Jesus is the Son of God. Amen.**

UNIT 2: GIVING BOLD TESTIMONY
TRUSTING THE SPIRIT

PREVIEWING THE LESSON

Lesson Scripture: Acts 11:1-18
Background Scripture: Acts 11:1-18
Key Verse: Acts 11:17

Focus of the Lesson:
When people's actions are contrary to community norms, they will be required to explain the reasons for their actions. How can they justify what they have done? Peter's report of how the Holy Spirit had converted the Gentiles gave rise to the Jerusalem church's endorsement of his actions.

Goals for the Learners:
(1) to learn that Peter's preaching to the Gentiles was affirmed by the believers in Jerusalem.
(2) to feel comfortable reaching out to persons who are different from themselves.
(3) to identify and live out New Testament Scriptures that emphasize inclusion of all people in the body of Christ.

Supplies:
Bibles, newsprint and marker, paper and pencils, hymnals

READING THE SCRIPTURE

NRSV

Lesson Scripture: Acts 11:1-18

¹Now the apostles and the believers who were in Judea heard that the Gentiles had also accepted the word of God. ²So when Peter went up to Jerusalem, the circumcised believers criticized him, ³saying, "Why did you go to uncircumcised men and eat with them?" ⁴Then Peter began to explain it to them, step by step, saying, ⁵"I was in the city of Joppa praying, and

CEB

Lesson Scripture: Acts 11:1-18

¹The apostles and the brothers and sisters throughout Judea heard that even the Gentiles had welcomed God's word. ²When Peter went up to Jerusalem, the circumcised believers criticized him. ³They accused him, "You went into the home of the uncircumcised and ate with them!"

⁴Step-by-step, Peter explained what had happened. ⁵"I was in the city of

in a trance I saw a vision. There was something like a large sheet coming down from heaven, being lowered by its four corners; and it came close to me. ⁶As I looked at it closely I saw four-footed animals, beasts of prey, reptiles, and birds of the air. ⁷I also heard a voice saying to me, 'Get up, Peter; kill and eat.' ⁸But I replied, 'By no means, Lord; for nothing profane or unclean has ever entered my mouth.' ⁹But a second time the voice answered from heaven, 'What God has made clean, you must not call profane.' ¹⁰This happened three times; then everything was pulled up again to heaven. ¹¹At that very moment three men, sent to me from Caesarea, arrived at the house where we were. ¹²The Spirit told me to go with them and not to make a distinction between them and us. These six brothers also accompanied me, and we entered the man's house. ¹³He told us how he had seen the angel standing in his house and saying, 'Send to Joppa and bring Simon, who is called Peter; ¹⁴he will give you a message by which you and your entire household will be saved.' ¹⁵And as I began to speak, the Holy Spirit fell upon them just as it had upon us at the beginning. ¹⁶And I remembered the word of the Lord, how he had said, 'John baptized with water, but you will be baptized with the Holy Spirit.' **¹⁷If then God gave them the same gift that he gave us when we believed in the Lord Jesus Christ, who was I that I could hinder God?"** ¹⁸When they heard this, they were silenced. And they praised God.

Joppa praying when I had a visionary experience. In my vision, I saw something like a large linen sheet being lowered from heaven by its four corners. It came all the way down to me. ⁶As I stared at it, wondering what it was, I saw four-legged animals—including wild beasts—as well as reptiles and wild birds. ⁷I heard a voice say, 'Get up, Peter! Kill and eat!' ⁸I responded, 'Absolutely not, Lord! Nothing impure or unclean has ever entered my mouth.' ⁹The voice from heaven spoke a second time, 'Never consider unclean what God has made pure.' ¹⁰This happened three times, then everything was pulled back into heaven. ¹¹At that moment three men who had been sent to me from Caesarea arrived at the house where we were staying. ¹²The Spirit told me to go with them even though they were Gentiles. These six brothers also went with me, and we entered that man's house. ¹³He reported to us how he had seen an angel standing in his house and saying, 'Send to Joppa and summon Simon, who is known as Peter. ¹⁴He will tell you how you and your entire household can be saved.' ¹⁵When I began to speak, the Holy Spirit fell on them, just as the Spirit fell on us in the beginning. ¹⁶I remembered the Lord's words: 'John will baptize with water, but you will be baptized with the Holy Spirit.' **¹⁷If God gave them the same gift he gave us who believed in the Lord Jesus Christ, then who am I? Could I stand in God's way?"**

¹⁸Once the apostles and other believers heard this, they calmed down. They praised God.

UNDERSTANDING THE SCRIPTURE

Acts 11:1-3. In the previous chapter (Acts 10), Peter baptizes the first Gentiles into the messianic community. Chapter 11 continues this story, but moves the setting from Joppa and Caesarea back to Jerusalem, the headquarters for the new community. Before Peter arrives, word that Gentiles had accepted the word of God has already reached the whole church, referred to in verse 1 as "the apostles and the believers." (The Greek is literally just "brothers," but "believers" is used inclusively for all members in the NRSV; the inclusive familial metaphor of "brothers and sisters" is used in the CEB.)

In verse 2, then, the mention of "the circumcised" signals a change of reference. All Christians up to this point were Jewish, so all were part of "circumcised" Israel. The term, however, is used here to refer to a subset of the church, over against the whole of the community of faith and over against the apostolic leaders. "The circumcised" does not refer to the state of being of the subgroup but to their attitude. They are observant of Torah and expect others in the church to be observant in the same manner.

Their identification as the circumcised, along with their accusation that Peter has failed to observe the Torah by engaging in table-fellowship with Gentiles (11:3), makes clear that this is a trial scene. Readers of Acts are familiar with trial scenes at which the apostles defend themselves before the powers that be (4:1-22; 5:17-40; 6:8–7:60). But this trial is a church trial.

We should be clear that "the circumcised" are not accusing the Gentiles of doing something wrong. They are accusing their fellow Jewish-Christians of improper conduct. And we should avoid describing their motivation as being characterized by some kind of strict legalism. Peter's initial response to the vision in Joppa was also one of rejection and puzzlement (10:14, 17). The issue is not legalism but identity: The assumption at play is that to be Christian is to be Jewish.

Acts 11:4-12a. Peter defends himself simply by narrating and commenting on what happened to him. The repetition of this story in such detail shows how important it is for Luke's plot and theology. (Compare the repetition of Paul's conversion in chapters 9, 22, 26.)

Peter's recitation starts with the occurrences in Joppa, particularly his vision of the sheet lowering with animals previously considered unclean and the Lord instructing him to eat them (11:5-7). He names his own resistance to follow the instructions (11:8). This description invites those accusing him to identify with him. In a sense he says to them, "When I first received these new instructions, I thought about the dream exactly as you are thinking about me now." But the Lord will not be resisted, and Peter continues on to describe the Lord's insistence and the recurrence of the dream (11:9-10).

Peter concludes this section of his defense narrative by telling of Cornelius's men arriving to take him to Caesarea. But when one is a witness giving testimony to something that happened, new insights and details are revealed. Such is the case here. Two such new details are especially interesting to note in Peter's recollection of the visit versus the way the narrator described it in 10:17-23.

First, Peter says, "The Spirit told me to go with them *and not to make a distinction between them and us*" (11:12, emphasis added). The last part of these instructions did not appear in the original version (see 10:19-20). In light of his whole experience, Peter now interprets the Spirit's instructions as explicitly concerning the issue of partiality.

Second, Peter does not simply say that he goes with the men to see Cornelius, but that "*these* six brothers" (emphasis added) went with him (11:12). In 10:23, the narrator only vaguely mentions that "some of the believers [Greek: brothers] from Joppa accompanied him." This new reference to six specific Christians (who are presumably with Peter still as he makes his defense in Jerusalem), makes clear that there are other members of the community of faith who can give testimony to what happened in Caesarea and that Peter did not act independently of the Christian community.

Acts 11:12b-17. Peter's version of what occurred in Joppa is simply the setup for what occurs in Caesarea. Note that Peter gives his accusers no details about Cornelius. He is simply "the man" (11:12)—no name, no occupation, no rank in the military or in society. Just the man, the Gentile man. Peter does, however, recount the man's version of his own dream. Peter is laying the groundwork for his jury to acquit him on the basis that neither he nor "the man" did anything of their own accord, but only in obedience to divine prodding.

In narrating the man's dream, Peter again adds a key detail not found in the original. Peter's summary of Cornelius's speech describing why he sent for the apostle has the Spirit say, "He [Peter] will give you a message by which you and your entire household will be saved" (11:14; compare 10:4-6, 31-32). In the original version, Peter first arrives at Cornelius's house and then interprets the dream concerning food to be about all people being clean (10:28). Here he moves that interpretation back to Joppa and has it explicitly named by the Holy Spirit. Peter has raised the stakes of his case by doing this. This places the accusers in the position of being against God by criticizing Peter and the man's actions.

This assertion is punctuated all the more strongly with the conclusion to Peter's defense (11:17; compare 10:44-48). Notice how Peter phrases this conclusion. He makes clear that what he did in Caesarea was to humbly recognize that he should not resist God if God decided that the Gentiles were worthy of being given the Spirit. This conclusion is an invitation to his accusers to take the same posture.

Acts 11:18. And they do. The narrator's description of the accusers being "silenced" (a better translation than the CEB's "calmed down") is not meant to indicate that they were speechless, but that the conviction turned on them and they had no more criticism in them. But they did not simply drop the case. Their praise offered to God shows they joined Peter in celebrating this new thing.

INTERPRETING THE SCRIPTURE

Holy Spirit = Paradigm Shift

Congregations and denominations are filled with decision-making bodies. How they do their work is dependent on a range of things, from the personalities of those who make up the specific committees and boards to the politics of the larger body, from the history of the group to the future for which they hope. The diverse moral values and personal commitments, worldviews and theologies, found in communities of faith make decision-making a difficult process.

But in the body of Christ, we do not believe we make whatever decisions we make alone. We find in Acts 11 (and later in the related story of the Jerusalem Council in chapter 15) a model for discernment in the church. It is a model less for how the church should *make* decisions and more for how we should *confirm* decisions already made by the Holy Spirit.

The Jerusalem church has a conflict. Peter has baptized Gentiles without first consulting them. "The circumcised" implicitly question whether he should have done this by explicitly accusing the apostle of breaking the Torah. Which direction should the church follow: Include Gentiles in the messianic community or maintain the tradition that formed Peter and the Jewish Christians in the faith?

Peter's defense is simply to tell the story of what happened rather than present an argument for his actions. But of course there is no such thing as a neutral witness. Luke presents Peter as choosing a particular theological lens through which to narrate the event: The Holy Spirit is the main character of the story and initiated the radical change that occurred. Peter, the man, and his household responded in the only way they could: obediently. And the others in the church are persuaded by his story.

We should be clear that Peter is not the hero of this passage. "The circumcised" are. They began the court case criticizing Peter (11:2) but end the story glorifying God for that in which Peter participated. They are the heroes of this scene because they faithfully argued Peter was wrong in his actions and then faithfully changed their mind based on the evidence. Instead of deciding what they desire for the church or what they think is right for the church and refusing to budge, they humbly submit to the will of God, just as Peter, on the one hand, and Cornelius and his household, on the other, did in the story Peter narrates. The circumcised are willing to make a complete paradigm shift in their understanding of their self-identity, the church, salvation, and God if that is the direction God leads.

Paradigm Shift = New Members

The 180-degree turn the church makes in Acts 11 has to do with who is welcomed into the community of faith.

What is required for inclusion has already been made clear in Acts. At Pentecost, when the crowds ask Peter what they must do to be saved, Peter tells them to repent and be baptized so that they might be forgiven of their sins and receive the Holy Spirit (Acts 2:38). This requirement does not change in Acts 10–11. Peter's recognition that God shows no partiality and his proclamation to Cornelius and his household does not, however, translate into a claim that all are welcome without any boundaries or expectations of those invited. Repentance and forgiveness, baptism and the gift of the Spirit, are both gifts and requirements. Any who would join the messianic community must become a new person.

The turn the church makes is not *what* is required for entry into the community of faith, but rather the turn involves *who* is allowed to take the path to salvation and membership in the Christian community. Before this moment in the narrative, those invited were only Jews. Now Gentiles are also invited to become new persons, to experience the salvation of Jesus the Christ as part of the church. They are invited to repent of their sinfulness and experience the forgiveness of their sins. They are invited to be baptized and receive the Holy Spirit. And the reason the church invites them into Christ in this way is because God gave them the Spirit *before* the church baptized them. In other words, they had no choice if they were going to respond faithfully to what God had done.

New Members = New Church

"The circumcised" in the story are wise to be concerned about letting Gentiles into the church. In our modern, individualistic culture, we may too easily miss what is at stake in admitting people who are radically different from the current membership. We focus on what the individual gets from joining or how joining may affect that individual. "The circumcised" recognized, however, that admitting someone who is different from those already in the community would change the very nature and identity of the community.

In the past the church has been aware of this potential change in community and has resisted accepting those who are different. African Americans were allowed in worship—as long as they watched from the balcony. If European Americans allowed them to be full and equal participants in the body of Christ, then they would become "brothers and sisters" in Christ.

Women have always been a part of the church, but men have not always allowed them to be full members in the sense of sharing power and leadership roles in the church. If men allowed women to be ordained or hold lay offices in the church, then they would have to distribute power in the community in wider circles than they preferred.

The circumcised recognized that admitting Gentiles into the messianic community would change the very nature and identity of the community. Yet they did it anyway. Not out of the goodness of their hearts but out of faithfulness to the directive of the Holy Spirit. They went kicking and screaming into the new day, but they went. They let go of the idea that the Jewish Messiah was the messiah of only Israel. They let go of the idea that salvation in Jesus Christ was offered only to Jews who would repent and be baptized. They let go of the idea that to be in the church meant to observe Torah. They were able to let go of these things because they had faith that God would not give away the Holy Spirit willy-nilly. They trusted God so much that they were willing to abandon the boundaries between "us" and "them" that had defined so much of their existence. God created a new "us." Peter recognized it as a firsthand witness in Caesarea, and the circumcised recognized it through Peter's testimony in Jerusalem.

For the church to be faithful to God's providential guidance, we must always be ready to open our doors wider than we have opened them in the past. This does not mean that we should have no standards of membership and accept anyone simply because we are concerned about the loss of members in twenty-first century. It does mean, however, that we should be ready to invite anyone who receives the Holy Spirit to repent, be baptized, receive forgiveness, and become our sister or brother without first having to look or act exactly like we do. The Spirit moves where the Spirit will and we should follow faithfully.

SHARING THE SCRIPTURE

PREPARING TO TEACH

Preparing Our Hearts

Ponder this week's devotional reading from 1 Thessalonians 1:1-7. Written in about A.D. 50, 1 Thessalonians is thought to be the oldest book of the New Testament. What do you learn about Paul's relationship with the church at Thessalonica from these first seven verses? If the apostle were to write a letter to your congregation, what might he say to you?

Pray that you and the students will be open to the leading of the Holy Spirit that the good news of Jesus may enliven you.

Preparing Our Minds

Study the background Scripture and the lesson Scripture, both of which are from Acts 11:1-18.

Consider this question as you prepare the lesson: *How can people who have stepped beyond the boundaries of the faith community's norms on behalf of Christ justify what they have done?*

Write on newsprint:

❏ questions listed for Goal 3 in Sharing the Scripture.

❏ information for next week's lesson, found under Continue the Journey.

❏ activities for further spiritual growth in Continue the Journey.

Review the Introduction, The Big Picture, Close-up, and Faith in Action, which all precede the first lesson of this quarter. Consider how you might use any of this material in today's lesson.

LEADING THE CLASS

(1) Gather to Learn

❖ Welcome the class members and guests.

❖ Pray that those who have come today will trust God's Spirit to lead them.

❖ Read: **At times, people have marched or demonstrated in large numbers, held letter-writing campaigns, staged sit-ins, even waged revolutions to protest the status quo of what they think are harmful policies, actions, or attitudes. The American Revolution, civil rights movement of the 1950s and 1960s, Occupy Wall Street, and Arab Spring are just a few examples of such protests. Those involved were often arrested** and had to give an account of why they challenged the accepted norms of the community. What are some reasons people may have given to justify their participation in behaviors contrary to the community's norms? (Hear several ideas.)

❖ Read aloud today's focus statement: **When people's actions are contrary to community norms, they will be required to explain the reasons for their actions. How can they justify what they have done? Peter's report of how the Holy Spirit had converted the Gentiles gave rise to the Jerusalem church's endorsement of his actions.**

(2) Goal 1: Learn That Peter's Preaching to the Gentiles Was Affirmed by the Believers in Jerusalem

❖ Choose a volunteer to read Acts 11:1-18 and then ask:

1. **Why did the believers in Jerusalem criticize Peter?** (See Acts 11:1-3 in Understanding the Scripture.)
2. **What assumptions do these believers in Jerusalem make about who can be a Christian?** (See Acts 11:1-3 in Understanding the Scripture.)
3. **Recall that you have already heard Peter's story in chapter 10. Do you note any differences in details as he retells the story in chapter 11? If so, what are they and why might they be important?** (See Acts 11:4-12a and 11:12b-17 in Understanding the Scripture.)
4. **How do the believers from Jerusalem respond once they hear what Peter has to say?** (See Acts 11:18 in Understanding the Scripture.)

5. **How does the Holy Spirit influence the events that have occurred?** (See "Holy Spirit = Paradigm Shift" in Interpreting the Scripture.)

(3) Goal 2: Feel Comfortable Reaching Out to Persons Who Are Different From the Learners

❖ Read "New Members = New Church" from Interpreting the Scripture.

❖ Read at least one of these scenarios and discuss how the people who are currently in the church could reach out to those who are in close geographic proximity but who would not likely just show up. Also identify steps that could be taken to help those who are already in the church feel comfortable about reaching out to those who are in some way different from them.

• **Scenario 1: A small, rural church, composed mostly of farmers who had known each other for decades, finds itself in the middle of a housing boom. Former farm land is being sold to developers, and the new residents are young families with two working parents who commute long distances to their jobs.**
• **Scenario 2: A once stately city church has fallen into disrepair as its congregation has died or moved away. New residents in this community are reluctant to come into what seems to be a forbidding stone fortress. The few original members who are left no longer live in the area and do not know how to reach those now in the**

community. To complicate matters further, many of the new residents do not speak or read English fluently.

(4) Goal 3: Identify and Live Out New Testament Scriptures That Emphasize Inclusion of All People in the Body of Christ

❖ Post these four Scriptures on newsprint. Form four or more groups and assign each group one Scripture: 1 Corinthians 12:12-13; Galatians 3:27-28; Ephesians 4:1-6; Ephesians 4:11-13. Each group is to discuss these questions, which you may wish to post on newsprint:

1. What does this passage say to you about who is to be included in the body of Christ?
2. What suggestions does this passage give for how people can be included?

❖ Bring everyone together to hear ideas from each group.

❖ Challenge the class members to consider ways that they can invite and include people who may in some way be different from them.

(5) Continue the Journey

❖ Pray that as the learners depart, they will look for opportunities to welcome others in the name of Jesus.

❖ Post information for next week's session on newsprint for the students to copy:

- Title: God Rescues Peter
- Background Scripture: Acts 12:1-24
- Lesson Scripture: Acts 12:1-11
- Focus of the Lesson: In the midst of perilous life situations, deliverance sometimes appears to come through miraculous means. How

might the faithful be rescued from dangerous life circumstances? Acts shows that the fervent prayer of the church and the work of an angel provided Peter's deliverance.

❖ Post the following information on newsprint and provide paper and pencils for the students to copy it. Challenge the adults to grow spiritually by completing one or more of these activities related to this week's session.

(1) Praise and thank someone for work he or she has done to bring new believers into the church. Talk with this person about how the Holy Spirit's leading empowered him or her to act.
(2) Go with a friend to a service or event at a house of worship that is different from your own. How did people there welcome you and make you feel at home? How was this experience similar to and different from the way you experience God in your own congregation?
(3) Review the story of Peter and Cornelius in Acts 10–11. Where do you see yourself and your congregation in this story? If you are like the believers in Jerusalem, what steps might you take to overcome your narrow assumptions concerning who can join the church?

❖ Sing or read aloud "Filled with the Spirit's Power."

❖ Conclude today's session by leading the class in this benediction, which is adapted from Acts 9:20, the key verse for October 11: **Let us go forth to boldly proclaim that Jesus is the Son of God. Amen.**

UNIT 3: SPREADING THE GOSPEL
GOD RESCUES PETER

PREVIEWING THE LESSON

Lesson Scripture: Acts 12:1-11
Background Scripture: Acts 12:1-24
Key Verse: Acts 12:5

Focus of the Lesson:
In the midst of perilous life situations, deliverance sometimes appears to come through miraculous means. How might the faithful be rescued from dangerous life circumstances? Acts shows that the fervent prayer of the church and the work of an angel provided Peter's deliverance.

Goals for the Learners:
(1) to explore the story of Peter's deliverance from prison.
(2) to recognize and appreciate the power of prayer, especially in difficult circumstances.
(3) to commit to praying for those whose witness puts them in difficult or life-threatening situations.

Supplies:
Bibles, newsprint and marker, paper and pencils, hymnals, optional map

---

READING THE SCRIPTURE

NRSV

Lesson Scripture: Acts 12:1-11

¹About that time King Herod laid violent hands upon some who belonged to the church. ²He had James, the brother of John, killed with the sword. ³After he saw that it pleased the Jews, he proceeded to arrest Peter also. (This was during the Festival of Unleavened Bread.) ⁴When he had seized him, he put him in prison and handed him over to four squads of soldiers to guard

CEB

Lesson Scripture: Acts 12:1-11

¹About that time King Herod began to harass some who belonged to the church. ²He had James, John's brother, killed with a sword. ³When he saw that this pleased the Jews, he arrested Peter as well. This happened during the Festival of Unleavened Bread. ⁴He put Peter in prison, handing him over to four squads of soldiers, sixteen in all, who guarded him. He planned to charge him publicly after

him, intending to bring him out to the people after the Passover. **⁵While Peter was kept in prison, the church prayed fervently to God for him.**

⁶The very night before Herod was going to bring him out, Peter, bound with two chains, was sleeping between two soldiers, while guards in front of the door were keeping watch over the prison. ⁷Suddenly an angel of the Lord appeared and a light shone in the cell. He tapped Peter on the side and woke him, saying, "Get up quickly." And the chains fell off his wrists. ⁸The angel said to him, "Fasten your belt and put on your sandals." He did so. Then he said to him, "Wrap your cloak around you and follow me." ⁹Peter went out and followed him; he did not realize that what was happening with the angel's help was real; he thought he was seeing a vision. ¹⁰After they had passed the first and the second guard, they came before the iron gate leading into the city. It opened for them of its own accord, and they went outside and walked along a lane, when suddenly the angel left him. ¹¹Then Peter came to himself and said, "Now I am sure that the Lord has sent his angel and rescued me from the hands of Herod and from all that the Jewish people were expecting."

the Passover. **⁵While Peter was held in prison, the church offered earnest prayer to God for him.**

⁶The night before Herod was going to bring Peter's case forward, Peter was asleep between two soldiers and bound with two chains, with soldiers guarding the prison entrance. ⁷Suddenly an angel from the Lord appeared and a light shone in the prison cell. After nudging Peter on his side to awaken him, the angel raised him up and said, "Quick! Get up!" The chains fell from his wrists. ⁸The angel continued, "Get dressed. Put on your sandals." Peter did as he was told. The angel said, "Put on your coat and follow me." ⁹Following the angel, Peter left the prison. However, he didn't realize the angel had actually done all this. He thought he was seeing a vision. ¹⁰They passed the first and second guards and came to the iron gate leading to the city. It opened for them by itself. After leaving the prison, they proceeded the length of one street, when abruptly the angel was gone.

¹¹At that, Peter came to his senses and remarked, "Now I'm certain that the Lord sent his angel and rescued me from Herod and from everything the Jewish people expected."

UNDERSTANDING THE SCRIPTURE

Introduction. While Acts certainly presents persecution as a horrific response by powers that be to the mission and well-being of the church, it also portrays persecution as ultimately powerless to stop advance of the messianic community. After Stephen was brutally stoned and those calling on the name of Jesus were hunted down (6:8–8:3), Christians were scattered beyond Jerusalem (8:4) and began witnessing to Christ in accordance with the command of 1:8. We should expect the same sort of divine table-turning in chapter 12, in which Herod kills James and tries to kill Peter. Indeed, this chapter marks a major transition for the whole of Acts.

Acts 12:1-2. The lesson opens with the sudden appearance of King Herod. This Herod is Herod Agrippa, grandson of Herod the Great (mentioned in Luke 1:5). Even though Agrippa has played no role in Acts up to this point, the reader has a negative response to the mention of the name Herod due to the role Herod Antipas (simply called "Herod the tetrarch") plays as a persecutor of Jesus in the Gospel of Luke (see Luke 3:1, 19-20; 9:7-9; 13:31; 23:7-12; and yet another member of this family, Agrippa, will appear as a persecutor of Paul in Acts 25:13–26:32).

As suddenly as Herod appears, James is killed. The brevity of the reference to his martyrdom should not lead us to underestimate its importance for Luke's plot. Earlier Luke goes into great detail to show that after Judas's betrayal and death, the community was intent on keeping the number of apostles at twelve (Acts 1:15-26). With James's death, the days of the Twelve as the official leadership group of the church draw to a close.

Acts 12:3-4. Herod, who gains favor with the Jewish authorities (referred to here as simply "the Jews") by killing James, decides to kill Peter to gain more favor. The references to the "Festival of Unleavened Bread" and "Passover" are reminiscent of the timing of Jesus' passion. The reference to "four squads" of guards (along with the expanded description in verse 6 of the chains and guards on both sides of Peter and at the door) establishes how serious Herod is about keeping Peter in prison. These measures are surely meant to compensate for the fact that Peter has escaped from prison before (5:19). This exaggerated language functions in the same way

details of illness function in miracle stories in the Gospels. There, the more severe the symptoms, the more miraculous the cure. Here, the stronger the forces keeping Peter in prison, the more awesome the rescue. Escape appears to be impossible.

Acts 12:5-11. There is the impossible—and then there is God. The church is in fervent prayer for Peter (12:5), so the reader expects God to respond. (Luke–Acts speaks of prayer often, but this is the only occasion in which the author modifies praying with "fervently." Both the seriousness of the persecution and the intensity of the community's concern are highlighted.)

God does respond as expected. An angel appears, wakes Peter, and leads him out of the jail. The miraculous nature of the rescue is highlighted not only by the strength of the guard, chains, and gate imprisoning Peter but also by Peter's own unawareness that what appears to be happening is really happening. Perhaps the author wants the reader to think Peter assumes he is dreaming, but his actions are a little comical. After waking, the angel must give him step-by-step instructions on getting dressed; and only after Peter is out of the jail and the angel has left does Peter realize that God had rescued him.

Acts 12:12-17. The comical nature of that rescue scene is trumped by the humor in this one. Peter goes to Mary's house where the church is gathered. When Rhoda recognizes Peter's voice, she fails to let him into safety, but leaves him at the door and runs to tell the church that he is there (12:14). Those who have gathered specifically to pray for him refuse to believe that their prayers have been answered and think Rhoda is out of her mind (12:15; compare the reaction to the women who told the apostles of the empty tomb—they considered it an "idle tale," Luke 24:11).

Once Peter is finally admitted to Mary's house, he tells them of his rescue and concludes, "Tell this to James [likely the brother of Jesus as compared to the apostle who died in verse 2] and to the believers." And then the narrator concludes, "Then he left and went to another place." The instruction to pass the story on to James and Peter's departure (he is still a fugitive!) signals a passing of the torch of leadership of the Jerusalem church from the first generation of apostles to the next generation.

Acts 12:18-19a. Meanwhile back at the prison, Peter's escape is discovered. The result is that the guards are given the sentence intended for Peter—they are executed.

Acts 12:19b-24. The threat of Herod against the church comes to a swift end. Herod is in conflict with the cities of Tyre and Sidon. To appease Herod, the cities come to Caesarea, bribe a trusted servant of the king, and then flatter him in public, calling him a god. Herod does not deflect the praise and is immediately struck down by God and dies a grotesque death.

The Jewish historian Josephus tells a similar story of Agrippa's death at the hands of God for accepting praise as if he were divine (*Antiquities* 19.343-50). But for Acts, this death is not only related to his behavior in Caesarea. It is clearly retribution for his persecution of the church. This is signaled first by the contrast between Herod's actions and Peter's. Herod accepted praise from those calling him a god, but Peter rejected such praise when those who saw him heal a man in the Temple thought he was divine (Acts 3:12; compare a similar response from Paul and Barnabas in 14:11-18). It is signaled second by the fact that his death results in the word of God advancing and the church growing (12:24).

INTERPRETING THE SCRIPTURE

What Prayer Is Not

We must pay close attention to the way the narrator describes the church's prayer in Acts 12 if we are to avoid forcing our preconceived notions of prayer onto this scene. Luke writes, "The church prayed fervently to God for him [Peter]" (12:5, key verse) and then two verses later says, "Suddenly an angel of the Lord appeared." We people with a twenty-first-century, scientific mind-set are prone to think in terms of cause and effect even when reading ancient stories about supernatural occurrences.

In other words, we consciously or unconsciously assume the prayer is the cause and God taking action is the effect.

Our scene in Acts, however, makes no such connection. The church does what it does. And God does what God does. The two are related but the former does not result in the latter.

First of all, in prayer we do not inform God about situations of human suffering of which God is unaware since God knows all. God knew of Peter's imprisonment before the church named the persecution in prayer. God knew of the imprisonment before the church did. So the church praying for Peter tells God nothing new.

Second, prayer does not cajole, persuade, change, guilt, or force God into doing anything. It does not do this because it need not do this. God already cares and provides for us as is fitting to the character of God. And God's character is not subject to human desires and motivations, even the best of our desires and motivations. God is not a genie in a bottle, which if rubbed just right in our prayers will force God to come out and grant us our wish. So multiplying the number of people praying does not influence God. The right person saying the right words in the right place at the right time does not influence God. God does not need to be influenced. As the ancients said, God is by definition "for us." God is already, always, everywhere on our side. So the church praying for Peter did not convince God to be concerned with Peter's situation. God cared about Peter's persecution before the church ever spoke a word or breathed a sigh too deep for human words on Peter's behalf (Romans 8:26). In fact, the text signals that the rescue is God's initiative by the way it presents Peter as being completely at the mercy of the angel. Peter does not even get dressed without being instructed to do so. God acts of God's own accord, not because the community of faith prayed for Peter.

In other words, when we pray in times of distress, prayer is not about God and what God is or is not thinking, feeling, or doing.

What Prayer Is

If God is neither informed by our prayers nor persuaded to act on our or someone else's behalf by our prayers, what does prayer do? Why do we pray in times of distress? Why did the church pray *fervently* to God for Peter even after James was executed (12:2, 5)? In our praying, the church certainly uses language that sounds like we are telling God something God does not know yet. We certainly ask, beseech, and plead as if we might influence God's will. Why do we do this if prayer is not the human cause that brings about a divine effect?

We do so because humans are linguistic creatures. Our primary way of relating to ourselves, to others, to the world, and (yes) to God is through language. Informing God of what God already knows and asking God for something for which God need not be asked is our finite, human manner of relating to God as the anchor of our existence when something in life or the world has gone awry. In other words, prayer is not about God; it is about us.

Prayer can be defined as naming our finite human concerns to the Divine One who concerns us ultimately. We all have a multitude of concerns: health, school, livelihood, career, family, property, and so on. Some are small concerns and others occupy a great deal of our attention, energy, and personhood. For Christians, our greatest concern is (or should be) God. Prayer, then, is placing anything and everything that concerns us at any level in relationship to the One with whom we are concerned completely. To not do so risks either idolatry in which we think we can handle our concerns on our own or hopelessness in which we assume dire situations have the last word in defining the meaning of our circumstances and our ultimate fate.

The church prays for Peter not because God needs prayer to be God but because the church needs prayer to be the church. As the community of faith places our concerns before God, we place ourselves (and those for whom we pray) before God. In this way we lift God above all else. When the church prays, in other words, it fulfills the gift God has given us to love God with our whole heart, soul, strength, and mind (Luke 10:27).

What Prayer Also Is

As prayer is an expression of our love for God, it is also a gift from God to us, allowing us to love our neighbors (Luke 10:27). The church was offering Peter its love by praying fervently for him to God when he was in prison awaiting execution. By placing their concern for Peter in relation to their Ultimate Concern, they named Peter as being in relationship with God, as being under God's love. They did not cause the relationship to come into being, but acknowledged it—indeed, even celebrated it—by expressing their anguish over his situation.

Such a prayer is not a naive prayer. Because we do not assume we cause God to act on someone's behalf when we pray for that person, the church can pray for Peter in faith even as the community mourns the loss of James. Whether Peter dies at the hand of Herod as did James or is rescued from the tyrant, Peter has still been lovingly named as being under God's providential care in the church's prayers.

Prayer is not a substitution for Christian works of charity and justice in which we meet the needs of those we are able to meet. It is not a replacement for the church working to transform the world in accordance with the reign of God. But neither is prayer a way of avoiding caring for our neighbors. It is not escapism or a turning away from our responsibilities. John presents Jesus as saying, "No one has greater love than this, to lay down one's life for one's friends" (John 15:13). We might add that a pretty close second is to lay a neighbor down at God's feet in prayer. To pray fervently for those in need is a significant act of love and should never be dismissed as unimportant. Indeed, such prayer empowers the church to focus energy on the very concerns it raises up to God.

SHARING THE SCRIPTURE

PREPARING TO TEACH

Preparing Our Hearts

Ponder this week's devotional reading from Psalm 18:1-9. According to the heading, this psalm gives thanks for God's deliverance of David "from the hand of all his enemies, and from the hand of Saul." Which of the words in verse 2 would you use to describe God? What did the psalmist do to summon God for help? How did God respond?

Pray that you and the students will recognize that God is willing and able to come to your rescue.

Preparing Our Minds

Study the background Scripture from Acts 12:1-24 and the lesson Scripture from Acts 12:1-11.

Consider this question as you

prepare the lesson: *How might the faithful be rescued from life's perilous circumstances?*

Write on newsprint:

❏ information for next week's lesson, found under Continue the Journey.

❏ activities for further spiritual growth in Continue the Journey.

Review the Introduction, The Big Picture, Close-up, and Faith in Action, which all precede the first lesson of this quarter. Consider how you might use any of this material in today's lesson.

Check out websites where you can find information, including maps, about the persecution of Christians in countries around the world. Two helpful websites (as of 2014) are www.christianfreedom.org/persecuted-christians-map/ and www.opendoorsusa.org/persecution/about-persecution. Note several specific countries where persecution is occurring. If the website suggests specific prayers for people in any of these nations, take note of those. If your classroom does not have Internet access, try to make contact information available for the session.

LEADING THE CLASS

(1) Gather to Learn

❖ Welcome the class members and guests.

❖ Pray that those who have come today will recognize the value of fervent prayer.

❖ Invite volunteers to tell stories to the group (or small groups) of people and situations for which they have offered fervent prayers. Suggest that they say what they had hoped would happen and what the eventual

outcome was. What did these volunteers learn about what prayer was—and was not?

❖ Read aloud today's focus statement: **In the midst of perilous life situations, deliverance sometimes appears to come through miraculous means. How might the faithful be rescued from dangerous life circumstances? Acts shows that the fervent prayer of the church and the work of an angel provided Peter's deliverance.**

(2) Goal 1: Explore the Story of Peter's Deliverance From Prison

❖ Read or retell the Introduction, Acts 12:1-2, and Acts 12:3-4 in Understanding the Scripture to orient the students to the context of this lesson.

❖ Choose volunteers to read the parts of the narrator, an angel, and Peter. Ask them to read Acts 12:5-17; the class is to read the two quotations in verse 15. Although this passage extends into the background Scripture, we are reading these verses to provide a full account of how God orchestrated Peter's escape.

❖ Discuss these questions. Add to the discussion by using information from Understanding the Scripture as you find it helpful.

1. **Why might Luke have described the security surrounding Peter in such detail?** (See Acts 12:4-6)

2. **What does the fact that Herod's tight security is breached suggest to you about who God is and how God works?**

3. **Acts 12:5 (key verse) reports that "the church prayed fervently to God for [Peter]." How did the church members who gathered at Mary's house react**

when Peter appeared? What does their response suggest about their expectations regarding their fervent prayers?

4. Why might people find part of this story funny?
5. What do you learn about prayer from this story?

(3) Goal 2: Recognize and Appreciate the Power of Prayer, Especially in Difficult Circumstances

❖ Post of sheet of newsprint on which you have written "Prayer Is" and "Prayer Is Not." Draw a line down the center of the sheet to separate the two columns. Encourage the adults to state briefly what for them does—and does not—constitute true prayer. (You will find ideas to add in "What Prayer Is Not," "What Prayer Is," and "What Prayer Also Is" in Interpreting the Scripture. If copies of *The New International Lesson Annual* are available, assign three students to check out the information under the headings above so that they can comment.)

❖ Review the list and ask: **Are any of these comments surprising to you? Why?**

(4) Goal 3: Commit to Praying for Those Whose Witness Puts Them in Life-Threatening or Difficult Situations

❖ Read: **Note that Peter's life was definitely threatened, but he was just a forerunner of untold people who face persecution because of their belief in Jesus Christ. "Open Doors," an organization devoted to serving persecuted Christians, defines persecution against Christians as "any hostility, experienced from the world, as a result of one's** identification with Christ. From verbal harassment to hostile feelings, attitudes and actions, believers in areas with severe religious restrictions pay a heavy price for their faith. Beatings, physical torture, confinement, isolation, rape, severe punishment, imprisonment, slavery, discrimination in education and in employment, and even death are just [a] few examples they experience on the daily basis."

❖ Invite class members to call out places in the world where professing Christ threatens one's life. (Be prepared to add other countries from the research you did prior to the session. If you were able to find a map with the countries highlighted, show that now.)

❖ Distribute paper and pencils. Encourage each student to choose one country and write a prayer for those who are suffering persecution for the faith in that place.

❖ Challenge the adults to commit themselves to praying this prayer on a daily basis. Perhaps they will add other countries as well.

(5) Continue the Journey

❖ Pray that as the learners depart, they will give thanks for the freedom that they have to worship and remember those who face a constant struggle to practice their faith.

❖ Post information for next week's session on newsprint for the students to copy:

- **Title: God Makes No Distinction**
- **Background Scripture: Acts 15:1-35**
- **Lesson Scripture: Acts 15:1-12**
- **Focus of the Lesson: Conflicts and controversies, even**

within the community of faith, are often rooted in different interpretations as to "the right way to do things." How can such differences be resolved? In dealing with the questions of if and how Gentiles were to be included in the church, the Council of Jerusalem determined that God makes no distinctions in offering salvation to both Jews and Gentiles and therefore made accommodations so that Gentiles would not be required to undergo the Jewish ritual of circumcision.

❖ Post the following information on newsprint and provide paper and pencils for the students to copy it. Challenge the adults to grow spiritually by completing one or more of these activities related to this week's session.

(1) Pray this week for chaplains in war zones. If possible, write to at least one Christian chaplain and let this courageous servant of God know that he or she is in your prayers.

(2) Lift up Christians in a specific country who are being persecuted for their faith in Jesus. Be alert to media reports of places where persecution has begun or become more serious. Add these people to your prayers.

(3) List situations in your own life that require fervent prayer. Consider sharing these concerns with a prayer partner or several Christians with whom you have a solid relationship.

❖ Sing or read aloud "Prayer Is the Soul's Sincere Desire."

❖ Conclude today's session by leading the class in this benediction, which is adapted from Acts 9:20, the key verse for October 11: **Let us go forth to boldly proclaim that Jesus is the Son of God. Amen.**

UNIT 3: SPREADING THE GOSPEL
GOD MAKES NO DISTINCTION

PREVIEWING THE LESSON

Lesson Scripture: Acts 15:1-12
Background Scripture: Acts 15:1-35
Key Verses: Acts 15:8-9

Focus of the Lesson:

Conflicts and controversies, even within the community of faith, are often rooted in different interpretations as to "the right way to do things." How can such differences be resolved? In dealing with the questions of if and how Gentiles were to be included in the church, the Council of Jerusalem determined that God makes no distinctions in offering salvation to both Jews and Gentiles and therefore made accommodations so that Gentiles would not be required to undergo the Jewish ritual of circumcision.

Goals for the Learners:

(1) to analyze the story of how the Jerusalem Council listened to Paul and Barnabas as they told of the signs and wonders God did among the Gentiles.
(2) to reflect on ways in which their interpretation of who God is and how God acts may exclude others from the church.
(3) to practice resolving conflict in ways that honor God's love for those on all sides of an issue.

Supplies:

Bibles, newsprint and marker, paper and pencils, hymnals

READING THE SCRIPTURE

NRSV

Lesson Scripture: Acts 15:1-12

¹Then certain individuals came down from Judea and were teaching the brothers, "Unless you are circumcised according to the custom of Moses, you cannot be saved." ²And after Paul and Barnabas had no small

CEB

Lesson Scripture: Acts 15:1-12

¹Some people came down from Judea teaching the family of believers, "Unless you are circumcised according to the custom we've received from Moses, you can't be saved." ²Paul and Barnabas took sides against these

dissension and debate with them, Paul and Barnabas and some of the others were appointed to go up to Jerusalem to discuss this question with the apostles and the elders. [3]So they were sent on their way by the church, and as they passed through both Phoenicia and Samaria, they reported the conversion of the Gentiles, and brought great joy to all the believers. [4]When they came to Jerusalem, they were welcomed by the church and the apostles and the elders, and they reported all that God had done with them. [5]But some believers who belonged to the sect of the Pharisees stood up and said, "It is necessary for them to be circumcised and ordered to keep the law of Moses."

[6]The apostles and the elders met together to consider this matter. [7]After there had been much debate, Peter stood up and said to them, "My brothers, you know that in the early days God made a choice among you, that I should be the one through whom the Gentiles would hear the message of the good news and become believers. [8]And God, who knows the human heart, testified to them by giving them the Holy Spirit, just as he did to us; [9]and in cleansing their hearts by faith he has made no distinction between them and us. [10]Now therefore why are you putting God to the test by placing on the neck of the disciples a yoke that neither our ancestors nor we have been able to bear? [11]On the contrary, we believe that we will be saved through the grace of the Lord Jesus, just as they will."

[12]The whole assembly kept silence, and listened to Barnabas and Paul as they told of all the signs and wonders that God had done through them among the Gentiles.

Judeans and argued strongly against their position.

The church at Antioch appointed Paul, Barnabas, and several others from Antioch to go up to Jerusalem to set this question before the apostles and the elders. [3]The church sent this delegation on their way. They traveled through Phoenicia and Samaria, telling stories about the conversion of the Gentiles to everyone. Their reports thrilled the brothers and sisters. [4]When they arrived in Jerusalem, the church, the apostles, and the elders all welcomed them. They gave a full report of what God had accomplished through their activity. [5]Some believers from among the Pharisees stood up and claimed, "The Gentiles must be circumcised. They must be required to keep the Law from Moses."

[6]The apostles and the elders gathered to consider this matter. [7]After much debate, Peter stood and addressed them, "Fellow believers, you know that, early on, God chose me from among you as the one through whom the Gentiles would hear the word of the gospel and come to believe. [8]God, who knows people's deepest thoughts and desires, confirmed this by giving them the Holy Spirit, just as he did to us. [9]He made no distinction between us and them, but purified their deepest thoughts and desires through faith. [10]Why then are you now challenging God by placing a burden on the shoulders of these disciples that neither we nor our ancestors could bear? [11]On the contrary, we believe that we and they are saved in the same way, by the grace of the Lord Jesus."

[12]The entire assembly fell quiet as they listened to Barnabas and Paul describe all the signs and wonders God did among the Gentiles through their activity.

UNDERSTANDING THE SCRIPTURE

Introduction. The previous lesson dealt with Acts 12, in which James was beheaded and Peter escaped from prison but essentially steps down from the role of main character of the narrative. In chapters 13 and 14, the reader notices that Saul (now called Paul in the narrative) is rising to the position of main character. Paul and Barnabas set off from Antioch on a missionary tour and find themselves following in Peter's footsteps of preaching the gospel to Gentiles and bringing them into the fellowship of believers. Chapter 14 ends with the two returning to Antioch, reporting what God had done through them, and staying there "for some time" (14:28).

What follows in chapter 15 is sometimes called "the Council of Jerusalem." It is important to note that Paul refers to this event as well in his Letter to the Galatians (2:1-10). The version there does not fit completely with this version. For example, Paul presents Peter as the apostle to the circumcised in contrast to himself as the apostle to the uncircumcised (Galatians 2:7), whereas Acts presents the two as joined in defending the inclusion of Gentiles (Acts 15:6-12). Moreover, while in neither version is circumcision required of Gentile converts, Paul says that only "remembering the poor" (Galatians 2:10) was required of the Gentiles, but in Acts James requires of them "to abstain only from things polluted by idols and from fornication and from whatever has been strangled and from blood" (15:20). We will not try to reconcile these historical differences, but simply read Acts as it stands for the theology Luke wishes to offer the readers.

Acts 15:1-5. There in Antioch believers from Judea came teaching that Gentiles must be circumcised to be saved. Paul and Barnabas engage them in debate. The church in Antioch sends Paul and Barnabas to Jerusalem to continue the debate there and seek a ruling from the "apostles and elders" (15:2). This might seem to be a superfluous debate, since the matter seemed resolved in chapter 11 after Peter converted Cornelius and his household. Remember, however, that in that scene Peter was on trial for converting the Gentiles. Here is the issue: Once converted, must the Gentiles be circumcised to be saved? In other words, must they become Jews to be Christians so that the men are circumcised and the women marry only circumcised believers?

It is important to remember that what is at stake here is no mere ritual; nor is it an issue of legalism. The question before the church is one of identity.

Acts 15:6-12. Even though Peter has moved off center stage, he returns for a significant role in one last scene before disappearing from the story of Acts completely. His role is so important in the discernment of the "apostles and the elders" that his witness for the defense is presented in direct speech in five verses (15:7-11) while the defense of Paul and Barnabas is simply referred to in a single verse (15:12).

Peter again recounts what God did in Caesarea, referring to the fact that God sent him to the household of Cornelius and gave the Spirit to the Gentiles before they had even been baptized, signaling that God shows no partiality between Jews and Gentiles (15:7-9). But then Peter applies this story to the new issue before the community. The logic is simple: God saves (both Jew and Gentile) by grace; therefore no extra burden (of an added layer of identity) should be added to the Gentiles.

Acts 15:13-21. While Luke shows us Peter and Paul and Barnabas presenting their case for why the Gentiles should not be required to be circumcised, he does not show those on the other side of the issue presenting their case. Instead, the author moves straight to James to make a pronouncement on the case. The fact that James is given this prominent voice in the scene shows that the gavel has passed from Peter to him.

James does not simply say yes or no to requiring circumcision. He makes his ruling based on Peter's (not Paul and Barnabas's) testimony *as confirmed by* Scripture. In verses 16-18 he cites Amos 9:11-12, which refers to the rebuilding of the Temple. What is significant in the citation is the vision that the new Temple will be a place at which "even all the Gentiles" (15:17) can seek God. There is no requirement in the vision that the Gentiles become Jews to find God in the Temple. By analogy, the church is also to be a welcoming place for the Gentiles without requiring them to become something they are not.

This does not mean there are no requirements of the Gentiles, however. James requires of them "to abstain only from things polluted by idols and from fornication and from

whatever has been strangled and from blood" (15:20; repeated in slightly different form in 15:29 and 21:25). This list that seems odd to modern readers basically calls the Gentiles to no longer participate in other religions. In other words, Gentiles are not required to become Jews to become Christians, but they cannot continue to worship other gods alongside God-in-Christ if they become Christian.

Acts 15:22-29. Even though James declares the judgment, his word is not absolute. The "apostles and elders, with the consent of the whole church" (15:22) confirm his ruling. They do so by sending representatives of the Jerusalem church to Gentile converts in Antioch with Paul and Barnabas and a letter detailing the ruling of the community.

Note that the letter is addressed from the brothers (in Jerusalem) to the Gentile believers in Antioch. The apostles and elders call themselves the brothers of the addressees, making clear that they consider the Gentiles full members of the messianic community.

Acts 15:30-35. The scene concludes with the Gentile community in Antioch receiving the representatives and letter with rejoicing. The implication is that not only are they pleased that they are under no obligation to be circumcised but they also receive "the exhortation" (15:31) to "abstain from what has been sacrificed to idols and from blood and from what is strangled and from fornication" (15:29) as good news.

INTERPRETING THE SCRIPTURE

The Unchanging God

God is perfect. This is one of the basic tenets of Judeo-Christian thought. God's perfection means God need not change to better God's self. Thus God does not change God's mind, because being perfect, God cannot have been wrong at some point that needs correction.

God's perfection is a problem for Luke. In the past God made promises to and covenants with Israel that established the nation as a unique community of the children of God. Since God made covenant with Abraham—signified through circumcision—and codified this covenant further with the commandments God gave to Moses, then the Torah that establishes the unique identity of the Jewish people as God's people cannot be flawed. But by the late first century, Luke's church includes Gentiles. How can the community of those whom God saved through the ministry, death, and resurrection of Israel's Messiah include the uncircumcised unless God changed God's mind, unless God was wrong?

Those who come from Judea to Antioch preaching a gospel that requires circumcision of Gentile converts say the community can't include them. That is, they argue the church cannot include Gentiles and be God's people. God cannot have been wrong, so for them the church must be a subcommunity of Jews who believe Jesus is the Messiah in order to be God's people. This in turn means for them that Gentiles must become Jews in order to be in the church (which they welcome!). Otherwise, God was mistaken when all those promises and covenants were made with Israel, and that simply cannot be the case.

So those who believe circumcision is required need not be viewed as legalists or traditionalists. They need not be seen as racists who hate non-Jews. Indeed, they need not even be interpreted as ones resistant to change in general—after all, they have accepted that God has acted anew in Jesus the Christ. No, they seek what all people of faith should seek—a consistent theology. They are defenders of God's holy, divine perfection.

So is Luke. He also wants to protect God's perfection theologically, but his church is packed with Gentiles. So Luke has a problem.

The Ever-Changing World

God is perfect and unchanging, but we are not. The world around us changes and humanity changes with it. Cultures evolve. Relationships grow. Science expands. Political conflict waxes and wanes. Technology advances. We are finite and thus flawed. We need to change to better ourselves in light of changes around us. We need to change our minds because new evidence proves that at times in the past we have been wrong.

God as creator is not changed by the changing creation. But *our* experience of and thoughts concerning God are mediated by the changing world. Therefore, just as we once thought the world was flat but new experience and knowledge led us (kicking and screaming) to acknowledge the world is round, so must we also be willing to modify earlier assertions about God and God's will based on new knowledge and experiences of the divine.

The church in Acts knows God is unchanging, but the world around them is changing quickly. The radical changes began when Jesus the Messiah ministered, died, and rose again. This resulted in the birth of the church on Pentecost with thousands being baptized. And the world continued to change at a rapid pace (as the narrative presents it) as the word spread across the empire (Acts 1:8) and grew under the impetus of the Holy Spirit. Nothing dramatized that a full-blown paradigm shift was underway more than the inclusion of Gentiles in this growing church. The changing world made the believers begin to question old perceptions of God and thus the perceptions of what God wanted them to do and be.

But how does one know whether it is the old understandings of God and God's will or the new ones that are flawed and need to be reconsidered? Luke has a problem.

The Apostolic Church: Reformed and Always to Be Reformed

Luke also has an answer to the problem. In some ways the whole of Acts is a narrative answer to this problem, but we can stay focused on Acts 15 to see the way he thinks through the question.

Luke obviously wants to defend and support the inclusion of Gentiles in the community of believers. He does this through a mode of reinterpretation. And in the story of the Council of Jerusalem he presents two ways this is done.

The first is Peter's reinterpretation of his experience with Cornelius's household (15:7-10). Every retelling of a story is, in a sense, a reinterpretation of that story. Luke allows most of the retelling to be implied, but what he credits Peter as saying explicitly offers a new interpretation of what happened in Caesarea. For instance, in verse 8, Peter seems to refer to what happened rather directly—the Gentiles received the Holy Spirit just as the Jews in the church had (see 10:44). But in verse 9, Peter goes a step further by using language that did not show up in chapter 10: God cleansed their hearts by faith. Note that it is not by faith they had that they were cleansed but by faith God gave them. This is the evidence of God holding no distinction between Jews and Gentiles in the church. This detail in no way contradicts the earlier telling of the story; it simply adds a new interpretive layer to it.

Verses 10-11 continue extending the earlier story in this slightly new direction. Recalling a theme from Peter's defense of his decision to baptize the Gentiles (11:1-18) but making it more explicit and applying it now to the issue of circumcision, Peter asserts that to require something more of the Gentiles is to go against God. The logic is clear: God did not require the Gentiles to be circumcised before giving them the Holy Spirit, so why should we require that of them now? God shows no distinction among people; we are all saved through the grace of Christ.

In Acts 15:13-21, James acknowledges Peter's reinterpretation and adds his own. He does not reinterpret Peter's encounter with Cornelius; he reinterprets Scripture. In verses 15-18, he applies a text dealing with rebuilding the Temple to rebuilding the people of God. In light of new circumstances, he finds something new in the text.

Thus Luke addresses his problem

by drawing on two essential theological criteria of the church: experience and Scripture. By portraying them as being in accord once interpreted anew in light of the changing situation, Luke shows that the inclusion of the Gentiles without requiring them to be circumcised is actually the way God keeps God's promises to Israel, not a breaking of those promises.

Acts 15 is a model for how the church can struggle with the ambiguities of knowing God's will as it tries to adjust and live out its mission faithfully in ever-changing circumstances. In the creeds, we claim the church is apostolic, that it exists in continuity with the apostolic proclamation and practice of the faith still today. But this continuity is not stagnation. Like the apostles, we must be open to new interpretations as we fit the church for new days ahead. So we claim with the Protestant Reformation, "*Ecclesia semper reformanda est*," "the church is always to be reformed."

SHARING THE SCRIPTURE

PREPARING TO TEACH

Preparing Our Hearts

Ponder this week's devotional reading from Revelation 21:1-5. This passage looks ahead to a time when God will be "making all things new" (21:5). What changes are coming? People often fear and resist change. What attitude does the writer seem to have about the promised new heaven and earth? What do you need to do to get ready for this new day?

Pray that you and the students will be prepared to change as the Holy Spirit leads you in new directions.

Preparing Our Minds

Study the background Scripture from Acts 15:1-35 and the lesson Scripture from Acts 15:1-12.

Consider this question as you prepare the lesson: *How can differences be resolved when conflicts arise?*

Write on newsprint:
- ❏ the eight principles for Holy Conferencing found under Goal 3 in Sharing the Scripture.
- ❏ information for next week's lesson, found under Continue the Journey.
- ❏ activities for further spiritual growth in Continue the Journey.

Review the Introduction, The Big Picture, Close-up, and Faith in Action, which all precede the first lesson of this quarter. Consider how you might use any of this material in today's lesson.

Prepare a brief lecture using ideas from the entire Interpreting the Scripture portion to explain the problems that Luke needs to address because his community includes Gentiles. (Look for "Luke has a problem.")

LEADING THE CLASS

(1) Gather to Learn

❖ Welcome the class members and guests.

❖ Pray that those who have come today will be aware of ways in which God is moving among all people.

❖ Read aloud the following information: **The Church of the Holy Sepulchre in Jerusalem is an ancient building constructed at the site where most Christians believe Jesus was crucified, buried, and resurrected. What** should be one of the holiest sites in all of Christendom is also the place where conflicts break out among the six Christian communities that are responsible for carefully designated spaces there: the Armenian Orthodox, Syrian Orthodox, Greek Orthodox, and Roman Catholic (represented by the Franciscan Order), the Copts, and the Ethiopian Tawahedo Church. Due to disputes, much needed maintenance cannot be attended to. Even tasks that should be simple, such as who rings the church bells first, must be negotiated. Fist fights have occurred among clergy. The situation is and has been so tenuous that over several centuries a Muslim family has been the church gate-keeper. What message is being sent, both to believers and nonbelievers, when the Christian leaders here just cannot resolve conflicts about a building?

❖ Read aloud today's focus statement: **Conflicts and controversies, even within the community of faith, are often rooted in different interpretations as to "the right way to do things." How can such differences be resolved? In dealing with the questions of if and how Gentiles were to be included in the church, the Council of Jerusalem determined that God makes no distinctions in offering salvation to both Jews and Gentiles and therefore made accommodations so that Gentiles would not be required to undergo the Jewish ritual of circumcision.**

(2) Goal 1: Analyze the Story of How the Jerusalem Council Listened to Paul and Barnabas as They Told of the Signs and Wonders God Did Among the Gentiles

❖ Invite a volunteer to read Acts 15:1-5 immediately followed by another volunteer for verses 6-12.

❖ Discuss these questions using information from Understanding the Scripture to fill in gaps.

1. **What is the heart of the issue under debate?** ("It is important to remember that what is at stake here is no mere ritual; nor is it an issue of legalism. The question before the church is one of identity." See Acts 15:1-5 in Understanding the Scripture.)
2. **What points does Peter make?**
3. **Do you think this debate is "putting God to the test" as Peter claims in verse 10? Why or why not?**
4. **How did the audience respond to Peter's argument?**

(3) Goal 2: Reflect on Ways in Which the Learner's Interpretation of Who God Is and How God Acts May Exclude Others From the Church

❖ Introduce the lecture you have prepared by pointing out that the interpretation of the Pharisees concerning who God is and how God acts created problems for Luke, whose community included Gentiles. Present your lecture.

❖ Ask these questions:

1. **What are some issues that challenge today's church because believers rely on different interpretations of who God is and how God acts?**
2. **Name some groups of people who have been excluded from full participation in the church because some in the church are unwilling or unable to make reforms?**

(4) Goal 3: Practice Resolving Conflict in Ways That Honor God's Love for Those on All Sides of an Issue

❖ Read: **We saw in today's reading from Acts 15 how believers were** able to gather together, listen respectfully, and reach agreement on what had been a contentious issue. The Wesleyan tradition recognizes "holy conferencing" as a guideline and means of grace for talking together in ways that demonstrate love for one another, despite differences. According to Bishop Sally Dyck's "Eight Principles of Holy Conferencing," participants in such conversations need to (1) recognize that each person is God's child; (2) listen before speaking; (3) seek to understand from another's point of view; (4) accurately reflect other viewpoints; (5) disagree without being disagreeable; (6) discuss issues without defaming people; (7) pray before making decisions; (8) allow prayer to interrupt our busy-ness. (Post these eight principles on newsprint.)

❖ Choose one of the issues you identified in the previous activity. Form small groups and discuss the issue using these principles.

❖ Call time and provide a few moments for participants to say how the process worked for them.

(5) Continue the Journey

❖ Pray that as the learners depart, they will approach issues, especially of who is or is not Christian, with humility, respect, and love for those who may hold points of view that differ from theirs.

❖ Post information for next week's session on newsprint for the students to copy:

- **Title: From Derbe to Philippi**
- **Background Scripture: Acts 16:1-15**

- **Lesson Scripture: Acts 16:1-5, 8-15**
- **Focus of the Lesson: Sometimes what starts as a small project turns out to be much larger, having an unexpected effect on the lives of others. How do such results come about? Because Paul respected the decisions of the apostles and elders, and because of his response to the vision he received from God, his preaching resulted in the good news being spread into new regions.**

❖ Post the following information on newsprint and provide paper and pencils for the students to copy it. Challenge the adults to grow spiritually by completing one or more of these activities related to this week's session.

(1) Reread Acts 15. What ideas can the modern church adopt to more faithfully address "hot-button" topics that cause divisions today?

(2) Try to serve as peacemaker in the midst of a dispute within your own congregation.

(3) Use the principles of holy conferencing to guide a discussion on a topic about which you and another person disagree.

❖ Sing or read aloud "Go Forth for God."

❖ Conclude today's session by leading the class in this benediction, which is adapted from Acts 9:20, the key verse for October 11: **Let us go forth to boldly proclaim that Jesus is the Son of God. Amen.**

UNIT 3: SPREADING THE GOSPEL
FROM DERBE TO PHILIPPI

PREVIEWING THE LESSON

Lesson Scripture: Acts 16:1-5, 8-15
Background Scripture: Acts 16:1-15
Key Verse: Acts 16:10

Focus of the Lesson:

Sometimes what starts as a small project turns out to be much larger, having an unexpected effect on the lives of others. How do such results come about? Because Paul respected the decisions of the apostles and elders, and because of his response to the vision he received from God, his preaching resulted in the good news being spread into new regions.

Goals for the Learners:

(1) to recall how Paul added Timothy to his missionary teams and their labors in spreading the gospel from Derbe to Philippi.
(2) to reflect on characteristics needed for members of a successful evangelism team.
(3) to challenge them to be alert for opportunities to spread the gospel.

Supplies:

Bibles, newsprint and marker, paper and pencils, hymnals, map of Paul's second missionary journey

---

READING THE SCRIPTURE

NRSV

Lesson Scripture: Acts 16:1-5, 8-15

¹Paul went on also to Derbe and to Lystra, where there was a disciple named Timothy, the son of a Jewish woman who was a believer; but his father was a Greek. ²He was well spoken of by the believers in Lystra and Iconium. ³Paul wanted Timothy to accompany him; and he took him and had him circumcised because of

CEB

Lesson Scripture: Acts 16:1-5, 8-15

¹Paul reached Derbe, and then Lystra, where there was a disciple named Timothy. He was the son of a believing Jewish woman and a Greek father. ²The brothers and sisters in Lystra and Iconium spoke well of him. ³Paul wanted to take Timothy with him, so he circumcised him. This was because of the Jews who lived in those areas,

the Jews who were in those places, for they all knew that his father was a Greek. ⁴As they went from town to town, they delivered to them for observance the decisions that had been reached by the apostles and elders who were in Jerusalem. ⁵So the churches were strengthened in the faith and increased in numbers daily.

⁸So, passing by Mysia, they went down to Troas. ⁹During the night Paul had a vision: there stood a man of Macedonia pleading with him and saying, "Come over to Macedonia and help us." **¹⁰When he had seen the vision, we immediately tried to cross over to Macedonia, being convinced that God had called us to proclaim the good news to them.**

¹¹We set sail from Troas and took a straight course to Samothrace, the following day to Neapolis, ¹²and from there to Philippi, which is a leading city of the district of Macedonia and a Roman colony. We remained in this city for some days. ¹³On the sabbath day we went outside the gate by the river, where we supposed there was a place of prayer; and we sat down and spoke to the women who had gathered there. ¹⁴A certain woman named Lydia, a worshiper of God, was listening to us; she was from the city of Thyatira and a dealer in purple cloth. The Lord opened her heart to listen eagerly to what was said by Paul. ¹⁵When she and her household were baptized, she urged us, saying, "If you have judged me to be faithful to the Lord, come and stay at my home." And she prevailed upon us.

for they all knew Timothy's father was Greek. ⁴As Paul and his companions traveled through the cities, they instructed Gentile believers to keep the regulations put in place by the apostles and elders in Jerusalem. ⁵So the churches were strengthened in the faith and every day their numbers flourished.

⁸Passing by Mysia, they went down to Troas instead. ⁹A vision of a man from Macedonia came to Paul during the night. He stood urging Paul, "Come over to Macedonia and help us!" **¹⁰Immediately after he saw the vision, we prepared to leave for the province of Macedonia, concluding that God had called us to proclaim the good news to them.**

¹¹We sailed from Troas straight for Samothrace and came to Neapolis the following day. ¹²From there we went to Philippi, a city of Macedonia's first district and a Roman colony. We stayed in that city several days. ¹³On the Sabbath we went outside the city gate to the riverbank, where we thought there might be a place for prayer. We sat down and began to talk with the women who had gathered. ¹⁴One of those women was Lydia, a Gentile God-worshipper from the city of Thyatira, a dealer in purple cloth. As she listened, the Lord enabled her to embrace Paul's message. ¹⁵Once she and her household were baptized, she urged, "Now that you have decided that I am a believer in the Lord, come and stay in my house." And she persuaded us.

UNDERSTANDING THE SCRIPTURE

Introduction. At the conclusion of the Council of Jerusalem (Acts 15:1-21), church leaders sent representatives to accompany Paul and Barnabas to Antioch with a letter telling of their decision not to require circumcision of the Gentile converts (15:22-33). Afterward, Paul and Barnabas remained in Antioch until deciding to journey to the cities in which they had previously preached the good news (15:35-36). But the two of them disagreed about whether to take John Mark with them and so parted ways (15:37-41).

John Mark is introduced in 12:12, and is said to accompany Barnabas and Paul on their first missionary journey in 13:5. In 13:13, Luke states in a matter-of-fact tone that John left them and returned to Jerusalem. But now the readers learn that Paul interpreted his departure as abandonment. It is not clear whether Barnabas interpreted it that way or not, but in accordance with his name meaning "son of encouragement" (4:36), he gives John Mark another chance. This conflict sets the stage for Paul to become the leader of his own missionary team as he immediately chooses Silas to accompany him (15:40) and will choose Timothy in today's lesson.

Acts 16:1-5. Paul sets off to Derbe and Lystra (16:1). Students of Acts can profit from examining Paul's itinerary in relation to a map of the ancient Mediterranean region. What can be noticed easily is that in 14:6, these two cities are first mentioned in the opposite order near the end of Barnabas and Paul's first missionary journey. The significance of the reversal is simply a reminder that Paul is heading out in reverse order on this second trip.

At this first stop, Paul meets Timothy (16:1-3). Deciding to take Timothy with him as an assistant along with Silas, Paul has him circumcised. This is the same Paul who just testified in Jerusalem that Gentiles should not be required to be circumcised. It

is important to recognize that Luke would not tell this story if he thought there was a conflict with that ruling, especially since he goes on to report on that ruling in his continued travels (16:4). Timothy's mother is a Jewish-Christian and his father is Gentile. Luke, therefore, presents Paul as having Timothy circumcised to satisfy the Jews that Timothy, being of Jewish birth (by his mother), fulfilled the Jewish law. This incident serves as another reminder to the modern reader that the early Jewish-Christians did not reject the Torah. It was a part of their identity as Christians. They simply reinterpreted it in light of their messianic faith and did not require it of Gentile-Christians who shared that messianic faith.

As Paul sets out on this missionary journey, his intention is to see how those who accepted the word he and Barnabas preached are doing (15:36). But 16:4 adds a new layer to this pastoral visit. Paul reports to the brothers and sisters of the faith the ruling from Jerusalem concerning Gentile-Christians. This is significant because the apostles and elders made the ruling specifically for the Gentiles in Antioch, as seen by the fact that they send them a letter by way of representatives who have now returned to Jerusalem. They did not send the representatives to other cities in which Barnabas and Paul had preached. Paul seems to assume that their decision applies universally. And indeed Luke agrees, as shown by the note that the word continues to grow across the Roman Empire in ways and places the earliest followers of Jesus never could have imagined.

Acts 16:6-8. In these verses, Luke briefly informs the reader of the northwest direction Paul's missionary team travels. The language used to convey this, however, is striking. They travel through "Phrygia and Galatia" (an ambiguous reference since these terms can be used interchangeably) but the Holy Spirit forbids them to speak in Asia. They attempt to enter Bithynia but the "Spirit of Jesus" does not allow them to do so. There are likely lost historical reasons for Luke's mention that Paul does not go to these areas (possibly that they were evangelized by others), but the theological claim behind this odd description is clear enough: The church's expansion, even the direction of that expansion, is not by human initiative but by divine initiative.

Acts 16:9-12. The fact that Paul is not in charge of his own missionary journey is narrated in an even more dramatic way in this section. In the previous verses, the Spirit told Paul where he should *not* go. Now the Spirit, through a vision (compare Peter's vision from God in Acts 10:9-16) instructs Paul where he *is* to go. Even though Paul does not act on his own initiative, verses 10-12 make clear that he interprets the vision as God's will and acts obediently.

In verse 10 a striking stylistic change occurs in Acts. Without calling attention, the narrator simply starts referring to Paul's missionary team in the first-person plural ("we"). Since Luke provides no explanation for the "we-narratives" in Acts, scholars have taken it upon themselves to propose numerous theories. One of the older ones, now rejected by almost all, is that these sections represent Luke's own voice as one who accompanied Paul. It is more likely that Luke is imitating the practice of ancient historians who employed the first person to make accounts more engaging for the reader.

Acts 16:13-15. In this section readers see for the first time Paul offering the word to specific individuals. Lydia comes to the forefront: She is a "worshiper of God" (an ambiguous term that could refer to either a faithful Jew or a Gentile "god-fearer" like Cornelius; see 10:2) and a trader of purple cloth (implying wealth). Lydia is significant as a strong and faithful woman, in a narrative in which few women are mentioned explicitly. Her act in compelling Paul to stay with her indicates that she becomes a supporter of his work, and possibly a leader in the church in that geographical area.

INTERPRETING THE SCRIPTURE

Barnabas Goes His Own Way

Barnabas is a minor but intriguing character in The Acts of the Apostles. He first appears in a brief reference in 4:36 as an example of obedient stewardship in the Jerusalem church in contrast to Ananias and Sapphira (see the lesson for September 13). There Luke describes his name as meaning "son of encouragement."

Barnabas does not show up again until 9:27 when he brings Saul to the apostles and describes his conversion experience so they might accept him. When the Jerusalem church hears that there are new converts in Antioch they send Barnabas there to encourage them in the faith (11:19-24). He was successful in doing this and in bringing others to the Lord. Whether it is because he needs help in light of his success or because he wishes to keep Saul under his wing is unclear, but Barnabas goes to Tarsus and brings Saul to Antioch where they are in ministry together for a whole year (11:25-26).

At the conclusion of this work, Barnabas and Saul (along with John Mark) are sent by the church and Holy Spirit on a missionary tour (12:25–14:28). Across this section, Luke presents Paul as more and more in the spotlight with Barnabas taking more of a background role.

Thus when Paul and Barnabas split ways (Acts 15:36-39) it is no wonder that Barnabas disappears from the Acts narrative altogether and Paul becomes the main character throughout the rest of the book. But Luke makes clear in Barnabas's appearances in Acts that without him, there would have been no Paul. He mediated Paul's relationship with the apostles; he brought Paul to Antioch, which supported his mission; and he took Paul on his first missionary tour. Behind Paul's great ministry with Gentiles across the Roman Empire was Barnabas's encouragement. Behind those who evangelize the world is a church that supports and trains the evangelist.

Silas and Timothy Join Paul

Once Paul parts ways with Barnabas, he follows Barnabas's model of taking fledgling ministers with him. Silas's inclusion in Paul's team is simply noted in a matter-of-fact manner (15:40), but Timothy's inclusion takes some explanation (16:3-5). As previously noted, Timothy had not been circumcised as a child because his father was Gentile, but Paul now has him circumcised due to the fact that

his mother is Jewish. Luke, however, does not make the point that this is essential for Timothy's identity or faith even though it is appropriate because of his Jewish heritage. The reason Paul has Timothy circumcised is for the sake of their ministry: Paul "had him circumcised because of the Jews who were in those places, for they all knew that his father was a Greek" (16:3). Even though during this missionary tour they deliver the leaders' decision that Gentiles not be required to be circumcised (16:4), Luke presents Paul as removing any hindrance his ministry might have with the Jews. Even though Acts represents Luke's theology, here his view of ministry accords with that of Paul in 1 Corinthians 9:18-23:

What then is my reward? Just this: that in my proclamation I may make the gospel free of charge, so as not to make full use of my rights in the gospel. For though I am free with respect to all, I have made myself a slave to all, so that I might win more of them. To the Jews I became as a Jew, in order to win Jews. To those under the law I became as one under the law (though I myself am not under the law) so that I might win those under the law. To those outside the law I became as one outside the law (though I am not free from God's law but am under Christ's law) so that I might win those outside the law. To the weak I became weak, so that I might win the weak. I have become all things to all people, that I might by all means save some. I do it all for the sake of the gospel, so that I may share in its blessings.

When proclaiming the faith outside the church, we must not bend the gospel (or ourselves) to the ways of the world in ways that go against our faith, but we must shape how we present ourselves so that the word can get a hearing and be a blessing to those who would receive it.

Silas and Timothy never become key characters in Acts in the sense that they present major speeches or part ways with Paul to go off on missionary tours of their own. But Paul is rarely in ministry alone. Over and over again Luke presents Silas and Timothy as being co-ministers with Paul and others in phrases like "Paul and Silas" and "Silas and Timothy" (16:19, 25, 29; 17:1, 4, 5, 10, 14, 15; 18:5; see also 19:22 and 20:4). Silas is presented as closer to Paul in Acts; but in other parts of the New Testament, Timothy is presented as working very closely with him and as coauthor of some letters (Romans 16:21; 1 Corinthians 4:17; 16:10; 2 Corinthians 1:1, 19; Philippians 1:1; 2:19; Colossians 1:1; 1 Thessalonians 1:1; 3:6; 2 Thessalonians 1:1; Philemon 1:1) and as the recipient of two of Paul's letters (1 and 2 Timothy). Needless to say, we should picture these three as an incredible team of evangelists spreading the word to a whole new population throughout the Mediterranean world. Evangelism is not a task to be done alone.

Lydia Joins the Faith

Luke presents Paul as parting ways with Barnabas, forming his own missionary team, and setting off on a missionary tour. He summarizes the team's success in verse 5: "So the churches were strengthened in the faith [internal success] and increased in numbers daily [evangelistic success]."

Luke often uses such summaries to give the sense of the growth of the Way alongside individual stories as examples of that success. Such is the case here with the opening story of Paul in Philippi (16:12). What is intriguing about this example scene is that Paul and his team are not the real focus of it. Lydia, one of those being evangelized, is. When he introduces her in verse 14, Luke tells us about her spirituality ("a worshiper of God"), place of residence (Thyatira), and trade ("dealer in purple cloth"). But as Paul's movements are directed by God, so also is Lydia's openness to receiving Paul's proclamation: "The Lord opened her heart to listen eagerly" (16:14). She assertively and graciously responds to the Word. She and her household (parallel to Cornelius and his household in 10:2; 11:14) are baptized and then she urges Paul's team to accept her support in the form of hospitality.

It is uncustomary in the ancient world for a woman to be portrayed as such a strong character. The fact that Luke presents her with so much detail and gives her such a voice (when Paul does not speak directly in the scene at all) may signal that she became a leader in the church and/or a financial supporter of Paul's ministry. Luke's portrayal of Lydia reminds the reader that evangelism is contagious and results in others doing God's work besides the evangelists who began the work.

SHARING THE SCRIPTURE

PREPARING TO TEACH

Preparing Our Hearts

Ponder this week's devotional reading from Matthew 8:18-22. What do these verses suggest about Jesus' expectations for his followers? Do you think you could live such an itinerant lifestyle? What happens to other priorities in our lives when we choose to follow Jesus?

Pray that you and the students will examine your priorities and realign them, as needed, to meet Jesus' standards.

Preparing Our Minds

Study the background Scripture from Acts 16:1-15 and the lesson Scripture from Acts 16:1-5, 8-15.

Consider this question as you prepare the lesson: *What happens to cause seemingly small projects to have a large impact on the lives of others?*

Write on newsprint:

❏ information for next week's lesson, found under Continue the Journey.

❏ activities for further spiritual growth in Continue the Journey.

Review the three sections for November 15 of Close-up: Highlights of Paul's Second Missionary Journey, A.D. 49–52, which precedes the first lesson of this quarter. Although not all of this information is spotlighted in the lesson, this material will give you a good overview of the beginning of Paul's second trip.

Find a map showing Paul's second missionary journey. Familiarize yourself with the location of the cities mentioned in today's reading.

LEADING THE CLASS

(1) Gather to Learn

❖ Welcome the class members and guests.

❖ Pray that those who have come today will stand ready to spread the gospel.

❖ Read: **Sometimes a trash-strewn urban lot can be transformed from an eyesore to productive land. The process may begin almost imperceptibly. A few people start collecting the trash. Soil is added to enrich the degraded dirt. Some folks plant several vegetables or herbs. Others come to weed. Soon community members have access to fresh food that otherwise would not be available. Not only does the community benefit by the removal of a dangerous space that may attract vermin and be peppered with glass but it also gains a beautiful area, perhaps including benches, where people can enjoy a pretty garden that provides nutritious food for area residents.**

❖ Read aloud today's focus statement: **Sometimes what starts as a small project turns out to be much larger, having an unexpected effect on the lives of others. How do such results come about? Because Paul respected the decisions of the apostles and elders, and because of his response to the vision he received from God, his preaching resulted in the good news being spread into new regions.**

(2) Goal 1: Recall How Paul Added Timothy to His Missionary Teams and Their Labors in Spreading the Gospel From Derbe to Philippi

❖ Introduce today's lesson by reading or retelling "Barnabas Goes His Own Way" in Interpreting the Scripture. Note that although the split between Barnabas and Paul occurred in Acts 15:36-39, this change in ministry companions is important as Paul sets out with Silas on his second missionary trip (15:40-41).

❖ Select one volunteer to read Acts 16:1-5 and another to read verses 8-15.

❖ Use the map you have located, plus information in Close-up for November 15, to help the learners envision where Paul went and what was happening.

❖ Discuss these questions using additional information to expand the discussion:

1. **The Council at Jerusalem had recently agreed with Paul that Gentiles need not be circumcised to become Christian believers. Yet when Paul invites Timothy to join him, Paul insists that Timothy be circumcised. Why?** (See Acts 16:1-5 in Understanding the Scripture and "Silas and Timothy Join Paul" in Interpreting the Scripture.)

2. **What message did Paul deliver as he traveled, and how was that message received?** (See the last paragraph of Acts 16:1-5 in Understanding the Scripture.)

3. **How does the Holy Spirit play the role of travel agent in Paul's journey?** (See Acts 16:6-8 and Acts 16:9-12 in Understanding the Scripture.)

4. **What do you learn about Lydia?** (See Acts 16:13-15 in Understanding the Scripture and "Lydia Joins the Faith" in Interpreting the Scripture.)

(3) Goal 2: Reflect on Characteristics Needed for Members of a Successful Evangelism Team

❖ Post a sheet of newsprint and ask the students: **What characteristics made Paul, Silas, and Timothy evangelists who were able to win others to Christ?** Record answers. (Here are some possibilities: personal relationship with Jesus, dedication to Jesus and his church, well thought of by others, willing to leave home and travel, able to communicate well, sensitive to the leading of the Holy Spirit, willingness to talk with anyone who will listen.)

❖ Continue adding ideas to the list by asking, **What other personal characteristics, talents, and skills do you think are necessary for people who are serious about winning others to Christ?** (Here are some possibilities: good listening skills to hear the cries of people's hearts, solid grasp of the biblical story, willingness to be a partner in ministry by going out with others to witness.)

❖ Distribute paper and pencils. Invite the students to review the ideas and make two lists on their papers. On the left side they are to list characteristics, talents, and skills they think they already possess; on the right side, characteristics, talents, and skills that they would like to develop. On the back of the paper they are to list any barriers that prevent them from freely sharing God's good news.

❖ Conclude by asking: **How do you think our church could help you** to be better prepared to go and make new disciples?

(4) Goal 3: Challenge the Learners to Be Alert for Opportunities to Spread the Gospel

❖ Ask: **What groups in our community need to hear of God's love for them? How can we share that message in both word and deed?**

❖ Challenge the adults to be alert for opportunities to spread the gospel as they go about their daily business within the community.

(5) Continue the Journey

❖ Pray that as the learners depart, they will be aware of those who need to hear the good news—and be willing to share it.

❖ Post information for next week's session on newsprint for the students to copy:

- **Title: Thessalonica, Beroea, and Athens**
- **Background Scripture: Acts 17:1-32**
- **Lesson Scripture: Acts 17:1-4, 10-12, 22-25, 28**
- **Focus of the Lesson: Some people accept messages proclaimed with conviction while others reject them. How do Christians respond when those they hope will accept their messages reject them? Luke shows that**

Paul was undeterred and continued telling the good news story and preaching with strong passion and conviction.

❖ Post the following information on newsprint and provide paper and pencils for the students to copy it. Challenge the adults to grow spiritually by completing one or more of these activities related to this week's session.

(1) **List the cities cited in Acts 16:1-15 that Paul visited. Research several of these places to get a flavor for the people who lived there and the challenges that Paul might have faced in teaching them about Jesus.**

(2) **Meet with church members who may be interested in forming a new ministry team to reach out to others in order to make disciples. Pray and study together to discern where the Spirit is leading. Once you have some clear direction, begin to take bold action.**

(3) **Pray for missionaries and evangelists around the world.**

❖ Sing or read aloud "We've a Story to Tell to the Nations."

❖ Conclude today's session by leading the class in this benediction, which is adapted from Acts 9:20, the key verse for October 11: **Let us go forth to boldly proclaim that Jesus is the Son of God. Amen.**

UNIT 3: SPREADING THE GOSPEL

THESSALONICA, BEROEA, AND ATHENS

PREVIEWING THE LESSON

Lesson Scripture: Acts 17:1-4, 10-12, 22-25, 28
Background Scripture: Acts 17:1-32
Key Verse: Acts 17:23

Focus of the Lesson:
Some people accept messages proclaimed with conviction while others reject them. How do Christians respond when those they hope will accept their messages reject them? Luke shows that Paul was undeterred and continued telling the good news story and preaching with strong passion and conviction.

Goals for the Learners:
(1) to learn that, although Paul and Silas's message was accepted by some but not all, God received the glory.
(2) to reflect upon the effects of rejection in the lives of those who serve God.
(3) to seek out and use spiritual resources that support perseverance in the midst of rejection.

Supplies:
Bibles, newsprint and marker, paper and pencils, hymnals

READING THE SCRIPTURE

NRSV

Lesson Scripture: Acts 17:1-4, 10-12, 22-25, 28

¹After Paul and Silas had passed through Amphipolis and Apollonia, they came to Thessalonica, where there was a synagogue of the Jews. ²And Paul went in, as was his custom, and on three sabbath days

CEB

Lesson Scripture: Acts 17:1-4, 10-12, 22-25, 28

¹Paul and Silas journeyed through Amphipolis and Apollonia, then came to Thessalonica, where there was a Jewish synagogue. ²As was Paul's custom, he entered the synagogue and for three Sabbaths interacted with

argued with them from the scriptures, [3]explaining and proving that it was necessary for the Messiah to suffer and to rise from the dead, and saying, "This is the Messiah, Jesus whom I am proclaiming to you." [4]Some of them were persuaded and joined Paul and Silas, as did a great many of the devout Greeks and not a few of the leading women.

[10]That very night the believers sent Paul and Silas off to Beroea; and when they arrived, they went to the Jewish synagogue. [11]These Jews were more receptive than those in Thessalonica, for they welcomed the message very eagerly and examined the scriptures every day to see whether these things were so. [12]Many of them therefore believed, including not a few Greek women and men of high standing.

[22]Then Paul stood in front of the Areopagus and said, "Athenians, I see how extremely religious you are in every way. [23]**For as I went through the city and looked carefully at the objects of your worship, I found among them an altar with the inscription, 'To an unknown god.' What therefore you worship as unknown, this I proclaim to you.** [24]The God who made the world and everything in it, he who is Lord of heaven and earth, does not live in shrines made by human hands, [25]nor is he served by human hands, as though he needed anything, since he himself gives to all mortals life and breath and all things. . . . [28]For 'In him we live and move and have our being'; as even some of your own poets have said, 'For we too are his offspring.'"

them on the basis of the scriptures. [3]Through his interpretation of the scriptures, he demonstrated that the Christ had to suffer and rise from the dead. He declared, "This Jesus whom I proclaim to you is the Christ." [4]Some were convinced and joined Paul and Silas, including a larger number of Greek God-worshippers and quite a few prominent women.

[10]As soon as it was dark, the brothers and sisters sent Paul and Silas on to Beroea. When they arrived, they went to the Jewish synagogue. [11]The Beroean Jews were more honorable than those in Thessalonica. This was evident in the great eagerness with which they accepted the word and examined the scriptures each day to see whether Paul and Silas' teaching was true. [12]Many came to believe, including a number of reputable Greek women and many Greek men.

[22]Paul stood up in the middle of the council on Mars Hill and said, "People of Athens, I see that you are very religious in every way. [23]**As I was walking through town and carefully observing your objects of worship, I even found an altar with this inscription: 'To an unknown God.' What you worship as unknown, I now proclaim to you.** [24]God, who made the world and everything in it, is Lord of heaven and earth. He doesn't live in temples made with human hands. [25]Nor is God served by human hands, as though he needed something, since he is the one who gives life, breath, and everything else. . . . [28]In God we live, move, and exist. As some of your own poets said, 'We are his offspring.'"

UNDERSTANDING THE SCRIPTURE

Acts 17:1-9. Luke portrays Paul as traveling the Via Egnatia (17:1), a major Roman highway connecting the eastern and western parts of the empire. He stops at urban centers along the way, preaching the gospel in the synagogues "as was his custom" (compare Luke 4:16). Paul's initial visit is to Thessalonica.

The pattern of Paul's preaching that Luke offers (17:2b-3) is to argue from Scripture that the Messiah must suffer and be raised from the dead and, given those requirements, Jesus therefore must be the Messiah. In other words, Paul's argument starts with that which his hearers consider to be an accepted authority (the Scriptures) and then he applies it to that which is radically new and difficult to accept (Jesus as the Christ).

A diverse group of people hears Paul and is persuaded by his argument: Jews, Gentiles connected to the synagogue, and leading women (17:4). But "the Jews," that is, leaders in the synagogue, grew jealous of Paul. Luke does not tell us whether they argued against Paul, but he does describe them as foregoing argument and plotting to persecute him without being directly involved. They stir up "ruffians" in the marketplace (17:5). Luke intends the reader to see a class difference between the "leading" citizens who accept Paul's message and the day laborers looking for mischief in the marketplace who are stirred to action against him, even without hearing him.

Jason, presumably one who was persuaded by Paul (although Luke does not state this explicitly) becomes the target of the crowd (17:5b-7). They come to his house seeking Paul; but not finding him there, they turn their attention to Jason. They take him and others before the city rulers and accuse them of political conspiracy. Of course, no such direct political conspiracy has occurred, but in truth accepting and committing to Jesus as the Messiah *is* a political stance over against other political powers. The magistrates do not give in to the crowd, but simply make the believers pay a fine and release them (17:8-9; contrast the previous scene in 16:19-40).

Acts 17:10-15. The fact that the magistrates follow appropriate legal procedure does not mean Paul and Silas are safe, so the newly formed church sends them off from Thessalonica to Beroea, some fifty miles away. Paul again goes to the synagogue, presumably following the same pattern of proclamation. As in Thessalonica, many in Beroea are convinced, including leading women of the city. This time, however, the local Jewish leadership is more receptive to Paul's message. They do not necessarily accept his argument but are willing to consider it (17:10-12).

This does not mean, however, that Paul is safe. The religious authorities from Thessalonica follow him to Beroea and stir up trouble again (17:13). As before, the believers send Paul away for his own good, but this time Silas and Timothy stay behind to nurture the new community of faith (17:14-15).

Acts 17:16-21. Paul is sent further this time, to Athens, some 300 miles from Beroea. The fame of Athens as the philosophical center of Greek thought would not be lost on ancient readers. It would be no surprise to them, then, that added to Paul's custom of arguing in the synagogues (17:17a) is the necessity of his arguing in the marketplace with the likes of Epicureans and Stoics (two popular philosophical schools of the day; 17:17b-18).

Paul has a negative impression of Athens as being a place of idolatry (17:16), and the philosophers have a negative impression of Paul as a babbler and proclaimer of foreign deities (17:18). In Greek, babbler is *spermalogos* (seed + word). The metaphor is of a bird who picks up seed and spits out the shells. A babbler (or gossip) picks up bits and pieces of information and spits out nonsense. So the philosophers see Paul as trying to speak above his level. But the second accusation (proclaimer of foreign deities) is more serious. This is similar language to how Socrates was accused, tried, and executed. Luke hints at both the seriousness of Paul's situation and at his stature.

Nevertheless, the philosophers wish to hear more of Paul's word about Jesus and the resurrection because, as Luke disparagingly notes, Athens is always looking for the "new" (17:21). But there is ambiguity in Luke's language here. The philosophers "took him and brought him to the Areopagus" (17:19). "Areopagus" can either refer to a place, Mars'/Ares' Hill, or the Athenian council. If the first is intended, then "took him" simply means they led him to the place where philosophical argument takes place. If the second is intended, the "took him" means they arrested him and what follows is a formal defense speech at a trial.

Acts 17:22-32. By referring to Paul's message as "Jesus and the resurrection" earlier in verse 18, Luke signals to the reader that Paul preaches the same message to the Greek philosophers that he preaches to the synagogues. The same message, however, cannot translate into the same rhetorical pattern in this new setting. Paul cannot begin with Scripture and then move to Jesus because the Greek philosophers do not accept Jewish Scripture as authoritative.

Instead Paul begins with the experience of his hearers. To make them receptive to his message, he first praises them as religious (17:22) and then names an altar in Athens "To an unknown god" (17:23). Paul claims to know who this is, and immediately makes a connection with his hearers.

What follows is, of course, Paul's description of the God of Israel ultimately revealed in the resurrection of Jesus (17:24-31). We need not go into detail analyzing this speech for our purposes, but it is important to recognize that Luke presents Paul as offering this description in phrases and imagery drawn from Greek philosophy of the day. Paul is consistent in his message but adapts his technique as necessary for the context.

As Paul's message is consistent, so is the response to his message. Some accepted his word, and others rejected it.

INTERPRETING THE SCRIPTURE

Realistic Success

When Peter completed his Pentecost sermon, three thousand persons were added to the messianic community (Acts 2:41). As the first sermon in The Acts of the Apostles, this response sets a pretty high mark. One reading through that story too quickly might expect every example of proclamation of the gospel that follows in the narrative to be met with similar unanimous acclamation. But a careful reader would notice that even when the several thousand are baptized on Pentecost, Luke identifies them as "those who welcomed [Peter's] message." The use of "those" implies there are others who did not accept Peter's message.

Anyone who has read through the Gospel of Luke before moving into Acts would have known better than to expect that everyone who heard the good news would accept it. After all, Jesus himself is presented as being accepted and followed by some and rejected by others, especially religious leaders. As it was for the Messiah, so would it be for those sent out on behalf of the Messiah (see Luke 9:5).

All of this is to say that Luke took the perspective of a realist in writing his two-volume narrative. There is no resurrection without death. There is no advancement of the gospel without resistance to it. There is no growing church without many who refuse to enter.

By the time readers get to the stories of Paul in Thessalonica, Beroea, and Athens in chapter 17, they have already read of apostles being arrested, the church in Jerusalem scattered, James beheaded, and Peter on the run. Indeed, they have already seen Paul's message resisted. And indeed, after this phase of the story, they will see that resistance increase until Paul finally ends up under house arrest awaiting trial before the emperor (28:16-31).

In Thessalonica, Beroea, and Athens, Paul's message is received by some and rejected by others. It is especially rejected by those whose political status is challenged by devotion to Jesus as the Christ. It is rejected to the point that Paul's very life is threatened.

But this rejection does not have the last word. While the gospel is rejected by many, it is also received by many. At the end of this chapter, three new messianic communities have been formed in major urban centers. The fact that the Thessalonians have resources to send Paul safely on his way (17:10), there is need for Silas and Timothy to stay behind in Beroea (17:15), and that even those who reject Paul in Athens promise to hear Paul again about this message (17:32) signals that the stories we read in chapter 17 are only the beginning of success in these three locales. The work Paul began will be continued by others. And their work will meet with both continued acceptance— and continued rejection.

"To God Be the Glory, Great Things God Has Done"

As we read about Paul's preaching ministry, we appropriately admire his preaching abilities, his agility at adapting his speaking strategies for different audiences, and his ability to influence audiences in significant ways. Luke, however, does not see Paul as ultimately responsible for the achievements of his own ministry. Both acceptance and rejection of the gospel by those in Paul's audiences are works of God.

First, the acceptance. Consider Acts 17:4. Both the NRSV and CEB translations blur a nuance found in the Greek. Both say some "joined" Paul and Silas. The Greek, however, uses the passive voice here. Literally, the line should read that some "were joined to" Paul and Silas. The verb is a passive one but no clear subject is provided. It is as if one said, "The ball was thrown," without indicating who did the throwing. While English teachers might cringe at such grammatical ambiguity, it is quite common in the Bible and is often referred to by scholars as the divine passive. In other words, an author using such a passive verb implicitly claims that God is doing the acting. So in Acts, Paul did not join these people to himself nor did they join themselves to Paul. God joined them.

Second, the rejection. Luke never presents God as desiring that some reject the gospel. He does, however, make it clear that God's good news is such that some will not be able to accept it. In the Christ event, God is turning the world on its head. Recall Mary's prophetic speech in the Magnificat:

> He [God] has shown strength
>   with his arm;
>   he has scattered the proud in
>   the thoughts of their hearts.
> He has brought down the
>   powerful from their
>   thrones,
>   and lifted up the lowly;
>   he has filled the hungry with
>   good things,
>   and sent the rich away
>   empty. (Luke 1:51-53)

In order for the gospel of Jesus Christ to lift up the oppressed, it must topple the oppressors. Those who benefit from the status quo, then, naturally reject the gospel, because to accept it would require of them to give up an identity and status that come from standing on the necks of others. Religious, political, economic,

and philosophical leaders are rightfully threatened by the new word of Jesus the Christ. They barter power using the currency of death. Resurrection takes away any power they think they possess.

Thus both acceptance of the gospel by the lowly and the hungry and rejection of the gospel by the proud, the rich, and the enthroned point to the power of God acting through the good news of Jesus Christ.

"If You Can't Preach Like Peter, If You Can't Pray Like Paul"

While Luke presents God, and not Paul, as ultimately responsible for some people accepting and others rejecting the gospel when Paul preaches, Paul is clearly a hero of the narrative. Luke wants readers to admire, and even aspire to follow, the example of Paul.

It may seem odd to claim that Paul is a role model for us when Luke tells us so little about him as an individual in Acts. When he preaches he sounds just like Peter. We are told nothing about his physical attributes, his family of origin, or his inner self. He is in many ways a stock character for Luke. But it is in this very stereotype of a Christian witness that Paul is an example to follow.

Without being able to claim success or wallow in failure (since neither are his, but God's alone), Paul simply keeps on. He perseveres and preaches continually. If he must leave Thessalonica, he keeps preaching in Beroea. If he must leave Beroea, he keeps preaching in Athens. He interprets Christ through the lens of Scripture in the synagogue and through the lens of philosophy in the Areopagus.

We should expect no less. After all, this is the same Paul who shared the gospel with the very jailer who kept him imprisoned after the magistrates in Philippi had him beaten (16:27-34). Indeed, it is the same Paul who, while under house arrest in Rome awaiting trial (and beheading) before the emperor, continues "proclaiming the kingdom of God and teaching about the Lord Jesus Christ with all boldness and without hindrance" (28:31). And Luke expects no less of his readers.

SHARING THE SCRIPTURE

PREPARING TO TEACH

Preparing Our Hearts

Ponder this week's devotional reading from Psalm 47, a hymn of praise. For what specific reasons are people called to offer praise? How are they to praise God? How would you describe the worship setting where this psalm might have been sung?

Pray that you and the students will praise the God who rules over all the earth.

Preparing Our Minds

Study the background Scripture from Acts 17:1-32 and the lesson Scripture from Acts 17:1-4, 10-12, 22-25, 28.

Consider this question as you prepare the lesson: *How do you respond when you are rejected by those you hope will accept your message about Christ?*

Write on newsprint:

❏ information for next week's lesson, found under Continue the Journey.

❏ activities for further spiritual growth in Continue the Journey.

Review the Introduction, The Big Picture, Close-up, and Faith in Action, which all precede the first lesson of this quarter. Consider how you might use any of this material in today's lesson.

LEADING THE CLASS

(1) Gather to Learn

❖ Welcome the class members and guests.

❖ Pray that those who have come today will recognize that good things can come out of adversity.

❖ Read: **Throughout history people who "marched to the beat of a different drummer" have shared their messages with conviction. Through their work in many different arenas, people such as Copernicus, Galileo, Columbus, Newton, Martin Luther, Dr. Martin Luther King Jr., Gandhi, Bill Gates, Steve Jobs, and Mother Teresa changed the way we viewed the world, our relation to it, and how people might live together. Yet most people who saw or heard things in a new way were rebuffed or outright rejected, at least at the beginning, and perhaps executed for their convictions. How do those who truly make a difference respond to rejection?**

❖ Read aloud today's focus statement: **Some people accept messages proclaimed with conviction while others reject them. How do Christians respond when those they hope will accept their messages reject them? Luke shows that Paul was undeterred and continued telling the** good news story and preaching with strong passion and conviction.

(2) Goal 1: Learn That Although Paul and Silas's Message Was Accepted by Some but Not All, God Received the Glory

❖ Choose one or more volunteers to read Acts 17:1-4, 10-12, 22-25, 28 and ask: **How would you characterize people's reception of the message that Paul and his companions proclaimed?**

❖ Read or retell "Realistic Success" in Interpreting the Scripture to help the adults recognize that neither Jesus nor those who spread the good news about him were completely successful in winning people.

❖ Discuss these questions:

1. **What criteria does your church use to determine the effectiveness of a program or ministry?** (Note that numerical participation may be one yardstick, but spiritual growth, greater presence of the church in the community, and care for those who are vulnerable are examples of other measurements that can be used.)

2. **In a Jewish synagogue in Thessalonica, Paul focused his message on Jesus' suffering and death as proof that he was the Messiah. In Athens, where gods of the Greek pantheon were worshiped, Paul shaped his message to attract and win over the Greek philosophers. How might the message of God's redeeming love in Jesus Christ be framed in your community so as to attract people to him?**

3. **What strategies might you use to reach those who have**

no religious affiliation to proclaim the good news of Jesus to them?

(3) Goal 2: Reflect Upon the Effects of Rejection in the Lives of Those Who Serve God

❖ Discuss these questions:

1. **What are some ways in which people experience rejection?** (Here are possible answers: Some people believe others are making fun of them; a potential mate turns down a marriage proposal; a bank refuses to consider a loan; an artist's work is panned by reviewers; an employee is passed over for a promotion; a player is not chosen for a team.)

2. **What are some ways in which you or people you know respond to an instance of rejection?** (Here are some ideas: Some people such as Paul will persevere; others will become despondent; some will withdraw from or abandon the person or project that prompted the rejection.)

3. **How might you help a servant of God who feels that his or her message has been rejected?** (Consider using Paul as a role model, for he persevered no matter what the situation. Use ideas from "If You Can't Preach Like Peter, If You Can't Pray Like Paul" in Interpreting the Scripture.)

❖ Wrap up this activity by explaining that God is in charge of whatever successes or failures one experiences in trying to win others to Christ. Read or retell "To God Be the Glory, Great Things God Has Done" from Interpreting the Scripture.

(4) Goal 3: Seek Out and Use Spiritual Resources That Support Perseverance in the Midst of Rejection

❖ Look again at Acts 17:11-12, which describes how the Beroeans "welcomed the message very eagerly and examined the scriptures every day to see whether these things were so." Ask: **How does the Bible help you not only to determine the truth of any message about Jesus that you hear but also to support you if you feel the message you have shared about him has been rejected?**

❖ Review Acts 17:16-34, which tells the story of Paul's preaching and interactions with Greek philosophers. Ask: **What strategies does Paul use to reach these people who do not know Christ, some of whom rejected his message, but others of whom accepted it (17:32-34)?**

❖ Recall that Paul and his team were subjected not only to verbal rebuff but also became the target of "ruffians" (17:5) and mobs (17:5, 13). **How did believers support Paul in the midst of this threat? What are some other ways that those who are physically or psychologically threatened might be supported?**

(5) Continue the Journey

❖ Pray that as the learners depart, they will be ready not only to declare good news but also to bolster those whose message about God is rejected.

❖ Post information for next week's session on newsprint for the students to copy:

- **Title: Teaching God's Word**
- **Background Scripture: Acts 18**
- **Lesson Scripture: Acts 18:1-11, 18-21**

■ **Focus of the Lesson: People can be persistent when they really believe what they are doing and saying is the right thing. How do people sustain their enthusiasm for their work or vocation? Luke points out that the success in Paul's Corinthian mission and God's affirmation led Paul to extend his mission of proclaiming the good news to Syria and Ephesus.**

❖ Post the following information on newsprint and provide paper and pencils for the students to copy it. Challenge the adults to grow spiritually by completing one or more of these activities related to this week's session.

(1) **Offer an encouraging word to someone who has experienced the sting of rejection.**

(2) **Use the Internet, a Bible dictionary, or other resources to research Silas and Timothy to learn more about the roles they played in supporting Paul's ministry.**

(3) **Recall that Paul's preaching got to the heart of the gospel. Identify three to five points that you would be certain to make when you have an opportunity to present the good news of Jesus Christ.**

❖ Sing or read aloud "By Gracious Powers."

❖ Conclude today's session by leading the class in this benediction, which is adapted from Acts 9:20, the key verse for October 11: **Let us go forth to boldly proclaim that Jesus is the Son of God. Amen.**

UNIT 3: SPREADING THE GOSPEL
TEACHING GOD'S WORD

PREVIEWING THE LESSON

Lesson Scripture: Acts 18:1-11, 18-21
Background Scripture: Acts 18
Key Verses: Acts 18:9-10

Focus of the Lesson:
People can be persistent when they really believe what they are doing and saying is the right thing. How do people sustain their enthusiasm for their work or vocation? Luke points out that the success in Paul's Corinthian mission and God's affirmation led Paul to extend his mission of proclaiming the good news to Syria and Ephesus.

Goals for the Learners:
(1) to explore Paul's zeal for teaching the gospel message to the Gentiles, after he was rejected by the Jews.
(2) to identify feelings after making a vocational transition.
(3) to pray for the success of those whom God has placed in a new and challenging situation.

Supplies:
Bibles, newsprint and marker, paper and pencils, hymnals, candles, lighter

---

READING THE SCRIPTURE

NRSV

Lesson Scripture: Acts 18:1-11, 18-21

¹After this Paul left Athens and went to Corinth. ²There he found a Jew named Aquila, a native of Pontus, who had recently come from Italy with his wife Priscilla, because Claudius had ordered all Jews to leave Rome. Paul went to see them, ³and, because he was of the same trade, he stayed with them, and they

CEB

Lesson Scripture: Acts 18:1-11, 18-21

¹After this, Paul left Athens and went to Corinth. ²There he found a Jew named Aquila, a native of Pontus. He had recently come from Italy with his wife Priscilla because Claudius had ordered all Jews to leave Rome. Paul visited with them. ³Because they practiced the same trade, he stayed and worked with them. They all

worked together—by trade they were tentmakers. [4]Every sabbath he would argue in the synagogue and would try to convince Jews and Greeks.

[5]When Silas and Timothy arrived from Macedonia, Paul was occupied with proclaiming the word, testifying to the Jews that the Messiah was Jesus. [6]When they opposed and reviled him, in protest he shook the dust from his clothes and said to them, "Your blood be on your own heads! I am innocent. From now on I will go to the Gentiles." [7]Then he left the synagogue and went to the house of a man named Titius Justus, a worshiper of God; his house was next door to the synagogue. [8]Crispus, the official of the synagogue, became a believer in the Lord, together with all his household; and many of the Corinthians who heard Paul became believers and were baptized. [9]One night the Lord said to Paul in a vision, "Do not be afraid, but speak and do not be silent; [10]for I am with you, and no one will lay a hand on you to harm you, for there are many in this city who are my people." [11]He stayed there a year and six months, teaching the word of God among them.

[18]After staying there for a considerable time, Paul said farewell to the believers and sailed for Syria, accompanied by Priscilla and Aquila. At Cenchreae he had his hair cut, for he was under a vow. [19]When they reached Ephesus, he left them there, but first he himself went into the synagogue and had a discussion with the Jews. [20]When they asked him to stay longer, he declined; [21]but on taking leave of them, he said, "I will return to you, if God wills."

worked with leather. [4]Every Sabbath he interacted with people in the synagogue, trying to convince both Jews and Greeks. [5]Once Silas and Timothy arrived from Macedonia, Paul devoted himself fully to the word, testifying to the Jews that Jesus was the Christ. [6]When they opposed and slandered him, he shook the dust from his clothes in protest and said to them, "You are responsible for your own fates! I'm innocent! From now on I'll go to the Gentiles!" [7]He left the synagogue and went next door to the home of Titius Justus, a Gentile God-worshipper. [8]Crispus, the synagogue leader, and his entire household came to believe in the Lord. Many Corinthians believed and were baptized after listening to Paul.

[9]One night the Lord said to Paul in a vision, "Don't be afraid. Continue speaking. Don't be silent. [10]I'm with you and no one who attacks you will harm you, for I have many people in this city." [11]So he stayed there for eighteen months, teaching God's word among them.

[18]After Paul stayed in Corinth for some time, he said good-bye to the brothers and sisters. At the Corinthian seaport of Cenchreae he had his head shaved, since he had made a solemn promise. Then, accompanied by Priscilla and Aquila, he sailed away to Syria. [19]After they arrived in Ephesus, he left Priscilla and Aquila and entered the synagogue and interacted with the Jews. [20]They asked him to stay longer, but he declined. [21]As he said farewell to them, though, he added, "God willing, I will return."

UNDERSTANDING THE SCRIPTURE

Acts 18:1-4. Paul departs from Athens and heads to Corinth, more than forty miles west. Luke says that upon arriving Paul sought out a couple, Aquila and Priscilla, who had come to Corinth because of a recent expulsion of the Jews by Claudius. This little notice has been the object of much scholarly interest for a number of different reasons.

First, the fact that Paul already knew Aquila and Priscilla and that they later correct Apollos's Christian theology in Ephesus (18:26) implies that they were part of a Christian community in Rome before coming to Corinth. This means Paul had association with Christians in communities that he had not founded and to which he had not even traveled. (This picture accords with what we know of the situation behind Paul's writing of his Letter to the Romans.) On the other hand, the fact that Paul shares a profession with Aquila (tentmaking, which may mean, more broadly, something like leatherworking) may mean their connection is simply through a professional guild. Such guilds were important ways people found social and economic support in the ancient Mediterranean world.

Second, Aquila and Priscilla (sometimes Prisca) are always mentioned together in the New Testament (Acts 18:2, 18, 26; Romans 16:3; 1 Corinthians 16:19; 2 Timothy 4:19). This pairing gives the impression that they are co-leaders/co-missionaries in the church. This is a rare insight into the role of women in leadership of the early church.

Third, the mention of the expulsion by Claudius may give a historical grounding to part of the Acts narrative that is rarely present. The expulsion is mentioned in the Roman historian's work *Life of Claudius* 25:4. The reference there would date the expulsion to A.D. 49 and the reason given for it is a disturbance caused *impulsore Chresto*. This may well be a reference to preaching about Christ, in which case "Jews" would have been expelled because of Christian proclamation, showing that the Roman government at this point did not distinguish between the church and the rest of Judaism.

The fact that Luke does not offer more detail about any of these issues shows that (1) they are not his primary concern, and (2) he assumes his original readers understand the references in ways difficult for modern readers to catch.

Paul's main concern is to write a good theological story. This introduction to Paul's visit to Corinth offers a glimpse into Paul's missionary methodology: He enters a new location, finds a host, and works to support himself, all the while debating in the synagogue each week.

Acts 18:5-8. Paul's methodology in Corinth shifts as his success allows. We are not told how long Paul works under the conditions mentioned in verses 3-4, but once Silas and Timothy arrive, Paul "devoted himself fully to the word" (18:5; the CEB is a better translation here than the NRSV). The implication may be that Aquila and Priscilla's support, with a growing number of converts to provide support, and with Silas and Timothy there to work, Paul no longer needs to earn an income through "tentmaking" but can devote full time to his missionary work.

But a more significant change in the apostle's work in Corinth is signaled in this paragraph. As Paul increased his missionary work, so the resistance to that work increased. Therefore, following Jesus' instructions, Paul shakes the dust from his clothes as a sign of prophetic judgment against the Jewish leadership resisting him (Luke 9:5; 10:11; see also Acts 13:51) and he leaves the synagogue to offer the gospel to the Gentiles. He does so by setting up directly across the street from the synagogue!

This turning toward the Gentiles does not mean Paul is not concerned with offering the gospel to Jews who would hear it. His judgment is against those leaders who reject the gospel and hinder the path for others to accept it. After all, in an irony of ironies, Paul's first convert after leaving the synagogue (or the first convert of which Luke tells us) is Crispus, a leader in the synagogue! This notice of the conversion of Crispus is significant because such a leader becoming convinced of Paul's argument paves the way for others to be so persuaded. Indeed, the Greek of 18:8b literally says that "many of the Corinthians who heard had faith and were baptized." The NRSV and the CEB add that they heard Paul. The implication is of course that Paul's preaching was that which led them to faith, but the grammar of the sentence better signals that what they "heard" was that Crispus had become a believer, and they then followed suit.

Acts 18:9-17. The opposition to Paul should not be taken lightly. It was serious, and only divine providence would keep him from harm. As at other times in Acts, God's self-revelation comes to Paul through a vision or dream (9:3, which is called a vision in 10:10; 16:9; 26:19). Read too quickly, the divine promise offered in verse 10—that "no one will lay a hand on you to harm you"—may seem to be broken as quickly as two verses later when "the Jews made a united attack on Paul and brought him before the tribunal." But while they did lay hands on Paul, they were not able to do him harm in that the proconsul Gallio dismissed the case before it began (18:14-15). God's protection allows Paul to stay in Corinth for a year and a half, reminding us that while much of the second half of Acts details Paul's travels, in truth the image is of one who settles in a city for a while to ground a community firmly in the faith.

Acts 18:18-23. While divine guidance led to Paul staying in Corinth for "a considerable time" (18:18), it was also divine guidance that prevented him staying longer in Ephesus. God's will, and God's will alone, would determine whether Paul would return to the city (and he does in 19:1), but for now God was leading him back home to Antioch by way of Jerusalem (18:22) and then on yet another missionary journey (18:23).

Acts 18:24-28. A new missionary appears in verse 24: Apollos. In 1 Corinthians, Apollos seems not to be part of Paul's missionary team but someone whose work Paul appreciates (see 1 Corinthians 1:12; 3:4-6, 22; 4:6; 16:12). That picture is similar in Acts, but what is striking is that members of Paul's team—Priscilla and Aquila—correct Apollos's theology (which he seems to welcome) and then offer him support in the form of sending him to Corinth in the region of Achaia (18:27; 19:1) from which Paul's team has just come.

INTERPRETING THE SCRIPTURE

Finding a Way

Barriers are constantly put in Paul's way. In city after city as the apostle tries to proclaim the good news of Jesus Christ and bring people into the Way, there are always troubles that accompany his work. "The Jews," that is, the synagogue leaders, oppose him. Political authorities persecute him. But where there is God's will, there is a way—God's way.

In chapter 18 Paul comes to Corinth. The first problem he encounters is implied but not directly narrated by Luke. Paul must eat. He must make money to live on. So Paul finds a tentmaker like himself, joins forces with him, and works Sunday through Friday. He does this so that on the Sabbath, he can present evidence in the synagogue that Jesus is the Christ.

The second problem is more serious. It is that the powers that be at the synagogue will have nothing to do with Paul's message. They do not simply disagree with him; they "revile" him (18:6). Consequently, Paul leaves the synagogue with the prophetic action of shaking the dust from his clothes and goes across the street to set up shop. Luke clearly presents the church at this point as being in competition with the synagogue leadership . . . and the church wins in a big way when Paul converts Crispus, one of the leaders of the synagogue. (Luke's description of Crispus as "the" official of the synagogue in verse 8 probably refers to him as part of the team of leadership instead of the sole leader. There are still other leaders in place to resist Paul's work.)

A third implied but not explicitly named problem is that once Paul's mission becomes successful in Corinth, he no longer has time to work in the leather industry throughout the week to fund the work. But the arrival of Silas and Timothy, the continued support of Aquila and Priscilla, the patronage of Titius Justus (in whose house the new church met), and likely the financial support of new converts like Crispus allow him to shift his work schedule.

A fourth problem Paul faces (found in background verses 12-17) is that the Jewish authorities stir up enough opposition to carry Paul before the magistrate in Corinth. Paul stands ready to defend himself, but Gallio, the Roman-appointed official, will not allow it because he does not consider the dispute a civil matter.

Support

Paul's success was not his achievement alone. Throughout Acts, Luke reminds readers that God is the one really at work through the church and its representative missionaries. Paul does not act of his own initiative. No mere puppet, Paul is a willing servant of the will of God. And the Lord (that is, Christ) guides him in his actions—in this case, revealing divine care and support of Paul in the form of a vision (18:9-10). No greater promise can Christ offer than "I am with you." So Paul need not back down, silence himself, or fear any barrier or opposition that gets in the way of his sharing the good news of Jesus Christ.

While divine support of Paul's

work is central to any success Paul has, Luke makes clear that this is not the only form of support the apostle receives. Paul is part of a team. As he first went out as part of Barnabas's missionary team (11:25; 13:2), so now he heads a team of his own that includes Silas and Timothy (18:5). But Paul also adds members to his team when appropriate, as seen in the fact that Aquila and Priscilla accompany him when he leaves Corinth (18:18). Thus, without taking anything away from Paul as an individual, there is a sense that every time Luke presents Paul as being successful, readers are really to recognize that Paul's *team* has met with success. Luke's emphasis is on the work of the church as a community doing God's bidding instead of simply on telling the story of an individual's accomplishments.

Finally, Paul's success is supported by those whom he successfully converts to the Way. Financial (and thus moral) support is implied in the way Luke tells the story of the growing community in Corinth. Note for instance the mention of wealthy women (and men) who are converted (16:14-15; 17:4, 12; compare Luke 8:1-3). But even more important for today's lesson is the fact that when a leader of the synagogue, Crispus, and his household join the messianic community, many others are willing to follow him into the faith (18:8).

Luke presents Paul as an extraordinary figure with exemplary faith, deep devotion to his ministry, and great skill as a preacher and church planter. But for all the language in Acts presenting Paul as the main character and referring to Paul in the singular, the apostle never works or succeeds alone. Every time Paul is mentioned in Acts the reader should think of Paul's whole team and network of support. He and the many who work with him serve God *together*. This missionary community goes a long way to giving Paul the ability to persevere through the constant problems he faces and to succeed in spreading God's good news throughout the Roman Empire.

An Expanded "People"

When Paul faces severe resistance from the powers that be in the synagogue, he makes a dramatic turn in verse 6 to the Gentiles of Corinth (although the very next convert mentioned in verse 8 is a Jew!). Bringing the Word to the Gentiles was, of course, defined as Paul's primary purpose as an apostle from the moment of his call/conversion (Acts 9:15). Moreover, Paul has made such a claim about turning to the Gentiles before (13:46-49) while continuing to also preach to Jews.

Still, Luke signals something significant in this shift that can easily be missed. When the Lord speaks to Paul in a vision and tells him not to be afraid, Christ not only mentions his presence as reason that Paul should persevere. Christ also assures Paul that "there are many in this city who are *my people*" (18:10, emphasis added).

Luke has consistently used the Greek word *laos* (people) as a theological term referring to Israel as the people of God (for example, Luke 1:10, 17, 68, 77; 2:10, 31-32; 24:19; Acts 2:47; 3:12, 23; 4:2, 10, 21). Having just presented Paul as turning from the synagogue to the Gentiles, the use of "people" here seems to indicate that the Lord considers Gentiles to be part of God's people now. This assurance then is quite ironic: The rejection of

Paul's message of God's good news by the Corinthian synagogue authorities leads to Paul preaching to the Corinthians Gentiles and their being included with the Jews in the people of God.

Bringing people into God's people makes all of the difficulties of Paul and his team worthwhile. They are instruments of God's salvation, changing lives and thus changing the world.

SHARING THE SCRIPTURE

PREPARING TO TEACH

Preparing Our Hearts

Ponder this week's devotional reading from Matthew 28:16-20. In this very familiar passage, known as the Great Commission, Jesus charges the disciples to go into the world to make disciples, baptize, and teach. How are you fulfilling this commission as a disciple of Jesus? What lessons about Jesus can you share this week?

Pray that you and the students will do whatever you can, wherever you are, to spread the gospel

Preparing Our Minds

Study the background Scripture from Acts 18 and the lesson Scripture from Acts 18:1-11, 18-21.

Consider this question as you prepare the lesson: *How do people sustain their enthusiasm for their work or vocation?*

Write on newsprint:

❏ questions listed for Goal 2 in Sharing the Scripture.
❏ information for next week's lesson, found under Continue the Journey.
❏ activities for further spiritual growth in Continue the Journey.

Review the Introduction, The Big Picture, Close-up, and Faith in Action, which all precede the first lesson of this quarter. Decide if information for today's lesson in Close-up would be helpful for the class to review.

Set candles (or tealights) and a lighter on a small table for use at the end of the session.

LEADING THE CLASS

(1) Gather to Learn

❖ Welcome the class members and guests.

❖ Pray that those who have come today will work enthusiastically for God.

❖ Read: **This is the first Sunday in Advent, a season during which believers prepare spiritually for the coming and coming again of Jesus Christ. It is also a season when nonbelievers may be especially aware of their spiritual lives.**

❖ Ask these questions:

1. **How can we, as individual Christians and as the body of Christ, use this first season of the church year as an opportunity to witness enthusiastically for God and the Beloved Son?**

2. **What can we say or do to help differentiate between the commercial meaning that the media trumpets and the real reason for this season?**

❖ Read aloud today's focus statement: **People can be persistent when** they really believe what they are doing and saying is the right thing. How do people sustain their enthusiasm for their work or vocation? Luke points out that the success in Paul's Corinthian mission and God's affirmation led Paul to extend his mission of proclaiming the good news to Syria and Ephesus.

(2) Goal 1: Explore Paul's Zeal for Teaching the Gospel Message to the Gentiles, After He Was Rejected by the Jews

❖ Introduce today's lesson by reading or retelling "Finding a Way" in Interpreting the Scripture. Help participants understand that Paul faced rejection and obstacles as he worked tirelessly to fulfill his call to share the good news.

❖ Choose three volunteers to read Acts 18:1-4, 5-11, 18-21 and then discuss these questions:
1. **What do you learn from this passage about how Paul handles resistance to his work?** (See Acts 18:5-8 in Understanding the Scripture.)
2. **How did God reassure Paul that he was on the right track, despite the rejection and resistance he had encountered?** (See Acts 18:9-17 in Understanding the Scripture.)
3. **What kind of support system did Paul have, and how did this support impact his ministry?** (See "Support" in Interpreting the Scripture.)
4. **What lessons can the church in our day learn from Paul and his team about how to reach others for Christ?**
5. **How might your congregation put these lessons into practice?**

(3) Goal 2: Identify Feelings After Making a Vocational Transition

❖ Read or retell "An Expanded 'People'" from Interpreting the Scripture. Note that Paul made a vocational transition in terms of the target audience for his message. After his own Jewish people resisted his message of good news about Jesus, he reached out to Gentiles.

❖ Note that many people today may change focus within their vocations, or turn to completely new vocations. Form small groups and post these questions for discussion:
1. **If you have ever made a vocational change, what prompted you to explore a new vocation or change your focus within the job you had?**
2. **If you or someone close to you has ever made a vocational transition, what feelings surfaced during the journey from one vocation (or focus) to another?**
3. **When you settled into your new vocation, did you feel that the effort and sacrifice to make the transition had been worth it? Why or why not?**

❖ Bring participants together and close by asking: **Based on your discussions, what might you conclude about the challenges that Paul faced and the emotions he may have felt as he refocused his preaching and teaching on a Gentile audience?**

(4) Goal 3: Pray for the Success of Those Whom God Has Placed in a New and Challenging Situation

❖ Move the table with candles and lighter to a place where students can gather around it, if possible.

❖ Read these directions: **Each participant is invited to name an individual or team that is working in a challenging situation and then light a candle. The situation need not be a ministry as such; whatever people do in the name of Jesus is their vocation even if it is not connected with the church. We will observe a moment of silence followed by this unison response: "Empower this servant to work boldly and without fear."**

(5) Continue the Journey

❖ Continue with the candle lighting until each person has had an opportunity to lift a name for prayer. Then pray that as the learners depart they will go forth to spread God's word without fear and to support others.

❖ Post information for next week's session on newsprint for the students to copy:

- **Title: The Lord's Day**
- **Background Scripture: Exodus 16:23; 20:8-11; 31:12-18; Leviticus 23:3-8; Deuteronomy 5:12-15; Matthew 12:1-14; Acts 13:42**
- **Lesson Scripture: Exodus 20:8-11; 31:12-17**
- **Focus of the Lesson: Some people have turned away from those traditions that provide firm underpinnings for their lives. How can they maintain spiritual stability in a rapidly changing world? Scripture informs them of a God who set aside the**

Sabbath as a day to remember and to recommit to holy living.

❖ Post the following information on newsprint and provide paper and pencils for the students to copy it. Challenge the adults to grow spiritually by completing one or more of these activities related to this week's session.

(1) **Offer support to someone who is considering a call to ministry or who is engaged in a challenging ministry. Provide this support through prayer, financial giving, a listening ear, and by doing whatever you can to bolster the ministry.**

(2) **Be alert for God's call on your own life. Perhaps God has a specific task for you; maybe you are being called into a deeper ministry commitment. Talk with your pastor and others who could provide a support team for you.**

(3) **Pray for members of your Sunday school class by name, asking God to give them the boldness to share the good news without fear, even if they are rejected by some.**

❖ Sing or read aloud "Break Thou the Bread of Life."

❖ Conclude today's session by leading the class in this benediction, which is adapted from Acts 9:20, the key verse for October 11: **Let us go forth to boldly proclaim that Jesus is the Son of God. Amen.**

SECOND QUARTER
Sacred Gifts and Holy Gatherings

DECEMBER 6, 2015–FEBRUARY 28, 2016

The thirteen lessons of the winter quarter focus on holy celebrations in the Jewish tradition. We see Jesus participate in some of these events as he practices the traditions of his faith. The first unit, "What We Bring to God," opens on December 6 with "The Lord's Day," a lesson that includes extensive background Scripture from Exodus 16:23; 20:8-11; 31:12-18; Leviticus 23:3-8; Deuteronomy 5:12-15; Matthew 12:1-14; Acts 13:42 to help us explore the meaning of the Sabbath. "Acceptable Offerings," the session for December 13, looks at sacrificial giving that honors God as explained in Leviticus 22:17-33; 23:9-14, 31-32; Deuteronomy 22:6-7; Isaiah 1:10-20; Micah 6:6-8; Romans 12:1-2; 1 Corinthians 10:14-22. The lesson for December 20 reflects the excitement of the infant Jesus' presentation at the Temple with "Dedication of Firstborn," which draws on background from Exodus 13:11-16; Leviticus 12; Numbers 3:5-13; Luke 2:21-39. On December 27 we will consider "A Generous Gift," which explores a widow's offering as found in Matthew 23:1-12 and Mark 12:38-44.

Unit 2, "Four Weddings and a Funeral," looks at how the Bible handles two special life events. "A Bride Worth Waiting For," the session for January 3, examines Jacob's commitment to marry Rachel, as told in Genesis 28–30. The lesson for January 10, "The Most Beautiful Bride," looks at love and adoration through the lens of Song of Solomon and John 10:1-11. Israel's unfaithfulness is mirrored in the life of "An Unfaithful Bride," Hosea's wife, Gomer, whom we will encounter on January 17 as we study Hosea 1–3. The familiar story of "A Wedding in Cana," told in John 2:1-12, is the focus on January 24. The unit ends on a somber note on January 31 with "The Death of a Friend," as the death of Jesus' friend Lazarus is recounted in John 11:1-44.

Unit 3, "Holy Days," investigates four important Jewish holidays. We will study the first, "Passover," on February 7 as we delve into Exodus 12:1-14; Numbers 28:16-25; Mark 14:12-26. On February 14 we turn to the spring harvest festival of new grain known as "Feast of Weeks," which is detailed in background from Leviticus 23:15-22; Numbers 28:26-31; Acts 2:1-36. "Day of Atonement" is the featured holy day in background Scripture from Leviticus 16; 23:26-32; Numbers 29:7-11; Hebrews 7:26-28; 9:24; 10:4-18, which we will study on February 21. The quarter concludes on February 28 with an exploration of background Scripture from Leviticus 23:33-43; Numbers 29:12-40; Deuteronomy 16:13-17; 1 Corinthians 15:20-29; Revelation 14:1-5, to help us understand the "Feast of Booths," a festival celebrating the fall grain harvest.

MEET OUR WRITER

ANNE CRUMPLER

Anne Crumpler is a freelance editor and writer who lives in Nashville, Tennessee.

Anne comes from a long line of preachers, teachers, and writers. She learned theology and biblical interpretation, as well as a smattering of English grammar, over the dinner table. She also has a bachelor of arts in philosophy and religion from Chatham College. After studying at Pittsburgh Presbyterian Seminary, Louisville Presbyterian Seminary, and Phillips Theological Seminary, she earned a master of religious education degree from St. Meinrad School of Theology. Her educational background is ecumenical.

Anne has worked for both The United Methodist Church and the Presbyterian Church (U.S.A.). She was an assistant editor in the Department of Youth Publications of The United Methodist Publishing House until 1996. Since then, she has been a contract editor for *The Upper Room Daily Devotional Guide* and for *Devo'Zine*, a devotional magazine for youth published by The Upper Room.

Her writing includes Bible lessons for *Mature Years* magazine, *Daily Bible Studies*, and *The Present Word*; commentary for the 2003–2004 edition of *The New International Lesson Annual*; articles for *Devo'Zine* and *Alive Now*; devotions for *The Upper Room Disciplines*, *365 Meditations for Families*, and *Reflections: Devotions for the Present Day*; study guides for Lent and Advent offered online by The Upper Room; and lessons on the Kingdom of God for volume 3 of *The Pastor's Bible Study*.

Anne is married. She and David have two spectacular children, Rachel and Benjamin.

The Big Picture: Rituals, Holy Days, Connections

Rituals Define Us

Ordinarily, when we talk about setting aside time to be with the Lord, we mean personal devotional time. Our relationship with God involves prayer, Bible study, silent reflection—all of which compose a ritual of sorts, a way of being alone with God. Of course, our relationship with God is broader than one-on-one spirituality. The Bible talks about times appointed by God as sacred occasions. They are times when the people of God—in families, households, communities, nations—are ritually connected with the Lord. The religious calendar includes the weekly Sabbath, Passover, the Day of Atonement, Feast of Booths, and more. Holy days not only mark time—notes on a calendar—but they also define our relationship with God. Rituals also mark the patterns of our lives—love and marriage, birth and death—and remind us that all our times belong to God. Rituals and holy days connect us with God. The purpose of this article is to explore some of the ways ritual and sacred occasions provide a framework for our lives and describe us as the people of God.

Looking from the outside, rituals and holidays begin to define who we are. We are Christians: we are people who go to church on Sunday. We celebrate Christmas, Good Friday, Easter, Pentecost. We baptize our children and celebrate Holy Communion. We get married in the church. Funerals are a "Witness to the Resurrection." We are Jews: we are people who honor the Sabbath. We celebrate *Rosh Hashanah*, *Yom Kippur* (Day of Atonement), Passover, *Sukkoth* (Feast of Booths). When our children come of age, we have a bar mitvah or bat mitzvah. We marry under a canopy. We are buried within one day of our death. We are Muslims: we are people who pray five times a day. We fast during the month of Ramadan. Our holy days and rituals single us out and define us: we are people who. . . . Religious rituals and sacred occasions identify us as people of faith.

God the Creator

Rituals and holy days remind us that God is the creator of the natural world and the human community. Every new harvest is a gift of God, who provides the rain, warms the land, and gives the growth. Each new child is God's creature. Many of the sacred occasions appointed by the Lord in Scripture relate the people of God to God's creation. Observation of the Sabbath, a weekly day of rest, is commanded: "Remember the Sabbath day, and keep it holy . . . for in six days the Lord made heaven and earth . . . but rested the seventh day;

therefore the Lord blessed the sabbath day and consecrated it" (Exodus 20:8-11). During the Offering of First Fruits and Feast of Weeks, the first grain harvested is offered to the Lord before the rest is eaten (Leviticus 23:9-21). The festivals are rituals of thanksgiving because in the last analysis, the land, the seeds, the harvest all belong to God, as does the whole of creation. Even weddings are a celebration of God's creation—of God's gifts of male and female, physical attraction, love, the human need to live together in families. Rituals observe that God is the source of our lives and provides all we need; we are entirely dependent on God, who creates and keeps on creating.

Rituals often use what God has created as part of sacred observances. So, for example, farmers offer to God animals from their flocks. The animal may be a freewill offering, a gift of the firstborn, or a sacrifice on the Day of Atonement. Passover, celebrated for generations, includes lamb, bitter herbs, bread, wine— all gifts of God's creation. The Feast of Booths is celebrated with branches from a variety of different trees. Consider the rituals of the Christian community: baptism, which uses water, and communion, which uses bread and wine. These, too, are gifts of God's creation.

God of History: Past, Present, Future

Through rituals and holy days, we remember what God has done for us in the past. Observing the Sabbath is one of the Ten Commandments and grounded in God's saving act: "I am the LORD your God, who brought you out of the land of Egypt, out of the house of slavery" (Deuteronomy 5:6). Sabbath distinguishes life as slaves of Pharaoh from life as the people of God. God, unlike Pharaoh, gives people a day off. The Feast of Weeks is both a harvest festival and a commemoration of God's revelation at Sinai. The Feast of Booths celebrates the harvest, asks God's continued blessing on the crops, and also commemorates the Israelites' wandering in the wilderness. Passover remembers the Exodus, God's mighty act of salvation, in which God rescued the Israelites from slavery in Egypt and identified them as God's people. As the firstborn of Egypt were killed, God protected the Israelites and set them free for a new life. For Christians, the festivals also help us remember God's saving acts in the life of Christ. Jesus ate the Last Supper with his disciples on the Feast of Passover. We remember his death on Good Friday and celebrate his resurrection on Easter. Pentecost (the Greek name of Feast of Weeks) commemorates the gift of the Holy Spirit to the church.

Rituals and sacred occasions are, however, more than remembrances. Though we look at the past, we do not simply stand in the present looking backward. Ritual involves us in God's saving acts. Participating in the Passover ritual identifies us as the people of God, who were freed from slavery and now belong to God. During the Seder, the Passover meal, a child asks, "Why is this night different from all other nights?" The rest of the participants respond by saying, "We were slaves to Pharaoh in Egypt, and God brought us out with a strong hand and an outstretched arm." The ritual is commemoration but it also brings God's salvation into the present: This is what God has done for *us*. The Passover celebration, the present ritual, is as much God's saving act as the historic event.

During the Feast of Booths, Jews build temporary shelters and live in them for a week. They remember how the Israelites journeyed through the wilderness. At the same time, through the seven-day ritual, they get a sense of what it means to depend on God for food and shelter. Think of how the Christian holy days—Holy Thursday, Good Friday, Easter—draw us into union with Christ and take us through his death and resurrection. Ritual is reenactment of past events; but God also acts through the ritual itself, in the present, to make us God's people.

Most holy days also look to the future. God promises the people of God a new creation, a new life, a new covenant, a new social order. God promises to establish peace and justice on earth. Sabbath involves remembering God's rest at creation (past), resting from the work we ordinarily do (present), and also looking forward to eternal rest in God's presence. The ritual on the Day of Atonement symbolizes the purgation of the Temple and removal of sin from the community, but it also looks forward to a day when God will dwell among us and we can freely enter God's presence. During the Feast of Booths, people gather branches from a variety of different trees and bind them together. They represent different kinds of people united in faith and also call to mind the promised new age, in which all the nations will come together "year after year to worship the King" (Zechariah 14:16). The Passover concludes with "a final prayer asking God to bring the Messianic Era, when all of us will be gathered to Jerusalem as all humankind dwells in peace." The Christian ritual of the Lord's Supper looks back to Jesus' Last Supper; it represents the worldwide communion of saints, present; and it also looks forward to a time when all people will come together for a messianic banquet. Today, through rituals and sacred occasions, we participate in God's mighty acts of salvation in the past and we look forward to the coming of God's kingdom. Rituals are themselves an act of salvation, making us the *future* people of God.

Ceremonies that mark the events of our lives follow the same pattern. At weddings, we look to the past, to the marriages of grandparents and parents and to the lives of the bride and groom before they met. Remember the song from *Fiddler on the Roof*: "Is this the little girl I carried? Is this the little boy at play?" The wedding brings together two people, two families, two pasts into a present covenant. But by definition, a wedding looks to the future, to marriage, to growing old together, and maybe to a little happily ever after. Funerals act in much the same way. They look backward to the life of the person who has died and forward to his or her resurrection. In the ritual, in the present, they unite an individual with both a community of faith—the communion of saints—and with Christ who stands waiting to welcome us all into new life.

God of the Covenant

In Exodus and Leviticus, rituals and holy days are commanded. The Sabbath is part of the Ten Commandments. Other observances are established in Scripture that typically begin with the words "The LORD spoke to Moses" (for instance Leviticus 23:9, 26, 33). Sometimes Moses mediates for God, relaying God's message to the people. Other Scripture related to the festivals and rituals ends with the words "I am the LORD your God" (for example, Leviticus 23:43).

The words are shorthand for the revelation at Sinai, where God spoke to the people through Moses, and promised that they would be "a priestly kingdom and a holy nation" if they obeyed and kept the covenant (Exodus 19:4-6a). The people agreed and God gave them the law, speaking through Moses, "I am the LORD your God" (20:2). The Hebrew Bible understands that the rituals, offerings, and festivals are part of God's law, given at Sinai. Their observance is part of covenant obedience.

The covenantal relationship between God and God's people is summed up in Exodus 6:7, "I will take you as my people, and I will be your God." Rituals and holy days describe the relationship. Passover: God is the One who saves us, who delivers us from slavery and makes us God's own. The Harvest Festivals: God is the Creator, who made us, male and female, and created the world we live in. The whole earth belongs to God; God provides for us, sustains us. The Day of Atonement: God is holy and commands our obedience. God is merciful and takes away our sins. God is always God. And we are God's people, saved, created, loved, forgiven. Sanctuary rituals describe our relationship to God. People bring before the Lord a variety of offerings, which, like prayers, are always a response to what God has done. Rituals, like the covenant itself, begin with God. The people's offerings say, "Thank you," "Help," "Have mercy," "Bless us."

Be Holy as God Is Holy

The theology at the heart of the Book of Leviticus—and perhaps at the heart of Jewish and Christian practice—is summed up in Leviticus 19:2: "You shall be holy, for I the LORD your God am holy." At Sinai, God chooses us and set us apart from the rest of the world; we are to be a holy nation. We not only belong to God and are blessed by God; but by our obedience, we are to be a blessing to the world. The people of God are called to be like God.

Observing the rituals and holy days appointed by the Lord are a way of being holy. Remembering the Sabbath, keeping it holy, means setting aside a day for rest, a day when our lives are not caught up in our daily work, but instead focus on what God has done. On the seventh day, God rested, surveyed all the work of creation completed, and said, "Very good!" To be holy is perhaps to rest and enjoy God's gifts. The Feast of Weeks includes a word about gleaning. When farmers harvest, they are to leave uncut the last rows of wheat and leave in the field whatever falls, so that the poor and the alien have food for their tables. Gleaning is not a charitable donation, but an act of holiness. God lifts up the poor and feeds the hungry. Obedience requires that we do the same. Weddings: The Scripture often uses marriage as a metaphor for the relationship of God and God's people (for example, Hosea 2:16-23). God is faithful; God's "steadfast love endures forever" (Psalm 136:1). To be holy as God is holy is to be faithful to one another and to the covenant established in marriage. Funerals: The Scripture understands God as life-giving; death is contrary to God and God's purpose. When someone dies, our rituals and liturgies celebrate life—the life of the person who has died and also the life God gives, the resurrection of Christ, the new life God promises. To be holy as God is holy is not to suddenly become saintly—most of us cannot pull that off—but to witness to the holiness of God.

Back to the Calendar

Calendars are ways of keeping track of our all-too-busy lives. We scribble in appointments, meetings, deadlines, birthdays, reminders. The calendar, filled up, represents the world we live in. It connects us to work, family, friends, church, and a larger community. It gives us a day-to-day routine, week-to-week routine. In a sense, the calendar reveals and defines us. We are the people who work, go to parties, take the dog to the vet.

What would change if the calendar was filled in for us—with sacred occasions appointed by God? We might discover a new world, connected to God and the people of God, our time marked off by rituals and holy days. Perhaps, we would find that in the Lord "we live and move and have our being" (Acts 17:28).

Close-Up: Jewish Holidays

Hebrew Name	English Name	Biblical References	Dates in 2015–2016	Reason for Holiday
Rosh Hashana	Jewish New Year	Leviticus 23:23-32; Numbers 29:1-11	September 14–15, 2015	To rest on a day that celebrates God's creation of the world and God's kingship
Yom Kippur	Day of Atonement	Leviticus 23:26-32; Numbers 29:7-11	September 23, 2015	To fast and attend worship services during which people ask God and one another for forgiveness
Sukkot	Feast of Tabernacles (or Feast of Booths)	Leviticus 23:33-44	September 28–October 4	To recall the temporary shelters the Israelites lived in while in the Sinai desert with Moses; also to celebrate the fall harvest
Chanukah (also spelled Hanukkah)	Festival of Lights	2 Maccabees 5:1–6:1; 10:1-9 (in Apocrypha)	December 7–14, 2015	To recall the rededication of the Temple after Judas Maccabeus had defeated the Syrian king Antiochus IV Epiphanes (165 B.C.) (A small amount of oil was all that was available to relight the menorah candles, but that oil miraculously lasted the eight days it took to make a round-trip journey to obtain new oil.)
Pesach	Passover	Exodus 12:1-28; Exodus 23:14-15	April 23–30, 2016	To recall when God "passed over" the doorposts of the Hebrew slaves and Moses led them out of Egypt
Shavuot	Feast of Weeks; Pentecost	Leviticus 23:15-21	June 12–13, 2016	Celebrated seven weeks (fifty days) after Passover, Shavuot began as a spring agricultural festival. After the fall of the Temple in A.D. 70, it gradually became a feast celebrating the gift of the Ten Commandments.

FAITH IN ACTION: CELEBRATIONS IN THE CHRISTIAN TRADITION

As we focus on "Sacred Gifts and Holy Gatherings" this quarter, we also journey through the Christian seasons of Advent, Christmas, Epiphany, and conclude on the third Sunday of Lent. Faith in Action provides ideas for the class and their families to mark sacred time. You will find additional information about how these special days and seasons are celebrated within the church in the teacher enrichment article titled "Traditions of the Community," which is found near the beginning of this book. You may want to post the following information on newsprint that can be viewed throughout the quarter, or you may prefer to suggest a different activity each week that is appropriate to the season.

1. Purchase or handcraft an Advent calendar for use in your home. These calendars may be made of cardboard, paper, felt, wood, or other materials. You will find twenty-four "doors" on most of these calendars, one of which is to be opened from the beginning of Advent (or December 1) through Christmas Eve. Behind the "doors" you will see pictures of Christian symbols or toys or other objects related to the season. The opening of the "door" each day indicates that you are moving through the period of preparation for the coming of Jesus. Parents and grandparents especially like to use these calendars to help children count the days until Christmas.

2. Create a Jesse Tree by using a dead branch, a tree made of wooden dowels, or a small artificial tree. Based on Isaiah 11:1, the Jesse Tree uses biblical symbols to tell the salvation story. Beginning with a symbol for creation, a symbol that has been handmade or purchased is added each day throughout Advent. As the symbol is hung, a verse or two of Scripture may be read, followed by a brief prayer. The Jesse Tree is a way to mark the time of the Advent season while also reviewing the people and events throughout history that led to a Savior coming "from the stump of Jesse" (11:1).

3. Brighten the sidewalk of your home or church on Christmas Eve with luminaries, which are easy to make by putting sand in a paper bag and setting a tea light or votive candle in the sand. Real candles or LED-powered ones may be used. This tradition, which dates back to the sixteenth century, not only provides light to guide people as they walk but also symbolically reminds us that Jesus is the light of the world.

4. Set up a nativity scene, also known as a crèche, late on Christmas Eve or on Christmas morning. If you have a set with movable figures, you may wish to set it up earlier during Advent and add the Holy Family.

This sacred time is to be used to strengthen your relationship with God through prayer, meditation, or journaling.

Pronunciation Guide

Ahaz (ay' haz)
Azazel (uh zay' zuhl')
Baal (bay' uhl) or (bah ahl')
Beeri (bee' uhr i)
Bilhah (bil' huh)
Cana (kay' nuh)
Diblaim (dib lay' im)
ephah (ee' fuh)
Hallel (hal' el)
Haran (hair' uhn)
Hezekiah (hez uh ki' uh)
Hittite (hit' tite)
Jehu (jee' hyoo)
Jeroboam (jer uh boh' uhm)
Jezreel (jez' ree uhl)
Joash (joh' ash)

Jotham (joh' thuhm)
kapporet (kap po' reth)
Laban (lay' buhn)
lepta (lep' tuh)
Lo-ammi (loh am' i)
Lo-ruhamah (loh roo ha' muh)
Mahalath (may' huh lath)
Nisan (nee sawn')
Nunc Dimittis (noonk di mit'is)
paschal (pas' kuhl)
phylactery (fi lak' tuh ree)
Succoth (sook kohth')
Tirzah (tihr' zuh)
Uzziah (uh zi' uh)
Yom Kippur (yom kip' uhr)
Zilpah (zil' puh)

UNIT 1: WHAT WE BRING TO GOD
THE LORD'S DAY

PREVIEWING THE LESSON

Lesson Scripture: Exodus 20:8-11; 31:12-17
Background Scripture: Exodus 16:23; 20:8-11; 31:12-18; Leviticus 23:3-8; Deuteronomy 5:12-15; Matthew 12:1-14; Acts 13:42
Key Verse: Exodus 20:8

Focus of the Lesson:
Some people have turned away from those traditions that provide firm underpinnings for their lives. How can they maintain spiritual stability in a rapidly changing world? Scripture informs them of a God who set aside the Sabbath as a day to remember and to recommit to holy living.

Goals for the Learners:
(1) to explore the meaning of the Sabbath as expressed in Exodus.
(2) to recognize and appreciate the importance of Sabbath.
(3) to discover ways to practice Sabbath in the twenty-first century.

Supplies:
Bibles, newsprint and marker, paper and pencils, hymnals

READING THE SCRIPTURE

NRSV
Lesson Scripture: Exodus 20:8-11

8Remember the sabbath day, and keep it holy. 9Six days you shall labor and do all your work. 10But the seventh day is a sabbath to the LORD your God; you shall not do any work—you, your son or your daughter, your male or female slave, your livestock, or the alien resident in your towns. 11For in six days the LORD made heaven and earth, the sea, and all that is in them, but rested the seventh day; therefore the LORD blessed the sabbath day and consecrated it.

CEB
Lesson Scripture: Exodus 20:8-11

8Remember the Sabbath day and treat it as holy. 9Six days you may work and do all your tasks, 10but the seventh day is a Sabbath to the LORD your God. Do not do any work on it—not you, your sons or daughters, your male or female servants, your animals, or the immigrant who is living with you. 11Because the LORD made the heavens and the earth, the sea, and everything that is in them in six days, but rested on the seventh day. That is why the LORD

Lesson Scripture: Exodus 31:12-17

¹²The LORD said to Moses: ¹³You yourself are to speak to the Israelites: "You shall keep my sabbaths, for this is a sign between me and you throughout your generations, given in order that you may know that I, the LORD, sanctify you. ¹⁴You shall keep the sabbath, because it is holy for you; everyone who profanes it shall be put to death; whoever does any work on it shall be cut off from among the people. ¹⁵Six days shall work be done, but the seventh day is a sabbath of solemn rest, holy to the LORD; whoever does any work on the sabbath day shall be put to death. ¹⁶Therefore the Israelites shall keep the sabbath, observing the sabbath throughout their generations, as a perpetual covenant. ¹⁷It is a sign forever between me and the people of Israel that in six days the Lord made heaven and earth, and on the seventh day he rested, and was refreshed."

blessed the Sabbath day and made it holy.

Lesson Scripture: Exodus 31:12-17

¹²The LORD said to Moses: ¹³Tell the Israelites: "Be sure to keep my sabbaths, because the Sabbath is a sign between me and you in every generation so you will know that I am the LORD who makes you holy. ¹⁴Keep the Sabbath, because it is holy for you. Everyone who violates the Sabbath will be put to death. Whoever does any work on the Sabbath, that person will be cut off from the people. ¹⁵Do your work for six days. But the seventh day is a Sabbath of complete rest that is holy to the LORD. Whoever does any work on the Sabbath day will be put to death. ¹⁶The Israelites should keep the Sabbath. They should observe the Sabbath in every generation as a covenant for all time. ¹⁷It is a sign forever between me and the Israelites that in six days the LORD made the heavens and the earth, and on the seventh day the LORD rested and was refreshed."

UNDERSTANDING THE SCRIPTURE

Introduction. The Hebrew word *sabbath* comes from a verb meaning "to cease," "to rest," "to be at an end." Sabbath observance is the fourth of the Ten Commandments. Originally, it was simply the end of the week, the seventh day, and a day to abstain from work; but over time, the Sabbath became a day dedicated to the Lord, a day of rest, relaxation, community worship, and celebration.

Exodus 16:23. God's commandment in this verse, "Tomorrow is a day of solemn rest, a holy sabbath to

the LORD," is part of a larger story. The people of God, wandering in the wilderness, have worked for six days gathering manna, their daily bread. On the sixth day, they are surprised to collect twice as much. When they ask, "What's going on?" Moses responds with the commandment. God has provided food for tomorrow, the Sabbath, a day of rest. Sabbath is a gift of God's providence. Days of work and rest are built into the created order.

Exodus 20:8-11. Remembering is more than mental recall; it implies, according to Terence E. Fretheim, "an active observance." To "keep it holy" means "to set it apart" from other days: The Sabbath belongs to God. Abstaining from work on the seventh day was an early tradition in the ancient world, based on the idea that the seventh day belonged to evil spirits, who would sabotage any attempts at constructive work. The Hebrew people took up the tradition and did no work on the seventh day, but they transformed it into a day dedicated to the Lord. The explanation of the Sabbath in Exodus 20:11 refers to the story of creation in Genesis 1:1–2:3, in which God created the world in six days and rested on the seventh (2:3). The first implication of Sabbath is that it is a reminder that God is God. God is greater than all our days. Second, observing the Sabbath is imitating God's rest on the seventh day. We make the day holy in the same way God "blessed the sabbath day and consecrated it" (20:11). Part of keeping the Sabbath is relaxing, knowing that all our work is done, and enjoying the created order as God did. Third, the commandment to observe the Sabbath involves the whole created order: "heaven and earth, the sea, and all that is in them" (20:11).

Exodus 31:12-18. This Scripture finishes God's directions for building the tabernacle, which is understood as a dwelling place for God. It fulfills God's promise in Ezekiel 37:27: "My dwelling place shall be with them; and I will be their God, and they shall be my people." Notes in the *The Harper Collins Study Bible* (NRSV) point out that "the sacred time of the Sabbath is analogous to the sacred space of the tabernacle." The Sabbath is a sign of the covenant, a pledge of God's faithfulness from one generation to another. It is intended for the people God has chosen and sanctified, or set apart, as God's own people. "Profane" (31:14) is the opposite of "sanctify" (31:13), so violating the Sabbath is like saying, "We are not God's people." The penalty is excommunication, to be cut off from the people of God, and death because to be in God's presence is life. Verse 18 concludes God's conversation with Moses on the mountain, which began at 24:15.

Leviticus 23:3-8. The weekly celebration of the Sabbath heads a list of festivals celebrated annually in Israel. The work prohibited on the Sabbath probably began with agricultural work. As commerce increased and cities grew, the prohibition expanded to include occupational work and buying and selling. Later, it included household labor. Verse 3 describes the Sabbath as a time of "complete rest." With the growth of the cult and worship in the Temple, the community assembled on the Sabbath to worship God, "a holy convocation" (23:8).

Deuteronomy 5:12-15. Deuteronomy emphasizes God's authority. The Sabbath is to be observed because God says so. The Scripture relates the Sabbath not to creation but to the Exodus (5:15). Israel remembers that they were slaves in Egypt, owned by Pharaoh and working long hours every day, making a profit for the king. But God brings the people out of Egypt and makes them God's own. God's authority is not like Pharaoh's. God's power frees the people and divine commandments benefit the people. God gives the people a day of rest. Israel's election and the covenant at Sinai are implied in the language of the commandment.

Matthew 12:1-14. Jesus tangles with the Pharisees. Confident in their knowledge and application of God's law, they accused Jesus' disciples of breaking the Sabbath law. Jesus answers them with reference to Scripture. When David was hungry, he ate the bread of the Presence, loaves of bread reserved for the priests (1 Samuel 21:1-6). Moreover, he points out, priests work on the Sabbath. Then he announces in verse 6, "Something greater than the temple is here," and quotes Hosea 6:6: "I desire mercy and not sacrifice" (12:7). Mercy is greater than the Temple and greater than Sabbath observance. "Son of Man" generally refers to Jesus, but verse 8 may mean simply that "the sabbath was made for humankind, and not humankind for the sabbath" (Mark 2:27). Jesus defines the Sabbath in terms of mercy, subsuming all of God's law under the law of love.

In the second story (12:9-14), the question is whether healing breaks the Sabbath law. Jesus asks: Would one of you pull your only sheep out of a ditch on the Sabbath? The question no doubt sends the Pharisees into a turmoil. Jesus clarifies: It is lawful to do good on the Sabbath. Then he heals the man. Again the issue is love. Does God desire jot-and-tittle obedience to the law, or does God command us to love one another? These two examples of work on the Sabbath—feeding and healing, both of which meet basic human needs—cause the Pharisees to plot to kill Jesus (12:14).

Acts 13:42. Christians adopted the Sabbath as a day of worship. In time, they would worship on the first day of the week, looking both to creation, when God created light, and to the resurrection of Jesus Christ.

INTERPRETING THE SCRIPTURE

Day-to-Day

God commands us: For six days, work. On the seventh day, do not do any work. The seventh day, the Sabbath, is a day of rest. To observe the Sabbath is, first of all, to take the day off; but the commandment addresses every day: For six days, work. For one day, rest. At its most basic, the commandment is a way of ordering our time, of establishing the rhythm and the routine of daily life. We work for a living. We till the soil, teach children to read, crunch numbers, manage companies, mop floors, conduct experiments. Occupations determine our day-to-day routine. Retirement is difficult because suddenly the structure of our days disappears. But we find ways to work: Three days a week, we exercise; afternoons, we tend the garden; Tuesday and Thursday, we volunteer; Wednesday, we go to choir practice. Remember the children's song that outlines work done on each day: "Monday, washday; Tuesday, roast beef; Wednesday, soup." The commandment sets aside one day, the last day of the week, to do no work. On the Sabbath, all work ceases. We can put our feet up and relax. God gives us not only a day off but seven days, well ordered. Terence E. Fretheim in his commentary on Exodus points out: "The will of God for Israel is a 'discipline of dailyness.'"

Creation

Exodus 20:11 offers an explanation: In six days, God created the world—"heaven and earth, the sea, and all that is in them"—but on the seventh day, God rested. The Scripture ties the commandment to creation. First, the connection with creation makes Sabbath a reminder that God is Creator. God keeps chaos at bay and orders our lives. God is bigger than all our days. God is in charge. God provides. For six days, we labor, under the impression that we can make a living. On the seventh day, we remember that only God gives life; and actually, only God's work matters. Sabbath levels all our social-economic-political hierarchies and calls a halt to our ambitions because all people are God's creatures and God is the Lord of our lives. So the Sabbath is a day of rest—a day when we can rest in the knowledge that God is God.

Second, for humans created in the divine image to "remember the Sabbath day, and keep it holy" (20:8) is to imitate God, who "blessed the sabbath day and consecrated it" (20:11; see also Genesis 1:31–2:3), by living a godly life. How did the Lord spend the seventh day? Imagine God, looking around at all creation, enjoying this brand-new world. God worked hard. Perhaps God sighs with contentment, settling in to an easy day, knowing that the work of creation is good. Making the Sabbath holy is setting it apart from other days. It a day to rest and to enjoy God's good creation—not only the natural world but also the conversation of the human community—to settle in to an easy day, at peace with the world and one another.

Third, Sabbath rest is built into the structure of creation. It is not, fundamentally, a religious ritual imposed on or by a human community. Rhythms of work and rest define the whole universe. The law doesn't ask us to hole up for a day alone with our Bibles, but to participate in the world, to see ourselves connected with people outside our own families and communities as well as with the natural world—animals, birds, sky, land. It raises questions: How do we honor God's intentions for creation? How does our activity or inactivity affect the rest of the world? If I rest, do I ask someone else to work?

Fourth, creation brings to mind the new creation and God's promise of new life founded on love, mercy, and peace. Sabbath gathers all of creation into God's blessed rest. The commandment in Exodus 20:8-11 suggests meaning for the day and ways to "remember the sabbath day, and keep it holy."

Covenant

"Covenant" is sometimes defined as an agreement or a contract, sometimes as a promise. In Scripture, covenant describes the relationship between God and God's people. It includes the great promises of God for a new land and a new life, as well as the law. Covenant is played out in the lives of God's people as they struggle to love God and one another and to find their way in the world. According to Ezekiel 37:24-28, God promises a new life, a new social-political order founded on God's law, peace, and blessings for generation upon generation of God's people. The covenant is summed up: "My dwelling place shall be with them; and I will be their God, and they shall be my people. Then the nations shall know that

I the LORD sanctify Israel" (37:27-28a). God chooses a people, teaches them a way of life, blesses them, and expects them to live in ways that will enable other people to see and recognize God's gracious love.

The Sabbath, says Exodus 31:16-17, is a sign of the covenant. It marks the chosen people of God and serves as a reminder of the promise: God is our God; we are God's people. It defines the community of faith. Other people look and see that the people of God are different. Every week, they set aside one day to rest and to celebrate God's goodness. The Sabbath, passed from generation to generation, speaks to God, to the people of God, and to the nations, saying, "God is with us, and God is good." Observing the Sabbath is not only a reminder of God's faithfulness but also a witness to God's promises and love. What we do on the Sabbath matters. Even in Exodus 31:12-17, which follows God's directions concerning the important work of building the tent of meeting and its furnishings (31:1-11), God commands Moses to remind the people that Sabbath must be observed as a day set apart to rest.

All work must cease under penalty of death (31:14).

Sabbath Rest

Six days we work—at our jobs, at home, in the yard. More often than not, six days of work spills over into the seventh day. Clothes need to be washed, bathrooms cleaned, food prepared. We are busy people and fill up all our days with work. Do we know how to rest? God's law speaks to our busyness: "The seventh day is a sabbath to the LORD your God; you shall not do any work" (Exodus 20:10). Setting aside one day dedicated to the Lord does not mean spending twenty-four hours in prayer, trying to find God in holy words or silent meditation. Sabbath is a day to enjoy God's good creation, to laugh together, to sing God's praises, to celebrate, to play. It's a day to remember that we are God's people, blessed with God's love, sure of God's promises for new life. The Sabbath law is not law at all but grace, a gift of God that allows us the freedom to live for a day soaking up God's blessings.

SHARING THE SCRIPTURE

PREPARING TO TEACH

Preparing Our Hearts

Ponder this week's devotional reading from Hebrews 4:1-11. What do you learn about God's promise of rest? How do you observe the Sabbath? How is—or how could be—the observance of Sabbath a way of life for you?

Pray that you and the students will

take seriously God's promise of rest and act accordingly on the Sabbath.

Preparing Our Minds

Study the background Scripture from Exodus 16:23; 20:8-11; 31:12-18; Leviticus 23:3-8; Deuteronomy 5:12-15; Matthew 12:1-14; Acts 13:42. The lesson Scripture is from Exodus 20:8-11; 31:12-17.

Consider this question as you prepare the lesson: *How can we maintain spiritual stability in a rapidly changing world?*

Write on newsprint:

❏ steps listed under Goal 2 in Sharing the Scripture.

❏ information for next week's lesson, found under Continue the Journey.

❏ activities for further spiritual growth in Continue the Journey.

Review the Introduction, The Big Picture, Close-up, and Faith in Action, which all precede the first lesson of this quarter. Consider how you might use any of this material in today's lesson.

LEADING THE CLASS

(1) Gather to Learn

❖ Welcome the class members and guests.

❖ Pray that those who have come today will be faithful to God's command to keep the Sabbath.

❖ Begin to focus on today's topic, the Sabbath, by inviting participants to say what comes to mind when they hear the word "Sabbath." List their ideas on newsprint, but do not affirm or question any of them at this point.

❖ Read aloud today's focus statement: **Some people have turned away from those traditions that provide firm underpinnings for their lives. How can they maintain spiritual stability in a rapidly changing world? Scripture informs them of a God who set aside the Sabbath as a day to remember and to recommit to holy living.**

(2) Goal 1: Explore the Meaning of the Sabbath as Expressed in Exodus

❖ Read Introduction from Understanding the Scripture to define "Sabbath."

❖ Choose one volunteer to read Exodus 20:8-11 and another to read Exodus 31:12-17.

❖ Clarify these passages by reading or retelling the entries for Exodus 20:8-11 and Exodus 31:12-18 in Understanding the Scripture.

❖ Discuss these questions:

1. **Why are humans commanded to observe the Sabbath?** (See "Creation" in Interpreting the Scripture where you will find four explanations.)

2. **How is Sabbath rest connected to God's covenant with the people of Israel?** (See "Covenant" in Interpreting the Scripture. Note in the second paragraph that Sabbath is a sign of the covenant.)

3. **What options do people have for observing the Sabbath?** (See "Sabbath Rest" in Interpreting the Scripture.)

4. **Look again at the ideas listed in the Gather to Learn portion. What modifications might we need to make to bring our ideas more in line with the biblical purpose and meaning of Sabbath?**

(3) Goal 2: Recognize and Appreciate the Importance of Sabbath

❖ Read: **Old Testament scholar Walter Brueggemann writes in his book *Journey to the Common Good*: "Sabbath, in the first instance, is not about worship. It is about work stoppage. It is about withdrawal** from the anxiety system of Pharaoh, the refusal to let one's life be defined by production and consumption and the endless pursuit of private well-being." Recall that Sabbath was part of the covenant God gave to the people on Sinai *after* they had been liberated from Pharaoh and the grinding pace of work he required of these slaves. As you consider the notions of "work stoppage" and "withdrawal from the anxiety system" of Pharaoh or any other ruler or economic system, how are people's lives radically different when they are able to observe the Sabbath as a day of rest?

❖ Distribute paper and pencils and challenge the students to consider their appreciation of this gift of Sabbath that God has given by taking the following steps, which you will post on newsprint.

Step 1: Draw a circle and divide it into six sections. Each section represents approximately four hours. In each section write the kinds of activities that you regularly engage in. Perhaps two sections will be devoted to sleep. Perhaps two sections will be devoted to work, while another section represents time for self-care, such as bathing, dressing, eating, and interacting with friends and family.

Step 2: Draw another circle and divide it into six sections, each representing four hours. In this circle you are only considering activities that you engage in on Sundays. (Recall that the Jewish Sabbath runs from sundown on Friday through sundown on Saturday. However, many Christians refer to Sunday as their Sabbath. Those who work on Sunday may have another day set aside for rest.)

Step 3: Compare the two circles. How do your actions show that you do or do not recognize and practice Sabbath rest? What changes will you make?

❖ Bring the group together and invite volunteers to comment on their findings.

(4) Goal 3: Discover Ways to Practice Sabbath in the Twenty-first Century

❖ Read: **Writing in the November 11, 2013, edition of *The Washington Post*, Cecilia Kang begins, "And on the seventh day, there was delivery." Kang's reference was to Amazon. com's plan to make deliveries on Sunday, though she also could have focused on Amazon's competitors who are all rushing to get products to customers in just hours. In her article Kang demonstrates how the long-standing tradition of Sunday as a day of rest has been eroding as "blue laws" banning commercial activities have largely disappeared and the increasing use of technology means that people are connected not just socially but also to the workplace. In the words of MIT economics and labor professor Jonathan Gruber, "we are moving toward a society where e-mail and social media have caused the week and weekend to blur."**

❖ Form small groups to discuss this question: **How can we practice Sabbath, God's day of rest promised to us, amid the dizzying pace of the twenty-first century?**

❖ Call the groups together to hear some of their responses.

(5) Continue the Journey

❖ Pray that as the learners depart they will seek ways to be

Sabbath-keepers in a society where finding time to enjoy God's promised rest is difficult.

❖ Post information for next week's session on newsprint for the students to copy:

- **Title: Acceptable Offerings**
- **Background Scripture: Leviticus 22:17-33; 23:9-14, 31-32; Deuteronomy 22:6-7; Isaiah 1:10-20; Micah 6:6-8; Romans 12:1-2; 1 Corinthians 10:14-22**
- **Lesson Scripture: Leviticus 22:17-25, 31-33**
- **Focus of the Lesson: Enticing ads and commercials convince people that sacrificial material gifts are evidence of their love toward others. What gifts are better than those things that can be purchased? Leviticus informs God's people that the best gift one can give is obedience to God's commandments.**

❖ Post the following information on newsprint and provide paper and pencils for the students to copy it.

Challenge the adults to grow spiritually by completing one or more of these activities related to this week's session.

(1) **Make a special effort during this season of Advent to enjoy Sabbath rest as a means of preparing yourself to welcome Jesus.**

(2) **Read Abraham Joshua Heschel's classic, *The Sabbath*, to better understand this special day from the viewpoint of Judaism.**

(3) **Think about the rhythm of time of your own week. How does this ordering of time each day help you?**

❖ Sing or read aloud "Praise to the Lord, the Almighty."

❖ Conclude today's session by leading the class in this benediction, which is adapted from Leviticus 22:31 in the lesson for December 13: **As we go forth, we commit ourselves to keep the commandments of the Lord. Amen.**

UNIT 1: WHAT WE BRING TO GOD
ACCEPTABLE OFFERINGS

PREVIEWING THE LESSON

Lesson Scripture: Leviticus 22:17-25, 31-33
Background Scripture: Leviticus 22:17-33; 23:9-14, 31-32;
Deuteronomy 22:6-7; Isaiah 1:10-20; Micah 6:6-8; Romans 12:1-2;
1 Corinthians 10:14-22
Key Verse: Romans 12:1

Focus of the Lesson:
Enticing ads and commercials convince people that sacrificial material gifts are evidence of their love toward others. What gifts are better than those things that can be purchased? Leviticus informs God's people that the best gift one can give is obedience to God's commandments.

Goals for the Learners:
(1) to learn what Leviticus says about God's requirement for acceptable sacrifices that bring honor to God's holy name.
(2) to examine the connection between obedience to God and sacrificial giving of self and possessions.
(3) to pledge to make a self-sacrifice to God.

Supplies:
Bibles, newsprint and marker, paper and pencils, hymnals

READING THE SCRIPTURE

NRSV

Lesson Scripture: Leviticus 22:17-25, 31-33

¹⁷The LORD spoke to Moses, saying: ¹⁸Speak to Aaron and his sons and all the people of Israel and say to them: When anyone of the house of Israel or of the aliens residing in Israel presents an offering, whether in payment of a vow or as a freewill offering that

CEB

Lesson Scripture: Leviticus 22:17-25, 31-33

¹⁷The LORD said to Moses: ¹⁸Tell Aaron, his sons, and all the Israelites: Whenever someone from Israel's house or from the immigrants in Israel presents their offering to the LORD as an entirely burned offering—whether it is payment for a solemn promise or a

is offered to the LORD as a burnt offering, [19]to be acceptable in your behalf it shall be a male without blemish, of the cattle or the sheep or the goats. [20]You shall not offer anything that has a blemish, for it will not be acceptable in your behalf. [21]When anyone offers a sacrifice of well-being to the LORD, in fulfillment of a vow or as a freewill offering, from the herd or from the flock, to be acceptable it must be perfect; there shall be no blemish in it. [22]Anything blind, or injured, or maimed, or having a discharge or an itch or scabs—these you shall not offer to the LORD or put any of them on the altar as offerings by fire to the LORD. [23]An ox or a lamb that has a limb too long or too short you may present for a freewill offering; but it will not be accepted for a vow. [24]Any animal that has its testicles bruised or crushed or torn or cut, you shall not offer to the Lord; such you shall not do within your land, [25]nor shall you accept any such animals from a foreigner to offer as food to your God; since they are mutilated, with a blemish in them, they shall not be accepted in your behalf.

[31]Thus you shall keep my commandments and observe them: I am the LORD. [32]You shall not profane my holy name, that I may be sanctified among the people of Israel: I am the LORD; I sanctify you, [33]I who brought you out of the land of Egypt to be your God: I am the LORD.

Key Verse: Romans 12:1

[1]I appeal to you therefore, brothers and sisters, by the mercies of God, to present your bodies as a living sacrifice, holy and acceptable to God, which is your spiritual worship.

spontaneous gift— [19]for it to be acceptable on your behalf, it must be a flawless male from the herd, the sheep, or the goats. [20]You must not present anything that has an imperfection, because it will not be acceptable on your behalf. [21]Whenever someone presents a communal sacrifice of well-being to the LORD from the herd or flock—whether it is payment for a solemn promise or a spontaneous gift—it must be flawless to be acceptable; it must not have any imperfection. [22]You must not present to the LORD anything that is blind or that has an injury, mutilation, warts, a rash, or scabs. You must not put any such animal on the altar as a food gift for the LORD. [23]You can, however, offer an ox or sheep that is deformed or stunted as a spontaneous gift, but it will not be acceptable as payment for a solemn promise. [24]You must not offer to the LORD anything with bruised, crushed, torn, or cut-off testicles. You must not do that in your land. [25]You are not allowed to offer such animals as your God's food even if they come from a foreigner. Because these animals have blemishes and imperfections in them, they will not be acceptable on your behalf.

[31]You must keep my commands and do them; I am the LORD. [32]You must not make my holy name impure so that I will be treated as holy by the Israelites. I am the LORD—the one who makes you holy [33]and who is bringing you out of the land of Egypt to be your God; I am the LORD.

Key Verse: Romans 12:1

[1]So, brothers and sisters, because of God's mercies, I encourage you to present your bodies as a living sacrifice that is holy and pleasing to God. This is your appropriate priestly service.

UNDERSTANDING THE SCRIPTURE

Leviticus 22:17-33. These instructions are grounded in the relationship or covenant between God and God's people and in the commandments given to Moses. They have the authority of God's law. The Scripture is part of the Holiness Code (17:1–26:46), which is concerned not only with the purity of the sanctuary and the activity of priests ("Aaron and his sons," 22:18) but also with the holiness of those within the boundaries of Israel ("all the people of Israel . . . [and] aliens residing in Israel," 22:18). The text concerns several different kinds of sacrifices and offerings. A *votive offering* fulfills a vow—for example, "If you, Lord, bring me home safe from my travels, I will offer a sacrifice at the sanctuary." A *freewill offering* is given spontaneously out of joy: A shepherd, at the birth of a lamb, praises God, saying, "This one's for God!" The primary purpose of the *well-being offering* is to provide meat for the table, for the common people a celebratory meal. The *thanksgiving offering* is for a particular occasion (see Psalm 107) and must be eaten on the day it is offered.

To be "acceptable in your behalf" (22:19), the sacrificial animal must be unblemished. Malachi 1:8 says, "When you offer blind animals in sacrifice, is that not wrong? And when you offer those that are lame or sick, is that not wrong? Try presenting that to your governor; will he be pleased with you or show you favor?" Offering an unblemished animal for sacrifice is simply practical. We would not offer a second-best gift. Malachi also notes that the purpose of the offering is for God's pleasure and in hopes that God will bless the person who makes the offering. Beyond the practical reason is the theological issue: God is holy. God's people are, according to the covenant, to reflect God's holiness, to be holy as God is holy (see 1 Peter 1:16). Leviticus 22:19-22 describes blemishes that keep animals from being offered to the Lord. Leviticus 21:16-23 suggests a similar list of defects that keeps a priest from offering sacrifices to the Lord. All of Israel is included in the exhortation in Leviticus 22:31-33. Holiness is not a given. God is at work among the people making them holy because they are the people of God. These last verses bring the reader back to Moses, the Exodus, and the covenant at Sinai. Keeping the commandments entails being the people of God and also becoming a holy nation, sanctified by the Lord, who chose the people and brought them out of Egypt to the Promised Land.

Leviticus 23:9-14. The Scripture prescribes offering to the Lord the first fruits of the harvest. The farmer brings the first sheaf or armful of barley, the first crop, to the sanctuary, where the priest offers it to God. The offering includes grain mixed with oil, a lamb for a burnt offering, and wine. Its purpose is both to thank God for the harvest and to ask God's blessing on next year's harvest. Only after the offering may the farmer and his family partake of the harvest.

Leviticus 23:31-32. On the Day of Atonement, the people do no work and practice self-denial, abstaining from eating food, bathing, anointing, and having sexual intercourse. Samuel E. Balentine, in his commentary on Leviticus, says that the fast gives people an opportunity "to recognize where they have erred and to seek God's forgiveness" and "to embark on a new beginning with the refurbished hope that they may now live in ways that more faithfully honor the holiness of God."

Deuteronomy 22:6-7. Like Leviticus 22:28-29, this Scripture discusses a mother animal and her children. Commentaries variously explain the Scripture with humanitarian and environmental reasons, as well as a concern for motherhood.

Isaiah 1:10-20. God rejects ritual—sacrifice, festivals, holy days, worship—and refuses to accept the offerings or to hear the prayers of God's people. Isaiah calls the people—as individuals, a community, a nation—"to do good, seek justice, rescue the oppressed" (1:17). Isaiah 1:10-20 may be an outright rejection of the sacrificial system. Certainly it is a call to return to the covenant, to become a community that reflects the purposes of God. Ritual life has become a shield, as Otto Kaiser observes, "against God's claim upon their whole life," but finds a place in the context of life grounded in God's justice and love.

Micah 6:6-8. At issue is the covenant between God and God's people. Evidence of divine faithfulness is in God's mighty acts of deliverance. When God calls Israel to account, Israel responds, *What can we offer as evidence of our faithfulness? What can we offer to atone for our sins?* Burnt offerings, thousands of sacrifices, rivers of oil, firstborn children—the list becomes increasingly ludicrous. God is clear: Evidence of Israel's faithfulness is in the community's righteousness. To be faithful is "to do justice and to love kindness, and to walk humbly with your God" (6:8). The people of God are to reflect the holiness of God by living God's mercy and love.

Romans 12:1-2. This Scripture describes Christian life as an offering of ourselves to God in order to be transformed. Paul uses the language of the sacrificial system (sacrifice, holy, acceptable, perfect) and also of contemporary religions in his day and our own (spiritual worship, this world), but gives it new meaning. We are not to be transferred to a transcendent or spiritual plane; but to offer our bodies, doing God's will in down-to-earth ways. Our holiness is in living for God's purposes, for the new age or the new social order God promises in Jesus Christ.

1 Corinthians 10:14-22. Animals were slaughtered, and their blood, the animal's life, was given to God. Bread and wine were offered, the first fruits of the harvest. Part of the sacrificial system involved eating together in the presence of God, which bound people to one another and to the Lord. Similarly, Holy Communion binds us together in one body with Christ our Lord.

INTERPRETING THE SCRIPTURE

Authority

We tend to think of Leviticus as an instruction manual for priests. It includes how to perform a variety of sacrifices, how to arrange bread on the altar, how to purify the sanctuary, how to say prayers, how to celebrate the holy days and seasons, how to come before the Lord—so many how-tos!

We also assume that Leviticus compiles a lot of regulations—rules about foods to eat or avoid, for example—that may or may not be valid for our lives.

Leviticus 22:17-33 begins by saying, "The LORD spoke to Moses," who in turn spoke to the priests and to "all the people of Israel." The first sentence calls into question our assumptions about Leviticus. First of all, it speaks not only to priests but also to people. All the people of God are included; so in some sense, the Scripture is addressed to us. Second, we know something about Moses. We've heard about the Exodus, when through Moses' sometimes inept leadership, God brought the people out of slavery in Egypt and led them to the Promised Land. We know about God's revelation on Mount Sinai, and we believe in the Ten Commandments. God speaks to Moses, who speaks to us. What follows in Leviticus will have the same authority as the commandments given at Sinai.

The bulk of Leviticus 22:17-33 concerns offerings in the sanctuary. It's about ritual, a variety of offerings to God (freewill, votive, well-being, thanksgiving), and the characteristics that make animals unacceptable for sacrifice. We have a problem. The text seems to say that the laws in Leviticus are commandments grounded in the covenant, with the same authority as the Ten Commandments. They are addressed to us as the people of God. What do we do with laws about ritual sacrifice?

Our Take on Sacrifice

Ritual sacrifice: an animal slaughtered, its blood offered on an altar. We see in our minds scenes from blood-and-guts movies: a dark room; smoky incense; an altar; animals and perhaps a struggling maiden, laid out for killing; a knife; a man with a twisted grasp on reality. Or we think about primitive tribes and ancient customs no longer practiced. The fact is that ritual sacrifice makes us a little squeamish, and we are grateful to live in a time when sensible religion involves sitting in pews, reading the Bible, putting a check in the offering plate, and participating in ordered worship.

We have read Scripture, such as Isaiah 1:10-20 and Micah 6:6-8, in which God looks askance at the sacrifices of God's people and calls them to live with justice and righteousness. Though the prophets may well have accepted the sacrificial system as part of Israel's worship, they also required a return to faithfulness that involved the whole life of God's community: justice, mercy, love, and concern for the poor. We have interpreted the words of the prophets to mean that sacrifice is passé if not downright wrong. True offerings to God, we think, involve good deeds and love of neighbor.

Given our understanding of the sacrificial system, what do we do with Leviticus 22:17-33?

The Sacrificial System: Theology

Jacob Milgrom, in his commentary on Leviticus, explains, "Theology is what Leviticus is all about. . . . It is not expressed in pronouncements but embedded in rituals." Theological meaning lies under the offerings, requirements, sacrifices, and ritual.

God created the world by separating light and darkness, dry land and water, animals and people. By separating, God brought order out of chaos. Creation reveals God's nature as well as God's way of ordering the world. The sacrificial system also separates. Animal are unclean and clean, blemished and unblemished. The sanctuary is a place set apart for God, as is the land of Israel. Time is separated into ordinary time and Sabbath. An animal is separated from the flock and offered to God. An armful of barley is separated from the harvest as a gift to the Lord. Ritual separations express God's order. They also relate the lives of God's people to the Lord; their lives are in sync with God's ordering of creation.

Another theological tenant of the sacrificial system is holiness. Related to separation, holiness defines the nature of God and distinguishes God from everyone else. Holiness also means "to be set apart for God." Only God can make a person, nation, or place holy. So at Sinai, God speaks to the people: "If you obey my voice and keep my covenant, you shall be my treasured possession out of all the peoples. Indeed, the whole earth is mine, but you shall be for me a priestly kingdom and a holy nation" (Exodus 19:5-6). God separated from all the nations a people, Israel, to be God's own holy, set-apart, people.

Once God designates Israel a "holy nation," God sanctifies the people, making them more like God. To be holy is to be separated from the profane or impure. Holiness involves removing the stain of impurity or sin; even the priests purify themselves before they come before God. Holiness not only entails movement away from the profane but also toward God. Leviticus 19:2 says, "You shall be holy, for I the LORD your God am holy." What follows, in Leviticus

19, is a list of commandments, both ethical and ritual. By learning and obeying, the people—as individuals, as a community, and as a nation—begin to look like God's people. They become godlier. The commandments are the way of sanctification, the way God makes God's people holy. Holiness, then, is becoming "dead to sin and . . . alive to all that is good" (1 Peter 2:24a, J. B. Philips Translation).

What Do We Do?

The purposes of the sacrificial system—ritual commandments, offerings, sacrifices—are (1) to synchronize the way God's people live with the ordering of creation, which reveals God's nature, and (2) to provide a way of sanctification so that the people of God become more like God. We accept the meanings that lie under Leviticus. We understand ourselves as God's people. We try to live according to God's will. We try to resist sin and to be alive to what is good. But what do we do with the requirements of Leviticus 22:17-33? We are not about to offer up to God an animal, blemished or unblemished.

Consider two possibilities: First, we can begin to think about what makes us unique. How are we different from everyone else? What makes us God's people? The Scripture shows a people whose lives are dedicated to God. They talk to God, bargaining, singing God's praises, asking God's protection. They honor God before they sit down to eat. They give their best to the Lord. All of life is dedicated to God. Second, we can reflect on what makes us holy. What rituals purify us from sin? What do we do that helps us turn our lives to God? The Scripture shows people following the rules, putting God first; and it exhorts them to "keep my commandments and observe them" (Leviticus 22:31). The Scripture also gives the ritual a context: the covenant between God and God's people at Sinai. Our lives are built on ritual.

We worship. We pray. We find ways to dedicate our lives to God. We learn holiness both at home—a mother's stern word—and at church, where we find God's rules as well as God's love and discover that we are God's people.

SHARING THE SCRIPTURE

PREPARING TO TEACH

Preparing Our Hearts

Ponder this week's devotional reading from Hebrews 11:4-16. What do you learn about the faith of Abel, Enoch, Noah, Abraham, Isaac, and Jacob? What has God done for them? What connections can you draw between their faith and their willingness to give to God?

Pray that you and the students will be willing to offer your faith—and yourselves—unto God.

Preparing Our Minds

Study the background Scripture from Leviticus 22:17-33; 23:9-14, 31-32; Deuteronomy 22:6-7; Isaiah 1:10-20; Micah 6:6-8; Romans 12:1-2; 1 Corinthians 10:14-22. The lesson Scripture is from Leviticus 22:17-25, 31-33; the key verse is Romans 12:1.

Consider this question as you prepare the lesson: *What gifts are better than those things that can be purchased?*

Write on newsprint:
- ❏ information for next week's lesson, found under Continue the Journey.
- ❏ activities for further spiritual growth in Continue the Journey.

Review the Introduction, The Big Picture, Close-up, and Faith in Action, which all precede the first lesson of this quarter. Consider how you might use any of this material in today's lesson.

LEADING THE CLASS

(1) Gather to Learn

❖ Welcome the class members and guests.

❖ Pray that those who have come today will be willing to give of themselves to serve God and others.

❖ Chat informally with the students about the types of gifts they are planning to give for Christmas. Ask: **In what ways do these gifts represent a sacrifice of yourself, not in terms of money, but in terms of your time and talent?** Encourage participants to think about giving sacrificial gifts, such as a handcrafted or home-baked gift, or a gift of time to take someone to lunch or clean house or just sit and talk.

❖ Read aloud today's focus statement: **Enticing ads and commercials convince people that sacrificial material gifts are evidence of their love toward others. What gifts are better than those things that can be purchased? Leviticus informs God's people that the best gift one can give is obedience to God's commandments.**

(2) Goal 1: Learn What Leviticus Says About God's Requirement for Acceptable Sacrifices that Bring Honor to God's Holy Name

❖ Read "The Sacrificial System: Theology" in Interpreting the Scripture to set the stage for today's lesson.

❖ Select a volunteer to read Leviticus 22:17-25, 31-33.

❖ Discuss these questions:

1. **Several types of sacrifices are mentioned in this passage. What is the purpose of each type?** (See first paragraph of Leviticus 22:17-33 in Understanding the Scripture.)

2. **What are the characteristics of a sacrificial animal that pleases God?** (See second paragraph of Leviticus 22:17-33 in Understanding the Scripture.)

3. **What relationship does the character of God have with the sacrifices people bring?** (Notice comments on God's holiness in the second paragraph of Leviticus 22:17-33 in Understanding the Scripture and in "The Sacrificial System: Theology" in Interpreting the Scripture.)

(3) Goal 2: Examine the Connection Between Obedience to God and Sacrificial Giving of Self and Possessions

❖ Read or retell "What Do We Do?" in Interpreting the Scripture.

❖ Talk together about these questions:

1. **Since we no longer offer animal sacrifices, what acceptable offerings can we bring to God?** (Worship, prayer, service to others, and our whole selves are possible answers. Be aware that we will discuss Romans 12:1 under Goal 3, so do not linger

on the idea of offering our bodies if that is suggested here.)

2. **Leviticus 22:31-32 tells us to keep God's commandments and reminds us that God is the one who sanctifies us. What relationship do you see between obeying God and being the holy person that God intends for you to be?**

3. **In Leviticus 22:33 we are reminded that God liberated the Israelites from Egypt "to be your God; I am the LORD." In what ways has God worked in your life so that you might affirm God as Lord?**

(4) Goal 3: Pledge to Make a Self-sacrifice to God

❖ Lead the class in reading today's key verse from Romans 12:1.

❖ Form groups and invite the adults to consider the meanings of the words "living sacrifice," "holy," "acceptable," and "spiritual worship," which appear in the NRSV. Suggest that they look at this verse in several translations to find alternate words, which may help them better understand Paul's meaning. For example, in the CEB, the words are "living sacrifice," "holy," "pleasing," and "appropriate priestly service." Also suggest that those who have study Bibles check the footnotes for help in interpreting this verse.

❖ Distribute paper and pencils and direct the learners to rewrite part of this verse in words that are meaningful to them. They are to begin by writing: I pledge to present . . .

❖ Call on volunteers to read their pledge. Recommend that the adults take their pledges home and refer to them throughout the week.

(5) Continue the Journey

❖ Pray that as the learners depart they will follow through on the pledges they have made so as to be the kind of living sacrifices that God desires.

❖ Post information for next week's session on newsprint for the students to copy:

- **Title: Dedication of Firstborn**
- **Background Scripture: Exodus 13:11-16; Leviticus 12; Numbers 3:5-13; Luke 2:21-39**
- **Lesson Scripture: Exodus 13:13-15; Luke 2:22-32**
- **Focus of the Lesson: People today celebrate holidays and special occasions as if they are routine and ordinary. Are there still times for great excitement and celebration? Luke captures the overflowing joy the priest, Simeon, experienced as he dedicated Jesus according to the law of Moses.**

❖ Post the following information on newsprint and provide paper and pencils for the students to copy it. Challenge the adults to grow spiritually by completing one or more of these activities related to this week's session.

(1) **Review the pledge you made concerning yourself as a living sacrifice. What action will you take to fulfill that promise?**

(2) **Read the Holiness Code found in Leviticus 17:1–26:46. What can you glean from these chapters that could help you as a contemporary Christian better understand what it means to live a holy life before God?**

(3) **Plan to give sacrificially to others this Christmas so that they are receiving part of you, not just a purchased gift. Many people crave the gift of your time, so consider who on your Christmas list would enjoy a visit, perhaps spending time sharing memories with you.**

❖ Sing or read aloud "What Gift Can We Bring."

❖ Conclude today's session by leading the class in this benediction, which is adapted from Leviticus 22:31 in today's lesson: **As we go forth, we commit ourselves to keep the commandments of the Lord. Amen.**

UNIT 1: WHAT WE BRING TO GOD
DEDICATION OF FIRSTBORN

PREVIEWING THE LESSON

Lesson Scripture: Exodus 13:13-15; Luke 2:22-32
Background Scripture: Exodus 13:11-16; Leviticus 12;
Numbers 3:5-13; Luke 2:21-39
Key Verse: Luke 2:22

Focus of the Lesson:
People today celebrate holidays and special occasions as if they are routine and ordinary. Are there still times for great excitement and celebration? Luke captures the overflowing joy the priest, Simeon, experienced as he dedicated Jesus according to the law of Moses.

Goals for the Learners:
(1) to explore the story of Simeon at the presentation of Jesus at the Temple.
(2) to imagine the immense joy that Simeon felt when centuries of waiting finally culminated in the birth of the Messiah.
(3) to commit to making Jesus the center of attention during the secular busyness of the season.

Supplies:
Bibles, newsprint and marker, paper and pencils, hymnals, optional white paper bags, sand, tea lights or votive candles, newspaper, scissors

---

READING THE SCRIPTURE

NRSV

Lesson Scripture: Exodus 13:13-15

¹³"Every firstborn male among your children you shall redeem. ¹⁴When in the future your child asks you, 'What does this mean?' you shall answer, 'By strength of hand the LORD brought us out of Egypt, from the house of slavery. ¹⁵When Pharaoh stubbornly refused to let us go, the

CEB

Lesson Scripture: Exodus 13:13-15

¹³"You should ransom every oldest male among your children. ¹⁴When in the future your child asks you, 'What does this mean?' you should answer, 'The LORD brought us with great power out of Egypt, out of the place we were slaves. ¹⁵When Pharaoh refused to let us go, the LORD killed

LORD killed all the firstborn in the land of Egypt, from human firstborn to the firstborn of animals. Therefore I sacrifice to the LORD every male that first opens the womb, but every firstborn of my sons I redeem.'"

all the oldest offspring in the land of Egypt, from the oldest sons to the oldest male animals. That is why I offer to the LORD as a sacrifice every male that first comes out of the womb. But I ransom my oldest sons.'"

Lesson Scripture: Luke 2:22-32

²²**When the time came for their purification according to the law of Moses, they brought him up to Jerusalem to present him to the Lord** ²³(as it is written in the law of the Lord, "Every firstborn male shall be designated as holy to the Lord"), ²⁴and they offered a sacrifice according to what is stated in the law of the Lord, "a pair of turtledoves or two young pigeons."

²⁵Now there was a man in Jerusalem whose name was Simeon; this man was righteous and devout, looking forward to the consolation of Israel, and the Holy Spirit rested on him. ²⁶It had been revealed to him by the Holy Spirit that he would not see death before he had seen the Lord's Messiah. ²⁷Guided by the Spirit, Simeon came into the temple; and when the parents brought in the child Jesus, to do for him what was customary under the law, ²⁸Simeon took him in his arms and praised God, saying,

²⁹"Master, now you are dismissing
your servant in peace,
according to your word;
³⁰for my eyes have seen your
salvation,
³¹which you have prepared in the
presence of all peoples,
³²a light for revelation to the
Gentiles
and for glory to your people
Israel."

Lesson Scripture: Luke 2:22-32

²²**When the time came for their ritual cleansing, in accordance with the Law from Moses, they brought Jesus up to Jerusalem to present him to the Lord.** (²³It's written in the Law of the Lord, "Every firstborn male will be dedicated to the Lord.") ²⁴They offered a sacrifice in keeping with what's stated in the Law of the Lord, *A pair of turtledoves or two young pigeons.*

²⁵A man named Simeon was in Jerusalem. He was righteous and devout. He eagerly anticipated the restoration of Israel, and the Holy Spirit rested on him. ²⁶The Holy Spirit revealed to him that he wouldn't die before he had seen the Lord's Christ. ²⁷Led by the Spirit, he went into the temple area. Meanwhile, Jesus' parents brought the child to the temple so that they could do what was customary under the Law. ²⁸Simeon took Jesus in his arms and praised God. He said,

²⁹"Now, master, let your servant
go in peace according to your
word,
³⁰because my eyes have seen your
salvation.
³¹You prepared this salvation in the
presence of all peoples.
³²It's a light for revelation to the
Gentiles
and a glory for your people Israel."

UNDERSTANDING THE SCRIPTURE

Exodus 13:11-16. Israel adopted the customs of the surrounding culture, and interpreted them in new ways. Sacrificing firstborn children and animals was commonplace in many ancient societies. Exodus 13:1 states God's command: "Consecrate to me all the firstborn; whatever is the first to open the womb among the Israelites, of human beings and animals, is mine." Gradually, consecrating the firstborn became a way to remember and to experience anew the Passover and the Exodus (13:11-12). Notice that the Scripture picks up on future rituals in which a child asks, "What does this mean?" (13:14). The offering of the firstborn became a sign, across generations, that God "brought us out of Egypt" (13:16). In the context of God's mighty acts, the meaning of the offering expanded in two ways. First, the firstborn belong to God. In the Exodus event, God chose the Israelites as God's own people. They were all, in a sense, the firstborn. Jeremiah 31:9 describes the relationship between God and God's people as like that of a father and his firstborn son: "I have become a father to Israel, and Ephraim is my firstborn." Second, *The American Heritage Dictionary* defines "redeem" as "to set free; rescue or ransom." In the Scripture, it also conveys a sense of God's protection. Having claimed the Israelites as God's own children, God set them free from slavery in Egypt. In the final plague (Exodus 11; 12:29-32), God killed the firstborn of Egypt and passed over the firstborn of Israel. They were ransomed, bought and paid for, by the death of Egyptian children. In the offering, the firstborn are sacrificed but the firstborn of God's children are redeemed.

Leviticus 12:1-8. This passage sets forth the process by which a woman is ritually purified after childbirth. Differences regarding the child's gender also existed in other cultures, including that of the Hittites. Israel's purification rites do not involve the child, but the time of the mother's ceremonial uncleanness varies from seven days for a male child (12:2) to fourteen days for a female (12:5). The process essentially involves waiting for postpartum bleeding to slow and eventually to stop. The rites were based on the idea that God gives life and that life is in the blood. The loss of blood equates with death and so is counter to God's holiness, which is life-giving. The "blood purification" time will be thirty-three days for a male child (12:4) and sixty-six days for a female (12:5). Then the woman may touch anything common and conjugal relations may resume, but she may not touch anything holy or enter the sanctuary. "When the days of her purification are completed" (12:6), she brings to the priest a lamb and a dove for the offering. Substitutions (12:8) were allowed so that the poor could bring offerings to God. The burnt offering of the lamb is for thanksgiving for God's protection of mother and child; the pigeon or turtledove is a "sin offering." The woman's sin is not moral but ritual.

Numbers 3:5-13. The Scripture establishes a hierarchy. The descendants of Aaron will be priests. Levites will assist by guarding the tabernacle and transporting the tent of meeting. In verses 11-13, the Levites seem to increase in importance. They become substitutes for the firstborn of Israel. They belong to God and are dedicated to God's service.

Luke 2:21-39. Mary and Joseph were faithful, following the rules and rituals that defined Jewish religious life. Jesus was circumcised on the eighth day. Circumcision was the sign of the covenant with Abraham and incorporated Jesus into the people of God. Jesus' name, given by the angel in Luke 1:31, comes from the name Joshua, which means "God saves." Luke says in verse 22 that the whole family comes to the Temple for "their purification," though in Leviticus 12:1-8, only the woman comes. Unable to afford a lamb, they bring two turtledoves or two young pigeons to present to the priest. Luke conflates the rites of purification after childbirth with the offering of the firstborn. Jesus is presented to the Lord, in accordance with Exodus 13:2: "Consecrate to me all the firstborn." The offering of the firstborn, a sign of God's choosing and redeeming Israel, includes Jesus in the covenant with Moses. Though not always accurate, Luke is clear that Mary and Joseph are faithful to the law and that Jesus is part of the people of God. Jesus, who is the Messiah, is dedicated to God in the context of the law and God's covenantal relationship with Israel.

Simeon is "righteous and devout" (2:25) and anticipates "the consolation of Israel" (2:25). Consolation, deliverance, and redemption all point toward "salvation" (2:30), a new order of life and a new covenant inaugurated by the coming of the Messiah. Simeon shows up in the Temple, receives the child in his arms, and sings praises to God. The Holy Spirit had promised Simeon that "he would not see death before he had seen the Lord's Messiah" (2:26), and the Holy Spirit guided him to the Temple at the right time. Simeon's song (2:29-32) is praise for God's salvation, which has come in Jesus Christ for "all peoples" (2:31). Salvation is light, revealing God's purpose to the nations; it is also the glory of God for God's chosen people; and peace on earth. In verse 34, Simeon's words change from praise to warning: Jesus will be a sign of God's will, but public opinion will be divided. In the furor, families will be disrupted and "the inner thoughts of many will be revealed" (2:35). How will Mary's heart be pierced? Although the meaning of Simeon's words is not clear to Mary at the time, his comment is generally understood to refer to Mary's suffering at Jesus' crucifixion.

Anna is eighty-four and spends day and night worshiping the Lord. This pious prophetess praises God, confirming Simeon's joy. She also tells everyone who will listen about Jesus Christ, who fulfills their expectations of the Lord's Messiah.

INTERPRETING THE SCRIPTURE

The Context of Salvation

Jesus was born into an observant Jewish family. Mary and Joseph participated in rituals that made them part of the community of the faithful, the people of God. Jesus was circumcised according to the law (Luke 2:21). Later, Mary and Joseph brought him to the Temple and dedicated him to the Lord. Together, the rituals—circumcision and the offering of the firstborn—spoke of God's relationship with Israel: God's covenants with Abraham and Moses, the Passover, and the Exodus from Egypt. God chose the people as God's own. God blessed them, protected them, guided them, and saved them. Their lives were to be a blessing to the rest of the world so that all people would know the power and love of God.

Christians have similar laws and customs. We go to church, say prayers, sing hymns. We observe the church calendar—Advent, Christmas, Epiphany, Lent, Easter—that each year walks us through the life of Christ. We baptize our children and promise to raise them up in the "nurture and admonition of the Lord" (Ephesians 6:4 KJV). We partake of the Lord's Supper. Our rituals remind us that we belong to God.

The laws and rituals Luke mentions point to larger theological ideas and may foreshadow what is to come in the gospel. For example, in Exodus 13:14-15, the dedication of the firstborn refers to the story of Passover, when children of Egypt were killed so that the children of Israel would be redeemed. Substitution and redemption are ways of understanding the death of Christ. The firstborn are "designated as holy to the Lord" (2:23), which raises the issue of Jesus' relationship to God. Again, the language, "the firstborn," brings to mind Jesus' resurrection and the idea that he is "the firstborn of all creation" (Colossians 1:15) and "the firstborn from the dead" (1:18).

We tend to think of law and gospel as opposites; but in fact, law defines us as people of God, a religious community built on the knowledge of God's mighty acts and the promise of future salvation.

Expectations of Salvation

Simeon was "looking forward to the consolation of Israel" (2:25) and sings of "salvation . . . prepared in the presence of all peoples" (2:30, 31). Anna spoke to "all who were looking for the redemption of Jerusalem" (2:38). *Consolation, salvation, redemption*—what were they expecting?

We tend to think of salvation as an individual's hope for life after death. Certainly Simeon hints at personal salvation. He sings the Nunc Dimittis, which is sung at compline, the last prayers of the day, and also before death. Simeon is assured that he will die in peace, having seen beyond death to salvation.

Simeon also sees a wider vision. Israel looked forward to salvation for the whole world, a time when the glory of God would return to Jerusalem and all the nations would see the light of God's new life. In fact, when we pray, "Thy kingdom come; thy will be done," we are looking forward to a new life in the future when God's purposes are fulfilled "on earth as in heaven."

Joseph Fitzmyer, in his commentary on Luke, says, "'Salvation' denotes the deliverance of human beings from evil, physical, moral, political, or cataclysmic. It connotes a victory, a rescue of them from a state of negation and a restoration to wholeness or integrity." Israel was looking forward to a day when God would establish a new social-political-economic order based on love, righteousness, faithfulness, justice, generosity, and peace. They were longing for a new world in which the lame would be healed and the hungry fed, when death would be no more, enemies would make peace, the natural world would sprout green and fresh, and all things would be set right according to God's purposes. Salvation includes for people both a new inclination to moral obedience and a world where God lives with God's people, comforting them and teaching them God's way of life. Simeon and Anna were hoping to see, before they died, the "Lord's Messiah," the one God set apart and chose to usher in a brand-new world.

Responses to Jesus

Simeon was an elderly man who was looking forward to the "consolation of Israel" (2:25). He was a true believer. But the Holy Spirit is the actor in the story. The Holy Spirit promises Simeon that he will see the Messiah and then leads him to the Temple at the same time Mary and Joseph arrive. Perhaps the Spirit also gives voice to his joy when he receives the child and realizes that this newborn is the Lord's Messiah. How did he know? Jesus was an ordinary baby being brought to the Temple by parents of modest means. The Holy Spirit was apparently busy or Simeon might not have recognized who Jesus was.

Simeon sings. In the first chapters of Luke, everyone seems to burst into song. The birth of Jesus is rather like a locally staged musical, with Mary, Zechariah, the angels, Simeon, and Anna belting out praises to God for salvation. You might imagine Simeon and Anna hobbling into the Temple, seeing the baby Jesus, tapping their feet to the music, and thumping out a Broadway show tune. Think of their joy, knowing that God's promises were certain and the world would see the bright light of God's new world. Simeon sang the Scripture. Anna clapped along, singing background and telling everyone she saw: "Hey! Would you believe it? I have seen for myself the Lord's Messiah." "Hey! Listen! I have seen God's salvation."

Joy is tempered. Jesus is a sign of salvation, but not everyone will rejoice. Jesus, who will preach God's kingdom, will also be a threat. The truth is people are not always pleased with the purposes of God. Consider Mary's song, in which the powerful are dumped from their thrones and the lowly are lifted up, the poor are fed, and the rich are sent away empty (1:46-55). Or think of Jesus reading from Isaiah: "He has anointed me to bring good news to the poor. He has sent me to proclaim release to the captives" (4:18). Jesus tells us to love our enemies and to invite to our next party the lame, the blind, the unpopular, the homeless. We aren't always pleased with Jesus' visions of God's kingdom. Simeon warns Mary and Joseph that their child will be the center of opposing opinions; even they will struggle with what he says.

What about us? How do we respond to the coming of Jesus Christ? Sometimes we completely miss the point. We get wrapped up in Christmas rituals—cookies, Christmas trees, candlelight worship. When we get to the end of the endless to-do list, we have forgotten that Jesus is not just a baby in a stable strewn with warm hay but also the Lord's Messiah, who challenges our faith and promises the joy of a brand-new world filled with righteousness and peace.

SHARING THE SCRIPTURE

PREPARING TO TEACH

Preparing Our Hearts

Ponder this week's devotional reading from 2 Chronicles 30:5-12. The context of this passage is Judean king Hezekiah's proclamation that regular worship is being restored in the Temple. What actions and attitudes of their ancestors does Hezekiah want his fellow Israelites to turn away from? What does he want them to do instead? How did the various people who heard the king's proclamation respond? What lessons are in this passage for you?

Pray that you and the students will worship and serve the Lord.

Preparing Our Minds

Study the background Scripture from Exodus 13:11-16; Leviticus 12; Numbers 3:5-13; Luke 2:21-39. The lesson Scripture is Exodus 13:13-15; Luke 2:22-32.

Consider this question as you prepare the lesson: *As you reflect on the holidays, are there still times for great excitement, or have such celebrations become routine?*

Write on newsprint:

❑ information for next week's lesson, found under Continue the Journey.

❑ activities for further spiritual growth in Continue the Journey.

Review The Big Picture and Faith in Action: Celebrations in the Christian Tradition where you will find information that may be especially useful for the Gather to Learn activity.

Option: Obtain white paper bags, sand, tea lights or votive candles, newspaper, and scissors if you choose to make the luminaries suggested as an option in Gather to Learn.

LEADING THE CLASS

(1) Gather to Learn

❖ Welcome the class members and guests.

❖ Pray that those who have come today will be spiritually ready to celebrate the coming of Jesus.

❖ Read: **Today is the fourth Sunday in Advent. Christmas is less than one week away. As you make final preparations for this joyous holy day, what traditions in your church and home make this an especially meaningful time for you? Why?** (Read or post ideas from Faith in Action and The Big Picture: Rituals, Holy Days, Connections to add to the discussion.)

❖ **Option:** Instead of just talking about traditions, consider making luminaries that the adults can take home and use on Christmas Eve. Distribute white paper bags, about the size of a lunch bag or a little larger, and tea lights or votive candles. Have sand available on a table covered with newspaper so that the adults can put about two inches of sand in each bag and place a candle in the sand. For a fancier luminary, students can cut out or punch out designs on the bag. Try to have enough supplies so that each person can make two bags for use on a driveway or walkway at home. On Christmas Eve the adults can light the candles to create the light of Christ in front of their homes. Caution participants to be sure the area is free from leaves or other debris that could catch fire.

❖ Read aloud today's focus statement: **People today celebrate holidays and special occasions as if they are routine and ordinary. Are there still times for great excitement and celebration? Luke captures the overflowing joy the priest, Simeon, experienced as he dedicated Jesus according to the law of Moses.**

(2) Goal 1: Explore the Story of Simeon at the Presentation of Jesus at the Temple

❖ Provide the context for today's story of Jesus' presentation at the Temple by reading or retelling Exodus 13:11-16 in Understanding the Scripture. Link this information to the Gospel reading by pointing out that Luke's story clearly demonstrates that Mary and Joseph were devout Jews who wanted to bring up Jesus in a way that was consistent with their faith.

❖ Call on a volunteer to read Luke 2:22-32.

❖ Discuss these questions:

1. **What do you learn about Simeon?**
2. **How would you describe Simeon's expectations?** (See "Expectations of Salvation" in Interpreting the Scripture.)
3. **How does Simeon respond to Jesus?** (See "Responses to Jesus" in Interpreting the Scripture.)
4. **What role does the Holy Spirit play in this story?**

(3) Goal 2: Imagine the Immense Joy that Simeon Felt When Centuries of Waiting Finally Culminated in the Birth of the Messiah

❖ Enlist two people, one to play the role of Simeon and another to play the role of a friend of Simeon's.

Simeon is to tell his friend, in his own words, about the experience he had in the Temple with Mary, Joseph, and Jesus—and how that experience had fulfilled his expectations for God's Messiah. The friend may ask questions. Encourage Simeon not only to tell about his joy but also to demonstrate that joy in the way he talks and interacts with his friend.

❖ Invite the students to imagine themselves as Simeon. In response to his joy upon meeting the baby Jesus, he praised God (2:29-32). Ask: **How do you demonstrate your joy as you welcome the Messiah?** List their ideas on newsprint.

❖ Provide time for quiet reflection on these questions: **Am I really expressing my joy in the arrival of the Messiah, or am I just concerned about making Christmas a "good holiday" with little regard to the true meaning of Jesus' coming?**

(4) Goal 3: Commit to Making Jesus the Center of Attention During the Secular Busyness of the Season

❖ Read: **As the final countdown to Christmas has begun, our lives become more hectic. We have last minute gifts to buy or finish making and wrap. Cards need to be sent and cookies baked. We need to attend or plan a party. These are all important ways that we celebrate the holiday, we tell ourselves. And to a certain extent, we are right. But what happens when we are so focused on our busyness that we forget that Jesus is the reason for the season? Talk with a partner or small group about ways that you can keep the main thing *being* the main thing this Christmas. In other words, what can you do to keep your eyes focused** on Jesus? That does not mean you have to forego decorations, holiday food, cards, and so on. But it does mean that Jesus needs to take center stage—and these other things that seem so important must fit in.

❖ Call on volunteers to tell others whatever strategies they have discerned for keeping Jesus at the center of their holiday preparations and celebrations.

(5) Continue the Journey

❖ Pray that as the learners depart they will experience the excitement of the arrival of Jesus, God's Messiah.

❖ Post information for next week's session on newsprint for the students to copy:

- Title: A Generous Gift
- Background Scripture: Matthew 23:1-12; Mark 12:38-44
- Lesson Scripture: Matthew 23:2-12; Mark 12:38-44
- Focus of the Lesson: Integral to the human condition is that deep-seated craving to be recognized and held in high esteem by others. Will the adulation of others bring confirmation of a person's real importance? While Jesus denounced the scribes' and Pharisees' obsession with receiving recognition, he affirmed the acts of selfless

compassion and humility as exhibited by the poor widow, who gave all she had.

❖ Post the following information on newsprint and provide paper and pencils for the students to copy it. Challenge the adults to grow spiritually by completing one or more of these activities related to this week's session.

(1) Read Charles Dickens' *A Christmas Carol*. Who seems to be joyful in this familiar tale published in 1843? What is the reason for joy? Who lacks joy? Why?

(2) Plan a low-cost event for close friends or family that does not include presents. Spend time giving everyone an opportunity to say how at least one other person in the group has brought joy to their lives.

(3) Set up a crèche and use it to tell the story of Jesus' birth and dedication, particularly if children will be present.

❖ Sing or read aloud "My Master, See, the Time Has Come."

❖ Conclude today's session by leading the class in this benediction, which is adapted from Leviticus 22:31 in the lesson for December 13: As we go forth, we commit ourselves to keep the commandments of the Lord. Amen.

UNIT 1: WHAT WE BRING TO GOD
A GENEROUS GIFT

PREVIEWING THE LESSON

Lesson Scripture: Matthew 23:2-12; Mark 12:38-44
Background Scripture: Matthew 23:1-12; Mark 12:38-44
Key Verse: Matthew 23:12

Focus of the Lesson:

Integral to the human condition is that deep-seated craving to be recognized and held in high esteem by others. Will the adulation of others bring confirmation of a person's real importance? While Jesus denounced the scribes' and Pharisees' obsession with receiving recognition, he affirmed the acts of selfless compassion and humility as exhibited by the poor widow, who gave all she had.

Goals for the Learners:

(1) to observe the contrast that Jesus drew between the arrogance of religious leaders and the piety of a humble poor woman.
(2) to reflect upon the tension between wanting recognition and selfless giving that often receives no recognition.
(3) to resolve to become more selfless in giving.

Supplies:

Bibles, newsprint and marker, paper and pencils, hymnals

READING THE SCRIPTURE

NRSV
Lesson Scripture: Matthew 23:2-12

²"The scribes and the Pharisees sit on Moses' seat; ³therefore, do whatever they teach you and follow it; but do not do as they do, for they do not practice what they teach. ⁴They tie up heavy burdens, hard to bear, and lay them on the shoulders of others; but they themselves are unwilling to lift a finger to move them. ⁵They do all

CEB
Lesson Scripture: Matthew 23:2-12

²"The legal experts and the Pharisees sit on Moses' seat. ³Therefore, you must take care to do everything they say. But don't do what they do. ⁴For they tie together heavy packs that are impossible to carry. They put them on the shoulders of others, but are unwilling to lift a finger to move them. ⁵Everything they do, they do

their deeds to be seen by others; for they make their phylacteries broad and their fringes long. ⁶They love to have the place of honor at banquets and the best seats in the synagogues, ⁷and to be greeted with respect in the marketplaces, and to have people call them rabbi. ⁸But you are not to be called rabbi, for you have one teacher, and you are all students. ⁹And call no one your father on earth, for you have one Father—the one in heaven. ¹⁰Nor are you to be called instructors, for you have one instructor, the Messiah. ¹¹The greatest among you will be your servant. **¹²All who exalt themselves will be humbled, and all who humble themselves will be exalted.**

to be noticed by others. They make extra-wide prayer bands for their arms and long tassels for their clothes. ⁶They love to sit in places of honor at banquets. ⁷They love to be greeted with honor in the markets and to be addressed as 'Rabbi.'

⁸"But you shouldn't be called Rabbi, because you have one teacher, and all of you are brothers and sisters. ⁹Don't call anybody on earth your father, because you have one Father, who is heavenly. ¹⁰Don't be called teacher, because Christ is your one teacher. ¹¹But the one who is greatest among you will be your servant. **¹²All who lift themselves up will be brought low. But all who make themselves low will be lifted up.**

Lesson Scripture: Mark 12:38-44

³⁸As he taught, he said, "Beware of the scribes, who like to walk around in long robes, and to be greeted with respect in the marketplaces, ³⁹and to have the best seats in the synagogues and places of honor at banquets! ⁴⁰They devour widows' houses and for the sake of appearance say long prayers. They will receive the greater condemnation."

⁴¹He sat down opposite the treasury, and watched the crowd putting money into the treasury. Many rich people put in large sums. ⁴²A poor widow came and put in two small copper coins, which are worth a penny. ⁴³Then he called his disciples and said to them, "Truly I tell you, this poor widow has put in more than all those who are contributing to the treasury. ⁴⁴For all of them have contributed out of their abundance; but she out of her poverty has put in everything she had, all she had to live on."

Lesson Scripture: Mark 12:38-44

³⁸As he was teaching, he said, "Watch out for the legal experts. They like to walk around in long robes. They want to be greeted with honor in the markets. ³⁹They long for places of honor in the synagogues and at banquets. ⁴⁰They are the ones who cheat widows out of their homes, and to show off they say long prayers. They will be judged most harshly."

⁴¹Jesus sat across from the collection box for the temple treasury and observed how the crowd gave their money. Many rich people were throwing in lots of money. ⁴²One poor widow came forward and put in two small copper coins worth a penny. ⁴³Jesus called his disciples to him and said, "I assure you that this poor widow has put in more than everyone who's been putting money in the treasury. ⁴⁴All of them are giving out of their spare change. But she from her hopeless poverty has given everything she had, even what she needed to live on."

UNDERSTANDING THE SCRIPTURE

Introduction. In both Matthew 23:1-12 and Mark 12:38-44, Jesus denounces the scribes and Pharisees. They don't practice what they teach, and they practice piety for the sake of appearances. The context of both Scripture passages begins with the great commandment (Matthew 22:37-38; Mark 12:30-31) and ends with Jesus' foretelling the destruction of the Temple. Both inform the meaning of the Scripture reading for today.

Matthew 23:1-7. Scribes were lawyers, administrators, and interpreters of the law. Pharisees applied the law to everyday living. Matthew lumps the two groups together; they were religious leaders and Jesus' opponents. "Moses' seat" may have been an actual seat in the synagogue, but Jesus uses the phrase to indicate that scribes and Pharisees taught with the authority of Moses. Jesus commends their teaching, but condemns their practice: "They do not practice what they teach" (23:3). The religious leaders spoke of loving God and neighbor, but they burdened ordinary people with laws they could not possibly observe. Ulrich Luz, in his commentary on Matthew, points out, "Simple, uneducated poor people . . . not only will scarcely have been able to penetrate the many regulations of the scribes and priests; they will scarcely have been able to pay many of the sacrifices and tithes required by the laws. . . . Jesus spoke precisely for these social classes." Although burdening the poor, religious leaders did not follow the laws they preached. Jesus further denounces the scribes and Pharisees for exaggerating their piety to be seen by others.

Phylacteries were small boxes containing verses of Scripture, worn on the forehead and left arm. Fringes were tassels worn as a reminder to observe God's commandments (Numbers 15:38-39). The best seats at the synagogue and at banquets were places of honor, respect, social status. Matthew condemns "public relations piety" that seeks not the glory of God but the praise of other people.

Matthew 23:8-12. In verse 8, the audience changes; Jesus addresses his disciples, and by inference, the church. Each verse begins with an admonition not to acquire titles or to claim the honor or power they bestow. "Rabbi," before it referred to a religious teacher, was a title of respect, literally "my master" or "my great one." "Father" referred to an older adult who was honored for passing on the tradition and was often the benefactor or founding father of a church. "Instructor" may mean "guide" or "leader" as well as "academic teacher." The end of each verse is an explanation that describes what the church should be. Do not take on titles of respect, says Jesus, because you are all students of one teacher; God is your only Father; and Christ, the Messiah, is your only guide. The Scripture tells how the commandments to love God and neighbor play out in the church, where all people are equals, brothers and sisters in God's family, living in mutual respect and affection and worshiping one God, the only "great one." The last two verses in the passage add a larger theological context. Christians and Jews look forward to God's coming kingdom, a new social order grounded in God's righteousness and love. God's kingdom is characterized by reversals: The lame walk, the dead live. The reversals extend to authority, power, and social status. Jesus preaches God's coming kingdom in which "the meek . . . will inherit the earth" (5:5). Reversals overturn the hierarchy of both church and society. Thus, Jesus can preach the destruction of the Temple, the center of power in Israel, and call his followers to live in God's kingdom now.

Mark 12:38-40. The first part of the Scripture is comparable to the denunciation of the scribes and Pharisees in Matthew. In Mark, Jesus accuses the scribes specifically of "walk[ing] around in long robes" (12:38), a sign of social status; glad-handing in the marketplace; and taking the seats of honor in the synagogue and at banquets. They like their power, and they flaunt their piety. Commentaries differ. Some say that the scribes' reputation in the community recommended them to wealthy widows, who hired them to execute and run their estates. Jesus' warning was about turning piety into profit. Others say that verse 40 is a more general statement about scribes who "say long prayers" for the sake of appearances, but disregard the law, which commands them to take care of widows and orphans, the poorest in their community. Because the scribes make a show of their faith, they will be condemned more than ordinary religious people who try to love their neighbors but fail.

Mark 12:41-44. Jesus watches people contribute to the Temple treasury. Thirteen trumpet-shaped receptacles were in the sanctuary. They reverberated when coins were tossed into them, calling attention to both the gift and the giver—the louder the clanging, the larger the gift. Widows in Israel had no inheritance and lived from hand to mouth, relying on the generosity of their sons. "Widows and orphans" were the poorest people in the society, and God's law commands the community to take care of them. The widow contributed two lepta, which was the smallest denomination of money in circulation; it was considerably less than a day's wage but "all she had to live on" (12:44). Jesus calls his disciples to him and begins by saying, "Truly I tell you" (12:43). Both are clues that Jesus is about to say something important, probably on the subject of discipleship. The wealthy give of their abundance; the widow gives all she has. The phrase translated "all she had to live on" is also translated "livelihood" and can refer to her whole life and all the activities associated with it. Jesus' description of what the widow gives harkens back to the Great Commandment to love God with your whole heart, soul, mind, and strength. Though the scribe in Mark 12:28-34 *knows* the commandment, the widow *fulfills* it, giving her whole life to God.

INTERPRETING THE SCRIPTURE

Hypocrisy

Love God with all your heart, soul, mind, and strength. Love your neighbor as yourself. Two commandments sum up the whole law of God. Although they are intended to guide the actions of God's people, some of the religious leaders ignore them. Thus, in Matthew 23:1-12 and Mark 12:38-40, Jesus denounces religious leaders for hypocrisy. The criticism falls into two categories: The scribes and Pharisees do not practice what they teach, and their motivation is not true piety but concern for their own reputation and social status. The scribes and Pharisees teach the law of God and its interpretation for daily life. The problem is not with their knowledge of the law but with its practice. They do not love their neighbors, as evidenced by their treatment of the poor. They do not love God. True piety glorifies the one true God; but the religious leaders are misdirected, calling attention to themselves and hoping that other people will see their piety and praise them. They know the words of the Scriptures, but do not live their faith.

Everyone struggles with hypocrisy at some time. We teach our children to love God and neighbors; but when it comes to living day-to-day, we forget what we believe. Our lives are busy—filled up with work, chores, and family responsibilities. For many of us, loving God means going to church and saying a prayer before dinner. Neighbor love translates into a little feel-good volunteer work. We don't practice what we preach. The truth is we are hypocrites too. We talk about God and live for ourselves.

Personal Giving

Some statistics reveal the extent of personal giving in the United States. Surveys based on Internal Revenue Service records from 2008 show that middle-class Americans give away an average of 7.6 percent of their discretionary income. Wealthier people give less, an average of 4.2 percent of their income. America's poor are the most generous. According to a US Bureau of Labor Statistics survey, in 2007 people in the lowest income group gave away 4.3 percent of the income while people in the highest income group gave only 2.1 percent. Religious giving varies. Calculated as a percentage of gross income, Presbyterians, Episcopalians, and Methodists give 1.2 percent; evangelicals or members of nondenominational churches give 2.6 percent to their churches. Congregations, in turn, spend 85 percent of their income on themselves, paying for salaries, utility bills, and Sunday school materials.

Jesus was watching people contribute to the Temple treasury (Mark 12:41). Collection boxes lined the sanctuary and reverberated whenever someone tossed in a few coins. Rich people dropped in handfuls of money, and other people were no doubt impressed by their generosity. The clang and rattle of money called attention to both the gift and the giver. But when the poor widow dropped in a few pennies, no one noticed except Jesus. When billionaires write checks for thousands of dollars, people pay attention; sometimes philanthropy makes the news. But no one pays attention to a few dollars tossed in a collection plate—except perhaps to criticize: "Surely she could give a little more."

Jesus is clear: The rich gave of their abundance, but the widow gave all she had. Who followed the commandment to love God with heart, soul, mind, and strength? Jesus calls us to do the same, to give until we can give no more, to express our love for God not with a tiny percentage of our discretionary income, but with all that we have. Jesus calls us to over-the-top generosity.

Sermons, Sunday school lessons, and stewardship speeches interpret Mark 12:38-44, calling us to give generously and joyfully, to commit our lives and our pocketbooks to loving God and neighbor. The widow in the story set the standard, demonstrating true humility and piety, quietly giving all she had. We are called to do the same.

Another Interpretation

Some students of Scripture ask other questions: Should the widow give all she has to the upkeep of the Temple? Is the widow an example of Christian piety, or is she an example of how religious institutions take advantage of the poor, how the scribes "devour widows' houses" (12:40)? Perhaps we should take a second look at the socioeconomic implications of the story.

Jesus sets up the contrast between rich and poor: The rich put large sums into the treasury; the poor widow puts in two coins. The rich give of their abundance; the poor widow gives all she has to live on. Ched Myers, in his commentary *Binding the Strong Man*, says that Jesus passes judgment on the religious establishment: "The temple has robbed this woman of her very means of livelihood (12:44). Like the scribal class, it no longer protects widows, but exploits them." We may have misinterpreted Scripture by looking at issues of personal giving rather than at the political, social, and economic issues that keep the rich rich and the poor poor. Perhaps Jesus is telling us again to love our neighbors and, as churches, to give generously to the poor.

A farmer talked to a preacher, "I lost $70,000 this year. I don't know if I can keep my farm." The preacher wondered, "What can the church do to help?" The farmer was surprised. "I just wanted to let you I can't give my tithe this year. I don't have the money." This interchange raises some points to ponder in light of Jesus' teaching. First, as statistics show, most Christians do not tithe, so that's the first interesting point. Second, if parishioners are in financial need, how many are willing to let the church know of their hardship, much less expect any assistance? Finally, how many churches would jump to offer serious help to a member in need?

Are our churches truly practicing the commandment to love neighbors? Or do we tend to be so concerned about the survival of the church (paying salaries, keeping up buildings) that we forget about Jesus' commandment to love one another? Maybe the story of the widow's mite is a judgment on us.

A Wider Community

When we think of the way society is structured, we think of the government and people who are governed; institutions such as schools, churches, businesses—all of which tend to be hierarchical. We also think of divisions in society: rich and poor, black and white, urban and rural. We might consider social values, summed up in bumper sticker sayings: "Take care of your own." "The person with the most toys wins."

In Matthew 23:8-12, Jesus describes a new way of living together. He preaches the kingdom of God, which is a new social order based not on power but on love. The kingdom of God is often described in terms of reversals: The hungry are filled, the lonely are embraced, the poor hear good news, the humble are exalted, the powerful are humbled. The kingdom of God levels all social, political, and economic hierarchies because only God is God. Only God rules; only Christ instructs. When Jesus tells his listeners to call no one "teacher," "father," or "instructor," he is describing a society in which all people are equal. The division between scribe and widow disappears because both live under the power of God.

The church is called to live in ways that look forward to God's kingdom. So in the church, no one claims power and people live together in mutual respect and affection. The commandments tell us to love God and to love our neighbors. They suggest a social order in which all people live as brothers and sisters in the family of God. Perhaps the church's greatest gift is to live as God commands.

SHARING THE SCRIPTURE

PREPARING TO TEACH

Preparing Our Hearts

Ponder this week's devotional reading from John 1:10-18, the concluding verses of John's Prologue. What does John the Baptist reveal about who Jesus is and why he came? How does John describe the relationship between the Word and God the Father?

Pray that you and the students will give thanks during this season of Christmas for the One who humbled himself and was exalted by God.

Preparing Our Minds

Study the background Scripture from Matthew 23:1-12; Mark 12:38-44. The lesson Scripture is from Matthew 23:2-12; Mark 12:38-44.

Consider this question as you prepare the lesson: *Although humans crave to be recognized, will the adulation of others bring confirmation of our real importance?*

Write on newsprint:
❑ information for next week's lesson, found under Continue the Journey.
❑ activities for further spiritual growth in Continue the Journey.

Review the Introduction, The Big Picture, Close-up, and Faith in Action, which all precede the first lesson of this quarter. Consider how you might use any of this material in today's lesson.

LEADING THE CLASS

(1) Gather to Learn

❖ Welcome the class members and guests.

❖ Pray that those who have come today will consider the importance of giving generously to God.

❖ Read the first paragraph of "Personal Giving" in Interpreting the Scripture and ask: **Although we may think that those who have the most give the most, studies have shown that those who earn the least are** more inclined to give the most in terms of percentage of their income. What might motivate these poorer people to give so generously?

❖ Read aloud today's focus statement: **Integral to the human condition is that deep-seated craving to be recognized and held in high esteem by others. Will the adulation of others bring confirmation of a person's real importance? While Jesus denounced the scribes' and Pharisees' obsession with receiving recognition, he affirmed the acts of selfless compassion and humility as exhibited by the poor widow, who gave all she had.**

(2) Goal 1: Observe the Contrast that Jesus Drew Between the Arrogance of Religious Leaders and the Piety of a Humble Poor Woman

❖ Choose two volunteers, one to read Matthew 23:2-12 and the other to read Mark 12:38-44.

❖ Discuss these questions:

1. **Why does Jesus denounce the religious leaders for hypocrisy?** (See the first paragraph of "Hypocrisy" in Interpreting the Scripture.)
2. **What lesson is Jesus teaching by pointing out the contribution of a very poor widow?** (See the second and third paragraphs of "Personal Giving" in Interpreting the Scripture.)
3. **In today's key verse, Matthew 23:12, Jesus said, "All who exalt themselves will be humbled, and all who humble themselves will be exalted." How would you relate this teaching to his observations about the religious leaders and the widow?**

4. **What does Jesus have to say in Mark 12:41-44 about how the religious leaders treat widows?** (See the first and second paragraphs of "Another Interpretation" in Interpreting the Scripture.)
5. **Jesus said that the two greatest commandments are to love God with our whole being and love our neighbors as ourselves. What relationship do you see between the fulfillment of these commands and one's giving habits?** (See "A Wider Community" in Interpreting the Scripture.)

(3) Goal 2: Reflect Upon the Tension Between Wanting Recognition and Selfless Giving that Often Receives No Recognition

❖ Brainstorm reasons that people voluntarily give money to the church and other organizations. Write responses on newsprint. Here are possible answers, only some of which would please God: to show gratitude to God, to be a faithful steward of the money God has entrusted to me, to encourage God to bless me more, to ensure that God does not punish me for withholding money, to impress others with my generosity.

❖ Form several small groups and give each a sheet of newsprint and marker. Direct the students to list motivations that they feel are important for Christians. Then they are to discuss how the church could teach people to give to the kingdom of God for reasons that God would approve of, rather than for the reasons that society often touts, such as recognition. Think of ways to help people overcome their need to have a plaque on the wall or their names listed in a program.

❖ Call on a spokesperson from each group to report.

❖ **Option:** Appoint one or more students to pass these ideas along to the pastor and committees in the church responsible for financial stewardship.

(4) Goal 3: Resolve to Become More Selfless in Giving

❖ Enlist volunteers to read Jesus' words in the Sermon on the Mount from Matthew 6:1-4, 19-21, 24 as class members follow along in their Bibles.

❖ Distribute paper and pencils. Invite participants to consider their own motivations for giving and jot them down. Are they seeking recognition and praise from those who are aware of their generous giving? Are they giving as a means of demonstrating where their true allegiance is? Which master are they serving—God or wealth? Perhaps some responses listed for Goal 2 are their motivations as well. Encourage the adults to write a sentence or two affirming their resolve to become more aware of their motives and more selfless in their giving.

(5) Continue the Journey

❖ Pray that as the learners depart they will cheerfully give generously without seeking the recognition of others.

❖ Post information for next week's session on newsprint for the students to copy:

- **Title: A Bride Worth Waiting For**
- **Background Scripture: Genesis 28–30**

■ **Lesson Scripture: Genesis 29:15-30**

■ **Focus of the Lesson:** Marriages can be marred by unforeseen circumstances. How might husbands and wives patiently work through tradition and undesirable circumstances to reach their personal goals? After Laban tricked Jacob into marrying his older daughter Leah, Jacob willingly agreed to work for seven additional years in order to marry his beloved Rachel.

❖ Post the following information on newsprint and provide paper and pencils for the students to copy it. Challenge the adults to grow spiritually by completing one or more of these activities related to this week's session.

(1) Review your charitable giving for 2015, including money you gave to your church, educational and cultural institutions, and nonprofit organizations. How much of your money (in real dollars or as a percentage of giving) went to support the kingdom of God by supporting the church and those in need?

(2) Create a plan for charitable giving for 2016. What percentage of your income will you commit to give away? Estimate how many dollars this will be. Make a list of those organizations that you want to support and assign a dollar value to each one. Pray about this plan, seeking confirmation from God that this is the way the money entrusted to you can best be allocated.

(3) Examine your own motives for giving. Are you trying to help those in need? Is your main interest a tax write-off? How important is it to you that others know what you give? Bring these motives before God in prayer and make changes as needed.

❖ Sing or read aloud "Bless Thou the Gifts."

❖ Conclude today's session by leading the class in this benediction, which is adapted from Leviticus 22:31 in the lesson for December 13: **As we go forth, we commit ourselves to keep the commandments of the Lord. Amen.**

UNIT 2: FOUR WEDDINGS AND A FUNERAL
A Bride Worth Waiting For

PREVIEWING THE LESSON

Lesson Scripture: Genesis 29:15-30
Background Scripture: Genesis 28–30
Key Verse: Genesis 29:30

Focus of the Lesson:

Marriages can be marred by unforeseen circumstances. How might husbands and wives patiently work through tradition and undesirable circumstances to reach their personal goals? After Laban tricked Jacob into marrying his older daughter Leah, Jacob willingly agreed to work for seven additional years in order to marry his beloved Rachel.

Goals for the Learners:

(1) to examine the story of Jacob's love for and commitment to marry Rachel.
(2) to reflect upon marital relationships and how unforeseen circumstances may or may not affect the strength of the relationship.
(3) to commit to finding faith-based resolution to difficulties before abandoning relationships.

Supplies:

Bibles, newsprint and marker, paper and pencils, hymnals

READING THE SCRIPTURE

NRSV

Lesson Scripture: Genesis 29:15-30

¹⁵Then Laban said to Jacob, "Because you are my kinsman, should you therefore serve me for nothing? Tell me, what shall your wages be?" ¹⁶Now Laban had two daughters; the name of the elder was

CEB

Lesson Scripture: Genesis 29:15-30

¹⁵Laban said to Jacob, "You shouldn't have to work for free just because you are my relative. Tell me what you would like to be paid."

¹⁶Now Laban had two daughters: the older was named Leah and the

Leah, and the name of the younger was Rachel. [17]Leah's eyes were lovely, and Rachel was graceful and beautiful. [18]Jacob loved Rachel; so he said, "I will serve you seven years for your younger daughter Rachel." [19]Laban said, "It is better that I give her to you than that I should give her to any other man; stay with me." [20]So Jacob served seven years for Rachel, and they seemed to him but a few days because of the love he had for her.

[21]Then Jacob said to Laban, "Give me my wife that I may go in to her, for my time is completed." [22]So Laban gathered together all the people of the place, and made a feast. [23]But in the evening he took his daughter Leah and brought her to Jacob; and he went in to her. [24](Laban gave his maid Zilpah to his daughter Leah to be her maid.) [25]When morning came, it was Leah! And Jacob said to Laban, "What is this you have done to me? Did I not serve with you for Rachel? Why then have you deceived me?" [26]Laban said, "This is not done in our country— giving the younger before the first-born. [27]Complete the week of this one, and we will give you the other also in return for serving me another seven years." [28]Jacob did so, and completed her week; then Laban gave him his daughter Rachel as a wife. [29](Laban gave his maid Bilhah to his daughter Rachel to be her maid.) [30]So Jacob went in to Rachel also, and he loved Rachel more than Leah. He served Laban for another seven years.

younger Rachel. [17]Leah had delicate eyes, but Rachel had a beautiful figure and was good-looking. [18]Jacob loved Rachel and said, "I will work for you for seven years for Rachel, your younger daughter.

[19]Laban said, "I'd rather give her to you than to another man. Stay with me."

[20]Jacob worked for Rachel for seven years, but it seemed like a few days because he loved her. [21]Jacob said to Laban, "The time has come. Give me my wife so that I may sleep with her." [22]So Laban invited all the people of that place and prepared a banquet. [23]However, in the evening, he took his daughter Leah and brought her to Jacob, and he slept with her. [24]Laban had given his servant Zilpah to his daughter Leah as her servant. [25]In the morning, there she was—Leah! Jacob said to Laban, "What have you done to me? Didn't I work for you to have Rachel? Why did you betray me?"

[26]Laban said, "Where we live, we don't give the younger woman before the oldest. [27]Complete the celebratory week with this woman. Then I will give you this other woman too for your work, if you work for me seven more years." [28]So that is what Jacob did. He completed the celebratory week with this woman, and then Laban gave him his daughter Rachel as his wife. [29]Laban had given his servant Bilhah to his daughter Rachel as her servant. [30]Jacob slept with Rachel, and he loved Rachel more than Leah. He worked for Laban seven more years.

UNDERSTANDING THE SCRIPTURE

Genesis 28:1-5. In Genesis 27, Jacob, the younger son of Isaac and Rebekah, pretends to be his twin Esau in order to trick their father into receiving the blessing meant for the firstborn Esau. When Esau discovers the deception, he threatens to kill Jacob. In Genesis 28:1-5 Isaac tells Jacob to go to his uncle Laban, his mother's brother, and to marry one of his daughters. Afraid for Jacob because of Esau's threat, Rebekah had planted the seed of this idea by questioning Isaac as to why she should go on living if Jacob married one of the local Hittite women as Esau had done (27:46; 26:34-35). Actually, Esau had two Hittite wives, who "made life bitter for Isaac and Rebekah" (26:35).

Following directions, Jacob takes off to find a bride. The idea of marrying within the family probably came from a later time, after Israel's exile, when the community was disrupted and the family was responsible for keeping the faith alive. Before Jacob leaves, Isaac blesses him (28:1). Instead of a typical blessing before a journey ("safe travels"), Isaac refers to God's blessing at creation ("Be fruitful and multiply and fill the earth," 1:28) and God's promise to Abraham (12:1-8). Jacob will inherit the promises of God.

Genesis 28:6-9. In response to Isaac's blessing of Jacob and sending him to seek a wife from among their family, Esau recognized that his two Hittite wives did not please his parents (26:34-35; 27:46). He then took a third wife, Mahalath, who was the daughter of Abraham's son Ishmael.

Genesis 28:10-22. Jacob discovers a holy place. The "ladder" is a ramp or stairway extending from earth to heaven. Angels, who are messengers from God that keep an eye on the earth and its people, were going up and down the stairs. The God of his father and grandfather stands beside Jacob and reiterates the promise to Abraham:

Jacob will have land and children; in him, God will bless all the families of the earth. God adds a promise: "Know that I am with you and will keep you wherever you go, and will bring you back to this land" (28:15). Jacob vows that if God will be with him and keep him, then this God will be his God. Worship and tithing look forward to a future sanctuary at Bethel.

Genesis 29:1-14. Arriving in Haran, Jacob stops at a well where shepherds are waiting to water their herds. He asks about the well-being and peace of Laban's household. A meeting at a well typically signals a coming betrothal (Genesis 24:15-33; Exodus 2:15-21). When Rachel arrives to water her father's sheep, we assume that she will be Jacob's wife. Jacob performs a feat of Herculean strength, moving the stone from the well by himself. Then he kisses Rachel and weeps with relief that he has arrived and found her. Rachel runs to her father, Laban, who comes to welcome his nephew Jacob.

Genesis 29:15-30. Laban begins bargaining for Jacob's service. Ordinarily, a meeting at the well is followed by negotiations for a bride. The groom presents gifts, not actually a bride-price, but evidence of his ability to care for his wife and a sign of good intentions. Since Jacob has arrived empty-handed, he agrees to serve Laban for seven years for Rachel.

The stage is set for another deception. After Jacob's seven years of service, he marries. On the first day of the wedding feast, which lasted a week, Laban escorted his daughter, heavily veiled, to her groom; and the marriage was consummated. In the morning, Jacob wakes up to find Leah, not Rachel, in his bed. Enraged, Jacob demands an explanation. Laban summons tradition, "This is not done in our country—giving the younger before the firstborn" (29:26). Laban's deception is commonly understood as Jacob's comeuppance for deceiving his father. Perhaps more important: In the story of Jacob and Esau, Jacob—and God who chooses him—ignores custom. The firstborn, Esau, does not receive Isaac's blessing and will not carry the promises of God. Laban, on the other hand, is bound by custom. God works in both ways, breaking with tradition to do something new, but also working through the customs of human life. After a week, Jacob also marries Rachel, whom he loved more than her sister, and works another seven years for Laban.

Genesis 29:31–30:24. These verses are about the rivalry between Leah and Rachel. Though custom makes Leah Jacob's principle wife, she is "unloved" (29:31), a technical term for an unfavored co-wife. She, however, is bearing sons for Jacob while Rachel remains barren. The plot revolves around the birth and naming of Jacob's sons, who become the heads of the twelve tribes of Israel. In Scripture, names often reveal a child's destiny, but in Genesis 29:31–30:24, the names reflect the family situation and the emotional concerns of the women. Rachel first has children through a surrogate mother (30:4-5), as Sarah did (Genesis 16). The

practice may have been criticized, as Jacob asks, Am I to give you children when God, the giver of life, denies them? In Scripture, a barren woman often indicates that God is about to act in a decisive way. However, Joseph's birth is simply part of the story, perhaps the result of Reuben's mandrakes, commonly thought to be an aphrodisiac and able to increase fertility.

Genesis 30:25-31. Jacob has worked for more than fourteen years and is ready to move on. Laban is happy with the situation as it is. He has children and grandchildren, and Jacob's work has made him prosper. Laban and Jacob both evaluate the situation in terms of God's promise: "All the families of the earth will be blessed in you and in your offspring" (28:14). Legally, Jacob is working for Laban and has no property. His wives and children were born into Laban's household, and Laban claims them as his own (31:43). Laban offers to pay Jacob wages. Jacob says that he will take as his wages all the off-color sheep and goats. Laban agrees, but gives all the spotted, speckled, and striped animals into the care of his sons, leaving Jacob with no flock and no wages. Jacob turns the tables on Laban, breeding the animals in Laban's flock and, with a little magic and the help of recessive genes, producing off-color sheep and goats.

INTERPRETING THE SCRIPTURE

Boy Meets Girl

A love story: Boy meets girl. Boy loses girl. Boy finds girl. Boy and girl get married and live happily ever after. Genesis 29:15-30 is a love story.

Courtship and marriage customs vary. Marriages are arranged, bartered, chosen, or forced. They are monogamous or polygamous, marriages of convenience, and marriages of love. In many cultures, husband

and wife meet on their wedding night; in others, long courtships hope to ensure a couple's compatibility. In America, 2016, courtship customs are changing; but we still believe in happily ever after.

When the people of God were nomads or farmers, marriages were apt to be polygamous; their purpose was to produce lots of children who would watch the flocks and work the land. At times in the history of Israel, people were encouraged to marry outside their families and to settle down in the land where they lived. At other times, marriages were confined to families—cousins married—to ensure the continuing faith and religious practices of the community. Marriage customs changed as the society changed.

The love story in Genesis 29 begins when Jacob goes to Laban, his uncle, to marry one of his daughters. He arrives at the well outside of town and meets Rachel.

If romantic comedies were produced when the Bible was written, the first scene would picture a well, where townspeople gathered, shepherds watered their flocks, and boys met girls. The meeting at the well was followed by negotiations between the two families, usually the father of the woman and the man who hoped to marry her. The man brought gifts, which proved his ability to care for his wife. Jacob, who came to Laban empty-handed, offered instead seven years of service for Rachel's hand. Once arranged, the date for the wedding was set and preparations made. The marriage celebration lasted a week. On the first night, the bride was dressed in veils and escorted to her husband's tent, where the marriage was consummated. The meeting at the well led to marriage and, everyone hoped, to happily ever after.

Deception and Conflict

Although Genesis 29:15-30 is a love story, it is also a story of greed, ambition, stubbornness, deception, and conflict. It's a human story about people who are far from perfect. Jacob is portrayed as a callow youth, head over heels in love, and completely flabbergasted by Laban's deception. But recall the story in which Jacob stole his brother's birthright for a pot of beans (Genesis 25:29-34). Consider Jacob, pretending to be Esau, taking advantage of his blind, elderly father and receiving the blessing meant for the firstborn (Genesis 27). In fact, Jacob was arrogant, deceitful, and ambitious, grasping for a place in the world, playing every angle. He was not a saint. Laban was impressed by wealth and status; and he was rigid, holding on to custom. But he was ready to back out of agreements, twist the truth, and sacrifice his daughters' dignity to get what he wanted. Rachel and Leah, who seem like pawns in the story, show their character once they are married. Leah becomes bitter because she is unloved. Rachel is demanding; and she luxuriates in Jacob's love at Leah's expense.

Jacob works for Rachel's hand in marriage. Laban switches the brides, and Jacob unknowingly marries Leah. Laban's explanation, "This is not done in our country—giving the younger before the firstborn," sets Genesis 29:21-30 against Genesis 27, in which Jacob, the younger brother, receives through deception the blessing meant for the firstborn. Jacob cannot say a word. Custom and law are on Laban's side. So Jacob works another seven years for Rachel.

Marriage is difficult. Marriage means living with another person who has grown up in another family, whose routines, assumptions, ideas, and sense of humor are different from those of the spouse. Statistics show that in Western cultures, 40 to 50 percent of first marriages end in divorce. Subsequent marriages carry an even higher risk of divorce. Common reasons for divorce include lack of commitment, arguing, and unrealistic expectations. The basic issue is learning to live together. Money, job security, family demands, medical issues, politics, and all the difficulties of just getting by day-to-day create a land mine waiting to explode. Yes, spouses love each other—if they don't get too angry or stressed out to remember that they love each other.

Jacob's life with Leah and Rachel, living in Laban's household, is not what he expected. Jacob's partiality—"he loved Rachel more than Leah" (29:30)—plays out in bitter rivalry, a marriage and a household in which everyone is looking out for his or her own needs and dismissing the rest of the family. So much for happily ever after!

Understandings of God

Notice: God isn't mentioned in Genesis 29:15-30. The Scripture is basically a secular story about the messiness of love and marriage that somehow never lives up to expectations. Where does God fit in? Genesis 29:15-30 tells a story within a story within a story. Together with its context, the Scripture offers us different understandings of who God is and how God operates in our lives.

In Genesis 28:10-22, Jacob sees a holy place, where heaven meets earth. God, whose dwelling is in heaven, directs the affairs of human life from a distance, though God may occasionally appear in a vision. The people of God are awed by God's presence and worship God with ritual and gifts.

Another understanding sees God in a relationship with the patriarchs—Abraham, Isaac, Jacob. The relationship is defined by the promises to Abraham, which are carried from one generation to the next. When God meets Jacob at Bethel (Genesis 28:13-14), God reiterates the promise for land and offspring. In Jacob, God will bless all the families of the earth. God adds to the promise: "Know that I am with you and will keep you wherever you go" (28:15). It is a promise for Jacob's journey but also extends throughout the generations: God is with us wherever we go.

A third understanding of God is revealed in Genesis 29:31-34. God is the giver of life, opening wombs and closing them. God promises children. God doesn't perform miracles in the story of Jacob's wives, but keeps the promise, working through the rivalry, superstition, bargaining, bed-hopping, love, hate, ambition of the people involved. Compare Genesis 25 and 27 with Genesis 29:21-30. In chapter 25, Jacob, the younger child, ignores tradition and grabs hold of his brother's birthright. In chapter 27, Jacob deceives his father, Isaac, so as to get the blessing reserved for the firstborn. Yet God chooses Jacob and so disregards human custom to do something new. In chapter 29, God works through Laban's insistence on tradition, giving Jacob two wives and ultimately fulfilling God's promise for children. God works through the deceit, the intrigue, the something-less-than-righteous ambitions of the

people, to fulfill the promises first made to Abraham.

SHARING THE SCRIPTURE

PREPARING TO TEACH

Preparing Our Hearts

Ponder this week's devotional reading from 1 Timothy 1:12-17. Why does the writer, traditionally thought to be Paul, give thanks to Christ? What does the writer say about himself, both before and after he met Christ? What words of praise does he offer to God?

Pray that you and the students will recognize and give thanks for the love and mercy of God that you experience in your life.

Preparing Our Minds

Study the background Scripture from Genesis 28–30 and the lesson Scripture from Genesis 29:15-30.

Consider this question as you prepare the lesson: *How might husbands and wives patiently work through tradition and undesirable circumstances to reach their personal goals?*

Write on newsprint:
- information concerning case studies for Goal 2 in Sharing the Scripture.
- information for next week's lesson, found under Continue the Journey.
- activities for further spiritual growth in Continue the Journey.

Review the Introduction, The Big Picture, Close-up, and Faith in Action, which all precede the first lesson of this quarter. Consider how you might use any of this material in today's

lesson.

Use information from Understanding the Scripture to plan two brief lectures for Goal 1: one to provide background information for Genesis 28:1–29:14 and the other to provide background for Genesis 29:31–30:31. One of these will be given prior to discussion of today's Scripture; the other will wrap up the lesson. You need not include every detail, but try to give the class a broad picture of what happens before and after today's Scripture passage from Genesis 29:15-30.

LEADING THE CLASS

(1) Gather to Learn

❖ Welcome the class members and guests.

❖ Pray that those who have come today will think about the value and the challenges of following traditions.

❖ Read: **Although 90 percent of adults living in the Western world are married by age 50, in the United States a staggering 40 to 50 percent of first marriages end in divorce. That rate is even higher for subsequent marriages.**

❖ Ask: **What do these statistics suggest about the challenges of keeping a long term marriage on track?**

❖ Read aloud today's focus statement: **Marriages can be marred by unforeseen circumstances. How might husbands and wives patiently work through tradition and undesirable circumstances to reach their personal goals? After Laban tricked Jacob into** marrying his older daughter Leah, Jacob willingly agreed to work for seven additional years in order to marry his beloved Rachel.

(2) Goal 1: Examine the Story of Jacob's Love for and Commitment to Marry Rachel

❖ Present the first of the two lectures you have prepared to set the scene for today's story.

❖ Call on a volunteer to read Genesis 29:15-30.

❖ Present the second lecture to help the class members see how the story unfolded.

❖ Discuss these questions:

1. **How would you characterize Laban?** (See "Deception and Conflict" in Interpreting the Scripture.)
2. **How is Jacob like his mother's brother Laban?** (See "Deception and Conflict" in Interpreting the Scripture. Recall that Jacob was the trickster who cheated his brother, Esau, out of his birthright.)
3. **How would you have felt about your father, Laban, had you been Leah? Rachel?**
4. **How would you have felt about Jacob had you been Leah? Rachel?**
5. **What lessons might Jacob have learned from this experience?**
6. **Where do you see God at work in this story?** (See "Understandings of God" in Interpreting the Scripture.)
7. **The marriage customs depicted in this story are quite different from those with which most Americans are familiar. How can you as a Christian discern the timeless principles of** marital relationships from this story—or is it just too different to be of any help to you? Explain your answer.

(3) Goal 2: Reflect Upon Marital Relationships and How Unforeseen Circumstances May or May Not Affect the Strength of the Relationship

❖ Form two groups (or more if the class is large) and assign each group to one of the following case studies. Either read this material aloud or post it on newsprint.

Case 1: Jill and Jake Hill decided it was time to purchase a home. From the minute the decision was made, there was conflict. She wanted a sleek, modern, move-in ready house. He wanted a fixer-upper that they could work on, even though they had no basic knowledge of home renovation. They also disagreed on a budget for the home. The discussions have become so heated that they are almost ready to split. What help could you give this couple to strengthen their relationship and move forward together?

Case 2: Paul and Pam Merson were enjoying a stable life together with their two children when Paul's father died. His mother was recently diagnosed with cancer and could not handle the situation by herself. She was always calling and begging Paul to come to her home, which was 200 miles away from his. The stress was tearing at Paul and Pam's relationship. What course of action might be useful in keeping this marriage together, while also ensuring that Paul's mom was adequately cared for?

(4) Goal 3: Commit to Finding Faith-based Resolution to Difficulties Before Abandoning Relationships

❖ Invite the students to call out situations that have the potential to cause couples to walk away from their marriage. List these ideas on newsprint.

❖ Form several small groups. Ask each group to select one situation and talk about ways in which one's faith in God and one's church could play a role in salvaging this relationship.

❖ Call on one volunteer from each group to state the situation they chose and the ideas they have for resolving the problem.

(5) Continue the Journey

❖ Pray that as the learners depart they will recognize that God can help them maintain a marriage relationship even under difficult circumstances that may—or may not—have been caused by anything either partner did.

❖ Post information for next week's session on newsprint for the students to copy:

- **Title: The Most Beautiful Bride**
- **Background Scripture: Song of Solomon; John 10:1-11**
- **Lesson Scripture: Song of Solomon 6:4-12**
- **Focus of the Lesson: When marriages are grounded in love, adoration can become the lens through which a couple perceives one another. How does one adequately describe what is most likely in the eye of the beholder? The writer of Song of Solomon eloquently describes mutual adoration for the matchless inner and physical beauty of one another.**

❖ Post the following information on newsprint and provide paper and pencils for the students to copy it. Challenge the adults to grow spiritually by completing one or more of these activities related to this week's session.

(1) Do what you can to help repair a broken marriage. If it is your own, consider seeking counseling with your spouse. If it is someone else's, try to lend support without making judgments about the actions or attitudes of either party.

(2) Look around at couples who have been married for several decades. From what you can tell, why are they still married? If they seem to have a happy, successful relationship, what behaviors have promoted this? If they seem unhappy, why do you think they are staying together?

(3) Recall that Laban deceived Jacob, and Jacob had also deceived his brother, Esau. How do you feel when you realize that you have been tricked? What kinds of actions might you take against the deceiver? How can God help you through this situation?

❖ Sing or read aloud "Your Love, O God, Has Called Us Here."

❖ Conclude today's session by leading the class in this benediction, which is adapted from Leviticus 22:31 in the lesson for December 13: **As we go forth, we commit ourselves to keep the commandments of the Lord. Amen.**

UNIT 2: FOUR WEDDINGS AND A FUNERAL
THE MOST BEAUTIFUL BRIDE

PREVIEWING THE LESSON

Lesson Scripture: Song of Solomon 6:4-12
Background Scripture: Song of Solomon; John 10:1-11
Key Verse: Song of Solomon 6:9a

Focus of the Lesson:
When marriages are grounded in love, adoration can become the lens through which a couple perceives one another. How does one adequately describe what is most likely in the eye of the beholder? The writer of Song of Solomon eloquently describes mutual adoration for the matchless inner and physical beauty of one another.

Goals for the Learners:
(1) to explore love and adoration as pictured in the Song of Solomon.
(2) to reflect upon romantic relationships and how to nurture them.
(3) to seek ways to recognize and express appreciation, in appropriate ways, for inner and physical beauty in others.

Supplies:
Bibles, newsprint and marker, paper and pencils, hymnals

READING THE SCRIPTURE

NRSV

Lesson Scripture: Song of Solomon 6:4-12

⁴You are beautiful as Tirzah, my love,
   comely as Jerusalem,
   terrible as an army with banners.
⁵Turn away your eyes from me,
   for they overwhelm me!
Your hair is like a flock of goats,

CEB

Lesson Scripture: Song of Solomon 6:4-12

[Man]
⁴You are as beautiful, my dearest, as Tirzah,
   as lovely as Jerusalem,
   formidable as those lofty sights.
⁵Turn your eyes away from me,
   for they overwhelm me!

moving down the slopes of
Gilead.
⁶Your teeth are like a flock of ewes,
that have come up from the
washing;
all of them bear twins,
and not one among them is
bereaved.
⁷Your cheeks are like halves of a
pomegranate
behind your veil.
⁸There are sixty queens and eighty
concubines,
and maidens without number.
⁹My dove, my perfect one, is the
only one,
the darling of her mother,
flawless to her that bore her.
The maidens saw her and called her
happy;
the queens and concubines also,
and they praised her.
¹⁰"Who is this that looks forth like the
dawn,
fair as the moon, bright as the sun,
terrible as an army with banners?"
¹¹I went down to the nut orchard,
to look at the blossoms of the
valley,
to see whether the vines had budded,
whether the pomegranates were
in bloom.
¹²Before I was aware, my fancy set
me
in a chariot beside my prince.

Your hair is like a flock of goats
as they stream down from Gilead.
⁶Your teeth are like a flock of ewes as
they come up
from the washing pool—
all of them perfectly matched,
not one of them lacks its twin.
⁷Like a slice of pomegranate is the
curve of your face
behind the veil of your hair.
⁸There may be sixty queens
and eighty secondary wives,
young women beyond counting,
⁹but my dove, my perfect one,
is one of a kind.
To her mother she's the only one,
radiant to the one who bore her.
Young women see her and declare
her fortunate;
queens and secondary wives
praise her.
¹⁰Who is this, gazing down like the
morning star,
beautiful as the full moon,
radiant as the sun,
formidable as those lofty sights?
¹¹To the nut grove I went down
to look upon the fresh growth in
the valley,
to see whether the vine was in
flower,
whether the pomegranates had
bloomed.
¹²I hardly knew myself;
she had set me in an official's
chariot!

UNDERSTANDING THE SCRIPTURE

Song of Solomon 1:1. The title of the book attributes it to King Solomon, who was known for both his wisdom and his romantic exploits.

Song of Solomon 1:2-8. The Song of Solomon is poetry, expressing the feelings, desire, fantasy, and hopes of a young man and woman in love. The woman does most of the talking, though the Song is a dialogue between the two. The Hebrew word for love (*dodim*) in verse 2 means physical expressions of love—lovemaking. Much of the Song is about physical attraction and sexual desire. In verses 5-6, the woman describes herself as "black and beautiful" (1:5) as a result of being exposed to the sun (1:6). Verse 6 introduces her brothers, who have tried to keep her secluded. Taking action independently of her brothers, in verse 7 she speaks to the man, proposing a rendezvous, to which he responds.

Song of Solomon 1:9–2:7. Images of royalty (the king on his couch, 1:12) are a recurrent theme. Though some students of Scripture have argued that the Song is a narrative about Solomon and his Egyptian bride, the references to royalty are more likely terms of endearment and playful fantasy. The "daughters of Jerusalem" (1:5) are never identified, but serve primarily as a foil for the woman's reflections. The refrain in 7b ("Do not stir up or awaken love until it is ready!") is often used alone to dissuade sexual activity or young love, but it suggests other meanings (see 3:5; 8:4). Roland Murphy, in his commentary on the Song of Songs (another name for Song of Solomon) writes: "Love has its own laws. . . . Only when it is truly present ('until it is ready') can the participants enjoy it." Love should be genuine and fully enjoyed. Other commentators say that the refrain asks that the lovers not be disturbed until they have had their fill of lovemaking.

Song of Solomon 2:8-17. The woman recalls a visit from her lover, when he appeared at her window and invited her to come away with him, now that the spring was in full bloom. Throughout the Song, images of springtime and the verdant countryside are images of love awakened and fertile. The ditty about the foxes in the vineyard is a bit of sexual

teasing. Possession—"My beloved is mine and I am his" (2:16)—is a recurrent theme. The lovers' desire is to belong to each other, in marriage and in physical union.

Song of Solomon 3:1-5. The woman searches for her lover and finds him. She tells a similar story in 5:2-8. These verses may be descriptions of a dream or a daydream, a fantasy about her longing to be with her absent lover. Loss and discovery or rediscovery, absence and presence, define a love relationship.

Song of Solomon 3:6-11. Out of nowhere comes a procession: Solomon and his entourage crossing the desert. Ordinarily, these verses are understood as a royal wedding procession. Some commentaries suggest they are part of the lovers' fantasy.

Song of Solomon 4:1–5:1. These verses constitute a *wasf*, the Arabic name for a description of a loved one's physical beauty, often from head to toe. The images are intended to represent physical qualities and to evoke a personal response. For example, "your eyes are doves" (4:1) is a commonplace in ancient love poetry, but the image brings to mind a glance and perhaps the flutter of an eyelash. Verse 8 is an invitation; verses 9-11 are a love song. Verses 4:12–5:1 revolve around the garden, an image for the woman herself, which she offers and the man enjoys. Michael V. Fox writes that to "be drunk with love" (verse 5:1b) means "to give oneself over to sexual ecstasy."

Song of Solomon 5:2–6:3. The dream is different from the one in chapter 3. This time the woman, looking for her love, runs into watchmen who strip off her mantle (or "shawl," CEB, 5:7) and beat her. She almost shrugs off the watchmen's abuse and turns to the daughters of Jerusalem, begging their help in finding her beloved. Their questions offer her an opportunity to describe her lover's physical charms. The lover is apparently found (6:2), and the section ends with another statement of possession.

Song of Solomon 6:4-12. The man speaks first, praising his love. Tirzah was, for a time, the capital of the Northern Kingdom of Israel; Jerusalem was the capital of the Southern Kingdom. Why would the youth compare his love to a city and then say that she is "terrible as an army with banners" (6:4)? The phrase has been translated "formidable as those lofty sights" (CEB), "more powerful than all the stars" (CEV), "majestic as troops with banners" (NIV), "awesome with trophies" (Marvin Pope). The woman combines beauty and power, as awesome as a city decked out for victory. Verses 5-7 repeat some compliments of the *wasf* in 4:1-7. The youth concludes that among queens, concubines, maidens, no matter their number, his own love is "my perfect one . . . the only one" (6:9). She is unique, and she belongs to him. Verse 11 shifts the focus from the woman's beauty to the garden, a symbol of love, either an invitation or a remembered rendezvous.

Song of Solomon 6:13–8:4. Verses 7:1-5 are a *wasf*, this time from the feet up; the man praises the woman's beauty and, in verses 6:6-9, expresses his yearning for her. She responds, offering her love. The section ends with the refrain.

Song of Solomon 8:5-14. The woman works out issues with her brothers, asserting her maturity and independence. The man restates his love for the woman. Verses 6-7 sum up the poem's intent: "Love is strong as death." This is not a reference to the destructiveness of death but as Roland E. Murphy states, its "sheer force and relentlessness." "Raging flame" (8:6, NRSV) is also translated "divine flame" (CEB), comparing the intensity of human love to divine love.

John 10:1-11. Jesus is the gate that keeps the flock safe and also opens onto the abundance of life found in salvation: an abundance of life. Jesus is also the good shepherd. The Scripture describes the relationship of love and trust between Christ and the church, believers who recognize his voice and follow. Some interpret the Song of Songs as a love song expressing the relationship between Christ and the church, the good shepherd and his flock. The image of the shepherd pasturing his flocks is seen just prior to today's reading in Song of Solomon 6:2.

INTERPRETING THE SCRIPTURE

Young Love

The Song of Solomon is a poem sung by a young man and woman head over heels in love. The song is sensual, evocative—a bawdy romp through the lush fields of passion. The man speaks to the woman, praising her beauty and her strength. She is like a city turned out in victory. Picture city streets filled with people, markets, skyscraper glass, flashes of light and color. Think of ticker-tape parades, brass bands, old men dancing in the streets, children waving flags—a city in love. Other images are rural: Her hair is like a flock of goats, her teeth like tiny fresh-scrubbed sheep. Pictures capture the woman's winsome beauty and her strength.

Of all the women on earth—no matter how grand or how many—she is the one, "my perfect one," "the only one" (6:9). Could love blossom between the young man and another woman? Probably. But love is in some sense a choice; it is saying, "You are the one." It also involves a sense of ownership. "My beloved is mine and I am his," says the woman in Song of Solomon 2:16. Here in chapter 6 the man claims her as his own.

Like other passages in the song, verses 11 and 12 hint at sexual activity. References to natural abundance—blossoming valleys, budding vines, fruit in season—are symbols of fertility and sexual awakening. The relationship between the man and woman is passionate and physical; they choose each other and become one. The themes in the Scripture are themes of young love: adoration, belonging, possession, sexuality, passion. Song of Solomon is a love song.

Love Songs

Sing "One Hand, One Heart" from *West Side Story* or "Some Enchanted Evening" from *South Pacific*. The Song of Solomon is a lot like a Hollywood love song. Lovers see each other singled out in a crowd. They exchange a glance, a word. They fall in love, and the whole world seems to come alive. Generations have not changed the sweetness of love's first song.

At the same time, Hollywood love stories are not quite real; and neither is the Song of Solomon. It could have been written as entertainment, plain and simple.

Though true love may begin at first sight and blossom into the state where "I only have eyes for you," sooner or later, lovers face the realities of day-to-day life. They have bills to pay, an apartment to clean, food to fix, deadlines to meet. Love that begins with a romp in the hay or the back seat of a car may well produce children with diapers, runny noses, schoolwork, and soccer games. As we get older, the enthusiasm of new love wanes. We see each other's faults. We get angry. Respect dwindles. How do we continue to adore each other when, after thirty-five years, the children leave home; we retire from busy jobs; and suddenly across a crowded kitchen table, we see a stranger with gray hair and wrinkles?

Perhaps the Song of Solomon is a reminder that through it all, old married people are still one body, chosen and consummated. Love matures. We make commitments. We learn to live together. We get to know each other. We have a history—rich and poor, sickness and health. The Song is a reminder that we can still be tender with each other. Perhaps we will discover new love songs or we can sing the song "Do You Love Me?" from *Fiddler on the Roof*: "Twenty-five years my bed is his. If that's not love, what is?"

The Wisdom of God

Some readers question why the Song of Solomon is in the Bible. After all, the Song seems to be a pretty secular enterprise. The young man and woman are not married, though they would like to be. They are not following typically religious rules of behavior. The Song is about young people in love, discovering their sexuality. They express their feelings, desires, fantasies, whims. They lay claim to each other. Why is a book of love poetry in the Bible?

The Song of Solomon has been interpreted in a variety of ways. Jewish tradition has seen the Song in terms of the covenantal history between God and God's chosen people. Christians have tended toward an allegorical understanding of the relationship between Christ and the church or between God and the individual's soul. Students of Scripture have seen in the Song a romantic narrative or drama, a wedding liturgy, an anthology of ancient love poems. Some commentators have looked at the Song as love poetry without allegorical or spiritual meaning—though they are apt to tag on a note about God and God's love. Though the Song of Solomon is clearly love poetry, to see it as simply a secular book about human sexuality is not fair to the tradition of interpretation.

The first verse states the title of the book: "The Song of Songs, which is Solomon's." Attributed to King Solomon, the song is part of Jewish Wisdom Literature, which also includes Job, Proverbs, and Ecclesiastes. The Hebrew understanding of wisdom includes book learning, yes; but wisdom is also skill; common sense; the ability to navigate a business deal, a social engagement, the complexities and the courtesies of daily life. Wisdom is morality, living in ways that are both right and righteous, synchronized with the righteousness of God. Wisdom Literature understands that God made the world—not only nature but also the human community. God designed the ways we live together so that God's purposes are ultimately fulfilled. Wisdom is the ability to discern God's reasoning, which moves human life along.

At first glance, the Song of Solomon does not fit in. Young love is anything but common sense. Lovers caught up in a passionate embrace seldom discuss the vast purposes of God. On the other hand, God designed human life, including human sexuality. So love's embrace is part of God's plan for creation. Awakening love is as much a part of creation as spring's bloom; the intensity of hormonal urges is part of God's design for human life. God created humanity, male and female, and blessed them saying, "Be fruitful and multiply and fill the earth" (Genesis 1:28). Human sexuality, like all of God's good creation, serves God's purposes. "Love," says Song of Solomon 8:6, "is strong as death. . . . Its flashes are flashes of fire, a raging flame." Love—in all its variations—moves creation toward fulfillment in the love of God. Love pursues us, fills us with desire, leads us to physical union. "They become one flesh" (Genesis 2:24). Perhaps the commandment that reflects God's blessing at creation is in Song of Solomon 5:1: "Eat, friends, drink, and be drunk with love." Love poetry is included in Scripture because it is part of human life and essential to God's purposes.

SHARING THE SCRIPTURE

PREPARING TO TEACH

Preparing Our Hearts

Ponder this week's devotional reading from John 10:7-15. In this passage, Jesus tells his listeners that he is "the gate" (10:9) and "the good shepherd" (10:11). What actions does the shepherd take to care for the sheep? How is the shepherd different from the hired hand? How would you describe the relationship between the good shepherd and the sheep?

Pray that you and the students will seek the care of the good shepherd and attune your ears to hear his voice.

Preparing Our Minds

Study the background Scripture from Song of Solomon and John 10:1-11. The lesson Scripture is from Song of Solomon 6:4-12.

Consider this question as you prepare the lesson: *How does one adequately describe what is most likely in the eye of the beholder?*

Write on newsprint:
❏ information for next week's lesson, found under Continue the Journey.
❏ activities for further spiritual growth in Continue the Journey.

Review the Introduction, The Big Picture, Close-up, and Faith in Action, which all precede the first lesson of this quarter. Consider how you might use any of this material in today's lesson.

Select key points from Understanding the Scripture for Song of Solomon 1:1–8:4 to introduce the lesson.

Caution: This lesson may cause real discomfort for some class members. Be aware of people who have never been in a significant relationship or whose partner is now permanently separated from them due to divorce or death. Feelings of loss, emptiness, loneliness, and even anger may emerge. Also recognize that those who do not consider themselves physically attractive may have negative feelings about this love poem.

LEADING THE CLASS

(1) Gather to Learn

❖ Welcome the class members and guests.
❖ Pray that those who have come today will be aware of the beauty in others.
❖ Invite class members to call out names of popular love songs. They may even want to sing a few lines. (Several songs are mentioned in "Love Songs" in Interpreting the Scripture.)
❖ Ask: **How is romantic love often portrayed in these popular songs?**
❖ Read aloud today's focus statement: **When marriages are grounded in love, adoration can become the lens through which a couple perceives one another. How does one adequately describe what is most likely in the eye of the beholder? The writer of Song of Solomon eloquently describes mutual adoration for the matchless inner and physical beauty of one another.**

(2) Goal 1: Explore Love and Adoration as Pictured in the Song of Solomon

❖ Introduce the Song of Solomon by selecting several key points from Understanding the Scripture to enable class members to recognize the purpose and main features of this poem.

❖ Select a volunteer to read today's lesson from Song of Solomon 6:4-12.

❖ Ask these questions:

1. **What are some of the descriptive words or phrases that the poet uses?**
2. **What kinds of words or phrases do you think a young American woman would prefer to hear?**
3. **How realistic do you think the writer's descriptions of beauty and love are, especially over the long haul of life?** (See "Young Love" in Interpreting the Scripture.)
4. **How do you think this love poem filled with sexual imagery fits into the Bible story?** (Read "The Wisdom of God" in Interpreting the Scripture to discern how Jewish and Christian commentators relate this poem to the wisdom of God. Invite comments concerning these understandings.)

(3) Goal 2: Reflect Upon Romantic Relationships and How to Nurture Them

❖ Read again these words from last week's lesson: **Statistics show that in Western cultures, 40 to 50 percent of first marriages end in divorce. Subsequent marriages carry an even higher risk of divorce.**

❖ Ask: **Why are romantic relationships so difficult to sustain?** You may wish to list ideas on newsprint.

❖ Look at the list and try to help the adults discern some underlying causes. For example, are spouses' expectations of each other so unrealistic that no one could ever live up to them? Have one or both members of the couple not yet learned how to live within their means? Have the diverse upbringings of the couple caused them to see child-rearing practices from different vantage points? Are the individual goals of the spouses so at odds with one another that reasonable compromise cannot be reached? Do the two parties have different ways of handling conflict?

❖ Invite group members to suggest ways that some of these underlying causes could be addressed so that a couple can nurture their relationship rather than destroy it.

❖ **Option:** If the class includes couples who have been happily married over several decades, encourage them to identify strategies they have used to nurture their relationship through the years.

(4) Goal 3: Seek Ways to Recognize and Express Appreciation, in Appropriate Ways, for Inner and Physical Beauty in Others

❖ Note that although our lesson has focused on physical beauty, we can recognize and appreciate inner as well as physical beauty in others. Read these words of Ralph Waldo Emerson (1803–82): **Beauty is God's handwriting—a wayside sacrament. Welcome it in every fair face, in every fair sky, in every fair flower, and thank God for it as a cup of blessings.**

❖ Distribute paper and pencils and form small groups. Set a time limit (perhaps three minutes). Tell the groups to write down as many ideas as they can for appropriately expressing thanks for physical and inner beauty in others. Have each group read their list. If you want to make this into a game, declare the group with the most ideas to be the winner.

(5) Continue the Journey

❖ Pray that as the learners depart they will see and appreciate beauty around them, particularly the beauty of a special person in their lives.

❖ Post information for next week's session on newsprint for the students to copy:

- **Title: An Unfaithful Bride**
- **Background Scripture: Hosea 1–3**
- **Lesson Scripture: Hosea 1**
- **Focus of the Lesson: Unfaithfulness in covenant relationships leads to brokenness and alienation. How can brokenness and alienation be remedied? God uses Hosea and Gomer's marriage and the naming of their children as symbolic of Israel's alienation from God and God's plan for restoration.**

❖ Post the following information on newsprint and provide paper and pencils for the students to copy it. Challenge the adults to grow spiritually by completing one or more of these activities related to this week's session.

(1) **Speak words of adoration to your significant other. Let this person know how much you love him or her.**

(2) **Praise God for the beauty that you see around you—in a person, nature, or any of God's creation.**

(3) **Enter into a mentoring relationship. If you are a younger adult who wants to create a successful marriage, see if a married couple that has lived happily together for decades will share their "secrets" for a solid marriage. If you are an older adult who enjoyed a good relationship (even if your spouse is now deceased), be willing to help a younger couple get on the right track.**

❖ Sing or read aloud "Jesus, Joy of Our Desiring."

❖ Conclude today's session by leading the class in this benediction, which is adapted from Leviticus 22:31 in the lesson for December 13: **As we go forth, we commit ourselves to keep the commandments of the Lord. Amen.**

UNIT 2: FOUR WEDDINGS AND A FUNERAL
AN UNFAITHFUL BRIDE

PREVIEWING THE LESSON

Lesson Scripture: Hosea 1
Background Scripture: Hosea 1–3
Key Verse: Hosea 1:2

Focus of the Lesson:
Unfaithfulness in covenant relationships leads to brokenness and alienation. How can brokenness and alienation be remedied? God uses Hosea and Gomer's marriage and the naming of their children as symbolic of Israel's alienation from God and God's plan for restoration.

Goals for the Learners:
(1) to learn how God commanded Hosea to marry an unfaithful Gomer as a model for God's love for Israel despite the people's unfaithfulness.
(2) to reflect on the meaning of marriage and unfaithfulness and God's desire for the restoration of broken relationships.
(3) to demonstrate faithfulness to God through a commitment to maintain faithful friendships, relationships, and/or marriages.

Supplies:
Bibles, newsprint and marker, paper and pencils, hymnals

READING THE SCRIPTURE

NRSV
Lesson Scripture: Hosea 1

¹The word of the Lord that came to Hosea son of Beeri, in the days of Kings Uzziah, Jotham, Ahaz, and Hezekiah of Judah, and in the days of King Jeroboam son of Joash of Israel.

²When the LORD first spoke through Hosea, **the LORD said to Hosea, "Go, take for yourself a wife of whoredom and have children of**

CEB
Lesson Scripture: Hosea 1

¹The LORD's word that came to Hosea, Beeri's son, in the days of Judah's Kings Uzziah, Jotham, Ahaz, and Hezekiah, and in the days of Israel's King Jeroboam, Joash's son.

²When the LORD first spoke through Hosea, **the Lord said to him, "Go, marry a prostitute and have children of prostitution, for the people of the**

whoredom, for the land commits great whoredom by forsaking the Lord." ³So he went and took Gomer daughter of Diblaim, and she conceived and bore him a son.

⁴And the LORD said to him, "Name him Jezreel; for in a little while I will punish the house of Jehu for the blood of Jezreel, and I will put an end to the kingdom of the house of Israel. ⁵On that day I will break the bow of Israel in the valley of Jezreel."

⁶She conceived again and bore a daughter. Then the LORD said to him, "Name her Lo-ruhamah, for I will no longer have pity on the house of Israel or forgive them. ⁷But I will have pity on the house of Judah, and I will save them by the Lord their God; I will not save them by bow, or by sword, or by war, or by horses, or by horsemen."

⁸When she had weaned Lo-ruhamah, she conceived and bore a son. ⁹Then the LORD said, "Name him Lo-ammi, for you are not my people and I am not your God."

¹⁰Yet the number of the people of Israel shall be like the sand of the sea, which can be neither measured nor numbered; and in the place where it was said to them, "You are not my people," it shall be said to them, "Children of the living God." ¹¹The people of Judah and the people of Israel shall be gathered together, and they shall appoint for themselves one head; and they shall take possession of the land, for great shall be the day of Jezreel.

land commit great prostitution by deserting the LORD." ³So Hosea went and took Gomer, Diblaim's daughter, and she became pregnant and bore him a son. ⁴The LORD said to him, "Name him Jezreel; for in a little while I will punish the house of Jehu for the blood of Jezreel, and I will destroy the kingdom of the house of Israel. ⁵On that day I will break the bow of Israel in the Jezreel Valley." ⁶Gomer became pregnant again and gave birth to a daughter. Then the LORD said to Hosea, "Name her No Compassion, because I will no longer have compassion on the house of Israel or forgive them. ⁷But I will have compassion on the house of Judah. I, the LORD their God, will save them; I will not save them by bow, or by sword, or by war, or by horses, or by horsemen." ⁸When Gomer finished nursing No Compassion, she became pregnant and gave birth to a son. ⁹Then the LORD said, "Name him Not My People because you are not my people, and I am not your God."

¹⁰Yet the number of the people of Israel will be like the sand of the sea, which can be neither measured nor numbered; and in the place where it was said to them, "You are not my people," it will be said to them, "Children of the living God." ¹¹The people of Judah and the people of Israel will be gathered together, and they will choose one head. They will become fruitful in the land. The day will be a wonderful one for Jezreel.

UNDERSTANDING THE SCRIPTURE

Hosea 1:1. Hosea speaks and lives God's word as it comes to him. Prophecy is God's word for a particular people in a particular time and place. Hosea delivers God's message to Israel, beginning when Jeroboam II was king of the Northern Kingdom (786–746 B.C.). The reign of Jeroboam II was prosperous (though the gulf between rich and poor was wide) and relatively quiet. But Assyria was gathering its forces along Israel's borders, ready to attack and to send the people into exile. Hosea spoke against Israel's political and religious apostasy.

Hosea 1:2-9. The Scripture tells about Hosea's marriage to Gomer and the birth or their children. God commands Hosea, "Go, take for yourself a wife of whoredom and have children of whoredom, for the land commits great whoredom by forsaking the LORD" (1:2). Students of Scripture argue variously that Hosea's family was only a symbol, or that he did in fact marry a promiscuous woman or a woman who later committed adultery, or that he married a woman involved in the local Canaanite fertility cult. Whatever the actual situation, Hosea's marriage is interpreted as a symbolic action. He marries a "wife of whoredom" because Israel is promiscuous, forsaking the Lord to worship other gods. Hosea's marriage is an image for the relationship between God and Israel. Gomer's adultery is Israel's idolatry.

The names of the three children carry God's message to the people. The first is Jezreel. The message is directed to Jeroboam II, threatening his rule and the rule of future kings in Israel. The line of Jehu (Jeroboam's great-grandfather) began with a bloodbath. God anointed Jehu king and sent him to destroy King Ahab's line and family (2 Kings 9–10). Ahab had done "evil in the sight of the LORD" (1 Kings 16:30), particularly by introducing to Israel the worship of Baal and making it an official religion,

side by side with the worship of God. As the line of Ahab ended at God's command, so would the line of Jehu—and for the same reasons.

Gomer's second child is a girl named Lo-ruhamah, which means "Not Pitied" or "No Mercy." This name signifies that God will not have mercy on the Northern Kingdom of Israel (1:6) when it is attacked by Assyria. According to verse 7, God will save the Southern Kingdom of Judah, which did in fact escape from destruction by the Assyrians when Israel was destroyed in 722 B.C.

Gomer's third child is Lo-Ammi, "Not My People." Israel has chosen to be people of other gods. Yahweh's final word, "You are not my people and I am not your God" (1:9) reverses the words of God's covenant with Israel (Exodus 6:7). The Hebrew translated "your God" is "Ehyeh," the name of God revealed to Moses in Exodus 3:14, a name the Israelites would recognize and accept. Hans Wolff, in his commentary on Hosea, translates the phrase, "And I—I-Am-Not-There for you."

The threats in Hosea 1:1-9 are more and more severe. The monarchy will end. God will have no mercy on Israel. The covenant is broken. Verse 9 should be the end of the story.

Hosea 1:10–2:1. Hosea is grounded in the promises to the patriarchs, the Exodus, the covenant at Sinai. Whether or not the people return to God—and they show no signs of doing so—God is faithful. Hosea 1:10-11 recalls God's promises to Abraham for children and land (Genesis 12:1-9). On "the day of Jezreel" (1:11) God will act decisively to renew both land and people. The people will be as many as "the sand of the sea" (1:10; see also Genesis 15:5). Once they were "not my people"; now they are "children of the living God." Standing outside the mercy of God, they are as good as dead; but in God's embrace, they find new life. The people of God, the divided kingdom, will be united under one ruler. This restoration is seen in the children's names: "Ammi" means "My People" and "Ruhamah" means "Pitied." The verse may also be the beginning of a call to respond to the covenant. In God's love, we are all brothers and sisters.

Hosea 2:2-13. Gomer's response to her family in verse 5 is Israel's response: "I will go after my lovers; they will give me my bread and my water; my wool and my flax." Although the Israelites gave lip service to Yahweh, the God of their ancestors, they worshiped other gods. In the cult of Baal, sexual activity was thought to ensure fertility for the community and the land. Baal provided the basic necessities of life: bread, water, oil, clothing, children. The threats outlined in chapter 2 take away the necessities. God's hope is that without them, the Israelites will see that Yahweh, not Baal, provides for them and they will return to the Lord. But Israel rejects the covenant relationship with Yahweh. Verse 13 ends in despair: "'Me she forgot,' declares the LORD" (NIV).

Hosea 2:14-23. When all is lost and Israel shows no sign of repentance, God acts. Hosea 2:14-23 recalls Israel's election, the Exodus, their wandering in the wilderness, and their entering the Promised Land. God will start again, walking the people through their history and teaching them to be God's people. Verses 16-23 describe a new covenant as a marriage between God and Israel. "Baal" in verse 16 has a double meaning: both "my master" and the name of the Canaanite god. The people will no longer confuse an idol with God, and their relationship with God will be more intimate—they will know the Lord. God reverses the threats made in verses 2-13, promising to provide in abundance and to keep Israel secure. The image expands to include heaven and earth in a celebration of the marriage of God and God's renewed people.

Hosea 3:1-5. Chapter 3 begins with a command. "Go, love a woman who has a lover and is an adulteress, just as the Lord loves the people of Israel, though they turn to other gods." Hosea buys back his wife (the Scripture does not explain why or from whom) and keeps her as his own. She can no longer "play the whore" (3:3). In the same way, Israel will have no king and no idols, but only the Lord God; and they will stand in awe of God's goodness.

INTERPRETING THE SCRIPTURE

Idolatry

The *Ladies' Home Journal* includes a column called "Can This Marriage Be Saved?" This column suggests that we have a commitment to marriage and want our relationships to be strong. It offers advice for couples trying to work through troubled marriages by drawing on psychology, conflict resolution, and communication therapy to help couples change from "bickering couples into loving teams."

We tend to stuff our lives into

compartments, each of which has its own authorities and philosophical underpinnings. For example, we turn to psychology to build solid relationships. Concerned about money, we look to financial advisors and market analysis. Medical arts, practiced by doctors, dieticians, and physical trainers, provide for our physical well-being and may even keep death at bay. Consider the variety of compartments in our lives, all with their own rules, their own authorities, and sometimes their own shrines.

Unfortunately, for many people, God resides in a compartment too. We name it "spirituality," "church," "religion," "Bible." The rules include the Ten Commandments and a smattering of theology. Instead of permeating our entire selves and all of our lives, God is stuffed into a compartment and brought out as occasions seem to demand. When we fail to make God the center of our lives and trust God in all situations, we commit idolatry.

Idolatry is not a recent invention. Hosea speaks to Israel's idolatry. The Israelites' lives, like ours, were divided into compartments. For food, water, clothing, and fields ripe to harvest, as well as for productive marriages, they looked to Baal. For national security, they looked to political alliances and the military might of neighboring nations. Yahweh was the God of their ancestors—Abraham, Isaac, Jacob—the God of history, time past. Israel relied on the tradition of God's love; but for day-to-day needs, they looked elsewhere. We are a lot like Israel. Consequently, God's word, spoken by Hosea, is for us.

Hosea, Gomer, and the Kids

God commanded Hosea: "Go, take for yourself a wife of whoredom and have children of whoredom, for the land commits great whoredom by forsaking the LORD" (1:2). Hosea chose Gomer; and whether or not she was promiscuous at first, she became an adulterous woman. Hosea watched, helpless, as his marriage fell apart. He tried everything; but finally he had to admit, "She is not my wife, and I am not her husband" (2:2). Marriage vows were broken. Nothing was left for Hosea but anger, alienation, bitter longing as Gomer, with a backward glance, walked away, decked out and looking for lovers.

The marriage of Hosea and Gomer is an image for the relationship between God and Israel. God chose Israel and made her God's own people. Before promises could be kept or a land settled, Israel lusted after other gods. The people broke their marriage vows ("You shall have no other gods before me," Exodus 20:3). As soon as they said "I do," they turned their backs on God, not trusting God to provide, and danced around a golden calf (Exodus 32). The history of Israel's idolatry is long. Right from the start, Israel was a "wife of whoredom" (Hosea 1:2). We can imagine God, like Hosea, watching God's people walk away.

God's word was spoken to Israel in the names of Hosea's children. The first child was Jezreel. God would end the monarchy, the rule of Jeroboam II, as God had ended the previous line of kings. Jezreel was a catchword, reminding Israel that God had destroyed the house of Ahab, his line and his family, because he had established the cult of Baal as an official religion in Israel. He had built shrines and allowed the people to worship God and Baal side by side. Ahab met a bloody death. God's word for Israel was "Jezreel." Like Ahab, the kings in the line of Jehu allowed the people to worship Baal side by side with Yahweh. Like Ahab, they would meet a bloody end.

The second child's name was "Not-Pitied." Though God's nature is love, mercy, and forgiveness, God would no longer have mercy on Israel. When the armies of Assyria lined up on the borders of Israel and Judah, when they bore down on the land and scattered the people, God would have no mercy. God would allow Assyria to destroy God's people.

We tend to think that we are secure in God's love. After all, no matter who we are or what we have done, God loves us. We can throw ourselves on the mercy of God, and God will forgive. In much the same way, Israel was sure of God's love. They were God's chosen people. They were prosperous and at peace—sure signs of God's favor. How would they have responded to God's word "Not-Pitied"? Maybe they would brush off the prophecy and keep walking, unafraid, sure that God would protect them.

The third child's name was "Not-My-People." God's word reversed God's election and the covenant established at Mount Sinai. Israel had gone too far for too long. Israel had chosen not to be God's people and had refused to return. The first two names threatened the monarchy and the nation. They were meant to urge Israel's repentance. But "Not-My People" signaled the end of the relationship between God and Israel. Like Hosea's marriage, the covenant between God and Israel was over, with no second chances, no possibilities of return.

New Beginnings

One of the theological issues that divides us involves interpretations of sin and salvation. Some people say that God saves us only when we repent, turn away from evil, and return to the Lord. We come confessing our sins and accept God's forgiveness. Then our relationship with God is restored. Other people say that we are not able to repent. We sin and sin and sin, without a second glance at God. We are so corrupt that we cannot return to God. But in God's grace, we are forgiven. God loves us and gathers us up in God's embrace, no matter what we do. Repentance is an act of gratitude not a condition of salvation.

Of these two interpretations, Hosea stands in the second camp. Only when all is lost and the covenant is irreparably broken does the light of salvation shine on Israel. The people refuse to repent, seeming to enjoy their apostasy. God announces, "You are not my people" (1:9). Then everything becomes new. God remembers the promises to Abraham for land and for children and makes new promises. The people of God will be as numerous as the sands of the sea, and they will become the children of the living God. God will gather them up and make them one people, and God will give them the land. In the ancient promises, Hosea finds hope. The names of the children are reversed. Jezreel, once a day of bloody destruction, will be a day of rejoicing and new life. "Not-Pitied" will be "Pitied" and "Not My People" will be "My People." Israel has not changed, but God is good. In Hosea 2:1 is the hint of repentance. In a new relationship with God, the people can begin to be new people, seeing one another as brothers and sisters in the Lord.

Question: Can this marriage be saved? Answer: Only by the grace of God.

SHARING THE SCRIPTURE

PREPARING TO TEACH

Preparing Our Hearts

Ponder this week's devotional reading from Psalm 89:24-29, which concerns God's covenant with David. What promises does God make to David in these verses? As you think about Israel's history with God, where do you see these promises being fulfilled?

Pray that you and the students will maintain a strong, unbroken relationship with God through Jesus Christ.

Preparing Our Minds

Study the background Scripture from Hosea 1–3 and the lesson Scripture from Hosea 1.

Consider this question as you prepare the lesson: *How can brokenness and alienation be remedied?*

Write on newsprint:
- ❏ questions for Goal 3 in Sharing the Scripture.
- ❏ information for next week's lesson, found under Continue the Journey.
- ❏ activities for further spiritual growth in Continue the Journey.

Review the Introduction, The Big Picture, Close-up, and Faith in Action, which all precede the first lesson of this quarter. Consider how you might use any of this material in today's lesson.

Option: Invite a family therapist or marriage counselor or pastoral counselor to talk with the class during the Goal 2 segment of Sharing the Scripture. Determine in advance the amount of time you expect to have. Be clear about any financial arrangements before the person arrives.

LEADING THE CLASS

(1) Gather to Learn

❖ Welcome the class members and guests.

❖ Pray that those who have come today will repent of broken relationships and work toward reconciliation.

❖ Introduce today's lesson by reading "Idolatry" from Interpreting the Scripture. Encourage participants to comment on how we twenty-first-century Christians can be as unfaithful to our relationship with God as the Israelites were by idolizing things, people, and ideas other than God alone.

❖ Read aloud today's focus statement: **Unfaithfulness in covenant relationships leads to brokenness and alienation. How can brokenness and alienation be remedied? God uses Hosea and Gomer's marriage and the naming of their children as symbolic of Israel's alienation from God and God's plan for restoration.**

(2) Goal 1: Learn How God Commanded Hosea to Marry Unfaithful Gomer as a Model for God's Love for Israel Despite the People's Unfaithfulness

❖ Read or retell Hosea 1:1 from Understanding the Scripture to give the class a context for today's reading.

❖ Choose a volunteer to read Hosea 1.

❖ Discuss these questions:
1. **How does Hosea 1:2-9 describe the broken relationship**

between Israel and God, who had been forsaken by Israel? (See Hosea 1:2-9 in Understanding the Scripture to clarify the severity of the breach in this relationship.)

2. How is the broken relationship between Israel and God demonstrated in the marriage of Hosea and Gomer and in the naming of their children? (Read or retell "Hosea, Gomer, and the Kids" from Interpreting the Scripture.)

3. Does the prophet have any good news from God? If so, what is it? (See Hosea 1:10-11. Also see "New Beginnings" in Interpreting the Scripture.)

❖ Invite several volunteers to sit together at the front of the room and debate this statement: **Adultery is an apt metaphor for spiritual unfaithfulness to God.**

(3) Goal 2: Reflect on the Meaning of Marriage and Unfaithfulness and God's Desire for the Restoration of Broken Relationship

❖ Reflect on the meaning of marriage by discussing these questions:

1. In a society where many people prefer to live together rather than enter into marriage, why do other people decide that they will commit themselves to marriage?

2. What kinds of commitments do both the man and woman make when they enter into marriage in the church? (You may wish to check your denomination's marriage vows, but most services ask the two parties to pledge themselves to one another "for better, for worse,

for richer, for poorer, in sickness and in health, to love and to cherish, until we are parted by death.")

3. What are some of the causes of a marital break-up, which statistics show occurs in 40 to 50 percent of first marriages in Western societies?

4. Although break-ups likely involve the violation of one or more vows, often the cause is that one person has "found someone new," someone "who will better meet my needs." How does unfaithfulness in the marriage affect not only the partner who has been cheated on but other people as well?

❖ **Option:** Invite a person who is professionally involved in helping spouses work through broken relationships to talk with the class about how such relationships can be healed if the couple is willing to work together.

(4) Goal 3: Demonstrate Faithfulness to God Through a Commitment to Maintain Faithful Friendships, Relationships, and/or Marriages

❖ Distribute paper and pencils. Invite the participants to write the name of someone with whom they once had a close relationship but from whom they are now alienated. Suggest that they answer these questions, which you will post on newsprint. Note that the adults will not be asked to share any of their confidential information.

1. What happened to cause this rupture in the relationship?

2. What can you do now to try to recommit yourself to this relationship?

3. **What first step will you take to repair the relationship, regardless of whomever was at fault for causing the breakdown?**

❖ Bring the group together. Without disclosing the details of what they have written, invite volunteers to talk about how difficult or easy this assignment was. In other words, could they think of steps they could take to forgive and move on? What obstacles stood in the way of their making such a commitment?

(5) Continue the Journey

❖ Pray that as the learners depart they will do all in their power to restore broken relationships.

❖ Post information for next week's session on newsprint for the students to copy:

- **Title: A Wedding in Cana**
- **Background Scripture: John 2:1-12**
- **Lesson Scripture: John 2:1-12**
- **Focus of the Lesson: A hospitality tradition requires that the bride and groom make sure there is adequate food and beverage for invited wedding guests. How can the bride and groom accommodate their guests when there is a shortage? As an invited guest at the wedding in Cana, Jesus performed his first miracle when the wine ran out by turning ordinary** water into a wine unsurpassed in its quality, revealing his glory and causing his disciples to believe.

❖ Post the following information on newsprint and provide paper and pencils for the students to copy it. Challenge the adults to grow spiritually by completing one or more of these activities related to this week's session.

(1) **Support someone whose marriage is failing. Refrain from offering advice, but be willing to listen without making judgments and let the person know that you are praying for God to guide him or her.**

(2) **Research the prophet Hosea and the political and social circumstances in Israel during the mid-eighth century** B.C. **How does this information help you better understand the rupture in the relationship between Israel and God?**

(3) **Pray that God will lead you to find ways to restore a broken relationship in your own life.**

❖ Sing or read aloud "When Love Is Found."

❖ Conclude today's session by leading the class in this benediction, which is adapted from Leviticus 22:31 in the lesson for December 13: **As we go forth, we commit ourselves to keep the commandments of the Lord. Amen.**

UNIT 2: FOUR WEDDINGS AND A FUNERAL
A WEDDING IN CANA

PREVIEWING THE LESSON

Lesson Scripture: John 2:1-12
Background Scripture: John 2:1-12
Key Verse: John 2:10

Focus of the Lesson:

A hospitality tradition requires that the bride and groom make sure there is adequate food and beverage for invited wedding guests. How can the bride and groom accommodate their guests when there is a shortage? As an invited guest at the wedding in Cana, Jesus performed his first miracle when the wine ran out by turning ordinary water into a wine unsurpassed in its quality, revealing his glory and causing his disciples to believe.

Goals for the Learners:

(1) to understand that Jesus performed his first miracle in the lives of ordinary people when he met an important hospitality need at a wedding.
(2) to reflect on the meaning and practice of hospitality.
(3) to identify ways to demonstrate hospitality at weddings and other occasions.

Supplies:

Bibles, newsprint and marker, paper and pencils, hymnals, tape

READING THE SCRIPTURE

NRSV

Lesson Scripture: John 2:1-12

¹On the third day there was a wedding in Cana of Galilee, and the mother of Jesus was there. ²Jesus and his disciples had also been invited to the wedding. ³When the wine gave out, the mother of Jesus said to him, "They have no wine." ⁴And Jesus said to her, "Woman, what concern

CEB

Lesson Scripture: John 2:1-12

¹On the third day there was a wedding in Cana of Galilee. Jesus' mother was there, and ²Jesus and his disciples were also invited to the celebration. ³When the wine ran out, Jesus' mother said to him, "They don't have any wine."

⁴Jesus replied, "Woman, what does

is that to you and to me? My hour has not yet come." [5]His mother said to the servants, "Do whatever he tells you." [6]Now standing there were six stone water jars for the Jewish rites of purification, each holding twenty or thirty gallons. [7]Jesus said to them, "Fill the jars with water." And they filled them up to the brim. [8]He said to them, "Now draw some out, and take it to the chief steward." So they took it. [9]When the steward tasted the water that had become wine, and did not know where it came from (though the servants who had drawn the water knew), the steward called the bridegroom [10]and said to him, **"Everyone serves the good wine first, and then the inferior wine after the guests have become drunk. But you have kept the good wine until now."** [11]Jesus did this, the first of his signs, in Cana of Galilee, and revealed his glory; and his disciples believed in him.

[12]After this he went down to Capernaum with his mother, his brothers, and his disciples; and they remained there a few days.

that have to do with me? My time hasn't come yet."

[5]His mother told the servants, "Do whatever he tells you." [6]Nearby were six stone water jars used for the Jewish cleansing ritual, each able to hold about twenty or thirty gallons.

[7]Jesus said to the servants, "Fill the jars with water," and they filled them to the brim. [8]Then he told them, "Now draw some from them and take it to the headwaiter," and they did. [9]The headwaiter tasted the water that had become wine. He didn't know where it came from, though the servants who had drawn the water knew.

The headwaiter called the groom [10]and said, **"Everyone serves the good wine first. They bring out the second-rate wine only when the guests are drinking freely. You kept the good wine until now."** [11]This was the first miraculous sign that Jesus did in Cana of Galilee. He revealed his glory, and his disciples believed in him.

[12]After this, Jesus and his mother, his brothers, and his disciples went down to Capernaum and stayed there for a few days.

UNDERSTANDING THE SCRIPTURE

Introduction. The Gospel of John is filled with symbolism and layered with meaning. The wedding at Cana is a story about Jesus at a wedding feast, but it also reveals who Jesus is and what God promises to those who believe.

John 2:1-2. These two verses provide the setting and characters of a story that takes place at a wedding. Jesus' mother is there, as are Jesus and his disciples. Jesus, who is often referred to as the "bridegroom" (see,

for example, John 3:29) is an invited guest. "On the third day" may have symbolic meaning. Some students of Scripture tally up the days in chapter 1, in which Jesus is baptized and calls his first disciples. By the time of the wedding, the days total seven, which may refer to the week of creation. Here, "the third day" is understood as three days after the day cited in verse 43, which itself is last in a sequence of "next days" (1:29, 35, 43). Other commentators suggest that "the third day" calls to mind the resurrection. Either could be a reference to the new creation inaugurated by Christ's death, resurrection, and ascension. The wedding feast, in both Old and New Testaments, is a symbol for the messianic banquet, an image of the coming new age. (See, for example, the great feast in Isaiah 25:6-10 or the story of the banquet in Matthew 22:1-14, which begins, "The kingdom of heaven may be compared to a king who gave a wedding banquet for his son.") Marriage also serves as a metaphor for the new relationship between God and God's people (Hosea 2:16-23). The Gospel of John is concerned not only with the coming new age at Christ's resurrection, but especially with the person of Jesus Christ, who embodies both divine and human, the marriage of God and human.

John 2:3-5. The wine runs short. Hospitality would require the couple to provide for their guests. Mary tells Jesus the problem. For Jesus to call Mary "Woman" seems disrespectful to us. (Note, though, that the only other time Mary appears in the Gospel of John is at the cross, and Jesus addresses her in the same way, John 19:26-27.) Jesus' use of the word "woman" is not rude. Rather, Jesus is making clear that family ties, even to his own mother, will not cause him to act. The Hebrew idiom, read literally, is "What to me and to you?" In this context the phrase may mean "What's it to me?" "My hour has not yet come" refers both to the hour of Jesus' death, resurrection, and ascension—when Christ is glorified and the new age begins—and to the beginning of his ministry, which will reveal who he is and the salvation God offers to those who believe in him. The conversation between Jesus and his mother here is not unlike the conversation between Jesus and his mother in Luke 2:49: "Did you not know I must be in my Father's house?" He distances himself from his mother, letting her know that he will do God's work in God's time—at the appointed hour.

John 2:6-10: The six stone jars hold water for "Jewish rites of purification," for washing hands and vessels. Some commentators suggest that part of the story is about the inadequacy of Jewish law and ritual, compared to the abundance of God's grace given in Christ Jesus. Others point out that the focus is not on lack but on abundance: The jars hold twenty or thirty gallons of water, filled to the brim. The servants draw out the water and take it to the head steward, who tastes it and finds that it is not water at all, but good wine. Notice that the miracle itself is not mentioned; no one but Jesus and the servants know what happened. The steward comments to the bridegroom: "Everyone serves the good wine first, . . . but you have kept the good wine until now" (2:10). "Bridegroom" refers both to the man getting married and also to Jesus. Wine is a good gift of God. In abundance, it is commonly a symbol of the coming new age. For example, Isaiah 25:6 describes salvation: "On this mountain the LORD of hosts will make for all peoples a feast of rich food, a feast of well-aged wines." Luke 5:33-38 pulls together the images of the wedding feast, the bridegroom, and new wine to describe the new life in Jesus Christ.

John 2:11-12. The story of the wedding at Cana concludes with the climax in verse 10. When the wine ran short, an embarrassment to hospitality, Jesus intervened; and suddenly good wine flowed in abundance. Verse 11 tells the reader the purpose of the story. It is not referred to as a miracle but "the first of his signs." The signs include, among others, the turning water into wine at Cana, the healing of the blind man, the feeding of the five thousand, and the raising of Lazarus. These signs point to salvation, the beginning of God's new age, when the lame walk, the blind see, the dead are raised, and God's gifts are given in abundance. The signs also reveal Jesus' glory, which is the glory of God. John 1:14 says, "The Word became flesh and lived among us, and we have seen his glory, the glory as of a father's only son, full of grace and truth." The signs reveal Jesus as the Messiah, the incarnate Word of God who inaugurates the new age.

His ministry is self-revelation, manifesting the glory of God's grace both in the future and in himself. Only the eyes of faith can see the power and the light of God's grace in Jesus Christ. The steward sees only the wedding party, whom he praises for the gift of good wine. The disciples went further and "believed in him" (2:1). They had seen him as a teacher (John 1:38), the Messiah (1:41), the one promised by Moses and the prophets (1:45), the "Son of God . . . the King of Israel" (1:49). Now their faith is deepened, for they have seen in him the glory of God. Jesus serves as the mediator of salvation between God and humanity. Those who believe in him receive the abundance of eternal life.

INTERPRETING THE SCRIPTURE

A Wedding Feast

Something unplanned often happens at a wedding. The groom is late. The bride forgets her vows. The best man drops the ring, which skitters down the air-conditioning vent. The flower girl needs to go to the bathroom. The cake is awful. Nonetheless, a wedding is a celebration. Two people make a commitment to live together in joy and sorrow, to be faithful, to love each other for a lifetime. Prayers ask that their marriage be a witness to God's faithfulness and that they live in the Spirit of Christ's love, forgiveness, and joy. A wedding is a feast to celebrate the present union of two people and the promise of their future together. A wedding is a party, but it also points beyond itself.

Weddings in the Bible are often symbols of the new age, God's new creation. In fact, weddings celebrate a new creation: Two people are joined together and "become one flesh" (Genesis 2:24). From that day forward, they are not their own, but live together as a married couple. The new age promises a new social order, a new way of living, defined by God's astonishing love that heals, forgives, protects, comforts, and gives more than we can imagine. So Jesus tells the parable of the wedding feast (Matthew 22:1-14): "The kingdom of heaven may be compared to a king who gave a wedding banquet" (22:2).

Weddings in Scripture also serve as metaphors for the relationship between God and God's people or Christ and the church. God makes covenants with God's people. To assure the people of their deliverance from slavery in Egypt, God vows, "I will take you as my people, and I will be your God." In Hosea 2:16-20, God renews the covenant in a glad celebration of a new relationship with God's people: "You will call me, 'My husband' . . . I will take you for my wife in faithfulness; and you shall know the LORD" (2:20). Through generations, in joy and sorrow, God is faithful to the covenant. Jesus is often called the bridegroom and the union of Christ and the church is described as a wedding: "I saw the holy city, the new Jerusalem, coming down out of heaven from God, prepared as a bride adorned for her husband" (Revelation 21:2).

Weddings point beyond themselves. So when we learn that Jesus attended a wedding, we should be ready to read about the new age and the new relationship between God and God's people.

Good Wine in Abundance

Something unplanned often happens at a wedding. At the wedding at Cana, the wine ran short. Jesus told the servants to fill the water jugs; and when they drew the water out for tasting, it had turned to wine. What do we know about the wine? It was apparently good. The astonished headwaiter told the bridegroom, "Everyone serves the good wine first, and then the inferior wine after the guests have become drunk. But you have kept the good wine until now" (2:10). It is good wine, served up now, at the end of the party; and the wine fills six twenty- to thirty-gallon jugs—a lot of wine. The sign points to the promises for salvation at the end of time. Rudolf Schnackenburg, in his commentary *The Gospel According to St. John*, points out, "As a gift of Jesus, however, the wine also is significant; it is given at the end, and it is so precious and copious that it

is the eschatological gift of the Messiah." The wine is a free gift of God in Jesus Christ. It is a symbol of the messianic banquet, the new age, and eternal salvation. Isaiah describes salvation, at the end of time, as a party for the nations, where good food is served up in abundance and good wine flows freely. Imagine the banquet table stretched across centuries; dishes passed; glasses filled; laughter, storytelling, singing, and toasts for the bridegroom, who is Jesus Christ. Imagine the joy of salvation poured out and overflowing like the good wine at Cana.

The Person of Jesus

The Gospel of John does not understand salvation at the end of time apart from Jesus, who stands in time as the incarnate Word of God. The story of Cana is grounded firmly in everyday life: Mary, Jesus, the disciples go to a wedding at a town not far from Nazareth. At the wedding are guests, servants, a headwaiter, a bride, a groom, their friends, and family. Water, used for ritual cleansing but also for routine washing up, is turned to wine; and the headwaiter says, "Hey! You saved the best for last!" It's a down-to-earth story. Verse 2:11 explains that it is also a sign that reveals the glory of Jesus Christ. It points to salvation at the end of time, yes; but it also points to the person of Jesus, who is himself the marriage of God and humanity. "He reveals himself as the Messiah," according to Schnackenburg, "as the Son of Man come down from heaven, as the Son of God sent by the Father and united to him, bringing revelation and light"— the glory of God, which is power and light and promise. In the marriage of

God and humanity, in Jesus, is the promise of salvation, the gift of wine overflowing. Jesus says in John 10:10, "I came that they may have life, and have it abundantly." In Cana, the gift of abundant good wine points to the One who gives abundant life.

Belief

This sign at Cana, the first of many, revealed the glory of Jesus Christ—but not to everyone. The servants and presumably Mary knew where the wine came from. The sign prompted the disciples to believe in Jesus. But the headwaiter had no clue. He spoke not to Jesus but to the bridegroom, complimenting his choice of fine wine. And the party continued. Jesus not only is the giver of salvation and abundant good life but he also mediates salvation. The Gospel of John assumes that the only way to the Father is through the Son. Jesus says in John 14:6, "I am the way, and the truth, and the life.

No one comes to the Father except through me." Salvation hinges on faith. Jesus' self-revelation is for the purpose of sorting out those who believe that he is the Son of God and those who don't. The disciples come to the party with Jesus. They have been called and are ready to believe (1:35-50). Jesus has promised them a glimpse of God's glory (1:51). They see and believe; their faith is deepened. What do the other people see? Maybe without thinking twice about a glass placed in their hand, they keep on swaying to the music, celebrating the bride and groom, and having a good time. Maybe if they see him at all, they see only the man, Jesus, without the radiance of God's glory all around him. Jesus came so that we would believe, be saved, and have eternal abundant life. But for many of us a single miracle, especially one as hidden as the miracle at Cana, isn't enough. The Scripture promises other signs. The wedding at Cana is only the first.

SHARING THE SCRIPTURE

PREPARING TO TEACH

Preparing Our Hearts

Ponder this week's devotional reading from Matthew 5:12-16 in the Sermon on the Mount. In what ways do you see yourself as the salt of the earth? How do you let your light shine so that others can see what you do and, as a result, give glory to God? How would you say that salt and light can transform the world?

Pray that you and the students will be ready at all times to act as the people of God.

Preparing Our Minds

Study the background Scripture and the lesson Scripture, both of which are from John 2:1-12.

Consider this question as you prepare the lesson: *How can a bride and groom accommodate their guests when the food or beverage supplies run out?*

Write on newsprint:
❏ information for next week's lesson, found under Continue the Journey.
❏ activities for further spiritual growth in Continue the Journey.

Review the Introduction, The

Big Picture, Close-up, and Faith in Action, which all precede the first lesson of this quarter. Consider how you might use any of this material in today's lesson.

LEADING THE CLASS

(1) Gather to Learn

❖ Welcome the class members and guests.

❖ Pray that those who have come today will be aware of and accept the miracles that God performs in their everyday lives.

❖ Read this information from The-Knot.com concerning their Real Wedding Study in 2013, which surveyed thirteen thousand brides and grooms in the United States: **Couples are spending more than ever before on their weddings with the average wedding costing $29,858 (plus the honeymoon). About one in eight couples spent more than $40,000. About one in four did not even have a budget. Costs continue to mount despite the fact that more couples are choosing casual weddings. Why? Many couples are interested in providing a unique experience for their guests. They want to put their own stamp on this event and are looking for ways to do that. In 2013, only 33 percent of couples married within a house of worship. Since the average age of the bride is now twenty-nine while the groom is thirty-one, and since 74 percent of couples have lived together prior to the wedding, times and traditions are changing. But for many couples, the need to provide lavish hospitality remains constant, even though the price has risen dramatically.**

❖ Read aloud today's focus statement: **A hospitality tradition requires that the bride and groom make sure there is adequate food and beverage for invited wedding guests. How can the bride and groom accommodate their guests when there is a shortage? As an invited guest at the wedding in Cana, Jesus performed his first miracle when the wine ran out by turning ordinary water into a wine unsurpassed in its quality, revealing his glory and causing his disciples to believe.**

(2) Goal 1: Understand that Jesus Performed His First Miracle in the Lives of Ordinary People When He Met an Important Hospitality Need at a Wedding

❖ Read John 2:1-2 and then read or retell John 2:1-2 in Understanding the Scripture to set the scene for today's lesson.

❖ Call on a volunteer to read John 2:3-12 and then discuss these questions:

1. **Running out of wine at a wedding was a serious social gaff that would have caused embarrassment to the newly married couple and their families. What motivated Jesus to act?** (See John 2:3-5 in Understanding the Scripture.)

2. **In addition to the joining of a couple, what kinds of meanings do weddings reveal in the Bible?** (See "A Wedding Feast" in Interpreting the Scripture.)

3. **What does the sheer amount of wine (2:6-7) suggest about Jesus?** (See "Good Wine in Abundance" in Interpreting the Scripture.)

4. **Today's story recounts a miracle, but it is more than that. It is a sign that points beyond itself. What is this sign pointing**

to? (See "The Person of Jesus" in Interpreting the Scripture.)

5. **Although Jesus' action provided wine for the wedding guests, it provided something far greater for the disciples who were aware of what he had done. What was it?** (See "Belief" in Interpreting the Scripture.)

(3) Goal 2: Reflect On the Meaning and Practice of Hospitality

❖ Distribute half sheets of paper and pencils to participants. Ask each person to write a word or phrase to complete this sentence: **For me, a sign of good hospitality is . . .** Provide space on a wall or table top (if the group is small) where the students can place their slips of paper. As they do so, they are to explain in a few words why this sign is so important to them.

❖ When everyone has had an opportunity to speak, see if there are common threads among the responses. For example, perhaps many people included food or convivial conversation.

❖ Conclude by asking:

1. **In what ways is our congregation practicing the kind of hospitality that people expect— and that may prompt them to return?**
2. **If we seem to be lacking in hospitality, what can we do to change that?**

(4) Goal 3: Identify Ways to Demonstrate Hospitality at Weddings and Other Occasions

❖ Form several small groups and provide newsprint and a marker for each group. Challenge one group to plan a party in the church parlor to celebrate the reception of new members. Challenge another group to plan a community Thanksgiving dinner that will be held at the church. Challenge a third group to plan a Sunday school rally to energize classes of all ages. Tell each group that their focus is on providing hospitality for everyone who attends.

❖ Provide time for the groups to report back. Affirm those ideas that can be put into practice to demonstrate Jesus' gracious and abundant hospitality.

(5) Continue the Journey

❖ Pray that as the learners depart they will treat others with the abundant hospitality that Jesus showed by turning water into wine.

❖ Post information for next week's session on newsprint for the students to copy:
- **Title: The Death of a Friend**
- **Background Scripture: John 11:1-44**
- **Lesson Scripture: John 11:38-44**
- **Focus of the Lesson: Although some believe that science will be able to bring people back to life, the traditional rituals of burial recognize the common belief that physical death is final. Is physical death really final? Jesus performed a miracle in which Lazarus, who had been dead for four days, was raised from the dead.**

❖ Post the following information on newsprint and provide paper and pencils for the students to copy it. Challenge the adults to grow spiritually by completing one or more of these activities related to this week's session.

(1) Offer hospitality to a new-comer in your church or community. Find out what this person needs and do what-ever you can to meet that need in a warm, friendly manner.

(2) Use a Bible dictionary and search the Internet to deter-mine how hospitality was practiced in both Old and New Testament times. How did the people of God show their hospitality? What expe-riences had they already had with God's hospitality? What expectations did they have for God's hospitality in the age to come?

(3) Observe how hospitality is offered in your own congre-gation. Are people welcomed and given an opportunity to feel at home? If not, how can you institute change?

❖ Sing or read aloud "As Man and Woman We Were Made."

❖ Conclude today's session by leading the class in this benediction, which is adapted from Leviticus 22:31 in the lesson for December 13: **As we go forth, we commit ourselves to keep the commandments of the Lord. Amen.**

UNIT 2: FOUR WEDDINGS AND A FUNERAL

THE DEATH OF A FRIEND

PREVIEWING THE LESSON

Lesson Scripture: John 11:38-44
Background Scripture: John 11:1-44
Key Verse: John 11:43

Focus of the Lesson:

Although some believe that science will be able to bring people back to life, the traditional rituals of burial recognize the common belief that physical death is final. Is physical death really final? Jesus performed a miracle in which Lazarus, who had been dead for four days, was raised from the dead.

Goals for the Learners:

(1) to review the story of Jesus' raising of Lazarus from the dead.
(2) to reflect on how they can comfort those who mourn.
(3) to remember and celebrate the lives of those now deceased who had an impact on their faith.

Supplies:

Bibles, newsprint and marker, paper and pencils, hymnals

READING THE SCRIPTURE

NRSV

Lesson Scripture: John 11:38-44

³⁸Then Jesus, again greatly disturbed, came to the tomb. It was a cave, and a stone was lying against it. ³⁹Jesus said, "Take away the stone." Martha, the sister of the dead man, said to him, "Lord, already there is a stench because he has been dead four days." ⁴⁰Jesus said to her, "Did I not tell you that if you believed, you would see the glory of God?" ⁴¹So they

CEB

Lesson Scripture: John 11:38-44

³⁸Jesus was deeply disturbed again when he came to the tomb. It was a cave, and a stone covered the entrance. ³⁹Jesus said, "Remove the stone."

Martha, the sister of the dead man, said, "Lord, the smell will be awful! He's been dead four days."

⁴⁰Jesus replied, "Didn't I tell you that if you believe, you will see God's

took away the stone. And Jesus looked upward and said, "Father, I thank you for having heard me. ⁴²I knew that you always hear me, but I have said this for the sake of the crowd standing here, so that they may believe that you sent me." ⁴³When he had said this, **he cried with a loud voice, "Lazarus, come out!"** ⁴⁴The dead man came out, his hands and feet bound with strips of cloth, and his face wrapped in a cloth. Jesus said to them, "Unbind him, and let him go."

glory?" ⁴¹So they removed the stone. Jesus looked up and said, "Father, thank you for hearing me. ⁴²I know you always hear me. I say this for the benefit of the crowd standing here so that they will believe that you sent me." ⁴³Having said this, **Jesus shouted with a loud voice, "Lazarus, come out!"** ⁴⁴The dead man came out, his feet bound and his hands tied, and his face covered with a cloth. Jesus said to them, "Untie him and let him go."

UNDERSTANDING THE SCRIPTURE

John 11:1-6. The story begins with allusions to Jesus' death. Lazarus, Mary, and Martha live in Bethany, outside of Jerusalem. According to John's Gospel, Mary is the woman who anointed Jesus' feet, thereby preparing his body for burial even before his crucifixion (John 12:1-8).

Lazarus is ill. His sisters send a message to Jesus, apparently hoping that he will heal their brother. Jesus' response is startling. He stalls, waiting two days before leaving a place "across the Jordan" (10:40) where he was staying, because "this illness does not lead to death; rather it is for God's glory, so that the Son of God may be glorified through it" (11:4). In fact, the illness does lead to death; and Jesus intends to wait until it has. Then God, through the Son, will give Lazarus life. The miracle will reveal that Jesus is the life-giver. When the time is right, he will go to Bethany.

John 11:7-16. By going to Judea, where Jerusalem is located, it is clear that Jesus is on his way to the cross. The disciples express concern that going to Judea is risky (see 10:31-39). Jesus answers with a parable, assuring

them that traveling during the day will be safe. The parable also says that although Jesus' work is almost done, it isn't finished yet. The darkness of death has not closed around him; the light of God's glory still shines. God will keep him safe until all is revealed. "The light of the world" (7:9) typically refers to Jesus himself; so the parable may also speak to believers, who walk in the light of Christ and not in darkness. Jesus announces, "Our friend Lazarus has fallen asleep, but I am going there to awaken him" (11:11). "Falling asleep" is a euphemism for death, but the disciples misunderstand. If Lazarus sleeps, "he will be all right," they insist (11:12). The word translated "he will be all right" is literally "he will be saved." The Gospel is not short on irony. The disciples, in their confusion, say what will actually happen and point to a deeper meaning of Lazarus's recovery. Then Jesus speaks plainly: "Lazarus is dead" (11:14). In verse 16, Thomas hurries the disciples to Judea with what sounds like cynicism, saying in essence, "We might as well go and die with him." But he focuses attention on the journey, which finally leads to the cross, and speaks theological truth without knowing it: As believers, they will die with Christ.

John 11:17-27. Lazarus has been dead four days. People commonly believed that the soul hovered near the body for three days; on the fourth day, death was final. Jesus' conversation with Martha explains what is about to happen. Martha begins, "Lord, if you had been here, my brother would not have died" (11:21). Her comment is generally assumed to be a statement of faith in Jesus' power to heal, not criticism. She still assumes that Jesus will do something, but does not expect Jesus to raise a dead man. Martha misconstrues Jesus' answer, "Your brother will rise again" (11:23), as comfort for the grieving and responds with common beliefs: At the end of the age, God will raise the dead. Jesus brings hope for the future into the present by proclaiming: "I am the resurrection and the life" (11:25). Rudolf Schnackenburg, in his commentary on John, says, "Jesus is bearing witness to himself as the one who has been given and fully possesses (5:26) the power which belongs to God alone to 'give life.'" The restoration of Lazarus to his mortal body "is only a feeble reflection of that true life which Jesus calls forth in believers." The sentences in John that follow do not promise an end to physical death. Rather, they promise believers God's gift of eternal life after death as well as a new kind of life here and now. Salvation, which is a relationship with God through Jesus Christ, extends beyond physical death. The verses are also an invitation to believe and to live the new life Jesus promises. Martha believes. She confesses, responding not to what Jesus says

but to who he is: "I believe that you are the Messiah, Son of God, the one coming into the world" (11:27).

John 11:28-37. Mary's words in verse 33 seem intended to recall Jesus' whole conversation with Martha. The crowd follows, weeping and wailing, as they would at a burial. When Jesus sees them, he is "greatly disturbed in spirit" (11:33), words generally used to indicate anger. Why would Jesus be angry? Some commentators suggest that the cost of death and its toll on human relationships prompts his indignation. With the mourners, he sheds tears over the loss of his friend. Other scholars point out that the story of Lazarus foreshadows Jesus' death and resurrection and that his weeping anticipates his agony in the garden of Gethsemane. Jesus asked, "Where have you laid him?" (11:34). The response, "come and see" (11:34), recalls words Jesus earlier spoke to his disciples (1:39); seeing leads to belief. The story then moves to the tomb.

John 11:38-44. The tomb is a "cave," with "a stone lying against it" (11:38). Martha's concern about the smell is not a lack of faith but realism and underscores the fact of Lazarus's death. Verse 40 reiterates: This is a sign. The glory of God, the giver of life, will be revealed in what Jesus does. The Jews believed that miracles happened only by the power of God. Jesus prays, asking that they will see and believe. Jesus knows that God will hear his prayer because he is with God and acts on God's will. Jesus calls out with a loud voice, which indicates his power and authority and recalls traditions in which the voice of God raises the dead on the last day. It may also be a call to believers to live new life, unbound and free. Lazarus comes out, still in his grave clothes, which are like the clothes in which Jesus will be buried. Lazarus, whose life is still in this world, will need them again. Jesus, whose new life is eternal, can leave them folded up in the tomb.

INTERPRETING THE SCRIPTURE

Dead Is Dead

Seldom does anyone say, "He died." We speak in euphemisms: "Father passed away" or simply "He passed." "God called Grandmother home." "She is with God now." "My friend is resting in the arms of Jesus." Someday, as Hamlet reminds us, we will all "shuffle off this mortal coil." Even Jesus says, "our friend Lazarus has fallen asleep" (John 11:11), though he finds the need to speak literally to clear up the disciples' confusion: "Lazarus is dead" (11:14).

The language we use says a lot about how we feel about death and what we believe. Most of us are scared of dying; we would rather not talk about it. Death conjures up horror-film images: creepy cobwebby falling-down mansions and corpses laid out, surrounded by candles, as well as ghosts, half-decayed bodies, zombies walking city streets. More realistically, thinking about death, we relive grief, seeing in our mind's eye the faces of those we love, images of last moments, a sentence stopped, a sleep without waking, a shout in the night and silence. "He looked like my Daddy except he wasn't breathing." We remember a grave, flowers, snatches of prayers. When we talk about death, we skip over the hard parts. "He passed away." Well, yes, the person who died is gone, no longer physically present. But the statement raises the question, "Where did he go?" Sometimes we don't talk about death at all, but say what we believe about resurrection. "God called Grandmother home" reassures us that death is simply a way station on her journey to be with the Lord.

Perhaps in believing, we have passed over the reality of death. We should speak plainly. We live a little while, and then we die. We don't actually know what happens next, except that our mortal bodies decay. Senses that allowed us to see, hear, feel, touch, and taste no longer exist. Can we think or feel without consciousness? Death, for all we know, is a long, silent, dark, emptiness. The Scripture is pretty realistic. When Jesus says, "Take away the stone," Martha counters, "Lord, already there is a stench because he has been dead four days" (John 11:39). The prospect of opening a grave is frightening. Decay begins almost immediately. All we really know is that death is the end of life as we have experienced it. Death is final. It is not a stop on the journey or a passing over from one realm to another. From a strictly human perspective, dead is dead—period, the end.

Theological Conversation

Jesus is about to raise a man who has been dead four days. This miracle is a sign that points beyond itself to the glory of God in Jesus Christ. Jesus explains the miracle ahead of time in John 11:4, 23-26, 40. Jesus' raising

Lazarus from the dead will reveal the power of God to give life, in the future and also now, in and through the person of Jesus. The basic meaning of the word "glory" is "good opinion" or "praise." It also means "splendor" and is associated with light or radiance. Glory refers to the power, majesty, and goodness of God that is revealed in God's mighty acts. In the raising of Lazarus, Martha, the disciples, and at least some people in the crowd will see the glory of God. What will they see, other than a dead man, alive and walking out of a cave that has entombed him? Martha already knows that God promises a general resurrection (11:24); and Jesus' sign points to the last days, the end of time, when God will once and for all establish God's new creation. God will raise the dead, with a shout, and give them new life. But Jesus says that resurrection is not only a someday promise but is happening now: "I am the resurrection and the life" (11:25). In Jesus, the future is brought into the present. The glory of God is revealed in the acts of a human Jesus in a human situation. The act of raising Lazarus will reveal that Jesus has been given the power and the goodness of God to raise the dead and to give new life. The raising of Lazarus is a manifestation of God's power and purpose, which is new life. This event reveals Jesus, who is one with the Father (10:30). The miracle is a promise for the future: The dead will be raised to new life. It is also a promise for salvation now in relationship to Jesus Christ.

Belief

The signs, including the miracle at Bethany, are for believers. "If you believed," says Jesus, "you would see the glory of God" (11:40). Not everyone believes, but for those who do, the miracle is a sign that reveals God's power. Jesus prays for the crowd, that in the raising of Lazarus, "they may believe that you [God] sent me" (11:42). The saying "seeing is believing" is true, but only if seeing is with the eyes of faith. Believers see through the human situation to a manifestation of God's future, happening before their eyes, and they see also in Jesus the power of God to give life.

Belief in Jesus is the condition for new life. In John 11:25-26, Jesus explains, "Those who believe in me, even though they die, will live; and anyone who lives and believes in me will never die." Believers will not escape physical death—life on earth is transient—but they will receive eternal life. Moreover, belief is not only setting our hearts on a distant hope. It is trust and reliance in a person: Jesus. It is knowledge of God and Jesus, a relationship that unites us so that we are one with Jesus, who is one with God (17:22-23). Eternal life is grounded in belief and is lived out day to day. Eternal life is a new way of life, a moral obligation, a call to live in every human situation the life God gives for eternity.

Lazarus is a prototype of the believer. Jesus calls him to new life with a shout. He has died but lives again on earth unbound by the grave, at least for a time.

The Miracle and the Cross

The story of Jesus' raising Lazarus from the dead, found only in the Gospel of John, provides the impetus for the official decision to have

Lazarus killed (see John 12:9-11). John traces the work of Jesus through a series of signs that reveals who he is and what he has come to do. Jesus reveals the power and glory of God, which finally is the triumph of life over death and the promise of new life in God's presence for all who believe. The raising of Lazarus illustrates Jesus' self-identification in John 10:10-11: "I have come that they may have life, and have it abundantly. I am the good shepherd. The good shepherd lays down his life for the sheep." Jesus gives his own life so that Lazarus—and all who believe— will live. The story prepares us for Jesus' death and resurrection.

SHARING THE SCRIPTURE

PREPARING TO TEACH

Preparing Our Hearts

Ponder this week's devotional reading from Isaiah 25:6-10. How will God, who will hold a feast in Jerusalem on Mount Zion, deal with death? How are verses here used in 1 Corinthians 15:54 and Revelation 7:17? Why do you—or don't you—believe that God "will swallow up death forever" (Isaiah 25:8)?

Pray that you and the students will recognize that even though death is part of our earthly journey, we live as hopeful, Easter people because of what God has done through Jesus Christ.

Preparing Our Minds

Study the background Scripture from John 11:1-44 and the lesson Scripture from John 11:38-44.

Consider this question as you prepare the lesson: *What is your understanding of the finality of death?*

Write on newsprint:

❏ information for next week's lesson, found under Continue the Journey.

❏ activities for further spiritual growth in Continue the Journey.

Review the Introduction, The Big Picture, Close-up, and Faith in Action, which all precede the first lesson of this quarter. Consider how you might use any of this material in today's lesson.

Prepare a brief introductory lecture for Goal 1 in Sharing the Scripture by using information from John 11:1-6 through John 11:28-37 in Understanding the Scripture.

Caution: Discussion about the death of a loved one may be especially difficult for class members who have recently lost someone close. If anyone has experienced a death very recently, you may want to advise that student of the topic for discussion prior to class.

LEADING THE CLASS

(1) Gather to Learn

❖ Welcome the class members and guests.

❖ Pray that those who have come today will be open to an astonishing miracle.

❖ Read this true account as told by Randi Kaye and Chelsea J. Carter of CNN: **In January 1999, orthopedic surgeon Mary Neal was pinned in** her kayak while boating in Chile. Although she had taken her four children to Sunday school and tried to incorporate spirituality into her life, she would run out of time to devote to her spiritual life. Yet, realizing that she was helplessly trapped, she "really gave it all over to God" and said, "Your will be done." She had an out-of-body experience, watching friends frantically trying to rescue her. She also was met by spirits who told her that she still had work to do, so it was not her time to die. The spirits told her that her son Willie had already finished his work and would soon die. Having been without oxygen for about thirty minutes, she spent months recovering. But time took on new meaning. In June 1999, nineteen-year-old Willie was out with a friend when he was hit by a car and killed. Dr. Neal, who chronicled her story in *To Heaven and Back*, believes not only "that every person can look at their life and see the hand of God" but also that "most miracles are quiet."

❖ Read aloud today's focus statement: **Although some believe that science will be able to bring people back to life, the traditional rituals of burial recognize the common belief that physical death is final. Is physical death really final? Jesus performed a miracle in which Lazarus, who had been dead for four days, was raised from the dead.**

(2) Goal 1: Review the Story of Jesus' Raising of Lazarus from the Dead

❖ Set the context for today's reading by presenting the introductory lecture you have prepared on John 11:1-37 from Understanding the Scripture.

❖ Choose a volunteer to read the climax of this story from John 11:38-44 and discuss these questions:

1. **Why is Jesus performing this miracle?** (See "Theological Conversation" in Interpreting the Scripture.)

2. **What is the difference between Jesus' restoring Lazarus to life and God resurrecting Jesus?** (Lazarus will continue to live as a mortal, but eventually he will die. Jesus, however, has been raised to eternal life. Be sure that the adults understand that the resuscitation of Lazarus and the resurrection of Jesus are two different actions.)

3. **Why did Jesus have to tell onlookers to "unbind" Lazarus?** (Lazarus was still bound by the trappings of death. Note that when Jesus arose from the dead, cloths were left behind in the tomb, according to John 20:5.)

4. **Suppose you had been present at the tomb. What would have been your reaction to Lazarus—and to Jesus?**

5. **Suppose you had been Lazarus. How might your relationship with Jesus change as a result of this event?**

❖ **Option:** Compare the stories of Lazarus and the resurrection of Jesus, found in John 19:38–20:10. What similarities and differences do participants note? What do these stories teach the adults about death and new life?

(3) Goal 2: Reflect on How the Learners Can Comfort Those Who Mourn

❖ Discuss ways in which people in the United States express their beliefs about death by the way they speak about it. Add to the discussion by reading or retelling "Dead Is Dead" in Interpreting the Scripture.

❖ Invite participants to recall words spoken to them when they were mourning the loss of a loved one and ask:

1. **What words gave you comfort and hope? Why?**
2. **What words seemed unhelpful, insensitive, or upsetting? Why?**

❖ Conclude by asking the learners to identify ways that well-wishers can offer tangible help to those who mourn.

(4) Goal 3: Remember and Celebrate the Lives of Those Who Had an Impact on the Learners' Faith

❖ Distribute paper and pencils. Suggest that participants think of someone who is now deceased whose life had an impact on their faith. This person may have been a family member, perhaps a grandparent or parent; or a mentor in their church, such as a teacher, counselor, pastor, or choir director; or a community member who was a coach, coworker, or club member. Write a letter to this person stating how his or her life touched yours in ways that helped to shape your faith.

❖ Enlist volunteers to read or retell the major points in their letters. Give thanks for these special people.

❖ Suggest that the learners review their letters during the week and ask themselves: When I no longer walk this earth, what will people remember about how I helped to shape and strengthen their faith?

(5) Continue the Journey

❖ Pray that as the learners depart they will give thanks for those whose memories continue to live on in the hearts and minds of their loved ones and friends.

❖ Post information for next week's session on newsprint for the students to copy:

- **Title: Passover**
- **Background Scripture: Exodus 12:1-14; Numbers 28:16-25; Mark 14:12-26**
- **Lesson Scripture: Exodus 12:1-14**
- **Focus of the Lesson: People love to commemorate historic events by creating traditional days of celebration. What makes these commemorations so important? God gave Moses and the people instructions for the first Passover, commemorating their deliverance from Egyptian bondage.**

❖ Post the following information on newsprint and provide paper and pencils for the students to copy it. Challenge the adults to grow spiritually by completing one or more of these activities related to this week's session.

(1) **Comfort someone who has lost a loved one.**
(2) **Read accounts of people who have experienced death and returned, such as Dr. Mary Neal's book, To *Heaven and Back*.**
(3) **Make a gift in memory of someone who has had an impact on your spiritual life.**

❖ Sing or read aloud "Come, Let Us Join Our Friends Above."

❖ Conclude today's session by leading the class in this benediction, which is adapted from Leviticus 22:31 in the lesson for December 13: **As we go forth, we commit ourselves to keep the commandments of the Lord. Amen.**

UNIT 3: HOLY DAYS
PASSOVER

PREVIEWING THE LESSON

Lesson Scripture: Exodus 12:1-14
Background Scripture: Exodus 12:1-14; Numbers 28:16-25; Mark 14:12-26
Key Verse: Exodus 12:14

Focus of the Lesson:
People love to commemorate historic events by creating traditional days of celebration. What makes these commemorations so important? God gave Moses and the people instructions for the first Passover, commemorating their deliverance from Egyptian bondage.

Goals for the Learners:
(1) to recall events surrounding the institution of the Passover feast.
(2) to reflect on the meaning of Passover and what it reveals about God to them.
(3) to praise God for salvation.

Supplies:
Bibles, newsprint and marker, paper and pencils, hymnals

READING THE SCRIPTURE

NRSV
Lesson Scripture: Exodus 12:1-14
¹The Lord said to Moses and Aaron in the land of Egypt: ²This month shall mark for you the beginning of months; it shall be the first month of the year for you. ³Tell the whole congregation of Israel that on the tenth of this month they are to take a lamb for each family, a lamb for each household. ⁴If a household is too small for a whole lamb, it shall join its closest neighbor in obtaining one; the lamb

CEB
Lesson Scripture: Exodus 12:1-14
¹The Lord said to Moses and Aaron in the land of Egypt, ²"This month will be the first month; it will be the first month of the year for you. ³Tell the whole Israelite community: On the tenth day of this month they must take a lamb for each household, a lamb per house. ⁴If a household is too small for a lamb, it should share one with a neighbor nearby. You should divide the lamb in proportion to the number

shall be divided in proportion to the number of people who eat of it. ⁵Your lamb shall be without blemish, a year-old male; you may take it from the sheep or from the goats. ⁶You shall keep it until the fourteenth day of this month; then the whole assembled congregation of Israel shall slaughter it at twilight. ⁷They shall take some of the blood and put it on the two door-posts and the lintel of the houses in which they eat it. ⁸They shall eat the lamb that same night; they shall eat it roasted over the fire with unleavened bread and bitter herbs. ⁹Do not eat any of it raw or boiled in water, but roasted over the fire, with its head, legs, and inner organs. ¹⁰You shall let none of it remain until the morning; anything that remains until the morning you shall burn. ¹¹This is how you shall eat it: your loins girded, your sandals on your feet, and your staff in your hand; and you shall eat it hurriedly. It is the passover of the LORD. ¹²For I will pass through the land of Egypt that night, and I will strike down every firstborn in the land of Egypt, both human beings and animals; on all the gods of Egypt I will execute judgments: I am the LORD. ¹³The blood shall be a sign for you on the houses where you live: when I see the blood, I will pass over you, and no plague shall destroy you when I strike the land of Egypt.

¹⁴**This day shall be a day of remembrance for you. You shall celebrate it as a festival to the LORD; throughout your generations you shall observe it as a perpetual ordinance.**

of people who will be eating it. ⁵Your lamb should be a flawless year-old male. You may take it from the sheep or from the goats. ⁶You should keep close watch over it until the fourteenth day of this month. At twilight on that day, the whole assembled Israelite community should slaughter their lambs. ⁷They should take some of the blood and smear it on the two doorposts and on the beam over the door of the houses in which they are eating. ⁸That same night they should eat the meat roasted over the fire. They should eat it along with unleavened bread and bitter herbs. ⁹Don't eat any of it raw or boiled in water, but roasted over fire with its head, legs, and internal organs. ¹⁰Don't let any of it remain until morning, and burn any of it left over in the morning. ¹¹This is how you should eat it. You should be dressed, with your sandals on your feet and your walking stick in your hand. You should eat the meal in a hurry. It is the Passover of the LORD. ¹²I'll pass through the land of Egypt that night, and I'll strike down every oldest child in the land of Egypt, both humans and animals. I'll impose judgments on all the gods of Egypt. I am the LORD. ¹³The blood will be your sign on the houses where you live. Whenever I see the blood, I'll pass over you. No plague will destroy you when I strike the land of Egypt.

¹⁴**"This day will be a day of remembering for you. You will observe it as a festival to the LORD. You will observe it in every generation as a regulation for all time."**

UNDERSTANDING THE SCRIPTURE

Exodus 12:1-14. The context of the Scripture is God's mighty act of deliverance, in which God frees the Israelites from slavery in Egypt and in the covenant at Sinai that makes them God's people. In this passage we learn about the institution of the Feast of Passover just prior to the Exodus. The Scripture describes both a liturgical and a historical event.

Today's passage begins in verse 1 with a formula: "The LORD said to Moses." These words precede directions that God will give through Moses to the people. God proclaims, "This month shall mark for you the beginning" (12:2), not only the first month of the year but also the beginning of a new way of life. The Exodus is the decisive event in the life of Israel. Brought out from slavery in Egypt, the Hebrew slaves become the people of God. Verse 3 defines the Passover and the Exodus as a community event. God's redemption is not for individuals but for the "whole congregation," the whole people of God. Passover is a family celebration; but the lamb is to be shared among neighbors so that no one eats alone, everyone has enough to eat, and nothing is left over. The lamb chosen for the feast is to be a year-old male, without blemish, an animal suitable as a sacrifice or offering to God; and as with a sacrificial animal, the blood is given to God and the meat is eaten. The Hebrew word translated in 12:6 as "twilight" encompasses several meanings: the time between noon and night (when the sun begins to go down in the sky and darkness); or dusk, the time between sunset and darkness. Lamb, unleavened bread,

and bitter herbs are a full meal, though the bread represents the haste with which the Israelites left Egypt, taking "their dough before it was leavened" (12:34). The bitter herbs in the Passover meal represent the embittered lives of the slaves in Egypt. The family is to eat "with your loins girded, your sandals on your feet, and your staff in your hand," prepared and ready to leave at a moment's notice (12:11). The Hebrew word translated as "hurriedly" not only means "haste" but also implies an element of fear. What about the blood of the lamb? Verse 12 may imply that the blood is for God's benefit, "when I see the blood, I will pass over you, and no plague shall destroy you," but verse 13 clarifies that the blood smeared on the doorposts is a sign, not for God, but "for you," the people of God. Blood is lifeblood, the life of the animal, which belongs to God. It is used as a sign for the people that God will protect them. It also signifies that they belong to God, that God is their God and they are God's people. The blood is a sign of God's covenant faithfulness and, in a sense, consecrates the people. The killing of the firstborn is judgment on both Egypt and the gods of Egypt, including Pharaoh, for refusing to recognize God's authority and prohibiting God's people from worship. (The Scripture allows for the existence of other gods, but they have no power.) The firstborn whose households are consecrated, or set apart for the Lord, will be set free to be the people of God. Moreover, although the Exodus event will occur only once, verse 14 makes clear that it is to be observed "as a perpetual ordinance" so that all generations will know what happened.

Numbers 28:16-25. This passage is part of a cultic calendar, describing the offerings for each of the holy days, seasons, and festivals. Passover is to be observed "on the fourteenth day of the first month" with "a Passover offering to the LORD" (28:16). This date falls in the Jewish month of Nisan, which overlaps our March and April. The next day begins the seven-day Feast of Unleavened Bread. Over time this agricultural feast was combined with Passover. The Feast of Unleavened Bread, which begins and ends with a day of rest and a "holy convocation," includes a variety of sacrifices as specified in verses 19-24. These sacrifices were offered by the priests on all seven days, whereas Passover is observed by a family in the home.

Mark 14:12-26. This passage describes both a historical event detailing Jesus' last meal with his disciples and the institution of what Christian congregations refer to as Holy Communion. The early church quickly linked Jesus with the paschal lamb and saw his sacrificial death within the context of Passover. However, the connection Mark draws in 14:12 between "the first day of Unleavened Bread" with the time "when the Passover lamb is sacrificed" is questionable in light of the fact that the lambs would have been slaughtered during the afternoon prior to the Passover meal in the evening. (Recall that for Jews the day ends at sundown, so "evening" would have been a new day.) Just as Exodus was God's mighty act of deliverance, in which the Israelites were identified as God's people, freed from slavery, and brought into a covenantal relationship with God, the death and resurrection of Jesus Christ creates a new people, freed from sin and brought into a new relationship with God. Jesus eats the Passover meal with his disciples; they are his household, his family. In the midst of this celebratory meal Jesus announces, "one of you will betray me" (14:18) to which the distressed disciples respond, "Surely not I?" (14:19). Verses 22-24 are the words of institution used in the liturgy of the Lord's Supper: "This is my body" (14:22) and "this is my blood of the covenant" (14:24) recalling the covenant at Sinai, which was sealed when Moses sprinkled the congregation of Israel with blood (see Exodus 24:5-8). Jesus' comment in verse 25 looks ahead to a new messianic age, the kingdom of God, when all people will sit together as one family, and everyone will have enough. But for now, it is time to go. The Passover meal traditionally concludes with the Hallel Psalms (Psalms 114–118), which are probably "the hymn" referred to in verse 26.

INTERPRETING THE SCRIPTURE

Celebrations

National and worldwide celebrations are listed on the calendar: New Year's Day, Martin Luther King Jr. Day, Passover, Easter, Independence Day, Labor Day, Halloween, Thanksgiving, Christmas. Add birthdays and anniversaries. On the surface, holidays commemorate events in our personal, national, or religious history. An anniversary celebrates a wedding. The Fourth of July commemorates the adoption of the Declaration of Independence. Seldom are holidays simple memories. Anniversaries are celebrated within a marriage. Remembering the wedding takes second place to the couple's continuing relationship and their future together. Think about the historical events holidays commemorate and the ways they have expanded to include the present and future. Consider how celebrating a holiday comes to define the day. For example, Independence Day is marked with fireworks, parades, and picnics. Celebrations often commemorate historical events, but the history is sometimes forgotten in the wider meaning of the day. Think about how the meaning of a celebration may have changed. Thanksgiving, for example, is not just a reminder of Pilgrims and Native Americans eating together in 1621. It is, according to Abraham Lincoln's proclamation, "a day of Thanksgiving and Praise to our beneficent Father who dwelleth in the Heavens." And more recently, it has become a day of parades, football, and shopping.

Passover: The Texts

Just as the Fourth of July celebrates a major turning point in the history of the United States, so too Passover is a foundational celebration for the Jews. The accounts of how the Passover came to be stretch back to ancient texts. The stories of the plagues in Egypt and the Passover are compiled from different sources. In Exodus 11:4-8 Moses warns that the firstborn in Egypt will die. His words from

the Lord are enacted in 12:29-39 as the final plague is unleashed. God passed through the land, and all the firstborn of Egypt died. In the night, as a wail of grief rose from the land, Pharaoh told the Hebrew people to leave. They left in a hurry with the clothes on their backs and the food they could carry. The story is told with urgency, capturing the horror, grief, and fear that sent the Israelites running. The historical event is Israel's liberation from Egypt.

The story of Passover in Exodus 12:1-14 sounds more like instructions for worship, as if the ritual of Passover, celebrated for generations, were projected back onto the historical event. The story is told with precision. It includes dates and times; the selection of the Passover lamb and how it should be cooked, divided, and eaten; and the ritual of putting blood on the doorposts. Exodus 12:14 says, "This day shall be a day of remembrance for you. You shall celebrate it as a festival to the LORD; throughout your generations you shall observe it as a perpetual ordinance." The purpose of the Passover ceremony is to commemorate the Exodus. But its meaning has expanded. The ritual and liturgy of the Passover ceremony have become part of the event itself.

Liturgy and History

What is the relationship between liturgy and history? Brevard S. Childs, in his commentary The Book of Exodus, says that the biblical writer "does not see the exodus as an 'act of God' distinct from 'the word of God' which explains it. In theological terms, the relation between act and interpretation, or event and word, is one which cannot be separated."

The word of God interprets the act of God. The Passover celebration tells us what the historical event means. Celebrated in the first month, Passover defines the Exodus as the beginning, the decisive event in Israel's life as the people of God. The lamb is both a sacrificial offering to God and food for a common meal. The blood of the lamb identifies and protects the households of Israel. They are consecrated, set apart for God, who gives them life in the turmoil of judgment and death that takes the firstborn of Egypt. The haste with which the meal is eaten and the use of unleavened bread simulates the Israelites' hurry to leave, following God into the wilderness to worship.

Terence E. Fretheim, in his commentary on Exodus, suggests that the opposite is true. The act of God, he says, is the Passover celebration itself. The word of God is the story of the Exodus. He points out that during the Passover celebration, a child in the family asks for interpretation: "Why is this night different from all other nights?" The question refers to the celebration: Why is this meal different? Then the story is told: "We were slaves to Pharaoh in Egypt, and God brought us out with a strong hand and an outstretched arm." The primary event is worship, a celebration in which the story of the Exodus is told.

Word and act, interpretation and event, inform each other. Worship is part of our immediate experience. We celebrate Christmas, Holy Week, Easter, Pentecost—days and seasons that are different from all others. We participate in sacraments. If we ask why, someone is apt to tell a story, which is based on a historical event. "Why do we break bread and share a cup?" "Jesus, before his death and resurrection, broke bread with us and poured out for us the cup of salvation." "Why do we light candles at Christmas?" "When Jesus was born, God brought light into our darkness." "Why is this night different?" "God brought us out of Egypt and made us God's own people."

Past, Present, Future

We ordinarily think that God acted in the past, in history, for our salvation. The mighty acts of God are recorded in the Bible. But if we believe that God's activity ended with the last chapter of Revelation, we can't help wondering: *Why isn't God still acting? What does an event that happened thousands of years ago have to do with us?* We think of then and now, of salvation wrapped up in the past and fulfilled in the future. What about now?

The Exodus was an event in the past. The Israelites were slaves to Pharaoh, set free to become the people the God. Exodus 12:1-14 tells about the Passover in Egypt; but Passover happens year after year, generation after generation. Each time Passover is celebrated, families participate in the saving act of God. The Exodus event does not literally happen again, but celebrants are drawn into it. The language of the Passover liturgy is first-person plural: "We were slaves to Pharaoh in Egypt. God brought *us* out with a strong hand." Fretheim says of the Passover celebration: "The saving power of the original event is made available ever anew to the community by God's redeeming activity within the context of worship."

The Passover is past and present. It is also promise for new life in new order. Passover marks people as

God's own. Chosen, they are saved from death and freed from slavery. They will become a new people in a new land. The promise of the Exodus is salvation, which ultimately is for all people. Salvation is a new relationship with God and a whole new way of life. Often in Scripture it is pictured as a meal, a messianic banquet, in which people from every time and place come to celebrate and praise the Lord. In the liturgy for Passover, a final prayer asks God "to bring the Messianic Era, when all of us will be gathered to Jerusalem as all humankind dwells in peace. . . . Next year in Jerusalem! Next year, may we all dwell in peace!"

SHARING THE SCRIPTURE

PREPARING TO TEACH

Preparing Our Hearts

Ponder this week's devotional reading from Matthew 26:20-30. What might have been the mood among the disciples as they ate this last Passover with Jesus? Why might Judas ask a question (26:25) to which he already knows the answer? How does Jesus reinterpret the symbolism of the Passover meal?

Pray that you and the students will recognize the importance of Passover for the Jewish community and the meaning that this meal has within the Christian community.

Preparing Our Minds

Study the background Scripture from Exodus 12:1-14; Numbers 28:16-25; Mark 14:12-26. The lesson Scripture is from Exodus 12:1-14.

Consider this question as you prepare the lesson: *What makes commemorating historic events so important?*

Write on newsprint:

❏ questions for Goal 3 in Sharing the Scripture.
❏ information for next week's lesson, found under Continue the Journey.
❏ activities for further spiritual growth in Continue the Journey.

Familiarize yourself with the information in Close-Up: Jewish Holidays. You may want to write some of this information on newsprint so that the class can see it.

LEADING THE CLASS

(1) Gather to Learn

❖ Welcome the class members and guests.

❖ Pray that those who have come today will praise God for salvation.

❖ Invite the students to call out names of Jewish holidays and say a brief word about their meaning. Use the chart on the page Close-Up: Jewish Holidays. If you have written any information on newsprint, leave this posted throughout the unit so that you can easily refer to it again.

❖ Read aloud today's focus statement: **People love to commemorate historic events by creating traditional days of celebration. What makes these commemorations so important? God gave Moses and the people instructions for the first Passover, commemorating their deliverance from Egyptian bondage.**

(2) Goal 1: Recall Events Surrounding the Institution of the Passover Feast

❖ Select a volunteer to read Exodus 12:1-14, which records the institution of the first Passover as the Hebrew people are instructed to prepare for their liberation from Egyptian slavery.

❖ Discuss these questions:

1. **What instructions does God give the people so that they will be properly prepared for this event?** (See Exodus 12:1-14 in Understanding the Scripture.)

2. **Which instructions would have suggested to the people that they would be leaving quickly?** (Note that their loins were to be girded; sandals were to be on their feet; their staffs were to be in their hands; they were to eat hurriedly; the bread was to be made without leaven, indicating that there was not enough time for yeast bread to rise.)

3. **What do the instructions suggest about the importance of the community and family?**

4. **God said that the people were to remember this event "as a perpetual ordinance"** (12:14, key verse). **What does this command suggest about the importance of the Passover event for Israel's past, present, and future?** (See "Past, Present, Future" in Interpreting the Scripture.)

5. **Had you been one of the Hebrew people who heard Moses give these instructions from God, what would you have thought about God?**

(3) Goal 2: Reflect Upon the Meaning of Passover and What It Reveals About God to the Learners

❖ Choose someone to read Mark 14:12-26 from the background Scripture.

❖ Recall that Jesus was a Jew, as were his disciples. Celebrating Passover would have been very important to them. Notice that Jesus tells two disciples how to make preparations for this meal that Jesus would host. Form several small groups and ask these questions, allowing time between each one for the groups to formulate answers:

1. **How would the joy of recalling liberation from enslavement been overshadowed during this Passover meal?** (pause)

2. **Two common foods—bread and wine—were an integral part of the Passover. Unleavened bread signified the haste with which the slaves were to depart, and the four cups of wine were each blessed with the words "Blessed are You, Lord our God, King of the Universe, who creates the fruit of the vine." How did Jesus reinterpret the meanings of these familiar foods?** (pause)

❖ Bring the groups together and encourage them to comment on any insights they gleaned about God and about the connection between the celebration of Passover and the celebration of Holy Communion.

(4) Goal 3: Praise God for Salvation

❖ Read: **Recall that God's purpose for the Passover event was to liberate the people from generations of oppression in Egypt. They were,** indeed, saved and free at last! On Wednesday, February 10, we Christians will enter into the season of Lent. During this time we look ahead to our own salvation, which is brought about by the death and resurrection of Jesus. The season of Lent calls us to make time and space to examine our relationship with God through the Beloved Son, Jesus.

❖ Distribute paper and pencils. Note that this activity will be confidential, so urge the adults to be open and honest with God. Suggest that they write this question at the top of the page: **In what ways does God need to remold me so that I can say to God as Jesus said in Gethsemane, "not what I want but what you want" (Matthew 26:39)?** Provide quiet time.

❖ Recommend that the students take their papers home to continue reflecting and writing. Suggest that as ideas come to them as to how they can do God's will, they write them, perhaps keeping a journal. On Easter, they may want to review their Lenten journey to see how God has worked in their lives to continue to bring about salvation.

(5) Continue the Journey

❖ Pray that as the learners depart they will remember all that the Lord has done.

❖ Post information for next week's session on newsprint for the students to copy:

- Title: Feast of Weeks
- Background Scripture: Leviticus 23:15-22; Numbers 28:26-31; Acts 2:1-36
- Lesson Scripture: Leviticus 23:15-22
- Focus of the Lesson: People celebrate the harvest of

their labors with thanksgiving and share the fruits with others. Why do they respond in this way? The Lord commanded the Hebrews to offer God joyful praise and thanksgiving, as they shared their harvest with the needy.

❖ Post the following information on newsprint and provide paper and pencils for the students to copy it. Challenge the adults to grow spiritually by completing one or more of these activities related to this week's session.

(1) Find a copy of "The Passover Haggadah," which is a guide to the Seder meal. (Here is one that you can find on the Internet: www.jewishfederation. org/images/uploads/holiday_ images/39497.pdf.) What do you learn about how the Passover is celebrated and who is included in this celebration? How would this liturgy help people of all ages to remember and participate in what God has done?

(2) Plan to attend an Ash Wednesday service this week to start the season of Lent.

(3) Renew and strengthen your relationship with God by setting aside time to practice a spiritual discipline such as prayer, meditation, or journaling.

❖ Sing or read aloud "Shalom."

❖ Conclude today's session by leading the class in this benediction, which is adapted from Leviticus 22:31 in the lesson for December 13: **As we go forth, we commit ourselves to keep the commandments of the Lord. Amen.**

UNIT 3: HOLY DAYS
FEAST OF WEEKS

PREVIEWING THE LESSON

Lesson Scripture: Leviticus 23:15-22
Background Scripture: Leviticus 23:15-22; Numbers 28:26-31; Acts 2:1-36
Key Verse: Leviticus 23:16

Focus of the Lesson:
People celebrate the harvest of their labors with thanksgiving and share the fruits with others. Why do they respond in this way? The Lord commanded the Hebrews to offer God joyful praise and thanksgiving, as they shared their harvest with the needy.

Goals for the Learners:
(1) to examine the Feast of Weeks found in Leviticus.
(2) to celebrate with joy and thanksgiving times of giving to God what belongs to God and to the needy.
(3) to commit to a life plan of returning to God a portion of what one has received from God and sharing with those in need.

Supplies:
Bibles, newsprint and marker, paper and pencils, hymnals

READING THE SCRIPTURE

NRSV

Lesson Scripture: Leviticus 23:15-22

¹⁵And from the day after the sabbath, from the day on which you bring the sheaf of the elevation offering, you shall count off seven weeks; they shall be complete. **¹⁶You shall count until the day after the seventh sabbath, fifty days; then you shall present an offering of new grain to the LORD.** ¹⁷You shall bring from

CEB

Lesson Scripture: Leviticus 23:15-22

¹⁵You must count off seven weeks starting with the day after the Sabbath, the day you bring the bundle for the uplifted offering; these must be complete. **¹⁶You will count off fifty days until the day after the seventh Sabbath. Then you must present a new grain offering to the LORD.** ¹⁷From wherever you live, you will bring two

your settlements two loaves of bread as an elevation offering, each made of two-tenths of an ephah; they shall be of choice flour, baked with leaven, as first fruits to the LORD. [18]You shall present with the bread seven lambs a year old without blemish, one young bull, and two rams; they shall be a burnt offering to the LORD, along with their grain offering and their drink offerings, an offering by fire of pleasing odor to the LORD. [19]You shall also offer one male goat for a sin offering, and two male lambs a year old as a sacrifice of well-being. [20]The priest shall raise them with the bread of the first fruits as an elevation offering before the LORD, together with the two lambs; they shall be holy to the LORD for the priest. [21]On that same day you shall make proclamation; you shall hold a holy convocation; you shall not work at your occupations. This is a statute forever in all your settlements throughout your generations.

[22]When you reap the harvest of your land, you shall not reap to the very edges of your field, or gather the gleanings of your harvest; you shall leave them for the poor and for the alien: I am the LORD your God.

loaves of bread as an uplifted offering. These must be made of two-tenths of an ephah of choice flour, baked with leaven, as early produce to the LORD. [18]Along with the bread you must present seven flawless one-year-old lambs, one bull from the herd, and two rams. These will be an entirely burned offering to the LORD, along with their grain offerings and drink offerings, as a food gift of soothing smell to the LORD. [19]You must also offer one male goat as a purification offering and two one-year-old lambs as a communal sacrifice of well-being. [20]The priest will lift up the two sheep, along with the bread of the early produce, as an uplifted offering before the LORD. These will be holy to the LORD and will belong to the priest. [21]On that very same day you must make a proclamation; it will be a holy occasion for you. You must not do any job-related work. This is a permanent rule wherever you live throughout your future generations. [22]When you harvest your land's produce, you must not harvest all the way to the edge of your field; and don't gather every remaining bit of your harvest. Leave these items for the poor and the immigrant; I am the LORD your God.

UNDERSTANDING THE SCRIPTURE

Leviticus 23:15-22. The discussion of two agricultural feasts—the Feast of Firstfruits (23:9-14) and the Feast of Weeks (23:15-22)—begins with Leviticus 23:10: "When you enter the land that I [God] am giving you and you reap its harvest, you shall bring the sheaf of the first fruits of your harvest to the priest." Offerings are to be made because the land belongs to God, who has entrusted the people with the task

of planting and harvesting it as stewards. (Think of God's planting a garden in Eden and putting Adam there "to till it and keep it," Genesis 2:15.) As the people are making their offerings, they are giving back a portion of what rightfully belongs to God. The rest is God's gift to God's people.

The one-day Festival of Weeks begins seven weeks after the Feast of Firstfruits for the barley harvest, described in Leviticus 23:9-14. The days and weeks are counted as the farmers await a ripe harvest of wheat, which matures after barley, hoping the weather will be favorable and the harvest plentiful. The Festival of Weeks, also known in Greek as Pentecost, celebrates the gathering of the wheat harvest, an "offering of new grain to the LORD" (23:16). The offering of wheat is not a sheaf, as the barley was (23:10), but rather is made into two loaves of leavened bread. The name of the offering comes from the ritual; the priest lifts or "elevates" the bread toward heaven. The offering of bread is accompanied by "an offering by fire of pleasing odor to the LORD" (23:18); seven lambs, a bull, and two rams are the "burnt offering" (23:18). The offering is completely burned up, turned to smoke that rises. Its purpose is to please God, in hopes that God will bless both the land and the people with abundance.

Besides the problem of too many animals lined up at the sanctuary, farmers about to harvest their wheat did not have time for a day off and a holy convocation, much less a pilgrimage to Jerusalem. Jacob Milgrom, in his commentary on Leviticus, traces the development of the feast from a harvest celebration by farmers, who brought their offerings to a local sanctuary; to a regional celebration; to a ceremony with fixed dates, sacrifices, and offerings (Numbers 28:26-31); to a public sacrifice in Jerusalem, in which the offerings were provided not by the farmer but by the cult. Later, the Feast of Weeks was cast as a commemoration of the events at Sinai, God's revelation and the giving of the law.

The final verse returns to the idea that the land belongs to God. God's people, farming God's land, are to behave as God would behave, caring for the poor and the alien. Those whom God has blessed with abundance are to be a blessing to others. This is not an exhortation to be charitable, but according to Jacob Milgrom, "a reminder to the landowner that sharing the grain harvest with the poor and the alien is not just an ethical desideration [that is, requirement], but a specific, time-bound, yearly obligation." "Gleanings" comes from a word meaning "collect, gather piecemeal." When the wheat is harvested, some is dropped and some is left standing, which the poor will be able to gather. Although concern for the poor was common in the ancient Near East, Israelite law added "the alien."

Numbers 28:26-31. This passage is part of a calendar of holy days and seasons. It prescribes the sacrifices and offerings for each celebration. Numbers 28:26 describes "the day of the first fruits," probably a private offering brought by each farmer, and "your festival of weeks," a public ceremony at either the Temple in Jerusalem or a regional sanctuary. Numbers assumes a previous offering of the first fruits. Barley is harvested first; the "new grain" is an offering of wheat. The Festival (or Feast) of Weeks is a one-day celebration featuring a day of rest from one's normal occupation and a "holy convocation," which was a solemn assembly held in conjunction with Israel's festivals. The first fruits of the harvest are offered as flour mixed with oil. Verses 28-30 also list animals that are to be offered. Note that this list is slightly different from the one in Leviticus 23. A burnt offering and a drink offering are also to be offered to the Lord. The offering is both a gift of thanks and a hope for God's continued blessings.

Acts 2:1-36. This passage describes the gift of the Holy Spirit given to Jesus' followers and Peter's proclamation of the good news. The setting is Pentecost—the Feast of Weeks—during which "devout Jews from every nation under heaven" (2:5) were in Jerusalem. Fifty days after Jesus' resurrection, the disciples were all together as a community when a sound like the wind filled the house and a tongue, likened to fire, "rested on each of them" (2:3). Fire and wind are symbols of God's presence. The disciples began to speak in languages that were known to the crowds but which Jesus' Galilean disciples would not have known. Hearing words describing "God's deeds of power" (2:11), those in the crowd were both "amazed and perplexed" (2:12). Groping to make sense of this event, some assumed that the disciples were drunk. To interpret the event to the crowd Peter spoke, tying the gift of the Spirit at Pentecost to promises for the end of time made by the prophet Joel (2:17-21). Peter points out in verse 22 that God performed "deeds of power" through Jesus, yet they handed him over to "those outside the law" (2:23), that is, the Roman government, to be crucified. According to Luke 2:23, humans bear responsibility for Jesus' death, but his death is in keeping with God's plan. By God's will and design, Jesus was raised from the dead and made "both Lord and Messiah" (2:36). The testimony of Peter, who was among those who witnessed these events (2:32), was "welcomed" (2:41) by three thousand persons who chose to be baptized (2:41). Thus, the community of faith begins on Pentecost with the Holy Spirit and the present word of God.

INTERPRETING THE SCRIPTURE

God's Land

"This land is your land. This land is my land. . . . This land was made for you and Me." Woody Guthrie's folk song has been sung across the land. Think of families traveling cross-country; youth groups singing on a bus; children marching across playgrounds; a lone folksinger, guitar thrown over his shoulder, humming along with the beat of his shoes hitting the pavement. This land is our land.

Or is it? The Scripture is clear: We may inhabit the earth, but this land is not ours. The land belongs to God. God is creator, marking out the edges of continents, rolling out hills and pushing up mountains, flattening out farmland, dotting the land with trees and filling fields with grass. God sustains the land. God waters the land. God establishes seasons for planting and harvest and brings forth on the earth every kind of vegetation. God's land is made for farming. In addition, God created human beings and put them to work tilling the soil. God promised God's people a land, where they would settle down in agricultural communities to till the soil, to plant, and to reap an annual, bountiful harvest. The land belongs to God, and so does the harvest. In Leviticus 23:10, God establishes the harvest festivals by saying, "When you enter the land that I am giving you and you reap its harvest, you shall bring the sheaf of the first fruits of your harvest to the priests." God gives the land to God's people to tend as careful stewards; but the land still belongs to God.

The First Fruits, the Countdown, the Feast of Weeks

In Israel, the first grain to be harvested was barley, the second was wheat. The harvest festivals began with the offering of the first fruits—an armful of barley brought to the priest and dedicated to the Lord. Nothing from the harvest could be eaten before the offering. Dedicating the first fruits was a way of acknowledging that both the land and the harvest were the Lord's; it was a reminder that we eat and drink only because of God's gracious provision.

After the offering of the first fruits, the counting begins. The farmer, having sown the wheat, counts fifty days until the harvest. Maybe he reads the *Farmers' Almanac* and checks the weather reports. Too much rain might rot the fields. Too little might mean the beginning of hot east winds that blow across the land dry, killing the crops. The fifty days were a time to wait and pray, perhaps a prayer each day, that God would bless the harvest. Jacob Milgrom, in his commentary on Leviticus, writes: "God commanded to count these days, to keep the anxiety of the world in mind and to turn to him in wholehearted repentance, to plead with him to have mercy upon us, on mankind and on the land, so that the crops should turn out well, for they are our life." The emphasis is on God's provision. We rely entirely on God because the land, the rain, the wind, and the harvest all belong to the Lord.

On the fiftieth day, the Festival of Weeks, the farmer brings the first fruits of the wheat harvest, baked into two loaves of bread, and presents them to the priest, who in turn dedicates them to God. The gift acknowledges that the first fruits belong to God. Verses 18-19 add animals and a drink offering to the farmer's grain offering. As offerings were burnt, "an offering by fire of pleasing odor to the LORD" (23:18) would have filled the sanctuary. The Feast of Weeks, according to Leviticus 23:21, is a day of rest from one's customary occupation and celebration. It is also a day to hold a solemn assembly, "a holy convocation."

The church recalls one particular Feast of Weeks, which in Greek was known as Pentecost. On that day in about A.D. 33, as throngs of people gathered in Jerusalem to celebrate this festival, God poured out the Holy Spirit on Jesus' disciples, who, in turn, proclaimed the good news by speaking in languages unknown to them so that all might hear about Jesus. Peter interpreted this amazing event for the crowd. As a result of his sermon, in which he testified to God's mighty deeds and acts in Jesus the Messiah, three thousand people stepped forward for baptism. This, indeed, was a bountiful harvest that inaugurated the church. Today we still celebrate this one day in May or June (depending on the date of Easter) and give thanks not only for the birth of the church but also for how it continues to grow and spread. God is still pouring out abundant blessings.

Thanksgiving

After weeks of waiting and praying, the harvest was ready; and Israel was ready to celebrate. The Feast of Weeks was Israel's thanksgiving, a time to rejoice and give thanks for the abundant blessings of God. A harvest festival is celebrated in nearly every nation in the world. In the United States, we gather together parents, children, grandchildren, aunts, uncles, cousins, and friends and eat until we think we'll burst. The fruits of the harvest weigh down our tables. Aunt Mary always brings her famous sweet potatoes. Granny brings corn pudding. Uncle Bob tells about his tomato crop. Warren brags about his apple tree, the one Jamie climbed every year to pick the first apple. Thanksgiving is a time of joy and laughter, celebrating the year's blessings. And before we sit to eat, someone starts singing: "Come ye thankful people, come; raise the song of harvest home." Thanksgiving is not too different from the Feast of Weeks. When the harvest is over, the celebrations begin.

Gleaning

Leviticus 23:22 looks like a second thought, a nod, to charitable giving. In fact, the provision for gleaning is central to Leviticus and an essential part of God's covenant with God's people. Gleaning expresses compassion and justice among people who take seriously God's command to be holy. Leviticus 19 begins with God's word to the people: "You shall be holy; for I the LORD your God am holy" (19:2). Leviticus 23:22 repeats Leviticus 19:9, one of the requirements for holiness, and ends with a reminder: "I am the LORD your God." Providing for the poor is part of covenant holiness. To be the people of God is to be like God, who feeds the hungry and cares for the poor. So at harvest, landowners did not harvest the last rows of grain, pick up grain that was dropped, or cut shafts of grain left standing. All that was left in the field after the harvest was for the poor, the widows, the orphans, the aliens. Perhaps our Thanksgiving feasts should always include gifts to the poor—shopping bags filled with turkey and all the fixings. Maybe we should set places at our tables for the needy or spend our Thanksgivings at shelters for the homeless, serving dinner. Of course, nations, as well as families, celebrate the harvest. The Feast of Weeks is a celebration of God's good gifts, an abundance of food to be shared with neighbors in need.

SHARING THE SCRIPTURE

PREPARING TO TEACH

Preparing Our Hearts

Ponder this week's devotional reading from Romans 7:14-25. Can you identify with Paul's concern? Do you feel yourself divided—wanting to do one thing but feeling pulled to do something else? What help do you need from God?

Pray that you and the students will be able to overcome the internal struggle that you, like all of God's people, experience from time to time.

Preparing Our Minds

Study the background Scripture from Leviticus 23:15-22; Numbers 28:26-31; Acts 2:1-36. The lesson

Scripture is from Leviticus 23:15-22.

Consider this question as you prepare the lesson: *When people have worked hard, what motivates them to share the fruits of their labor with others?*

Write on newsprint:

❏ information for next week's lesson, found under Continue the Journey.

❏ activities for further spiritual growth in Continue the Journey.

Review Close-Up: Jewish Holidays and use any information you might find helpful today.

LEADING THE CLASS

(1) Gather to Learn

❖ Welcome the class members and guests. Wish everyone a happy Valentine's Day.

❖ Pray that those who have come today will be willing to share their material blessings with others.

❖ Read "God's Land" in Interpreting the Scripture and discuss these questions:

1. **When we acknowledge that God is the creator and owner of all, what difference does that make in terms of how we view ourselves?** (We are stewards, that is, caretakers, not owners.)

2. **How is our understanding of distribution of food among peoples of the world affected when we recognize that we are not owners but rather that God has entrusted us to act as faithful stewards?**

3. **Option:** If your group includes members of the farming community, call on them to talk about their feelings when, after months of hard work, their crops have been harvested.

How do they celebrate? How do they share their bounty?

4. Read aloud today's focus statement: **People celebrate the harvest of their labors with thanksgiving and share the fruits with others. Why do they respond in this way? The Lord commanded the Hebrews to offer God joyful praise and thanksgiving, as they shared their harvest with the needy.**

(2) Goal 1: Examine the Feast of Weeks Found in Leviticus

❖ Read today's key verse, Leviticus 23:16, and ask if anyone knows which holy day this refers to. ("Fifty days" may call to mind the Greek name for the feast, which is Pentecost.)

❖ Choose a volunteer to read Leviticus 23:15-22. Note that Feast (or Festival) of Weeks (Deuteronomy 16:9-10) is also referred to as Festival of Harvest (Exodus 23:16).

❖ Read or retell "The First Fruits, the Countdown, the Feast of Weeks" in Interpreting the Scripture to further explain the Feast of Weeks.

❖ Distribute hymnals and form pairs or threesomes. Page through your hymnal to find songs that thank God for blessings, creation, God's care, and especially a fruitful harvest. Talk with your partners about how you see these themes in the hymn(s) you select, as well as in the Feast of Weeks.

(3) Goal 2: Celebrate with Joy and Thanksgiving Times of Giving to God What Belongs to God and to the Needy

❖ Ask: **What are some ways that we as a class could give to God by**

giving to those in need? List ideas on newsprint. (Encourage the group to think not only of monetary gifts to worthwhile projects but also of ways that they can give of themselves. For example, members may be able to provide relief kits for people whose lives have been shattered by a natural disaster. One denominational group, The United Methodist Committee on Relief (UMCOR) has specific directions for needed supplies (www.umcor.org/UMCOR/Relief-Supplies). Class members may be able to volunteer to serve as foster grandparents or tutors who assist schoolchildren.

❖ Review the list and select one or two projects that class members will agree to support. Form a task force to get necessary information and work out logistics.

❖ Begin to talk about how the class will celebrate and give thanks to God for ways that they have been able to give back their time, talent, and treasure.

(4) Goal 3: Commit to a Life Plan of Returning to God a Portion of What One Has Received from God and Sharing with Those in Need

❖ Form small groups to consider this question: **Since most people in the United States do not have agricultural bounty to return to God and share with other people, what are some ways in which we can share the fruit of whatever labor we do?** List ideas on newsprint.

❖ **Option:** Ask farmers to form their own groups to discuss this question: **How can we ensure that a portion of the fruit of our harvest is distributed to those in need?**

❖ Call everyone together to present their ideas.

❖ Invite each person to select one or more ideas that they will commit to trying in order to return to God a portion of what God has given them and share with those in need. Suggest that they evaluate the idea(s) they have selected during the harvest season. At that time, they are to confirm their commitment or decide to try other ideas. The point here is that participants are to find a way of giving and sharing that they can continue and build on over time.

(5) Continue the Journey

❖ Pray that as the learners depart they will give thanks to God for the food they have and willingly share their bounty with others.

❖ Post information for next week's session on newsprint for the students to copy:

- **Title: Day of Atonement**
- **Background Scripture: Leviticus 16; 23:26-32; Numbers 29:7-11; Hebrews 7:26-28; 9:24; 10:4-18**
- **Lesson Scripture: Leviticus 16:11-19**
- **Focus of the Lesson: Often people regret wrongful actions committed against another and because of their guilt seek to make amends. What are some ways atonement can be made? In Leviticus, God commanded the Israelites to set aside a day in which to sacrifice animals for payment of sin's debt; Hebrews says that the blood of animals is no longer sufficient and that God has provided Jesus as the supreme sacrifice for atonement.**

❖ Post the following information

on newsprint and provide paper and pencils for the students to copy it. Challenge the adults to grow spiritually by completing one or more of this week's session.

(1) Start a "savings plan" for food-related missions by placing a jar or coin box wherever you eat. Agree on an amount that each family member will contribute daily. Determine which hunger-fighting program(s) you will give this money to and when you will make your donation. Consider programs that your church supports, groups that do gleaning, such as the Society of Saint Andrew (www.endhunger.org/gleaning_network.htm), or groups that provide food to those in need, such as Stop Hunger Now (www.stophungernow.org).

(2) Find ways to fight hunger by volunteering your time. Consider volunteering at a soup kitchen, working with a food pantry, salvaging food from a grocery store or farmers' market that can be given to a local agency that feeds hungry people, or becoming a hunger advocate through an organization such as Bread for the World (www.bread.org).

(3) Plan to grow some herbs, vegetables, or fruits in your own yard or on a balcony with containers. Give thanks to God for whatever you can grow and harvest with the time and space you have available. Give a portion of your harvest to someone in need.

❖ Sing or read aloud "Come, Ye Thankful People, Come."

❖ Conclude today's session by leading the class in this benediction, which is adapted from Leviticus 22:31 in the lesson for December 13: **As we go forth, we commit ourselves to keep the commandments of the Lord. Amen.**

UNIT 3: HOLY DAYS
DAY OF ATONEMENT

PREVIEWING THE LESSON

Lesson Scripture: Leviticus 16:11-19
Background Scripture: Leviticus 16; 23:26-32; Numbers 29:7-11; Hebrews 7:26-28; 9:24; 10:4-18
Key Verse: Leviticus 16:16

Focus of the Lesson:
Often people regret wrongful actions committed against another and because of their guilt seek to make amends. What are some ways atonement can be made? In Leviticus, God commanded the Israelites to set aside a day in which to sacrifice animals for payment of sin's debt; Hebrews says that the blood of animals is no longer sufficient and that God has provided Jesus as the supreme sacrifice for atonement.

Goals for the Learners:
(1) to explore the Day of Atonement found in Leviticus.
(2) to reflect on the meaning of atonement for their sins and its relevance today.
(3) to identify those things in their lives needing repentance and to seek atonement.

Supplies:
Bibles, newsprint and marker, paper and pencils, hymnals

READING THE SCRIPTURE

NRSV
Lesson Scripture: Leviticus 16:11-19

¹¹Aaron shall present the bull as a sin offering for himself, and shall make atonement for himself and for his house; he shall slaughter the bull as a sin offering for himself. ¹²He shall take a censer full of coals of fire from the altar before the LORD, and two

CEB
Lesson Scripture: Leviticus 16:11-19

¹¹Aaron will offer the bull for his purification offering to make reconciliation for himself and his household. He will slaughter the bull for his purification offering. ¹²Then he will take an incense pan full of burning coals from the altar, from before

handfuls of crushed sweet incense, and he shall bring it inside the curtain [13]and put the incense on the fire before the LORD, that the cloud of the incense may cover the mercy seat that is upon the covenant, or he will die. [14]He shall take some of the blood of the bull, and sprinkle it with his finger on the front of the mercy seat, and before the mercy seat he shall sprinkle the blood with his finger seven times.

[15]He shall slaughter the goat of the sin offering that is for the people and bring its blood inside the curtain, and do with its blood as he did with the blood of the bull, sprinkling it upon the mercy seat and before the mercy seat. **[16]Thus he shall make atonement for the sanctuary, because of the uncleannesses of the people of Israel, and because of their transgressions, all their sins; and so he shall do for the tent of meeting, which remains with them in the midst of their uncleannesses.** [17]No one shall be in the tent of meeting from the time he enters to make atonement in the sanctuary until he comes out and has made atonement for himself and for his house and for all the assembly of Israel. [18]Then he shall go out to the altar that is before the LORD and make atonement on its behalf, and shall take some of the blood of the bull and of the blood of the goat, and put it on each of the horns of the altar. [19]He shall sprinkle some of the blood on it with his finger seven times, and cleanse it and hallow it from the uncleannesses of the people of Israel.

the LORD, and two handfuls of finely ground perfumed incense and bring them inside the inner curtain. [13]He will put the incense on the fire before the LORD so that the cloud of incense conceals the cover that is on top of the covenant document, or else he will die. [14]He will take some of the bull's blood and sprinkle it with his finger on the cover from the east side. He will then sprinkle some of the blood with his finger seven times in front of the cover. [15]Then he will slaughter the goat for the people's purification offering, bring the blood inside the inner curtain, and do with it as he did with the bull's blood: he will sprinkle it on the cover and in front of the cover. **[16]In this way, he will make reconciliation for the inner holy area because of the pollution of the Israelites and because of their rebellious sins, as well as for all their other sins. Aaron must do the same for the meeting tent, which is with them among their pollution.** [17]No one can be in the meeting tent from the time Aaron enters to make reconciliation in the inner holy area until the time he comes out. He will make reconciliation for himself, for his household, and for the whole assembly of Israel.

[18]Aaron will then go to the altar that is before the LORD and make reconciliation for it: He will take some of the bull's blood and some of the goat's blood and put it on each of the altar's horns. [19]He will sprinkle some of the blood on the altar with his finger seven times. In this way, he will purify it and make it holy again from the Israelite's pollution.

UNDERSTANDING THE SCRIPTURE

Leviticus 16:1-2. Aaron's sons defiled the sanctuary by bringing "unholy fire before the LORD"; and they died, consumed by the holiness of God (Leviticus 10:1-3). Leviticus 16:1 refers to that event. God tells Moses to warn Aaron to enter the sanctuary only according to prescriptions laid down by God. The "sanctuary inside the curtain" (16:2) is the Holy of Holies, the inner sanctuary, which contains the ark of the covenant. *Kapporet*, translated as "mercy seat" (NRSV) or "cover" (CEB), may have come from a word meaning "sole of foot," bringing to mind the footstool of God's holy throne. The name may also be related to its place in the ritual of Yom Kippur. The verb *kipper*, most often translated "atone," is more accurately translated "purge," "purify," or "decontaminate." The ritual is for purification, and the day is sometimes called the Day of Purgation. God appears in "the cloud upon the mercy seat" (16:2). The cloud is the subject of debate. Some students of Scripture argue that the cloud is fire and smoke that descended on Sinai and, in Exodus 40:34-35, on the tent of meeting when Israel made camp. The cloud signified the presence of the Lord. Others argue that the cloud was created by the incense or something added to the incense the priest brought into the inner sanctuary. To see God is to die. To touch the ark is fatal (see 2 Samuel 6:7). Aaron takes the necessary precautions and follows the prescribed ritual to the letter.

Leviticus 16:3-10. Aaron collects animals for sacrifice, washes, and dresses in linen. The clothing is less ornate than robes the high priest wears when serving at the altar and more like that of angels in the heavenly council (Ezekiel 9:2-3, 11). He first offers sacrifices for himself and for the other priests. The word translated "sin offering" is also rendered "purification offering" (CEB). The sins of the people pollute the sanctuary; the offering purifies it. The high priest takes two goats from the congregation, the community of Israel. Drawing lots allows God to choose which goat will be sacrificed for purification and which will carry the community's sins into the wilderness. Azazel is variously understood to mean scapegoat, wilderness, and a demon that inhabits the wilderness. Though Azazel may once have been a demon, with powers of evil, it is now no more than a name to identify the goat. The Scripture reiterates that the Azazel goat is "presented alive before the LORD" (16:10).

Leviticus 16:11-19. Purification of the sanctuary is the center of the ritual. Impurity is ritual uncleanness, described in chapters 11–15: the consumption of unclean foods, unclean animals, disease, bodily discharges. "Transgressions" (16:16) is "rebellion," open and intentional defiance against God. "All of their sins" (16:16) is a catchall term; all kinds of sin pollute the sanctuary. The degree of sin determines how far into the sanctuary the contamination reaches. So an individual's inadvertent sins reach only to the courtyard, inadvertent sins of the high priest or of the whole community reach into the outer sanctuary, and transgressions pollute the inner sanctuary. The fear is that too much sin will make the sanctuary uninhabitable and God will leave, abandoning the community of Israel to its death. The priest slaughters the bull, then takes the incense into the Holy of Holies, creating a cloud to screen himself from the Lord's presence. The blood sprinkling is directed toward the *kapporet* seven times, to cleanse the sanctuary. The priest purges the inner sanctuary, then the outer sanctuary. The blood daubed on the horns of the altar cleanses it; the sprinkling consecrates it, making it holy to the Lord so that it can be used for sacrifices.

Leviticus 16:20-28. The priest lays hands on the Azazel goat and confesses the sins of Israel, transferring them to the goat. Then the goat is sent away into the wilderness, where it and the sins it carries can do no harm. The scapegoat takes away the "iniquities of the people" (16:21). Originally, the goat may have taken away the sins purged from the sanctuary. The blood ritual removes the consequences of sin; the Azazel goat takes away the sin itself. The ritual concludes with washing, changing, and cleaning up.

Leviticus 16:29-34. Originally, the ritual of purgation may have been an emergency measure, cleansing the sanctuary in times when Israel was in danger. In these verses, the day is observed once a year by Israel and Aaron's successors. It includes purging the sanctuary and also fasting and rest, the community's acts of repentance.

Leviticus 23:26-32. The Scripture says that the Day of Atonement involves "holy convocation" (23:27), "self-denial" (23:27), and complete rest (23:28). Anyone who does not practice self-denial is cut off from the community; working on the Day of Atonement brings down the judgment of God.

Numbers 29:7-11. The Day of Atonement, Yom Kippur, falls in the seventh month, ten days into the New Year. Yom Kippur is a day of self-denial, fasting and abstinence, as well as complete rest. Numbers specifies the offerings for the day. The purpose of the Day of Atonement is purification from sin. Specific offerings are enumerated in verses 8-11.

Hebrews 7:26-28; 9:24; 10:4-18. Hebrews compares the sacrificial system of Israel with the sacrifice of Jesus Christ. While the priests offer sacrifices for their own sin, Christ, though tempted, is sinless. He is both the perfect high priest and the perfect sacrifice, without sin or blemish. Though the priests make sacrifices for atonement year after year, Christ's sacrifice is "once and for all" (7:27). He serves not in a humanly made sanctuary, but in a heavenly sanctuary, where he sits at the right hand of God (10:12). Jesus Christ makes access to God possible for those who draw near. His self-sacrifice on the cross and his willing obedience to all that God commands leads to a new covenant. Hebrews sets up a contrast to show Jesus' superiority, but Leviticus informs our understanding of Jesus as the great high priest, who atones for the sins of the people and comes into the presence of God to intercede for them.

INTERPRETING THE SCRIPTURE

God's Holiness

The sanctuary represents God's presence on earth. What happens there describes the relationship between God and the community of God's people. The sanctuary is divided into specific areas to which different people—Gentiles, female Israelites, male Israelites, and priests—have access. Moving from the outside farther into the interior, the sanctuary space becomes increasing holy, with the holiest area being "inside the curtain" (16:2). In the inner sanctuary, the high priest stands before the Lord, not in direct contact with God, but in God's presence. Coming into the sanctuary was a little like walking a labyrinth, prayerfully entering the outer circle and moving slowly closer to God, until in the center, the worshiper—or the priest—comes into God's presence. The inner sanctuary, like the center of the labyrinth, is not God's home. God is not confined to a place. But in some sense, the place is where we come before the Lord. In the inner sanctuary, the Holy of Holies, was the ark of the covenant, which contained the law of God and was considered almost an "extension or embodiment of the presence of Yahweh." Above the ark was the kapporet or "mercy seat," a slab of solid gold, with cherubim on each side, facing each other with heads bowed and wings outstretched. The kapporet may have been seen as the footstool of God's throne.

Leviticus 16 emphasizes the importance of holiness. The high priest could not come before the Lord on just any day or without significant preparation. For the Day of Atonement, the priest spent seven days in preparation, quarantined from impurities, reading Scripture, rehearsing the ritual. The priest changed into linen clothes because entering the inner sanctuary was like being admitted to the heavenly council, where the membership included angels, dressed in linen, and God presided. Another explanation for the use of linen garments was that they represented the garb of an ordinary priest. The high priest washed before and after the ritual, cleaning up to present himself before the Lord. Before the priest entered the sanctuary, he sacrificed a bull to "make atonement for himself" (16:6). He took coals and finely ground incense inside the curtain. The incense created a cloud that screened him from seeing the Lord's presence (16:13). To see God was to die; to see the kapporet, God's footstool, was fatal. The reason for taking precautions was that the ritual was a gift of God that, followed precisely, allowed the priest to enter God's holy presence. God is holy; meeting up with holiness is dangerous.

"Holy" means "set apart," "sacred," "separate." God is completely beyond us, completely other than us. We struggle to believe in God's holiness. We like having God close. God walks beside us. God comes near to comfort us and carries us through times of trouble. But in Scripture, God is set apart. God is most present in the inner sanctuary, which is closed off from the people. Coming into God's presence is a matter of life and death and, therefore, requires caution.

Sin

In his commentary on Leviticus, Samuel E. Balentine, points out that in our society, people are isolated. Though we may long for community, we have trouble seeing too far beyond ourselves. "We succeed alone, we fail alone," Balentine writes. "To use religious terms, we are righteous alone, and to the extent that we use the language any more, we sin alone." What do we mean by sin? We think of really bad sins: murder, stealing, and other ways of breaking God's Ten Commandments. We think of bad words, bad thoughts, drinking, drugs, sexual impropriety. We think of gossip, lying, hurtful words spoken between friends. And there we stop. Sin, for us, stays in our own minds and in our personal relationships. We see no real connection between our sins and a larger community. Do we imagine that our sins have any effect on those around us? We are basically isolated. We sin alone.

Leviticus believes in all kinds of sin. It expands our definition by showing us connections. No one lives an isolated life. Our sins affect not only ourselves and the people closest to us but also other people. Think of the spread of disease from one person to another; similarly, sin spreads like contagion. I hurt you, you hurt another person, who hurts someone else. Sin affects institutions. Think of what happens when we take our unethical behavior to work. Consider the sin of a government mired in political divisiveness or a religious group turned in on itself. Sin is bigger than individuals and institutions. The Scripture believes in collective sin for which the whole community is responsible and in iniquities that multiply and spread. Sin affects who we are as a human community and as the people of God.

The sanctuary represents God's presence on earth and the relationship between God and God's people. Leviticus understands that sin contaminates the sanctuary. It skews or corrupts our relationship with God and threatens God's presence on earth. If sin makes the sanctuary uninhabitable, will God leave? Can we fill the earth and the human community with so much corruption that God will give up and abandon us? The fear underlying the Day of Atonement is that God will leave us to our own devices and we will no longer be God's people—we will no longer be. Jacob Milgrom, in his commentary on Leviticus, sums up: "The sanctuary symbolized the presence of God; impurity represented the wrongdoing of persons. If persons unremittingly polluted the sanctuary they forced God out of the sanctuary and out of their lives."

Atonement

The ritual prescribed by Leviticus 16:11-19 involved slaughtering a bull for the priests and a goat for the people and then sprinkling their blood in the sanctuary. The blood functions as a detergent. The question is, Why blood? The Bible understands blood as life. The symbolism makes sense: When we lose too much blood we die. Sin leads to death, but life is from God. Jacob Milgrom observes, "The blood of the purification offering symbolically purges the sanctuary by symbolically absorbing its impurities . . . another victory of life over death." Purging the sanctuary with blood purges the contamination of sin. The purification ensures that God will continue to dwell on earth. It also reestablishes God's purpose in the community because God's purpose is life.

The rest of the ritual involves the other goat. The collective sins of the community are confessed and ritually transferred to the goat who is sent out into the wilderness where it and the sin it carries can do no harm. Blood purges the sanctuary of impurities caused by sin. The other goat carries away the sin itself, the iniquities of the people.

The Day of Atonement, when it

became an annual ritual, included fasting, self-denial, and complete rest in the community. It was a day for the community to repent and to begin again to live in obedience to God. As life and holiness were restored to the sanctuary, they were reestablished in the community of God's people.

SHARING THE SCRIPTURE

PREPARING TO TEACH

Preparing Our Hearts

Ponder this week's devotional reading from Hebrews 3:1-6. Hebrews was likely written to persecuted Jewish-Christians who were tempted to renounce their Christian faith. What comparisons and contrasts does the writer draw between Jesus and Moses? What does the reference to Jesus as "high priest" (3:1) suggest about his work on behalf of the people? Would this writer's arguments have convinced you to remain true to the Christian faith? Why or why not?

Pray that you and the students will examine your relationship with God and call upon the "high priest" to help you make confession and receive forgiveness.

Preparing Our Minds

Study the background Scripture from Leviticus 16; 23:26-32; Numbers 29:7-11; Hebrews 7:26-28; 9:24; 10:4-18. The lesson Scripture is from Leviticus 16:11-19.

Consider this question as you prepare the lesson: When people regret wrongful actions, what are some of the ways that they can atone and make amends?

Write on newsprint:
- ❏ information for next week's lesson, found under Continue the Journey.
- ❏ activities for further spiritual growth in Continue the Journey.

Prepare two brief lectures from Understanding the Scripture, one for Leviticus 16:1-10 and the other to include verses 20-34.

LEADING THE CLASS

(1) Gather to Learn

❖ Welcome the class members and guests.

❖ Pray that those who have come today will consider their own sins, ask forgiveness, and seek to make amends.

❖ Read: **First performed in 1611, *Macbeth* is not only a masterful tragedy but also William Shakespeare's most popular play. Lady Macbeth convinces her husband to murder the king, Duncan, but then she becomes deeply disturbed by the sin she has committed. In Act 5, Scene 1 she insists on sleeping with a lit candle next to the bed and rises to walk and talk in her sleep. A doctor and gentlewoman who see her sleepwalking note that she frequently washes her hands. They hear her speak: "Yet here's a spot . . . Out, damned spot! Out, I say! . . . Yet who would have thought the old man to have had so much blood in him. . . . What, will these hands ne'er be clean? . . . Here's the smell of the blood still. All the perfumes of Arabia will not sweeten this little hand. Oh, Oh, Oh!" Once she returns to bed, the** doctor makes this observation: "More needs she the divine than the physician. God, God forgive us all! Look after her, Remove from her the means of all annoyance, And still keep eyes upon her."

❖ Ask: **What truths does Shakespeare reveal about sin?**

❖ Read aloud today's focus statement: **Often people regret wrongful actions committed against another and because of their guilt seek to make amends. What are some ways atonement can be made? In Leviticus, God commanded the Israelites to set aside a day in which to sacrifice animals for payment of sin's debt; Hebrews says that the blood of animals is no longer sufficient and that God has provided Jesus as the supreme sacrifice for atonement.**

(2) Goal 1: Explore the Day of Atonement Found in Leviticus

❖ Present the brief lecture on Leviticus 16:1-10 to introduce the Scripture.

❖ Choose a volunteer to read Leviticus 16:11-19.

❖ Follow up the reading by presenting the brief lecture on Leviticus 16:20-34 that you prepared.

❖ Ask: **How might you relate the need to atone for sin and the careful preparations required for making atonement to the holiness of God?** (See "God's Holiness" in Interpreting the Scripture.)

❖ Form two groups and assign one to review background Scripture from Hebrews 7:26-28 and 9:24 and the other to review Hebrews 10:4-18. Ask: **What do these verses say about Jesus' role as high priest and the sacrifice he made?**

❖ Bring the groups together to report and then ask: **How would you compare and contrast Jesus' actions and sacrifice with those of the high priest on the Day of Atonement?**

(3) Goal 2: Reflect on the Meaning of Atonement for the Learners' Sins and Its Relevance Today

❖ Note that on this Second Sunday in Lent we are studying the Day of Atonement (Yom Kippur). Read "Atonement" from Interpreting the Scripture and ask: **What connections can you draw between the Christian season of Lent and the Jewish Day of Atonement?**

❖ Read these words penned by T. W. Wilson: **The Old Testament Hebrew word that we translate** atonement **means literally "to cover up." The animal sacrifices were intended to "cover" a man's sins. In the New Testament, however, the meaning of atoning sacrifice is conveyed by the word** expiate, **which means "to put away." The blood that Jesus shed in our behalf on the cross at Calvary does not merely cover up our sin, it puts away our sin as though it had never been committed.**

❖ Ask: **How does the distinction that Wilson makes help you to understand the difference between the annual Day of Atonement and Jesus' work on the cross?**

(4) Goal 3: Identify Those Things in the Learners' Lives Needing Repentance and Atonement

❖ Ask: **How do you define "sin"?** (Add information from "Sin" in Interpreting the Scripture.)

❖ Lead the students in this guided imagery activity:

1. Envision yourself in a familiar

place seated on a chair or wherever you feel most comfortable. Let your mind wander to an action for which you need to repent. (*pause*)

2. As you mull over whatever you have identified, think about who may have been hurt by your behavior. Imagine yourself talking with this person to say how sorry you are and seeking forgiveness. Hear the person's response. (*pause*)

3. Think about steps you can take to atone for your action. Is there anything you can do to make things right? If so, offer to do whatever you can. (*pause*)

4. Hear Jesus say to you, "In my name, you are forgiven."

❖ Suggest that the adults look for opportunities this week to ask God for forgiveness and make amends with those they have wronged.

(5) Continue the Journey

❖ Pray that as the learners depart they will continue to be aware of their sins and seek forgiveness from God, others, and self for their missteps.

❖ Post information for next week's session on newsprint for the students to copy:

- Title: Feast of Booths
- Background Scripture: Leviticus 23:33-43; Numbers 29:12-40; Deuteronomy 16:13-17; 1 Corinthians 15:20-29; Revelation 14:1-5
- Lesson Scripture: Leviticus 23:33-43
- Focus of the Lesson: Families need rituals of celebration to remember their heritage and to pass it on to their children.

How can their heritage be remembered and passed on to succeeding generations? The Israelites' celebration of the Festival of Booths assisted them in renewing their commitment to their guiding and protecting God and in passing on their faith to their children.

❖ Post the following information on newsprint and provide paper and pencils for the students to copy it. Challenge the adults to grow spiritually by completing one or more of these activities related to this week's session.

(1) Set aside extra time to spend with God during Lent to strengthen your relationship with God through prayer, meditation, or journaling.

(2) Review each day before you go to bed. Ask: What have I done to share the love of Jesus? What have I done for which I need forgiveness? Ask God for that forgiveness and rest assured that through the atoning work of Jesus you are forgiven.

(3) Research Yom Kippur (Day of Atonement) to learn more about the meaning of this holy day and how it is marked.

❖ Sing or read aloud "Just as I Am, Without One Plea."

❖ Conclude today's session by leading the class in this benediction, which is adapted from Leviticus 22:31 in the lesson for December 13: **As we go forth, we commit ourselves to keep the commandments of the Lord. Amen.**

UNIT 3: HOLY DAYS
FEAST OF BOOTHS

PREVIEWING THE LESSON

Lesson Scripture: Leviticus 23:33-43
Background Scripture: Leviticus 23:33-43; Numbers 29:12-40; Deuteronomy 16:13-17; 1 Corinthians 15:20-29; Revelation 14:1-5
Key Verses: Leviticus 23:42-43

Focus of the Lesson:
Families need rituals of celebration to remember their heritage and to pass it on to their children. How can their heritage be remembered and passed on to succeeding generations? The Israelites' celebration of the Festival of Booths assisted them in renewing their commitment to their guiding and protecting God and in passing on their faith to their children.

Goals for the Learners:
(1) to understand all aspects of the Festival of Booths, a fall grain festival.
(2) to appreciate a faith heritage in which they are guided and protected by a patient, forgiving, and merciful God.
(3) to make a commitment to pass on to the next generation a legacy of faith that God will always guide and protect.

Supplies:
Bibles, newsprint and marker, paper and pencils, hymnals, commentaries

READING THE SCRIPTURE

NRSV

Lesson Scripture: Leviticus 23:33-43

³³The LORD spoke to Moses, saying: ³⁴Speak to the people of Israel, saying: On the fifteenth day of this seventh month, and lasting seven days, there shall be the festival of booths to the LORD. ³⁵The first day shall be a holy convocation; you shall not work at your occupations. ³⁶Seven days you shall present the Lord's offerings

CEB

Lesson Scripture: Leviticus 23:33-43

³³The LORD said to Moses: ³⁴Say to the Israelites: The Festival of Booths to the LORD will start on the fifteenth day of the seventh month and will last for seven days. ³⁵The first day is a holy occasion. You must not do any job-related work. ³⁶For seven days you will offer food gifts to the LORD. On the eighth day you will have a

by fire; on the eighth day you shall observe a holy convocation and present the Lord's offerings by fire; it is a solemn assembly; you shall not work at your occupations.

37These are the appointed festivals of the LORD, which you shall celebrate as times of holy convocation, for presenting to the LORD offerings by fire— burnt offerings and grain offerings, sacrifices and drink offerings, each on its proper day— 38apart from the sabbaths of the LORD, and apart from your gifts, and apart from all your votive offerings, and apart from all your freewill offerings, which you give to the LORD.

39Now, the fifteenth day of the seventh month, when you have gathered in the produce of the land, you shall keep the festival of the LORD, lasting seven days; a complete rest on the first day, and a complete rest on the eighth day. 40On the first day you shall take the fruit of majestic trees, branches of palm trees, boughs of leafy trees, and willows of the brook; and you shall rejoice before the LORD your God for seven days. 41You shall keep it as a festival to the LORD seven days in the year; you shall keep it in the seventh month as a statute forever throughout your generations. **42You shall live in booths for seven days; all that are citizens in Israel shall live in booths, 43so that your generations may know that I made the people of Israel live in booths when I brought them out of the land of Egypt: I am the LORD your God.**

holy occasion and must offer a food gift to the LORD. It is a holiday: you must not do any job-related work.

37These are the LORD's appointed times that you will proclaim as holy occasions, offering food gifts to the LORD: entirely burned offerings, grain offerings, communal sacrifices, and drink offerings—each on its proper day. 38This is in addition to the LORD's sabbaths and in addition to your presents, all the payments for solemn promises, and all the spontaneous gifts that you give to the LORD.

39Note that on the fifteenth day of the seventh month, when you have gathered the land's crops, you will celebrate the LORD's festival for seven days. The first day and the eighth day are days of special rest. 40On the first day you must take fruit from majestic trees palm branches, branches of leafy trees, and willows of the streams, and rejoice before the LORD your God for seven days. 41You will celebrate this festival to the LORD for seven days each year; this is a permanent rule throughout your future generations. You will celebrate it in the seventh month. **42For seven days you must live in huts. Every citizen of Israel must live in huts 43so that your future generations will know that I made the Israelites live in huts when I brought them out of the land of Egypt; I am the LORD your God.**

UNDERSTANDING THE SCRIPTURE

Leviticus 23:33-36. The Festival of Booths is a pilgrimage festival, the last harvest festival of the year. It begins with a day of rest, followed by seven days of celebration. "Offerings by fire" are the offerings and sacrifices specified in Numbers 29:12-40. The eighth day was an addition to the original festival. On that day people participated in a "solemn assembly," the purpose of which was to pray for rain so that the next year's crops would thrive.

Leviticus 23:37-38. These verses begin to conclude the annual calendar of festivals, which began in Leviticus 23:4. They are holy days, appointed by the Lord and proclaimed "as holy occasions" (23:37, CEB). Leviticus 23 is addressed to the people of Israel (Leviticus 23:2); its primary emphasis is on "natural and agricultural data" and on the rituals and offerings of ordinary people. The annual feasts are to be celebrated in addition to Sabbath observances. Offerings on feast days are in addition to regular Sabbath sacrifices and other public and private offerings to the Lord.

Leviticus 23:39-43. The last verses give us a glimpse into how the Festival of the Booths was celebrated. Like Leviticus 23:33-36, this section starts out with dates and times: the fifteenth day, the seventh month, lasting for seven days, the first and the eighth days of complete rest. (Notice that the eighth day is now part of the festival, not an add-on.) The Festival of Booths is also called the "Harvest Festival" (Exodus 23:16, CEB), the "festival of ingathering" (Exodus 23:16, NRSV), the "festival of the LORD" (Leviticus 23:39; Judges 21:19,

NRSV), and simply "the festival" (1 Kings 8:2). It takes place after harvest (the last crops harvested were fruits and olives) and after the produce has been prepared for storage—the grain separated from the chaff, the grapes pressed for wine and the olives for oil. When the harvest is gathered in, the farmer has time to celebrate.

Students of Scripture differ in their interpretation of 23:40. What are the trees listed? Some suggest, for example, that the "fruit of majestic trees" is citrus fruit, frond of date palm tree, myrtle tree, or olive. Others say that the word "fruit" should be translated "branches." How are the branches used? In Nehemiah 8:14-15, Ezra interprets the text to mean that the branches should be used in the construction of booths for the festival. Leviticus 23:42 instructs the people to "live in booths for seven days." Sadducees followed this tradition, but Pharisees tied together four branches to be carried in the right hand, along with a branch of citron in the left as they processed to their synagogues on each of the seven days. Booths were temporary shelters. Some commentators say that booths were used by farmers during the harvest so that they could use every minute of daylight and protect their fields at night. Jacob Milgrom suggests that the first booths were used precisely for the festival. Because pilgrims filled Jerusalem to overflowing, many built temporary shelters on the hillsides around the city. Later, the booths became a permanent part of the festival and were interpreted as a way of remembering God's providential care during Israel's trek through the wilderness. Leviticus 23:43 links the Festival of Booths to the early days of freedom from the Egyptians. According to Exodus 12:37 and Numbers 33:5, the first place that the newly liberated Hebrew slaves encamped was called Succoth. The Hebrew word *sukkah* actually means "booth."

Numbers 29:12-40. The Festival of Booths is a seven-day celebration of thanksgiving for the harvest and supplication for the blessings of rain. Numbers 29:12-40 enumerates the sacrifices for each day. The festival begins and ends with a day of rest. An eighth day is added in verse 35 to the seven prescribed in verse 12.

Deuteronomy 16:13-17. The timing of the seven-day Festival of Booths is specified: "when you have gathered in the produce from your threshing floor and you wine press" (16:13). Deuteronomy emphasizes inclusivity, so everyone—children, slaves, priests, strangers, orphans, widows—is to keep the "festival to the LORD." Verse 16 reflects an older tradition that specified that "all your males" were to keep the festival. Offerings here are not specified, as they are in Numbers; but verse 17 states, "all shall give as they are able," according to their wealth and the success of their harvest.

1 Corinthians 15:20-29. The resurrection of Jesus Christ is the beginning. He is the first fruits, which belong to God, the promise of an abundant harvest: the resurrection of all who have died. Both Adam and Christ stand for all of humanity. In Adam is death, which is both physical

death and, because God's purpose is life, also the violation of God's will. In Christ is life. Verses 24-28 begin, "Then comes the end," which may mean simply "conclusion" or "the dissolution of the world" but may also mean "completion, success, or attainment." The Scripture describes the purposes of God fulfilled in the kingdom of God. Christ reigns until all things are subject to his rule—except God, who is "all in all" (15:28).

Revelation 14:1-5. The context of the Scripture is the final battle between good and evil. Christ, the lamb, stands firmly on Mount Zion; and the armies of the Lord, the 144,000, prepare for battle. J. Massyngberde Ford, in her commentary on Revelation, unpacks the symbolism. Zion is Jerusalem, the city of God, the seat of God's judgment, and the center of the messianic new age. Verse 2 combines God's voice, which is like water and thunder, "a welcome sound in a land which often suffered from drought," with the voices of angels (harps) and human beings (song). "Redeemed" is from the Greek word meaning "purchase." Unblemished, the 144,000 are acceptable gifts offered before the Lord. Some commentaries indicate that "first fruits" means "servants devoted to God" and here specifically references the sacrifice of martyrs. Others point out that the offering of the first fruit was necessary before any of the crop was consumed. Without this offering to God, the rest of the crop would not be blessed (see Leviticus 23:14; Deuteronomy 26:1-16; Proverbs 3:9-10).

INTERPRETING THE SCRIPTURE

The Harvest Festival

Farming communities have their own calendars: times for plowing, seeding, harvesting, turning the soil, fertilizing, replanting. As each field is harvested, the produce is processed and stored. Grain is milled. Corn fills up silos for winter feed. Green beans, pears, olives, pickles, tomatoes, and jam in canning jars line pantry shelves. Potatoes, carrots, and turnips fill up the root cellar. Figs are dried and nuts poured into burlap bags. Grapes are pressed for wine and juice. When the harvest is over for the year, then farmers have a few weeks for tinkering—fixing the tractor, cleaning tools, replacing barn wood—and time to relax before the next year's plowing and planting begins.

The Festival of the Booths was celebrated in autumn. Deuteronomy 16:13 refers to the time "when you have gathered in the produce from your threshing floor and your wine press." Leviticus 23:34 sets a date: the fifteenth day of the seventh month. When all the year's produce was processed and stored, the farmers gathered up their families and went to Jerusalem to celebrate the end of the agricultural year.

The Festival of the Booths was a seven-day celebration (23:33) to which an eighth day was added (23:39). It begins and ends with a day of rest, but in between is a party. The word that defines the feast is "rejoice." "Rejoice before the LORD your God," says Leviticus 23:40. Numbers 29:12 says, "You shall celebrate a festival to the LORD." Deuteronomy 16:14-15 says, "Rejoice during your festival. . . .

The Lord your God will bless you in all your produce and in all your undertakings, and you shall surely celebrate."

Branches

On each day of the festival, the people took branches from a variety of trees and, as part of daily worship, processed around the altar seven times. The liturgy followed Psalm 118. Reciting the psalm as they processed, the Israelites waved the branches with verse 1, "O give thanks to the LORD, for he is good" and verse 25, "Save us, we beseech you, O LORD! O LORD, we beseech you, give us success!" The purpose of the ritual was thanksgiving for the completion of the agricultural year and supplication for rain, so that next year's crops would thrive.

The ritual using the branches is ancient, attributed in some sources to Abraham. It has continued, generation after generation; and even today, observant Jews celebrate the Festival of Booths in the same way. Over time, the meaning of the ritual has changed. When Israel was a settled, agricultural community, the ritual was directly related to the agricultural calendar: praise for the harvest and supplication, asking God to bless the next round of plowing and planting. In exile, the ritual was probably discontinued; the people had no land to plow and no altar to process around. On their return, the festival was reinstated and the branches were used for constructing booths (Nehemiah 8:13-18). Today, the branches are waved in all six directions (east, south, west, north, up and down) in recognition of the fact that God is everywhere. They are also used in daily processions around the pedestal where the Torah is read as a way of remembering the ancient rites of the people and their prayers for rain. A further interpretation says that the different branches represent different people and their need to be united in one community of faith. Perhaps the idea of one community comes from Zechariah 14:16-18, which uses the festival as an image for describing the future, God's promise for a new age. All the nations of the earth will go to Jerusalem to worship God, and God will give them rain in abundance.

Notice the interplay between the ritual and its meaning in the lives of the people. The ritual is an expression of faith in God, who provides the land, the rain, the growth, the harvest. But as generations pass, the ritual becomes a way of remembering the past and teaching the children. The ritual itself becomes the center of meaning. Question: Why do we do this? Why do we wave around the branches? Answer: Because God is everywhere.

Booths

Booths are temporary shelters. Jacob Milgrom, in his commentary on Leviticus, suggests that the booths were an integral part of the festival itself. Pilgrims came to Jerusalem. The city was crowded, so many people built booths, temporary shelters where they could live for the seven day of the festival—hence the name: Festival of Booths. Even today, observant Jews build booths of cardboard or cloth with roofs made of branches, open to the sky. They decorate with dried corn and squash and children's artwork and live or at least eat their meals in the booth for the seven days of the festival. Imagine Jerusalem with booths lining the streets, covering rooftops, setting on balconies, dotting the hillsides.

Booths took on meaning. They were temporary shelters during the harvest, where the farmer lived, ready to capture every second of sunlight and to protect the crops at night. So booths brought to mind the agricultural meanings of the festival, the fact that we depend on God, who gives rain for planting and growth for the harvest. The booths also took on historical meaning: "You shall live in booths for seven days . . . so that your generations may know that I made the people of Israel live in booths when I [God] brought them out of the land of Egypt" (Leviticus 23:42-43). They were a way to remember the years after the Exodus from Egypt, when the people wandered in the wilderness for forty years. The wilderness was a training ground for the Israelites, the place where they learned how to be the people of God, entirely dependent on God for shelter and protection. The booths may also have resembled the shanties the Israelites lived in when they were slaves in Egypt and when they were exiles in Babylon and so were a way of remembering their lives both before and after God's mighty acts of salvation.

Pulling together the historical interpretation of the booths with the ritual using the branches, Samuel Balentine, in his commentary on Leviticus, adds further meaning: "Each of the trees cited . . . seems to be associated with the bounty of the promised land, not the barrenness of the wilderness. In terms of creation theology, the bounty of the earth that surpasses barrenness, like the divine order that exceeds primordial chaos, is reason to praise God." Meaning expands as ritual is interpreted.

The Festival of Booths, like many of the holy days appointed by God, has layers upon layers of meaning. It is a harvest festival. It remembers God's act of salvation in the Exodus and the forty years when the Israelites wandered in the wilderness, a temporary way of life when they learned to be God's people. Now, perhaps it is a way of teaching children as they raise questions and come to understand the rituals associated with the holy days of their faith.

SHARING THE SCRIPTURE

PREPARING TO TEACH

Preparing Our Hearts

Ponder this week's devotional reading from Deuteronomy 8:1-11. The writer reminds readers of the ways that God has humbled and disciplined them. What experiences have you had that have taught you to depend upon God? In what ways have experiences during lean times prompted you to remember and thank God during prosperous times?

Pray that you and the students will remember God not only when you need help but also in good times.

Preparing Our Minds

Study the background Scripture from Leviticus 23:33-43; Numbers 29:12-40; Deuteronomy 16:13-17; 1 Corinthians 15:20-29; Revelation 14:1-5. The lesson Scripture is from Leviticus 23:33-43.

Consider this question as you prepare the lesson: *How can our heritage be remembered and passed on to succeeding generations?*

Write on newsprint:
❏ information for next week's lesson, found under Continue the Journey.

❏ activities for further spiritual growth in Continue the Journey.

Gather several commentaries on Leviticus and Bible dictionaries to be used to answer questions raised under Goal 1 in Sharing the Scripture.

LEADING THE CLASS

(1) Gather to Learn

❖ Welcome the class members and guests.

❖ Pray that those who have come today will appreciate the faith that has been passed on to them.

❖ Read or retell portions of The Big Picture: Rituals, Holy Days, Connections to introduce today's lesson and sum up Unit 3, "Holy Days."

❖ Talk with the students about how rituals, holy days, and connections in their own faith traditions enable them to better understand and more faithfully relate to both God and the community of faith. Also discuss how they pass these faith traditions on to the next generation.

❖ Read aloud today's focus statement: **Families need rituals of celebration to remember their heritage and to pass it on to their children. How can their heritage be remembered and passed on to succeeding** generations? The Israelites' celebration of the Festival of Booths assisted them in renewing their commitment to their guiding and protecting God and in passing on their faith to their children.

(2) Goal 1: Understand All Aspects of the Festival of Booths, a Fall Grain Festival

❖ Choose a volunteer to read Leviticus 23:33-43.

❖ Make a list on newsprint of all that the students learn about this festival from their Bible reading. Include dates, offerings, and actions that are prescribed.

❖ Invite the adults to raise questions about the items on the list. For example, they may wonder about the significance of the branches or the purpose of this feast or why booths were constructed or what a "holy convocation" entails.

❖ Form small groups and assign each group one of the questions that the class has raised. Provide commentaries on Leviticus and Bible dictionaries to answer these questions. Distribute paper and pencils so group members can make notes. Answers will likely also be found in Understanding the Scripture and Interpreting the Scripture, so give the groups any copies of *The New International Lesson Annual* that you have available if the students do not have their own copies. Also suggest that students look at background Scripture from Numbers 29:12-40 and Deuteronomy 16:13-17.

❖ Call the groups together and ask each to report. See what questions remain and try to answer them based on Understanding the Scripture and Interpreting the Scripture.

(3) Goal 2: Appreciate a Faith Heritage in which the Learners Are Guided and Protected by a Patient, Forgiving, and Merciful God

❖ Recall that the Feast of Booths helped—and continues to help—Jewish people appreciate their relationship with God who led and cared for them in the wilderness.

❖ Ask these questions:
1. **Which holy days in the Christian tradition help you to remember and appreciate how God has been patient, forgiving, and merciful toward you?** (Easter will be a likely choice for many students. Remind the group that today is the third Sunday in Lent, about halfway to Easter.)
2. **Why are these holy days so important to you?**
3. **As you think about the history of your own congregation, what were the watershed moments, the times when the church needed God's protection and guidance to get through a challenging time?**
4. **What challenge is your congregation facing right now that calls for God's guidance and protection?**
5. **How does the memory of God's past dealings with this congregation give us hope for the future?**

(4) Goal 3: Make a Commitment to Pass on to the Next Generation a Legacy of Faith that God Will Always Guide and Protect

❖ Invite the adults to talk with a partner or small group about how they learned about Jesus. What role did parents and other family members play? What role did the Sunday school, confirmation class, choirs, fellowship groups, camps, worship services, retreats, or other church-based groups play? What role did their personal seeking after God play?

❖ Call everyone together and ask these questions:

1. **How many of you came into a relationship with Jesus with no help from anyone else?** (Likely, no one will respond affirmatively.)
2. **Given that we all had someone to teach and mentor us, what are you willing to do to help members of the next generation(s) come into a relationship with Jesus?**
3. **What else could we, as a congregation, do to help our young people?** (This would be an opportunity to discuss the addition or expansion of a Sunday school or other programming for children and teens. Note that although there are some communities that have no younger people, most communities do. They just may not be part of the church. What can you do to draw them in?)

❖ Provide quiet time for students to determine how they can help younger generations and then make a silent commitment to God to pass on their faith using whatever strategy or talent they have identified.

(5) Continue the Journey

❖ Break the silence by praying that as the learners depart they will cherish the heritage of the past and look ahead to the church's future, especially as that future is in the hands of younger generations.

❖ Post information for next week's session on newsprint for the students to copy:

- **Title: Powerful Faith**
- **Background Scripture: Mark 9:14-29**
- **Lesson Scripture: Mark 9:14-29**
- **Focus of the Lesson: It is commonly accepted that people are able to accomplish great things only by changing self-doubt to believing in themselves. How can people believe they can accomplish great things? Jesus encouraged his disciples to believe that with his help they could accomplish great things and then demonstrated that by casting out the boy's evil spirit.**

❖ Post the following information on newsprint and provide paper and pencils for the students to copy it. Challenge the adults to grow spiritually by completing one or more of these activities related to this week's session.

(1) **Talk with a younger person about holy day traditions that are important to you as a Christian. You may include days that are special to your particular congregation, such as Homecoming, and explain why these holy days are important.**

(2) **Volunteer to meet with a confirmation or youth Sunday school class to talk about an event in your church's history that needs to be honored and remembered. Include pictures if you have access to them.**

(3) Continue your Lenten times of prayer, meditation, or journaling. What new insights have you discovered about your relationship with God through Jesus Christ?

❖ Sing or read aloud "Pass It On."

❖ Conclude today's session by leading the class in this benediction, which is adapted from Leviticus 22:31 in the lesson for December 13: **As we go forth, we commit ourselves to keep the commandments of the Lord. Amen.**

THIRD QUARTER
The Gift of Faith

MARCH 6, 2016–MAY 29, 2016

The lessons during the spring quarter will focus on the theme of faith as it is seen in the Gospels of Mark and Luke. "The Gift of Faith" is divided into three units: "Tests of Faith," comprising four lessons from Mark, including the story of Jesus' resurrection; "Restorative Faith," which includes four lessons from Luke; and "Fullness of Faith," a five-session unit from Luke.

Unit 1, "Tests of Faith," opens on March 6 with an exploration of Mark 9:14-29 where we see the "Powerful Faith" of the father of a demon-possessed boy who is healed by Jesus. We continue in the Gospel of Mark on March 13, this time looking at "Simple Faith" in 10:17-31 where a rich man questions Jesus about how he can inherit eternal life. In "Struggling Faith," the lesson for Palm Sunday from Mark 14:26-31, 66-72, Jesus tells Peter that he will deny him three times. On Easter we will examine "Resurrection Faith" from Mark 16:1-8 to see the women's response to the empty tomb.

On April 3 we move into Unit 2 with a lesson of healing from Luke 7:1-10 titled "Renewed Health." Luke 7:36-50 is the basis for our study on April 10, "A Reversal of Shame," which shows the loving response of a woman whom Jesus had forgiven. "A Sound Mind," the session for April 17 from Luke 8:26-39, explores the change in a demon-possessed man when Jesus heals him. The familiar parable of the prodigal son is the focus for the lesson from Luke 15:11-32 on April 24 in which we see "A Family Reunion" as the wayward son returns home.

Unit 3, "Fullness of Faith," opens on May 1 with "Increased Faith," a teaching of Jesus from Luke 17:1-10 concerning how members of the community of faith are to interact with one another. On May 8 we turn to a story of "Grateful Faith" in Luke 17:11-19, where a Samaritan who was one of ten lepers Jesus has healed returns to give thanks. "Humble Faith," the lesson for May 15, examines the actions of a Pharisee and tax collector in the Temple and Jesus' reactions to them, as told in Luke 18:9-14. In the two background Scriptures for May 22, Luke 18:15-17 and Mark 10:13-16, we see Jesus welcoming youngsters and hear his commendation of "Childlike Faith." The quarter closes on May 29 with "Joyous Faith," the story of the Jewish tax collector Zacchaeus as told in Luke 19:1-10.

MEET OUR WRITER

DR. JERRY L. SUMNEY

Dr. Jerry L. Sumney is a member of the Society of Biblical Literature and is past president for the Southeastern Region of the Society. At the national level, he also served as chair of the steering committee for the Theology of the Disputed Paulines Group from 1996 through 2001 and currently serves as the chair of the steering committee for the Disputed Paulines Section. He is also currently chair for the Pauline Epistles and Literature Section of the International Meeting of the Society of Biblical Literature. He was elected to membership in the Studiorum Novi Testamenti Societas (SNTS) in 2005.

Dr. Sumney has written six books: *The Bible: An Introduction* (2010); *Colossians: A Commentary*, New Testament Library Series (2008); *Philippians, A Handbook for Second-Year Greek Students* (2007); *Servants of Satan, False Brothers, and Other Pauline Opponents* (1999); *Preaching Apocalyptic Texts* (coauthored with Larry Paul Jones [1999]); and *Identifying Paul's Opponents* (1990). He is editor of *The Order of the Ministry; Equipping the Saints* (2002) and coeditor of *Theology and Ethics in Paul and His Interpreters* (1996), *Paul and Pathos* (2001), and *Romans* in the Society of Biblical Literature Bible Resources series (2012). Dr. Sumney also has written more than thirty articles in journals and books. He also contributed entries to the *New Interpreter's Dictionary of the Bible* and the *Dictionary of the Later New Testament and Its Developments*, and the forthcoming *Dictionary of Scripture and Ethics*. In addition, he is a contributor to *The College Study Bible* and the *CEB Study Bible*.

Prior to joining the faculty of Lexington Theological Seminary (LTS), where he is professor of biblical studies, he taught in the religion department at Ferrum College from 1986 through 1997. He received his BA from David Lipscomb University in 1978, his MA from Harding University in 1982, and his PhD from Southern Methodist University in 1987.

Dr. Sumney has presented papers at regional, national, and international academic conferences. He has also led numerous workshops for elders and deacons; Bible study workshops and series, including in the Lay School of Theology at LTS and in the school for licensed ministers sponsored by the Kentucky region of the Christian Church. He is the regular teacher of an adult Sunday school class in his home church, Central Christian Church (Disciples of Christ) in Lexington.

Jerry and his wife, Diane, have three daughters: Elizabeth, Victoria, and Margaret.

THE BIG PICTURE: THE GOSPELS OF MARK AND LUKE

Our texts for this spring quarter come from two of the four Gospels: Mark and Luke. As we prepare to study texts from the Gospels, it may be helpful to remind ourselves about the nature of the Gospels and how we go about reading them. As we look at these stories from the life of Jesus, we will be looking for what they intend us to believe and how they intend us to live. Fortunately, that is exactly what the Gospels were written to do. Although we sometimes read the Gospels as though they are history texts, they are really theological texts. That is, the Gospels are most concerned about helping their readers understand God, Christ, the world, and ourselves. These writers were telling their stories so that their churches would have proper understandings of God and of Christ and what Christ has done for us. So as we read the Gospels, we will be looking for those important truths that can help us live as faithful Christians.

Most scholars think that Mark was the first of our four New Testament Gospels to be written. Some think that Mark is the first author to construct a narrative of the life of Jesus. If that is right, we have in Mark the first running account of the ministry of Jesus. Up until that point, some people had collected and memorized, and perhaps written, stories about what Jesus did or things that Jesus said. But no one had set them out as a story that flows from the beginning of his ministry in Galilee to its end in Jerusalem. So we owe this way of telling the story of Jesus to Mark.

There is also broad agreement that Luke had a copy of Mark as he wrote his Gospel. So Luke generally follows the chronology of Mark, but adds a good deal of material. Most of the material Luke adds are things that Jesus says. Much of this added material is also in Matthew. The added material is so much alike in Matthew and Luke that it seems likely that it was also in written form. The document that contained this teaching material is usually called Q. Unfortunately, no one has found a copy of Q, so its existence remains hypothetical. Still, most scholars think it existed and that Matthew and Luke had copies of it. In addition to material from Mark and Q, Luke also has some stories that are unique to this Gospel and its understanding of Jesus.

While it may seem strange to think that Luke had and used a copy of Mark, that is consistent with what Luke says about how he went about his task of writing. Luke begins his Gospel with a short prologue that tells how he did the work of writing this Gospel. He says that he read what others had written and he talked to eyewitnesses and ministers who told stories about Jesus (1:1-4). Luke says that he has done research to prepare for his writing. This does not make Luke less inspired. Rather, it tells us that God chose to be known through the stories that Luke found while conducting his research.

Knowing that Luke had read Mark helps us again think about how to read the Gospels. As we pay careful attention to what each Gospel says, it becomes evident that they tell the story of Jesus somewhat differently. Since Luke had a copy of Mark, we can be sure that when he tells things differently from Mark he has a reason. We can be sure of this because of all the places where Luke follows what Mark says. The differences in what these Gospels tell us about Jesus are there because the Gospels are primarily theological writings. The Gospels tell their stories in the ways they do to help us understand religious truths and to build faith. So when we see them relate some things differently, the question we need to ask is not about who got it right but about what different idea each one wants us to hear. As we read the Gospels we will ask what lesson they want us to learn.

Mark was written around the year A.D. 70, the year that the Romans destroyed the Temple in Jerusalem. The loss of the Temple was a not only a shock to Judaism but also to the church. The one Temple of the God the church said is the most powerful of all has just fallen. What does that say about the power of God? The insurrection in Judea that led to the Temple's destruction may well have led to some persecution of Christians who were now devotees of the same God as those causing the disturbance in Palestine. Whether related to the problems in Judea or not, Mark's church has experienced persecution so severe that it has led some to wonder why this powerful God allowed it to happen. Consequently, in his presentation of Jesus, Mark needs to help his church interpret the fall of the Temple and their persecution. How are they to keep their faith under these circumstances? This social setting helps us understand much about Mark.

Mark's presentation of the disciples has often left readers wondering. In his Gospel the disciples do not understand Jesus. The more they hear, the less they seem to understand his teachings or the direction of his ministry. Early in his ministry, Jesus says they are being given the keys to understanding how God is now working to bring the Kingdom into existence (4:10-11). By the time we pick up the story in our first lesson, things have gone downhill. The disciples no longer seem to be able to understand Jesus' mission. Even when it seems that Peter understands Jesus and proclaims him to be the Messiah, we see that he so badly misunderstands what that means that Jesus calls him Satan (8:27-33). In the end all the disciples desert Jesus, with only Peter staying around, and he finally denies knowing Jesus. Unlike the other Gospels, there are no scenes of reconciliation or forgiveness after the resurrection. Peter's denial is the last appearance the disciples make in Mark. Readers have often asked why Mark paints such a dismal portrait of the disciples. Many interpreters think that Mark presents the disciples in this way to help his church think about what to do with members who denied their faith in a time of persecution. Seeing this weakness in the disciples and knowing that they became great champions of the faith enables Mark's church to forgive those who failed in the face of persecution. If Peter could be forgiven, so could those in Mark's church who had denied their faith.

Of course, the central character in Mark and all the Gospels is Jesus. Mark presents Jesus as the one who brings the Kingdom into the world. Mark summarizes Jesus' preaching as the proclamation that the Kingdom is "near," so people need to repent and accept this good news (1:14-15). When Jesus says the

Kingdom is near, he means that it is close by in the person of Jesus and that it is coming soon. So the kingdom of God makes its entry into the world with the ministry of Jesus. As the one who inaugurates the Kingdom, Jesus is more powerful than evil, as his exorcisms show. Mark also emphasizes that this Kingdom is for both Jews and Gentiles. Especially in chapters 5–8, Mark has Jesus interact with Gentiles to demonstrate that they are among those Jesus loves and calls to be the people of God. They are as important in the Kingdom as the Jews. This is an important message because most of the people in Mark's church are Gentiles. So Mark shows that they were part of the plan from its inception.

The most important affirmation Mark wants his readers to make about Jesus is that he is the Son of God. By this he means that Jesus is the person who represents God in the world and the one through whom God acts. Jesus as Son is the one who brings in the Kingdom. He is the One who is the presence of God and the One who brings salvation. But Mark wants readers to know that being the Son of God is not just about wielding power. Mark certainly presents Jesus as the One who has the power of God, but if you want to see what the ministry and mission of Jesus is about you must also see his suffering and death. The person who finally understands that Jesus is the Son of God is the centurion at the foot of the cross. He sees both the power and the suffering of Jesus. This act of self-giving for the good of others is a vital aspect of Jesus' identity. According to Mark, without seeing it, we cannot understand who Jesus is. This act of giving oneself for the good of others provides both the means for a right relationship with God and the model for how believers should act in relation to one another (10:41-45).

Luke affords us a different angle on the ministry and identity of Jesus. If we remember that Luke had read Mark, then we can look for what he wants us to see about Jesus when he tells the story differently. Like Mark, one of the most important ways Luke identifies Jesus is as the Son of God. For Luke, this means that Jesus has a more intimate relationship with God than anyone else does. Jesus is the fulfillment of what God always wants humans to be. You see this in part through the genealogy he gives for Jesus. Luke traces Jesus' ancestors all the way back to "Adam, son of God" (3:38). So the originating ancestor of Jesus is God. The virgin birth story (which Mark does not have) also identifies Jesus as the unique son of God. It is through Jesus, the unique son, that people are forgiven—granted God's forgiveness and given access to the presence of God. Jesus not only has the relationship with God that God wants with all people but he also makes that relationship possible for others.

One of the most distinctive aspects of Luke is his concern for the marginalized, for outcasts and those who were considered of little or no importance. He sees the poor and outcasts as the real focus of the ministry of Jesus. While the salvation he brings is for all, it is especially for those whom others reject. This emphasis is evident from the beginning of his Gospel to its end. At the beginning Luke identifies Jesus with the poor by having him be born in the stable and having his birth announced to shepherds, night-shift shepherds at that. Compare that with Matthew, who has the king and the wealthy magi take notice of Jesus' birth. In addition, the principal characters in the birth story in Luke are the women. At the end of Luke, the women are among those who stay to witness the crucifixion.

Luke lays out the importance of the marginalized in the story that sets the theme for the whole ministry of Jesus: that of his return to Nazareth (4:14-30). In Matthew and Mark, this is a relatively minor episode in the middle of Jesus' ministry in Galilee. Luke, however, moves this story to be the first one that he tells about the ministry of Jesus, and he expands it so that he can tell readers who the ministry of Jesus is for. In Luke, Jesus reads the passage from Isaiah that has him say that God's Spirit has come upon him to bring good news to the poor and to set the oppressed free. When Jesus says this passage is fulfilled in him, the crowd assumes that they are the poor and oppressed. After all, the Romans have been dominating them for decades. Jesus then makes it clear that those God is coming for are those who are not present, those who have not been recognized as God's people. The good people in worship then want to kill him.

This theme also comes through in stories that only appear in Luke. Only Luke has the parable of the rich man and Lazarus. In this parable Lazarus has no particular virtue; he is just poor. Still, he is saved. The only thing we hear about the rich man is that he is rich, and he is condemned. This is not a comforting parable to those of us who are financially comfortable. Only Luke has the parable of the good Samaritan (10:25-37). In this parable, the hero is the least likely and least respected person the crowd could have imagined. Samaritans were outcasts to Jews, yet Jesus tells the man who had asked how he should live to go be like a Samaritan. When Luke tells the parable of the great supper (14:15-24), only his version has the servants bring in the poor to replace the wealthy who had refused their invitation. More than in the other Gospels, Luke has Jesus identify himself with tax collectors and sinners. Luke also has many warnings about the dangers of wealth and how it can lure us into unfaithfulness, perhaps even hiding our need for God.

As it does in all the Gospels, the crucifixion shows how we are to understand the ministry and mission of Jesus. In Luke, Jesus knows what his mission is and what he "must" do. In these places Jesus is acknowledging that there is a plan for what he is to do. His job is to follow the plan, to be obedient, and so to be in a position to grant forgiveness and salvation. Luke sees a great reversal of fortunes coming for the oppressed. The first will be last, the last first. The crucifixion and resurrection of Jesus is the pattern and proof of this coming act of God. Jesus is seemingly defeated and everyone thought that any plan to bring salvation through him must have ended at the cross. But the resurrection demonstrates that God is determined to overcome evil and give salvation to God's people. Through the resurrection, Jesus is exalted to the place of authority in heaven. From there, he has the authority to forgive sins in the name of God and to grant people access to God and thereby to the relationship with God that gives life and meaning.

These two Gospels, then, give us different angles of vision on this ministry and mission of Jesus. The images they give us are not in competition. Rather, each Gospel gives us a window into the meaning of Jesus. Each writer tries to describe the significance of something that is beyond his ability to capture. Having both accounts gives us a wider and deeper understanding of how God is present in and acted through Jesus than either would give by itself.

Close-up:
Quotations of Faith

People of many religious traditions—as well as skeptics who claim no religious traditions—have written about faith. Here are some quotations that you may wish to use as you discuss the theme of faith throughout the quarter. Consider posting one or two quotations each week for the students to discuss as they assemble prior to the beginning of the session.

- Sir Thomas Browne, *Religio Medici*
  "To believe only possibilities, is not faith, but mere Philosophy."

- Emily Dickinson, "I Never Saw a Moor," *Complete Poems*
  I NEVER saw a moor,
  I never saw the sea;
  Yet know I how the heather looks,
  And what a wave must be.
  I never spoke with God,
  Nor visited in heaven;
  Yet certain am I of the spot
  As if the chart were given.

- Havelock Ellis, *The Dance of Life*
  "No faith is our own that we have not arduously won."

- John Gunstone, *The Lord Is Our Healer*
  "One of the deepest mysteries of faith is that, although it constitutes our deepest response to God for what he has done for us in Jesus Christ, yet it is, at the same time, a gift from him when we lift our eyes beyond ourselves. He meets us with faith when we want to have faith."

- St. John of the Cross, *The Ascent of Mount Carmel*
  "Faith tells us of things we have never seen, and cannot come to know by our natural senses."

- Martin Luther, preface to his translation of St. Paul's Epistle to the Romans
  "Faith is a living and unshakeable confidence, a belief in the grace of God so assured that a man would die a thousand deaths for its sake."

- Michel de Montaigne, *Essays*
  "'Tis faith alone that vividly and certainly comprehends the deep mysteries of our religion."

- John Locke, *An Essay Concerning Human Understanding:* Book 4: Chapter 18, "Of Faith and Reason, and their Distinct Provinces"

"Faith . . . is the assent to any proposition, not thus made out by the deductions of reason, but upon the credit of the proposer, as coming from God, in some extraordinary way of communication."

- Edmond Rostand, *Chanticler*, Act II, Scene 3
  "It is at night that faith in light is admirable."

- John-Paul Sartre, *Words*
  "Faith, even when profound, is never complete."

- John Lancaster Spalding, *Means and Ends of Education*
  "Your faith is what you believe, not what you know."

- Miguel de Unamuno, *The Agony of Christianity*
  "Faith which does not doubt is a dead faith."

- Voltaire, *Philosophical Dictionary*
  "Faith consists in believing not what seems true, but what seems false to our understanding."

Faith in Action: Living as Faithful People

During the spring quarter all of our lessons are centered on the theme of faith. Post the following activities and encourage the students to complete them at home.

Activity 1: Define "faith" by using information from Bible dictionaries and from Scripture passages, which you can locate in Bible concordances. What is faith? Who has faith? Name ways that believers can demonstrate by their words and deeds that they are faithful followers of Jesus Christ.

Activity 2: Review the story of the father who sought healing for his demon-possessed son in Mark 9:14-29. The father asked Jesus to help him overcome his unbelief. Meditate on Jesus' willingness to use even a grain of faith to transform our lives.

Activity 3: Page through a hymnal looking for songs about faith. What points do the hymn writers make about faith? Which of these hymns speaks most clearly to you about what faith is and how believers can exercise faith?

Activity 4: Look at the Scriptures for this quarter's lessons. Which of these stories or parables best illustrates your understanding of faith? Why?

Activity 5: Think about challenges in your own life over the past months. What has tested your faith? How were you able to hang on to your faith and grow from the experiences?

Activity 6: Read James 1:22 and 2:14-19. Here James insists that we must be "doers of the word" (1:22), that is, people who show their faith by their works. Although we are saved by grace through faith (see Ephesians 2:8-9), not works, the works that we do enliven our faith. James specifically mentions caring for those who lack the basic necessities of life—food and clothing. In what ways are you demonstrating your faith by helping those in need? What more can you do?

Activity 7: Consider how faith in Jesus is made manifest by one's loyalty to him and one's willingness to bear witness to him, no matter what the cost. Where can you express your loyalty to Jesus by bearing witness to him?

Activity 8: Grow in faith by making a commitment to practice at least one spiritual discipline each day. Spend time praying, studying the Bible, meditating, observing a fast (from food, entertainment, or something else important to you) to devote time to God, journaling, or simplifying your life. How does your practice of a discipline empower you to grow spiritually?

Activity 9: Focus on the story of Jesus' resurrection on Easter morning. Recognize that although a heavenly messenger brings tidings that Jesus has risen, no human actually witnessed that event. Yet this event is fundamental to Christian belief. How is your faith formed and strengthened by the news that God has raised Christ from the dead?

Pronunciation Guide

Capernaum (kuh puhr′ nay uhm)
denarii (di nair′ ee i)
Gerasene (ger′ uh seen)
mikvah (mik vaw′)

Naaman (nay′ uh muhn)
Salome (suh loh′ mee)
Sanhedrin (sah hee′ druhn)
Zacchaeus (za kee′ uhs)

UNIT 1: TESTS OF FAITH
POWERFUL FAITH

PREVIEWING THE LESSON

Lesson Scripture: Mark 9:14-29
Background Scripture: Mark 9:14-29
Key Verse: Mark 9:24

Focus of the Lesson:

It is commonly accepted that people are able to accomplish great things only by changing self-doubt to believing in themselves. How can people believe they can accomplish great things? Jesus encouraged his disciples to believe that with his help they could accomplish great things and then demonstrated that by casting out the boy's evil spirit.

Goals for the Learners:

(1) to explore the details of the failure of the disciples to heal the child, even though Jesus was then able to do so.
(2) to contemplate the faith it takes to use the power of Jesus Christ to minister to others.
(3) to pray for those who need healing.

Supplies:

Bibles, newsprint and marker, paper and pencils, hymnals

READING THE SCRIPTURE

NRSV

Lesson Scripture: Mark 9:14-29

¹⁴When they came to the disciples, they saw a great crowd around them, and some scribes arguing with them. ¹⁵When the whole crowd saw him, they were immediately overcome with awe, and they ran forward to greet him. ¹⁶He asked them, "What are you arguing about with them?" ¹⁷Someone from the crowd answered him, "Teacher, I brought you my son;

CEB

Lesson Scripture: Mark 9:14-29

¹⁴When Jesus, Peter, James, and John approached the other disciples, they saw a large crowd surrounding them and legal experts arguing with them. ¹⁵Suddenly the whole crowd caught sight of Jesus. They ran to greet him, overcome with excitement. ¹⁶Jesus asked them, "What are you arguing about?"

¹⁷Someone from the crowd

he has a spirit that makes him unable to speak; [18]and whenever it seizes him, it dashes him down; and he foams and grinds his teeth and becomes rigid; and I asked your disciples to cast it out, but they could not do so." [19]He answered them, "You faithless generation, how much longer must I be among you? How much longer must I put up with you? Bring him to me." [20]And they brought the boy to him. When the spirit saw him, immediately it threw the boy into convulsions, and he fell on the ground and rolled about, foaming at the mouth. [21]Jesus asked the father, "How long has this been happening to him?" And he said, "From childhood. [22]It has often cast him into the fire and into the water, to destroy him; but if you are able to do anything, have pity on us and help us." [23]Jesus said to him, "If you are able!—All things can be done for the one who believes." **[24]Immediately the father of the child cried out, "I believe; help my unbelief!"** [25]When Jesus saw that a crowd came running together, he rebuked the unclean spirit, saying to it, "You spirit that keep this boy from speaking and hearing, I command you, come out of him, and never enter him again!" [26]After crying out and convulsing him terribly, it came out, and the boy was like a corpse, so that most of them said, "He is dead." [27]But Jesus took him by the hand and lifted him up, and he was able to stand. [28]When he had entered the house, his disciples asked him privately, "Why could we not cast it out?" [29]He said to them, "This kind can come out only through prayer."

responded, "Teacher, I brought my son to you, since he has a spirit that doesn't allow him to speak. [18]Wherever it overpowers him, it throws him into a fit. He foams at the mouth, grinds his teeth, and stiffens up. So I spoke to your disciples to see if they could throw it out, but they couldn't."

[19]Jesus answered them, "You faithless generation, how long will I be with you? How long will I put up with you? Bring him to me."

[20]They brought him. When the spirit saw Jesus, it immediately threw the boy into a fit. He fell on the ground and rolled around, foaming at the mouth. [21]Jesus asked his father, "How long has this been going on?"

He said, "Since he was a child. [22]It has often thrown him into a fire or into water trying to kill him. If you can do anything, help us! Show us compassion!"

[23]Jesus said to him, "'If you can do anything'? All things are possible for the one who has faith."

[24]At that the boy's father cried out, "I have faith; help my lack of faith!"

[25]Noticing that the crowd had surged together, Jesus spoke harshly to the unclean spirit, "Mute and deaf spirit, I command you to come out of him and never enter him again." [26]After screaming and shaking the boy horribly, the spirit came out. The boy seemed to be dead; in fact, several people said that he had died. [27]But Jesus took his hand, lifted him up, and he arose.

[28]After Jesus went into a house, his disciples asked him privately, "Why couldn't we throw this spirit out?"

[29]Jesus answered, "Throwing this kind of spirit out requires prayer."

UNDERSTANDING THE SCRIPTURE

Introduction. The disciples' reaction to the Transfiguration immediately precedes this story. Peter, James, and John have seen Jesus transformed but fail to understand it. Our reading begins as they and Jesus rejoin the other disciples. While the glory of Jesus is revealed in the Transfiguration, the disciples fail to understand who he is. This exorcism story seems to be one more piece of evidence that the disciples do not yet have the faith they need.

Mark 9:14-19. As Jesus returns to the nine disciples who were not present for the Transfiguration, a crowd has gathered. The crowd, which included some religious experts (scribes), was embroiled in an argument. Strangely, when they see Jesus they are "overcome with awe" (9:15). This reaction suggests that there is something extraordinary about the appearance of Jesus, even though the story of the Transfiguration has said that he has returned to his usual state. Nevertheless, the crowd approaches him with some expectation that he will be able to settle their dispute.

Their argument involves the exorcism of a demon. The disciples have tried to cast it out, but have failed. This is unexpected because earlier in Mark they are able to exorcise demons (6:13). Now they fail. If we have been following Mark's descriptions of the disciples, we know that he is painting a worsening portrait of them. The longer they are with Jesus, the less they understand him. Back in chapter 4 Jesus had identified them as the insiders who are given the secrets of the Kingdom (4:11). But from that point on they have more

and more trouble understanding Jesus. When he stills the storm they ask, "Who then is this?" (4:41). When they return from their preaching trip among Israelites, they want Jesus for themselves and do not imagine that Jesus can feed the crowd that has gathered (6:30-44). When Jesus walks on the water, they again do not understand (6:51). There is a second feeding that they do not understand (8:1-10). When Jesus accepts the title of Messiah, they reject the idea that it means he will die (8:27-33). Finally Peter, James, and John fail to understand the Transfiguration. Now it seems they are losing the powers they once had because they cannot defeat this demon.

The description of the demon's attacks reminds many readers of epilepsy. However we might understand his condition, Mark and all the characters in his story attribute these attacks to demonic forces. Jesus does not dispute this. Instead, he focuses on the lack of faith he sees in the disciples and, more broadly, in all the crowd. His response reminds us that the story of his ministry is drawing to a close. We know he is on his way to Jerusalem to die when he asks how much longer he will have to be with these people. Their lack of faith grieves him. Yet he responds to their need by having them bring the boy.

Mark 9:20-27. The story now follows the expected pattern of an exorcism story as we see them in first-century literature. There is a description of the condition caused by the exorcism, the request for healing, the conversation between the demon and the exorcist, the departure of the demon, and the evidence of the cure. The description of the demon's effect on the child seems particularly detailed and gruesome in comparison with other exorcism accounts in the New Testament. Not only does it cause the boy to be deaf and speechless but it also tries to kill him. The biggest difference between this exorcism and those found in other literature is the seeming ease with which Jesus dispatches the demon. As expected, the demon puts on a show of strength, but then Jesus simply sends him away and he complies. Mark adds another important element to the story, though. After the demon leaves, the boy seems dead (9:26). But Mark has Jesus take the boy's hand and then lifts him up. This description parallels that of the raising of the dead girl in Mark 5:41-42. So Mark suggests that this cure and restoration of the boy is like a resurrection from the dead. This, then, may be more than a simple exorcism. The Christ revealed in the Transfiguration has the power to overcome demonic forces and give life, even in the midst of the worst circumstances.

The heart of the story comes in verses 22-24, the exchange between Jesus and the father. The father asks Jesus to help them, "if you are able" (9:22). This lack of certainty seems reasonable, given that the disciples have just failed. But Jesus utterly rejects this doubt and says that all things are possible for those who have faith. The father's response reflects the outlook of the disciples at this point in Mark's narrative. It also reflects the faith of people in Mark's church. They have some faith, but also have some doubt. Since they are like this character, they will be listening carefully to what happens.

The father confesses his lack of faith and asks for the gift of more faith. Jesus responds to this incomplete faith by healing the son. Even an incomplete faith is enough to accept Christ's healing. The power of God is not limited by the weak or incomplete faith of the one who asks for Jesus' help.

9:28-29. When the disciples are alone with Jesus they want to know why they could not exorcise the demon. After the scathing response of Jesus in verse 19, we expect harsh recriminations. But there are none. Instead, Jesus now casts no blame on the disciples; he does not attribute their inability to a lack of faith or even a misunderstanding. With more than a touch of restraint, he says simply that this was a more powerful demon than they had faced before. Most New Testament scholars think that Jesus' response to the disciples reflects the exorcism practices of Mark's community. That is, when faced with a case of demon possession, they exorcise it with extended prayer. Readers with a King James Version will have "and fasting" added to the end of verse 29. Interpreters think that the later manuscripts that contain this addition probably also reflect the practice of the church in the fourth and fifth centuries. So exorcisms at that time included both prayer and fasting.

INTERPRETING THE SCRIPTURE

The Disciples Fail—Again

By the time we get to this story in Mark's narrative, it is no surprise that the disciples cannot exercise God's power. They have misunderstood nearly everything Jesus has done and said since chapter 4. So it is only a small step from their misunderstandings to being unable to perform wonders in his name. Mark does not explicitly tell us why they misunderstand and now cannot exercise the power of God as they once did. Still, some reasons are fairly clear from a reading of the whole of Mark.

In Mark, the disciples are not able to understand Jesus and are unable to exercise God's power because they have not yet seen the death and resurrection of Jesus. For Mark, no one can understand who Jesus is and what he means for the world without seeing his death and resurrection. It is only through the lens of those acts of God that the life and teachings of Jesus make sense. In the previous chapter, so just a few lines earlier in 8:29, Peter confesses that Jesus is the Messiah, but fails to comprehend the meaning of that identification of Jesus. As soon as Jesus accepts that title, he tells the disciples that he must suffer and die. When Peter rejects this definition of being Messiah, Jesus says, "Get behind me, Satan!" (8:33). Those who would know Christ and the power of God that comes through him must keep his death and resurrection in view. It is only through those events that Christians have access to the power of God in their lives. The death and resurrection of Christ show how much God loves us and demonstrate just how powerful God is. After the disgraceful death of Jesus, it is only the power of God that can raise him and give meaning to his life and teaching. In the church, we experience the presence of God through the crucified and risen Christ.

The disciples also misunderstand the nature of Christian leadership. Just after this episode, the disciples argue about who will be the greatest in the Kingdom (9:33-37). Jesus confronts them and asserts that Christian leadership must consist of being the servant of others. John's response in verse 38 confirms just how badly the disciples have failed to understand. He tells Jesus that they had told someone to stop exorcising demons in Jesus' name because he was not one of them. It appears that from John's perspective, the disciples may have to be servants to some, but surely they can tell some people what to do! Jesus will try to teach the disciples that leadership and God's power are to be used to help others, not to secure privilege or accolades for oneself.

Jesus' first response to the disciples' inability to cast out the demon is to bemoan the faithlessness of the "generation" (9:19). If the disciples were trying to exorcise the demon in the name of Jesus and failing, perhaps their argument with the scribes is about whether the name of Jesus is able to work such wonders. It may also be that this is the reason the child's father says, "*if you are able*" (9:22, emphasis added), cast it out. In any case, Jesus first seems to attribute the disciples' inability to exorcise the demon to a lack of faith. That viewpoint does not seem, however, to fit with the end of the story when they ask Jesus why they could not cast it out. There he simply indicates that this was a powerful demon.

Jesus Works Through Even Wavering Faith

As the story unfolds, we see that Jesus does mighty acts even for one with incomplete faith. Jesus rejects the doubt expressed with the request modified by *"if* you are able," saying that all things are possible for those who have faith. The father responds by confessing that he has only partial faith: "I believe; help my unbelief" (9:24, key verse). Jesus' declaration at first sounded as though correct and strong faith were needed to receive healing. But when Jesus heals the son after this admission by the father, it becomes clear that such is not the case. Even if faith is incomplete and struggling, it is still sufficient for the power of Jesus to be effective. The overwhelming power of Jesus subdues the demon with an unusually swift and dominating stroke. Here Jesus exercises that great power for one who has but little and uncertain faith.

We should note that the father does not ask for his own healing, but for that of another. He has faith on behalf of his son. Jesus responds to the father's faith to bless the one who is possessed. In this story, the faith of one person mediates the healing presence of Christ for another person. This is not the first time this has happened in Mark. In 2:1-12, Mark tells the story of men who carried their paralyzed friend to Jesus. Mark does not say that the paralyzed man has faith; rather, he says that when Jesus saw the faith of those who brought him, Jesus declares the man's sins forgiven and heals him (2:5). In both of these stories, the healing power of Jesus comes to people through the faith of others.

We do not often think of our faith as something that can bring the healing power of Jesus to others. But the story in today's lesson and the earlier healing of the paralyzed man suggest that this is possible. We are not, of course, in the physical presence of Jesus as they were, but we can mediate the healing presence and power of Jesus through our faith. Today's reading assures us that Christ can be present and work through our faith, even when it is weak or incomplete. We can take great comfort in knowing that Christ can work through us even if our faith is not perfect. Christ worked through a person who had weak faith but great love for the one in need. In our text the father acknowledges a partial lack of faith, and still Jesus can heal through his faith. This story can encourage us to use the faith we have to reach out to people who have needs. We can know that Christ can work in healing ways even when we are struggling with our faith.

"Only Through Prayer"

After the extraordinary show of power over the forces of evil, the disciples ask why they were unable to exorcise this demon. After all, they had been able to overcome demons in their earlier mission trip (6:12-13). From the initial response of Jesus to the problem (9:19), we expect him to point the finger of blame. Instead, Jesus says that this was a powerful demon that comes out only with prayer. Most interpreters of Mark think that this response reflects the way that Mark's community per-forms exorcisms: They pray over them. Mark, then, has Jesus affirm this way of bringing the healing power of God to those who are entrapped by evil and the forces that keep us from life with God and life as God wants people to experience it. Thus, Jesus affirms the power of faithful interces-sory prayer.

SHARING THE SCRIPTURE

PREPARING TO TEACH

Preparing Our Hearts

Ponder this week's devotional read-ing from Genesis 50:15-21. Recall the story of Joseph and his brothers. Fol-lowing the burial of their father, Jacob, the brothers are concerned that Joseph will seek revenge. How does Joseph respond to his brothers' plea for for-giveness? What would you have done?

Pray that you and the students will be ready to forgive whatever wrongs have been done to you.

Preparing Our Minds

Study the background Scripture and the lesson Scripture, both of which are from Mark 9:14-29.

Consider this question as you pre-pare the lesson: *What enables people to believe that they can accomplish great things?*

Write on newsprint:
❏ questions for Goal 2 in Sharing the Scripture.
❏ information for next week's les-son, found under Continue the Journey.
❏ activities for further spiritual growth in Continue the Journey.

Review the Introduction, The Big Picture, Close-up, and Faith in Action, which all precede the first lesson of this quarter. Consider how you might use any of this material in today's lesson.

LEADING THE CLASS

(1) Gather to Learn

❖ Welcome the class members and guests.

❖ Pray that those who have come today will believe that the prayers of the faithful have real power.

❖ Read this quotation from Anne Frank: **"Everyone has inside of him a piece of good news. The good news is that you don't know how great you can be! How much you can love! What you can accomplish! And what your potential is!"**

❖ Ask: **How can we help others to discover this good news about who they are and what they can become?**

❖ Read aloud today's focus state-ment: **It is commonly accepted that people are able to accomplish great things only by changing self-doubt to believing in themselves. How can people believe they can accomplish great things? Jesus encouraged his disciples to believe that with his help they could accomplish great things and then demonstrated that by cast-ing out the boy's evil spirit.**

(2) Goal 1: Explore the Details of the Failure of the Disciples to Heal the Child, Even Though Jesus Was Then Able to Do So

❖ Provide a context for today's story by reading Introduction in Un-derstanding the Scripture.

❖ Select five volunteers to read the parts of a narrator, Jesus, someone from the crowd, the boy's father, and a disciple (9:28). The class is to read "He is dead" in verse 26.

❖ Discuss these questions:

1. **Do you think Jesus was surprised by the disciples' failure? Why or why not?** (See "The Disciples Fail—Again" in Interpreting the Scripture.)

2. **How does this exorcism story relate to others known in the first century?** (See Mark 9:20-27 in Understanding the Scripture.)

3. **What role did the father's faith play in the healing of his son?** (See "Jesus Works Through Even Wavering Faith" in Interpreting the Scripture.)

4. **What role did prayer play in this healing?** (See "Only Through Prayer" in Interpreting the Scripture.)

❖ Choose several volunteers to roleplay the private discussion between Jesus and the disciples referred to in verses 28-29. Tell the "disciples" to raise questions.

❖ **Option:** Read Mark 9:28-29 in Understanding the Scripture if time is too short to do the roleplay. Note that Jesus' response to the disciples is not as harsh as we might expect.

(3) Goal 2: Contemplate the Faith It Takes to Use the Power of Jesus Christ to Minister to Others

❖ Form small groups and assign one of the following Scripture passages from Mark to each group.

- Mark 2:1-12: Jesus heals a paralyzed man
- Mark 4:35-41: Jesus calms a storm

- Mark 5:25-34: Jesus heals a woman
- Mark 10:46-52: Jesus heals blind Bartimaeus
- Mark 11:20-24: Jesus uses a withered fig tree to teach a lesson

❖ Give each group a sheet of newsprint and a marker to make notes as they answer these questions, which you will post:

1. **What did the person(s) here need from Jesus?**
2. **How did Jesus meet the need(s)?**
3. **What do you learn about the quantity and quality of faith that is necessary for Jesus to meet needs?**

❖ Reconvene the class and ask each group to report its findings.

❖ Conclude with this question: **What have these actions and teachings of Jesus revealed to you about your own faith?**

(4) Goal 3: Pray for Those Who Need Healing

❖ Invite students to call out the names of persons who need to be healed. List these names on newsprint. (**Caution:** Unless the person and his or her medical issues are well known to the group or the person has given permission for information to be disclosed, suggest that the adults use only a first name and not make any comment on the illness or injury itself. Many people want their privacy respected and do not want others to know that they are ill.)

❖ Encourage each person present to take two names and silently pray for these persons.

❖ Come together and suggest that if the students are praying for people whom they know, they send a "get well" or "thinking of you" card or a handwritten note this week to tell these individuals that they are being lifted up in prayer. If possible, perhaps the note could include an offer of tangible help, such as running errands or providing a meal.

(5) Continue the Journey

❖ Pray that as the learners depart, they will claim the powerful faith that is theirs in Christ Jesus.

❖ Post information for next week's session on newsprint for the students to copy:

- **Title: Simple Faith**
- **Background Scripture: Mark 10:17-31**
- **Lesson Scripture: Mark 10:17-31**
- **Focus of the Lesson: It is very difficult even for good people to be willing to give up all their possessions to follow some altruistic goal. What can persuade someone to forfeit his or her possessions for others? Jesus said that faith in God makes it possible for people to sacrifice all they have for the benefit of others.**

❖ Post the following information on newsprint and provide paper and pencils for the students to copy it. Challenge the adults to grow spiritually by completing one or more of these activities related to this week's session.

(1) **Pray each day for a particular person in need of healing. As suggested during the session, let this person know that he or she is being prayed for.**

(2) **Focus on your own faith on this Fourth Sunday in Lent. How strong do you believe your faith is? Think back over your life to recall circumstances in which you had to rely on your faith. Based on these circumstances, would you say that your faith is stronger or weaker than you had at first thought it to be?**

(3) **Use a Bible concordance to explore the word "faith" as it appears in the New Testament. Based on the verses you have read, how would you define "faith"? What examples did you find of people with little faith having their prayers answered? What conclusions can you draw about faith?**

❖ Sing or read aloud "Silence, Frenzied, Unclean Spirit."

❖ Conclude today's session by leading the class in this benediction, which is adapted from Mark 9:23 in today's lesson: **Together we affirm that all things can be done for the one who believes. Amen.**

UNIT 1: TESTS OF FAITH
SIMPLE FAITH

PREVIEWING THE LESSON

Lesson Scripture: Mark 10:17-31
Background Scripture: Mark 10:17-31
Key Verse: Mark 10:21

Focus of the Lesson:

It is very difficult even for good people to be willing to give up all their possessions to follow some altruistic goal. What can persuade someone to forfeit his or her possessions for others? Jesus said that faith in God makes it possible for people to sacrifice all they have for the benefit of others.

Goals for the Learners:

(1) to delve into the story of the encounter of the rich young man with Jesus.
(2) to reflect on the barriers that stand in the way of following Jesus without reservation.
(3) to make a commitment to follow Jesus, no matter what the cost.

Supplies:

Bibles, newsprint and marker, paper and pencils, hymnals

READING THE SCRIPTURE

NRSV
Lesson Scripture: Mark 10:17-31

[17]As he was setting out on a journey, a man ran up and knelt before him, and asked him, "Good Teacher, what must I do to inherit eternal life?" [18]Jesus said to him, "Why do you call me good? No one is good but God alone. [19]You know the commandments: 'You shall not murder; You shall not commit adultery; You shall not steal; You shall not bear false

CEB
Lesson Scripture: Mark 10:17-31

[17]As Jesus continued down the road, a man ran up, knelt before him, and asked, "Good Teacher, what must I do to obtain eternal life?"

[18]Jesus replied, "Why do you call me good? No one is good except the one God. [19]You know the commandments: Don't commit murder. Don't commit adultery. Don't steal. Don't give false testimony.

witness; You shall not defraud; Honor your father and mother.'" 20He said to him, "Teacher, I have kept all these since my youth." 21**Jesus, looking at him, loved him and said, "You lack one thing; go, sell what you own, and give the money to the poor, and you will have treasure in heaven; then come, follow me."** 22When he heard this, he was shocked and went away grieving, for he had many possessions.

23 Then Jesus looked around and said to his disciples, "How hard it will be for those who have wealth to enter the kingdom of God!" 24And the disciples were perplexed at these words. But Jesus said to them again, "Children, how hard it is to enter the kingdom of God! 25It is easier for a camel to go through the eye of a needle than for someone who is rich to enter the kingdom of God." 26They were greatly astounded and said to one another, "Then who can be saved?" 27Jesus looked at them and said, "For mortals it is impossible, but not for God; for God all things are possible."

28Peter began to say to him, "Look, we have left everything and followed you." 29Jesus said, "Truly I tell you, there is no one who has left house or brothers or sisters or mother or father or children or fields, for my sake and for the sake of the good news, 30who will not receive a hundredfold now in this age—houses, brothers and sisters, mothers and children, and fields, with persecutions—and in the age to come eternal life. 31But many who are first will be last, and the last will be first."

Don't cheat. Honor your father and mother."

20"Teacher," he responded, "I've kept all of these things since I was a boy."

21**Jesus looked at him carefully and loved him. He said, "You are lacking one thing. Go, sell what you own, and give the money to the poor. Then you will have treasure in heaven. And come, follow me."** 22But the man was dismayed at this statement and went away saddened, because he had many possessions.

23Looking around, Jesus said to his disciples, "It will be very hard for the wealthy to enter God's kingdom!" 24His words startled the disciples, so Jesus told them again, "Children, it's difficult to enter God's kingdom! 25It's easier for a camel to squeeze through the eye of a needle than for a rich person to enter God's kingdom."

26They were shocked even more and said to each other, "Then who can be saved?"

27Jesus looked at them carefully and said, "It's impossible with human beings, but not with God. All things are possible for God."

28Peter said to him, "Look, we've left everything and followed you."

29Jesus said, "I assure you that anyone who has left house, brothers, sisters, mother, father, children, or farms because of me and because of the good news 30will receive one hundred times as much now in this life—houses, brothers, sisters, mothers, children, and farms (with harassment)—and in the coming age, eternal life. 31But many who are first will be last. And many who are last will be first."

UNDERSTANDING THE SCRIPTURE

Introduction. Today's reading is difficult. It challenges ideas we have about how to please God and about how we can tell that a person is blessed. It is also another episode where the disciples' misunderstanding provides Mark the opportunity to instruct his readers about both the sacrifices that believers must make and the unexpected blessings they receive.

Mark 10:17-22. This story takes place while Jesus is "on the way," that is, during Jesus' trip from Galilee to Jerusalem. During this trip, Jesus continually tries to prepare his disciples for the Passion and help them understand what his death and resurrection mean. So this "on the way" reminds us that Jesus is on his way to his Passion and is teaching the disciples. A man runs to Jesus, kneels, and addresses him as "Good Teacher" (10:17). Unexpectedly, Jesus rejects this title and takes the opportunity to emphasize God's holiness. Then Jesus responds to the man's question with a traditional answer.

Asking how one can inherit eternal life seems to be just the kind of question Jesus would hope to hear. It means that the inquirer takes him seriously as a teacher and as one who knows the will of God. Jesus' response is what we would hear from any good Jewish teacher: Obey God's will as it is expressed in the Scripture. Jesus cites basic commandments from the Ten Commandments. The man's response indicates that he has been a good religious and moral person; he has kept the commandments. He has lived as he should.

Mark says that Jesus loves the man. Jesus recognizes his sincere desire to live for God and so adds the action that will complete his acceptance of God's will: Sell all you have and give it to the poor. No one would be surprised to hear a teacher call for fuller commitment to God's will, but this is not a command that anyone expected, nor is it one that people accept. How could this be a good idea? This command is as shocking to the disciples as it is to the man. It goes far beyond any reasonable expectation. It demands that one give up all of oneself and one's security and rely completely upon God.

But that is not all. The coming of Jesus makes new demands. The man must not only sell his possessions but he must also follow Jesus. The perceptive reader of Mark knows by now that following Jesus means acting as the servant to those who have less power and position (9:33-37) and even being willing to die for Jesus, to take up one's cross (8:34-35).

The man had come to Jesus for reaffirmation of his relationship with God. He was, after all, a religious person who was obviously blessed. Rather than hearing what he had hoped, he turns away, unwilling to commit himself to what Jesus demands of those who want to inherit eternal life.

Mark 10:23-27. If the story took an unexpected turn for the man who asked the question, it takes an even more unexpected turn for the readers as Jesus says it is hard for the wealthy to enter the kingdom of God. This comment takes the disciples by surprise (10:24), so Jesus elaborates: It is harder for a rich person to be saved than for a camel to go through the eye of a needle. There have been many attempts to lessen the starkness of this declaration. Some have asserted that Jesus is talking about a gate in the city wall of Jerusalem that was sized so that camels had to get on their knees to squeeze through. Thus, he says that it is difficult for rich people to be saved. The problem with this interpretation is that no such gate existed! This explanation makes us feel better but misses the point. Jesus says it is impossible for rich people to be saved. That meaning is explicit in verses 26 and 27, where the disciples ask who can be saved if not the rich. Jesus responds that salvation is impossible for humans; it is accomplished only by God.

In keeping with the conventional thinking of their day, the disciples think wealth is a sign of God's favor. Surely the rich are closer to God and God's blessings. Surely they are in line to receive eternal life and to be received into the Kingdom. When the disciples hear the rich cannot be saved, they are sure they have no chance; if the rich cannot be saved, no one can (10:26). Jesus says that is right. Salvation cannot be accomplished by humans, but God can overcome what keeps even the wealthy away from God's will. This passage contains both condemnation of those who do not commit themselves fully to God's service and the promise of grace for those who cannot make the expected commitment.

Mark 10:28-31. The passage ends with Peter trying to secure his place with Jesus. He reminds Jesus that he and the other disciples had left everything. While Jesus has just asserted that salvation is a gift of God, Peter tries to show that he deserves it. He misunderstands again. Yes, he and the other disciples have done outwardly what Jesus demanded of the rich man, but inwardly he is depending upon himself for his relationship with God.

Still, this comment by Peter gives Mark an opportunity to have Jesus assure his readers that the difficulties they endure as believers are not the last word. God does indeed bless those who commit themselves to God in Christ. Those who give up things for Jesus will receive more than they give up. He does not mean that faith brings wealth. The houses, possessions, and family that come to those who trust Jesus are the relationships they have with fellow-believers who become their families, their homes, and their possessions. These things come "in this age" (10:30) that is, in the present. While faith brings eternal life, it also brings the blessings of a fuller, more meaningful life in the present.

The passage also reaffirms the radical principle that the first will be last and the last first. Those who devote themselves to God and so accept disadvantage now are those who are richly blessed by God now and in "the age to come" (10:30). What Jesus has just said about the rich entering the Kingdom is an example of the first being last.

INTERPRETING THE SCRIPTURE

A Surprising Encounter

Today's reading is surprising on many accounts. First, we seldom see such deference to Jesus from the wealthy in Mark. This rich man kneels before Jesus and calls him "Good Teacher" (10:17) and "Teacher"

(10:20), thereby granting Jesus significant status. He has been impressed with what he has heard about Jesus. Readers need not see this person as self-righteous. He does not tell Jesus that he deserves eternal life; rather, he comes asking what he needs to do to receive it. To know that you have been faithful is not arrogance. The inquirer seems sincere. Even his sadness at hearing what Jesus says suggests that he is sincere. The next surprise for us is to hear that Jesus makes stricter demands than the law. The commands Jesus mentions stand for the whole of the law's expectations about how people treat one another. But that is not enough. Jesus demands more. We usually think that Jesus makes living for God easier. But that is not the impression you get from this story or from reading the whole of the Gospels carefully.

The Rich Cannot Be Saved?

Perhaps the most surprising element of the story is Jesus' assertion that the rich cannot be saved. This is completely unexpected. It violates all that we think about the world and what demonstrates that God is pleased with a person. We may not advocate the "prosperity gospel" that says God will make people rich if they will only give to a particular ministry, but we still see wealth as a blessing from God. In this text, wealth is not a sign of blessing, but an impediment to a saving relationship with God. This is shocking. The disciples have as hard a time hearing this as we do. Their immediate response is to assume that if rich people cannot be saved, then no one can. Even more shocking, Jesus agrees!

Some earlier interpreters tried to lessen the shock of what Jesus says

by interpreting his analogy of the camel going through the eye of a needle as something that could be done, if only with great difficulty (see the comments for verses 23-27 in the Understanding the Scripture section). But Jesus is making his point with an outrageous (and somewhat comical) image. A camel cannot get through the eye of a needle. That is how impossible it is for rich people, then all people, to be saved. At least it is impossible for people to be saved if they rely upon themselves for their relationship with God. But God is able to save all.

Giving Up Treasures

As we read this story, we want to ask, "What is so bad about being rich?" We are not told explicitly, but the story seems to point us to the rich being self-reliant. While the rich man who asks the question is not described as arrogant or self-righteous, his inability to give up his wealth suggests that it defines him and gives him a measure of self-assurance that he cannot do without. Selling everything would make him completely reliant on God for everything. He was not able to make that commitment. The problem was not that he was wealthy, but that he could not give up what gave him security in the world or in his relationship with God. Jesus called him to acknowledge and express his complete reliance on God for his life and salvation. What Jesus wants him—and everyone—to give up is all things that we think establish our place with God and our value in the world.

When Peter chimes in to say he has given up everything, he seems to be complying with what Jesus wants. But the very fact that he puts his commitment forward as evidence that he has done what Jesus commands shows that he has, again, missed the point. Peter wants to rely on his obedience to attain his place in the Kingdom. This is just what Jesus has said will not work and it is very close to the behavior of the man who could not sell his possessions. Even our commitment to do God's will can be a way to try to make a claim on God's grace. Jesus does not denigrate the sacrifice the disciples have made. Instead, he notes that their sacrifice will be more than worth it.

This passage also grants hope, even for a good life in the here and now. Jesus says that the disciples who have given up everything now have more family, homes, and possessions than they had before. This is obviously not true in a literal sense. They do not have more money or bigger families. What they do have is a new, larger family that comprises fellow believers. People in the church are their new family. The security they have with those of like faith is their new wealth. As much as Jesus has warned the disciples that following him will bring suffering and persecutions, there is more to be said. Jesus notes that the life of faith will involve persecution. But in the midst of that persecution, in the middle of hard times, Jesus promises comfort and goodness. Again, this is not in the form of material wealth. This new and larger family in the greater house is the joy and comfort that comes from the certainty of being accepted by, saved by, God. The life lived for God brings more meaning to the present because it conforms to the way God made us. We are living in the way that best suits what we are as the human creatures God made.

Believers accept some kinds of disadvantages, but those are more than compensated for by the fullness of life they receive from God. That fullness begins to be experienced now, but will only be complete in that life in the time to come.

Redefining All of Life

The blessings of a full life now and eternal life to come seem to come at a high price: Sell everything and give away the proceeds. But even that demand is too tame. This story ends with Jesus repeating the promise that the first will be last and the last first. This adage requires a complete reorientation. It requires us to reevaluate all things. Those who seem to be privileged will be last and those with the least claim on anyone or anything will be first in the Kingdom. If we are to take this story to heart, we will need to recognize that the things we thought were so valuable are not, and the things that have little value in our world may well be the most important. Jesus calls his followers to do more than give up all their possessions. Jesus wants their hearts and minds to be transformed. He wants possession of their values, not just their valuables. We know how hard it is to give up reliance on ourselves and our gifts. Indeed, as Jesus says, it is impossible for us on our own. The closing remark—the last will be first—points us to what is required: We have to reject the usual ways we value people and things and commit our whole selves to Jesus' way of evaluating all things. We can begin to orient ourselves toward that way of thinking and commit our whole selves to God because "for God all things are possible" (10:27).

SHARING THE SCRIPTURE

PREPARING TO TEACH

Preparing Our Hearts

Ponder this week's devotional reading from Galatians 5:1-13. How do you define freedom in Christ? In practical terms, what does this freedom mean in regard to how you live your life?

Pray that you and the students will have faith that enables you to live freely and generously.

Preparing Our Minds

Study the background Scripture from the lesson Scripture, both of which are from Mark 10:17-31.

Consider this question as you prepare the lesson: *What can persuade someone to forfeit possessions for others?*

Write on newsprint:

❏ information for next week's lesson, found under Continue the Journey.

❏ activities for further spiritual growth in Continue the Journey.

Review the Introduction, The Big Picture, Close-up, and Faith in Action, which all precede the first lesson of this quarter. Consider how you might use any of this material in today's lesson.

LEADING THE CLASS

(1) Gather to Learn

❖ Welcome the class members and guests.

❖ Pray that those who have come today will be willing to put a right relationship with God above all else, including their possessions.

❖ Read: **Oseola McCarty died in September 1999 of cancer at the age of ninety-one. This poor woman, who took in wash to support herself, only went out to buy groceries and attend Friendship Baptist Church. Yet she had quietly saved $150,000 over her lifetime. In 1995 she determined to make her money count by donating it to the University of Southern Mississippi in her hometown of Hattiesburg. She gave this money "so that the children won't have to work so hard, like I did." This unassuming woman's story spread quickly and she found herself receiving hundreds of awards, being honored by the United Nations, and shaking hands with President Bill Clinton. Her altruism attracted more scholarship money: $330,000 given by six hundred donors (as of September 1999). It also prompted media mogul Ted Turner to give away one billion dollars! Hers was truly a generous life.**

❖ Ask: **Jesus told a rich man to sell his possessions and give to the poor. Oseola McCarty was poor, yet she gave what she had to help others get an education. What motivates people to give so sacrificially for others?**

❖ Read aloud today's focus statement: **It is very difficult even for good people to be willing to give up all their possessions to follow some altruistic goal. What can persuade someone to forfeit his or her possessions for others? Jesus said that faith in God makes it possible for people to sacrifice all they have for the benefit of others.**

(2) Goal 1: Delve Into the Story of the Encounter of the Rich Young Man With Jesus

❖ Choose three volunteers, one to read Mark 10:17-22, a second to read verses 23-27, and a third to read verses 28-31.

❖ Discuss these questions:

1. **In some societies, including that of the United States, wealth and possession are seen as a sign of God's blessing. How does Jesus turn this notion on its head?** (See "The Rich Cannot Be Saved?" and "Giving Up Treasures" in Interpreting the Scripture.)

2. **What can you surmise about the rich man who approaches Jesus?** (See Mark 10:17-22 in Understanding the Scripture.)

3. **What seems to be the intent of Peter's comment in verse 28?** (See Mark 10:28-31 in Understanding the Scripture.)

4. **How is the man in this story different from you? How is he similar to you?**

5. **What is Jesus teaching you about your own life?**

❖ Close by reading "Redefining All of Life" in Interpreting the Scripture.

(3) Goal 2: Reflect on the Barriers that Stand in the Way of Following Jesus Without Reservation

❖ Distribute paper and pencils. Read the following statements and invite the students to complete them. There are no right or wrong answers. The purpose of this activity is to prompt the adults to think about barriers, not condemn their actions.

1. **I feel good about what I give because . . .**
2. **I would give more to others in need if only . . .**
3. **I expect to give more when . . .**
4. **I do not plan to give more because . . .**
5. **I think giving to people in need is a bad idea because . . .**

❖ Talk with the group about their answers, though be careful that people do not take it upon themselves to judge others either in the class or those who may be in need.

❖ Provide quiet time for the adults to reflect on their answers. Suggest that they seek God's guidance about any changes that they may need to make.

(4) Goal 3: Make a Commitment to Follow Jesus, No Matter What the Cost

❖ Read: **A man, his wife, and two children converted to Christ in the midst of a very hostile environment in India. Other villagers also professed Jesus, but the chief was so angry that he pressured the first family to renounce their faith, which they would not do. The four were executed but not before the man, led by the Holy Spirit, sang "I have decided to follow Jesus." He would not turn back even if alone; the cross was before him. Moved by this willingness to sacrifice all, the chief confessed that he too belonged to Jesus.**

❖ Challenge class members to silently make a commitment to Christ no matter what the cost.

(5) Continue the Journey

❖ Pray that as the learners depart, they will remain committed to Jesus.

❖ Post information for next week's session on newsprint for the students to copy:

- **Title: Struggling Faith**
- **Background Scripture: Mark 14:26-31, 66-72**
- **Lesson Scripture: Mark 14:26-31, 66-72**
- **Focus of the Lesson: People often overestimate their ability to remain loyal to a cause and bear witness to it. What happens when they discover they cannot do something they truly believed they could do? Peter was convinced of his faith, but he grieved mightily when he understood that his failure to stand up publicly as a follower of Jesus Christ was evidence of the weakness of his faith.**

❖ Post the following information on newsprint and provide paper and pencils for the students to copy it. Challenge the adults to grow spiritually by completing one or more of these activities related to this week's session.

(1) **Consider how attached you are to any of your possessions. Which ones could you easily part with? Which ones must you keep in order to feel secure? Pray about your relationship with your possessions and how they are affecting your relationship with Jesus.**

(2) **Recall the sacrificial giving of Oseola McCarty. How can she be a role model for you? What will you donate to help others?**

(3) **Think about your relationship with things and how that is helping or hurting your relationship with Jesus.**

❖ Sing or read aloud "I Have Decided to Follow Jesus."

❖ Conclude today's session by leading the class in this benediction, which is adapted from Mark 9:23 in the lesson for March 6: **Together we affirm that all things can be done for the one who believes. Amen.**

UNIT 1: TESTS OF FAITH
STRUGGLING FAITH

PREVIEWING THE LESSON

Lesson Scripture: Mark 14:26-31, 66-72
Background Scripture: Mark 14:26-31, 66-72
Key Verse: Mark 14:30

Focus of the Lesson:
People often overestimate their ability to remain loyal to a cause and bear witness to it. What happens when they discover they cannot do something they truly believed they could do? Peter was convinced of his faith, but he grieved mightily when he understood that his failure to stand up publicly as a follower of Jesus Christ was evidence of the weakness of his faith.

Goals for the Learners:
(1) to remember all that happened when Jesus foretold Peter's denial and when Peter acted as Jesus had said.
(2) to explore feelings and reactions when one fails to meet the expectations of those who are loved and respected.
(3) to practice spiritual disciplines in order to build a stronger relationship with God.

Supplies:
Bibles, newsprint and marker, paper and pencils, hymnals, optional palm branches

---

READING THE SCRIPTURE

NRSV

Lesson Scripture: Mark 14:26-31, 66-72

26When they had sung the hymn, they went out to the Mount of Olives. 27And Jesus said to them, "You will all become deserters; for it is written,

'I will strike the shepherd,
and the sheep will be scattered.'

CEB

Lesson Scripture: Mark 14:26-31, 66-72

26After singing songs of praise, they went out to the Mount of Olives.

27Jesus said to them, "You will all falter in your faithfulness to me. It is written, I will hit the shepherd, and the sheep will go off in all directions.

303

²⁸But after I am raised up, I will go before you to Galilee." ²⁹Peter said to him, "Even though all become deserters, I will not." ³⁰**Jesus said to him, "Truly I tell you, this day, this very night, before the cock crows twice, you will deny me three times."** ³¹But he said vehemently, "Even though I must die with you, I will not deny you." And all of them said the same.

⁶⁶While Peter was below in the courtyard, one of the servant-girls of the high priest came by. ⁶⁷When she saw Peter warming himself, she stared at him and said, "You also were with Jesus, the man from Nazareth." ⁶⁸But he denied it, saying, "I do not know or understand what you are talking about." And he went out into the forecourt. Then the cock crowed. ⁶⁹And the servant-girl, on seeing him, began again to say to the bystanders, "This man is one of them." ⁷⁰But again he denied it. Then after a little while the bystanders again said to Peter, "Certainly you are one of them; for you are a Galilean." ⁷¹But he began to curse, and he swore an oath, "I do not know this man you are talking about." ⁷²At that moment the cock crowed for the second time. Then Peter remembered that Jesus had said to him, "Before the cock crows twice, you will deny me three times." And he broke down and wept.

²⁸But after I'm raised up, I will go before you to Galilee."

²⁹Peter said to him, "Even if everyone else stumbles, I won't."

³⁰**But Jesus said to him, "I assure you that on this very night, before the rooster crows twice, you will deny me three times."**

³¹But Peter insisted, "If I must die alongside you, I won't deny you." And they all said the same thing.

⁶⁶Meanwhile, Peter was below in the courtyard. A woman, one of the high priest's servants, approached ⁶⁷and saw Peter warming himself by the fire. She stared at him and said, "You were also with the Nazarene, Jesus."

⁶⁸But he denied it, saying, "I don't know what you're talking about. I don't understand what you're saying." And he went outside into the outer courtyard. A rooster crowed.

⁶⁹The female servant saw him and began a second time to say to those standing around, "This man is one of them." ⁷⁰But he denied it again.

A short time later, those standing around again said to Peter, "You must be one of them, because you are also a Galilean."

⁷¹But he cursed and swore, "I don't know this man you're talking about." ⁷²At that very moment, a rooster crowed a second time. Peter remembered what Jesus told him, "Before a rooster crows twice, you will deny me three times." And he broke down, sobbing.

UNDERSTANDING THE SCRIPTURE

Introduction. This story of the prediction and then the reality of Peter's denial of Jesus is the high point, or better the lowest point, of Mark's description of the disciples. Mark has portrayed their increasing misunderstanding as the mission of Jesus progresses. They do not know who Jesus is (4:41) and misunderstand so badly that Jesus calls Peter Satan (8:27-33).

Jesus repeatedly tells the disciples he must suffer, and they continue to reject this and misunderstand his mission (8:31–9:1; 9:9, 30-32; 10:32-34). Peter's denial is the low point of the disciple's failures—and their last appearance in Mark.

Mark 14:26-31. In the first part of our reading, Jesus and the disciples are leaving the Last Supper. There, Jesus announced that one of them would betray him and instituted the Lord's Supper (Eucharist). Jesus now tells the disciples that they will all desert him. They have repeatedly failed to believe that his mission includes dying. Since this fate remains inconceivable for them, they cannot imagine a scenario in which they would desert him.

Peter leads all the disciples in rejecting the idea that they could turn their backs on Jesus. Jesus responds to Peter specifically, telling him that he would deny him three times before sunrise. Peter asserts that he is willing to die for Jesus. Of course, he did not think his commitment would be tested to that extent.

Mark 14:66-71. When our reading resumes, Jesus has been arrested and found guilty of blasphemy (14:64). All the disciples except Peter have run away. Even as we watch Peter fail, we should remember that all the others who affirmed their allegiance to Jesus left him at Gethsemane. Peter has remained, perhaps hoping for a mighty act of God that would convince the Sanhedrin to listen to Jesus or that would throw off the yoke of the Roman domination. Whatever he was thinking, he was close enough to see what Jesus would do. Standing outside the building where the trial is taking place indicates that Peter did not want to be identified with Jesus, even as he wanted to see if God would rescue him or the nation.

To envision the scene, we need to think of a large house or public building that has multiple outside areas for people to congregate. These could be places where people with some interest in a trial could gather or where the servants of the wealthy who were involved in a case would wait. It would not have been strange for people like Peter to be standing there, waiting. What might have made Peter's presence unusual is that this was at night. Sanhedrin trials were not usually conducted at night. Since the courtyard would not have been crowded, it may have been easy to see who was there.

The servant girl's identification of Peter as someone who was with Jesus may have been an accusation or just an observation. Whichever it was, it makes Peter uncomfortable enough to say he has no idea what she is talking about. He seems to deny even knowing there is a trial of anyone named Jesus going on. Then he moves on, perhaps not wanting anyone to think he had strong reasons for remaining there.

We do not know how the servant girl recognized Peter. As a servant of the high priest she would have spent most of her time in Jerusalem. Jesus and his disciples had only been there for about a week, so there were few opportunities for her to cross paths with Jesus, much less to remember what his disciples looked like. But Mark is not worried about such difficulties; he simply needs a character to recognize Peter so the plot can advance.

Peter did not move far enough to avoid the same servant. Now her identification seems like more of an accusation. He is "one of them" (14:69). Peter again denies that he is associated with Jesus. Identifying Peter as an associate of Jesus of Nazareth would imply that he was from Galilee. Now others who are standing around notice that he is a Galilean, perhaps because of his accent. Just as different regions have different accents now, so it was then. The dialect of northern and rural Galilee was noticeably different from that of the urban and southern Judea. Peter's identity as a Galilean confirms the accusation about his association with the person on trial.

Feeling more trapped, Peter's third denial is even more vehement. He swears that he does not know Jesus. In the space of a few hours Peter has gone from pledging that he would never desert Jesus to swearing that he does not know him. Peter sinks to this level because he was never able to understand that Jesus' commission as Messiah meant that Jesus must suffer. Peter, and all others who thought about what a messiah would be, thought of God acting through a messiah in mighty ways to save God's people. Being found guilty and turned over to the Romans for execution was an unthinkable fate for a messiah. But now Peter sees this happening to Jesus. So he swears that he does not know Jesus.

Mark 14:72. Just when all the evidence seems to suggest that Jesus was not who Peter thought he was and that allegiance to Jesus was foolish, the rooster crows a second time. When Peter remembers what Jesus had told him, he again knows that God is with Jesus because Jesus' prophecy comes true. Now he realizes that he has denied the One who had brought God's presence to the lives of so many and had even empowered Peter himself to heal and exorcise demons. It is a crushing blow. Peter weeps.

This is the last appearance Peter or any of the disciples make in Mark. They do not appear at the tomb and there are no scenes in which the risen Christ restores Peter or the other disciples. We will ponder this end of the disciples as we continue.

INTERPRETING THE SCRIPTURE

Peter Overestimates His Strength

As this story unfolds, we see Peter and the other disciples overestimating their own faithfulness. They resolve to be by Jesus' side no matter what, but they do not really think the worst can happen. They think they can stand beside a powerful Jesus to face enemies of any sort that may come. But their reliance on themselves is illusory. When their faith is put to the test, they do not persevere. They fail Jesus and they fail themselves. While Peter seems to stand out as the worst among them, that is only because he is the only one to have enough nerve to go to the trial of Jesus. The others have already completely deserted him. Now Peter's faith fails when put to the test of possible persecution.

We wonder why their faith failed. These are people who have seen the power and glory of Jesus. They have seen the sick healed, storms stilled, and Jesus glorified in the Transfiguration.

Still they fail. As Mark presents them, much of the reason they fail is that they misunderstand the mission and ministry of Jesus. They see power and expect Jesus to exercise that power in ways that will demand obedience. They expect mighty acts that place Jesus in power. That is a mission they can stand behind, one they are willing to give their lives for. But there is a shocking turn of events. Rather than conquering, Jesus submits to arrest, then to trial, which will soon result in his execution. None of the disciples expected this. In the face of this radical turn, they desert Jesus.

They do not have the strength to remain faithful because they have misunderstood Jesus. Their denials are linked directly to their misunderstanding of how God is present in Jesus. God's love is shown in willingness to suffer for those God loves, not in an exercise of military might. The depth of God's love is demonstrated in the willingness of Christ to give his life for those who desert him. Submitting to arrest and execution hardly seems like strength, but that is what Jesus had been telling the disciples since chapter 8 when Peter confesses that Jesus is the Messiah. Jesus acknowledges that he is the Messiah, but immediately begins to redefine that identity to mean that he will suffer and die. The disciples do not have the strength to accept this as the will of God or as the pattern for the way God acts in the world. Their faith fails because they expect the wrong things. They have trusted their own definitions of how God's power is wielded in the world. Their definition leads them to trust in their own power to be faithful rather than to depend upon the God who is with Jesus through his crucifixion.

God's Unfailing Love

The sad story in our text is not merely the tale of someone who is overly confident—though it is that. Jesus knows the weaknesses of his disciples; he knows them better than they know themselves. But even as he knows their failings, he loves them. Just before he tells them they will deny him, he has eaten his last meal with them and included them in his institution of a new covenant meal, the Lord's Supper. Immediately after the prediction of their denial, he asks them to pray with him in the garden of Gethsemane. Their weakness is no impediment to the love of God. They will fail, he knows it, but still he loves them. This should inspire great confidence in God's love. Here we see a desperate moment, the worst moment in all the ministry of Jesus, and the disciples are no help. Instead their denials must have been yet another burden for Jesus to bear at this point. But he bears it and continues to love them.

Our failures and denials of Jesus are much less dramatic, even though they may be just as real. This story assures us that Jesus can know our weaknesses and failures, but still love us. It should be a great comfort to see the unshakable love of God remaining with those who deny Christ in times of struggle.

Why Have Such Weak Disciples?

Mark's presentation of the disciples is far from flattering. They begin to misunderstand Jesus in chapter 4 and only get worse the longer they are with him. Finally, they desert and deny him. Mark does not even have any appearances of the disciples with the risen Christ in which he forgives them. After the denial by Peter, they never again appear in the story (though they are mentioned in 16:7). Interpreters have often wondered why Mark presents the disciples in such a negative light. After all, Mark's readers know that they went on to become the apostles, those interpreters of Jesus' life, death, and resurrection whose testimony is the foundation of the church's beliefs. The answer seems to lie in the situation the Gospel of Mark addresses.

Mark's church seems to have experienced some significant persecution. We do not know precisely what it was or when it happened, but it was severe enough that some members of this church capitulated. Some denied their faith. We do not know if it was a direct denial, as in the case of Peter, or if it consisted more in simply disassociating from the church, as the other disciples disappeared when Jesus was arrested. Whatever they did, all recognize that they had denied the faith. The persecution has now passed. Some of those who capitulated now want to be part of the church; they want to be received again into the fellowship of those who believe in Christ. The church is unsure about what they should do. If they allow those who denied the faith to return, it seems to be a slap in the face to those who endured the suffering. Indeed, it smacks of cheap grace and allows fair-weather loyalty, but makes no real demands.

Mark addresses this issue with his portrait of the disciples. Here are people who lived in the very presence of Jesus and were witnesses to his miracles. Yet their faith utterly fails. They desert and deny Jesus. And what becomes of them? Are they excluded from the love of God or the fellowship of the church? They obviously are not. After their miserable failings they because the foundation of the church. There is grace even after such horrific failure. Mark does not tell of their reinstatement; he does not have to because all of his readers already know about it. Instead, he makes the readers tell the story. Mark's readers, those who have to discern what to do with those who have denied the faith in their church, have to complete the tale of the forgiveness the disciples receive and the powerful faith they are given. There is no more powerful story of the unfailing love of God. There can be no more certain sign that those who have faltered are loved by God and need to be received by the church. There is no greater assurance we can receive that God wants us even when we have failed miserably.

SHARING THE SCRIPTURE

PREPARING TO TEACH

Preparing Our Hearts

. Ponder this week's devotional reading from Jeremiah 3:12-18, which records a call to repentance. What do you believe about God's willingness to take back those who fail if they are willing to repent? What do you need to repent of right now?

Pray that you and the students will obey God's voice by turning away from sin and toward God.

Preparing Our Minds

Study the background Scripture and the lesson Scripture, both of which are from Mark 14:26-31, 66-72.

Consider this question as you prepare the lesson: *How do you respond when you discover you cannot do something you truly believed you could do?*

Write on newsprint:

❏ information for next week's lesson, found under Continue the Journey.

❏ activities for further spiritual growth in Continue the Journey.

Review the Introduction, The Big Picture, Close-up, and Faith in Action, which all precede the first lesson of this quarter. Consider how you might use any of this material in today's lesson.

Become especially familiar with information in the lesson and in The Big Picture: The Gospels of Mark and Luke that describes the weaknesses and failures of the disciples.

Option: Have palm branches ready to distribute, if this is a tradition in your Sunday school.

LEADING THE CLASS

(1) Gather to Learn

❖ Welcome the class members and guests. If your class has a tradition of distributing palms, you may wish to give them to the students as they arrive. Note as you begin the lesson that while the palm branches call to mind Jesus' entry into Jerusalem, they also remind us that his trial, desertion of his disciples, and crucifixion are just days away.

❖ Pray that those who have come today will recognize that God knows we sometimes fail to live up to our expectations.

❖ Read: **Although many people think of biblical characters as giants of the faith who are perfect, we know that some of the most well-known characters experienced colossal failures. Who are some examples that you can name? How did they fail?** Here are some possible answers:

- Moses killed an Egyptian taskmaster and had to flee the Egyptian pharaoh who sought to kill him (Exodus 2:11-15).
- David committed adultery with Bathsheba and had her husband, Uriah, killed in battle to cover up the fact that she was pregnant with David's child (2 Samuel 11).
- Jonah disobeyed God's orders concerning the people of Nineveh (Jonah).
- Saul/Paul severely persecuted God's people until he met Jesus on the road to Damascus (Galatians 1:11-24).

❖ Read aloud today's focus statement: **People often overestimate their ability to remain loyal to a cause and bear witness to it. What happens when they discover they cannot do something they truly believed they could do? Peter was convinced of his faith; but he grieved mightily when he understood that his failure to stand up publicly as a follower of Jesus Christ was evidence of the weakness of his faith.**

(2) Goal 1: Remember All that Happened When Jesus Foretold Peter's Denial and When Peter Acted as Jesus Had Said

❖ Choose two volunteers, one to read Mark 14:26-31 and the other to conclude the story by reading verses 66-72.

❖ Recall that we have just discussed some biblical people who failed miserably. Now we see that Peter has failed Jesus at the very moment when he could be of most support to Jesus. Note, though, that the other disciples have actually deserted Jesus. At least Peter showed up to the place of the trial. Ask:

1. **According to Mark 14:31, Peter and the other disciples all claimed that they would willingly die with Jesus. Why might their faith have failed?** (See "Peter Overestimates His Strength" in Interpreting the Scripture.)

2. **How does Mark portray the disciples?** (See "Why Have Such Weak Disciples?" in Interpreting the Scripture.)

3. **The disciples do not appear as weak and ineffective in the other Gospels. Why might Mark portray them in this way?** (See the first seven paragraphs in The Big Picture: The Gospels of Mark and Luke.)

4. **In what kinds of situations might contemporary Christians deny Jesus?**

(3) Goal 2: Explore Feelings and Reactions When One Fails to Meet the Expectations of Those Who Are Loved and Respected

❖ Form small groups and ask participants to tell of a situation in which they failed to meet the expectations of a parent, other family member, pastor, teacher, coach, or some other significant person in their lives. Encourage them to talk about how they felt when they realized they had failed. Also encourage them to talk about how the person they failed responded.

❖ Reconvene the class and read or retell "God's Unfailing Love" in Interpreting the Scripture and ask:

1. **What assurance do you find here, even when you have failed to meet God's expectations?**

2. **How might knowing that God loves you, no matter how much you stumble, help you to deal with disappointment expressed by other people?**

(4) Goal 3: Practice Spiritual Disciplines in Order to Build a Stronger Relationship with God

❖ Read: **There are many spiritual disciplines that we can use to strengthen our relationship with God. Examples include worship, Bible study, meditation, prayer, living simply, and fasting. Today we are going to meditate on Isaiah 55:6-7. Follow along in your Bible as I read these words. Invite God to speak to you through them. Consider your openness to calling on God right now in order to return to God. Give thanks for God's mercy and pardon. Listen to whatever God has to say to you in the next three minutes.**

❖ Bring everyone together to discuss these questions:

1. **How difficult was it for you to concentrate for three minutes?**

2. **Were you able to sense God speaking to you?**

3. **What did you learn about yourself and/or God?**

❖ Encourage participants to try a brief meditation each day this week using verses they choose.

(5) Continue the Journey

❖ Pray that as the learners depart, they will find new depths in their relationship with Jesus during this Holy Week.

❖ Post information for next week's session on newsprint for the students to copy:

- **Title: Resurrection Faith**
- **Background Scripture: Mark 16:1-8**
- **Lesson Scripture: Mark 16:1-8**
- **Focus of the Lesson: People hold strong beliefs that may be severely tested and then come to an outstanding vindication. What can confirm strong beliefs? Jesus' closest followers were devastated when he was crucified, but their faith was validated when Jesus was raised from the tomb.**

❖ Post the following information on newsprint and provide paper and pencils for the students to copy it. Challenge the adults to grow spiritually by completing one or more of these activities related to this week's session.

(1) **Plan to attend some kind of observance (worship service,** community crosswalk, time of mediation) **of Jesus' crucifixion on Good Friday. Speak with Jesus about how you feel you have failed him. Repent—and forgive yourself as God has forgiven you.**

(2) **Recall from Mark 14:31 that Peter and all the disciples felt certain they were ready to die with Jesus if need be. Meditate on or journal about your own faith. How strong is it? Where do you see yourself struggling? Ask Jesus for help.**

(3) **Locate a picture of Jesus on the cross. Think about what his sacrifice on the cross accomplished for you and give thanks.**

❖ Sing or read aloud "Out of the Depths I Cry to You."

❖ Conclude today's session by leading the class in this benediction, which is adapted from Mark 9:23 in the lesson for March 6: **Together we affirm that all things can be done for the one who believes. Amen.**

UNIT 1: TESTS OF FAITH
RESURRECTION FAITH

PREVIEWING THE LESSON

Lesson Scripture: Mark 16:1-8
Background Scripture: Mark 16:1-8
Key Verse: Mark 16:6

Focus of the Lesson:
People hold strong beliefs that may be severely tested and then come to an outstanding vindication. What can confirm strong beliefs? Jesus' closest followers were devastated when he was crucified, but their faith was validated when Jesus was raised from the tomb.

Goals for the Learners:
(1) to remember details of the discovery by his followers of Jesus' resurrection and the promise for the future.
(2) to feel the devastating loss experienced by the women as well as the relief that comes from understanding how faith in God helps Christians survive their loss.
(3) to encourage and strengthen one another with assurance of good things to come through Jesus Christ.

Supplies:
Bibles, newsprint and marker, paper and pencils, hymnals

READING THE SCRIPTURE

NRSV

Lesson Scripture: Mark 16:1-8

¹When the sabbath was over, Mary Magdalene, and Mary the mother of James, and Salome bought spices, so that they might go and anoint him. ²And very early on the first day of the week, when the sun had risen, they went to the tomb. ³They had been saying to one another, "Who will

CEB

Lesson Scripture: Mark 16:1-8

¹When the Sabbath was over, Mary Magdalene, Mary the mother of James, and Salome bought spices so that they could go and anoint Jesus' dead body. ²Very early on the first day of the week, just after sunrise, they came to the tomb. ³They were saying to each other, "Who's going to roll the

roll away the stone for us from the entrance to the tomb?" [4]When they looked up, they saw that the stone, which was very large, had already been rolled back. [5]As they entered the tomb, they saw a young man, dressed in a white robe, sitting on the right side; and they were alarmed. [6]But he said to them, **"Do not be alarmed; you are looking for Jesus of Nazareth, who was crucified. He has been raised; he is not here. Look, there is the place they laid him.** [7]But go, tell his disciples and Peter that he is going ahead of you to Galilee; there you will see him, just as he told you." [8]So they went out and fled from the tomb, for terror and amazement had seized them; and they said nothing to anyone, for they were afraid.

stone away from the entrance for us?" [4]When they looked up, they saw that the stone had been rolled away. (And it was a very large stone!) [5]Going into the tomb, they saw a young man in a white robe seated on the right side; and they were startled. [6]But he said to them, **"Don't be alarmed! You are looking for Jesus of Nazareth, who was crucified. He has been raised. He isn't here. Look, here's the place where they laid him.** [7]Go, tell his disciples, especially Peter, that he is going ahead of you into Galilee. You will see him there, just as he told you." [8]Overcome with terror and dread, they fled from the tomb. They said nothing to anyone, because they were afraid.

UNDERSTANDING THE SCRIPTURE

Introduction. The joyous proclamation of Easter comes only after the misery of a weekend without hope. The disciples, including the women who were with Jesus, have endured his shameful death. No mighty act of God intervened; Jesus even felt deserted on the cross (15:34). It seemed that evil had won, that the message and ministry of Jesus had been overcome by those who would keep things as they were. Jesus has been mocked and executed. But then Easter Sunday arrives.

Mark 16:1-3. As our reading begins, it is a sad morning. Jesus had died on Friday and there had not been time for a decent funeral or preparation of the body for entombment because the Sabbath begins at sundown on Friday evening. The new week has begun as chapter 16 opens. Now loved ones can tend to the body of their deceased leader. We must note that the women who go to the tomb do not go expecting the resurrection. Rather, they are bringing spices to anoint a dead body. They think that the dream Jesus brought is now over. The Kingdom had not come, God had not intervened. All that is left to do is give their prophet and friend a proper burial.

Mark identifies the three women who go to the tomb as Mary Magdalene, Mary the mother of James, and Salome. We know Mary Magdalene from early stories, though there is no good reason to identify her with the woman who is caught in adultery. The identity of the other women is less clear. The mother of James may also be the mother of Jesus, but that is uncertain. We do not know for certain who Salome is, but she must have been well known in the early church as a witness to the resurrection.

The absence of any expectation of a resurrection is obvious from the chief worry the women expressed on the way to the tomb: Who would be strong enough to open the door? Jesus had been buried in a tomb that was carved out of soft rock and so was something of a cave. Such tombs were sometimes family burial chambers. Some were elaborately decorated and furnished, whereas others were more sparsely decorated. The most recent person to die would be on a stone bed in the chamber. That person would lie there for about a year. Then his or her bones would be gathered into a box or placed on a shelf to make room for the next person who died to occupy the bed. The body of the recently deceased would, then, be available for treatment such as anointing it with spices. There are still examples of such tombs from the first century and still some ancient burial chambers of this sort that have stone doors that can be rolled in a track to open and close them. These devoted followers of Jesus now simply want to grant him the proper respect of a decent treatment of his body and in their sorrow are concerned only about the details of how they would do that.

Mark 16:4-7. Much to their surprise, the tomb is open when they arrive. Rather than finding the body of Jesus, they see only a young man, who most identify as an angel. This young man tells the women that Jesus has been raised. We might expect relief and joy; instead they are alarmed. They do not know what to think. They had not expected a resurrection! But they are faced with an empty tomb and shown the place where the body of Jesus had been.

The messenger also gives them a task. He sends them to tell the disciples, especially Peter, that Jesus will meet them in Galilee. This instruction is full of hope, promise, and forgiveness. Jesus has risen and will meet with the disciples in the place where most of the ministry of Jesus was conducted—in Galilee. As they had seen him in earlier times, now they will see him there as the resurrected Christ.

The extreme love of God that provides forgiveness is also evident in this short instruction. The messenger mentions Peter explicitly. The last appearance of Peter in Mark was his denial of Jesus. The direct mention of him is the assurance that he is forgiven and will be received by the risen Christ. He will be restored to his relationship with Christ.

Mark 16:8. The last line of Mark may be the most surprising of all. The witnesses to the resurrection run away and tell no one because they are afraid! How can a Gospel end with those words? There is no appearance of the resurrected Christ, no recognition or proclamation of his resurrection, only fear and silence. Ancient copyists were as distressed by this ending as we are. So, several wrote alternative endings to Mark. These appear in some translations as alternative endings, and in some translations verses 9-16 still appear as the proper ending of Mark. The oldest manuscripts we have of Mark do not include verses 9-16.

Of course, the readers of Mark know that the story does not stop with the women leaving the empty tomb and telling no one. They are reading this Gospel because the proclamation of the death and resurrection of Christ has gone forward. So why does Mark leave readers hanging in such a way? Like the story of the failures of the disciples in Mark, many interpreters think Mark ends this way so that the reader has to finish the story. With this ending Mark encourages, even requires, his readers to be the ones who proclaim the resurrection of Christ and what God accomplishes through it. This account of Easter gives us good news that we have to tell others. If Mark and the original witnesses do not complete the task of sharing the good news, the readers of this Gospel are compelled by its ending to take up that task. So we proclaim, "Christ is risen."

INTERPRETING THE SCRIPTURE

The Faithful Women

Mark's account of the resurrection is the story of three faithful disciples returning to show their love for Jesus. While the Twelve had deserted Jesus, these women stayed at the foot of the cross and witnessed his death (15:40-41). Now they are the ones with courage enough to be identified with him even after his apparent defeat and death. They are not, at this point, a company filled with hope. They expect only to anoint Jesus' body, to take this one last chance to express their love and devotion to him.

Their devotion is rewarded with a surprise. When they arrive at the tomb, they find the door is open and the body of Jesus is gone. Rather than a lifeless Jesus, there is a young man dressed in white. This brightly clothed person seems to be an angel who delivers unbelievable news: Jesus has been raised from the dead. That same Jesus who died a shameful death has been raised to life. When all had seemed lost, God had acted in a way no one expected. Even though Mark has had Jesus speak of his resurrection, this news is completely unexpected to these disciples. This act of God was more powerful than anything they might have hoped for when Jesus confronted the Jerusalem authorities and was arrested. It is one thing to take over the Temple or to defeat the Romans; it is quite another to defeat death. The proof of the resurrection in Mark is the absence of a body. There will be no resurrection appearances in Mark, just the proclamation that Jesus has been raised. This proclamation changes everything. The other Gospels have stories of appearances of Jesus, including an encounter with Mary. Mark has none of these, only the proclamation and the empty tomb. That is enough to give hope and show that God has acted in the most powerful of ways.

Power and Love

One of the most moving elements of Mark's manner of telling about the resurrection is the message the young man (who is at the least a messenger of God) gives to the women. They are to proclaim this resurrection to the disciples. The disciples are those who only days before deserted Jesus in his time of trouble. They were too afraid to be present at his trial and crucifixion. But now they are the ones who are to be given the good news. Even more amazingly, the biggest offender of all, Peter, is singled out for special mention—not for reprimand, but for assurance. Jesus will meet the disciples, especially Peter, in Galilee. The messenger also sends a reminder that this is what Jesus had said would happen.

At this moment of the exercise of extraordinary power, when death is defeated, that power is used to offer forgiveness and reconciliation. The disciples had suffered loss, and had done it in a cowardly way. Their loss and failure, however, are overcome with the exceedingly great power of the resurrection. God's great power is shown to be an exercise of God's love. No loss is so great that the power of God cannot overcome it. No failure can be so harmful that God's love cannot forgive it. Jesus will lead them again in Galilee.

The Meaning of the Resurrection

Mark gives no explicit interpretation of the resurrection. We have seen that the young man provides assurance of forgiveness by telling the women to prepare the disciples to see Jesus. But beyond this, Mark says nothing about what the resurrection means. Other New Testament writers give further interpretations to this overwhelming act of God. One of the important ones is that the resurrection of Jesus has consequences for us all. It does not just proclaim forgiveness to the disciples; it does so for us as well. More broadly, it assures believers of the power and love of God that will be exercised for the good of God's people. As Paul talks about it in 1 Corinthians 15 (among other places), the resurrection of Christ is the assurance that God has more power than the forces of evil, even more power than death. While the world often looks as though evil forces have the most power, the resurrection demonstrates that God has more power than

all of those forces combined. Even after Jesus has been killed, God is able to raise him. Jesus endured the worst that evil could deal out and God overcame it to bring blessing and reconciliation to God's people.

As New Testament writers understand it, this power of God has a personal and a worldwide, even cosmic, dimension. The resurrection of Christ is the assurance that God will raise believers who are faithful. Whatever difficulties or losses believers endure, however difficult their lives, the resurrection of Christ is the assurance that God is not only with us in hardship but promises new life after all troubles. Paul sees the resurrection of Christ as the guarantee of the resurrection of believers. It is the assurance that God has the power and the will to overcome evil and grant the faithful life in God's presence. No loss is beyond the power of God to heal and give life. The despair of the women and the disciples is met with the power of resurrection. The genuine loss and death of Jesus is transcended by the exercise of God's resurrection power.

And They Told No One?

The conclusion Mark gives his resurrection account is nearly inconceivable. How could anyone see the empty tomb and hear the messenger of God give assurance and remain silent? As we have already noted, their silence was temporary. And we can prove that: Only if they tell of their experience would the message have gotten out. The natural response to such good news, even if it is beyond our full understanding, is to tell others. Mark wants his readers to finish the story, to tell others of the power of the resurrection in their lives. He wants them to share their experience of that power and the faith that they have in the future that God has in store for God's people. They will also need to tell of the restoration and empowerment the disciples receive from the resurrected Christ. The story of the unconquerable love of God must be told, even if the messengers are as afraid and uncertain as those first witnesses.

The Gospel of Mark ends abruptly on Easter morning. Mark has said all he thinks he needs to say. The stark and clear proclamation of the good news gives his church the foundation it needs to live as God's people. As we finish Mark's Gospel, it leaves us in the same place it left the original readers. We must continue to tell the story, that of the resurrection of Christ, that of his presence with us now, and that of the assurance of blessings to come for those who are in Christ.

SHARING THE SCRIPTURE

PREPARING TO TEACH

Preparing Our Hearts

Ponder this week's devotional reading from Psalm 23. Read this psalm, which you may have memorized years ago, as if this is the first time you are seeing it. What new insights come to mind? How is the image of the Lord as your shepherd helpful to you—or is it?

Pray that you and the students will seek the Good Shepherd, especially during Holy Week and on Easter.

Preparing Our Minds

Study the background Scripture and the lesson Scripture, both of which are from Mark 16:1-8.

Consider this question as you prepare the lesson: *What can confirm deeply held beliefs?*

Write on newsprint:
- ❏ litany for Goal 3 in Sharing the Scripture.
- ❏ information for next week's lesson, found under Continue the Journey.
- ❏ activities for further spiritual growth in Continue the Journey.

Review the Introduction, The Big Picture, Close-up, and Faith in Action, which all precede the first lesson of this quarter. Consider how you might use any of this material in today's lesson.

Prepare for Sunday's session with the Easter celebration in mind. Will the congregation follow a special schedule that may impinge on time for Sunday school? Will some class members be involved in special activities, such as a choir cantata, that may cause them to miss class or attend only part of the session?

LEADING THE CLASS

(1) Gather to Learn

❖ Welcome the class members and guests.

❖ Pray that those who have come today will affirm their beliefs in Jesus' resurrection.

❖ Read: **As this lesson is being**

written, *The Washington Post* reports that a prominent rabbi who leads a congregation in the Georgetown section of Washington, D.C., has been arrested on a charge of voyeurism. This charge stems from allegations that the rabbi had set up a video camera, disguised as a clock, to take pictures inside the synagogue's mikvah. This is an area used by women for ritual baths to purify themselves after they bleed, especially following menstruation. Use of the mikvah is considered highly private because it reveals details about a woman's sex life. This nationally known rabbi, who holds a doctorate and a law degree, is recognized for his efforts on behalf of converts. On hearing the allegations, an unidentified woman said, "I'll never be able to trust. . . . It makes this thing something dirty. . . . I'm devastated to think someone might have been watching me."

❖ Ask: **How are people affected when strongly held beliefs, especially about their spiritual lives, are severely tested?**

❖ Read aloud today's focus statement: **People hold strong beliefs that may be severely tested and then come to an outstanding vindication. What can confirm strong beliefs? Jesus' closest followers were devastated when he was crucified, but their faith was validated when Jesus was raised from the tomb.**

(2) Goal 1: Remember Details of the Discovery by His Followers of Jesus' Resurrection and the Promise for the Future

List on newsprint details that class members can recall about Easter morning from Mark 16:1-8, without checking their Bibles.

Call on a volunteer to read the account of Easter morning from Mark 16:1-8.

Review the list and ask:

1. **Are there details we have omitted that appear in Mark's Gospel?** (Add these details.)
2. **Are there details we have added that Mark did not include?** (Draw a line through those that are not from this Gospel. The completed list should include only details from Mark's Gospel.)

❖ Note that each of the four Gospel writers tells the story using details that may or may not appear in the other three Gospels. Also point out that a major difference between Mark and the other three is the ending of the story. Read Mark 16:8 from Understanding the Scripture to help explain this difference.

(3) Goal 2: Feel the Devastating Loss Experienced by the Women as Well as the Relief that Comes from Understanding How Faith in God Helps Christians Survive Their Loss

❖ Invite three volunteers to role-play the discussion among the three women as they make their way to Jesus' tomb on Easter morning. What is their mood? What troubles them? What are their expectations?

❖ Read or retell "The Faithful Women" from Interpreting the Scripture and ask: **Had you been with Mary Magdalene, Mary, and Salome, what thoughts would have crossed your mind or what emotions might you have experienced on the way to the tomb?**

❖ Recall that instead of finding

Jesus' lifeless body, the women were greeted by a heavenly messenger. Read his message in today's key verse, Mark 16:6.

❖ Ask: **If you believe the messenger reported good news about Jesus, why do you think the women were so terrified that they fled from the tomb?**

❖ Invite the students to talk with a partner (who is not related to them) about their own response to this news. What impact does it have on situations in their lives? How does this news help them to deal with their own losses?

❖ Bring the students together and ask: **Suppose you could bridge the two-thousand-year gap to talk with these women. How could you empathize with them and also let them know the impact that Jesus' resurrection has had on your life?**

(4) Goal 3: Encourage and Strengthen One Another with Assurance of Good Things to Come Through Jesus Christ

❖ Post the following litany and divide the group to read it responsively. Or read the litany yourself and invite the learners to respond with the phrase "Christ is risen indeed. Alleluia."

Creator of all life, we praise you for raising Jesus from the dead.
Christ is risen indeed. Alleluia.
We rejoice in Jesus' victory over sin and death.
Christ is risen indeed. Alleluia.
We give thanks that because he lives we too may have eternal life.
Christ is risen indeed. Alleluia.
As we live in this time between his resurrection and his coming again in glory

we are grateful for the Holy Spirit who guides us in the way we should go.
Christ is risen indeed. Alleluia.
Empower us to be the community of faithful believers who share this good news so that others may know Jesus and walk in his way.
Christ is risen indeed. Alleluia. Amen and Amen.

❖ Suggest that as the students go forth today, perhaps to visit with family and friends, they be ready to tell others about their own beliefs in the resurrection and what Jesus' dying and being raised by God to new life means for their lives.

(5) Continue the Journey

❖ Pray that as the learners depart, they will celebrate Jesus' victory over death.

❖ Post information for next week's session on newsprint for the students to copy:

- **Title: Renewed Health**
- **Background Scripture: Luke 7:1-10**
- **Lesson Scripture: Luke 7:1-10**
- **Focus of the Lesson: Everyone has desperate needs at times that cause him or her to wonder if any help is available. To whom can people turn for help that makes a difference? The centurion's faith in Jesus Christ as the great healer made all the difference in meeting his need to see his servant healed.**

❖ Post the following information on newsprint and provide paper and pencils for the students to copy it. Challenge the adults to grow spiritually by completing one or more of these activities related to this week's session.

(1) **Review all four Gospel accounts of Easter morning. Which one resonates most with you? Why?**

(2) **Comfort someone who is grieving. Being available to listen is a great gift.**

(3) **Use common symbols of Easter, such as butterflies and dyed eggs, to talk with a child about the meaning of Jesus' resurrection.**

❖ Sing or read aloud "He Lives."

❖ Conclude today's session by leading the class in this benediction, which is adapted from Mark 9:23 in the lesson for March 6: **Together we affirm that all things can be done for the one who believes. Amen.**

UNIT 2: RESTORATIVE FAITH
RENEWED HEALTH

PREVIEWING THE LESSON

Lesson Scripture: Luke 7:1-10
Background Scripture: Luke 7:1-10
Key Verse: Luke 7:9

Focus of the Lesson:

Everyone has desperate needs at times that cause him or her to wonder if any help is available. To whom can people turn for help that makes a difference? The centurion's faith in Jesus Christ as the great healer made all the difference in meeting his need to see his servant healed.

Goals for the Learners:

(1) to analyze the story of the centurion's faith and Jesus' healing of the centurion's servant.
(2) to experience strong faith for deliverance from illness like the faith of the centurion in the story.
(3) to commit (or recommit) to regularly visiting the sick to pray with them and to encourage them to believe God will heal according to God's will.

Supplies:

Bibles, newsprint and marker, paper and pencils, hymnals

READING THE SCRIPTURE

NRSV

Lesson Scripture: Luke 7:1-10

[1]After Jesus had finished all his sayings in the hearing of the people, he entered Capernaum. [2]A centurion there had a slave whom he valued highly, and who was ill and close to death. [3]When he heard about Jesus, he sent some Jewish elders to him, asking him to come and heal his

CEB

Lesson Scripture: Luke 7:1-10

[1]After Jesus finished presenting all his words among the people, he entered Capernaum. [2]A centurion had a servant who was very important to him, but the servant was ill and about to die. [3]When the centurion heard about Jesus, he sent some Jewish elders to Jesus to ask him to come

slave. ⁴When they came to Jesus, they appealed to him earnestly, saying, "He is worthy of having you do this for him, ⁵for he loves our people, and it is he who built our synagogue for us." ⁶And Jesus went with them, but when he was not far from the house, the centurion sent friends to say to him, "Lord, do not trouble yourself, for I am not worthy to have you come under my roof; ⁷therefore I did not presume to come to you. But only speak the word, and let my servant be healed. ⁸For I also am a man set under authority, with soldiers under me; and I say to one, 'Go,' and he goes, and to another, 'Come,' and he comes, and to my slave, 'Do this,' and the slave does it." **⁹When Jesus heard this he was amazed at him, and turning to the crowd that followed him, he said, "I tell you, not even in Israel have I found such faith."** ¹⁰When those who had been sent returned to the house, they found the slave in good health.

and heal his servant. ⁴When they came to Jesus, they earnestly pleaded with Jesus. "He deserves to have you do this for him," they said. ⁵"He loves our people and he built our synagogue for us."

⁶Jesus went with them. He had almost reached the house when the centurion sent friends to say to Jesus, "Lord, don't be bothered. I don't deserve to have you come under my roof. ⁷In fact, I didn't even consider myself worthy to come to you. Just say the word and my servant will be healed. ⁸I'm also a man appointed under authority, with soldiers under me. I say to one, 'Go,' and he goes, and to another, 'Come,' and he comes. I say to my servant, 'Do this,' and the servant does it."

⁹When Jesus heard these words, he was impressed with the centurion. He turned to the crowd following him and said, "I tell you, even in Israel I haven't found faith like this." ¹⁰When the centurion's friends returned to his house, they found the servant restored to health.

UNDERSTANDING THE SCRIPTURE

Introduction. The story of the healing of the centurion's servant is the first story Luke tells after Jesus' Sermon on the Plain. This sermon is much like the Sermon on the Mount in Matthew. Those two sermons have many of the same teachings, but they are set in different places. The story of the servant's healing serves as evidence of the validity of the teaching in the Sermon on the Plain. The healing story is proof that Jesus has authority from God to teach and to heal. Many interpreters compare this story with the healing of Naaman in 2 Kings

5:1-19. In 2 Kings an officer of a foreign army travels to the prophet Elisha and asks for healing. In addition, Elisha speaks to him through intermediaries rather than directly and the healing takes place at a distance. If Luke has this story in the back of his mind, then he wants his readers to see Jesus presented as a mighty prophet (Luke 7:16). While that is not a sufficient understanding of who Jesus is, it is an important aspect of Jesus' identity that will help the readers accept the teaching in the preceding sermon.

Luke 7:1-5. After the Sermon on the

Plain, Jesus returns to Capernaum, the city that seems to be his base of operation. He is met by a delegation of leaders of the Jewish community who come with a request from a Roman centurion. The centurion has a slave that he cares about who is so sick that he is about to die. This centurion is presented very sympathetically. He is a good person who loves the Jewish people and has built a place of worship for them. He is an officer in the occupying army who cares about the people he governs, and even about his slaves. If we remember that Luke was written not long after the Romans destroyed the Temple, this portrayal of a Roman soldier seems even more noteworthy. Some interpreters see this interchange between Jesus and the centurion as an indication that Jesus' concern includes those whom many would see as enemies.

Having the leaders of the Jewish community come to Jesus seems to reflect the centurion's willingness to respect any concern Jesus might have about associating with a Gentile. He may also be calling in the kind of favor the community owes him for building their synagogue. But if the elders are acting out of obligation and the soldier is respecting boundaries, Jesus responds without concern for those distinctions between Jews and Gentiles or between the Romans and those they ruled.

Luke 7:6-8. Jesus goes immediately to the centurion's house. But before he arrives, the officer sends more messengers, this time friends. There is an unexpected role reversal here. The representative of the ruling government says to one of the people he has authority over that he is not worthy to have Jesus come into his house. The centurion recognizes the difficulty it might cause Jesus to be in his house, and so gives Jesus a way to avoid any problems. We may note that Jesus does not seem worried about whatever may have made the centurion or others nervous about going into the house of a Roman soldier.

Jesus' openness to this Roman Gentile is important, but only a secondary concern of this story. The real point comes in the message that the centurion sends to Jesus. The centurion says he knows both what it means to be under someone's authority and what it means to wield authority. He is an officer with one hundred soldiers under his command, and he is under the authority of the officers above him. He sees Jesus in a similar position. Jesus is under the authority of God and he also wields authority on earth. He recognizes Jesus as the one who has the authority to grant healing. It is not a question of power, but of authority. Luke's story has already given accounts of Jesus healing lepers, a paralyzed person, and a man with a "withered hand." Jesus has already exorcised demons and been credited with healing everyone people bring to him. The issue Luke brings up explicitly in our reading today is about the *authority* of Jesus.

The centurion recognizes that Jesus has authority from God to heal his servant. Such authority does not require Jesus to touch or even see the servant. God has given Jesus the authority to use God's power and to represent God in the world. This is the central point of this story. Coming on the heels of the Sermon on the Plain, this story is the guarantee that the teaching in that sermon is the will of God. Jesus has authority to wield the power of God in the world, so readers must accept the teaching in the preceding sermon as God's will.

Luke 7:9-10. The resolution of this quest for healing comes in verses 9-10. Luke mentions the successful healing almost in passing. The servant is well when the messengers get back to the house. The emphatic element in this resolution is Jesus' assessment of the centurion's faith. He has a greater or a different sort of faith than anything Jesus has seen among his own people. While the people are at times amazed at the things Jesus does in Luke, here Jesus is amazed at the centurion's faith. This soldier has seen that Jesus has God's authority on earth.

We should not miss Luke's contrast between the centurion's faith and that of Jesus' own people. We should think of this in the context of Luke's church. It comprises both Jews and Gentiles, but is predominantly Gentile. Members of Luke's church may be wondering about how Gentiles fit in this church that worships the God of Israel, or even whether members of the Roman military should be welcomed. If that is a question, this story and Jesus' evaluation of the man's faith calls them to welcome and value Gentiles, even Roman conquerors, who have faith in Jesus.

INTERPRETING THE SCRIPTURE

The Centurion's Amazing Faith

In this week that follows Easter, our reading takes us back to a time early in the ministry of Jesus. Still, it is a time when people have heard of both his healings and his teachings. Jesus uses Capernaum as the place from which he goes out to do ministry. It is a good-sized city for the region and so a place of commerce and a place where there would be a Roman presence. The main character (other than Jesus) of this story never appears directly. We only hear descriptions of him and get messages sent by him. Yet Jesus says he has a faith that is superior to everyone he had met in his ministry. The centurion has obviously heard of Jesus' reputation as a healer. This is no surprise. Healing has been a significant part of Luke's description of Jesus' ministry to this point and a person charged with keeping the peace would have kept tabs on such events.

The centurion does not, however, view the healing power of Jesus as a threat. He judges it to be genuine, so genuine that he is willing to ask the community leaders to approach Jesus on his behalf. He is willing to use some of the political goodwill he had accumulated to have them go to Jesus to ask for the healing of one of his slaves. So he trusts the healing power, and perhaps the things he had heard about the teaching, of Jesus enough to use some hard-earned political capital.

By itself, believing that Jesus could heal would not be enough for Jesus to evaluate his faith as better than any he had seen before. What stands out about the centurion's faith is that it is an expression of his confidence that Jesus has the authority to use God's power. Other people had come to Jesus for healing. Perhaps they thought he was close enough to God that God granted him the ability to heal, at least on occasion. The centurion's faith goes beyond that. He sees Jesus as a person who stands under the authority of God, as he was under the authority of the emperor. But the place Jesus holds is one that also grants him authority to use the power of God. This recognizes a higher status for Jesus than just being able to heal. Jesus is the representative of God who has been granted God's authority. This is a very important theme for Luke. Not only does this place of authority grant Jesus power to heal, it also authorizes his teaching. (By the time we get to the end of Luke's Gospel, Luke will show that Jesus has the authority to grant salvation to those with faith.) So the faith of the centurion is a faith that Luke wants his readers to emulate.

The Faith of an Outsider

It is important for us to think about the original readers of Luke as we approach this passage. The church Luke writes for comprises mostly Gentiles, but also has some Jewish members. It is obvious in the narrative of the Gospel to this point that Jesus had spent most his time with fellow Jews. They have been the objects of his healings and the context for his teaching. But in this story the hero is a Gentile. Indeed, a Gentile who recognizes how hard it could be for some Jews to associate intimately with him.

Beyond being a Gentile, he is a Roman. Jews who read Luke would still be feeling the loss of the Temple in Jerusalem. For those readers, the centurion's office represents the often repressive Roman rule. Yet he comes to Jesus. And he comes in a rather humble way; he sends delegates whom he thinks will be more

acceptable to Jesus. The important parallels between this story and the healing of Naaman by Elisha are no accident. Luke wants readers to see the similarity between the power of God that worked in Elisha and that is at work in Jesus. But there are also differences. In the Elisha story, the military officer goes directly to the prophet, while the prophet sends a messenger. The officer is arrogant there, but humble in Luke's story. He says he is not worthy to have Jesus enter his house. The centurion in Luke is a better person than the general in the Elisha story. Luke emphasizes the goodness of the centurion. The leaders of the city tell Jesus that he loves their people (rather than being oppressive or cruel) and that he had even built a synagogue for them. These leaders say he is worthy to receive Jesus' help. This description makes him an attractive outsider. In Luke's day there were still questions in the church about how Gentiles were to be received into churches that have Jews who continue to keep the law. So Luke paints a sympathetic portrait of this outsider. Even Jews outside the church see him as worthy to receive the gifts of God that Christ offers.

Our Faith in Jesus

As much as the centurion is an outsider, he is also a character that Luke wants his readers (including us) to imitate. His faith is the kind of faith believers are to develop. While it may not be a complete and fully formed faith, it is a faith that recognizes that Jesus possesses and is authorized to use God's power. Jesus' authority is broader than the centurion imagined, but he embodies an important element of our faith. In the flow of Luke's Gospel, this affirmation of the authority of Jesus assures the readers that the teaching Jesus has just given in the Sermon on the Plain is the will of God. We can now see Jesus as the One authorized to reveal God's will; his teaching is, then, to be accepted as God's will.

Most explicitly in the story, Jesus has the ability to heal. As the Gospel progresses, Luke will show that the healing power of Jesus goes far beyond removing physical maladies. In fact, those healings are merely demonstrations of more important powers, especially of the power to heal our relationship with God. While we have turned away and done harm to our relationship with God, Jesus is authorized to forgive and so to heal that relationship. As Luke thinks about the way that Jesus brings us salvation and spiritual healing, he envisions Jesus as the one who is authorized to use the power of God to accomplish those tasks. This story begins to focus our attention on Jesus as the One given the power to grant God's forgiveness and salvation.

That is surely good news for us—and for others as well. The centurion's faith in Jesus was used for the good of someone other than himself. His example reminds us that we are to use our faith for the benefit of others. We can mediate our trust in God to those who find themselves in difficult situations. Our faith should be manifested in our own reaching out to those who need God's healing and saving power. We can share our trusting in God's goodness and love with those who need assurance that God cares. Using our faith to support others and to nurture trust in God can be a way for us to emulate the centurion's amazing faith.

SHARING THE SCRIPTURE

PREPARING TO TEACH

Preparing Our Hearts

Ponder this week's devotional reading from Malachi 3:16–4:2. In verse 15, the people charge that evildoers "prosper" and escape testing. How will the righteous be treated on the day of the Lord? How will evildoers be treated? How can one distinguish between these two types of people?

Pray that you and the students will be ready to serve God.

Preparing Our Minds

Study the background Scripture and the lesson Scripture, both of which are from Luke 7:1-10.

Consider this question as you prepare the lesson: *To whom can we turn for help that makes a difference in times of desperate need?*

Write on newsprint:
- ❏ information for next week's lesson, found under Continue the Journey.
- ❏ activities for further spiritual growth in Continue the Journey.

Review the Introduction, The Big Picture, Close-up, and Faith in Action, which all precede the first lesson of this quarter. Consider how you might use any of this material in today's lesson.

Option: Invite a class member or guest to talk with the class about a serious illness or injury from which he or she was healed in answer to prayer. Be sure to suggest a time limit.

Caution: God can and does heal people in response to prayer. However, not everyone who prays and has prayers said on his or her behalf is cured of an illness or disability. Some people who have prayed, but not been cured, feel either that God does not answer prayers or that they lack faith. Do not let such comments stand unchallenged. Recall that Paul had a "thorn" (2 Corinthians 12:6-9) that God did not remove despite Paul's appeals. No one can say why certain people are fully cured and others are not.

LEADING THE CLASS

(1) Gather to Learn

❖ Welcome the class members and guests.

❖ Pray that those who have come today will have faith in Jesus' ability to heal.

❖ Note that we have moved from Mark's Gospel to Luke's Gospel. Read or retell The Big Picture: The Gospels of Mark and Luke, beginning with the ninth paragraph ("Luke affords us") to provide an overview of his Gospel.

❖ Read aloud today's focus statement: **Everyone has desperate needs at times that cause him or her to wonder if any help is available. To whom can people turn for help that makes a difference? The centurion's faith in Jesus Christ as the great healer made all the difference in meeting his need to see his servant healed.**

(2) Goal 1: Analyze the Story of the Centurion's Faith and Jesus' Healing of the Centurion's Servant

❖ Select a volunteer to read Luke 7:1-10.

❖ Discuss these questions:

1. **What does Jesus (and the reader) know about the centurion before he agrees to go to his home?** (See Luke 7:1-5 in Understanding the Scripture.)

2. **What do we learn about the faith of the centurion?** (See "The Centurion's Amazing Faith" and "The Faith of an Outsider" in Interpreting the Scripture.)

3. **On what basis does the centurion believe that Jesus will heal the sick slave?** (See Luke 7:6-8 in Understanding the Scripture. Note the centurion's comparison between how his military authority operates and how Jesus' authority from God works.)

4. **Recall that Luke's community includes both Jews and Gentiles. How does Jesus' encounter with the centurion (through the messengers he sent) hint at the inclusion of Gentiles in Jesus' ministry?**

(3) Goal 2: Experience Strong Faith for Deliverance from Illness Like the Faith of the Centurion in the Story

❖ **Option:** If you invited a speaker, ask this person to give a testimony as to how faith and prayers enabled him or her to be healed from a serious illness or injury.

❖ Encourage class members to talk about healings they have experienced—or are aware of—that have occurred as a result of faith and prayer. Note that sometimes these cures can seem spontaneous, but people may need to be under a physician's care. Seeking medical help in no way indicates that faith is weak or prayers are ineffectual.

(4) Goal 3: Commit (or Recommit) to Regularly Visiting the Sick to Pray with Them and to Encourage Them to Believe God Will Heal According to God's Will

❖ Note that although in today's story the centurion's servant was healed instantly, often people need to be placed in a hospital or other facility for treatment. Invite participants to call out the names of health facilities in your community. Include hospitals, hospices, nursing homes, rehab centers, facilities for drug and alcohol rehab, residential treatment centers for those with psychiatric illnesses, and any other facilities. List the names of these places on newsprint. Add a word or two about the services offered at facilities.

❖ Review the list and ask for a show of hands of class members who would be willing to go to each facility. Be clear that not everyone will feel comfortable visiting in all types of facilities. Write volunteers' names next to each facility.

❖ Decide if there is one facility where class members could go not only to see individuals but also to conduct a Bible study, hymn sing, or short worship service on a regular basis. Another possibility would be for individuals to each visit in different facilities. Recognize that in some places, particularly public hospitals, spoken prayers for patients who are unknown to the visitor may be frowned upon, but that does not mean that the visitor could not pray after leaving the room.

❖ **Option:** Some class members may have well-trained dogs (or other animals) that could become involved with pet therapy. Visiting with a pet is a wonderful ministry, touching people's lives with the love of God even

if prayers cannot be spoken aloud. Suggest that those who are interested look into local pet therapy groups to see about their requirements and the facilities they visit.

❖ Encourage those who are able to make a commitment to visit the sick and minister to them in person. Encourage those who cannot visit to pray for those who are ill.

(5) Continue the Journey

❖ Pray that as the learners depart, they will give thanks that Jesus has authority from God to heal.

❖ Post information for next week's session on newsprint for the students to copy:

- **Title: A Reversal of Shame**
- **Background Scripture: Luke 7:36-50**
- **Lesson Scripture: Luke 7:36-50**
- **Focus of the Lesson: Sometimes in life, people are remorseful to the point of tears about something they did or said. Where can they turn for help? Jesus' response to a sinful woman provided real forgiveness and peace because she loved him so much.**

❖ Post the following information on newsprint and provide paper and pencils for the students to copy it. Challenge the adults to grow spiritually by completing one or more of these activities related to this week's session.

(1) **Compare the story of the healing of Naaman in 2 Kings 5 with that of the healing of the centurion's slave. What similarities do you notice? What differences? What do these stories suggest about God's**

desire that all people, including enemies, be healed?

(2) **Plan to visit one or more sick people on a regular basis. Be prepared to read a short Scripture and offer a prayer.**

(3) **Keep a list of sick or injured people who need prayer. Offer prayer on a regular basis for each person.**

❖ Sing or read aloud "Heal Me, Hands of Jesus."

❖ Conclude today's session by leading the class in this benediction, which is adapted from Mark 9:23 in the lesson for March 6: **Together we affirm that all things can be done for the one who believes. Amen.**

UNIT 2: RESTORATIVE FAITH
A REVERSAL OF SHAME

PREVIEWING THE LESSON

Lesson Scripture: Luke 7:36-50
Background Scripture: Luke 7:36-50
Key Verse: Luke 7:47

Focus of the Lesson:
Sometimes in life, people are remorseful to the point of tears about something they did or said. Where can they turn for help? Jesus' response to a sinful woman provided real forgiveness and peace because she loved him so much.

Goals for the Learners:
(1) to know the story of Jesus' tenderness for the repentant woman and his forgiveness of her sins.
(2) to express the great joy that comes from knowing their sins have been forgiven.
(3) to forgive others for their failures, shortcomings, and hurtful actions.

Supplies:
Bibles, newsprint and marker, paper and pencils, hymnals

READING THE SCRIPTURE

NRSV
Lesson Scripture: Luke 7:36-50

³⁶One of the Pharisees asked Jesus to eat with him, and he went into the Pharisee's house and took his place at the table. ³⁷And a woman in the city, who was a sinner, having learned that he was eating in the Pharisee's house, brought an alabaster jar of ointment. ³⁸She stood behind him at his feet, weeping, and began to bathe his feet with her tears and to dry them with her hair. Then she continued kissing

CEB
Lesson Scripture: Luke 7:36-50

³⁶One of the Pharisees invited Jesus to eat with him. After he entered the Pharisee's home, he took his place at the table. ³⁷Meanwhile, a woman from the city, a sinner, discovered that Jesus was dining in the Pharisee's house. She brought perfumed oil in a vase made of alabaster. ³⁸Standing behind him at his feet and crying, she began to wet his feet with her tears. She wiped them with her hair, kissed

his feet and anointing them with the ointment. [39]Now when the Pharisee who had invited him saw it, he said to himself, "If this man were a prophet, he would have known who and what kind of woman this is who is touching him—that she is a sinner." [40]Jesus spoke up and said to him, "Simon, I have something to say to you." "Teacher," he replied, "Speak." [41]"A certain creditor had two debtors; one owed five hundred denarii, and the other fifty. [42]When they could not pay, he canceled the debts for both of them. Now which of them will love him more?" [43]Simon answered, "I suppose the one for whom he canceled the greater debt." And Jesus said to him, "You have judged rightly." [44]Then turning toward the woman, he said to Simon, "Do you see this woman? I entered your house; you gave me no water for my feet, but she has bathed my feet with her tears and dried them with her hair. [45]You gave me no kiss, but from the time I came in she has not stopped kissing my feet. [46]You did not anoint my head with oil, but she has anointed my feet with ointment. [47]**Therefore, I tell you, her sins, which were many, have been forgiven; hence she has shown great love. But the one to whom little is forgiven, loves little."** [48]Then he said to her, "Your sins are forgiven." [49]But those who were at the table with him began to say among themselves, "Who is this who even forgives sins?" [50]And he said to the woman, "Your faith has saved you; go in peace."

them, and poured the oil on them. [39]When the Pharisee who had invited Jesus saw what was happening, he said to himself, If this man were a prophet, he would know what kind of woman is touching him. He would know that she is a sinner.

[40]Jesus replied, "Simon, I have something to say to you."

"Teacher, speak," he said.

[41]"A certain lender had two debtors. One owed enough money to pay five hundred people for a day's work. The other owed enough money for fifty. [42]When they couldn't pay, the lender forgave the debts of them both. Which of them will love him more?"

[43]Simon replied, "I suppose the one who had the largest debt canceled."

Jesus said, "You have judged correctly."

[44]Jesus turned to the woman and said to Simon, "Do you see this woman? When I entered your home, you didn't give me water for my feet, but she wet my feet with tears and wiped them with her hair. [45]You didn't greet me with a kiss, but she hasn't stopped kissing my feet since I came in. [46]You didn't anoint my head with oil, but she has poured perfumed oil on my feet. [47]**This is why I tell you that her many sins have been forgiven; so she has shown great love. The one who is forgiven little loves little."**

[48]Then Jesus said to her, "Your sins are forgiven."

[49]The other table guests began to say among themselves, "Who is this person that even forgives sins?"

[50]Jesus said to the woman, "Your faith has saved you. Go in peace."

UNDERSTANDING THE SCRIPTURE

Introduction. This text follows closely behind last week's lesson. Just as the question of the authority of Jesus was an issue in the healing of the centurion's servant, so Jesus' authority is a crucial topic of this text. Now the question is not who has authority to heal and teach, but who has authority to forgive sins.

Luke 7:36-38. As this story opens, Jesus has been invited to a formal dinner at the house of a Pharisee. There is a bit of irony here because just before (7:34), Jesus notes that he is sometimes accused of being a drunk and a glutton. He is then immediately invited to a lavish dinner at the house of a Pharisee.

The dinner envisioned here follows the pattern of the Greek Symposium. At these gatherings a rich dinner was followed by lively conversation and even debate. Participants in the meal reclined on couches with their heads close to the table and their feet behind them. That is why the woman could approach his feet from behind. The kind of repartee that we hear in this story between Jesus and Simon would be appropriate for this kind of setting.

We should note that Jesus is invited to the house of a Pharisee and that he accepts the invitation. Pharisees are not uniformly seen as enemies of Jesus in Luke. When they are mentioned in connection with scribes, they are usually opponents. But the Pharisee in this story is not an enemy. He is not sure what to make of Jesus, but he is not an opponent. He addresses Jesus as "teacher," but the story ends without telling us whether he is convinced by Jesus' argument.

When the woman enters the room, she engages in dramatic and outlandish behavior. She, an uninvited guest, interrupts the dinner party with crying and washing Jesus' feet with her hair and tears and anointing them with expensive ointment. At this point in the story we do not know why she behaves in this way. We know only that she lavishes extraordinary care on Jesus.

Luke 7:39-43. The host knows this woman as a sinner. We do not know what her offenses were, but Jesus does not dispute this evaluation. Jesus' acceptance of her attention causes the host to question Jesus' judgment and identity. Others have seen him as a prophet, but if he allows this kind of contact with such a notorious sinner, that assessment seems mistaken.

It is significant that Jesus calls this Pharisee by name. Few minor characters in Luke are given a name. Naming him seems to indicate that Jesus has a connection with him and hopes he will see the truth that Jesus is about to articulate. In response to Simon's judgment about Jesus' behavior, Jesus asks him to comment on a hypothetical situation. In essence, he asks him to participate in a parable. Who will love the benefactor more: a person who was forgiven a debt that was relatively small (about a month and a half in wages for a day laborer) or a person who owed so much (about a year and an half's wages) that he would never be able to repay it? Simon's seemingly reluctant response is that he supposed that the one who owed more would have more love for the one who forgave him. Jesus says Simon is right. While they agree about the point that the parable makes, Simon's reaction to Jesus' association with the woman shows that they disagree about how to treat sinners. After all, Simon does not yet know the application Jesus intends to give to the parable.

Luke 7:44-47. Now Jesus applies the parable to the situation at the dinner. He compares the treatment the woman gave him to that which he received from Simon. There is no suggestion here that Simon had failed to treat Jesus with respect or had failed in his duties as a host. But in comparison with the lavish treatment Jesus received from the woman, Simon's reception of Jesus seems unimpressive.

The explanation Jesus gives for the different treatments he got from Simon and from the woman not only confirms Simon's evaluation of the woman but also emphasizes how expansive God's love is. She is in fact a person with many and grievous sins, in contrast to Simon who is a good person. This difference allows her to experience the grace of God in ways that Simon does not know. It leads her to be grateful to God in ways that Simon can hardly plumb. She knows the depth of her sin and so how much grace God had extended to her. Her extravagant treatment of Jesus is the direct result of the experience of receiving the liberating and thrilling grace of God.

Luke 7:48-50. The interpretation that Jesus gives to the woman's behavior in verse 47 seems to assume that the woman's sins have already been forgiven, perhaps in a previous encounter with Jesus. But in verse 48 Jesus tells her that her sins are forgiven. This direct declaration moves us to the central affirmation about Jesus that Luke wants us to hear: Jesus has the authority to forgive sin. Those who are at the dinner with Jesus doubt that he has this authority, just as those who heard him forgive sin did when he healed the paralyzed man (5:21-25). Jesus remains undaunted by their doubt. He has authority to forgive and to save. He now tells the woman that her faith, that is, her faith in him, has saved her. She can now go in peace because her relationship with God has been restored by Jesus.

As the story ends, the woman is restored and forgiven. There is no closure in the Simon part of the narrative. He is challenged to understand Jesus and Jesus' actions in a new light. His guests are inclined to reject Jesus, but we do not hear what Simon thinks in the end. This open-ended story permits Luke to allow that some Pharisees may turn to Jesus.

INTERPRETING THE SCRIPTURE

Jesus Forgives Sins

The central point of this story about Jesus is that he has the authority and power to forgive sins, even for people who have been very sinful. Luke has made this point before (5:20-26), but it is one that he needs to make repeatedly. This is a powerful affirmation about who Jesus is. He is the one who mediates God's forgiveness. It is the woman's faith in Jesus that brings her forgiveness and salvation.

Importantly, attributing this power to Jesus does not mean that sin is unimportant or that it matters little to God. Just the opposite. Sin separates us from God. When we sin we reject the will of God and put ourselves at cross-purposes with God. When we sin we act in ways that harm ourselves and our fellow humans. This rejection of God and God's will keeps us from having the relationship with God that God wants and accrues real guilt. The good news of this passage is that God forgives us through Jesus, the One who was willing to die to attain the position that authorizes him to forgive. Jesus has this power from God during his ministry because it is assumed that he will give himself on the cross and be exalted to the place at God's side. The length to which God goes to offer forgiveness is a clear signal of the seriousness of sin.

While this story does not make the point, other places in Luke make it clear that sinners must change their behavior. Having Christ be able to forgive is not a license to sin. Forgiveness restores our relationship with God and allows us to live in peace with God. If we fail to try to live for God (and so try to stop sinning), however, we abuse God's gift. In accepting peace with God, we can begin to live at peace with others. Our treatment of them will begin to reflect the will of God.

The Joy of Being Forgiven

A second important point of this story is that the forgiveness that comes through Jesus brings joy to our lives. The woman in our story is aware of the sin that characterized her life. She knows that the name "sinner" fits her. As a result, she is exceedingly grateful for the forgiveness that she receives from Jesus. She knows what a great burden has been lifted. She knows how the way she had lived harms her own well-being and that of those around her. Because she knows how harmful sin is, she appreciates forgiveness as the wonderful gift that it is. Many of us in the church, however, are more like Simon—in a good way. Often our lives have not been characterized by obvious and hurtful sin. We see ourselves as people who have lived good lives. In fact, many do not see much need for Christ to do anything to attain forgiveness for us. We have been pretty good people who are quite likeable. We have not killed anyone or robbed a bank. We are just the kind of people God should like. Sure we have small sins, but any reasonable assessment would conclude that those are easy enough for God to forgive. We do not feel exhilaration when forgiveness is proclaimed because we think there was not much to forgive.

As the example of Simon shows, we are not the first people to think that our sins are small and inconsequential, especially in comparison with the sins of some people we could name. The eleventh-century monk and theologian Anselm said famously, "You have not yet considered how great the weight of sin is." His point was that our sins do matter, in our relationship with God and in how we relate to one another. Those of us who think we have sinned little simply have not recognized the harm done even by the kinds of sin we commit. Even when they are few, they are damaging.

This is not to say that all sin is the same or that we should feel free to sin a lot. Jesus recognizes the difference between Simon and the woman. She had many sins; he only a few. The number and type do matter. But all sin separates us from God. Still, it is natural that those who have been forgiven the most are more appreciative than those who have been forgiven less. We have seen the joy and the zeal of recent converts. Jesus finds this zeal good and appropriate. He also recognizes that the experience of forgiveness is less exhilarating to those without such a checkered history. Still his forgiveness is needed by all. Knowing of the forgiveness God gives in extreme cases can give us confidence that God forgives our sins. Thus we can live in a joyous relationship with God and with others who have experienced this forgiveness.

Receiving Sinners

Remembering that we have all sinned and need forgiveness can help us be forgiving. In our story, Simon needed to be reminded that he had sin that needed to be forgiven, even if the number and severity were fewer than those of the women. In the parable, there are two debtors. Both owe the creditor and both are expected to appreciate the release from debt they are granted. The debt owed by one was smaller, but no less real. So the forgiveness had to be just as real for the small debt as for the larger one.

We all know the sting of having someone sin against us or against those we care about. The shortcomings and failures of others may hurt feelings or even impede some good work. Such failures and offenses may leave deep scars. In these cases, the good news of forgiveness of sinners may seem undeserved. Indeed, it is always undeserved. Yet the story of the sinful woman demonstrates that Jesus brings God's forgiveness even to those people who publicly do things that harm others. This story also calls us to be forgiving. As we remember and are grateful for the forgiveness we receive, we can extend that forgiveness to others.

Simon knew he had sins that had been forgiven. As a good observant Jew he had honored the Day of Atonement, the day of forgiveness. Jesus suggests in this story that he should be forgiving, just as he had been forgiven. The forgiveness we have received from God and the joy it brings can enable us to begin to be forgiving. Part of the gift we are given in Christ is the power to forgive others. We can recognize that we all—those who accepted forgiveness long ago and those who have only recently received it, those who need forgiveness for much and those who need it for less—stand in need of God's grace. When the sin and failures of others harm us, we can forgive because we have been forgiven. The grace that we receive helps us to receive others. This does not mean that we act as though sin does not matter. It does mean that we live the words of the Lord's Prayer, "forgive us our sins as we forgive those who sin against us." Receiving God's forgiveness brings the responsibility of forgiving others. But this is also a blessing as it enables us to live lives that are not encumbered by resentment.

SHARING THE SCRIPTURE

PREPARING TO TEACH

Preparing Our Hearts

Ponder this week's devotional reading from Psalm 13 in which an individual prays to God to be delivered from his enemies. When have you felt that God had abandoned you? Why does the psalmist seem to have hope that God will act? What hope do you have?

Pray that you and the students will trust God to take care of you.

Preparing Our Minds

Study the background Scripture and the lesson Scripture, both of which are from Luke 7:36-50.

Consider this question as you prepare the lesson: *When we feel remorseful, where can we turn for help?*

Write on newsprint:

❏ information for next week's lesson, found under Continue the Journey.

❏ activities for further spiritual growth in Continue the Journey.

Review the Introduction, The Big Picture, Close-up, and Faith in Action, which all precede the first lesson of this quarter. Consider how you might use any of this material in today's lesson.

LEADING THE CLASS

(1) Gather to Learn

❖ Welcome the class members and guests.

❖ Pray that those who have come today will be open to receiving and extending forgiveness.

❖ Ask the students to recall the story of David's adulterous affair with Bathsheba as recorded in 2 Samuel 11. Also recall that when she became pregnant with David's child he resorted to having her husband, Uriah, stationed on the battlefield so that he would be killed. The prophet Nathan used a parable to show David his sin (2 Samuel 12). After reviewing the story, distribute hymnals (if they include a Psalter) and lead the class in reading Psalm 51 responsively. Point out the superscription: "A Psalm of David, when the prophet Nathan came to him, after he had gone in to Bathsheba." (Alternatively, have one person read the psalm.) Ask: **What does David pray for? Why?**

❖ Read aloud today's focus statement: **Sometimes in life, people are remorseful to the point of tears about something they did or said. Where can they turn for help? Jesus' response to a sinful woman provided real forgiveness and peace because she loved him so much.**

(2) Goal 1: Know the Story of Jesus' Tenderness for the Repentant Woman and His Forgiveness of Her Sins

❖ Choose four volunteers to read the parts of the narrator, Jesus, Simon, and a guest (7:49).

❖ Discuss these questions:

1. **What can we know or infer about the dinner party that Jesus attended?** (See Luke 7:36-38 in Understanding the Scripture.)

2. **What similarities and differences do you see between the way Simon the Pharisee and Jesus view the woman who has crashed the dinner party?** (See

Luke 7:39-43 in Understanding the Scripture.)

3. **To what does Jesus attribute the woman's lavish treatment of him?** (See Luke 7:44-47 in Understanding the Scripture.)

4. **What does this story teach about Jesus' authority?** (See Luke 7:48-50 in Understanding the Scripture and "Jesus Forgives Sins" in Interpreting the Scripture.)

5. **What does Jesus' authorization by God to forgive sin suggest about the seriousness of sin?** (See "Jesus Forgives Sins" and "The Joy of Being Forgiven" in Interpreting the Scripture.)

(3) Goal 2: Express the Great Joy that Comes from Knowing the Learners' Sins Have Been Forgiven

❖ Discuss: **If we were to take a poll of people in the church concerning their need for forgiveness, what do you think most people would say about the nature and severity of their own sins?**

❖ **Option:** Read the first and second paragraphs of "The Joy of Being Forgiven" in Interpreting the Scripture in addition to or instead of discussing the prior question.

❖ Read: **The woman in today's story shows the joy of her forgiveness by lavishing attention on Jesus by bathing his feet and massaging them with ointment. She was able to do something for the One who had forgiven her. In our day, we can do something in Jesus' name to demonstrate the joy we have in being forgiven. Try to think of things that we can do individually or as a group to show our gratitude to Jesus. Join with two or three other people and**

take a marker and sheet of newsprint to record your ideas. Let's see if as a class we can brainstorm at least ten ideas per group.

❖ Invite the groups to report on several ideas. Hang their sheets around the room, if possible. Affirm their ideas. Count to see how many ideas the total class generated. Here are some ideas: Fix lunch for someone who is ill, take a spring bouquet to a homebound friend, repair a screen door for an elderly neighbor, babysit children for a mom who needs a break.

❖ Close this portion by suggesting that the adults select at least one of these ideas that they can use to express their joy and gratitude to Jesus for his forgiveness of their sins.

(4) Goal 3: Forgive Others for Their Failures, Shortcomings, and Hurtful Actions

❖ Recall with the learners these words from the Lord's Prayer: "forgive us our sins as we forgive those who sin against us." (Use whatever words are familiar to your church: "debts / debtors" or "trespasses / trespass.")

❖ Read aloud the second and third paragraphs of "Receiving Sinners" in Interpreting the Scripture. The point you want to make is that God expects us to forgive others as we receive forgiveness from God.

❖ Distribute paper and pencils and encourage participants to think of one person whom they believe has wronged them. Suggest that they think of words to express their forgiveness and a setting in which to offer that forgiveness, even if the other person does not seek forgiveness. (Note that the other person may not even know that he or she has caused an offense either by something done or left undone.)

❖ Reconvene the group and challenge them to make arrangements to offer their forgiveness in person if at all possible, over the phone (or via Skype), or in writing.

(5) Continue the Journey

❖ Pray that as the learners depart, they will thank God for the forgiveness of sins that they have received through Jesus.

❖ Post information for next week's session on newsprint for the students to copy:
- Title: A Sound Mind
- Background Scripture: Luke 8:26-39
- Lesson Scripture: Luke 8:26-36
- Focus of the Lesson: Sometimes when people suffer from emotional or physical disorders affecting the mind, they might behave abnormally and even be a threat to themselves or others. Who can clear their minds and give them something to shout about? Jesus once healed a man who was **demon-possessed and then told him to go home and tell everyone how much God had done for him.**

❖ Post the following information on newsprint and provide paper and pencils for the students to copy it. Challenge the adults to grow spiritually by completing one or more of these activities related to this week's session.

(1) **Seek forgiveness from someone you have wronged. Recognize that you can only ask for forgiveness; you cannot force the other person to accept your offer.**

(2) **Forgive someone who has wronged you.**

(3) **Use a concordance to find New Testament references to Jesus' authority. For what purposes does Jesus use this authority? What difference does his authority make in your life?**

❖ Sing or read aloud "Forgive Our Sins as We Forgive."

❖ Conclude today's session by leading the class in this benediction, which is adapted from Mark 9:23 in the lesson for March 6: **Together we affirm that all things can be done for the one who believes. Amen.**

UNIT 2: RESTORATIVE FAITH
A SOUND MIND

PREVIEWING THE LESSON

Lesson Scripture: Luke 8:26-36
Background Scripture: Luke 8:26-39
Key Verse: Luke 8:35

Focus of the Lesson:

Sometimes when people suffer from emotional or physical disorders affecting the mind, they might behave abnormally and even be a threat to themselves or others. Who can clear their minds and give them something to shout about? Jesus once healed a man who was demon-possessed and then told him to go home and tell everyone how much God had done for him.

Goals for the Learners:

(1) to learn the details of Jesus' healing of the Gerasene man from demons.
(2) to empathize with those who have great troubles and to remember their own times of trial.
(3) to support persons with mental health issues.

Supplies:

Bibles, newsprint and marker, paper and pencils, hymnals

READING THE SCRIPTURE

NRSV

Lesson Scripture: Luke 8:26-36

²⁶Then they arrived at the country of the Gerasenes, which is opposite Galilee. ²⁷As he stepped out on land, a man of the city who had demons met him. For a long time he had worn no clothes, and he did not live in a house but in the tombs. ²⁸When he saw Jesus, he fell down before him and shouted at the top of his voice, "What have you to do with me, Jesus, Son of

CEB

Lesson Scripture: Luke 8:26-36

²⁶Jesus and his disciples sailed to the Gerasenes' land, which is across the lake from Galilee. ²⁷As soon as Jesus got out of the boat, a certain man met him. The man was from the city and was possessed by demons. For a long time, he had lived among the tombs, naked and homeless. ²⁸When he saw Jesus, he shrieked and fell down before him. Then he shouted, "What

the Most High God? I beg you, do not torment me"— [29]for Jesus had commanded the unclean spirit to come out of the man. (For many times it had seized him; he was kept under guard and bound with chains and shackles, but he would break the bonds and be driven by the demon into the wilds.) [30]Jesus then asked him, "What is your name?" He said, "Legion"; for many demons had entered him. [31]They begged him not to order them to go back into the abyss.

[32]Now there on the hillside a large herd of swine was feeding; and the demons begged Jesus to let them enter these. So he gave them permission. [33]Then the demons came out of the man and entered the swine, and the herd rushed down the steep bank into the lake and was drowned.

[34]When the swineherds saw what had happened, they ran off and told it in the city and in the country. **[35]Then people came out to see what had happened, and when they came to Jesus, they found the man from whom the demons had gone sitting at the feet of Jesus, clothed and in his right mind.** And they were afraid. [36]Those who had seen it told them how the one who had been possessed by demons had been healed.

have you to do with me, Jesus, Son of the Most High God? I beg you, don't torture me!" [29]He said this because Jesus had already commanded the unclean spirit to come out of the man. Many times it had taken possession of him, so he would be bound with leg irons and chains and placed under guard. But he would break his restraints, and the demon would force him into the wilderness.

[30]Jesus asked him, "What is your name?"

"Legion," he replied, because many demons had entered him. [31]They pleaded with him not to order them to go back into the abyss.[32]A large herd of pigs was feeding on the hillside. The demons begged Jesus to let them go into the pigs. Jesus gave them permission, [33]and the demons left the man and entered the pigs. The herd rushed down the cliff into the lake and drowned.

[34]When those who tended the pigs saw what happened, they ran away and told the story in the city and in the countryside. **[35]People came to see what had happened. They came to Jesus and found the man from whom the demons had gone. He was sitting at Jesus' feet, fully dressed and completely sane.** They were filled with awe. [36]Those people who had actually seen what had happened told them how the demon-possessed man had been delivered.

UNDERSTANDING THE SCRIPTURE

Introduction. This exorcism story occurs as Jesus enters Gentile territory for the first time. Jesus has had interactions with Gentiles, but this is the first time he has ventured into an area

that is predominantly Gentile. Luke says he went "to the other side of the lake" (8:22) and that it is "opposite Galilee" (8:26). Furthermore, we hear of a herd of pigs, a food Jews do not eat. So we have clearly moved into Gentile country. The first miracle of Jesus among Gentiles is an exorcism. As Jesus steps out into the world that does not recognize God, he is met by the forces of evil. Luke here gives a more detailed account of an exorcism than anything we have seen so far.

Luke 8:26-30. Luke describes the manifestations of this man's demon possession in graphic ways. The demon makes him go naked, empowers him to break chains, and forces him to live in the cemetery. It has dehumanized him. Demon possession exemplifies the most personal experience of evil. As people of the first century understood it, a malevolent power took possession of one's body and even mind. Possessed persons were left without free will, forced to do things that harmed themselves and others. And as people of the first century saw it, a personal force came into those who were possessed and controlled them. So Jesus faces this most personal and powerful manifestation of evil.

This detailed description of the power of the demon makes the ease of the exorcism that much more remarkable. In most exorcism stories there is at least a verbal battle before the demon leaves. All we hear in this case is the demon asking a favor: Please don't torment me. The demon knows it has no power in comparison with Jesus.

This demon immediately recognizes Jesus. The contrast with the previous story is shocking. After Jesus stilled the storm in the boat, the disciples had asked who he was. Now a demon has no trouble recognizing him. It knows that Jesus is the "Son of the Most High God" (8:28). This way of designating God is appropriate

for a Gentile who would have recognized many gods. Still, even the demon acknowledges the one true God. It is interesting to note that the demons are the only ones in this story to understand Jesus this fully. They have knowledge from a realm beyond this world to know who Jesus is. For Luke's story, a raw exercise of power is not sufficient for people to know who Jesus is. It will finally take his death and resurrection for that identity to be fully understood. But even at this early time, the demons know his identity and his power; they know that he wields the power of God to defeat evil and bring salvation.

A part of the contest between a demon and an exorcist often involved discovering the name of the opponent. Whoever knew the true name of the other one had an advantage. This demon knows who Jesus is, but it does not matter. Further, Jesus has control before he knows the demon's name, but Luke wants us to hear that name. It is "Legion." This is the name for a company of Roman soldiers. We should not miss the implication that the Roman Empire was a force that was empowered by evil and dehumanized its subjects just as the company of demons did this man.

Luke 8:31-33. The demons ask that they not be sent to the abyss, that realm where demons are punished. They at least want to avoid that fate in the short term. So they ask permission to enter the herd of pigs. But when that permission is granted, their presence drives the pigs to commit suicide. The demons end up in the lake of Galilee, which here probably serves as a symbol of the abyss. This is especially the case because in the previous story Jesus has stilled the lake's chaos just as God had stilled the original chaos (often thought of as an abyss) to create the world.

Luke 8:34-39. There are two basic reactions to this amazing miracle: fear and the desire to devote oneself to Jesus. Luke provides the usual ending to an exorcism by giving evidence of the cure. When the people get to the place where the pigs had run off the cliff, they see the person who had been possessed behaving rationally. He is dressed and calm. Those who had seen the exorcism tell the tale. Rather than being joyful, the inhabitants of the region are afraid. They see Jesus as a person with great power—power so great that he is to be feared. If he is able to defeat such powerful forces of evil, just imagine what he could do to regular people or a whole village if he were angry with them. So they ask him to leave. Jesus accommodates them. Perhaps their lack of comprehension is understandable if we remember that the disciples, who have now been with Jesus for some time and had just seen Jesus still a storm, still cannot discern who he is.

The story does not end on a note of rejection of Jesus. The man who had been healed comes to ask if he can join the company of Jesus. At this point, Jesus does not allow this Gentile to accompany him in his ministry in Galilee. But he does commission him to preach. Jesus tells him to go tell his people all that God had done for him. We should notice that Luke then says that the man tells everyone what *Jesus* had done for him. Thus, Luke identifies what Jesus does with acts of God.

This story is about both the power of Jesus and people's reaction to it. Luke indicates that the mighty acts of Jesus are the acts of God. Those who see this power may turn away in fear or lack of understanding. But some who see it recognize the work of God and so want to follow Jesus and are willing to proclaim what God does through him.

INTERPRETING THE SCRIPTURE

A Shocking Introduction

Jesus' first trip into Gentile territory begins in a dramatic fashion. A violent and dangerous demon-possessed man meets Jesus. Perhaps he represents the religious and moral world of Gentiles, a world that opposes the will of God. The effects of evil in this man's life are portrayed graphically to emphasize how much power and control evil exercised over his life. It keeps him from any real human contact. He lives among the dead. This seems symbolic of what has happened to his existence; it is no real human life. He is the extreme, even among the possessed.

As Luke presents it, this is a contest between competing powers: One brings destruction and alienation, the other offers reconciliation and wholeness. But there is really no contest. Jesus' power is so superior to the demons that Luke does not even tell the story as his readers would have expected to hear an exorcism story. Rather than telling of a confrontation in which the demon and the exorcist each try to gain an advantage, Luke has the demon's first words be a plea for mercy. Jesus' extraordinary power is demonstrated even more emphatically when Jesus requires the demon to reveal its name. It goes by "Legion" because it is really multiple demons. Jesus is not just superior to individual demons; he is more powerful than the combined forces of evil. With a single word Jesus dispatches the forces that have dominated and damaged this person's life. But even in this moment of exercising such overwhelming power, Jesus shows mercy. The demons ask for a reprieve and get it.

Despite the terrible things they had wrought on this man, Jesus has mercy even for them. Their punishment is delayed by their going into the herd of pigs. Perhaps being able to possess an entire herd also demonstrates just how many demons had possessed the man. Still, they were no match for Jesus, but neither were they beyond his mercy.

Demon Possession?

Few of us today would say that the behavior Luke describes is the result of demon possession. Our understanding of the world does not admit such explanations. We turn to medical or psychological explanations for such behavior. While some in the ancient world also looked to physical causes for such disturbing behavior, we have more tools of analysis than they had. We know about chemical imbalances and the long-lasting effects of traumatic experiences on one's psyche. We have techniques for helping people with post-traumatic stress disorder (PTSD) and drugs to help with depression and schizophrenia.

We should not too quickly identify what this text talks about as demon possession with some type of mental illness, though. The descriptions of demon-possessed people in other texts do not allow for a simple equation of the two. Sometimes those descriptions point to other kinds of maladies, some that we might describe as physical, others as psychosomatic. The ancients did recognize the effects that trauma could have on a person's behavior and outlook. They could distinguish some of those effects from what they called demon possession. Talk of demon possession should make us think of things that take over people's lives, things that rob them of who they are and what they could be. The ancients saw people's lives taken in ways that seemed too great to explain through the means they had to evaluate and think about such events. When they saw that level of dominance and taking over of people's identities and control of their bodies and minds, they spoke of demon possession. It was the extreme case and the deepest explanation for it.

Describing this taking of one's personhood as demon possession recognizes that it violates the way things should be. Such harm could only be explained by pointing to something beyond the world of usual existence. The ancients looked to malevolent beings who came into our world with the goal of doing harm and diminishing life. This belief gives expression to the sense that there is something drastically wrong with the world. We do not always see or experience it, but there are times and places at which that brokenness comes to overwhelming expression. When that brokenness is concentrated in a person, we can understand how a person could think about it as an invasion from outside. We know how inexplicable and seemingly inescapable difficulties and evils can be. There sometimes seems no adequate explanation and no avenue of escape from the grip some problems have on people.

So we know the feeling of standing in the face of seemingly unconquerable troubles of mind and body. We know how helpless it can feel to be trapped or to try to help someone who is trapped. We simply do not have the power, even with the miracles of modern medicine, psychiatry, and technology, to overcome these deep and hurtful powers. This story assures us that such circumstances are not beyond the power of God to redeem. We may not expect a miracle of the type the Gerasene demoniac experienced, but his story assures us that God is more powerful than the worst that can happen to us. God may not take away our problem, but neither will God leave us alone. God's presence does not take the form of simply removing the problem or illness, but God's love continually tries to enter our hearts. No loss of our powers can keep us from God's love. Luke gives us this assurance with a dramatic story. Paul, a person who knows troubles and affliction, expresses it poetically, telling us that nothing, neither "angels nor rulers, nor things present, nor things to come . . . nor anything in all creation, will be able to separate us from the love of God in Christ Jesus our Lord" (Romans 8:38-39).

Responding to God's Gift

The astounding power of Jesus evokes wonder in everyone who sees it in our reading. For some, that wonder causes them to fear. But the one who was touched by the healing knows what loving power it is that Jesus has. He wants to be with Jesus, but is given the task of sharing with others what God had done for him. The language that Luke uses for his healing in verse 36 is the same word that the New Testament commonly uses for "saved." This healing brought wholeness and salvation. He now shares that with others.

The released man's response to Jesus' healing power can be a model for us. We have, in various ways, experienced God's love and healing. Now we can turn to share that healing with others, in part by responding with God's love to those with significant needs. Among those who need assurance of God's care are those who suffer with problems that affect the mind. Whether those problems come from trauma or chemical imbalances or dementia, the story of this exorcism assures us that God's love is more powerful than such painful conditions. The caregivers for these people share in the pain and helplessness. They also experience the harm that comes from the loss of autonomy and even loss of self that the mentally ill endure. The healed man's example calls us to share that love with those who need assurance that their experiences and conditions cannot separate them from God's love, or from ours, because we have been touched with that powerful love ourselves.

SHARING THE SCRIPTURE

PREPARING TO TEACH

Preparing Our Hearts

Ponder this week's devotional reading from Philippians 2:1-11, which includes the familiar passage known as the Christ hymn. What do you learn about Christ and about God the Father? What connection does this hymn concerning Christ's humility have with Paul's teaching about unity?

Pray that you and the students will share in the mind of Christ so as to look to the interests of other people.

Preparing Our Minds

Study the background Scripture from Luke 8:26-39 and the lesson Scripture from Luke 8:26-36.

Consider this question as you prepare the lesson: *How can Jesus and the church help those who have mental health issues?*

Write on newsprint:
- ❏ information for next week's lesson, found under Continue the Journey.
- ❏ activities for further spiritual growth in Continue the Journey.

Review the Introduction, The Big Picture, Close-up, and Faith in Action, which all precede the first lesson of this quarter. Consider how you might use any of this material in today's lesson.

Caution: Although some examples in this lesson refer to mental illness because that concept is familiar to readers, and although symptoms and outward expressions of both may be similar, do not assume that demon possession and mental illness are synonymous.

LEADING THE CLASS

(1) Gather to Learn

❖ Welcome the class members and guests.

❖ Pray that those who have come today will empathize with those who have serious mental health issues.

❖ Read: **Since 2007, your editor, Nan, and her husband, Craig, have volunteered with their two Curly-Coated Retrievers, Ada and Bentley, to do animal-assisted therapy with both teens and adults who have psychiatric and conduct disorders. The Duerlings currently visit in a locked-down residential treatment center for teens. Behaviors can be very unpredictable: one resident is very withdrawn; another cannot sit still; a third is exuberant; another, thinking of suicide. Tempers can flare over the smallest matter. For some teens, especially as they begin their treatment program, a pet therapy group is the only place where they are successful. They feel calmed and reassured by the dogs, who offer unconditional love.**

❖ Read aloud today's focus statement: **Sometimes when people suffer from emotional or physical disorders affecting the mind, they might behave abnormally and even be a threat to themselves or others. Who can clear their minds and give them something to shout about? Jesus once healed a man who was demon-possessed and then told him** to go home and tell everyone how much God had done for him.

(2) Goal 1: Learn the Details of Jesus' Healing of the Gerasene Man from Demons

❖ Solicit a volunteer to read Luke 8:26-36. Direct the adults to imagine themselves as disciples who witnessed this event.

❖ Discuss these questions:

1. **What did you notice about the man who was tormented by demons?** (See Luke 8:26-30 in Understanding the Scripture.)

2. **How did Jesus' treatment of the demons surprise you?** (See Luke 8:31-33 in Understanding the Scripture and "A Shocking Introduction" in Interpreting the Scripture.)

3. **How did the man and those around him respond to this event?** (See Luke 8:34-39 in Understanding the Scripture and "Responding to God's Gift" in Interpreting the Scripture.)

❖ Conclude by inviting four adults to play the roles of two swineherds, who are upset about the economic loss of their pigs, and two disciples, who try to convince the swineherds that the healing of this man is worth the loss of the pigs.

(3) Goal 2: Empathize with Those Who Have Great Troubles and Remember the Learners' Own Times of Trial

❖ Read these representative headlines:

1. **Bullied teen opens fire on classmates, killing one and injuring four others.**

2. **Fired employee enters workplace and holds two coworkers hostage.**

3. **Mother secures children in car and drives into river.**

4. **Man sets fire to ex-girlfriend's apartment.**

❖ Point out that in each case an evil deed has been committed and there is certainly reason to suspect that the perpetrator of these crimes is mentally unstable. Ask: **What steps can we as a society and as a church take to help these people find ways to express their hurt or anger without acting violently?**

❖ Option: Invite volunteers to tell stories of times when they felt under siege for some reason. How did they respond? What help was the church able to offer? How did their faith in God enable them to act with love and forgiveness?

(4) Goal 3: Support Persons with Mental Health Issues

❖ Recall the example in the "Gather to Learn" portion of how one could volunteer to help people with mental health issues by doing pet therapy. Encourage the students to make a list of nearby hospitals, counseling centers, clinics, and other facilities that can aid those who have mental health issues.

❖ Discuss these questions:

1. **Is our congregation doing anything to offer a spiritual dimension to the treatment that people receive at these facilities? If so, what?**

2. **Is there anything we could be doing to help?** (Some facilities, such as where the Duerlings volunteer, are affiliated with a Christian denomination, making it possible to touch on spiritual issues with patients who want to discuss such matters,

provided there is no attempt to proselytize. However, that opportunity does not exist in all facilities, so you need to check.)

3. **Is there a school, business, or other facility where the actions of a person alleged to be mentally ill have harmed people? If so, in what ways might we offer support to those involved?**

4. **Are there professional mental health workers in our congregation whom we could support in prayer as they work with this very vulnerable population? If so, who are they?**

❖ Close by asking several people to do some research on any facilities the group has identified to see what, if anything, they could do there as volunteers to share the love of Christ with those facing mental health challenges.

(5) Continue the Journey

❖ Pray that as the learners depart, they will be willing to reach out to those who need to experience God's love.

❖ Post information for next week's session on newsprint for the students to copy:

- **Title: A Family Reunion**
- **Background Scripture: Luke 15:11-32**
- **Lesson Scripture: Luke 15:11-24**
- **Focus of the Lesson: Family relationships become too easily twisted and broken. What**

can be one ingredient that can keep families together? A Godlike love and forgiveness, given and accepted like the experience that happened between the father and the lost son, can mend and make the difference.

❖ Post the following information on newsprint and provide paper and pencils for the students to copy it. Challenge the adults to grow spiritually by completing one or more of these activities related to this week's session.

(1) **Research "demon" in a Bible concordance and Bible dictionary to discover what first-century people thought about demons and how Jesus responded to those who were demon-possessed.**

(2) **Learn all you can about how your community handles those who may be mentally ill. What help is available to these people? How is the community protected from such individuals if they may cause harm to themselves or others?**

(3) **Pray for those families touched by mental illness.**

❖ Sing or read aloud "Heal Us, Emmanuel, Hear Our Prayer."

❖ Conclude today's session by leading the class in this benediction, which is adapted from Mark 9:23 in the lesson for March 6: **Together we affirm that all things can be done for the one who believes. Amen.**

UNIT 2: RESTORATIVE FAITH
A FAMILY REUNION

PREVIEWING THE LESSON

Lesson Scripture: Luke 15:11-24
Background Scripture: Luke 15:11-32
Key Verse: Luke 15:24

Focus of the Lesson:
Family relationships become too easily twisted and broken. What can be one ingredient that can keep families together? A Godlike love and forgiveness, given and accepted like the experience that happened between the father and the lost son, can mend and make the difference.

Goals for the Learners:
(1) to examine a parable of a divided family reunited.
(2) to feel the need for reunion and forgiveness in families and to connect that to their relationship with God.
(3) to commit to helping broken families be restored by praying for them and giving any other assistance possible.

Supplies:
Bibles, newsprint and marker, paper and pencils, hymnals

READING THE SCRIPTURE

NRSV

Lesson Scripture: Luke 15:11-24

¹¹Then Jesus said, "There was a man who had two sons. ¹²The younger of them said to his father, 'Father, give me the share of the property that will belong to me.' So he divided his property between them. ¹³A few days later the younger son gathered all he had and traveled to a distant country, and there he squandered his property in dissolute living. ¹⁴When he had spent everything, a severe famine took

CEB

Lesson Scripture: Luke 15:11-24

¹¹Jesus said, "A certain man had two sons. ¹²The younger son said to his father, 'Father, give me my share of the inheritance.' Then the father divided his estate between them. ¹³Soon afterward, the younger son gathered everything together and took a trip to a land far away. There, he wasted his wealth through extravagant living.

¹⁴"When he had used up his

place throughout that country, and he began to be in need. [15]So he went and hired himself out to one of the citizens of that country, who sent him to his fields to feed the pigs. [16]He would gladly have filled himself with the pods that the pigs were eating; and no one gave him anything. [17]But when he came to himself he said, 'How many of my father's hired hands have bread enough and to spare, but here I am dying of hunger! [18]I will get up and go to my father, and I will say to him, "Father, I have sinned against heaven and before you; [19]I am no longer worthy to be called your son; treat me like one of your hired hands."' [20]So he set off and went to his father. But while he was still far off, his father saw him and was filled with compassion; he ran and put his arms around him and kissed him. [21]Then the son said to him, 'Father, I have sinned against heaven and before you; I am no longer worthy to be called your son.' [22]But the father said to his slaves, 'Quickly, bring out a robe—the best one—and put it on him; put a ring on his finger and sandals on his feet. [23]And get the fatted calf and kill it, and let us eat and celebrate; **[24]for this son of mine was dead and is alive again; he was lost and is found!' And they began to celebrate."**

resources, a severe food shortage arose in that country and he began to be in need. [15]He hired himself out to one of the citizens of that country, who sent him into his fields to feed pigs. [16]He longed to eat his fill from what the pigs ate, but no one gave him anything. [17]When he came to his senses, he said, 'How many of my father's hired hands have more than enough food, but I'm starving to death! [18]I will get up and go to my father, and say to him, "Father, I have sinned against heaven and against you. [19]I no longer deserve to be called your son. Take me on as one of your hired hands."' [20]So he got up and went to his father.

"While he was still a long way off, his father saw him and was moved with compassion. His father ran to him, hugged him, and kissed him. [21]Then his son said, 'Father, I have sinned against heaven and against you. I no longer deserve to be called your son.' [22]But the father said to his servants, 'Quickly, bring out the best robe and put it on him! Put a ring on his finger and sandals on his feet! [23]Fetch the fattened calf and slaughter it. We must celebrate with feasting **[24]because this son of mine was dead and has come back to life! He was lost and is found!' And they began to celebrate."**

UNDERSTANDING THE SCRIPTURE

Introduction. This parable, commonly called the parable of the prodigal son, appears in Luke as the third parable in a row about lost things. Jesus' telling of these parables is set up by the grumbling of some who observe that he associates with "sinners" (15:1-2). Each of the three parables about lost things ends with rejoicing over the lost being found. The first is about a lost sheep, the second about a lost coin, and our reading is about a lost son. These parables relate something important about God's love and the mission of Jesus. They show that God's love seeks those who have turned away. Indeed, the mission of Jesus is to bring those people into relationship with God. When the valued item is found in each parable, it leads to celebration. But our story has a more complicated ending.

Luke 15:11-16. The two sons of this parable behave very differently in relation to the father. The younger asks for his share of the inheritance early. According to expected inheritance practices, the oldest son would receive twice as much as other children. With just two sons, the older one is in line to receive two-thirds of his father's property. It was unusual and probably shameful to have a son ask for his inheritance before the father died. But the father is willing to suffer this disgrace. The younger son sells the property he inherited and moves away. In short order, he wastes all his inheritance. As a foreigner in a distant land, when he is out of money he has no safety net. To make things worse, there is a famine. He ends up taking a shameful job. We should assume that this character is Jewish because everyone in Jesus' audience is. So feeding the pigs is dishonorable work because he is taking care of unclean animals. He has sunk even lower; he thinks about eating the pigs' food.

This description is more extensive than what we find in most parables. Luke provides this vivid description of the man's degradation because this is still Jesus' response to those who complain about him eating with tax collectors and sinners. The parable is now about a person who is far more sinful than those with whom Jesus has been associating.

Luke 15:17-19. The story takes a dramatic turn at verse 17. The son now comes to his senses; he recognizes what he has done to himself and sees how far he has fallen. Remembering how much better servants have it at his father's business, he realizes what he has given up. So he decides to repent, confess his mistakes, and ask to be accepted as a servant. He knows he is no longer worthy to hold the status of a son. This repentance is an important element in the story. The son who returns does so as one who admits wrong and the harm he has done.

Luke 15:20-24. The focus of the parable now shifts to the father. He sees his son while he is far away and rushes to greet him in the most loving of ways, hugging and kissing him. Clearly the father loves him very much. The son does as he had planned: He confesses his sins and his unworthiness. The father's response is to receive him back as a son with all the rights and privileges that entails. He is given a robe appropriate for a celebration and a ring. This ring may well represent the authority of the father; it is certainly a sign that he is a member of the family who owns the business.

The ensuing celebration is extravagant. It has music and dancing; it includes a feast that features the best foods they have. The father calls the community to rejoice with him in the recovery of his son. He describes this recovery in the most extraordinary terms: The son was dead and now he is alive. The son had been lost to the family, but now he is rejoined to their life.

To this point, this parable, including this scene of celebration, fits the pattern of the two parables that precede it. That which was lost is recovered and the recovery leads to celebration. But this parable has one more segment that distinguishes it from the previous two.

Luke 15:25-32. If we remember how chapter 15 began, the last scene of this parable becomes particularly significant. The faithful religious people had complained about Jesus giving attention to sinners. The older brother represents those who have not rebelled against God. He is the one who has always been faithful. Now he wants to know why there is a huge celebration. Surely his faithfulness is more worthy of celebration than the return of a wretch. But he has gotten no recognition!

What the older son wants is justice. He wants to be treated fairly. If his brother gets a celebration, he deserves more. The older brother is right; what is happening is not fair. It is, rather, an expression of the abundant love of the father. What the older son fails to realize is that the love the father has for the younger son does not diminish the love he has for the older one. The return of the lost son is a cause for celebration. The joy is the natural response to the return of someone who is loved.

We should note that the father's love does not excuse the younger brother, but it does welcome his return. The father's love also comes to expression in what he gives the older son. All of the father's property is the older son's possession (15:31). The return of the lost son does not diminish the gifts of the father for the older son who had remained faithful.

Importantly, this parable has an open-ended conclusion. We do not know what the older brother does. We hear the father's repeated reason for joy (the return of the lost son), then the story ends. In the flow of Luke's narrative, those who criticized Jesus for eating with sinners are here offered the chance to rejoice as those who were lost are recovered.

INTERPRETING THE SCRIPTURE

Love in the Family

This parable is about love for people who repent and about how people who have been faithful should respond when God's love celebrates the return of one who has rejected God and God's will for life. The parable suggests that turning from the will of God brings degradation, but that God remains open to receiving those who will confess their sin and return to accept God's love.

Luke gives more attention to telling us about these characters than any others in his parables. Most people who appear in parables are flat characters; they have no personality and we know nothing of them except for the single characteristic that is needed for the parable to work. In this parable, we hear their thoughts, see the extravagant response of the father, hear of the emotions of the older son, and overhear the conversations between the father and sons. This parable can touch the hearers on many levels.

We do not learn about the relationships within the family before the younger son asks for his inheritance. We do not know how he had related to his father or whether he and his brother got along. Such details are not important to the points Luke wants to make. But our experience of family dynamics increases our empathies for one character or another. We may have felt the need to get away or the regret of having hurt others in the family. Perhaps we know how much courage it takes to admit wrong and ask forgiveness within the family. We may know how the older brother felt when the younger, who had caused all the turmoil, has love lavished on him when he decides to return. Or as parents we may know the heartbreak of seeing our children make decisions that harm themselves and all the other members of the family.

Regardless of which of these or other tensions within families we have experienced, we know the pain involved for all. We are tempted to add all kinds of descriptions of the father who loves his son, because we know how parents yearn for the best for their children. Luke describes for us the kind of reception an extraordinarily loving father would give to an idealized son. We see in this story all stereotyped characters, but our experiences of family always enter the story.

It may be hard to hear this story if our father was not so loving, indeed, if he harmed the family or us. In such cases we need to remember that the story is one about idealized characters who fit molds that move the story along. This is not a story about a literal father who has defects. This is a character about whom we are told only the things that help us understand the points Luke wants us to hear about God and the mission of Jesus.

Whatever our experience in our own families, this parable reminds us of the yearning we all have for loving families; for places where we are loved and forgiven. We want safe places to be loved and to love others.

We also are reminded of the pain that estrangement in families causes. It matters little who is at fault; all suffer when these ruptures occur in our families. The love shown by the father in this parable points us to the way to healing in our families.

The Church as the Family of God

The most common way that believers address one another in the New Testament is to call the other a brother or a sister. This form of address assumes that believers are taken into a new family, the family of God. Here, God is the loving parent who has prepared a place to live and love. We are all children whom God has claimed as God's own. Even if we are more like the older brother who has been on the path of obedience throughout our lives, we have known moments when we rejected God's will. We know the kind of loneliness and disappointment in ourselves that such moments contain. We may experience those times in ways that are rather like what we feel when we are estranged from family members.

In these moments we can know that God continually reaches out to us in love. God wants to renew that relationship with us, to return us to our place as full family members, and to celebrate our return. We have all received this undeserved love of God. God loves us simply because we are God's children. Those who recognize their sin, their rejection of God and God's will, also know the joy that their confession and repentance bring. Our parable asserts powerfully that there is nothing we could do to keep God from loving us. The runaway son here has squandered all the family's gifts, led a disreputable life, and returns with nothing. Even such callous disregard and irresponsible use of what he was given cannot inhibit his father's love. The parable declares that whatever we have done, whether it has harmed our families or the family of God, God's love is unfailing. God will celebrate the return of the lost.

Who Deserves a Celebration?

The parable intends us to think about how we receive those who have been offensive, those who have done harm to us or our church or what God wants for the world. The older brother here is the faithful person in the pew. He is the one who warily watches the person whose reputation is less than sterling come into the church. He is the good person who worries about how the person who has led such a disreputable life will damage the morals of the rest of the church. Those who questioned Jesus' choice of dinner companions did not want others to think that the behavior of those people was acceptable to God. They were right to want to protect the community against lowering their moral standards, but they were wrong to think that this meant excluding those who had done wrong.

It is important to remember that the parable is constructed so that the prodigal repents. He recognizes that his way of living has been foolish and determines to return humbly to his family's home. The older brother is now expected to receive him as a genuine brother, to accept his repentance and treat him with love—even to celebrate his return. In the same way, faithful members of the church are to welcome new or returning brothers and sisters who have turned from God and done harm. When those who have done harm and damaged the church's image express remorse, the faithful are to love them and celebrate their return. That love can take many forms, including helping them find ways of living that reflect God's will. The faithful can show this love because they have been the recipients of the same love that claims the one returning. It is the love of God that brings us all into God's household and makes us all brothers and sisters.

SHARING THE SCRIPTURE

PREPARING TO TEACH

Preparing Our Hearts

Ponder this week's devotional reading from Luke 15:1-7. Who is listening to Jesus? What point is Jesus trying to make by telling them this parable and the one that we will study today? What do you learn about the one who is doing the searching? What do you learn about how the shepherd and his neighbors respond? What lessons are here for you and your congregation?

Pray that you and the students will be open to assisting all those who seek God.

Preparing Our Minds

Study the background Scripture from Luke 15:11-32 and the lesson Scripture from Luke 15:11-24. Consider this question as you prepare the lesson: *What can help to keep families together?*

Write on newsprint:

- ❏ information for next week's lesson, found under Continue the Journey.
- ❏ activities for further spiritual growth in Continue the Journey.

Review the Introduction, The Big Picture, Close-up, and Faith in Action, which all precede the first lesson of this quarter. Consider how you might use any of this material in today's lesson.

LEADING THE CLASS

(1) Gather to Learn

❖ Welcome the class members and guests.

❖ Pray that those who have come today will be ready to mend fences within their own families.

❖ Read information from an article in 2008 by Olivia Gordon that appeared in *The Telegraph*, a British newspaper: "Inheritance Disputes: Where There's a Will There's a War" is an apt title for a news article concerning how families are handling quarrels about inheritances. One problem is that 75 percent of citizens in Britain do not have a will. About one-quarter of people expect contentious actions among relatives as a result of anticipated inheritances. Just as in the United States, divorces, remarriages, and blended families mean that more people will try to make claims against an estate. In addition to financial issues, families can fight over last wishes of a deceased family member. In one family, a dispute about whether to honor a grandmother's wishes to be cremated and have her ashes spread in a place that was dear to her or have her buried split a family of five grown children. Feelings of betrayal and who has the last word further complicate monetary matters.

❖ Read aloud today's focus statement: **Family relationships become too easily twisted and broken. What can be one ingredient that can keep families together? A Godlike love and forgiveness, given and accepted like the experience that happened between the father and the lost son, can mend and make the difference.**

(2) Goal 1: Examine a Parable of a Divided Family Reunited

❖ Set the context for today's lesson by reading Luke 15:1-2 and retelling the Introduction in Understanding the Scripture so that the students understand who the listeners were and what point Jesus was trying to make.

❖ Enlist a volunteer to read Luke 15:11-32.

❖ Discuss these questions:

1. **Had you been part of the prodigal son's extended family, what would you have thought about his asking for his inheritance while his father was still alive?** (See Luke 15:11-16 in Understanding the Scripture.)

2. **The prodigal likely felt that "the grass was greener on the other side of the fence." What did he do when he realized he had been wrong?** (See Luke 15:17-19 in Understanding the Scripture.)

3. **Had you been invited to the celebration when the prodigal returned, would you have attended? Why or why not?** (See "Who Deserves a Celebration?" in Interpreting the Scripture.)

4. How can the father's welcome be a model for the church when people who have been away for a long time decide to return "home"? (See Luke 15:20-24 in Understanding the Scripture and "The Church as the Family of God" in Interpreting the Scripture.)

(3) Goal 2: Feel the Need for Reunion and Forgiveness in Families and Connect That to the Learners' Relationship with God

❖ Read or retell "Love in the Family" in Interpreting the Scripture.

❖ Distribute paper and pencils. Suggest that each person write a short essay that begins, "If I could change a broken relationship within my own family I would . . ." Tell the students that they will not be asked to divulge the private information in this essay.

❖ Reconvene the class and suggest that they continue to probe ideas about how they might try to mend relationships, either with themselves and someone else or with two or more other family members. Note that no matter what someone else has done, the students can use the powerful love of God to forgive and mend fences.

(4) Goal 3: Commit to Helping Broken Families Be Restored by Praying for Them and Giving Any Other Assistance Possible

❖ Invite class members to call out the names of agencies or institutions in your community that help those who have experienced broken family relationships. Examples could include shelters for victims of domestic

violence, facilities for children who cannot live with their families, Court Appointed Special Advocates (CASA) for Children. List the names on newsprint. Perhaps some students will have firsthand knowledge about one or more of the agencies that they can share.

❖ Encourage all of the students to make a commitment to pray for those who need the services of a particular agency that they choose. Challenge those who are able to contact an agency to see if there are ways that they can help. The class as a whole may be able to collect toiletries or other items needed by the agency for those it serves.

❖ **Option:** Invite participants to brainstorm ways that they as a class can spearhead a churchwide effort to restore people who have fallen away from the church family. What can they do to help heal the brokenness that these church family members feel? How will they contact these people? What steps will they take to help the "older brothers" in the church celebrate their return?

(5) Continue the Journey

❖ Pray that as the learners depart, they will be open to family reunions within their personal families and the church family.

❖ Post information for next week's session on newsprint for the students to copy:

- **Title: Increased Faith**
- **Background Scripture: Luke 17:1-10**
- **Lesson Scripture: Luke 17:1-10**
- **Focus of the Lesson: Even though Christians may do their best, they may fail and**

require helpful correction from someone else. What kind of attitude would be appropriate as they seek to correct one another? Jesus teaches his followers that even the smallest amount of genuine faith will cause them to rebuke sin. If repentance occurs, then the fullness of faith leads to forgiveness and restoration; this is the very least of what God expects of God's followers.

❖ Post the following information on newsprint and provide paper and pencils for the students to copy it. Challenge the adults to grow spiritually by completing one or more of these activities related to this week's session.

(1) Act as a mediator and peacekeeper in your own family if there is strife between two or more family members.

(2) Help a longtime absent church member who has come to himself or herself return to the church and be welcomed back.

(3) Support parents who have "prodigal" sons or daughters who have physically or emotionally left their parents' values and teachings. Take the role of an active listener who will hear concerns and offer prayer.

❖ Sing or read aloud "Come Back Quickly to the Lord."

❖ Conclude today's session by leading the class in this benediction, which is adapted from Mark 9:23 in the lesson for March 6: **Together we affirm that all things can be done for the one who believes. Amen.**

UNIT 3: FULLNESS OF FAITH
INCREASED FAITH

PREVIEWING THE LESSON

Lesson Scripture: Luke 17:1-10
Background Scripture: Luke 17:1-10
Key Verse: Luke 17:3

Focus of the Lesson:
Even though Christians may do their best, they may fail and require helpful correction from someone else. What kind of attitude would be appropriate as they seek to correct one another? Jesus teaches his followers that even the smallest amount of genuine faith will cause them to rebuke sin. If repentance occurs, then the fullness of faith leads to forgiveness and restoration; this is the very least of what God expects of God's followers.

Goals for the Learners:
(1) to review what Jesus said about causing another to stumble, correcting the offender, accepting the offender's repentance, and forgiving.
(2) to appreciate the importance of correcting and receiving correction in a loving and gentle Christian manner.
(3) to study and improve our methods and style of godly correcting of others when necessary.

Supplies:
Bibles, newsprint and marker, paper and pencils, hymnals

READING THE SCRIPTURE

NRSV

Lesson Scripture: Luke 17:1-10

¹Jesus said to his disciples, "Occasions for stumbling are bound to come, but woe to anyone by whom they come! ²It would be better for you if a millstone were hung around your neck and you were thrown into the sea than for you to cause one of

CEB

Lesson Scripture: Luke 17:1-10

¹Jesus said to his disciples, "Things that cause people to trip and fall into sin must happen, but how terrible it is for the person through whom they happen. ²It would be better for them to be thrown into a lake with a large stone hung around their neck than to

these little ones to stumble. **³Be on your guard! If another disciple sins, you must rebuke the offender, and if there is repentance, you must forgive.** ⁴And if the same person sins against you seven times a day, and turns back to you seven times and says, 'I repent,' you must forgive."

⁵The apostles said to the Lord, "Increase our faith!" ⁶The Lord replied, "If you had faith the size of a mustard seed, you could say to this mulberry tree, 'Be uprooted and planted in the sea,' and it would obey you.

⁷"Who among you would say to your slave who has just come in from plowing or tending sheep in the field, 'Come here at once and take your place at the table'? ⁸Would you not rather say to him, 'Prepare supper for me, put on your apron and serve me while I eat and drink; later you may eat and drink'? ⁹Do you thank the slave for doing what was commanded? ¹⁰So you also, when you have done all that you were ordered to do, say, 'We are worthless slaves; we have done only what we ought to have done!'"

cause one of these little ones to trip and fall into sin. **³Watch yourselves! If your brother or sister sins, warn them to stop. If they change their hearts and lives, forgive them.** ⁴Even if someone sins against you seven times in one day and returns to you seven times and says, 'I am changing my ways,' you must forgive that person."

⁵The apostles said to the Lord, "Increase our faith!"

⁶The Lord replied, "If you had faith the size of a mustard seed, you could say to this mulberry tree, 'Be uprooted and planted in the sea,' and it would obey you.

⁷"Would any of you say to your servant, who had just come in from the field after plowing or tending sheep, 'Come! Sit down for dinner'? ⁸Wouldn't you say instead, 'Fix my dinner. Put on the clothes of a table servant and wait on me while I eat and drink. After that, you can eat and drink'? ⁹You won't thank the servant because the servant did what you asked, will you? ¹⁰In the same way, when you have done everything required of you, you should say, 'We servants deserve no special praise. We have only done our duty.'"

UNDERSTANDING THE SCRIPTURE

Introduction. Luke 17:1-10 is the conclusion of a section that focuses on the question of who the participants in the kingdom of God will be. This section has involved interactions with the Pharisees who are the foil for the teaching of Jesus. The immediately previous instructions and parable had the Pharisees as the main audience; now at 17:1 Jesus turns to the disciples.

Luke 17:1-4. Jesus warns his

disciples not to cause others to stumble, that is, to lose their faith or turn away from developing faith. This seems to be a direct contrast with those who have rejected Jesus' teaching (16:14-15). After that rejection, Jesus affirms the importance of keeping God's commands and tells the parable of the rich man and Lazarus. In this parable, the one who is privileged is rejected by God. He and his siblings are hopeless because they will not listen to God's messengers even if a person rises from the dead to call them to repent. It is just after that comment that Jesus warns the disciples not to cause others to stumble.

In our passage, causing others to stumble means to make them turn away from the faith. While it is inevitable that things will come along that do turn people from faith, Jesus issues a warning not to be the source of that loss of faith. Jesus says it would be better to die than to cause others to lose their faith. Given that his opponents have just been described as those who love money (16:14) and that the parable just before this suggests that the wealthy will not listen to God's word, this matter of causing others to stumble probably includes consideration of how the disciples should use wealth. So not only are they to be careful that their teaching and conduct do not lead people astray, they should be particularly careful about how they use money. This element of the warning becomes more prominent when Luke calls the people the disciples must not cause the "little ones" (17:2) to stumble. Luke uses this term to refer to the outcasts and poor. So disciples must give careful thought to how they relate to these people who are often cast aside.

Verse 3 shifts the focus so that Jesus is not just warning against doing something that turns others away. Now his instructions tell the disciples to correct people who are turning others away or who are sinning more broadly. But then the instruction becomes even more specific: The very people who are wronged are to give the rebuke. You can see that this is about a wrong done to the person who corrects the one who sins

because the person voicing the correction is told to forgive the offender. Verse 4 explicitly states that the sin is against "you."

Jesus demands that people forgive those who sin against them an extraordinary number of times. In the parallel in Matthew, the number is seventy times seven (Matthew 18:21-22); here in Luke it is seven times a day. Either asks more than what we would call reasonable. In essence, this is a call to forgive constantly, for it to be the believer's mode of existence. By calling these offenses sins, Luke implies that they are also offenses against God. This rebuking and forgiving is the explicit way that Jesus calls the disciples not to cause others to stumble. It is the responsibility of each disciple to correct and forgive.

Luke 17:5-6. This task of correcting and forgiving is weighty. When the apostles hear this instruction, they ask Jesus to give them the faith it takes to do it. Jesus responds with an exaggeration that emphasizes the power of just a little faith. If they have the tiniest bit of faith, they can do extraordinary things. The imagery Jesus uses is known in the ancient world: The mustard seed is proverbially small and the mulberry tree is known as deeply rooted. So the smallest bit of faith can move the most deeply rooted thing. Likewise, their faith can empower them to rebuke and forgive.

Luke 17:7-10. These verses use imagery that makes us nervous; they tell about how people treat slaves. While slavery was not race-based in the ancient world, slaves were still considered property. Slaves were found across the ancient world. They were essential to the economy of all urban areas and were commonly the agricultural workers on large farms.

In some cities, there were more slaves than free people. So this is imagery that all understand, whether or not they own or are slaves. Jesus' instructions here neither accept nor reject the institution of slavery. He simply draws on something everyone understands.

Everyone knows that slaves must wait on their masters and defer meeting their own needs until they have done what the master wants. When they do this, they are doing nothing extraordinary; it is just their job. That seems to be what Jesus is saying about forgiving your fellow Christian seven times a day: Forgiveness is nothing exceptional; it is your job.

There is an interesting change in the audience in verse 5. Jesus is now speaking to the "apostles" rather than the "disciples." This suggests that the conversation is now between Jesus and those who will be leaders in the church. The instructions in verses 7-10, then, may be directed specifically at leaders. They are the people directed to behave as slaves among their fellow church members. They are to put the needs and good of the others in the church ahead of their own good. This is not the only place in the Gospels where Jesus uses the term "slave" to describe how leaders are to relate to the church (Matthew 20:27; Mark 10:44). Giving priority to the good of others is not exceptional behavior for Christian leaders. They are to see it as their duty. It is the expected behavior for which they should anticipate no thanks. It is, in fact, the kind of leadership that Jesus modeled by being willing to give himself for the good of others.

INTERPRETING THE SCRIPTURE

Difficult Tasks

This passage is full of hard sayings. It calls Jesus' followers to refrain from causing others to stumble, to rebuke, to forgive, to strengthen the faith of others, and to be deferential to the needs of others. And these come with a stern warning: It would be better to be killed than to violate them. While leaders seem to be the special focus of verses 5-10, that is not the case in verses 1-4. There the instructions are for all believers, all disciples. So we cannot leave the attention to correction and instruction only to leaders. We cannot leave the forgiving only to leaders. All disciples of Christ are to care for fellow disciples in these ways—and we know from experience how difficult that is for us to do.

The demand that we not cause others to stumble means that we are not to say or do things that cause others to lose or violate their faith. Such a broad command includes, at times, refraining from some otherwise acceptable behaviors or activities that would lead someone else to sin. It means that the good of the other person's faith is more important than our "right" to do what we want. This command does not allow someone to manipulate the group or another person by simply saying that something offends him or her. This is not about whether a person likes something; it concerns things that turn people away from God or that causes them to be unfaithful.

This saying of Jesus makes us

responsible for one another. We must not cause people to be unfaithful to what they believe is right. The placement of these verses after a controversy with the Pharisees also implies that this responsibility for others includes being sure they believe the right kinds of things about God and about what God wants in the world.

This saying of Jesus also directs our attention to the weak and the outcast. The "little ones" in Luke are those who are disadvantaged physically, economically, and/or socially. After a parable about the danger of wealth, this saying includes a call to use our financial resources in ways that bring people to faith rather than in ways that hinder the development of faith among the disadvantaged. More generally, it tells us to conduct our lives so that we are examples to everyone of how to be faithful. That is, we are responsible to those who have a less mature faith as well as those we might more readily recognize as the disadvantaged.

If Someone Sins

Verse 3 begins with an exhortation to watch out!—or as the NRSV puts it, "Be on your guard!" It is hard to tell whether this warning goes with the preceding instructions about not causing the "little ones" to stumble or with the following instructions about rebuking and forgiving. We should probably see it applying to both. After noting that stumbling in faith is inevitable (17:1) and warning against being the cause of it, Jesus gives instructions about what to do when it happens. At first, the instruction seems to be about any sin that a person commits. Each disciple is responsible for fellow believers. Each is to be on guard about

the life of the others. Jesus calls disciples to be willing to call one another to account. These are difficult instructions for us. We do not like to have others notice our sins, and we do not like to confront others about theirs. We would prefer a relationship with God that involves just God and me. But Jesus does not allow that way of being a disciple. The Christian life is always a community matter; it is always about how we live in relationship with one another. Jesus here demands that a part of that relationship must entail loving others enough to let them know that their behavior is displeasing to God and harmful to them and to those around them.

"Rebuke" seems like a harsh word (17:3). It sounds judgmental and arrogant. Jesus does not unleash us to be abusive to those in whom we find a fault. We must remember that the warning in verses 1-2 is about causing others to lose or violate their faith. Any rebuking must be done in a way that moves people toward faithfulness. This means that it must be done in love and in gentleness. Any correction must be done in a manner that shows love for the person, and that demonstrates that we have only the good of the person and the church in view. Any response to the sins of others that expresses pride or belittles the other violates the whole thrust of this passage. As the slave analogy in verses 7-10 suggests, how we behave in this act of correcting others must be done as a service to them. We must see ourselves as their slaves, doing what is required for their good.

It is hard for us to imagine how rebuking someone can be done in this way. This interaction requires that we have relationships within the church that are built on love, trust, and mutual commitment. These are not strangers that we correct from a distance; these are brothers and sisters in our church. This task requires humility and love. We need to remember that the model for life within the church is the ministry and death of Jesus. He was willing to put our good ahead of his own to the extent that he died for us. That model demands that we prayerfully adopt the posture of doing what is good for others rather than for ourselves. This attitude may make it possible for us to approach those who need correction and instruction. Our desire for the good of others should be our known pattern of life and should be particularly obvious in this moment.

Sins Against You

While verse 3 at first seems to talk about sin generally, the focus is soon more personal. The person is not just sinning, but sinning "against you." These are not minor incidents; they are "sins." The person does you wrong. Now you must do more than correct; you must forgive. This person somehow harms you, and you are to take responsibility to make things right. There is not feigned talk about everyone being at fault. The disciple rebukes the one who has done the wrong to him or her. When the person acknowledges the wrong and promises to change, the person who was aggrieved must forgive. This is the moment when it is hardest to adopt the attitude required for a conversation that turns the person away from the sin and builds faith. Here the willingness of the person who was wronged to imitate Christ's willingness to put the good of others first and to forgive is tested mightily.

This expectation of the person who was wronged violates what we see as fairness. We think the one who did the wrong should make amends. But Jesus does not ask for fairness. He asks for an expression of love that goes beyond what could be fairly expected. But that is just the beginning. We are to offer forgiveness to a repeat offender! We must do it seven times a day for the same person. This seven is symbolic. The number seven stood for fullness or perfection. Here it means that we have to forgive as many times as it takes.

SHARING THE SCRIPTURE

PREPARING TO TEACH

Preparing Our Hearts

Ponder this week's devotional reading from Jeremiah 23:33–24:6. Note that there is a play on words here. The Hebrew word translated as "utterance" also means to "carry" or "lift." The noun form is "burden." In verse 33 when the prophet is asked, "What is the burden of the LORD," God's reply is that the people themselves are the "burden," which God will cast off. What do you make of God's message to Jeremiah? What is the meaning of the two baskets of figs?

Pray that you and the students will be aware of God's message for them.

Preparing Our Minds

Study the background Scripture and the lesson Scripture, both of which are from Luke 17:1-10.

Consider this question as you pre-pare the lesson: *What kind of attitude should believers have as they try to correct one another?*

Write on newsprint:

❏ information for next week's les-son, found under Continue the Journey.

❏ activities for further spiritual growth in Continue the Journey.

Review the Introduction, The Big Picture, Close-up, and Faith in Action, which all precede the first lesson of this quarter. Consider how you might use any of this material in today's lesson.

Caution: Correction—especially when it is not done in humility, or is based on secondhand information, or does not move another believer toward greater faith—can be coun-terproductive. Any correction must be done with the love, long-suffering patience, and personal knowledge of the situation.

LEADING THE CLASS

(1) Gather to Learn

❖ Welcome the class members and guests.

❖ Pray that those who have come today will be open to giving and re-ceiving correction that is offered in a loving, helpful manner.

❖ Invite participants to answer these questions: **As you think back to your childhood and teens years, can you recall an incident when you were harshly corrected? If so, how did you respond to that correction? Can you recall another incident when the correction really helped you to grow and change your ways? What was different about the way you were corrected this time?**

❖ Read aloud today's focus state-ment: **Even though Christians may do their best, they may fail and re-quire helpful correction from some-one else. What kind of attitude would be appropriate as they seek to correct one another? Jesus teaches his followers that even the smallest amount of genuine faith will cause them to rebuke sin. If repentance oc-curs, then the fullness of faith leads to forgiveness and restoration; this is the very least of what God expects of God's followers.**

(2) Goal 1: Review What Jesus Said About Causing Another to Stumble, Correcting the Offender, Accepting the Offender's Repentance, and Forgiving

❖ Call on a volunteer to read Luke 17:1-10.

❖ Discuss these questions:

1. **What are the tasks to which Jesus calls all believers?** (See "Difficult Tasks" in Interpreting the Scripture.)

2. **What are believers called to do if another believer sins?** (See "If Someone Sins" in Interpret-ing the Scripture.)

3. **How does Jesus expect those who are trying to correct an-other to act?** (See Luke 17:7-10 in Understanding the Scripture and "If Someone Sins" in Inter-preting the Scripture.)

4. **Although Jesus' use of slaves in his teaching may make us uncomfortable, he is not com-menting on the institution of slavery but rather is making a point about how slaves act. What is his point?** (See Luke 17:7-10 in Understanding the Scripture.)

5. What are Jesus' expectations when one believer sins against another believer? (See "Sins Against You" in Interpreting the Scripture.)

(3) Goal 2: Appreciate the Importance of Correcting and Receiving Correction in a Loving and Gentle Christian Manner

❖ Read Revelation 3:19 and ask:
1. How would you imagine Jesus correcting and disciplining those whom he loves? (Think about the tone of his voice, the look on his face, the words that he chooses, and his body language.)
2. How would you receive such correction from Jesus?

❖ Invite the learners to think silently about someone who has corrected them in a Christlike manner. Who was this person? What was it about the way that he or she acted that seemed so Christlike? How can you copy this person's example?

❖ Invite volunteers to comment on how they felt about receiving Christlike correction and the changes it made in them. What attitudes or behaviors will they try to imitate when they feel they must correct someone else?

❖ Close this section by reading in unison today's key verse, Luke 17:3.

(4) Goal 3: Study and Improve Methods and Style of Godly Correction of Others When Necessary

❖ Read one or both of these scenarios. Encourage the adults to say how each one will end. The students are to keep in mind how the one doing the correction acted and how the offender responded. If time permits,

try to create one ending that shows a Christlike correction and humble response and another ending that demonstrates a response to an inappropriate correction.

Scenario 1: Mrs. Smith has personally overheard Mr. Jones spreading false information about Smith's ethics in her financial planning business. Mrs. Smith has been wondering why several clients from Mr. Jones's church have moved their business from her company to that of Mr. Jones's spouse. She now has the proof she needs to confront Mr. Jones about his behavior.

Scenario 2: Mr. Brown has been a powerful finance chairperson in the church for many years, but a new pastor wants to replace Mr. Brown with Mrs. Johnson. Mr. Brown knows the pastor is very well liked, so instead of talking directly with her, Mr. Brown decides to badmouth Mrs. Johnson. She, in turn, has tried to ignore Mr. Brown's innuendoes and nasty comments, but feels it is time to talk with him.

(5) Continue the Journey

❖ Pray that as the learners depart, they will be open to giving and receiving correction as godly disciples.
❖ Post information for next week's session on newsprint for the students to copy:
- **Title: Grateful Faith**
- **Background Scripture: Luke 17:11-19**
- **Lesson Scripture: Luke 17:11-19**
- **Focus of the Lesson: Some people express their gratitude with sincerity; others find it**

difficult to express their gratitude, while still others are ungrateful for what is done for them. How can Christians grow a sincere, thankful spirit in their lives? By faith, one of the ten lepers that Jesus healed was able to express his gratitude and praise.

❖ Post the following information on newsprint and provide paper and pencils for the students to copy it. Challenge the adults to grow spiritually by completing one or more of these activities related to this week's session.

(1) **Practice offering forgiveness to those who ask, even if they ask repeatedly.**

(2) **Be open to receiving correction** for your own behavior. Was this correction warranted? If so, how will you seek to make amends and change your behavior?

(3) **Recognize that some adults use harsh tones and punitive measures to correct children. What can you as a Christian do to model loving-kindness and graciousness toward God's "little ones"?**

❖ Sing or read aloud "He Touched Me."

❖ Conclude today's session by leading the class in this benediction, which is adapted from Mark 9:23 in the lesson for March 6: **Together we affirm that all things can be done for the one who believes. Amen.**

UNIT 3: FULLNESS OF FAITH
GRATEFUL FAITH

PREVIEWING THE LESSON

Lesson Scripture: Luke 17:11-19
Background Scripture: Luke 17:11-19
Key Verses: Luke 17:15

Focus of the Lesson:
Some people express their gratitude with sincerity; others find it difficult to express their gratitude, while still others are ungrateful for what is done for them. How can Christians grow a sincere, thankful spirit in their lives? By faith one of the ten lepers that Jesus healed was able to express his gratitude and praise.

Goals for the Learners:
(1) to review the story of the ten healed lepers among whom only one was grateful for healing.
(2) to feel and express gratitude for all blessings, including healing, they have received.
(3) to celebrate and give thanks for the healing of others.

Supplies:
Bibles, newsprint and marker, paper and pencils, hymnals, offering container

READING THE SCRIPTURE

NRSV

Lesson Scripture: Luke 17:11-19

¹¹On the way to Jerusalem Jesus was going through the region between Samaria and Galilee. ¹²As he entered a village, ten lepers approached him. Keeping their distance, ¹³they called out, saying, "Jesus, Master, have mercy on us!" ¹⁴When he saw them, he said to them, "Go and show yourselves to the priests." And as they

CEB

Lesson Scripture: Luke 17:11-19

¹¹On the way to Jerusalem, Jesus traveled along the border between Samaria and Galilee. ¹²As he entered a village, ten men with skin diseases approached him. Keeping their distance from him, ¹³they raised their voices and said, "Jesus, Master, show us mercy!"

went, they were made clean. **15Then one of them, when he saw that he was healed, turned back, praising God with a loud voice.** 16He prostrated himself at Jesus' feet and thanked him. And he was a Samaritan. 17Then Jesus asked, "Were not ten made clean? But the other nine, where are they? 18Was none of them found to return and give praise to God except this foreigner?" 19Then he said to him, "Get up and go on your way; your faith has made you well."

14When Jesus saw them, he said, "Go, show yourselves to the priests." As they left, they were cleansed. **15One of them, when he saw that he had been healed, returned and praised God with a loud voice.** 16He fell on his face at Jesus' feet and thanked him. He was a Samaritan. 17Jesus replied, "Weren't ten cleansed? Where are the other nine? 18No one returned to praise God except this foreigner?" 19Then Jesus said to him, "Get up and go. Your faith has healed you."

UNDERSTANDING THE SCRIPTURE

Introduction. This story begins a new section in Luke. Jesus' trip from Galilee to Jerusalem began in Luke 9:51, but he has made little progress—he is still in Galilee. But now the pace picks up. In the earlier sections of Luke we have seen the power of Jesus. In this section, the healings and various interchanges with different kinds of people focus our attention on how people respond to Jesus. While the disciples are still struggling to understand Jesus, a rather unexpected person becomes the model for how to respond to the coming of the Kingdom in the person of Jesus.

Luke 17:11-14. The narrative opens with Jesus going through Galilee and Samaria. Even though he has been on his trip to Jerusalem since 9:51, he has not gotten out of his home region. Samaria lies between Galilee (the region in which Nazareth is located) and Judea (where Jerusalem is). So going through Samaria is the logical path for Jesus to go to Jerusalem.

At one village a group of lepers asks for healing. We do not know what kind of disease(s) these men may have had.

The label "leprosy" covered a wide range of skin diseases. Since at least some of these diseases were communicable, lepers were often required to stay out of the main areas of cities and may have banded together into communities. We should see them as people who were stigmatized and excluded from normal life. In this text they respectfully keep their distance. This may also be a sign that they have faith that Jesus can heal, even at a distance. They address him as a person with power, calling him "Master." In Luke the title often seems to suggest that Jesus has miraculous power (5:5; 8:24, 45; 9:33). Using this title for Jesus means that these supplicants identify themselves as his subordinates; he is one who has power over them. Their request is also interesting: They ask for mercy or compassion. Their request is really for healing, but that healing is more than an exercise of power; it is an act of compassion.

Jesus' response to their plea is remarkably brief. There is no pronouncement of healing, no contact with them, no prayer for them. They are simply told to go show themselves to the priest. Lepers were readmitted to full community life only after they got a clean bill of health from a priest. The Jewish lepers would not need to go to Jerusalem to do this. Priests only served part of the year in the Temple. The rest of the time they would be in their hometowns, often as teachers of the faith or perhaps employees at a synagogue. In those places they would also carry out duties for which a person needed a priest (such as inspecting lepers). So Jesus is not imposing a long trip, simply sending them to receive confirmation of their healing.

These ten lepers start their trip to the priests before they are healed. They are healed only as they are on their way. So they all had enough faith to begin the trip to the priest without having received their healing. But, of course, they are not disappointed. They are made clean on the way.

Luke 17:15-19. We do not know how far they had gone, but they notice they are healed. One of them stops and gives thanks to God. He proclaims his thanks in a loud voice—he yells his thanksgiving to God. Then he returns to Jesus and falls at his feet, giving Jesus thanks. We should not miss the parallel between the man thanking God and now thanking Jesus. The posture Luke describes is that of worship. He bows to the ground before Jesus, thanking him for this wonderful gift. Then Luke surprises his readers; he tells them that this man was a Samaritan. Samaritans and Jews did not get along. Samaritans were the descendants of the people who had been left behind when the nation of Israel fell in the eighth century B.C. These people then intermarried with the other native peoples of Palestine and with the Assyrians who were brought in when the people of Israel were exiled.

The nation of Judah (whose capital was in Jerusalem) did not fall until the sixth century B.C. Jews of Jesus' day (and today) are descendants of these people of Judah who maintained their identity as Judeans. They wanted little to do with the mixed-race people of Samaria—and the feeling was mutual. The Samaritans' religion was also a bit different. They continued to worship the God of Abraham, but their Scriptures were a bit different and their Temple was not in Jerusalem. Jews and Samaritans each saw themselves as the ones who pleased God. Luke's Gentile readers could also recognize Samaritans as outsiders because they were not quite Gentiles, just as they were not quite Jews.

So the hero of our story is an outcast. He is the only one of the ten who were healed who returned to thank Jesus and acknowledge him as one worthy of worship. Jesus' response emphasizes the low social standing of the one who was thankful. He refers to him as "this foreigner" (17:18) to shame those who had not stopped to thank God. If they are the people of God, they should be the ones to honor God, but it is the outsider who gives thanks who is the model for how to respond to God's blessings.

The story ends with Jesus saying, "You faith has made you well" (NRSV) or as The New Jerusalem Bible puts it, "You faith has saved you." Throughout the story, various words are used to refer to the healing. But here at the end, Luke uses a Greek word that means "saved." New Testament writers often use "saved" to speak of a healing. Yet this is the first time Luke uses it in this story. Its usage seems to suggest that his man has received more than those who did not return to give thanks.

INTERPRETING THE SCRIPTURE

Receiving God's Blessings

As this story begins, a group of people approaches Jesus. All have the same need, because they all suffer from the same disease. Furthermore, they are all kept away from a full life by their disease. Importantly, they all recognize the power of Jesus. When they call him "Master," Luke wants us to see them as people who believe that the power of God works through Jesus. We don't know how they know about Jesus, but they believe he has the power to heal. They see him as the one with the authority to send away the thing that inflicts them with pain and isolation. So they ask Jesus for mercy. Jesus' quick response demands that they trust him. And their trust is rewarded, for they are healed.

The healing here comes through their recognition of who Jesus is. He is the One who wields the power of God. He is the One who can overcome those things that diminish life. And he is the One who is willing to grant mercy—even to strangers. This is an extraordinary healing. It is done at a distance and seemingly after only a brief encounter. But in those moments they seem to know what they need to about Jesus.

Only One Was Grateful

It is only after the healing that this story takes a strange turn. Only one of those who is healed thanks God and returns to thank Jesus. His behavior here singles him out as the one who knows most clearly who Jesus is. He returns to bow before Jesus. This posture of worship suggests more than that Jesus exercises the power of God. It intimates that he is an appropriate object of worship. When John tries to bow like this before an angel in the Book of Revelation, he is told not to do it because such adoration is only due to God (Revelation 22:8-9). Similarly in Acts, Peter does not allow Cornelius to bow before him in this way because Peter is just a human (10:25-26). Here, however, bowing is the proper thing to do before Jesus. The healed man glorifies God and gives thanks to Jesus as he bows before him. As Luke presents him, this man who was healed seems to recognize the presence of God in Jesus. Beginning with this story, Luke has some characters (particularly those who are seen as powerless or outcasts) on the trip to Jerusalem understand and accept Jesus in ways that others do not. These people understand better than the disciples, who are still struggling to understand Jesus even as they enter Jerusalem for the Passion Week.

Thus, this healed leper becomes the example of how people should respond to Jesus and the gifts they receive through him. This Samaritan leper is the one who goes out of his way to thank God and Jesus for what he has been given. His disease had been no more debilitating than the others. The gift he received was not greater than what the others were given. But he responds in the way Jesus thinks is appropriate. He stops to give thanks to God. He does it in a rather extreme way. It would make good sense for him to see a priest, be readmitted to his family and community, and then make time to thank Jesus. Instead, he turns as soon as he knows he is healed and gives thanks to God. Knowing that he owes his healing and his regaining of his life to Jesus, he makes it his priority to offer God thanks. Responding immediately to the gift of God is more important than anything else in his life.

He serves as an example for how to respond to the blessings we receive from God. He recognizes that those blessings come through Christ, he honors Christ, and he glorifies God. To glorify God includes more than our private thanks. To glorify someone is to sing his praises, to increase the reputation of the other person by extolling her qualities. As this healed man gives thanks to Jesus and to God, he tells others of the wonderful thing God has done for him. He lets others know about the God who has blessed him so richly. The importance of giving thanks goes beyond the appropriate show of gratitude; it helps direct others to God. It lets them know about the care that God gives us. This kind of giving glory to God invites others to trust God because they hear about how God has made our lives richer.

Your Faith Has Saved You

This story ends with a proclamation about the healed man's faith. We should note that all the men with leprosy were healed. They all recognized the power of Jesus. But only this man is said to have faith. He has the faith in Jesus that Luke wants all his readers to develop. His thanksgiving expresses his faith in God. Following this example, we are to express our faith through thanksgiving that shows we recognize our dependence upon God for all good things. Thanking God gives voice to our trust in the goodness of God.

The healed man's faith that expresses itself in thanksgiving brought him more than release from the disease that had inflicted his body. The language used for the healing of this leprosy has varied. In verses 14 and 17 they are cleansed; in verse 15 they are healed. But as this story ends, Jesus says that this man's faith has "saved" him. As we noted previously, many New Testament writers use the word "saved" to describe a healing. But in this story, Luke has reserved this term until the end. Here it seems to include more than the remission of the man's leprosy. He is the one who acknowledges that this good thing in his life comes from God. This acknowledgment of dependence on God brings wholeness and healing that goes beyond the physical malady. Having faith of this type means that one relies on God and so is freed to live in peace in God's presence and invite others to experience the same kind of healing and salvation.

Yet Broader Thanksgiving

In the healing story in today's lesson, the man is able to voice only his own thanksgiving. We who live together as the church and who are bound together by the love of Christ can give thanks for the good things in the lives of our fellow Christians that we see God working in. Paul often calls his churches to rejoice with him or to give thanks with him for the blessings he has received. This multiplying of the thanksgiving to God can unite us as a community as we share in the joys of the lives of those around us. Such thanksgiving reminds us of how God's blessings of us can make us more joy-filled people. So even giving thanks is a blessing. As thanksgiving makes us more grateful, it glorifies God. Thus, when we give thanks, others can see how good God is and how being in relationship with God brings meaning and joy to our lives.

SHARING THE SCRIPTURE

PREPARING TO TEACH

Preparing Our Hearts

Ponder this week's devotional reading from Colossians 3:12-17. What does Paul (or the author who wrote in his name) say about how "God's chosen ones" (3:12) are to live together? Which of the traits listed here describe you? Which traits do you need more of? How do your actions reflect thanksgiving for the love that God has shown to you in Christ Jesus?

Pray that you and the students will express your faith with a grateful heart.

Preparing Our Minds

Study the background Scripture and the lesson Scripture, both of which are from Luke 17:11-19.

Consider this question as you prepare the lesson: *How can we grow a sincere thankful spirit in our lives?*

Write on newsprint:
❏ information for next week's lesson, found under Continue the Journey.
❏ activities for further spiritual growth in Continue the Journey.

Review the Introduction, The Big Picture, Close-up, and Faith in Action, which all precede the first lesson of this quarter. Consider how you might use any of this material in today's lesson.

LEADING THE CLASS

(1) Gather to Learn

❖ Welcome the class members and guests.

❖ Pray that those who have come today will respond with thanksgiving to God's gracious actions.

❖ Brainstorm answers to this question: **What are some creative ways that people have expressed their appreciation to you for something you said or did—or that you expressed appreciation to someone else?** Write these ideas on newsprint. (Here are some possible answers: send a card, possibly one you have made; make some baked goods; create a gift bag; pay the kindness forward by helping someone else; send a basket of flowers or fruit, perhaps using items from your own garden; take the person out for a meal; be there to help or listen to the other person.)

❖ Read aloud today's focus statement: **Some people express their gratitude with sincerity; others find it difficult to express their gratitude, while still others are ungrateful for what is done for them. How can Christians grow a sincere, thankful spirit in their lives? By faith, one of the ten lepers that Jesus healed was able to express his gratitude and praise.**

(2) *Goal 1: Review the Story of the Ten Healed Lepers Among Whom Only One Was Grateful for Healing*

❖ Choose a volunteer to read this familiar story from Luke 17:11-19.

❖ Discuss these questions:

1. **What do you know about the kind of life that those who had a skin disease were forced to live?** (See Luke 17:11-14 in Understanding the Scripture and "Receiving God's Blessings" in Interpreting the Scripture.)

2. **What attracted the lepers to Jesus as One who could heal them?** (See "Receiving God's Blessings" in Interpreting the Scripture.)

3. **What might you expect Jesus to do to heal the lepers? What does Luke say that Jesus actually did?** (See Luke 17:11-14 in Understanding the Scripture.)

4. **When the lepers realized they had been healed, how did they react?** (See Luke 17:15-19 in Understanding the Scripture.)

5. **How is the Samaritan leper a good role model for us?** (See "Only One Was Grateful" in Interpreting the Scripture.)

6. **What relationship do you see in this story between gratitude and faith?** (See "Your Faith Has Saved You" in Interpreting the Scripture.)

❖ Invite the students to suggest reasons why the nine lepers did not return to Jesus to give thanks. (Were they simply ungrateful? Did they find it difficult to express their thanks? Were they unsure that they had been fully healed, preferring to hear assurance from the priest before they thanked Jesus?)

❖ Ask: **How are the reasons that those "lepers" who did not express their gratitude to Jesus immediately similar to and different from excuses you may have used—or would you have gone back with the Samaritan?**

(3) *Goal 2: Feel and Express Gratitude for All Blessings, Including Healing, the Learners Have Received*

❖ Distribute paper and pencils. Suggest that the learners fold the paper into quarters and then tear it into four parts. On each piece the students are to write one blessing for which they have to be thankful. These blessings may be broad (such as "family") or very specific (such as God healed me from cancer). Tell the adults that you will be reading some of these blessings at random. If they want to remain anonymous, they will need to omit specific names or dates that might identify them.

❖ Pass around a container so that the students may offer their blessings by placing them in the container. Draw at random as many blessings as you have time to read.

❖ Close with several moments of silence so that the learners can give thanks for all the blessings that they and their classmates have received from God.

(4) *Goal 3: Celebrate and Give Thanks for the Healing of Others*

❖ Read: **In October 2014, nurse Nina Pham of Texas Health Presbyterian Hospital Dallas contracted Ebola while caring for a man from Liberia, who soon after his arrival at the hospital died from this highly contagious disease. Pham released a statement saying, "I'm doing well and want to thank everyone for their** kind wishes and prayers. . . . I am blessed by the support of family and friends and am blessed to be cared for by the best team of doctors and nurses in the world." A longtime friend of Pham's commented that she and her family have a strong Roman Catholic faith. This friend further noted that Pham views her work as a nurse as a calling, as a way to serve others. When released from the National Institutes of Health Clinical Center in Bethesda, Maryland, to which she had been transferred, Pham said, "Throughout this ordeal, I have put my faith in God and my medical team."

❖ Ask these questions:

1. **In what ways might Nina Pham's situation be compared to those lepers who asked Jesus to heal them?** (She was in isolation, apart from others, just as the lepers were.)

2. **How would you compare Nina Pham's attitude to that of the Samaritan leper?** (She exhibits a grateful spirit, just as he did.)

3. **Had you been a friend of one of these sick people, how would you celebrate and give thanks for healing?**

(5) Continue the Journey

❖ Pray that as the learners depart, they will remember to acknowledge and give thanks for all that God has done for them.

❖ Post information for next week's session on newsprint for the students to copy:

- **Title: Humble Faith**
- **Background Scripture: Luke 18:9-14**

- **Lesson Scripture: Luke 18:9-14**
- **Focus of the Lesson: The faithful wonder whether their words, which are sometimes uttered out of desperation, will make a difference. Is there an attitude or posture that can assure them that their words are heard? Jesus taught that effective words of prayer are infused with power when uttered with humility of spirit rather than out of self-righteousness.**

❖ Post the following information on newsprint and provide paper and pencils for the students to copy it. Challenge the adults to grow spiritually by completing one or more of these activities related to this week's session.

(1) **Prepare for bedtime by writing three to five reasons you have to be thankful to God and to other people. Express your gratitude in whatever ways seem most appropriate.**

(2) **Give thanks for someone else's healing, even if you do not know this individual personally.**

(3) **Pray for those who are sick. Give thanks when you hear that they have been healed.**

❖ Sing or read aloud "When Jesus the Healer Passed Through Galilee."

❖ Conclude today's session by leading the class in this benediction, which is adapted from Mark 9:23 in the lesson for March 6: **Together we affirm that all things can be done for the one who believes. Amen.**

UNIT 3: FULLNESS OF FAITH
HUMBLE FAITH

PREVIEWING THE LESSON

Lesson Scripture: Luke 18:9-14
Background Scripture: Luke 18:9-14
Key Verse: Luke 18:13

Focus of the Lesson:
The faithful wonder whether their words, which are sometimes uttered out of desperation, will make a difference. Is there an attitude or posture that can assure them that their words are heard? Jesus taught that effective words of prayer are infused with power when uttered with humility of spirit rather than out of self-righteousness.

Goals for the Learners:
(1) to hear what the Pharisee said that was so wrong and what the tax collector said that was right.
(2) to appreciate the difference between self-righteous platitudes and true gratitude for God's mercy and grace.
(3) to inspect, and if necessary to correct, the motivation for their own piety.

Supplies:
Bibles, newsprint and marker, paper and pencils, hymnals

READING THE SCRIPTURE

NRSV

Lesson Scripture: Luke 18:9-14

⁹He also told this parable to some who trusted in themselves that they were righteous and regarded others with contempt: ¹⁰"Two men went up to the temple to pray, one a Pharisee and the other a tax collector. ¹¹The Pharisee, standing by himself, was praying thus, 'God, I thank you that

CEB

Lesson Scripture: Luke 18:9-14

⁹Jesus told this parable to certain people who had convinced themselves that they were righteous and who looked on everyone else with disgust: ¹⁰"Two people went up to the temple to pray. One was a Pharisee and the other a tax collector. ¹¹The Pharisee stood and prayed about

I am not like other people: thieves, rogues, adulterers, or even like this tax collector. ¹²I fast twice a week; I give a tenth of all my income.' **¹³But the tax collector, standing far off, would not even look up to heaven, but was beating his breast and saying, 'God, be merciful to me, a sinner!'** ¹⁴I tell you, this man went down to his home justified rather than the other; for all who exalt themselves will be humbled, but all who humble themselves will be exalted."

himself with these words, 'God, I thank you that I'm not like everyone else—crooks, evildoers, adulterers— or even like this tax collector. ¹²I fast twice a week. I give a tenth of everything I receive.' **¹³But the tax collector stood at a distance. He wouldn't even lift his eyes to look toward heaven. Rather, he struck his chest and said, 'God, show mercy to me, a sinner.'** ¹⁴I tell you, this person went down to his home justified rather than the Pharisee. All who lift themselves up will be brought low, and those who make themselves low will be lifted up."

UNDERSTANDING THE SCRIPTURE

Introduction. This parable is closely related to the previous one (18:1-8) in which the persistence of the widow leads to her request being granted. But today's reading also opens a section that explores the question of who belongs in the kingdom of God. Specifically, it looks at a difference between true and false righteousness.

Luke 18:9. There are only a few places where the Gospel writers explicitly tell the readers who a parable of Jesus was intended for. This is one of those places. This parable identifies two characteristics of its intended audience: They trust in themselves to be righteous and they view others with contempt. These are people who know that they are good religious folks. They live moral lives that follow God's commandments. By all appearances, they are what good people should be. But they are condemned because of their attitude: They believe these things give them the status of being right with God. That is, they think they deserve to be

those God favors and those who are in a good relationship with God. It is important for us to remember that Jesus does not characterize all of his audience in this way. Christians have often been too quick to say that Jews of Jesus' day believed that they earned their place with God. The opening of this parable suggests that only some thought this, just as some think that in the church today.

The second characteristic of this group is that they look down on others who are not as good as they are. This attitude is the flip side of self-righteousness. If you believe you made yourself righteous, you can be judgmental about those who are not as faithful as you, or at least do not appear to be as faithful as you. This parable addresses both of these attitudes.

Luke 18:10-13. The parable identifies one character as a Pharisee and the other as a tax collector. It is rare that Luke identifies characters in his parables in this way. If we have been reading in Luke to this point, we know how each of these groups has been characterized. The Pharisees have not received Jesus and wonder why he associates with sinners, including tax collectors. Pharisees were generally recognized as good religious people in the first century. We have a bad view of them because they are always presented as Jesus' antagonists. Outside the New Testament, the Pharisees appear in a much different light. They are usually seen as faithful and conscientious interpreters of God's will. But in Luke they oppose Jesus' mission to the poor and outcasts. They are a necessary foil for Luke to present the ministry of Jesus as he wants readers to see it. So we should recognize that Luke has created a persona for them that does not fairly represent most Pharisees.

In this parable, this Pharisee is the personification of the self-righteous person. In his prayer, this character lists things he is proud of, each of which is a good thing. He lives a moral life, participates in devotional disciplines, and gives of his resources to support his religious community and help the poor. The problem is that he has a self-congratulatory attitude about these things. He believes that his performance of these things gives him something to boast about to God. He does not consider the idea that he is able to live in this way because God has enabled him to do so. He seems to think that he deserves to have God listen to him and accept him.

The other character in this parable, the tax collector, is the opposite of the Pharisee in many ways. First, tax collectors in first-century Palestine were looked down on and seen as traitors and as dishonest. They collected tax money for the oppressive Romans and so colluded with the enemy. Many seem to have demanded more than the just amount when they went to collect the taxes. In Luke, however, they have been objects of Jesus' special attention. He is often with them and they seem to accept him. They represent the outcasts that Luke has as the central concern of Jesus. So readers of Luke know that this is the kind of person Jesus calls and that they often welcome him. Still, the power of naming him a tax collector is that such people are obvious sinners. And that is who he is in this parable.

Even though he is a sinner, the tax collector knows the proper attitude to have before God. He knows that he does not deserve God's grace and love. His life has been a demonstration of his unworthiness. His posture is an indication of his humility, of his recognition of his dependence on God for forgiveness and acceptance. His prayer is simply that God will have mercy on him. He also knows himself to be a sinner. Beyond the common expectation that tax collectors are sinners, this confession may suggest that he knows his place before God better than the person who has done all the right things.

Luke 18:14. Jesus interprets this parable just to be sure no one misses the point. He says that the person who leaves the Temple in right relationship with God is the confessed and forgiven sinner. He is the one "justified," that is, made right with God. Like other "sinners" in Luke, he now finds himself a member of the people of God. The religious person who expects that God is with him is wrong. He does not have a right relationship with God, and so he remains in his sins. The only sins we know of are his self-righteousness and his disregard for the sinner. But these are enough to keep him away from God.

Jesus' final comment in relation to this parable repeats an earlier warning about those who exalt themselves and his privileging of those who are humble (14:11). In this case, the one who boasts before God is rejected, whereas the one who humbly begs for forgiveness is raised to the status of being in the kingdom of God.

INTERPRETING THE SCRIPTURE

A Dangerous Goodness

Our text today is addressed to a specific set of people: those who think they are right with God through their own doing and so look down on others. It is important to notice that all the things the Pharisee boasts of are good things. His personal, social, and religious behaviors are all exemplary. His problem is that he thinks these things show that he is a person who deserves to be accepted by God. His life has been good enough that he thinks he has little need for God's grace.

This Pharisee has more in common with many of us in the church today than we should be comfortable with. Many of us grew up in religious families and have usually been in some way associated with the church. Even those of us who have not been as closely attached to the church as lifelong members probably think of ourselves as fairly good people. We don't commit murder or rob banks, we are faithful within our families, we give to charity drives, and maybe even work on a Habitat for Humanity build. All these good things show the kinds of people we are. When we think of ourselves in these ways, we often see little need to come to God to ask for forgiveness. We are basically good people, so any fault should be overlooked easily.

This viewpoint shows itself in many ways in our churches. Some seldom have a confession of sin and prayer for forgiveness in their worship. Others have difficulty thinking about the death of Jesus as something that deals with sin. It is simply not needed, especially by good people like us. Yes, Jesus sets a good example and we as good people follow it fairly well, we think. But that business of needing someone to intervene because we have behaved in sinful ways, well, that seems unnecessary, maybe even offensive. We are good people!

This perspective has deep roots in our culture. We do not like to be dependent on anyone or anything. We honor those who are self-made people or who are clearly able to make their own way in the world. To acknowledge dependence is to show weakness. So we all work hard to demonstrate that we are independent, to show that we are dependent upon no one and nothing other than our own work and possessions. This outlook follows us into our churches. We are loath to admit that we need help—or that we do not deserve to have God be in relationship with us. We have all the evidence we need: faithful attendance, good works, decent lives. Of course, we do not explicitly brag about these things, at least not to God. Still, our reticence to profess our dependence on God and on Christ for our place with God and for the many gifts we possess shows that we have a good bit of this Pharisee in us.

A Contrast in Attitudes

The most important distinction between the two characters in this parable is their view of how their relationship with God is secured. The one who lists his good deeds thinks he deserves all the good things God gives. The tax collector knows better. We often think of him as someone who must have a lot of really bad sins to confess. Surely he is an embezzler, or at least he regularly misses worship. But all we really know is that he is a person looked down on by the good people and that in Luke's Gospel Jesus constantly seeks out his type of person. He knows himself to be a sinner. That is an attitude, not evidence that he has done all sorts of evil deeds.

The important contrast in this parable is between the person who thinks he deserves to be in God's presence and one who knows he does not. However bad or good his behavior has been, he recognizes his dependence on God and God's mercy.

We are quick to remind ourselves that all people are worthy because we are all made in the image of God. And this is correct; it grants us all value beyond calculation. But being this valuable does not keep us from being dependent on God for all good things. This value does not mean that we have not turned from God as we have sinned. Our value does not diminish our dependence on God for forgiveness and right relationship. The tax collector does not lack self-esteem; rather, he sees the truth of his

existence. He is completely dependent upon God, and he is a person who has sinned against God. He recognizes his guilt, but also his value. In humility, he asks God for forgiveness. We must assume that he believes that God grants that forgiveness.

He Went Home Justified

Jesus says at the end of this parable that it is the people who recognize their dependence on God and confess their sins who are justified. The term "justified" is used often in the New Testament as the word that means "salvation." It is a term often found in legal settings for being found not guilty, but its nuance in the first century was a bit different from what that means today. The not-guilty verdict then signaled that the parties were now to resume the relationship that had been interrupted by the offense. So in the New Testament it means that the offense that separated a person and God has been wiped out and that God and the sinner are again in right relationship. Jesus says that the person who recognizes his dependence on God and confesses his sin is the one who receives not just forgiveness but also that renewed relationship with God.

A Reversal of Fortunes

Our text ends with a proverb that gives a second angle on the results of the attitudes of each person in the parable and so on the attitude of those to whom it is addressed. The humble will be exalted and those who exalt themselves will be humbled. We may on occasion wish that this proverb came true more evidently than it does. The haughty often seem to get their way, while the humble are trampled. This saying of Jesus is a warning about final judgment, not a promise about what happens in this world. Jesus says that those who are humble before God, those who recognize their need for and dependence upon God's grace will be received by God in the end. They are the ones God will exalt at judgment. Those who think they deserve a place in God's presence have an unpleasant surprise awaiting them when God evaluates their lives. Their pride will bring them God's disapproval in the end. This concluding proverb is sobering. It warns us not to think that we are more deserving of God's love than those who do not seek to honor God in their lives. We all stand before God as sinners who are dependent on God for mercy. There is no room for self-righteousness in any of us. We have each turned away from God in our own ways and rely on God's grace in Christ for our restored relationship with God. It is this relationship that brings meaning and joy to life. Those gifts far outweigh anything we might make of ourselves.

SHARING THE SCRIPTURE

PREPARING TO TEACH

Preparing Our Hearts

Ponder this week's devotional reading from Micah 6:6-8; 7:18-19. In what ways do you walk humbly with God? What good news do you hear in these passages?

Pray that you and the students will recognize the value of a humble faith.

Preparing Our Minds

Study the background Scripture and the lesson Scripture, both of which are from Luke 18:9-14.

Consider this question as you prepare the lesson: *Is there an attitude or posture that can assure us that our words of desperation will be heard and make a difference?*

Write on newsprint:
❏ directions for Goal 3 in Sharing the Scripture.
❏ information for next week's lesson, found under Continue the Journey.

❏ activities for further spiritual growth in Continue the Journey.

Review the Introduction, The Big Picture, Close-up, and Faith in Action, which all precede the first lesson of this quarter. Consider how you might use any of this material in today's lesson.

LEADING THE CLASS

(1) Gather to Learn

❖ Welcome the class members and guests.

❖ Pray that those who have come today will appreciate a humble heart.

❖ Read this anecdote concerning the remarkable humility of Albert Einstein: **Soon after moving to America, Albert Einstein was persuaded by mathematicians at Princeton University to address them. Although he felt he had no new information to share with them, he finally chose as his topic tensor analysis, a mathematical tool needed in the study of relativity theory. A small notice posted on one** bulletin board announced this talk. When that date came, the entire campus was packed with cars more likely to be expected at a football game than a mathematical talk. People pushed to get into the small auditorium where Einstein anticipated addressing a select group of mathematicians. Seeing this huge crowd jockeying for position, Einstein remarked, "I never realized that in America there was so much interest in tensor analysis."

❖ Read aloud today's focus statement: **The faithful wonder whether their words, which are sometimes uttered out of desperation, will make a difference. Is there an attitude or posture that can assure them that their words are heard? Jesus taught that effective words of prayer are infused with power when uttered with humility of spirit rather than out of self-righteousness.**

(2) Goal 1: Hear What the Pharisee Said that Was So Wrong and What the Tax Collector Said that Was Right

❖ Solicit a volunteer to read Luke 18:9-14, which is the familiar parable of the Pharisee and the tax collector.

❖ Discuss these questions:

1. **How would you characterize the people for whom Jesus told this parable?** (See Luke 18:9 in Understanding the Scripture.)
2. **What do you learn about the Pharisee?** (See Luke 18:10-13 in Understanding the Scripture.)
3. **How might contemporary church members, like you and me, be like the Pharisee?** (See "A Dangerous Goodness" in Interpreting the Scripture.)
4. **What do you learn about the tax collector?** (See Luke 18:10-13 in Understanding the Scripture.)

5. **What enables one to stand in a right relationship with God?** (See Luke 18:14 in Understanding the Scripture.)
6. **What differences do you see between the way the Pharisee and the tax collector perceive themselves in relationship with God?** (See "A Contrast in Attitudes" in Interpreting the Scripture.)
7. **What attitudes characterize those who are put right with God?** (See "He Went Home Justified" and "A Reversal of Fortunes" in Interpreting the Scripture.)

(3) Goal 2: Appreciate the Difference Between Self-righteous Platitudes and True Gratitude for God's Mercy and Grace

❖ Read: **In the Sermon on the Mount, Jesus provided three examples of self-righteous piety: one concerning the giving of alms (Matthew 6:1-4), one concerning prayer (6:5-8), and the other concerning fasting (6:16-18).**

❖ Form small groups. Ask about one-third of the groups to review 6:1-4 to discern the difference between the self-righteous almsgiver and the one who gives with a godly motivation. Another third of the groups will study 6:5-8 to discover a way to pray that is pleasing to Jesus. The final third is to review 6:16-18 to determine how true fasting stands in contrast to fasting done to attract attention to oneself.

❖ Call the groups together and listen to their ideas.

❖ Invite participants to reflect silently on these questions, which you will read: **How do you think** observers would characterize your **behavior?** (pause) **Are you one of the self-righteous ones who wants everyone to see and laud your behavior, or are you one whom Christ would commend?** (pause) **How do your actions and attitudes support your self-evaluation?** (pause)

(4) Goal 3: Inspect, and If Necessary Correct, the Learners' Motivation for Their Own Piety

❖ Read this quotation from Billy Graham: **"I've never known a person whom I thought was truly filled with the Holy Spirit who went out and bragged about it or sought to draw attention to himself."** Suggest that most of us would not brag about our relationship with God to draw attention to ourselves. Yet what motivates one to act—even if the actions are commendable—may not be in keeping with the humility that Jesus expects of us.

❖ Distribute paper and pencils and ask the adults to answers these questions, which you will post on newsprint. State in advance that the learners will not be asked to share their responses.

1. Name one action you have performed within the last two weeks that you felt reflected your character as a Christian.
2. What reactions did this action bring forth from others?
3. How did you respond to those who praised you?
4. Looking back, do you think your motives were rooted in humility, or were you seeking to show others just how pious you are?

5. If you had the chance to take similar action, what if anything would you do differently?

❖ Suggest that the adults be aware of their motivations so that they are in keeping with whatever good deeds they might do.

(5) Continue the Journey

❖ Pray that as the learners depart, they will value humility in themselves and others.

❖ Post information for next week's session on newsprint for the students to copy:

- **Title: Childlike Faith**
- **Background Scripture: Luke 18:15-17; Mark 10:13-16**
- **Lesson Scripture: Luke 18:15-17; Mark 10:16**
- **Focus of the Lesson: Children's openness to life is a worthy model for everyone in society. What can be learned from children? Jesus taught that to receive the gift of the kingdom of God, the faithful must become as children: open, attentive, and receptive to what God has freely given.**

❖ Post the following information on newsprint and provide paper and pencils for the students to copy it. Challenge the adults to grow spiritually by completing one or more of these activities related to this week's session.

(1) Be aware of people who act with humility. Sometimes those who do brave deeds whom others hail as heroes do not see themselves in that light. What separates these people from so many others who do all they can to be recognized and praised?

(2) Research the Pharisees. Although they are often portrayed negatively in the Scriptures, they have many admirable qualities that made them worthy opponents of Jesus.

(3) Pray daily for God's grace and mercy to abound in your life.

❖ Sing or read aloud "Something Beautiful."

❖ Conclude today's session by leading the class in this benediction, which is adapted from Mark 9:23 in the lesson for March 6: **Together we affirm that all things can be done for the one who believes. Amen.**

UNIT 3: FULLNESS OF FAITH
CHILDLIKE FAITH

PREVIEWING THE LESSON

Lesson Scripture: Luke 18:15-17; Mark 10:16
Background Scripture: Luke 18:15-17; Mark 10:13-16
Key Verse: Luke 18:17

Focus of the Lesson:
Children's openness to life is a worthy model for everyone in society. What can be learned from children? Jesus taught that to receive the gift of the kingdom of God, the faithful must become as children: open, attentive, and receptive to what God has freely given.

Goals for the Learners:
(1) to recognize that Jesus valued children so highly that they were his models for Kingdom possessors.
(2) to believe that the best qualities of children are the very ones that they should seek to cultivate in themselves.
(3) to commit to self-examination and self-improvements with childlike faith.

Supplies:
Bibles, newsprint and marker, paper and pencils, hymnals, magazine pictures or photographs of small children

---

READING THE SCRIPTURE

NRSV

Lesson Scripture: Luke 18:15-17

15People were bringing even infants to him that he might touch them; and when the disciples saw it, they sternly ordered them not to do it. 16But Jesus called for them and said, "Let the little children come to me, and do not stop them; for it is to such as these that the kingdom of God belongs.

CEB

Lesson Scripture: Luke 18:15-17

15People were bringing babies to Jesus so that he would bless them. When the disciples saw this, they scolded them. 16Then Jesus called them to him and said, "Allow the children to come to me. Don't forbid them, because God's kingdom belongs to people like these children.

¹⁷Truly I tell you, whoever does not receive the kingdom of God as a little child will never enter it."

Lesson Scripture: Mark 10:16
¹⁶And he took [the little children] up in his arms, laid his hands on them, and blessed them.

¹⁷I assure you that whoever doesn't welcome God's kingdom like a child will never enter it."

Lesson Scripture: Mark 10:16
¹⁶Then he hugged the children and blessed them.

UNDERSTANDING THE SCRIPTURE

Introduction. The story of Jesus receiving the children has often been misinterpreted as a call for Christians to be satisfied with simplistic faith. As we will see, this misses the very important points that Luke wants readers to get from this episode. This story follows directly the parable of the Pharisee and the tax collector who pray in the Temple. As we read the Gospels, we need to keep in mind that the writers often placed together teachings on the same topic. We noted in the last lesson that the basic message of that parable was to teach that we are all dependent upon God's grace for our relationship with God. Thinking that we deserve to be saved or to be in God's presence is the sin that parable rejects. The story that follows Jesus receiving the children is that of the rich person who comes asking Jesus what he needs to do to be saved. He thinks that his keeping of the commandments has probably gotten him pretty close to what is needed. Like the Pharisee in the parable, he thinks he has done enough (or almost enough) that God should receive him gladly. If the material on each side of our text is on the topic of recognizing our dependence on God, we should expect that this one has something to do with the same topic.

Luke 18:15. This verse sets up the scene that has a saying of Jesus as its climax. This is a kind of story that appears often in the Gospels. It is called a pronouncement story because it ends with a saying, a pronouncement, from Jesus that is always the main point the story intends to make. However long the preceding story is, it is all set up for the short saying at the end. In this case, we have two closely related sayings at the end. So the form is a bit different, but those sayings still contain the central point of the passage.

As we saw in last week's lesson (18:9-14), Jesus has been teaching, even teaching some difficult things, when some people begin to bring their children to him to be blessed. They hope that a touch from Jesus will confer good things on their children. Luke heightens the nature of the disturbance by changing the story from the way he had read it in Mark (10:13-16). (Luke probably read Mark and used Mark's outline to structure his story of Jesus' ministry.) Mark has the people bring children; Luke has them bring infants. So the interruption may be even greater: It is not just children; it is crying babies! The disciples step in to be sure that people get to hear Jesus' teaching. After all, he has the word of God that everyone needs to hear. They tell the parents "sternly" to get the children away from Jesus. The disciples believe they are doing the right thing.

Luke 18:16-17. But Jesus takes this moment to make these infants an object lesson. He tells the disciples to let the children come to him because the people who are like children are those in the Kingdom. Further, he says that those who would be in the Kingdom must receive it as children. We have often misunderstood this text because we do not think of children the same way as people in the first century did and, therefore, have not read the passage in context.

In the ancient world, children were people without rights and without status. They could not make demands or make claims about what parents owed them. Everyone recognized children as those without position or power in the social or household structure. They had little value as humans. It was not until they reached the age of majority that they were seen to have any social status. By naming these children infants, Luke emphasizes their vulnerability. There was a very high infant mortality rate in the first century. It was somewhere near 50 percent. It is easy to see why people would want to have their babies blessed! So the ones Jesus receives as those to whom the Kingdom belongs are the vulnerable and weak, those with no claims to status or power or position. Luke's Gospel has Jesus focus his ministry on the outcasts and second-class people, those without power who were often disregarded. In many ways, Luke points readers to those people as the object of special concern for Jesus.

The second saying of Jesus (18:17) goes beyond observing that it is people who are like infants who do receive the Kingdom; it demands that those who want to get into the Kingdom must be like infants. The emphasis here is on the dependence of infants on others and the absence of any claim to status. The stories on each side of this episode have bad examples. In those stories, people assert their position; they think they deserve a place in the Kingdom. This scene with the children gives the good example: Be like babies, those who are dependent on others and who know they have no right to make demands.

Mark 10:13-16. Our readings for today's lesson include the same story from Mark, though the conclusion of this episode is different in Mark's Gospel. Luke does not conclude with the action of Jesus taking the children in his arms to bless them, but rather moves us to the bad example of the ruler who comes to Jesus so we do not get distracted from the point that the contrast is making. Mark also has the ruler come to Jesus immediately after the children come to him, but he adds another reaction of Jesus. Jesus embraces the children. Mark, then, has the episode conclude with a demonstration of Jesus' love and acceptance of the children (who are not called infants in Mark). The point of the story remains the same, but Mark gives readers an image of the way that Jesus receives the children and, by extension, those who come to him as children—he takes them lovingly into his arms.

INTERPRETING THE SCRIPTURE

Childlike Faith

When Jesus receives these infants and makes them examples, it is truly surprising behavior. No one would have guessed that children, much less babies, were examples of what Jesus' followers should be. Many people in recent times have talked about how this story means that we should have faith that is innocent or open or simple. This story has been understood through a romanticized view of children that gives them these characteristics. Once that view of children is presented, then we are told that we should be like that. It is always hard not to allow our cultural understandings to shape our reading of the New Testament. In the case of this passage, we have usually just capitulated and allowed our senti-mentalized thoughts about children to determine our reading. But when we do this, we will miss what Luke wants us to hear and what the actions of Jesus mean. Luke tries to make sure that we do not slip into those kinds of readings when he identi-fies the children brought to Jesus as infants. Whatever we might want to say about children as they get older, infants cannot really be characterized as open to new things or trusting or open-minded. We know infants are needy and dependent on others for all things. They cannot live without the support of others.

We place a very high value on infants. Things were rather different in the ancient world. People were often reticent to get attached to a child before some time had passed after his or her birth. Roman custom had the father wait about a week before even naming the child for fear that it would die. With the infant mortality rate somewhere around 50 percent, everyone recognized the fragility of the lives of children. Still, having children was valued. They were seen as help on the farm in lower-income settings and they were heirs to whom one could pass on one's wealth and property in upper-income settings. But while they remained children, they had few legal rights and were sometimes seen as property. Fathers could sell their children into slavery multiple times if the need arose. So when Jesus gives attention to chil-dren, especially infants, he is invest-ing them with status and value. They come as suppliants with no claim to attention, yet they are received as valuable.

The children represent the pow-erless who are without status in the world. When Jesus accepts them, he is accepting those who know they can make no claim on God. They are the ones who do not think they can assert any right or contend that they should be taken in to the presence of God.

When Jesus calls his disciples to have the faith of children, it is a call to acknowledge that we have no claims on God. All that we receive is a mat-ter of grace. We must accept that we have no claim on God to enter the Kingdom. Having the faith of chil-dren means that we come to God as complete dependents. A childlike faith is a faith that depends on God for all gifts and blessings. With child-like faith we know we are citizens of God's kingdom through the work of Christ rather than because of what we offer to God or because we have been good people.

Being called to a childlike faith does not suggest that we allow our faith to remain unexamined or that we do not have to develop responses to the hard questions of life that test faith. There is nothing of that meaning in the text. It does suggest that we accept the gifts of God in humility, trusting in the power and love of Christ to bring us into God's kingdom.

A Subversive Act

While it is hard for us to think of it in these terms, Jesus' receiving of these children is an act that challenges the values of the social system. We are similar to those living in the first century in that we pay more attention to and cater to the wishes of those who have power and status. In the flow of Luke's narrative, Jesus takes time away from addressing those who have power (those mentioned in 18:9 and the ruler who comes to him immediately after this story) to give attention to the ones who have no status. He is symbolically rejecting the system that values those with power above the helpless. The disciples know that it makes no sense for Jesus to be slowed down by babies when he has important people to meet and influence. But Jesus shows that these children who are without status or power are as important as and are as loved as those who seem more important by the standards of the world. Jesus says that the kingdom of God belongs to these who are powerless and who are in a position only to accept the gifts of God.

A Holy Hug

Our lesson texts for this week added to the story in Luke the conclusion of this story as it appears in Mark 10:16. The CEB translates what Jesus did by saying that he "hugged" them. Luke deletes this verse from his account so that he can directly oppose the ruler who comes to Jesus asking about eternal life with the description of the required perspective seen in children. But Mark took time to mention that Jesus not only blesses the children but picks them up and hugs them. As much as the children serve as symbols of those without power and status, Mark still lets us see them as children with whom Jesus interacts. His hug shows the love that he has for children. His attention to them has been a demonstration of their value, despite what the cultural norms were. Now we see that he not only values them but also loves them and shows that love in visible ways. As we read this touching scene we should see Jesus showing love for children and for all who are dispossessed, all who need to be supported in situations in which they are without the power to direct their own lives. These are the people Jesus takes up, enfolds in his arms, and blesses.

Having a Childlike Faith

This text drives us back to the point made with the parable of the Pharisee and the tax collector. In a different way it contends that those God receives are those who know they are dependent upon God for their lives and their relationships with God. The children and the tax collector are examples of the same kind of attitude toward God. As we noted in connection with the parable, this is a difficult posture to maintain in our culture where we value independence and autonomy. Jesus' receiving of the children shows that we must reject those cultural values if we are to be received into the Kingdom. Learning to live in dependence on God also entails learning to value others for the right reasons. When Jesus receives those who have no status and says they are the one who are in the Kingdom, he gives us an example to follow. As the church, we are to show our childlike faith by receiving those who have no status. We will not only help those in need, we will seek ways to invite them into our fellowship and help them to see that they are loved and valued by God and by us.

SHARING THE SCRIPTURE

PREPARING TO EACH

Preparing Our Hearts

Ponder this week's devotional reading from Isaiah 11:1-9, which is the familiar description of the ideal king who presides over the peaceable kingdom. What are the characteristics of this ideal king? What will be the characteristics of society once the ideal king begins his reign?

Pray that you and the students will seek to live peaceably as God's children.

Preparing Our Minds

Study the background Scripture from Luke 18:15-17; Mark 10:13-16. The lesson Scripture is from Luke 18:15-17; Mark 10:16.

Consider this question as you prepare the lesson: *What can we learn from children about receiving the gift of the kingdom of God?*

Write on newsprint:
❑ information for next week's lesson, found under Continue the Journey.
❑ activities for further spiritual growth in Continue the Journey.

Review the Introduction, The Big Picture, Close-up, and Faith in Action, which all precede the first lesson of this quarter. Consider how you might use any of this material in today's lesson.

Collect pictures from magazines or photographs of small children. Contact class members to assist you.

LEADING THE CLASS

(1) Gather to Learn

❖ Welcome the class members and guests.

❖ Pray that those who have come today will receive God's kingdom with the openness and dependency of a child.

❖ Show any pictures of small children that you have brought and invite those who have also brought pictures to show them. Remind class members to be careful handling any photographs. Ask: **What character traits or behaviors do you often associate with young children?** List these ideas on newsprint for use later in the session.

❖ Read aloud today's focus statement: **Children's openness to life is a worthy model for everyone in society. What can be learned from children? Jesus taught that to receive the gift of the kingdom of God, the faithful must become as children: open, attentive, and receptive to what God has freely given.**

(2) Goal 1: Recognize that Jesus Valued Children So Highly that They Were His Models for Kingdom Possessors

❖ Set the context for today's lesson by using information from Introduction in Understanding the Scripture.

❖ Select a volunteer to read Luke 18:15-17 and another to read Mark 10:16.

❖ Discuss these questions:

1. **How were children commonly regarded in the Roman Empire during the first century?** (See "Childlike Faith" in Interpreting the Scripture.)

2. **How did Jesus' willingness to receive children undercut the commonly held values of his day?** (See "A Subversive Act" in Interpreting the Scripture.)

3. **What does it mean to have a childlike faith?** (See "Having a Childlike Faith" in Interpreting the Scripture.)

4. **What connection does Jesus draw between receiving a child and receiving the kingdom of God?** (See Luke 18:16-17 in Understanding the Scripture.)

5. **How do the accounts of this story in Mark and Luke differ?** (See Mark 10:13-16 in Understanding the Scripture.)

6. **What can adult believers learn from children that will enable them to mature in their faith and grow closer to God?**

(3) Goal 2: Believe that the Best Qualities of Children Are the Very Ones that the Learners Should Seek to Cultivate in Themselves

❖ Look again at the character traits listed in the "Gather to Learn" activity. Note that some of these traits

we adults have outgrown or as Paul would say, "put an end to childish ways" (1 Corinthians 13:11). Other traits, however, will draw us closer to God. Ask: **Which of the traits that we have listed would help us to cultivate a close, personal relationship with Jesus?**

❖ Form two groups (or multiples of two) to write summaries of expectations for parents and children. Distribute newsprint and a marker and ask one group to list actions and attitudes that a parent of a small child could be expected to exhibit. Distribute newsprint and a marker to the second group and ask those participants to list behaviors and attitudes that a small child may exhibit.

❖ Call everyone back together to hear ideas.

❖ Ask: **What ideas can you glean about how Jesus interacts with us and how we are to interact with him?**

❖ Conclude by exploring how Jesus interacts with children by reading "A Holy Hug" in Interpreting the Scripture.

(4) Goal 3: Commit to Self-examination and Self-improvements with Childlike Faith

❖ Distribute paper and pencils. Tell the adults that you will read several incomplete sentences, which they are to complete. Before you begin, post the list of traits from "Gather to Learn" so that everyone can see them.

1. **The childlike qualities that I possess include . . .**
2. **I wish I could cultivate traits of _____ in order to trust God more.**
3. **The characters in today's reading include "people" (probably parents), infants, the disciples,**

and Jesus. If I were in this crowd, I would most likely be one of the _____ because. . .

4. Even though I am an adult, I can sense Jesus hugging me as a parent hugs a child when . . .

5. I know Jesus blesses me because . . .

❖ Ask the adults to consider ways in which they might mature in their faith by becoming more dependent on God's grace. They may want to write about a problem or situation that burdens them. What can they do to turn this problem over to God as a sign of their childlike faith and trust in God?

❖ Call everyone together. Invite volunteers to discuss any insights they have or what they intend to do to become more faithful by becoming more childlike in their faith, or both.

(5) Continue the Journey

❖ Pray that as the learners depart, they will be more open to God by allowing God to lead and nurture them.

❖ Post information for next week's session on newsprint for the students to copy:

- **Title: Joyous Faith**
- **Background Scripture: Luke 19:1-10**
- **Lesson Scripture: Luke 19:1-10**
- **Focus of the Lesson: All have experienced a loss of direction in their lives and the inability to make necessary changes and new plans. How can we remedy this loss of direction?**

After Zacchaeus gladly welcomed Jesus with great faith and repentance, Jesus declared that his own mission was to seek and save the lost.

❖ Post the following information on newsprint and provide paper and pencils for the students to copy it. Challenge the adults to grow spiritually by completing one or more of these activities related to this week's session.

(1) Observe a group of young children. How do they interact with each other? How do they interact with significant adults? What characteristics of children do you note that adults would do well to imitate?

(2) Read or recite Psalm 23. How would you compare God's caring for the sheep to a parent caring for a child? What characteristics of the sheep are similar to characteristics of children?

(3) Act as an advocate for children. Are there projects in your community that you could volunteer to assist with, perhaps tutoring or helping children navigate the legal system? Learn more about these projects to see if any of them might be a good fit for your personality and talents.

❖ Sing or read aloud "Jesus Loves Me."

❖ Conclude today's session by leading the class in this benediction, which is adapted from Mark 9:23 in the lesson for March 6: **Together we affirm that all things can be done for the one who believes. Amen.**

UNIT 3: FULLNESS OF FAITH
JOYOUS FAITH

PREVIEWING THE LESSON

Lesson Scripture: Luke 19:1-10
Background Scripture: Luke 19:1-10
Key Verse: Luke 19:10

Focus of the Lesson:
All have experienced a loss of direction in their lives and the inability to make necessary changes and new plans. How can they remedy this loss of direction? After Zacchaeus gladly welcomed Jesus with great faith and repentance, Jesus declared that his own mission was to seek and save the lost.

Goals for the Learners:
(1) to study the details of Zacchaeus's encounter with Jesus.
(2) to believe that with God's help they can make necessary changes in their lives.
(3) to repent of shortcomings and commit to living godly lives.

Supplies:
Bibles, newsprint and marker, paper and pencils, hymnals

READING THE SCRIPTURE

NRSV

Lesson Scripture: Luke 19:1-10

¹[Jesus] entered Jericho and was passing through it. ²A man was there named Zacchaeus; he was a chief tax collector and was rich. ³He was trying to see who Jesus was, but on account of the crowd he could not, because he was short in stature. ⁴So he ran ahead and climbed a sycamore tree to see him, because he was going to pass that way. ⁵When Jesus came to the place, he looked up and said

CEB

Lesson Scripture: Luke 19:1-10

¹Jesus entered Jericho and was passing through town. ²A man there named Zacchaeus, a ruler among tax collectors, was rich. ³He was trying to see who Jesus was, but, being a short man, he couldn't because of the crowd. ⁴So he ran ahead and climbed up a sycamore tree so he could see Jesus, who was about to pass that way. ⁵When Jesus came to that spot, he looked up and said, "Zacchaeus,

to him, "Zacchaeus, hurry and come down; for I must stay at your house today." ⁶So he hurried down and was happy to welcome him. ⁷All who saw it began to grumble and said, "He has gone to be the guest of one who is a sinner." ⁸Zacchaeus stood there and said to the Lord, "Look, half of my possessions, Lord, I will give to the poor; and if I have defrauded anyone of anything, I will pay back four times as much." ⁹Then Jesus said to him, "Today salvation has come to this house, because he too is a son of Abraham. **¹⁰For the Son of Man came to seek out and to save the lost."**

come down at once. I must stay in your home today." ⁶So Zacchaeus came down at once, happy to welcome Jesus.

⁷Everyone who saw this grumbled, saying, "He has gone to be the guest of a sinner."

⁸Zacchaeus stopped and said to the Lord, "Look, Lord, I give half of my possessions to the poor. And if I have cheated anyone, I repay them four times as much."

⁹Jesus said to him, "Today, salvation has come to this household because he too is a son of Abraham. **¹⁰The Human One came to seek and save the lost."**

UNDERSTANDING THE SCRIPTURE

Introduction. This story takes place as Jesus is going through Jericho, a city near Jerusalem, the place Jesus will fulfill his mission by submitting to the crucifixion. This story takes up a number of themes that have been a part of Luke's Gospel, including Jesus reaching out to the marginalized and bringing them salvation. Many things connect it to the preceding story. Not least among those things is the imagery of sight as a metaphor for seeking salvation. In the previous story Jesus gives sight to a blind man; in this one Zacchaeus is trying to see Jesus.

Luke 19:1-4. The initial description of Zacchaeus combines elements that are incongruous in Luke's account of Jesus ministry. Throughout this Gospel, those who have been receptive to Jesus are tax collectors and sinners; those who reject him are the wealthy and privileged. Zacchaeus is all of these things. He is a "ruler" or chief of tax collectors and he is wealthy. He probably has a group of lower-level

tax collectors working for him. He may be among those who contracted with the Romans to deliver the taxes and then hired others to do most of the actual collecting. All tax collectors in Palestine were, of course, working for the Romans and so were seen as collaborators. His precise job description, though, matters little for the story. We are to see him as a mix of the kinds of people who have accepted and rejected Jesus. This description intentionally defies the stereotypes Luke has constructed for us. Thus, Zacchaeus can be an example that shows that Jesus saves all kinds of people.

Zacchaeus is on a quest. In the preceding stories, the characters are each on a quest and are in some way blocked from attaining their goal: the widow who goes to the unjust judge, the children whom the disciples try to shoo away, and the blind man whom the crowd tries to quiet. Zacchaeus wants to see Jesus but the crowd will not allow him. Some interpreters think that calling him small here is a metaphor for his social location. Everyone looks down on him because of his job. He must overcome the obstacles of his height (literal and figurative) in order to get to know Jesus.

Luke 19:5-8. Zacchaeus's plan to see or get to know Jesus succeeds beyond his hopes. When he gets to the spot where Zacchaeus is up in the tree, Jesus stops and calls Zacchaeus down. The way Jesus invites himself to stay with Zacchaeus is important to notice. Throughout Luke, Jesus has spoken of elements of his ministry as things that he must do to complete the task God had set for him. Jesus uses that language to speak of staying at the home of Zacchaeus. Jesus says "I must" or "it is necessary that" he stay with Zacchaeus (19:5). It is a divine necessity that Jesus goes to his house to bring it salvation.

The crowd still tries to be an obstacle to this encounter with Jesus. The people grumble that Jesus is going to the house of a sinner. Of course, this is not a new criticism of Jesus in Luke. The response of Zacchaeus is the opposite of the crowd's. He recognizes Jesus as Lord and then becomes a role model for the wealthy.

Interpreters are divided over whether Zacchaeus is presented as a dishonest tax collector who repents when Jesus meets him or whether he is assuring Jesus of his character when he says that he gives half of his possessions to the poor and repays four times anyone who is defrauded (perhaps by those who work under him). The verbs are in the present tense. So they could indicate his regular practice or point to a moment of repentance. Perhaps the response of Jesus in verse 9 suggests that this is repentance because Jesus says

that salvation comes to Zacchaeus "today." If this is repentance, it does not show clearly that Zacchaeus was unscrupulous in the amount of tax he collected. If he was, he makes a very rash commitment. Indeed, some would say that giving away this much amounted to giving away all his possessions, just as Jesus had told the rich ruler to do only a few verses earlier (18:22-23). Whether he repents or refers to his usual practice, Luke makes him the example of the way the rich should respond to Jesus. They give their possessions to those who cannot repay them, and they do not use their status or position to treat those subordinate to them unfairly.

Luke 19:9-10. This story ends with an affirmation of the salvation of Zacchaeus and with a pronouncement about the ministry of Jesus. Hearing of Zacchaeus's conduct (probably his repentance), Jesus says that salvation has come to his house. This sinner who is a tax collector is now identified as a child of Abraham, that is, as one of the people of God. In both his acceptance of Jesus and in his manner of handling his wealth, he shows readers how the people of God are to conduct their lives. It is, of course, a surprise to the crowd (and perhaps us readers) to hear Jesus identify such a person as one of God's people. But it is just such unacceptable people that Luke makes the object of Jesus' special concern.

The concluding and most important pronouncement of the story is that Jesus (the Son of Man) has come to seek and save the lost. The mission of Jesus is to reach out to those who need to repent, who need salvation. This story begins with elements of a quest story, with Zacchaeus seeking Jesus but facing obstacles. At the end, we see that it has really been Jesus who is doing the seeking. His ministry is about finding people like Zacchaeus and bringing them salvation. Sinners and excluded, the lost, are the very ones for whom Jesus has come. The figure of Zacchaeus, with the many things he represents, signals that all people need the salvation Jesus gives.

INTERPRETING THE SCRIPTURE

Hope for Us All

The story of Zacchaeus and his brief encounter with Jesus should give us all hope. Throughout his Gospel, Luke has emphasized that the ministry of Jesus is particularly focused on the marginalized, those who are seen as less valuable than others. He even has stories and parables that make it seem that the wealthy and privileged have little hope of receiving salvation. But now, near the end of Jesus' ministry we have Zacchaeus. Luke's description of this character makes him represent all kinds of people: people who are powerful and those others look down on, people who have status and those who do not, people who are marginalized and those with wealth. All of those groups who have reacted to Jesus so differently throughout this Gospel now come together in this one person. The good news of this story is that Jesus came to bring salvation to all kinds of people. No one is beyond the saving love of God.

Seeking and Finding

This story begins with Zacchaeus wanting to see and know Jesus. He wants to see Jesus badly enough that he makes the effort to overcome multiple obstacles to do so. In this, Zacchaeus is like the characters in the stories of the previous chapter. They sought the presence of Jesus, as he does. You may note that in verse 3 the text does not just say that Zacchaeus wanted to see Jesus, but that he wanted to see who Jesus was. He wanted to understand what people saw in Jesus and why they were attracted to him. Zacchaeus goes to great lengths to demonstrate his determination to know and understand Jesus. When the crowd will not accommodate him, he runs ahead to a place that is not yet crowded and positions himself so they cannot deny him the chance to see Jesus.

Zacchaeus exemplifies the famous statement of St. Augustine who said, "our *hearts* are *restless till* they find *rest* in You." Something in Zacchaeus drove him to seek Jesus. But the story takes an unexpected turn. At first it seemed to be about someone wanting to know Jesus, but it becomes a story about Jesus seeking sinners. Jesus stops and calls Zacchaeus. Jesus says he *must* go to his house. It is a part of the mission of Jesus to seek people like Zacchaeus. As is always the case with pronouncement stories (stories in which Jesus makes a proclamation at the end of a narrative), the main point is the pronouncement. Here that pronouncement is that the mission of Jesus is to seek and save the lost. The central point of the story is not that Zacchaeus sought Jesus, but that Jesus seeks people like Zacchaeus, people who are sinners. Given the complex and multifaceted identity that Luke gives in his description of Zacchaeus, this pronouncement means that the mission of Jesus is to seek us all. It also suggests that we are all among the lost. We should see ourselves as people who belong among those who need the presence of Jesus and the salvation that he brings.

Repentance

As previously noted, a number of commentators think that Zacchaeus was already giving half of his income to the poor. But a majority continues to think that his brief encounter with Jesus changed his life. It does not seem that Jesus has even gotten to his house, but rather has only just headed off in the direction of the house of this sinner. The label "sinner" has different meanings in Luke. At times it designates people who ignore the word and will of God. But at other times, it is used for those whom the religious elite condemn as not dedicated enough to the ways they believe someone should live for God. It is a title some leaders use to look down on people who do not conform to their heightened expectations. It seems to have a broader meaning than this second definition here because it is the crowd that says this about Zacchaeus. Perhaps it is his profession and the general expectation that tax collectors are thieves that makes this plausible. In any case, Luke does not have anyone in the story refute the accusation. Indeed, the response of Zacchaeus may suggest that the charge was accepted.

Zacchaeus's encounter with Jesus immediately brings him to recognize Jesus as Lord and to commit himself to a new way of living. However he had gained his wealth, whether through honest or dishonest means, Zacchaeus now determines to use it in ways that Jesus approves. Earlier Jesus had told the rich ruler that he needed to sell all his possessions if he wanted to follow Jesus (18:18-23). Earlier Jesus had said that people who have a dinner party should invite people who cannot reciprocate so that God will receive them (14:12-14). Now Zacchaeus promises to give half of his possessions to the poor, to those who cannot repay him. In his repentance, he exemplifies what Jesus says wealthy people should do.

As a result of his encounter with Jesus, Zacchaeus takes up a new orientation of life. If he had been concerned about accumulating wealth, he is now more concerned to take care of the poor. If he had worried about elevating his status, he now helps those who cannot help him climb higher. He reaches out to those who can do him no good.

Coming into the presence of Jesus can reorient our lives. Repentance is not just about confessing sins; it is about changing how we live. Being in the presence of Jesus and recognizing him as Lord enabled Zacchaeus to conform his life to what God wants. It often seems like a monumental task when we think about changing the ways we live or leaving behind something that moves us to unfaithfulness to God. Zacchaeus is able to do this in our story because he sees how Jesus values him and he receives the salvation that Jesus brings. If we wonder where the strength to change our lives comes from, this story suggests that it comes from being in the presence of Christ and acknowledging that he is Lord.

A Child of Abraham

When he hears Zacchaeus commit himself to this way of life, Jesus declares that he is a child of Abraham, that is, one of the people of God. It is the combination of the confession of Jesus as Lord and the commitment to live in a way that recognizes that truth that is the evidence that Zacchaeus is among God's people. Whatever he had been before, his orientation of life now marks him as one who belongs among the saved. The salvation that he receives includes more than a promise of life to come. This salvation includes the expectation that we live in a new way. This expectation is part of the gift of salvation because this new way of living imbues our lives with meaning as we live as those created in God's image. At the same time, it gives dignity to those who need our help. This fullness of salvation is readily available to all as the gift that Christ gives all who seek him, for he is already seeking us.

SHARING THE SCRIPTURE

PREPARING TO TEACH

Preparing Our Hearts

Ponder this week's devotional reading from Isaiah 44:23-26. Why is creation called to sing and shout praise to God? How is your life affected by the redemption of Jacob (Israel)? What praises will you offer today? Whom will you ask to join you in praise?

Pray that you and the students will continuously sing praise and give thanks for who God is and for all that God has done.

Preparing Our Minds

Study the background Scripture and the lesson Scripture, both of which are from Luke 19:1-10.

Consider this question as you prepare the lesson: *How can we regain our bearings when we have lost our direction?*

Write on newsprint:
❏ a prayer of confession for Goal 3 in Sharing the Scripture.
❏ information for next week's lesson, found under Continue the Journey.
❏ activities for further spiritual growth in Continue the Journey.

Review the Introduction, The Big Picture, Close-up, and Faith in Action, which all precede the first lesson of this quarter. Consider how you might use any of this material in today's lesson.

LEADING THE CLASS

(1) Gather to Learn

❖ Welcome the class members and guests.

❖ Pray that those who have come today will joyously welcome Jesus and one another today.

❖ Ask: **Throughout the ages, what resources have travelers used to stay on course in order to reach their destinations?** Write ideas on newsprint. (Here are some examples: stars, landmarks, oral directions, signposts, maps, Global Positioning System [GPS].)

❖ Read aloud today's focus statement: **All have experienced a loss of direction in their lives and the inability to make necessary changes and new plans. How can they remedy this loss of direction? After Zacchaeus gladly welcomed Jesus with great faith and repentance, Jesus declared that his own mission was to seek and save the lost.**

(2) Goal 1: Study the Details of Zacchaeus's Encounter with Jesus

❖ Choose a volunteer to read Luke 19:1-10.

❖ **Optional:** If your group will engage in a lighthearted activity, sing "Zacchaeus Was a Wee Little Man," which many class members likely learned years ago in Sunday school. You can find words and directions for motions on websites such as www.makingmusicfun.net/htm/f_mmf_music_library_songbook/zacchaeus-lyrics.htm.

❖ Discuss these questions:

1. **Where in this story do you find words related to sight? What do these words suggest about Zacchaeus's intentions?** (See Luke 19:3, 4, 5, 7)

2. **How does Zacchaeus relate to the types of people that Jesus goes to seek?** (See Luke 19:1-4 in Understanding the Scripture.)

3. **In what ways were both Zacchaeus and Jesus seeking and finding?** (See "Seeking and Finding" in Interpreting the Scripture.)

4. **How does the crowd help or hinder Zacchaeus?** (See Luke 19:5-8 in Understanding the Scripture.)

5. **Why does Jesus say that Zacchaeus is a "son of Abraham"?** (See "A Child of Abraham" in Interpreting the Scripture.)

6. **How does the story of Zacchaeus's encounter with Jesus give you hope?** (See "Hope for Us All" in Interpreting the Scripture.)

(3) Goal 2: Believe that with God's Help the Learners Can Make Necessary Changes in Their Lives

❖ Recall the resources travelers used to reach their destinations discussed in "Gather to Learn" and ask: **What resources do believers have to stay on the course of their spiritual journeys?** (Answers may include Bible, prayer, worship, help from other believers, written records left by Christians through the centuries.)

❖ Distribute paper and pencils. Invite the adults to use a line to represent their own spiritual journeys. Encourage them to consider whether they are currently on the course that God wills for them. If not, recommend that they draw a line showing where they have veered off course and write a few words to state why they believe they are off course and, if they know, how they got lost. Suggest that they consider the changes that they must make to get back on course. They may want to write briefly about these intended changes.

❖ Conclude by inviting the learners to repeat after you these words from Philippians 4:13: **"I can do all things through [Christ] who strengthens me."**

(4) Goal 3: Repent of Shortcomings and Commit to Living Godly Lives

❖ Read "Repentance" from Interpreting the Scripture.

❖ Invite the adults to read in unison this prayer of confession from page 891 of *The United Methodist Hymnal* that you will read from the hymnal or have written on newsprint prior to the session:

**Almighty and most merciful God
we have erred and strayed from
    thy ways like lost sheep.
We have followed too much
the devices and desires of our
    own hearts.
We have offended against thy
    holy laws.
We have left undone
those things which we ought to
    have done,
and we have done
those things which we ought not
    to have done.
But thou, O Lord, have mercy
    upon us.
Spare thou those, O God, who
    confess their faults.
Restore thou those who are
    penitent,
according to thy promises
    declared in Christ Jesus our
    Lord.
And grant, O most merciful God,
    for his sake,
that we may hereafter live a godly,
    righteous, and sober life;
to the glory of thy holy name.
    Amen.**

(Pray in silence. Then one voice reads the following words taken from *The United Methodist Hymnal*, page 892)

**The saying is sure and worthy of
    full acceptance,
that Christ Jesus came into the
    world to save sinners.
(All) Thanks be to God.**

❖ Challenge the adults to recall these words of commitment throughout the week:

**May we hereafter live a godly,
righteous, and sober life for the
sake of Christ Jesus our Lord.**

(5) Continue the Journey

❖ Pray that as the learners depart, they will yearn, as Zacchaeus did, to see Jesus and repent of their sins.

❖ Post information for next week's session on newsprint for the students to copy:

- **Title: The Day of the Lord**
- **Background Scripture: Genesis 1:1–2:3; Zephaniah 1:2–2:4**
- **Lesson Scripture: Zephaniah 1:4-6, 14-16; 2:3**
- **Focus of the Lesson: People sometimes greatly damage strong and beautiful relationships with others and also with the earth. What can happen when someone does something that harms a relationship? Genesis tells that God created the heavens and the earth and all that lives on the earth, and declared creation to be good; Zephaniah describes the Israelites' marring of creation by sinning against God, thereby earning the Lord's promised punishment, and offers an opportunity for the people to seek righteousness to save their relationship with God.**

❖ Post the following information on newsprint and provide paper and pencils for the students to copy it. Challenge the adults to grow spiritually by completing one or more of these activities related to this week's session.

(1) Identify people that you believe are lost today. What might you do to seek out such people and lead them to Jesus? Take the first steps to reach out to them in a winning, nonjudgmental way.

(2) Study Isaiah 61:1-2 in which the prophet announces a message God has sent him to proclaim and Luke 4:18-19 in which Jesus states his own mission. Where do you see yourself fitting into this mission to the lost?

(3) Offer support to someone who yearns to see Jesus. Do whatever you can to help this person learn about Jesus and make a commitment to him.

❖ Sing or read aloud "Rejoice, the Lord Is King."

❖ Conclude today's session by leading the class in this benediction, which is adapted from Mark 9:23 in the lesson for March 6: **Together we affirm that all things can be done for the one who believes. Amen.**

FOURTH QUARTER
Toward a New Creation

JUNE 5, 2016–AUGUST 28, 2016

"Toward a New Creation," the course for the summer, examines selected passages from Zephaniah and Romans. These passages are set within the context of the broader theme of creation by using Genesis 1:1–2:3 as a portion of the background Scripture for Unit 1. Psalms 8; 104; 136:1-9, 26; and 148 are part of the background Scripture for Unit 2.

Unit 1, "Judgment and Salvation," comprises three lessons that each include background Scripture from Genesis 1:1–2:3 and the book of the seventh-century B.C. prophet Zephaniah. "The Day of the Lord," our lesson for June 5, examines Zephaniah 1:2–2:4, where the prophet implores the people to humble themselves and seek righteousness in preparation for the coming judgment. On June 12 we read in Zephaniah 3:1-8 about the wickedness of the people of Jerusalem, including its leading citizens, and "The Consequences of Disobedience" that the people must face. God offers "Assurances and Joy for the Faithful," according to Zephaniah 3:9-20, which we will study on June 19.

Unit 2, "A World Gone Wrong," begins on June 26 with background Scripture from Psalm 8 and Romans 1:18-32, which teaches that "Ignoring God's Plain Truth" will lead to disaster. On July 3 we turn to Psalm 104 and Romans 2:14-29 to see how we may be "Ignoring God's Truth Within Us." Psalm 136:1-9, 26 and Romans 3:9-20, the background Scripture for July 10, make clear that "We're All Under Sin's Power." As we learn on July 17 from Psalm 148 and Romans 3:21-31, sin is not the end of the story, for "God Set Things Right."

In the first lesson of Unit 3, "Life on God's Terms," on July 24, Paul tells us that we are "Not Without Hope," according to Romans 5:1-11. The background Scripture for July 31, Romans 6, speaks about baptism and shows us that "Death Becomes Life." We continue in Romans on August 7 with "Safe in God's Love," where we read in 8:28-39 that nothing can separate us from the love of God. "Living Under God's Mercy," the session for August 14 from Romans 9:6-29, helps us to know ourselves better as we consider our "spiritual family tree." In "God Prunes and Grafts" for the lesson from Romans 11:11-36 on August 21 Paul teaches that God has by no means rejected the Jews as Gentiles have been added to the "tree" of believers. The fourth quarter and Sunday school year end on August 28 with a session from Romans 12:1-2 and 13:8-14 where Paul sets forth the idea that "Love Fulfills the Law."

Meet Our Writer

REV. DAVID KALAS

David Kalas is the pastor of First United Methodist Church in Green Bay, Wisconsin, where he has served since 2011.

David grew up as the son of a United Methodist pastor, first in Madison, Wisconsin, and later in Cleveland, Ohio. After graduating from high school in Cleveland, he attended the University of Virginia, where he earned his bachelor's degree in English. He began his seminary work at Pittsburgh Theological Seminary and completed it at Union Theological Seminary of Virginia.

David felt his call to the ministry as a young teenager, and for the rest of his adolescent years his sense of purpose and preparation was for serving Christ and his church. He began his ministry while a college student, appointed as the student-pastor of two rural churches outside of Charlottesville, Virginia. He recalls with great fondness and gratitude the sweet and patient saints of Bingham's and Wesley Chapel United Methodist churches.

Because it was during his own teenage years that David came to Christ, began reading the Bible, and felt his calling, he has always had a heart for teens and for youth ministry. During the latter half of his college years and throughout his seminary training, David served as a youth minister. For six years, he worked with the youth of Church of the Saviour United Methodist Church in Cleveland, Ohio, followed by three years with the youth of Huguenot United Methodist Church in Richmond, Virginia. Even in his role as lead pastor of subsequent churches, he has made working with the youth of the church a personal priority.

Following seminary, David entered full-time pastoral ministry, serving a rural two-point charge in Virginia. A move to Wisconsin in 1996 was a happy return to his childhood home. For eight years, David served as pastor of Emmanuel United Methodist Church in Appleton, Wisconsin, followed by seven years in Whitewater, before moving to his current appointment in Green Bay.

In addition to *The New International Lesson Annual*, David has also contributed to a number of published collections of sermons, and is a regular writer for *Emphasis*, a lectionary-based resource for preachers.

David and his wife, Karen, have been married for thirty years. They met in their home church youth group when they were just teenagers in Cleveland and have been together ever since. They are the proud parents of three daughters: Angela, Lydia, and Susanna.

Another great love of David's life is the Holy Land. He has made six trips to that part of the world, and is always planning another pilgrimage. He has found his own reading of the Bible has been enriched by getting to know the land from which it came.

David is also an avid sports fan. He loves to play sports as recreation and to watch sports as relaxation. He is delighted to live and serve in Green Bay, the home of his beloved Packers. He also enjoys traveling, walking, tinkering with around-the-house projects, and spending as much time with his family as possible.

THE BIG PICTURE: THE GOOD, ACCEPTABLE, AND PERFECT WILL OF GOD

The text of The Lord's Prayer is not within the parameters of our readings for this upcoming quarter, but I would like for us to begin our study with one line from it. The prayer comprises a series of very brief, exemplary petitions. Along the way, Jesus teaches us to include in our praying this bold request: "Your will be done on earth as it is in heaven" (Matthew 6:10).

That phrase, like the prayer from which it comes, is so familiar to us that we may not give it much thought. Yet I believe that single, simple line contains profound implications for our understanding of God and of the gospel.

The petition is about the will of God, which is of immense importance to us. It reveals to us both God's heart and plan. And this particular prayer, "your will be done," includes two important implications. First, the request assumes that God's will is not done on earth. And, second, it suggests that God's will is done in heaven.

Now all of that may seem so obvious to us as to be truisms. Yet it is often the things that are obvious that deserve more careful attention from us. We pass quickly by the things that are familiar and self-evident, and in the process we miss their profundity and beauty. So let us examine what seems already familiar to discover more of the fullness of the gospel truth.

Thinking Bigger

We have an unhappy habit of domesticating the will of God. That is to say, we may think about it and talk about it only as it pertains to some particular matter or decision in our lives. Is it God's will for me to take this job? To marry? To move? To be healed?

These are not small matters, to be sure. They are certainly big to us. And yet, if those personal junctures are the only time we give serious thought to God's will, then we make it a smaller thing than it actually is. We think the sun is there to guarantee the warmth and pleasantness of the outdoor event we had planned, and we lose sight of the fact that it is a massive ball of fire so intensely hot that we need to be 93 million miles away from it in order to survive. The will of God is a bigger matter than just our individual decision points.

From time to time, therefore, perhaps we should set aside the question of what the will of God is and consider instead what the will of God is like. That is to say, rather than wondering only what that particular will is for some intersection in my life, let me wonder at the qualities of God's will in general. I may find that, once I have a clearer picture of what the divine will is like, I will be better positioned to perceive what that will is one situation at a time.

Jesus offers us a magnificent picture of what God's will is like. Pray for it to be done, he says, as it is done in heaven. Heaven, then, is put forward as the model for God's will, and that can be very helpful to us.

What do we know about heaven? Our space is too limited here, of course, to do an exhaustive examination of the subject as it is revealed in Scripture. At a minimum, though, we know that it is perfect. So it is that Jesus is encouraging us to pray for God's perfect will to be done. That kind of praying is no "weak resignation." It is not shrugging our shoulders and saying, "Que sera, sera." Rather, Jesus is encouraging us to think big and pray boldly: to petition for God's perfect will to be done here on earth as it is in heaven.

Heaven and Revelation

Since Jesus presents us with the prospect of heaven as a guide for our praying, let's think about heaven just a bit. The references and allusions to heaven over the sixty-six books of the Bible are too many to recite here. When we think of it, though, we think of radiance and glory. We know, too, that it will be free of sickness and sin. We think of abundance, freedom, and wholeness. When we ponder God's perfect someday, we remember the promise of natural adversaries in the animal kingdom laying down together (Isaiah 11:6-9) and swords being beaten into plowshares (Micah 4:3), prompting us to envision reconciliation and peace. We anticipate a perfect reign of justice and righteousness. We think of the Lord wiping away our tears, of endless day, of all things being made new, and of eternal life. And, most significant of all, when we think of heaven, we try to comprehend being in the very presence of God.

Historically, we see that the people of God tend to do more thinking about heaven and the culmination of the age when in the midst of troubles and suffering. That is to say, it is when the present life is bad that we think more about the life to come. We observe, for example, a lot of singing about heaven in the spirituals generated by the African slaves in the United States of the eighteenth and nineteenth centuries.

But we must not relegate the beauty of heaven to the future. It is a prospect to be anticipated, to be sure, but the perfection of heaven has implications for the present, as well. First, as we have noted, Jesus' model prayer invites us to make heaven our gauge when praying for God's will to be done in the here and now. And, second, inasmuch as heaven embodies God's will, it also reveals to us God's plan and heart.

From time to time in my pastoral counseling, I will try to help folks clarify their feelings about a situation by asking them, "What's your perfect picture?" For if individuals can articulate their perfect pictures, those visions can help them then to formulate a plan. And when you see a person's perfect picture, you also get a peek into his or her heart.

Of course, we human beings have so many limitations that we cannot guarantee our perfect picture simply by making a plan. You and I have made plenty of plans that did not come to fruition. God, however, does not suffer from those limitations. And so when Scripture offers us glimpses of God's perfect picture, we may count on it coming to pass in the end. And, as with human beings, that perfect picture offers insight into God's heart.

Consider heaven, therefore, and see God's perfect picture. It shows us what the Lord values and desires and intends to make happen. And if God values and desires it in the end, we may count on God to value and desire it in the present, as well.

I've Got Good News and Bad News

Heaven is the good news. It reveals God's heart and reflects the divine plan and promises. In short, it's all good.

But when Jesus said that we should pray for God's will to be done on earth as it is in heaven, he was indicating the bad news as well, namely, that God's will is not always done on earth. That should be self-evident, of course. Whether in the big picture of international conflict or the small-scale setting of broken relationships and personal tragedies, we need not look far for evidence that God's will is not always done on earth.

The heartache and irony of that fact, however, is that it represents such a departure from God's original design. Originally God's will was meant to be done on earth as it is in heaven. Perfection was not postponed by God, but rather it was derailed by us. Everything had been made altogether good (see Genesis 1:31), according to God's values and desires.

The way people use the term "paradise" is telling. What does the term bring to your mind? Probably one of two things, for it is used to refer both to Eden and to heaven. At both the beginning and the end, Scripture gives us glimpses of God's perfect picture. And since God's creation was perfect at the start and promises to be perfect at the end, the question for us to consider is what happens in between.

The Bible provides us with clear answers: In between comes the Fall. In between comes sin and rebellion. In between comes unresponsiveness and unfaithfulness on the part of humanity, including God's own covenant people. And in the face of all of that, what is a perfect God to do?

Make and Keep Me Pure

I think I have known two kinds of perfectionists in my life: those who are strong and those who are weak. The weak perfectionist is the one who wants everything to be perfect, but who is too easily discouraged. For this individual, perfection is a fragile thing, easily ruined. He wants the trip to be perfect, but waves the white flag as soon as something goes wrong. She wants everything around the house to be just so, but is quickly overwhelmed by messes or setbacks. They want their relationship to be perfect, but become despondent at the first sign of conflict or disagreement.

The weak perfectionist not only *wants* everything to be perfect but also *needs* everything to be perfect. But that type of person finds it so hard to cope with imperfection that he or she is no good at making or keeping things perfect.

The strong perfectionist, on the other hand, is better equipped to achieve the desired goal. This is the person who is not rattled by imperfections but rather is motivated by them. Such people have a clear sense of the way things ought to be. They neither buy into nor resign themselves to the status quo, but instead press on toward the objectives. These are the roll-up-their-sleeves-and-get-it-done types. These are people who revel in words like "reform" and "redemption."

The weak and the strong perfectionist want the same thing. They long for the same destination. The one is far better equipped to reach that destination, however. Ironically, the person who is better at coping with imperfection stands the best chance of achieving perfection.

In The Lord's Prayer, it seems to me that Jesus is encouraging us to be strong perfectionists. He concedes the reality that God's will is not done on earth, and yet he instructs us not to surrender to that reality. On the contrary, we are encouraged to pray against the grain, to pray upstream in this world. We keep our eyes on that perfect destination—heaven—and we pray for here to be like there, for now to be like then.

It should not surprise us, of course, that the Lord wants us to be strong perfectionists. That, after all, is one way that we become more like the Creator in whose image we were made. For God is not overwhelmed or deflated by the fallen world and its imperfect human beings. The Lord did not wave the white flag and surrender. On the contrary, our Creator is also our Redeemer, who keeps in view the perfect picture and endeavors to make it happen.

Something Old, Something New

You and I live in a disposable culture. In addition to all of the paper and plastic things that are specifically designed to be used once and discarded, we also find that a disposable mentality has crept into other areas of life as well, like our technology. We discover that it is cheaper to replace than to repair. When the device, appliance, or gadget is no longer working properly, the salesperson at the store does not encourage us to get it fixed. Instead, we are told to just toss it out and get a new one.

In contrast to that culture, see the priorities and the choices of our God. Certainly no one is more able to dispose of something that is broken. And no one is better equipped to start over with something new. God can, after all, create whatever is desired, and can do it for free. God has elected to do the costly thing: that which is unimaginably costly, costly beyond our measuring. God has chosen to repair what is broken, and to do it at great expense— the cost of the Beloved Son, Jesus. Rather than cast off the old, God makes it new (for example, 2 Corinthians 5:17; Revelation 21:5). It proves to be a long, slow process, yet God persists in our redemption. And our Creator patiently, strongly, lovingly works through all of the imperfections in order to realize the perfect picture.

During the coming thirteen weeks, we will watch this good news unfold. We will explore both Old and New Testament texts, which bear witness to the same truths. That should not surprise us, of course, since they reveal the same God, who does not change (see Malachi 3:6; Hebrews 13:8).

The story opens with a God who created everything to be perfect from the beginning. That perfect picture is marred, however, by human disobedience. All sorts of faithlessness, failure, and rebellion follow. And even when the human culprits themselves occasionally desire the same perfect picture that God intends, they still find themselves unable to achieve it.

It is left to God, then, to make things right. God does make things right by revealing what is right in creation and defining what is right in the law given through Moses to the Hebrew people when they were wandering in the desert. Where individuals or groups are determined to do wrong, God periodically steps in to make things right by acts of judgment. And, in Christ, God steps in to make things right by means of merciful and gracious justification.

In the weeks ahead, we will see how tightly knit together these matters are. Perfection, creation, righteousness, law, judgment, and justification—these are all natural and inseparable companions. And so it must be, for they are all extensions of the character of God, which is constant and pure.

So Jesus urges us to pray for God's will to be done. What does that look like? Well, it looks like heaven! It looks like the perfect picture we can see when we peek into God's heart. That heart of God is revealed in every aspect of the word of God: the commandments, the promises, and the divine activity within history. And it is that very heart of God that does not give up on the earth where the perfect will is not done, but rather sets out to make everything right.

CLOSE-UP: THE DAY OF THE LORD

This quarter's theme is "creation." The background Scriptures from Genesis 1:1–2:3 (Unit 1) and Psalms 8; 104; 136; and 148 (Unit 2) highlight God's work as the creator. The lesson Scriptures throughout the summer look forward to a new creation, a time after God has judged sin and set things right in a world that had gone terribly wrong.

This time when God will intervene in human history to punish evildoers, deliver the faithful ones, and establish divine rule is referred to sixteen times in the Old Testament as "the day of the LORD." Similar terms are also used to refer to this time of judgment and salvation: "on that day" (Zephaniah 1:9-10; Amos 8:9); "the day of the LORD's sacrifice" (Zephaniah 1:8); "the day of the wrath of the LORD" (Ezekiel 7:19).

Some scholars assert that this event is the main message of the prophets. On the day of the Lord, God will punish Israel and Judah, as well as neighboring nations that have committed atrocities. The books of Joel and Zephaniah particularly focus on this day. Amos is thought to be the first prophet to suggest that instead of their longed-for conquest of enemies, the Israelites themselves will face God's judgment (Amos 5:18-20). The way that God will bring about this punishment is through military defeat. God's purpose is not to destroy but rather to cleanse the covenant people from the evils of idolatry, pride, and injustice—evils for which Israel's leadership is especially responsible.

Isaiah, Zephaniah, and Zechariah see not only the destruction of Israel but also a global event. Zephaniah goes even further by depicting this event as a "reversal of creation" (see 1:2-3) that, as Greg A. King notes, will be "more vast than even that brought about by the Flood." But judgment is not the end of the story. As a result of judgment, a group of people known as "the remnant" will be cleansed and blessed because they humbly sought the Lord (see Zephaniah 3:11-13). This remnant will return to their homeland and live with God in their midst (Zephaniah 3:15, 20; Amos 9:14-15).

The New Testament reports that there will be a final judgment, a time when the faithful will be rewarded and evildoers will be punished. This time of accountability, often referred to as the day of our Lord Jesus Christ, is associated with the Second Coming of Christ (see, for example, 1 Corinthians 1:8; 2 Corinthians 1:14; Philippians 1:6; 1 Thessalonians 5:2; 2 Peter 3:10-13). As did Isaiah, Joel, and Zephaniah, Paul proclaimed that the day was near (Romans 13:11-12). In Mark 13, Jesus taught that although we would see signs, only God the Father knew the exact time. Consequently, Jesus called his followers to keep awake and live as the people of God while waiting for his return.

Faith in Action: Living Toward God's New Creation

During the summer quarter we are looking at God's creation, especially how human behavior has marred what God called "good." Consequently, all humanity will be judged so that God can set things right and people can live again on the terms that God has set forth. Post these activities on newsprint and suggest that the adults select several to complete at home over the next thirteen weeks. Note that all of them are rooted in the sessions for Unit 3 from Romans.

- Offer assurance to someone who is struggling so that he or she may have hope and experience reconciliation with God through Jesus and the peace that this relationship brings.
- "Boast" about what God has done for humanity through Jesus, who died for sinners that all may be put right (justified) with God and thereby saved.
- Ponder the meaning of your baptism. Even if you cannot remember the actual act, what does it mean to you to know that you have been made a new creature in Christ and are now identified with him?
- Keep a record of instances during this quarter when you know that Romans 8:28—God working for good in you because you love God and are called according to God's purposes—has been true. Use these instances to witness to others about God's unfailing love and care.
- Be alert for news about situations where evil appears to be working against people. Affirm the truth of Romans 8:31, 37-39, that if God is for us nothing can be against us. Surround with prayer those who are being beset by evil.
- Identify and give thanks for those people who are part of your "spiritual family tree." What did they do to help you make a commitment to Christ and grow closer to him? In what ways have you passed on their legacy to others?
- Think back over your life. Was there ever a time that you rejected Christ, perhaps due to pride or arrogance? What prompted your rejection? Having stumbled, what did you do to return to him? Who helped you?
- Perform a random act of kindness for a stranger. Do this not because you expect to receive thanks or a reward but because you want your love of God to flow out to others. How did this person respond to action?
- Follow Paul's command in Romans 12:1-2 by presenting your body as a "living sacrifice," as a way of worshiping God. Consider how this command may alter your concept of worship. Also discern how your way of living in the world is "holy and acceptable to God," not just when you are at church but at all times. What are some attitudes you need to hold, behaviors you need to engage in, and actions you need to avoid in order to be seen by God as "holy and acceptable"?

Pronunciation Guide

abodah (ab o daw')
Achan (ay' kan)
Apollinaris (apol li naris')
Baal (bay' uhl) or (bah ahl')
chronos (kroh' nohs)
Chrysostom (kris' uh stuh m) or (kri sos' tuh m)
dikaioo (dik ah yo' o)
dikaiosune (dik ah yos oo' nay)
elpis (el pece')
Gnostic (nos' tik)
hupernikao (hoop er nik ah' o)

Jabal (jay' buhl)
Jubal (joo' buhl)
kairos (ki' rohs)
koine (koi nay')
Korah (kor' uh)
Laodicea (lay od i see' uh)
Leviathan (li vi' uh thuhn)
Milcom (mil' kuhm)
nikao (nik ah' o)
Sennacherib (suh nak' uh rib)
shabbat (shab bawth')
Zephaniah (zef uh ni' uh)

UNIT 1: JUDGMENT AND SALVATION
THE DAY OF THE LORD

PREVIEWING THE LESSON

Lesson Scripture: Zephaniah 1:4-6, 14-16; 2:3
Background Scripture: Genesis 1:1–2:3; Zephaniah 1:2–2:4
Key Verse: Zephaniah 2:3

Focus of the Lesson:

People sometimes greatly damage strong and beautiful relationships with others and also with the earth. What can happen when someone does something that harms a relationship? Genesis tells that God created the heavens and the earth and all that lives on the earth, and declared creation to be good; Zephaniah describes the Israelites marring of creation by sinning against God, thereby earning the Lord's promised punishment, and offers an opportunity for the people to seek righteousness to save their relationship with God.

Goals for the Learners:

(1) to learn that on the Great Day of the Lord, the Creator of the universe will punish those who have not repented and humbled themselves under God's authority.
(2) to recognize the relationship between righteous living and one's responsibility to maintain "the good" found in God's created order.
(3) to encourage them to repent and reaffirm their faithfulness to God.

Supplies:

Bibles, newsprint and marker, paper and pencils, hymnals

READING THE SCRIPTURE

NRSV	CEB
Lesson Scripture: Zephaniah 1:4-6, 14-16	Lesson Scripture: Zephaniah 1:4-6, 14-16
⁴I will stretch out my hand against Judah,	⁴I will stretch out my hand against Judah
and against all the inhabitants of	and against all the inhabitants of

Jerusalem;
and I will cut off from this place
    every remnant of Baal
    and the name of the idolatrous
      priests;
⁵those who bow down on the roofs
    to the host of the heavens;
those who bow down and swear to
    the LORD,
    but also swear by Milcom;
⁶those who have turned back from
    following the LORD,
    who have not sought the LORD or
      inquired of him.
¹⁴The great day of the LORD is near,
    near and hastening fast;
the sound of the day of the LORD is
    bitter,
    the warrior cries aloud there.
¹⁵That day will be a day of wrath,
    a day of distress and anguish,
a day of ruin and devastation,
    a day of darkness and gloom,
a day of clouds and thick darkness,
    ¹⁶a day of trumpet blast and battle
    cry
against the fortified cities
    and against the lofty battlements.

Lesson Scripture: Zephaniah 2:3
³**Seek the LORD, all you humble of
    the land,
    who do his commands;
seek righteousness, seek humility;
    perhaps you may be hidden
    on the day of the LORD's wrath.**

Jerusalem.
I will eliminate what's left of Baal
    from this place
    and the names of the priests of
      foreign gods,
⁵those bowing down to the
    forces of heaven on the rooftops,
    those swearing by the LORD along
    with those swearing by Milcom,
⁶those turning away from the LORD,
    those who don't seek the LORD
    and don't pursue him.
¹⁴The great day of the LORD is near;
    it is near and coming very quickly.
The sound of the day of the LORD is
    bitter.
    A warrior screams there.
¹⁵That day is a day of fury,
    a day of distress and anxiety,
    a day of desolation and
      devastation,
    a day of darkness and gloominess,
    a day of clouds and deep
      darkness,
¹⁶a day for blowing the trumpet
    and alarm
against their invincible cities
    and against their high towers.

Lesson Scripture: Zephaniah 2:3
³**Seek the LORD, all you humble
    of the land who practice his
    justice;
seek righteousness;
seek humility.
Maybe you will be hidden
    on the day of the LORD's anger.**

UNDERSTANDING THE SCRIPTURE

Introduction. People who are products of a scientific age clamor for all sorts of information and details, but the biblical author is wiser. With an amazing economy of words, the writer offers deep insights into God, humanity, and creation. The questions that plague the modern mind are comparatively minor issues when set against the profound and eternal truths presented here.

Genesis 1:1-2. In this opening

chapter of Genesis the writer describes a cosmic before-and-after picture. It's not merely that nothing exists prior to God's creative act. Rather, there is a mysterious "deep," which is marked by three telling attributes: emptiness, darkness, and formlessness. As the story unfolds, however, the word of God introduces into that primordial mist light and order, color and variety, abundance and fruitfulness. And by the time this creative work is finished, God has established ongoing solutions to the prior deficiencies: sources of light, reproducing creatures to populate the earth, and human beings with dominion to preserve order.

Genesis 1:3-25. The account of creation is filled with so much beauty and insight. Our ambition in this small space can only be to highlight the broad patterns. First, we see that God creates with the divine word, which is emblematic of God's authority. We note, too, that the Bible understands a day as evening and morning, rather than morning and evening—a point that is later reflected in Jewish timekeeping. We observe separation as a recurring element of the creation process, perhaps as part of bringing order. We recognize that the living parts of creation are all designed to reproduce, and to do so abundantly. Finally, there is the inescapable refrain that it was all good. Of course it was, for God had made it.

Genesis 1:26-30. The creation of human beings emerges as unique within the larger story. The familiar "let there be" gives way to the much more personal "let us make." And, most significantly, while everything else had been fashioned according to God's will and pleasure, one part of creation is fashioned according to God's image and likeness. Even before the human beings have been made, they have been vested with authority and responsibility: "dominion over" all the elements of God's creation on earth. And once they are made, they are commanded both to "fill the earth and to subdue it" (1:28). While God's creating act is complete, there is evidently still work to be done in creation, and it remains for human beings to do it.

Genesis 1:31–2:3. Creation culminates with three acts by God that the reader likely cannot anticipate. First, there is the emphatic approval. All had been good before, each step along the way. But now that it was complete, God saw that it was all "very good." Then the Creator rests. Who would have imagined that God rested? And who could have been wise enough to suppose that rest is a necessary complement to work—that the week would be literally incomplete without it? And, finally, God hallowed the seventh day. Lest we overlook the day of rest as a curious detail in the larger creation story, we see that God's final action in that story is to single out that day and make it holy.

Zephaniah 1:2-3. Zephaniah was a judgment prophet, who lived in Judah during the late seventh century B.C., the era of King Josiah (reigned 640–609 B.C.) and the growing Babylonian Empire. In startling contrast to the loveliness of the creation story we had been reading, however, these first words from Zephaniah read like an anti-creation story. The Lord's judgment promises to be as thorough as creation. The destruction will be as comprehensive as the formation had been.

Zephaniah 1:4-6. After the universal calamity described in the first verses, we see the judgment of God more narrowly focused in these verses. Judah and Jerusalem are God's surprising targets, and specifically the idolaters in the land. The terror of the early verses indicates the seriousness of the idolatry identified here.

Zephaniah 1:7-13. Now the coming judgment of God is attached to a particular day, and the prophet paints a terrible picture of what will happen on that day. The Lord identifies those who will be punished "on that day," from the morally corrupt leaders to the spiritually complacent merchants. In contrast to the global calamity of the first verses, now the judgment of God has names and faces attached to it. Meanwhile, specific places are included, too, bringing the frightening prospect very close to home for Zephaniah's audience.

Zephaniah 1:14-16. The "day of the LORD" is a prominent and recurring theme in Scripture. It is not a single, twenty-four-hour day, nor is it characterized by a single mood or activity. Rather, the phrase anticipates the climactic time when God will step into history to make things right. For the righteous and those who suffer unjustly, that day is rightly anticipated. For those whose lives cut across the grain of God's will, however, that day is a dreadful prospect.

And for the audience of this judgment prophet, we see that the day of the Lord promised not only to be terrible but also close at hand.

Zephaniah 1:17-18. Three unsettling similes mark this judgment message. The people will become like the blind, their blood will be like dust, and their flesh will be like dung. Each image suggests degradation and disaster. The subsequent warning about their silver and their gold emphasizes the futility and hopelessness of their situation. And the concluding image of fire consuming the whole earth recalls the kind of global destruction described in the opening verses of the chapter.

Zephaniah 2:1-4. The warnings of chapter 1 painted a hopeless picture. The audience had cause only to despair, it seemed. But now, with the first verses of chapter 2, we meet a new opportunity. The invitations to "gather together" (2:1) and "seek the LORD" (2:3) suggest a reason for hope. "Perhaps you may be hidden on the day of the LORD's wrath," says the prophet in verse 3. Disaster is coming, to be sure, but the people of God may spare themselves from it if they will seek humility and righteousness.

INTERPRETING THE SCRIPTURE

Well Begun

The story of creation has a tragic poignancy to it. Reading the account in Genesis 1 is like looking at the wedding album of a couple who has since divorced. There is so much beauty, promise, and hope in the beginning, yet we know how sour and unhappy it turns after a time.

We are fond of saying that "well begun is half done," and perhaps that is especially true of God's creation. It was all well begun, indeed, for the Lord had made everything perfect. And yet it was only half-done in the sense that, by design, creation was not a static thing. It featured growth and change. It required tending and stewardship. It was designed to multiply and reproduce.

While God's work of creating was done after six days, there still remained work to do. And a portion of that work fell to the human beings, who were made in God's own image and given dominion over all of creation.

We know how unhappily the story unfolds from that point.

Disappointment, we find, is always in proportion to expectation. If you do not expect much, you cannot be very disappointed. But we observe that the part of God's creation with the greatest potential proves, in the end, to be the most profound disappointment. The man and the woman, who were originally vested with lordship over the garden, now cower and clutch at their coverings as they leave Eden in disgrace.

Yet the heart of God never changes. Creation changes, but its Creator does not. For the One who made all things perfect in the beginning does not lose the desire for everything to be just so. And so, again and again throughout the biblical story, we see that God's endeavor is to redeem the fallen creation. Just as God had made it all good to begin with, so God undertakes to make it all good again.

The Day God Makes Things Good

One of the hallmarks of the Creation account in Genesis is the recurring phrase: "God saw that it was good" (1:4, 10, 12, 18, 21, 25). Such was the nature of creation. It was good; indeed, altogether, "it was very good" (1:31). That's how God made it from the start.

That God made it good, however, is only the beginning of the good news about our Creator. The rest of the good news is revealed in how God responds when creation turns bad.

Certainly God had the capacity, after all, simply to wad it all up and throw it away. Who could have stopped the Creator of all things? Yet our Creator did not discard or destroy the fallen creation, but rather set out to redeem and re-create it.

Through the unfolding years of Old Testament history, the people of God came to recognize that the Lord would, from time to time, step into human affairs in order to make things right. The deliverance of the Hebrew slaves from their bondage in Egypt was such an occasion. So, too, the parting of the Red Sea. Punishment of the wicked and the elimination of the rebellious were also necessary parts of making things right, which Israel recalled in the stories of Sodom's destruction (Genesis 18–19), Korah's rebellion (Numbers 16), and Achan's sin (Joshua 7).

Later in the Old Testament, the prophets looked ahead toward a climactic moment when God would step into history again to make things right. That moment was called "the day of the Lord," and across the many messages of the prophets we see manifold facets of that day. On the day of the Lord, the oppressor will be defeated, the wicked will be judged, and the captive will be released. On the day of the Lord, the humble will be exalted, the righteous will be rewarded, and a new covenant will be established. And on the day of the Lord, a perfect king will come to reign forever, with a global rule of peace, justice, and prosperity.

The prophet Zephaniah spoke about the coming day of the Lord, and for his audience it was not good news. The promise that God is coming to make things right sounds good—unless you are part of what's wrong. And Zephaniah's audience is identified as part of what's wrong.

The description of the day of the Lord reads like a menacing forecast. If a meteorologist were able to show footage of a tornado's destruction before it arrived, that would be the look and feel of this prophecy. Zephaniah's warning not only puts the people on alert about the imminence of the calamity to come but it also paints a detailed picture of it.

Unlike a tornado with its many innocent victims, however, this forecasted calamity is targeted and deserved. The people have offended God with their idolatry and injustice. And so the disaster will truly be an act of God, for it is justified divine judgment. Yet such destructiveness is not inconsistent with God's character, for it is all part of a fervent desire to make things right. To destroy what is bad is just as important as to create what is good.

God of the Altar Call

Perhaps we are squeamish about the judgment of God. Perhaps we think it would be kinder not to bring the sort of destruction warned of by Zephaniah. Of course, we know better in other areas of life. We know it is not kindness for the doctor to leave a tumor in place just so that he can avoid for us the trauma of surgery. We know that it is not kindness for a

parent to leave a child uncorrected. So, too, it would be a great unkindness for God to let wickedness go unchecked and evil undefeated. We may rejoice, therefore, that God always endeavors to get rid of what is bad.

It turns out, however, that there is more than one way to get rid of what is bad. Judgment and destruction are not the only answers. Indeed, they are not even the preferred means. Rather, the Lord favors redemption.

Imagine a man who foolishly locks himself into a condemned building. The dilapidated and dangerous eyesore is scheduled for demolition. If only the hypothetical fool would move out and live elsewhere he would be safe. When the building comes down, he dies unnecessarily.

Such is the plight of the unrepentant sinner. Sin must be destroyed, and so the sinner who clings to it dooms himself. Ah, but if only he will move out. If he will let go of his sin and walk away from it, then he may be saved.

So it is that God's prophet is sent not only to warn of judgment; he also encourages the people to repent. "Seek the LORD," Zephaniah declares in today's key verse (2:3), and "seek righteousness, seek humility." Our God would rather cure than kill. And so, even in the face of calamity, the invitation of grace persists so that "perhaps you may be hidden on the day of the LORD's wrath" (2:3).

SHARING THE SCRIPTURE

PREPARING TO TEACH

Preparing Our Hearts

Ponder this week's devotional reading from Isaiah 25:6-10. What time is it? Where are we? What is happening here? What do you learn about God? What do you learn about humanity and God's intentions for us?

Pray that you and the students will

be ready to participate in this heavenly banquet.

Preparing Our Minds

Study the background Scripture from Genesis 1:1–2:3; Zephaniah 1:2–2:4. The lesson Scripture is from Zephaniah 1:4-6, 14-16; 2:3.

Consider this question as you prepare the lesson: *What can happen when someone does something that harms a relationship?*

Write on newsprint:
❏ prayer of confession for Goal 3 in Sharing the Scripture.
❏ information for next week's lesson, found under Continue the Journey.
❏ activities for further spiritual growth in Continue the Journey.

Review the Introduction, The Big Picture, Close-up, and Faith in Action, which all precede the first lesson of this quarter. Consider how you might use any of this material in today's lesson.

LEADING THE CLASS

(1) Gather to Learn

❖ Welcome the class members and guests.

❖ Pray that those who have come today will live so as to be prepared for the day of the Lord.

❖ Read: **Most of us have dealt with the tragedy of divorce, either within our families, within our circle of friends, or within our own marriages. She says, "I don't love you anymore" and walks out with the children in tow. He finds a younger woman and decides that she is more attractive and interesting than his wife of thirty years.**

The ripple effect draws extended family, friends, and colleagues into the circle of damaged relationships. Time and money may be spent on lawyers battling as a divorce settlement and custody arrangements are hammered out. Children, who are often pawns in this process, may suffer consequences over decades. What was once a loving relationship has been irreparably damaged.

❖ Read aloud today's focus statement: **People sometimes greatly damage strong and beautiful relationships with others and also with the earth. What can happen when someone does something that harms a relationship? Genesis tells that God created the heavens and the earth and all that lives on the earth, and declared creation to be good; Zephaniah describes the Israelites marring of creation by sinning against God, thereby earning the Lord's promised punishment, and offers an opportunity for the people to seek righteousness and save their relationship with God.**

(2) Goal 1: Learn that on the Great Day of the Lord, God the Creator of the Universe Will Punish Those Who Have Not Repented and Humbled Themselves Under God's Authority.

❖ Set today's lesson from the prophet Zephaniah within the context of the creation by reading or retelling "Well Begun" in Interpreting the Scripture.

❖ Select a volunteer to read Zephaniah 1:4-6, 14-16.

❖ Discuss these questions:
1. **What does Zephaniah reveal about the day of the Lord?** (Close-up includes information

about Zephaniah's view of the day of the Lord.)

2. **What do you believe about the day of the Lord?** (Read "God of the Altar Call" in Interpreting the Scripture to help the adults understand that judgment is a last resort. What God really wants from us is repentance.)

3. **Who does the prophet say will be punished on the day of the Lord—and why?** (See Zephaniah 1:4-6 and 7-13 in Understanding the Scripture.)

4. Lead the class in a unison reading of today's key verse, Zephaniah 2:3. **What hope does the prophet provide?**

(3) Goal 2: Recognize the Relationship Between Righteous Living and One's Responsibility to Maintain "the Good" Found in God's Created Order

❖ Read "The Day God Makes Things Good" in Interpreting the Scripture. Notice that God continues to work to make things good, even after the actions of humanity caused the good to go sour. Zephaniah warns about the day of the Lord that will come as judgment on the wicked. Yet God had created humanity to be stewards of creation—to take good care of it (Genesis 1:26). Stewardship of God's creation, therefore, is an integral part of righteous living.

❖ Post a sheet of newsprint and encourage participants to answer this question: **What actions can believers take to demonstrate by their stewardship the righteous living to which God calls them?** List ideas on newsprint.

❖ Review the list. Encourage the students to engage in at least one of these actions as individuals. Perhaps

the class will discover an idea that they want to put into practice as a group.

(4) Goal 3: Encourage the Learners to Repent and Reaffirm Their Faithfulness to God

❖ Remind the learners of God's call in Zephaniah 2:3 to seek the Lord in humility.

❖ Read in unison the following prayer of confession, which you will post on newsprint. Or, if you have access to *The United Methodist Hymnal*, you will find this prayer on page 890. Alternatively, you may choose to use again the prayer of confession from last week's lesson or a different prayer of repentance from another hymnal.

> **Most merciful God,**
> **we confess that we have sinned against you**
> **in thought, word, and deed,**
> **by what we have done,**
> **and by what we have left undone.**
> **We have not loved you with our whole heart;**
> **we have not loved our neighbors as ourselves.**
> **We are truly sorry and we humbly repent.**
> **For the sake of your Son Jesus Christ,**
> **have mercy on us and forgive us;**
> **that we may delight in your will,**
> **and walk in your ways,**
> **to the glory of your name. Amen.**

❖ Allow a few moments for silent prayer and then read: **Almighty God have mercy on you and forgive all your sins through our Lord Jesus Christ. Amen.**

❖ Challenge the adults to include

a prayer of confession, which they have found or written themselves, in their daily devotions.

(5) Continue the Journey

❖ Pray that as the learners depart, they will repent and live righteously as God's humble people.

❖ Post information for next week's session on newsprint for the students to copy:

- Title: The Consequences of Disobedience
- Background Scripture: Genesis 1:1–2:3; Zephaniah 3:1-8
- Lesson Scripture: Zephaniah 3:6-8
- Focus of the Lesson: Sometimes people persist in destroying something that has been created beautiful even when they know the grave consequences. What are some consequences of destroying a good thing? Genesis tells that God created the light and the swarms of living creatures and God declared creation to be good; Zephaniah recounts how God began punishing the people for their disobedience, hoping that they would respond by correcting their behavior.

❖ Post the following information on newsprint and provide paper and pencils for the students to copy it. Challenge the adults to grow spiritually by completing one or more of these activities related to this week's session.

(1) Research the term "day of the Lord." Where do you find it in the Bible? What is expected to happen on this day? What are your hopes and dreams for this day?

(2) Review the key verse from Zephaniah 2:3. How do you define the terms "righteousness" and "humility"? What are you doing to live as one who is both righteous and humble before the Lord?

(3) Read all three chapters of Nahum. How does the message of this prophet compare and contrast with that of Zephaniah? How do Nahum's words give you hope—or do they?

❖ Sing or read aloud "Creator of the Earth and Skies."

❖ Conclude today's session by leading the class in this benediction, which is adapted from Romans 8:31b, the key verse for August 7: Let us go forth rejoicing in the knowledge that since God is for us, nothing in all creation can be against us. Amen.

UNIT 1: JUDGMENT AND SALVATION

THE CONSEQUENCES OF DISOBEDIENCE

PREVIEWING THE LESSON

Lesson Scripture: Zephaniah 3:6-8
Background Scripture: Genesis 1:1–2:3; Zephaniah 3:1-8
Key Verse: Zephaniah 3:8

Focus of the Lesson:

Sometimes people persist in destroying something that has been created beautiful even when they know the grave consequences. What are some consequences of destroying a good thing? Genesis tells that God created the light and the swarms of living creatures and God declared creation to be good; Zephaniah recounts how God began punishing the people for their disobedience, hoping that they would respond by correcting their behavior.

Goals for the Learners:

(1) to discern from Zephaniah's prophesy that God wanted to save the people, but they refused to accept correction.
(2) to realize that the loving Creator will give rebellious people opportunities to repent and change their ways.
(3) to identify and repent of actions and attitudes displeasing to God.

Supplies:

Bibles, newsprint and marker, paper and pencils, hymnals

READING THE SCRIPTURE

NRSV

Lesson Scripture: Zephaniah 3:6-8
⁶I have cut off nations;
　　their battlements are in ruins;
I have laid waste their streets
　　so that no one walks in them;
their cities have been made desolate,

CEB

Lesson Scripture: Zephaniah 3:6-8
⁶I will cut off nations;
　　their towers will be destroyed;
I will devastate their streets.
　　No one will pass through.
Their cities will be laid waste.

without people, without
inhabitants.
⁷I said, "Surely the city will fear me,
it will accept correction;
it will not lose sight
of all that I have brought upon it."
But they were the more eager
to make all their deeds corrupt.
⁸**Therefore wait for me, says the**
LORD,
for the day when I arise as a
witness.
For my decision is to gather nations,
to assemble kingdoms,
to pour out upon them my
indignation,
all the heat of my anger;
for in the fire of my passion
all the earth shall be consumed.

There will be no person, no inhab-
itant left.
⁷I said, "Surely, she will fear me;
she will take instruction
so that her habitation won't be cut
off
because of everything I did to
her."
However, they rose early to corrupt
their deeds.
⁸**Therefore, wait for me, says the**
LORD,
wait for the day when I rise up as
a witness,
when I decide to gather nations, to
collect kingdoms,
to pour out my indignation upon
them,
all the heat of my anger.
In the fire of my jealousy,
all the earth will be devoured.

UNDERSTANDING THE SCRIPTURE

Genesis 1:1-5. The first act of God is to bring light. As the larger story of Scripture unfolds, we observe the profound associations made with both light and darkness. Light is linked with truth, knowledge, wisdom, glory, and life. Darkness, by contrast, is related to evil, ignorance, and death. This first creative act of speaking light into darkness is emblematic, therefore, of God's ongoing redemptive work.

Genesis 1:6-13. If we could physically portray God in the story of creation, hands would be conspicuously absent. We rightly cherish, both from Scripture and from song, lovely and powerful images of the hands of God. Yet the prominent physical features of God in the creation story are not hands but a mouth and eyes. The key actions throughout the creation story concern

what God said and saw. God's mouth speaks everything into being, and God's eyes see that it is good.

Genesis 1:14-19. We observed that God's first action is to bring light. That was on the first day. Interestingly, however, it is not until the fourth day that God creates what we customarily think of as the sources of light. It is as though God walked into a dark, empty room on day one and said, "Light," and the room was illuminated. It was not until a few days later, however, that the Creator finally got around to installing the wiring and fixtures. The story challenges us, therefore, to reconsider the real source of light (compare Isaiah 60:19; Revelation 21:23).

Genesis 1:20-25. In dramatic contrast to the "formless void" with which the scene began in verse 1, now the stage is filled with variety and abundance. Words and phrases such as "swarms," "fruitful," "multiply," and "every kind" bear witness to the eye-popping abundance of God's creativity, design, and will.

Genesis 1:26. Here God says, "let us make," thus indicating, as Terence Fretheim notes, that "God is not in heaven alone, but is engaged in a relationship of mutuality." Historically, Christian theologians, including John Wesley, have understood this to be a reference (or at least possible reference) to the Trinity. Other explanations—such as the use of the royal "we," or the notion that God is addressing a divine council—are also possible.

Genesis 1:27-31. The text does not explicitly list the way(s) that human beings were made in God's image. We are left to interpret and discern that for ourselves. One significant way that we were made in God's image is implied, namely, that man and woman were given dominion. Indeed, those two details of God's design—"make in our image" and "have dominion"—are set side by side in the text. Dominion, of course, is related to lordship. God has bequeathed to these particular creatures, it seems, a share of the Creator's own authority, which is to be used to care lovingly for what God has created. Thoughtful students of the Bible will recognize in this the concept of stewardship.

Genesis 2:1-3. God rested on the seventh day. The Hebrew word for "rested" (*shabbat*) is the word from which we get "Sabbath." In the Jewish calendar, a new day begins at sunset. This way of keeping mirrors creation: "And there was evening, and there was morning, the [first, second, and so on] day." The Sabbath begins at sunset on Friday and ends at sunset on Saturday. God also "blessed" and "hallowed" this day of rest. To "hallow" means to "set apart as sacred," "dedicate," or "consecrate."

Zephaniah 3:1-2. The city referred to in verse 1 is Jerusalem. God had chosen this city and had high expectations for it. Now, however, it has become a supreme disappointment. This brief indictment reflects that Jerusalem was completely wicked: impure, unjust, and unresponsive.

Zephaniah 3:3-4. The spiritual issue within a city, of course, is not found in its bricks and mortar, its infrastructure or its neighborhoods. We may judge a city by such externals, but "the LORD looks on the heart" (1 Samuel 16:7). If a city has a spiritual problem, the issue is the people. And in this case, we see that it is not merely the residents who are the culprits. Instead, as the Lord lists the offenders, we observe how utterly corrupt Jerusalem's leadership is. We see elsewhere in Scripture that the Lord entrusts people with positions of leadership and responsibility in order to help bring God's will to pass. Yet at every level—civic, legal, ritual, and spiritual—the key people within the city of Jerusalem are living and leading contrary to the will of God.

Zephaniah 3:5-7. The Lord is not an outsider or bystander. Nor does God merely look down on Jerusalem or pay an occasional visit. Rather, the Lord is within the city. And in contrast to those who were meant to be human partners there, the Lord "is righteous [and] does no wrong." Speaking in the first person, beginning in verse 6, God recounts the corrective measures taken in response to the wickedness of the people. God's correction was meant to encourage a change of heart and life, but it did not have the desired effect. When the Lord says that the people "were the more eager to make all their deeds corrupt" (3:7), we get a measure of how hopelessly recalcitrant they had become.

Zephaniah 3:8. Correction is not the same as judgment. The former may bring hardship and difficulty, but its purpose remains fundamentally a redemptive one. In the preceding verses, we read about measures the Lord had taken to correct the people. When they so stubbornly refuse to repent, however, then God begins to warn of coming judgment for Jerusalem; and for the nations. That is the sober turn and harsh message of this verse. Judgment is more severe than correction, and more final: For while the design of correction is to put an end to the people's wickedness, judgment will put an end to the wicked people.

INTERPRETING THE SCRIPTURE

Spoiled Rotten

We know the look of something that began good, but which has since turned bad. It can be as innocuous as that no-longer-identifiable food item in the back of a college student's refrigerator. Sadder are the once-stately buildings in some inner cities that are now characterized by graffiti and boarded-up windows. And then, most poignant of all, there are the relationships—parent-child, husband-wife—that have become hard, cold, and hurtful. They were full of sweetness and promise at the beginning, but now they are so sad and tragic.

This is the trajectory of God's experience with people. It is true in the big picture of humankind, and it plays itself out repeatedly, one generation and one individual at a time. We get a glimpse of both the bigger and the smaller pictures in our selected Scripture passages.

The bigger picture is found in Genesis. We read the familiar account of creation, and we see, with God, that it was good. Thoroughly good. Yet both the next chapters of the story and our own observations of the world around us reveal that it is no longer completely good. To be sure, we still rejoice in all that is beautiful, fruitful, and consistent with God's design. At the same time, however, we are grieved by so much that is to contrary to the perfect will of God. In both nature and civilization, in our relationships both international and interpersonal, in both our systems and our hearts, we show at every level that we are fallen and flawed.

The smaller picture, meanwhile, is found in Zephaniah. It is a snapshot in history: a picture of Jerusalem in the mid-seventh-century B.C. Jerusalem in particular, like creation in general, had been the object of God's high hopes and wonderful plans. The people of Israel recognized it as the place where the Lord had chosen to dwell, the site of the everlasting throne of David, and eventually the place to which all nations would come to worship the God of Israel. But the reality was far short of the vision. At every level of life, Jerusalem's leaders were corrupt and recalcitrant. And just as Genesis depicts creation as thoroughly good, so Zephaniah depicts Jerusalem as thoroughly bad. It was fallen and flawed, and something needed to be done.

A Serious Problem

The setting was a church committee meeting, perhaps thirty years ago. The committee was made up entirely of adults, but at the moment they were talking about the youth. And one of them, in the midst of making some point, referred to "the discipline problem with our youth group."

I interrupted to ask what he meant. I knew the youth of that church well, and I had never thought of them as having a discipline problem. But this gentleman on the committee cited a couple of things that had gotten broken around the church by kids in the youth group in recent months. That, he said, was evidence of a discipline problem.

I am probably now the age that that committee member was then, and I have grown more sympathetic to the kinds of concerns for a church building that he was reflecting. I still believe, however, that he had misdiagnosed the problem. I did not think the group had a discipline problem just because they occasionally made mistakes—much less because they occasionally had accidents. My experience with those kids was that they responded to instruction and correction. If they didn't respond to correction, I told the committee, then I would concur that there was a discipline problem.

In contrast to this youth group, Zephaniah's Jerusalem definitely had a severe discipline problem.

As we read the account of creation in Genesis 1, we are struck by the impact of God's word. God speaks, and things happen. Whether calling light into being or commanding the earth to bring forth vegetation, God spoke "and it was so." As the hymn writer Isaac Watts sings it, "The moon shines full at God's command, and all the stars obey."

Against that grand backdrop, then, see the oddity that is humankind. We are the only element of creation that does not promptly and completely respond to God's word. We debate and hesitate. We pick and choose. We even ignore. The celestial bodies in their epochal splendor must marvel at these audacious, dusty creatures: here today, gone tomorrow, yet filled with anxiety and rebellion in between.

So the Lord rebuked the people of Zephaniah's day because they did not respond to God's word. They had not heeded divine instructions in the first place, and they did not yield to God's correction in the second. And in the wake of that unresponsiveness, we hear his sober warning. In escalating language, the Lord speaks of "my indignation, all the heat of my anger, [and] the fire of my passion" (3:8). And in the end, "all the earth shall be consumed" (3:8).

Grace Upon Grace

Some verses never get embroidered.

I've been fortunate to spend my whole life in the church, and I have been in more different church buildings than I can count. From small rural churches to large urban and suburban complexes, from grand cathedrals to simple chapels, from ancient catacombs to modern coliseums, I have observed a tremendous variety of things that churches put on their walls. Yet for all of that exposure, I have yet to see that verse from Zephaniah about God's anger consuming all the earth on any church's wall.

I have seen a great many Scripture verses painted, posted, embroidered, crocheted, carved, and cross-stitched. I have often seen the Lord's Prayer and the Beatitudes, the Ten Commandments and the Twenty-third Psalm displayed. I have seen promises and blessings, instructions and challenges. But I have not seen the kinds of warnings issued by judgment prophets like Zephaniah.

And those prophetic warnings are not only neglected in our choice of wall hangings. It is equally true that they are omitted from what we hear preached and taught. And it is likely also true that these passages are not highlighted or underlined in our Bibles.

It's not that the judgment material is rare, mind you. The fact is that we find dozens of chapters of the very sort of message expressed here in Zephaniah. Our hesitation to highlight these passages is that we perceive them as bad news, and we would rather focus on good news. That preference is partly about our natural comfort, of course, but it is also a theological choice. We Christians believe in good news.

Yet all of it is good news, for all of it comes from the heart of God. It is a testimony to grace in the first place that God created everything good. Moreover, our Creator begins with high hopes and great plans for creation, for Jerusalem, and for you and me individually. By grace we humans are created as free, which makes our response to God's word even more splendid than the stars, which obey on cue. By grace God instructs us so that we may always know the way in which we should go. It is likewise by grace that God corrects us when we miss the mark or choose a wrong path. And, finally, it is by grace that God warns of judgment. For the warning tells us that our God is neither capricious nor out to get us. Yes, there are consequences for disobedience, but God repeatedly offers opportunities for us to repent.

SHARING THE SCRIPTURE

PREPARING TO TEACH

Preparing Our Hearts

Ponder this week's devotional reading from Deuteronomy 8:11-18. What does the writer call the people to remember? After outlining God's blessings on those who obey, Moses' listeners are warned not to forget God when they are settled in the Promised Land. Why is it easy to forget God when life is going our way?

Pray that you and the students will obey God, no matter what the circumstances.

Preparing Our Minds

Study the background Scripture from Genesis 1:1–2:3 and Zephaniah 3:1-8. The lesson Scripture is from Zephaniah 3:6-8.

Consider this question as you prepare the lesson: *What are some consequences of destroying a good thing?*

Write on newsprint:

❏ a list of Scripture references and questions for Goal 2 in Sharing the Scripture.

❏ information for next week's lesson, found under Continue the Journey.

❏ activities for further spiritual growth in Continue the Journey.

Review the Introduction, The Big Picture, Close-up, and Faith in Action, which all precede the first lesson of this quarter. Consider how you might use any of this material in today's lesson.

LEADING THE CLASS

(1) Gather to Learn

❖ Welcome the class members and guests.

❖ Pray that those who have come today will repent of their failure to obey God.

❖ Read: **James C. Dobson, founder of Focus on the Family, has this to say about parental attitude toward a disobedient child: "The proper attitude toward a child's disobedience is this: 'I love you too much to let you behave like that.'"** Ask:

1. **On what occasions have similar words been directed toward you?**

2. **On what occasions have you said similar words to a child?**

3. **How might God the Father's attitude be similar to or different from the attitude that Dobson recommends?**

❖ Read aloud today's focus statement: **Sometimes people persist in destroying something that has been created beautiful even when they know the grave consequences. What** **are some consequences of destroying a good thing? Genesis tells that God created the light and the swarms of living creatures and God declared creation to be good; Zephaniah recounts how God began punishing the people for their disobedience, hoping that they would respond by correcting their behavior.**

(2) Goal 1: Discern From Zephaniah's Prophecy That God Wanted to Save the People, but They Refused to Accept Correction

❖ Set the stage for today's lesson by describing the wickedness of Jerusalem. (See Zephaniah 3:1-2 and 3-4 in Understanding the Scripture.) Also discuss how God has responded to the evil. (See the corrective measures God has taken in Zephaniah 3:5-7 in Understanding the Scripture.)

❖ Select a volunteer to read Zephaniah 3:6-8.

❖ Discuss these questions:

1. **What does the text say about God?**

2. **What do you suppose would have happened if people had trusted in the Lord and accepted correction?**

3. **What is the difference between "correction" and "judgment"?** (See Zephaniah 3:8 in Understanding the Scripture.)

4. **What is God's ultimate intent?** (See Zephaniah 3:8, today's key verse, and "Grace Upon Grace" in Interpreting the Scripture.)

(3) Goal 2: Realize that the Loving Creator Will Give Rebellious People Opportunities to Repent and Change Their Ways

❖ Post this list of Scripture

references, which you have prepared prior to the session:

- Numbers 21:5-9
- 1 Samuel 7:3-4
- Ezra 10:1-5
- Jonah 3:1-9
- Luke 15:11-24
- Luke 18:9-14
- Acts 8:9-24

❖ Form several groups and assign each group one or more of these Bible passages, each of which concerns the story of repentance by an individual or a group. Refer them to the following questions, which you will also post, and set a time limit for discussion:

1. What can you discern from this passage concerning why an individual or group needed to repent?
2. Where do you see evidence that the person or group repented as a result of God's correction?
3. Based on what you have read, what would you say the motivation for this repentance was—for example, a desire to avoid punishment, a yearning to get right with God, a wish to impress others with one's piety?
4. What leads you to believe that this repentance is sincere and will have a life-changing effect?
5. How might the repentance of the individual or group affect others?

❖ Call everyone together and invite each group to report.

❖ Conclude by asking: **What lessons are in these stories for us?**

(4) Goal 3: Identify and Repent of Actions and Attitudes Displeasing to God

❖ Recall that the class has

previously offered corporate prayers of confession. Such prayers often encompass a variety of general sins, because these prayers are intended to be prayed by a group.

❖ Distribute paper and pencils. Read: **Today, you are to identify three or four personal actions or attitudes that are displeasing to God. These should be very specific sins for which you choose to seek repentance. You may want to write an individual prayer of confession, perhaps including steps you will take to avoid a certain action or attitude in the future. Be honest! You will not be asked to reveal to anyone else what you have written.**

❖ Close by reading again James Dobson's words, this time not as a word from parent to child but as a reassuring message from God to each person: **"I love you too much to let you behave like that."**

(5) Continue the Journey

❖ Pray that as the learners depart, they will continue to seek repentance, knowing that God loves them too much to let them act in ways that are contrary to the divine will and hold attitudes that are sinful.

❖ Post information for next week's session on newsprint for the students to copy:

- **Title: Assurances and Joy for the Faithful**
- **Background Scripture: Genesis 1:1–2:3; Zephaniah 3:9-20**
- **Lesson Scripture: Zephaniah 3:9-14, 20**
- **Focus of the Lesson: People will sometimes repent of their harmful, destructive ways and seek to restore what has been originally**

created beautiful. How can people turn from destruction to reconstruction? Genesis tells that God created cattle, creeping things, wild animals, and humankind, and God declared creation to be very good; Zephaniah recounts that God's intervention was required for the people to stop their rebellion and return to God with singing.

❖ Post the following information on newsprint and provide paper and pencils for the students to copy it. Challenge the adults to grow spiritually by completing one or more of these activities related to this week's session.

(1) Ponder your own behaviors, especially those that may harm others or yourself. What do you think motivates such destructive behavior? What changes can you make, with God's help?

(2) Scan the media for news of corporate, church, organizational, or governmental corruption. How have the corrupt deeds harmed people—and the organization itself? If the church is involved, how has the message of Jesus Christ been damaged?

(3) Review the corrective measures God took in Zephaniah 3:1-8. What corrective measures has God tried to take in your life? How are you responding to this correction? Given whatever you are doing now, how likely is it that God will look with favor on your response?

❖ Sing or read aloud "Out of the Depths I Cry to You."

❖ Conclude today's session by leading the class in this benediction, which is adapted from Romans 8:31b, the key verse for August 7: Let us go forth rejoicing in the knowledge that since God is for us, nothing in all creation can be against us. Amen.

UNIT 1: JUDGMENT AND SALVATION

ASSURANCES AND JOY FOR THE FAITHFUL

PREVIEWING THE LESSON

Lesson Scripture: Zephaniah 3:9-14, 20
Background Scripture: Genesis 1:1–2:3; Zephaniah 3:9-20
Key Verse: Zephaniah 3:14

Focus of the Lesson:
People will sometimes repent of their harmful, destructive ways and seek to restore what has been originally created beautiful. How can people turn from destruction to reconstruction? Genesis tells that God created cattle, creeping things, wild animals, and humankind, and God declared creation to be very good; Zephaniah recounts that God's intervention was required for the people to stop their rebellion and return to God with singing.

Goals for the Learners:
(1) to hear God's proclamation through Zephaniah that God would bring the people to obedience.
(2) to assure them that God will help them through their times of trouble and disobedience.
(3) to pray for each other and themselves for God's presence and involvement in their lives.

Supplies:
Bibles, newsprint and marker, paper and pencils, hymnals, envelopes (any size)

READING THE SCRIPTURE

NRSV	CEB
Lesson Scripture: Zephaniah 3:9-14, 20	Lesson Scripture: Zephaniah 3:9-14, 20
⁹At that time I will change the speech of the peoples to a pure speech,	⁹Then I will change the speech of the peoples into pure speech, that all of them will call on the

that all of them may call on the name
of the LORD
and serve him with one accord.
¹⁰From beyond the rivers of Ethiopia
my suppliants, my scattered ones,
shall bring my offering.
¹¹On that day you shall not be put to
shame
because of all the deeds by which
you have rebelled against me;
for then I will remove from your
midst
your proudly exultant ones,
and you shall no longer be haughty
in my holy mountain.
¹²For I will leave in the midst of you
a people humble and lowly.
They shall seek refuge in the name of
the LORD—
¹³the remnant of Israel;
they shall do no wrong
and utter no lies,
nor shall a deceitful tongue
be found in their mouths.
Then they will pasture and lie down,
and no one shall make them
afraid.
**¹⁴Sing aloud, O daughter Zion;
shout, O Israel!
Rejoice and exult with all your
heart,
O daughter Jerusalem!**
²⁰At that time I will bring you home,
at the time when I gather you;
for I will make you renowned and
praised
among all the peoples of the earth,
when I restore your fortunes
before your eyes, says the LORD.

name of the LORD
and will serve him as one.
¹⁰From beyond the rivers of Cush,
my daughter, my dispersed ones,
will bring me offerings.
¹¹On that day, you won't be ashamed
of all your deeds
with which you sinned against
me;
then I will remove from your
midst those boasting with
pride.
No longer will you be haughty on
my holy mountain,
¹²but I will cause a humble and
powerless
people to remain in your midst;
they will seek refuge in the name
of the LORD.
¹³The few remaining from Israel
won't commit injustice;
they won't tell lies;
a deceitful tongue won't be found
on their lips.
They will graze and lie down;
no one will make them afraid.
**¹⁴Rejoice, Daughter Zion! Shout,
Israel!
Rejoice and exult with all your
heart, Daughter Jerusalem.**
²⁰At that time, I will bring all of you
back, at the time when I gather
you.
I will give you fame and praise
among all the neighboring
peoples
when I restore your possessions
and you can see them—says the
LORD.

UNDERSTANDING THE SCRIPTURE

Genesis 1:1-4. What exactly is "a formless void"? "Formless" suggests that it has no shape. Void suggests that it has no content. It is a strange expression used to describe a mysterious scene, namely, that which was before God began to create. Verse 2 also refers to "darkness," described as "covering the face of the deep," and "the waters" over which the wind (or breath) of God blew.

Genesis 1:5-10. One way that we human beings demonstrate that we are made in God's image is that we name things. God called—that is, gave names to—the light and the darkness, the land and the waters, and more. For as sophisticated as we have discovered so much of animal communication to be, we have no clues to suggest that they name things. Yet we human beings, from so soon after we begin to talk, give names to things. And not only previously assigned names like "Mommy" and "Daddy." We see the creative naming that young children instinctively do with their toys, pets, and stuffed animals.

Genesis 1:11-13. Joyce Kilmer famously noted, "Only God can make a tree." I appreciate the sentiment, but the record suggests something different: "Let the earth put forth" and "the earth brought forth" represent a change in the creative process. Now creation itself is producing according to God's will.

Genesis 1:14-19. On day four, we see God ordaining the sun to "rule the day" and the moon to "rule the night." These two created lights help to separate the day from the night. The sun and the moon also mark days, years, and seasons.

Genesis 1:20-25. As we noted on the third day, when "the earth brought forth vegetation" (1:12), the text suggests that God's creation is participating in the creative act again on day six. While "God created" and "God made" are still factored into the account here, the Creator's initial commands are that the waters and the earth "bring forth . . . living

creatures" (1:20). Unlike the prior state of "a formless void," God's creation is not a static and impotent thing, but vital and productive.

Genesis 1:26-31. The earlier phenomenon of the earth or waters bringing forth life is not found here. There is no intermediary in the creation of human beings. The creation of man and woman is presented as a personal act of God, and that in contrast to some other elements of the creation.

Genesis 2:1-3. While our reflex may be to associate the Sabbath with the Ten Commandments, the origin of the holy day predates all the rest of the Old Testament laws. And the logic of the later commandment—"Six days you shall labor and do all your work" (Exodus 20:9)—is rooted here in the report that God had finished all work in six days. The completion of work is essential to the observance of the Sabbath—and is perhaps our greatest impediment to it.

Introduction to Zephaniah 3:9-20. The prophet Zephaniah preached to the people of Judah during the time of the Babylonian Empire. His message was primarily one of warning as the Lord prepared the people for the military, economic, and political catastrophe that was to come. Yet even in the face of such disaster, the Lord still had good news. For on the other side of that necessary judgment of God was a promise of hope and restoration. That is the happy and hopeful era anticipated by Zephaniah's references in chapter 3 to "at that time" (3:9) and "on that day" (3:11).

Zephaniah 3:9-10. Three good accomplishments of that post-judgment restoration are noted here. First, there is a purification of the people's speech, which Jesus might say indicates a purification of their hearts (see Matthew 15:10-20). Second, the people return to calling on and serving the Lord, which suggests repentance and recommitment. And, third, there is the happy prospect of peoples coming from great distances to worship at the Lord's altar.

Zephaniah 3:11-15. The purification of the people includes a winnowing of the people. The distinction between whom the Lord will "remove from your midst" (3:11) and whom the Lord will "leave in the midst of you" (3:12) is a succinct glimpse into what pleases and displeases God. Furthermore, the Lord promises to set them free from shame, fear, and judgment. In contrast to the threatening cloud under which Zephaniah's contemporaries lived, the Lord promises a time when they, like secure sheep, will feed and rest unafraid. And that good prospect, in turn, gives rise to rejoicing and singing.

Zephaniah 3:16-19. The next description of what will characterize "that day" includes a magnificent series of statements of what the Lord will do for the people of Jerusalem. The list has a marvelously personal quality, as the Lord will rejoice and exult over them. It is practical, too, as God promises to "remove disaster" from them and "deal with" their oppressors. Finally, the list has a spiritual quality, including God's promise to save them and to turn their shame to "praise and renown."

Zephaniah 3:20. The concluding "at that time" statement features the promise of return and restoration in a verse that recalls God's original promise to Abraham (Genesis 12:1-3). The land was part of that original promise, and now returning to that land is God's expressed will for these descendants of Abraham. Beyond the mere geography, though, God's good will is characterized by restoring the people to a certain quality of life. Peace and abundance are implicit. After being a target and a byword among the nations, now they will be "renowned and praised among all peoples of the earth." And we recall that God's promise to Abraham included making his name great and a similarly global statement of purpose: "in you all the families of the earth shall be blessed" (Genesis 12:3).

INTERPRETING THE SCRIPTURE

Cartoon Villains

When our children were young, my wife and I became well acquainted with the literature, movies, and music that were geared toward those ages. And as we watched—in some cases over and over—the shows and movies that our children especially enjoyed, I was struck by two very different approaches to villains.

On the one hand, the standard fare was to compose a happy ending that featured the villain's demise. Cruella de Vil, Gaston, Ursula, and Shere Khan all meet with disaster in the end. That prompts celebration among the other characters in the story, as well as a sense of satisfaction and relief within the readers.

In contrast to that pattern, however, stands Dr. Seuss's famous Christmas villain: the Grinch. He is as antisocial, as conniving, and as malevolent as any of the others. Yet in the end, the Grinch is not destroyed; he is changed. His is a story of conversion rather than defeat. And as the curtain closes, the other characters in the story embrace the redeemed Grinch, welcoming him into their lives and their world.

The contrast presents us with a personal question. What sort of ending do we prefer? What do we like to see happen to the villain in the end? Are we more pleased to see him battered or bettered?

The prophet Zephaniah was a judgment prophet. His somber calling was to warn the people of his time and place about the imminent disaster that was provoked by their sin. That righteous judgment would be the act of God, to be sure. And yet we discover that such destruction is not the perfect or final will of God. We may be satisfied when the antagonists are defeated. God is not satisfied, however, until they are redeemed.

God's Good Will

I remember a conversation with a girl from our church youth group. She shared with me her earnest, thirteen-year-old conviction about marriage. "I believe God has a man picked out for me," she said, but then added, "I'm just afraid I won't like him."

Her candor was characteristically youthful, but her experience was not. Young and old alike struggle with the same worry, namely, that we won't like God's will for us. We live with a nagging fear that what God has in store may be something undesirable.

That's a hard case to make, of course, when you look at creation. The beauty, splendor, and abundance with which the Lord surrounded

human beings are a living and ubiquitous witness to the goodness of God's will. At the end of each day of the multi-phase project, God saw that it was good. And when it was nearly complete, God handed it over to the man and the woman, graciously made in the divine image, so that they might enjoy and employ it.

Constitutional scholars and politicians sometimes use the phrase "original intent"—that is, what the framers of the Constitution meant by what they wrote. Sometimes that may seem unclear. But not so with God, whose original intent is marvelously evident in creation and testifies to the profound goodness of the divine will for human beings.

Ah, but what to do with those human beings when they themselves do not live up to their Creator's original intent? When people have strayed so far from God's good will, what then? That is the circumstance of Zephaniah's context.

Judgment was the immediate remedy, but it was not the final one. For destruction is never the perfect will of the Creator. When creation does not live up to its Maker's original intent, God does not abandon it, but rather redeems it.

In perhaps his most famous and cherished hymn, Isaac Watts captures that redemptive will of God for creation: "No more let sins and sorrows grow, nor thorns infest the ground," Watts sings, with an eye on the Fall (Genesis 3:18). But, instead, "He [God] comes to make his blessings flow far as the curse is found."

When people were not living up to God's original intent, God's perfect will was to redeem. Theodoret of Cyr, a bishop in fifth-century Syria, insisted that even the prophets' judgment message was an indication of God's preference for redemption. "After all, if he [God] wanted to punish," Theodoret wrote, "he would not threaten punishment; instead, by threatening he makes clear that he longs to save and not to punish."

And so the goodwill that the Lord demonstrated in creation was reaffirmed even in the face of judgment. For the judgment prophet Zephaniah revealed the plan that the Lord had in mind for the people on the other side of their impending disaster. It was a good plan, filled with the kind of beauty that is typical of God's goodwill toward us.

A Perfect Plan

To see a person's plans is to peek into his or her heart. Our plans reveal our interests and priorities. They show our allegiances and our ambitions. They express our fondest wishes and highest hopes. If you told me your plans for either your weekend or your life, they would likely give me a sense for what is really important to you and what you truly value.

So it is with the Lord, whose heart is revealed in godly plans. And in this passage from Zephaniah, God communicates part of that plan.

First, we observe God's gracious undoing of the people's past: "On that day you shall not be put to shame because of all the deeds by which you have rebelled against me" (3:11). Ever since Adam and Eve cowered behind Eden's bushes, we have experienced shame because of our misdeeds. Yet the Lord promises to take that away.

Likewise, God promises to bring the people home again. Their sinfulness had led to their eviction and dispersion. Yet now "my scattered ones shall bring my offering" (3:10) and "I will bring you home, at the time when I gather you" (3:20)

Moreover, the scope of God's perfect plan extends even beyond the covenant people. When the Lord promises to "change the speech of the peoples" (3:9), the vocabulary and the plural noun suggest a broader audience than just the people of Israel. The One who created the whole world seeks to redeem the whole world.

Also, we hear God's good plan to cleanse people. Promises to change their speech and remove evil from their midst sound like global sanctification. And the lovely end result is a faithful "remnant of Israel . . . [that] shall do no wrong and utter no lies" (3:13).

Finally, there is that perfect picture of a people who are at rest and unafraid. The Lord is in their midst and has restored to them the abundance that is God's good will. The people are characterized by their exultant worship and praise.

We do not list Zephaniah among the books of the New Testament, but this excerpt could easily fit there. It speaks of forgiveness and sanctification. And it anticipates a time and place of abundance, reunion, and rest; a setting of worship in the presence of the Lord. This is God's good and perfect will for us. It always has been.

SHARING THE SCRIPTURE

PREPARING TO TEACH

Preparing Our Hearts

Ponder this week's devotional reading from Hebrews 11:29-39. What does the writer have to say about those who are faithful? If you are unfamiliar with the stories of any of the heroes of faith listed in these verses, use a concordance to locate and read about how they had demonstrated their faith. How do their stories inspire you to greater faithfulness?

Pray that you and the students will live with such faith so as to be role models for others.

Preparing Our Minds

Study the background Scripture from Genesis 1:1–2:3; Zephaniah 3:9-20. The lesson Scripture is from Zephaniah 3:9-14, 20.

Consider this question as you prepare the lesson: *How can people turn from destruction to reconstruction?*

Write on newsprint:
❏ information for next week's lesson, found under Continue the Journey.
❏ activities for further spiritual growth in Continue the Journey.

Review the Introduction, The Big Picture, Close-up, and Faith in Action, which all precede the first lesson of this quarter. Consider how you might use any of this material in today's lesson.

LEADING THE CLASS

(1) Gather to Learn

❖ Welcome the class members and guests.

❖ Pray that those who have come today will feel assured of God's love in all circumstances of their lives.

❖ Read: **A young British woman reported that she had low self-esteem. Given that when she was just nine her dad died, when she was fourteen her mother was jailed, and when she was sixteen she had an abortion, her feelings of unworthiness seem understandable. At age eighteen, she started working in a prison and was flattered by attention from the male inmates. She smuggled drugs into the prison and at age twenty-one was arrested. She started praying to God and reading Psalm 27 regularly. Although she could have been sentenced to five years, she was sentenced to only two—and served only ten months. Her experience had sent her to God, where she found a sense of self-worth and freedom.**

❖ Read aloud today's focus statement: **People will sometimes repent of their harmful, destructive ways and seek to restore what has been originally created beautiful. How can people turn from destruction to reconstruction? Genesis tells that God created cattle, creeping things, wild animals, and humankind, and God declared creation to be very good; Zephaniah recounts that God's intervention was required for the people to stop their rebellion and return to God with singing.**

(2) Goal 1: Hear God's Proclamation Through Zephaniah that God Would Bring the People to Obedience

❖ Read Introduction to Zephaniah 3:9-20 in Understanding the Scripture.

435

❖ Choose a volunteer to read Zephaniah 3:9-14, 20.

❖ Discuss these questions:

1. **What good news do you hear in verses 9-10?** (See Zephaniah 3:9-10 in Understanding the Scripture.)

2. **Based on what God plans to do, what conclusions can you draw about what pleases—and displeases—God?** (See Zephaniah 3:11-15 in Understanding the Scripture.)

3. **Recall that when the Babylonians took the Israelites into captivity, they also destroyed the city of Jerusalem. What promises does God make about Jerusalem?** (See Zephaniah 3:16-19 in Understanding the Scripture. Note that many translations exist for verse 18 due to the difficulty of the Hebrew. Ask several participants who have different translations to read that verse to help clarify what is being said here.)

4. **How might the reversal of fortune promised in verse 20 relate to God's covenant with Abraham?** (See Zephaniah 3:20 in Understanding the Scripture.)

5. **Zephaniah prophesied judgment on God's people, but these verses at the end of chapter 3 show that the people have been restored. What does this restoration reveal about God's will?** (See "Cartoon Villains" and "God's Good Will" in Interpreting the Scripture.)

6. **What connections might you draw between Zephaniah and the good news of the New Testament?** (See "A Perfect Plan" in Interpreting the Scripture.)

(3) Goal 2: Feel Assurance that God Will Help the Learners Through Their Times of Trouble and Disobedience

❖ Distribute paper and pencils. Invite the students to recall at least one time of trouble they experienced as an adult. On the paper they are to list ways that they believe God helped them to get through this difficult time, being as specific as possible. Here are examples of specific responses: I felt God's presence; I experienced the love of Jesus in the care that a particular nurse gave me; the person whose car I hit was forgiving; my church family was praying for us when our daughter ran away.

❖ Invite volunteers to state ways that they felt God had cared for them. They need not divulge any of the circumstances, unless they choose to.

❖ Distribute envelopes. Suggest that the students label them as [Name's] Memory Bank. Tell them to put inside the papers on which they have written ways that God has helped them in the past and put these in a safe place at home where they can refer to them when they face another difficult situation.

(4) Goal 3: Pray for Each Other and Themselves for God's Presence and Involvement in Their Lives

❖ Form groups of three. Invite person A to state one prayer request for his or her own life. Persons B and C are then to offer a short prayer for person A, asking God to intercede. This pattern is to continue, with Person B stating a prayer request and being prayed for, followed by Person C. To ensure that each person has equal time, set a time limit and call time so that the groups can move on to the next person.

❖ Bring everyone together and ask: **How might your attitude toward whatever concern you had be different now that you know two other people are praying for you?**

❖ Suggest that the adults commit themselves to praying for their other two group members during the week. If the prayer was offered for something that was to happen during the week, such as receiving medical test results, recommend that the "pray-ers" call and check on the one for whom they offered intercession to offer words of thanksgiving and encouragement.

(5) Continue the Journey

❖ Pray that as the learners depart, they will trust God to care for them in all situations.

❖ Post information for next week's session on newsprint for the students to copy:

- **Title: Ignoring God's Plain Truth**
- **Background Scripture: Psalm 8; Romans 1:18-32**
- **Lesson Scripture: Romans 1:18-23, 28-32**
- **Focus of the Lesson: Some people do what they believe is right, while others constantly do what is wrong. Why do humans act this way? The psalmist says that some people live lives consistent with God's creation and even give praise constantly for all**

that God has done, while Paul points out that others disobey God and take pride in filling their lives with all kinds of actions that oppose God's decree.

❖ Post the following information on newsprint and provide paper and pencils for the students to copy it. Challenge the adults to grow spiritually by completing one or more of these activities related to this week's session.

(1) **Recall a time when you strayed from God. How did you feel when you returned? What did you do to show your joy and gratitude for restoration?**

(2) **Read a psalm of praise or sing a hymn of praise to express the joy of a reconciled relationship with God.**

(3) **Listen carefully to yourself as you speak. How pure is your speech? Do you use words that hurt or words that heal, words that are displeasing to God or pleasing? What changes might you need to make?**

❖ Sing or read aloud "Rejoice, Ye Pure in Heart."

❖ Conclude today's session by leading the class in this benediction, which is adapted from Romans 8:31b, the key verse for August 7: **Let us go forth rejoicing in the knowledge that since God is for us, nothing in all creation can be against us. Amen.**

UNIT 2: A WORLD GONE WRONG
Ignoring God's Plain Truth

PREVIEWING THE LESSON

Lesson Scripture: Romans 1:18-23, 28-32
Background Scripture: Psalm 8; Romans 1:18-32
Key Verse: Romans 1:20

Focus of the Lesson:
Some people do what they believe is right, while others constantly do what is wrong. Why do humans act this way? The psalmist says that some people live lives consistent with God's creation and even give praise constantly for all that God has done, while Paul points out that others disobey God and take pride in filling their lives with all kinds of actions that oppose God's decree.

Goals for the Learners:
(1) to explore Paul's message to the Roman church about all manner of human sinfulness.
(2) to accept that humans have the freedom to disobey God, but are subject to consequences.
(3) to discern God's will and follow it.

Supplies:
Bibles, newsprint and marker, paper and pencils, hymnals

READING THE SCRIPTURE

NRSV
Lesson Scripture: Romans 1:18-23, 28-32

[18]For the wrath of God is revealed from heaven against all ungodliness and wickedness of those who by their wickedness suppress the truth. [19]For what can be known about God is plain to them, because God has

CEB
Lesson Scripture: Romans 1:18-23, 28-32

[18]God's wrath is being revealed from heaven against all the ungodly behavior and the injustice of human beings who silence the truth with injustice. [19]This is because what is known about God should be plain to

shown it to them. **²⁰Ever since the creation of the world his eternal power and divine nature, invisible though they are, have been understood and seen through the things he has made. So they are without excuse;** ²¹for though they knew God, they did not honor him as God or give thanks to him, but they became futile in their thinking, and their senseless minds were darkened. ²²Claiming to be wise, they became fools; ²³and they exchanged the glory of the immortal God for images resembling a mortal human being or birds or four-footed animals or reptiles.

²⁸And since they did not see fit to acknowledge God, God gave them up to a debased mind and to things that should not be done. ²⁹They were filled with every kind of wickedness, evil, covetousness, malice. Full of envy, murder, strife, deceit, craftiness, they are gossips, ³⁰slanderers, God-haters, insolent, haughty, boastful, inventors of evil, rebellious toward parents, ³¹foolish, faithless, heartless, ruthless. ³²They know God's decree, that those who practice such things deserve to die—yet they not only do them but even applaud others who practice them.

them because God made it plain to them. **²⁰Ever since the creation of the world, God's invisible qualities— God's eternal power and divine nature—have been clearly seen, because they are understood through the things God has made. So humans are without excuse.** ²¹Although they knew God, they didn't honor God as God or thank him. Instead, their reasoning became pointless, and their foolish hearts were darkened. ²²While they were claiming to be wise, they made fools of themselves. ²³They exchanged the glory of the immortal God for images that look like mortal humans: birds, animals, and reptiles.

²⁸Since they didn't think it was worthwhile to acknowledge God, God abandoned them to a defective mind to do inappropriate things. ²⁹So they were filled with all injustice, wicked behavior, greed, and evil behavior. They are full of jealousy, murder, fighting, deception, and malice. They are gossips, ³⁰they slander people, and they hate God. They are rude and proud, and they brag. They invent ways to be evil, and they are disobedient to their parents. ³¹They are without understanding, disloyal, without affection, and without mercy. ³²Though they know God's decision that those who persist in such practices deserve death, they not only keep doing these things but also approve others who practice them.

UNDERSTANDING THE SCRIPTURE

Psalm 8:1-2. The author of Psalm 8 gives voice to an experience that we will recognize. He looks in two directions at once, and he marvels at the juxtaposition that he observes. His split screen is both a looking up and a looking down. He considers, at once, both God and humanity. He acknowledges the majesty of the Lord's name, yet that majesty is known "in all the earth." The Lord's glory is "above the heavens," yet proclaimed by "babes and infants."

Psalm 8:3-8. The psalmist looks in all directions. He looks up to consider the cosmos and down to fathom the sea. He contemplates the other creatures that inhabit the earth with him, and he takes account of the Creator who made it all. And in the midst of it all there are human beings, with their inexplicable rank. The Lord has favored them, exalted them, and put them in charge. "A little lower than God" is the psalmist's astonished conclusion in verse 5, and he is filled with wonder at God's design and sovereign choice.

Psalm 8:9. The psalm ends where it began, which offers both symmetry and perspective. The symmetry is found in the repetition. The perspective, meanwhile, is found in the content of what is repeated, namely, the global majesty of God. The psalmist has wondered at the elevated status of humankind, yet he knows that our importance must be understood against the divine backdrop. Apart from that, the cosmos might dwarf us into underestimating our role, or our role might tempt us into an inflated sense of self-importance.

Romans 1:18. This verse serves as a kind of thesis statement for the passage that follows. In a few words, Paul expresses several key themes. First, there is the hard fact of God's wrath. We prefer to put the accent on a different syllable, yet God would not be worthy of worship if God were indifferent to wickedness. Grace reaches out to the sinner, to be sure, and love embraces the penitent one. But holiness cannot wink at or turn a blind eye to entrenched and recalcitrant evil. And so the judgment of God is cited.

Second, the idea that the wrath of God is "revealed" is significant, for central to Paul's argument is the belief that so much of the nature and will of God has been revealed. That is precisely why humans are "without excuse." And that leads, finally, to the point that evil people "by their wickedness suppress the truth." The problem is more diabolical than mere ignorance. The issue is not that the truth is unknown, or even unacknowledged, but rather that it is suppressed.

Romans 1:19-21. Here we get a fuller picture of Paul's understanding with respect to what theologians call "general revelation." The principle is that God is revealed to humankind in both general and specific ways. The Lord speaking to Moses at the burning bush would be an example of special revelation. General revelation, on the other hand, refers to that which is universally available: the experiences and understanding of God that are accessible to every human being. And Paul's conviction is that creation itself offers such general revelation about the nature, character, and will of God. While much of humanity, therefore, might not have known about Abraham, Moses, David, or Jesus, they should still have known enough to give God glory.

Romans 1:22-25. It is truly a tragic irony when our wisdom proves to be counterfeit. Imagine the self-reliant driver who is absolutely certain that he knows the right way to reach his destination, but manages only to deliver himself and his companions into some lost place far from where they wanted to go. Such was the condition of the human beings Paul had in mind. They thought they were so clever, so enlightened, and yet the apostle reveals them for the fools that they are. For any time our wisdom leads us away from God, it is actually folly. And since they were committed to their folly, Paul writes in verse 24 that "God gave them up." This is not active and aggressive judgment from God; this is simply the sober choice to allow us to experience the natural consequences of our decisions. Perhaps it is the choice that the father of the prodigal son makes when he hands over the inheritance and permits the confident fool to walk out the door. And it is the hard choice that every parent has had to make when resigned to letting the stubborn child learn from his or her mistakes.

Romans 1:26-31. The apostle has traced the cause; now he itemizes the effects. He begins with a lament over unnatural behaviors, and that paradigm sets the stage for all that follows—"every kind of wickedness" (1:29). The underlying premise is that there is a way things ought to be done, according to the design of the Creator who brought order out of chaos. Yet everything about the behaviors Paul lists contradicts that natural design. Instead, just as the people

had exchanged the glory of God for other things, they subsequently make all sorts of other exchanges and thereby do "things that should not be done" (1:28). Meanwhile, we might take note of the particulars that Paul itemizes. Each culture—and for that matter, each individual—has a short list of taboos, of truly wicked behaviors. It may be instructive for us to see some of the things that are on the apostle's list, for it includes matters we may consider trivial (gossip), harmless (covetousness), and inevitable (strife). Yet these are lumped together by Paul with murder and hating God.

Romans 1:32. The passage concludes with one final, frank assessment from the apostle. He has pulled no punches in the preceding verses, and he remains no-nonsense here. The summary conclusion is simple: They knew both the will of God and the consequence of disobedience. In spite of that, they have not responded obediently to what they knew. And, as a kind of ultimate perversion, they delighted in and encouraged the disobedience of others.

INTERPRETING THE SCRIPTURE

Ignorance Is No Excuse

Perhaps you have tried to explain to the police officer standing beside your car that you didn't know. You didn't realize what the speed limit was on this stretch of road. You didn't see the no-left-turn sign. You weren't aware that it was a one-way street. And perhaps that officer has excused your mistake. More likely, though, the officer informed you that ignorance is no excuse for breaking the law.

We have an obligation to know the rules, after all. Whether on the playing field, in the workplace, or driving through town, a responsible person must take responsibility for knowing what is required and what is forbidden. That is the only way that we can keep ourselves safe. It is the only way to be fair to those around us. And it is the only way to please whoever the relevant authorities may be. While breaking a rule may seem to us occasionally desirable, it is ultimately in our own best interest to know the rules and to obey them. Ignorance is no excuse.

When it comes to the will of God, the apostle Paul would also say that ignorance is no excuse. In this case, though, we have no excuse precisely because we are not ignorant. Rather, "ever since the creation of the world," Paul says that the nature of God has "been understood and seen through the things he has made" (1:20).

The people of Israel had God's law carefully spelled out for them. But the rest of humanity was also equipped to discern God's character and will, for nature bears witness to both. The Creator's design reveals the Creator's intent. Nevertheless, some people cut across the grain of nature, and so "God gave them up to a debased mind and to things that should not be done" (1:28).

The Transaction of Sin

Every day you and I engage in countless exchanges. Many of them involve money, of course. We exchange our money for the food at the grocery store, the clothes at the dry cleaners, and the fuel at the filling station.

Beyond those financial transactions, however, we participate in a variety of other exchanges as well. The bride and groom exchange vows and rings. Perhaps angry drivers exchange words. And strangers in the checkout line exchange pleasantries.

It is the nature of an exchange to give something and to receive something else in return. At times, we have experienced an exchange as an unequal one. Perhaps we regret that the product was not worth the money we paid for it. It has been an unequal exchange.

In our excerpt from Paul's Letter to the Romans, the apostle is aware of the exchanges that fallen humanity has made. It is the transaction of sin. And it is always an unequal and regrettable exchange.

Adam and Eve sought the advertised benefits of the forbidden fruit. All it got them, though, was shame and disharmony. And as they fled Eden, clutching their coverings, I doubt that the exchange seemed profitable.

So it was for hungry Esau with his pottage, despising his birthright (Genesis 25:34). So, too, with those lured to destruction by the wayward woman's seduction (Proverbs 7). Charles Wesley captured the tragic exchange in song: "Ye, who have sold for naught/Your heritage above!" Such is the transaction of sin: It is all loss.

For the lost folks whom Paul had in mind, the exchange was an unthinkable one. They had forfeited "the glory of the immortal God" (1:23) in favor of puny and finite things. To any clear-eyed observer, this exchange seems nonsensical. And so Paul concludes about them that, though "claiming to be wise, they became fools" (1:22). Indeed, they did. For the transaction of sin is always a foolish exchange.

Devil's Advocate

We hear and use the expression casually. It is how we introduce an opposite opinion in a meeting of conversation. "Let me play devil's advocate for a moment," we say, and then proceed to offer a contrary perspective.

It is, of course, a perfectly awful expression. And it is misplaced too, for we are seldom actually doing the devil's work at the times we use the expression. Typically, we're just trying to see another side of a situation or decision.

The real trouble with misplacing the expression, however, is that we then fail to recognize or admit what we're doing when we are actually doing it. That is to say, there may be occasions when we actually do speak for the devil and do his bidding. That sounds like a terrible prospect, to be sure, yet anytime a person says the sort of thing the devil would say, that person is acting as the devil's advocate.

John Donne remorsefully reflected on one aspect of the phenomenon. In a poetic prayer of confession titled "A Hymn to God the Father," Donne wrote: "Wilt Thou forgive the sin which I won/Others to sin, and made my sins their door?" He saw, with regret, that he had effectively been the devil's advocate.

Meanwhile, the people whom Paul describes were inarguably devil's advocates. They did not honor or give thanks to God. They suppressed the truth. They replaced God with lesser things. They engaged in all manner of wickedness. And then, as the ultimate evil, they approved and encouraged the wickedness of others.

Surprising Grace

The boundaries of our passage do not include any overt message about the love and grace of God, nor of the salvation offered in Jesus Christ. Still, the gracious nature of God is implicit in the immediate text, and we know the gospel message is explicit in the larger context of this letter from Paul to the Romans. Yet against the backdrop of this sober passage, the truth that we know about God's saving grace is all the more amazing.

That God is generous toward us is implicit in our text at two points.

First, the very fact that God created us free is a testimony to the divine nature. God takes no pleasure in robotic obedience. Only as free agents are we capable of loving the Lord, and Scripture bears witness that that is most important to God (Deuteronomy 6:5; Matthew 22:37-38).

Second, the universal nature of God's self-revelation is also an indication of the divine character. Even though we insist on closing our eyes, still God has not turned off the lights. Instead, God endeavors to make known the divine will and way to everyone. The stubbornness of our rebellion does not surpass the tenacity of God's love and grace.

And, finally, even Paul's sober statement in verse 26 that "God gave them up" is its own kind of testament to God's gracious working in our lives. For in the most recalcitrant cases, perhaps only the desperation of sin's consequences will awaken the longing for salvation. Perhaps the prodigal has to live with the pigs before he knows enough to miss home. In a poem, Ruth Bell Graham poignantly prays for straying sheep, who have joined with a wolf pack, suggesting that they see for themselves "the companionship wolves give/to helpless strays." Even giving them up, therefore, may be done with a gracious eye toward getting them back, for that is always God's gracious and perfect will.

SHARING THE SCRIPTURE

PREPARING TO TEACH

Preparing Our Hearts

Ponder this week's devotional reading from Psalm 52. Note that this judgment speech is spoken by a human. What is this person saying? How would you characterize the one against whom this psalm is directed?

Pray that you and the students will avoid the kind of behavior that leads to accusations and a guilty verdict.

Preparing Our Minds

Study the background Scripture from Psalm 8; Romans 1:18-32; and the lesson Scripture from Romans 1:18-23, 28-32.

Consider this question as you prepare the lesson: *Why do some people do what they believe is right, whereas others often do what is wrong?*

Write on newsprint:
❏ information for next week's lesson, found under Continue the Journey.
❏ activities for further spiritual growth in Continue the Journey.

Review the Introduction, The Big Picture, Close-up, and Faith in Action, which all precede the first lesson of this quarter. Consider how you might use any of this material in today's lesson.

LEADING THE CLASS

(1) Gather to Learn

❖ Welcome the class members and guests.
❖ Pray that those who have come today will seek to do what God wills.

❖ Read: **As this lesson is being written, the world has again watched in horror as another Westerner was beheaded by jihadists claiming to be members of ISIS (Islamic State of Iraq and Syria), also referred to as ISIL (Islamic State of Iraq and the Levant). On November 17, 2014,** *The Telegraph* **reported that the father of a medical student from Cardiff (Wales) believes his son is one of the killers shown in video beheading Syrian soldiers. The father's grief and disbelief nearly leapt from the page of this British newspaper. Although he could not positively identify his twenty-year-old son, he proclaimed that if his son was among the executioners, "he must face up" to his inhuman actions. Adding that his son had changed, that he had not been brought up to do such things, the father candidly said that if his son was proven to be a killer, he "should face a death sentence."**

❖ Ask: **How is it possible for people to go against all that they have been taught to take actions that can only be described as evil?**

❖ Read aloud today's focus statement: **Some people do what they believe is right, while others constantly do what is wrong. Why do humans act this way? The psalmist says that some people live lives consistent with God's creation and even give praise constantly for all that God has done, while Paul points out that others disobey God and take pride in filling their lives with all kinds of actions that oppose God's decree.**

(2) Goal 1: Explore Paul's Message to the Roman Church About All Manner of Human Sinfulness

❖ Select a volunteer to read Romans 1:18-23, 28-32.

❖ Discuss these questions:

1. **What main points does Paul make in verse 18?** (See Romans 1:18 in Understanding the Scripture.)

2. **Why does Paul insist that even nonbelievers are without excuse when they fail to recognize God?** (See Romans 1:19-21 in Understanding the Scripture. Be sure to mention the theological principle known as general revelation. Also see "Ignorance Is No Excuse" in Interpreting the Scripture.)

3. **How do you interpret Paul's comment in verse 24 that "God gave them up"?** (See Romans 1:22-25 in Understanding the Scripture and "Surprising Grace" in Interpreting the Scripture.)

4. **What is Paul's conclusion in verse 32?** (See Romans 1:32 in Understanding the Scripture.)

(3) Goal 2: Accept that Humans Have the Freedom to Disobey God, but Are Subject to Consequences

❖ Segue into this portion of the lesson by noting that although people should know how to behave better than they often do, God has given each of us the freedom to disobey. Yet with that freedom comes the requirement that we accept the consequences of our actions. Recall from the Gather to Learn activity that the father of the young man allegedly involved in ISIS killings recognized that his son would have to face the consequences of his actions.

❖ Read aloud these quotations concerning "consequences." Invite class members to comment on how each quotation does—or does not—reflect their understanding of the relationship between what they freely choose to do and the consequences that follow as a natural result of their actions:

1. **"If a man gets drunk and goes out and breaks his leg so that it must be amputated, God will forgive him if he asks it, but he will have to hop around on one leg all his life."** (Dwight Lyman Moody, 1837–1899)

2. **You cannot unscramble eggs.** (American proverb)

3. **"Choices made, whether bad or good, follow you forever and affect everyone in their path one way or another."** (J.E.B. Spredemann, *An Unforgivable Secret*)

4. **"We are free to choose our paths, but we can't choose the consequences that come with them."** (Sean Covey, *The 7 Habits of Highly Effective Teens*)

❖ Conclude by asking: **How can we show others the importance of accepting the consequences of our actions?**

(4) Goal 3: Discern God's Will and Follow It

❖ Brainstorm answers to this question and write them on newsprint: **What guideposts do you use to discern the will of God?** Answers may include the Bible, circumstances, prayer, meditation, sense of inner peace when you know God's will, comments by mature believers.

❖ Challenge the adults to use these ideas to discern God's will for a decision they are facing. Suggest that they consider discussing the plan they have discerned with a trusted Christian before putting it into action.

(5) Continue the Journey

❖ Pray that as the learners depart, they will seek, discern, and follow God's will.

❖ Post information for next week's session on newsprint for the students to copy:

- **Title: Ignoring God's Truth Within Us**
- **Background Scripture: Psalm 104; Romans 2:14-29**
- **Lesson Scripture: Romans 2:17-29**
- **Focus of the Lesson: Many people talk about appreciating the world around them but do not demonstrate it with their actions. What causes such inconsistency? The psalmist sings praises that the earth is full of the wonders of God's creation; but Paul insists that, while some people teach others how to obey the law and live in ways consistent with God's creation, they do not obey the law themselves and do not have it written on their hearts.**

❖ Post the following information on newsprint and provide paper and pencils for the students to copy it. Challenge the adults to grow spiritually by completing one or more of these activities related to this week's session.

(1) **Help someone who is struggling with issues of right and wrong understand that actions have consequences. Offer support but allow this person to make his or her own mistakes and experience the consequences.**

(2) **Spend time in nature this week. You need not go to the mountains or a beach far away, but enjoy time in your own yard or a nearby park. Even if you were not a believer, what evidence can you find that God exists and is the Creator of all that is?**

(3) **Read and contemplate Psalm 8, part of this week's background Scripture. How does the reality of human behavior, expressed by Paul in Romans 1, compare with the way that God intended humans to be? How does that discrepancy make you feel?**

❖ Sing or read aloud "O God Who Shaped Creation."

❖ Conclude today's session by leading the class in this benediction, which is adapted from Romans 8:31b, the key verse for August 7: **Let us go forth rejoicing in the knowledge that since God is for us, nothing in all creation can be against us. Amen.**

UNIT 2: A WORLD GONE WRONG
IGNORING GOD'S TRUTH WITHIN US

PREVIEWING THE LESSON

Lesson Scripture: Romans 2:17-29
Background Scripture: Psalm 104; Romans 2:14-29
Key Verse: Romans 2:13

Focus of the Lesson:
Many people talk about appreciating the world around them but do not demonstrate it with their actions. What causes such inconsistency? The psalmist sings praises that the earth is full of the wonders of God's creation; but Paul insists that, while some people teach others how to obey the law and live in ways consistent with God's creation, they do not obey the law themselves and do not have it written on their hearts.

Goals for the Learners:
(1) to tell what Paul reveals about the people who claim to follow God's law while failing to keep it.
(2) to recognize the hypocrisy of claiming to belong to God while breaking God's law.
(3) to identify the hypocrisy in their beliefs and actions and commit to making words and actions match.

Supplies:
Bibles, newsprint and marker, paper and pencils, hymnals

READING THE SCRIPTURE

NRSV	CEB
Lesson Scripture: Romans 2:13 (key verse), 17-29	Lesson Scripture: Romans 2:13 (key verse), 17-29
13For it is not the hearers of the law who are righteous in God's sight, but the doers of the law who will be justified.	**13It isn't the ones who hear the Law who are righteous in God's eyes. It is the ones who do what the Law says who will be treated as righteous.**

[17]But if you call yourself a Jew and rely on the law and boast of your relation to God [18]and know his will and determine what is best because you are instructed in the law, [19]and if you are sure that you are a guide to the blind, a light to those who are in darkness, [20]a corrector of the foolish, a teacher of children, having in the law the embodiment of knowledge and truth, [21]you, then, that teach others, will you not teach yourself? While you preach against stealing, do you steal? [22]You that forbid adultery, do you commit adultery? You that abhor idols, do you rob temples? [23]You that boast in the law, do you dishonor God by breaking the law? [24]For, as it is written, "The name of God is blasphemed among the Gentiles because of you."

[25]Circumcision indeed is of value if you obey the law; but if you break the law, your circumcision has become uncircumcision. [26]So, if those who are uncircumcised keep the requirements of the law, will not their uncircumcision be regarded as circumcision? [27]Then those who are physically uncircumcised but keep the law will condemn you that have the written code and circumcision but break the law. [28]For a person is not a Jew who is one outwardly, nor is true circumcision something external and physical. [29]Rather, a person is a Jew who is one inwardly, and real circumcision is a matter of the heart—it is spiritual and not literal. Such a person receives praise not from others but from God.

[17]But, if you call yourself a Jew; if you rely on the Law; if you brag about your relationship to God; [18]if you know the will of God; if you are taught by the Law so that you can figure out the things that really matter; [19]if you have persuaded yourself that you are: a guide for the blind; a light to those who are in darkness; [20]an educator of the foolish; a teacher of infants (since you have the full content of knowledge and truth in the Law);

[21]then why don't you who are teaching others teach yourself? If you preach, "No stealing," do you steal? [22]If you say, "No adultery," do you commit adultery?

If you hate idols, do you rob temples?

[23]If you brag about the Law, do you shame God by breaking the Law? [24]As it is written: *The name of God is discredited by the Gentiles because of you.*

[25]Circumcision is an advantage if you do what the Law says. But if you are a person who breaks the Law, your status of being circumcised has changed into not being circumcised. [26]So if the person who isn't circumcised keeps the Law, won't his status of not being circumcised be counted as if he were circumcised? [27]The one who isn't physically circumcised but keeps the Law will judge you. You became a lawbreaker after you had the written Law and circumcision. [28]It isn't the Jew who maintains outward appearances who will receive praise from God, and it isn't people who are outwardly circumcised on their bodies. [29]Instead, it is the person who is a Jew inside, who is circumcised in spirit, not literally. That person's praise doesn't come from people but from God.

UNDERSTANDING THE SCRIPTURE

Psalm 104:1-4. Perhaps your church includes in its litanies a "call to worship." Traditionally, a call to worship is some statement or reading that invites the congregation to attitudes and acts of worshiping God. Here, at the beginning of Psalm 104, the psalmist essentially calls himself to worship—"Bless the LORD, O my soul"—and then launches into his expressions of praise of God.

Praise is sometimes distinguished from thanksgiving by the role of the worshiper. That is to say, thanksgiving usually indicates that the worshiper has benefited from the actions and attributes of God. Praise, on the other hand, does not assume any personal benefit to the worshiper; it merely adores who God is and what God has done. In these verses, the psalmist looks far beyond himself and praises the Creator for heavenly splendor, majesty, and might.

Psalm 104:5-9. In the first section, the psalmist looked up; now he looks around. He observes and praises the Almighty's deeds in the earth. Notice, though, that God's might is neither displayed in destruction nor in brutish or bullying behavior. Rather, God's might is manifested in orderliness. The Creator tames creation so that it is stable and secure: the earth "shall never be shaken" (104:5) and the waters will "not again cover the earth" (104:9).

Psalm 104:10-18. The movement of the psalmist's attention continues to descend. He began with the heavens, then moved to the large-scale elements of the earth, and now turns to its smaller inhabitants. And with the movement from great to small, the attributes of God become tenderer.

Earlier praised for splendor and power, God is now adored for providential care.

Psalm 104:19-23. The psalmist's praise of God's care prompts him next to ponder God's design, and that is a marvel, as well. With great economy of words, the poet offers a kind of time-lapse photography of how the world works for God's creatures. He walks us quickly from darkness to light, observing the creatures in their habits and habitats.

Psalm 104:24-26. Everywhere the psalmist looks, he is inspired to praise the Lord. All around him he sees God's creatures; and with those, he sees God's works; and with those, he sees God's wisdom. Then the worshiper turns in yet another direction, and he marvels at the activity in and on the seas.

Psalm 104:27-30. The last specific creature mentioned was the legendary Leviathan, which was understood to be a great and terrible sea monster. And yet, in this next breath, all creatures together are seen like pet kittens waiting for their owner to set down the dish of food on the kitchen floor. In ignorance, some of Israel's ancient neighbors set up images of selected creatures for worship. But the psalmist knows better. No creature can be confused with God, for they are all dependent upon the One who made them.

Psalm 104:31-35. As we noted, the psalm began with a kind of call to worship—that is, a line that did not address God, but rather directed the worshiper's attention to God. Then, throughout the body of this psalm, the Lord is addressed repeatedly with second-person pronouns "you" and "your." And now, in these final verses, the psalmist ends where he began. The Lord is referred to in the third person, while the poet pledges his lifelong praise to God. Meanwhile, the two uses of "rejoice in" provide a meaningful juxtaposition. On the one hand, in verse 34 the psalmist rejoices in the Lord. At the same time, though, he hopes that the Lord will "rejoice in his [God's] works" (104:31). That is the way that it ought to be, of course, and yet there is that fly in the ointment. Thus the psalmist prays for the elimination of sinners, possibly because of the damage they have done to the goodness and orderliness of God's creation.

Romans 2:13-16. The issue at hand for the apostle Paul is the presumed difference between Jews and Gentiles. The Jews were the people who had a covenant relationship with God—the ones who had experienced the revelation of God's own self in history. The terms of the covenant had been articulated by God in the law, and the covenant had been signified by the people in circumcision. Yet Paul asserts that the Gentiles, even without the benefit of that covenant relationship, instinctively know something of law and will of God. Paul declares that the Gentiles will be judged by the degree to which they lived in accordance to what they knew.

Romans 2:17-20. The Jews, on the other hand, have all the benefits of that covenant relationship. They know God and they know the law. They reasonably assume, therefore, that they are positioned and equipped to teach and correct others.

Romans 2:21-24. Yet the apostle observes a terrible disconnect. If a Jew knows the way of God yet does not walk in that way, is he truly in a position to instruct others about which way to go? If a Jew knows the right answer yet consistently gives the wrong answer in the daily test of life, can he correct the errors of others? The tragic result of this disconnect is that those who do know God provoke those who do not know God, namely, the Gentiles, to commit blasphemy.

Romans 2:25-29. Paul concludes his argument with the helpful example of circumcision. On the one hand, it signifies that covenant relationship. On the other hand, it is an external thing, and therefore potentially superficial. Since we are physical creatures, it is perhaps our natural tendency to focus on physical things: that which is visible, tangible, and external. But "God is Spirit" (John 4:24), and does not look on outward appearances but "looks on the heart" (1 Samuel 16:7). Consequently, a fixation on the physical while neglecting the spiritual (compare Matthew 23:23) can never please God. Paul's conclusion, while scandalous to his Jewish contemporaries, is entirely logical: that the Gentile whose life reflects the law of God wins God's praise, while mere physical circumcision (without inner transformation) may account for nothing but hypocrisy.

INTERPRETING THE SCRIPTURE

How Do You Become a Member of This Church?

In our time and place, it's a little hard for us to imagine a church that is mostly Jewish, or a Christianity that struggles to know what to do with Gentiles. Yet that was the scene in the first-century Mediterranean world. The original followers of Jesus were all Jewish, as Jesus himself was. His mission was expressly to the Jews (Matthew 15:24); the explosion of growth on the Day of Pentecost seems to have been among Jews there in Jerusalem (Acts 2:5), and even Paul's first stop when traveling in the Gentile world was customarily the local synagogue (Acts 17:1-2).

Accordingly, a number of chapters in our New Testament—particularly in Paul's epistles—are devoted to controversies that arose from the influx of Gentiles into the church. Because the first Christians were all Jewish, and because they understood that Jesus fulfilled rather than abolished the law that they had known (Matthew 5:17), a natural assumption evolved among many of those early Christians: They believed that a person had to become Jewish in order to be a Christian.

Perhaps your church has certain requirements for becoming a member. Baptism is probably required. Maybe there are classes to be completed or commitments to be made. Perhaps your incoming members take membership vows. Whatever the particulars, though, I doubt that any of us has been to a church where converting to Judaism was a requirement for membership, let alone being circumcised.

It seems like an odd concept to us. We might do well, therefore, to think in terms of college courses that have prerequisites. How can you take third-year French, for example, without completing first- and second-year French? The one, after all, builds and depends upon the other.

These early Jewish Christians did not believe that Judaism, with its rituals and requirements, was the end of the line. They did, however, understand it to be an essential part of the line. And so there was much discussion in the early church over what should be required of the Gentiles who were coming to Christ.

The congregation to which Paul wrote in Rome was a mixed group. There were both Jewish and Gentile Christians within that church family—both circumcised and uncircumcised. And so Paul explored with them the expectations of each and the salvation of both.

The More Things Change . . .

The whole issue seems quite far removed from us, of course. But it's risky business to dismiss any part of Scripture as dated or irrelevant. After all, it is the written word of God. And, too, while the backdrop and scenery may change on the stage, the characters always remain the same, namely, God and human beings.

When we read this passage from Romans, we may not recognize the assumptions and prejudices surrounding circumcision and uncircumcision. Upon closer examination, however, we will recognize some very familiar behavior patterns among people. And, more significantly, we will also recognize the heart and desires of God.

On the human side, Paul paints a portrait of someone we know well: the hypocrite. You and I know what he or she looks like. Perhaps from time to time we have even seen him or her in the mirror.

Hypocrites are those who claim to act or believe one way when in reality their actions or beliefs are contrary to what they say. Their claims often suggest that they know all the right answers. Furthermore, they insist on those right answers in other people's lives. That can be a little obnoxious, of course. But the truly troubling thing about them is what a little scrutiny reveals, namely, that their talk does not always match their walk. Even if they know what is right, they do not necessarily act on what they know.

Paul chides the hypocrites for this incongruity. "You, then, that teach others, will you not teach yourself?" (2:21). It's a strong challenge, and it rises above the immediate context of that first-century rift between the circumcised and the uncircumcised. It is the repugnant irony that marks every "do as I say, not as I do" lifestyle. And, worse still, it is the tragedy of every person who is repelled from the truth because of the one who claims to represent the truth.

This is the harsh indictment that Paul levels at those who were only superficially obedient to God. "The name of God is blasphemed among the Gentiles because of you," he writes (2:24). It is the complete opposite of evangelism. Rather than winning people to God, the religious hypocrite drives people away.

I remember the first time that I heard a certain song. I have come to appreciate it in the years since that time, but I remember that I didn't like it at all the first time that I heard it. The first time that I heard it was when a rather poor, amateur soloist attempted to sing it in church. In reality, there was nothing wrong with the song, of course, but it sounded awful to me. And, likewise, the truth of God will be unattractive if it is out of harmony with the life that purports to embrace it.

Aiming to Please

The student wonders what will be on the test. The job applicant imagines what the interview questions might be. And the contestants wish they knew exactly what the judges will be looking for.

For the man or woman of God, on the other hand, there is no guessing and no uncertainty. We need not wonder what delights the Lord, for it has been made clear. And so we may live with confidence as we aim to please God.

The law of God reveals the heart of God. With its concerns for holiness, purity, justice, and compassion, the law gives us a clear sense for what God desires. Obedience to the law is not our means of salvation, of course, but that law may inform our living as we endeavor to please the Lord.

It behooves the man or woman of God, therefore, to know the law in order to know the divine will. Yet merely knowing it is not enough. If we know it without doing it, we dishonor the God who gave this law.

And then there is yet one more layer. In addition to the knowing and the doing, we must also recognize the particular kind of doing that God finds pleasing. For God does not take delight in mere legalistic checklists or outward appearances.

Superficial obedience is always a

tempting detour, of course, because it is easy. It looks good, feels good, and is usually measurable. Yet "real circumcision is a matter of the heart" (2:29). And that truth written to a first-century audience is equally important to a twenty-first-century one.

You and I live in a superficial culture, and its prevailing winds drive us to be superficial as well. We are taught to focus on appearances and our "look." Status is often tied to that which is visible to the eye. But we belong to a God who sees what human eyes do not. Our aim is not to win praise from others but to please God.

Of course, living for a holy God in an unholy world is like swimming upstream. And living with an inward focus in a superficial world can be thankless. Yet "such a person receives praise not from others but from God" (2:29).

SHARING THE SCRIPTURE

PREPARING TO TEACH

Preparing Our Hearts

Ponder this week's devotional reading from 1 Peter 1:13-23. What does it mean to be holy as God is holy? What does Peter say about how believers are to live as God's holy people? Ponder what Peter may mean in verse 23 when he writes that "you have been born anew . . . of imperishable seed."

Pray that you and the students will hear and heed Peter's call to holy living.

Preparing Our Minds

Study the background Scripture from Psalm 104; Romans 2:14-29; and the lesson Scripture from Romans 2:17-29.

Consider this question as you prepare the lesson: *What causes some people to talk about appreciating the world around them but then failing to demonstrate that with their actions?*

Write on newsprint:
❏ Bishop Wheatley's words as found under Gather to Learn.
❏ information for next week's lesson, found under Continue the Journey.

❏ activities for further spiritual growth in Continue the Journey.

Review the Introduction, The Big Picture, Close-up, and Faith in Action, which all precede the first lesson of this quarter. Consider how you might use any of this material in today's lesson.

LEADING THE CLASS

(1) Gather to Learn

❖ Welcome the class members and guests.

❖ Pray that those who have come today will search their hearts for God's truth within them and live accordingly.

❖ Post and read these words by United Methodist bishop Melvin Wheatley (1915–2009):

"We are split spiritual personalities. We swear allegiance to one set of principles and live by another.

We extol self-control, and practice self-indulgence.

We proclaim brotherhood and harbor prejudice.

We laud character but strive to climb to the top at any cost.

We erect houses of worship, but our shrines are our places of business and recreation.

We are suffering from a distressing cleavage between the truths we affirm and the values we live by. Our souls are the battlegrounds for civil wars, but we are trying to live serene lives in houses divided against themselves."

❖ Ask: **On a scale of 1 to 10, how accurate do you think Bishop Wheatley's observations are? Why did you choose that rating?**

❖ Read aloud today's focus statement: **Many people talk about appreciating the world around them but do not demonstrate it with their actions. What causes such inconsistency? The psalmist sings praises that the earth is full of the wonders of God's creation; but Paul insists that, while some people teach others how to obey the law and live in ways consistent with God's creation, they do not obey the law themselves and do not have it written on their hearts.**

(2) Goal 1: Tell What Paul Reveals About the People Who Claim to Follow God's Law While Failing to Keep It

❖ Help the learners understand the context of today's passage—the question of whether one must become a Jew in order to follow Christ—by reading or retelling "How Do You Become a Member of This Church?" in Interpreting the Scripture.

❖ Recruit a volunteer to read Romans 2:17-29.

❖ Discuss these questions:
1. **Paul writes that because Jews have the benefit of God's law, they could teach others how to live. What observation does he**

make about how they live out what they teach? (See Romans 2:17-20 and 2:21-24 in Understanding the Scripture.)
2. **How does hypocritical behavior affect attempts at evangelism?** (See "The More Things Change . . ." in Interpreting the Scripture.)
3. **How does Paul define a true Jew?** (See Romans 2:25-29 in Understanding the Scripture.)
4. **What lessons can Christians learn from Paul's comments to the Jews?**

(3) Goal 2: Recognize the Hypocrisy of Claiming to Belong to God While Breaking God's Law

❖ Read "Aiming to Please" in Interpreting the Scripture.

❖ Read and discuss this scenario as an example of how people are affected when the actions of a hypocrite are unmasked: **Mr. Green generously gave his time to serve as church treasurer. He spoke often about how important it was to be a good steward of the church's money. How might his congregation react when they learn that he had been arrested for embezzling church funds? What might the community think of the church as a result of these allegations? What questions might Mr. Green raise about his own commitment to Christ?**

(4) Goal 3: Identify the Hypocrisy in the Learners' Beliefs and Actions and Commit to Making Words and Actions Match

❖ Refer to the newsprint with Bishop Wheatley's words, which you used in the Gather to Learn portion. Invite the adults to read these words again silently.

❖ Distribute paper and pencils.

Encourage the students to identify two or three recent situations in which their outward actions betrayed their inward beliefs. What did they do? Had they been true to their beliefs, what would they have done? Assure them that what they write will be confidential.

❖ Call everyone back together and ask:

1. **Why do you think we do not always act on what we believe?**
2. **What steps can we take to live so that what we confess with our lips we demonstrate in the way we live our lives?**

(5) Continue the Journey

❖ Pray that as the learners depart, they will be alert for times when they ignore the truth of God that is within them and take steps to reclaim that truth so that what they say they believe and how they act will be of one accord.

❖ Post information for next week's session on newsprint for the students to copy:

- **Title: We're All Under Sin's Power**
- **Background Scripture: Psalm 136:1-9, 26; Romans 3:9-20**
- **Lesson Scripture: Romans 3:9-20**
- **Focus of the Lesson: Many people are grateful for all that they have in life, but others take every opportunity to abuse each privilege that comes along. Why this wide variation? The psalmist says that God's people must give thanks for all the wonders God has done and for God's steadfast love that endures forever, while Paul laments that humans have corrupted God's creation almost from the beginning and that all human beings continue to be sinful and will be held accountable by God.**

❖ Post the following information on newsprint and provide paper and pencils for the students to copy it. Challenge the adults to grow spiritually by completing one or more of these activities related to this week's session.

(1) **Examine your day before retiring each night. Look for instances where your beliefs and actions were congruent with one another. Also look for those times that your walk did not match your talk. What changes will you make tomorrow?**

(2) **Listen to what other people are telling you about yourself. Are you a good Christian role model for them? Or do they sense a disconnect between what you say you believe and what you do? Bring their comments before God and prayerfully discern any action you need to take.**

(3) **Recall that some people avoid the institutional church because of hypocrisy there. Are there actions or attitudes within your congregation that a visitor may feel are hypocritical? What can you do to help the church identify and overcome these?**

❖ Sing or read aloud "Trust and Obey."

❖ Conclude today's session by leading the class in this benediction, which is adapted from Romans 8:31b, the key verse for August 7: **Let us go forth rejoicing in the knowledge that since God is for us, nothing in all creation can be against us. Amen.**

UNIT 2: A WORLD GONE WRONG

WE'RE ALL UNDER SIN'S POWER

PREVIEWING THE LESSON

Lesson Scripture: Romans 3:9-20
Background Scripture: Psalm 136:1-9, 26; Romans 3:9-20
Key Verse: Romans 3:20

Focus of the Lesson:
Many people are grateful for all that they have in life, but others take every opportunity to abuse each privilege that comes along. Why this wide variation? The psalmist says that God's people must give thanks for all the wonders God has done and for God's steadfast love that endures forever, while Paul laments that humans have corrupted God's creation almost from the beginning and that all human beings continue to be sinful and will be held accountable by God.

Goals for the Learners:
(1) to acknowledge Paul's claim that humankind began corrupting God's creation nearly from the beginning and that all humanity is under sin's power.
(2) to recognize that God holds each person accountable for sinful behavior.
(3) to show compassion in one's relationship with others, for all have sinned.

Supplies:
Bibles, newsprint and marker, paper and pencils, hymnals

READING THE SCRIPTURE

NRSV

Lesson Scripture: Romans 3:9-20

⁹What then? Are we any better off? No, not at all; for we have already charged that all, both Jews and Greeks, are under the power of sin, ¹⁰as it is written:

CEB

Lesson Scripture: Romans 3:9-20

⁹So what are we saying? Are we better off? Not at all. We have already stated the charge: both Jews and Greeks are all under the power of sin. ¹⁰As it is written,

"There is no one who is righteous,
not even one;
[11]there is no one who has
understanding,
there is no one who seeks
God.
[12]All have turned aside, together
they have become worthless;
there is no one who shows
kindness,
there is not even one."
[13]"Their throats are opened graves;
they use their tongues to
deceive."
"The venom of vipers is under
their lips."
[14]"Their mouths are full of curs-
ing and bitterness."
[15]"Their feet are swift to shed
blood;
[16]ruin and misery are in their
paths,
[17]and the way of peace they have
not known."
[18]"There is no fear of God
before their eyes."
[19]Now we know that whatever the
law says, it speaks to those who are
under the law, so that every mouth
may be silenced, and the whole world
may be held accountable to God. **[20]For
"no human being will be justified in
his sight" by deeds prescribed by
the law, for through the law comes
the knowledge of sin.**

There is no righteous person, not
even one.
[11]There is no one who
understands.
There is no one who looks for
God.
[12]They all turned away.
They have become worthless
together.
There is no one who shows
kindness.
There is not even one.
[13]Their throat is a grave that has
been opened.
They are deceitful with their
tongues,
and the poison of vipers is
under their lips.
[14]Their mouths are full of curs-
ing and bitterness.
[15]Their feet are quick to shed
blood;
[16]destruction and misery are in
their ways;
[17]and they don't know the way
of peace.
[18]There is no fear of God in their
view of the world.
[19]Now we know that whatever the
Law says, it speaks to those who are
under the Law, in order to shut every
mouth and make it so the whole
world has to answer to God. **[20]It follows that no human being will be
treated as righteous in his presence
by doing what the Law says, because
the knowledge of sin comes through
the Law.**

UNDERSTANDING THE SCRIPTURE

Introduction. This psalm of thanksgiving has a single, obvious thesis,
namely, that God's "steadfast love
endures forever." The psalmist insists
over and over that the lovely part of

the nature of God is utterly reliable:
never-failing and everlasting. What
we translate as "steadfast love" is
actually a single word in Hebrew, but
translators have often struggled to

duplicate it with any single word in English. In the first published English translation of the Bible, Myles Coverdale coined the term "loving-kindness" to try to capture the meaning.

Psalm 136:1-3. The chief characteristic of Hebrew poetry is parallelism: that is, the repetition of a statement or an idea in slightly different words. It goes beyond repetition, of course, inasmuch as the restating of the idea adds depth and nuance. And we see in the New Testament that this poetic way of thinking and speaking worked its way even into the prose of Jesus (for example, Matthew 7:7) and Paul (1 Corinthians 12:4-6). In these first verses of Psalm 136, the poet urges thanking the Lord for enduring loving-kindness in three ways. The first employs the actual name of God (rendered in English as "the LORD" in small capital letters). The second ("God of gods") and third ("Lord of lords"), meanwhile, employ the Hebrew superlative ("this of these," as in "Holy of holies" or "King of kings") to affirm that God is peerless, above all others.

Psalm 136:4-9. Every message features both form and content. Ideally, the form complements the content. In the case of this psalm, however, the poet achieves something still better, for the form itself becomes part of the content. That is to say, the very structure of the psalm is the message of the psalm. At first blush, the recurring refrain about God's steadfast love reads like an awkward and artificial intrusion into the text. It appears to interrupt and break the train of thought. In fact, however, that very interweaving bears witness to a truth about God's love: It does not stand off to the side as a separate and independent matter. Rather, it is woven

through all of life and touches all of creation.

Psalm 136:26. The psalm ends where it began. That is not always the case, of course, for some prayers and songs end in places very different from where they began. One psalm may begin in despair but end in hope. Another psalm may begin in guilt but end in forgiveness. In the spirit of its central affirmation, however, this psalm ends right where it began, namely, with the unending, unchanging love of God. And so, once again, the form is the content, the structure is the message.

Romans 3:9. The natural inclination among first-century Christians was to assume that the Jews had some advantage in their relationship with God. They were, after all, the people with whom God had a covenant relationship, and they were the ones to whom God had given the law and sent the prophets. Surely, therefore, they must have had some kind of a head start on the Gentiles with regard to their relationship with God. Well, yes and no. In terms of knowledge and understanding, yes, the Jews did have an advantage. But in terms of the core spiritual condition, which is Paul's concern here, no, the Jews did not have an advantage. Jew and Greek alike are sinners, and so the Jew and Greek alike require a Savior.

Romans 3:10-12. Such a message would have seemed inconceivable to the Jews in Paul's audience. How could it possibly be that God's chosen people are in the same spiritual condition as everyone else? And so the apostle deftly anticipates and answers the Jewish objection by quoting from the Jewish Scriptures in verse 12 (see Psalm 14:1-3). "As it is written," Paul says, as he cites Scripture in order to argue the principle of universal human guilt.

Romans 3:13-18. What follows is a veritable medley of Old Testament passages that Paul employs to further his point. It is an argument from authority, as the apostle continues to illustrate for the Jews from their own Scriptures the truth of what he is saying. Specifically, the excerpted passages itemize the details of human wickedness. And as Paul weaves together quotations from Psalms 5, 10, 36, and 140, as well as Isaiah 59, it is easy for us to imagine how nimbly he must have "reasoned with them [his Jewish listeners] from the Scriptures" (Acts 17:2 NIV) when preaching in the synagogues.

Romans 3:19. Paul's point that the law speaks to those who are under it makes immediate sense to us in the ordinary matters of daily life. The laws in the neighboring state, for example, do not apply to you for as long as you remain in your own state. The laws of Canada do not hold sway over me as I live in and am a resident of the United States. The question, then, is what law does Paul have in mind? If it is the law of Moses, then the ones to whom it speaks are the Jews. Early Christian theologian Origen, however, argued that "the apostle Paul is not speaking here about the law of Moses but about the natural law which is written on the hearts of men." That is why, then, Paul could contend, according to Origen, that "the whole world should be held accountable to God."

Romans 3:20. As the apostle concludes this section of his argument, he cites one more psalm. This time, he alludes to a line from Psalm 143:2 in order to make his point that human beings cannot be justified by the law. For human beings, as Paul sees us, are hopelessly in bondage to sin apart from the work of the Savior. The law cannot save us. Or, by way of analogy, the law is capable of diagnosing the human condition, but the law is incapable of curing it.

INTERPRETING THE SCRIPTURE

The Way Home

Imagine, for the sake of illustration, that home is in Chicago. You and your sister are both preparing to drive home, but you're coming from different places. You are starting your journey in Boston, but she is coming from San Diego.

The apostle Paul calls you both to help you make your travel plans. Along the way, he indicates that you will both be taking the same road to get to Chicago. Indeed, he insists on it! But how is that possible? You're starting in different places and coming from completely different directions. How can you take the same road?

The question at hand in Romans 3 seems far removed from us, yet we discover that Paul's answer to the question strikes very close to home. In that first-century context, Christianity had grown out of Judaism, and all of the earliest Christians were Jewish. As Gentiles began to hear the gospel and respond, however, the question arose about just how salvation in Christ worked for those who were not Jewish.

Paul offered his answer to that emerging question. And as we see in the larger body of the New Testament, he had to answer it again and again, for it proved to be a persistent question. He said that salvation worked the same way for both peoples. Both Jews and Gentiles take the same road to get to justification.

The concept must have seemed nonsensical to the Jews in Paul's audience. They began by being God's chosen people. They were the recipients of the law and the prophets. They were heirs of God's covenant. Surely they began in a different—probably closer—place than the Gentiles. And it may be that even some of those Gentiles in Paul's audience, who were sensitive to the Jewish heritage and claims, also thought that Paul's message was odd.

The mistake in logic did not belong to the apostle Paul, however. Rather, the mistake was in the assumption about the spiritual geography of the situation. For Paul's point is that Jews and Gentiles are not actually coming from different directions or different places. On the contrary, all of humanity—Jew and Greek alike—begins in the same place: sin.

If people are starting in the same place, it only makes sense that they would need to take the same road in order to arrive at the same destination. That road, as Paul explores in the larger context of his Letter to the Romans, is God's grace accessed by human faith. And he cites Old Testament examples to illustrate that faith has always been the way that people are made right with God—even before the law (see for example, 4:1-12 where Paul uses Abraham to make his point).

Shall We Throw Out the Old Directions?

If the Jews discover that they have no advantage over the Gentiles in the journey to God, then what is the use of the directions that they had received? After all, the children of Israel had, for generations, been cherishing and following the directions that God had given them through Moses. But if those instructions—that is, God's law—do not get us to the destination, then what good are they?

This is the sort of conundrum that Paul needed to address. If both Jews and Greeks are bound by sin, and if both are saved by grace through faith, then what was the usefulness of the Mosaic covenant? Should not the law be thrown out as an ineffectual and outdated thing?

As we noted in a previous week's lesson, and as Origen saw implicit in 3:19 this week, Paul believed that the Gentiles also had some knowledge of God and the law. In creation and in conscience, certain things about God's nature and will are revealed to all humankind. And so, even apart from the direct revelation of the law and the prophets, the Gentiles "are without excuse" (Romans 1:20).

Still, for the man or woman who wants to know God better and live more completely in line with God's will, there is an undeniable advantage to having that fuller revelation. Those of us who remember watching football games on black-and-white televisions with finicky antenna reception would not want to trade in our current experience with high-definition flat screens. Both units can show the very same game, to be sure, but one will show it so much more clearly. And so it is, too, that those who have the written law can see God's nature and will so much more clearly.

Nevertheless, that law cannot save. It shows people how to live, which is of great benefit. But when they recognize that they have not lived—and perhaps cannot live—according to God's perfect will, then what?

Augustine knew the answer, and it points to Christ:

> Under the law we struggle but are defeated. We admit that what we do is evil and that we do not want to do it, but because there is as yet no grace, we are defeated. In this state we discover how far down we lie, and when we want to rise up and yet we fall, we are all the more gravely afflicted. . . . So when the man who has fallen realizes that he cannot raise himself, let him cry to his Deliverer for help.

The Beauty of Helplessness

We are not fond of feeling helpless, though the fact is that helplessness is a rather common human experience. We are, after all, born helpless. While so many other creatures are up and walking, eating, and even fending for themselves within a few minutes, hours, or days of being born, human beings are conspicuously dependent upon their parents for years. And as we age toward the end of life, we often find ourselves increasingly helpless again, depending upon the love and care of those around us.

Even collectively and at our strongest, we human beings are frequently reminded of our fundamental helplessness. Think of the sophisticated technology we have in place to help us anticipate and cope with inclement weather. For all of that, though, we still discover that entire cities and regions can be shut down by snow or wiped out by wind, water, or fire.

The spots on the sun and the gravity of the moon impact us in ways that we cannot control. Our hands still hang limp in the face of so many diseases. And as hard as we push the edges of our lifespan, we cannot escape death.

That inevitability of death, meanwhile, brings us to our ultimate helplessness: sin. No matter what the coroner's report may say, sin, according to Scripture, is the real "cause of death." And the apostle Paul declares that we are all "under the power of sin" (3:9).

We are helpless. But from infancy on, we learn that helplessness makes for dependence. And we discover that, while we are unable to help ourselves, there may well be someone around us—specifically, someone who loves us—who is capable of helping us. There is no pride or boasting among babies. They are beautifully dependent upon the loving parent who helps them. And so are we.

SHARING THE SCRIPTURE

PREPARING TO TEACH

Preparing Our Hearts

Ponder this week's devotional reading from 1 John 1:5-10. What does John say about sin and how it can be remedied? Why do you suppose that even though God offers forgiveness, we often want to say, as verse 10 claims, "that we have not sinned"?

Pray that you and the students will

confess your sins and be cleansed by the blood of Jesus.

Preparing Our Minds

Study the background Scripture from Psalm 136:1-9, 26; Romans 3:9-20. The lesson Scripture is from Romans 3:9-20.

Consider this question as you prepare the lesson: *Why are some people grateful for all that they have, whereas others abuse every privilege that comes along?*

Write on newsprint:

❑ information for next week's lesson, found under Continue the Journey.

❑ activities for further spiritual growth in Continue the Journey.

Review the Introduction, The Big Picture, Close-up, and Faith in Action, which all precede the first lesson of this quarter. Consider how you might use any of this material in today's lesson.

LEADING THE CLASS

(1) Gather to Learn

❖ Welcome the class members and guests.

❖ Pray that those who have come today will hold themselves accountable to God for overcoming sin's grip on their lives.

❖ Read: **In November 2014, Sue Ann Hamm was awarded cash and assets totaling more than $1 billion as part of her divorce settlement from oil magnate Harold Hamm, the chief executive officer of Continental Resources. Reuters reports that Mrs. Hamm, a lawyer and economist herself, is disappointed with the judgment and plans to file an** appeal because the money awarded "grossly undervalues the marital wealth she is entitled to" after their twenty-six years of marriage. Although Continental stocks had dropped in price, as of November 2014, Mr. Hamm's stocks were worth about $13.5 billion. The judge ruled that the "$1.4 billion of the growth in [Mr. Hamm's] Continental shares during the marriage was 'marital capital' to be split with Sue Ann." You be the judge: If you were Sue Ann Hamm, would you be grateful for the settlement you received or would you seek additional money in order to have what you think is a more equitable share?

❖ Read aloud today's focus statement: **Many people are grateful for all that they have in life, but others take every opportunity to abuse each privilege that comes along. Why this wide variation? The psalmist says that God's people must give thanks for all the wonders God has done and for God's steadfast love that endures forever, while Paul laments that humans have corrupted God's creation almost from the beginning and that all human beings continue to be sinful and will be held accountable by God.**

(2) Goal 1: Acknowledge Paul's Claim that Humankind Began Corrupting God's Creation Nearly from the Beginning and that All Humanity Is Under Sin's Power

❖ Choose a volunteer to read Romans 3:9-20.

❖ Discuss these questions:

1. **What question might Jews have asked after reading Romans 3:9-10?** (See "Shall We Throw Out the Old Directions?"

in Interpreting the Scripture. Note that the concern is the usefulness of God's law as given to Moses.)

2. **Why did Paul summon so many quotations from the Old Testament?** (See Romans 3:10-12, Romans 3:13-18, and Romans 3:19 in Understanding the Scripture. In short, his purpose is to show that humans are unrighteous and, as such, cannot earn salvation by their works. Paul stitched together several Old Testament quotations to make his point. If time permits, you may want to have students look up the verses from the Old Testament that Paul uses.)

3. **What does the law make available to humanity? Why is this knowledge insufficient?** (See Romans 3:20 in Understanding the Scripture.)

(3) Goal 2: Recognize that God Holds Each Person Accountable for Sinful Behavior

❖ Read: **Those of a "certain age" will remember comedian Flip Wilson's unforgettable character Geraldine Jones, whose phrase, "the devil made me do it," quickly found its way into the national vocabulary. While Geraldine's antics were hilarious, there are others who are quite serious when they use her phrase as a defense for crimes:**

1. Accused of stealing $73,000 from her church in 2009, the defendant insisted, "Satan had a big part in the theft."

2. Accused of stabbing to death one child and injuring another in 2014, the defendant claimed, "The devil made me do it."

3. Accused of raping and sexually assaulting numerous children while volunteering at a missionary children's home in Kenya, the alleged perpetrator claimed that "a demon made him do it."

❖ Ask these questions:

1. **Based on today's reading, what do you think Paul would say to those who try to shift blame for their sins onto others, even the devil?**

2. **What does the fact that "the whole world may be held accountable to God" (3:19) suggest about God's way of dealing with the pervasiveness of sin?**

(4) Goal 3: Show Compassion in One's Relationship with Others, for All Have Sinned

❖ Lead the students in this guided imagery activity. Suggest that they sit in a relaxed, comfortable position as you read these scenes.

1. **See in your mind's eye someone who has wronged you or people you care about. Think about what this person said or did to cause harm.** (*pause*)

2. **Now see yourself putting on this person's shoes. Begin to walk beside this person to get a feel for his or her life. What stresses confront him? What advantages do you have that she lacks?** (*pause*)

3. **Speak to this person about the harm that he or she caused. Make clear the nature of the offense and how it has damaged you or those you care about. Listen to any explanation about this unacceptable behavior. Offer forgiveness if possible.** (*pause*)

4. Think about someone you have harmed. What would you want this person to say to you or do for you? (*pause*)

❖ Bring the group together and discuss this question: **How does remembering that you too have sinned and fallen short affect the way that you treat someone who has harmed you?**

(5) Continue the Journey

❖ Pray that as the learners depart, they will remember to show compassion to others, for no one is without sin.

❖ Post information for next week's session on newsprint for the students to copy:

- **Title: God Set Things Right**
- **Background Scripture: Psalm 148; Romans 3:21-31**
- **Lesson Scripture: Romans 3:21-31**
- **Focus of the Lesson: Some people give thanks for all that is good in life, while others seem to have no hope. Where can they find hope? While the psalmist sings praises for all that God has done in creation, Paul holds out hope that those who continue in sin can be saved through faith in Jesus Christ.**

❖ Post the following information on newsprint and provide paper and pencils for the students to copy it. Challenge the adults to grow spiritually by completing one or more of these activities related to this week's session.

(1) **Ponder Paul's statement in Romans 3:10 that not even one person is righteous. Where in your life do you see evidence of unrighteousness? Hold yourself accountable before God by identifying and repenting of your sin.**

(2) **Offer to help someone who is having difficulty owning up to a mistake and, therefore, not holding himself or herself accountable. Be gentle and compassionate in your approach.**

(3) **Recall that the law provides knowledge of sin but cannot take away that sin. Give thanks to Jesus for his atoning work on the cross that does have the power to cleanse you from sin and all unrighteousness.**

❖ Sing or read aloud "Grace Greater than Our Sin."

❖ Conclude today's session by leading the class in this benediction, which is adapted from Romans 8:31b, the key verse for August 7: **Let us go forth rejoicing in the knowledge that since God is for us, nothing in all creation can be against us. Amen.**

UNIT 2: A WORLD GONE WRONG
GOD SET THINGS RIGHT

PREVIEWING THE LESSON

Lesson Scripture: Romans 3:21-31
Background Scripture: Psalm 148; Romans 3:21-31
Key Verses: Romans 3:22b-24

Focus of the Lesson:
Some people give thanks for all that is good in life, while others seem to have no hope. Where can they find hope? While the psalmist sings praises for all that God has done in creation, Paul holds out hope that those who continue in sin can be saved through faith in Jesus Christ.

Goals for the Learners:
(1) to recall Paul's good news that God provided Jesus Christ as a way for humankind to reestablish its loving, obedient relationship with God.
(2) to feel hope because of one's belief in Jesus Christ.
(3) to affirm their belief in Jesus Christ as Savior and pledge anew to follow him.

Supplies:
Bibles, newsprint and marker, paper and pencils, hymnals, optional string

---

READING THE SCRIPTURE

NRSV

Lesson Scripture: Romans 3:21-31

²¹But now, apart from law, the righteousness of God has been disclosed, and is attested by the law and the prophets, ²²the righteousness of God through faith in Jesus Christ for all who believe. **For there is no distinction, ²³since all have sinned and fall short of the glory of God; ²⁴they are**

CEB

Lesson Scripture: Romans 3:21-31

²¹But now God's righteousness has been revealed apart from the Law, which is confirmed by the Law and the Prophets. ²²God's righteousness comes through the faithfulness of Jesus Christ for all who have faith in him. **There's no distinction. ²³All have sinned and fall short of God's**

now justified by his grace as a gift, through the redemption that is in Christ Jesus, 25whom God put forward as a sacrifice of atonement by his blood, effective through faith. He did this to show his righteousness, because in his divine forbearance he had passed over the sins previously committed; 26it was to prove at the present time that he himself is righteous and that he justifies the one who has faith in Jesus.

27Then what becomes of boasting? It is excluded. By what law? By that of works? No, but by the law of faith. 28For we hold that a person is justified by faith apart from works prescribed by the law. 29Or is God the God of Jews only? Is he not the God of Gentiles also? Yes, of Gentiles also, 30since God is one; and he will justify the circumcised on the ground of faith and the uncircumcised through that same faith. 31Do we then overthrow the law by this faith? By no means! On the contrary, we uphold the law.

glory, 24but all are treated as righteous freely by his grace because of a ransom that was paid by Christ Jesus. 25Through his faithfulness, God displayed Jesus as the place of sacrifice where mercy is found by means of his blood. He did this to demonstrate his righteousness in passing over sins that happened before, 26during the time of God's patient tolerance. He also did this to demonstrate that he is righteous in the present time, and to treat the one who has faith in Jesus as righteous.

27What happens to our bragging? It's thrown out. With which law? With what we have accomplished under the Law? 28No, not at all, but through the law of faith. We consider that a person is treated as righteous by faith, apart from what is accomplished under the Law. 29Or is God the God of Jews only? Isn't God the God of Gentiles also? Yes, God is also the God of Gentiles. 30Since God is one, then the one who makes the circumcised righteous by faith will also make the one who isn't circumcised righteous through faith. 31Do we then cancel the Law through this faith? Absolutely not! Instead, we confirm the Law.

UNDERSTANDING THE SCRIPTURE

Psalm 148:1-4. The psalmist serves as a cosmic choir director. The universe's choir has several sections, though not the traditional soprano, alto, tenor, and bass. The psalmist begins by pointing to the celestial section, urging everything from stars to angels to join in praising the Lord.

Psalm 148:5-6. Now the psalmist offers a rationale for the participants'

praise. It's an important thematic move, for praise must not be mindless exuberance. Rather, there is good reason to praise the Lord. And, in the case of the aforementioned elements of creation, the reason for praise is that God created them and built them into the grand design and order.

Psalm 148:7-10. Next, the psalmist points to the "earth" section of the choir. And, just as with the heavenly participants in verses 1-4, both creatures and inanimate elements of creation are called upon to join the universal chorus of praise. To the modern mind, it may seem naive to think of snow, mountains, and trees as being able to praise the Lord. It may be, however, that we have either underestimated these inanimate parts of creation or that we have too narrowly understood praise. In any case, whatever is part of God's work is evidently capable of singing praise. And that should not surprise us since, as we gather from the larger testimony of Scripture, all of God's works are capable of reflecting, pleasing, and serving their creator.

Psalm 148:11-12. Perhaps echoing the order of the story of creation, the final group to be included in this choir of praise is human beings. The psalmist makes it clear that all human beings are involved. Not one should be silent. While human civilizations may tend to divide their citizens by class, caste, status, demographics, and such, everyone is lumped together here. The praise of God is marvelously egalitarian. And the psalmist's all-encompassing vision reminds us of Paul's later understanding of the church (Galatians 3:28).

Psalm 148:13-14. Once again, the psalmist offers the rationale for praise. Specifically, he cites the Lord's name, the Lord's glory, and the Lord's deeds. A larger examination of the psalms of praise would find that these are all recurring themes, and we might do well, therefore, to contemplate and internalize this approach to praise. Meanwhile, though the "choir" has been universal, in the final verse the psalmist brings the worship of God up close

and personal: The faithful people of Israel are close to the Lord. Drawing close is a right move to make, lest our praise become an arm's-length enterprise. Our God is relentlessly personal and our experience with God is meant to be very personal, as well. Our praise and worship, therefore, are offered not merely because we are part of that larger universe of praise, but specifically because we want to be near to God.

Romans 3:21. This verse picks up in the middle of a larger case that Paul is making. We have been introduced to that larger case in previous weeks, and we recognize the continuation here. The potential scandal in this verse comes with the phrase "apart from law." The law was regarded by the Jews as the fullest expression of God's will and the articulation of their covenant with the One who chose them. Yet Paul is quick to affirm that he is not jettisoning the law, for the message he brings is "attested by the law," as well as the prophets.

Romans 3:22-23. The issue is the righteousness of God. It is not, however, a righteousness that is obtained through compliance with the law, but rather "through faith in Jesus Christ." Paul will shortly address whether or not such faith nullifies the law. For the present, his point is that both those who had and knew the Mosaic law and those who did not are in the same position. "There is no distinction," he says in today's key verses, "since all have sinned." Even those who had the benefit of knowing God's law, therefore, need the righteousness of God that is "apart from law" (3:21).

Romans 3:24-26. A righteousness that is accomplished through compliance with the law would be based on self-righteousness or a works-righteousness. If, however, we cannot earn that righteousness by our own accomplishment, then being made right with God must be a gift. Paul declares that it is a gift of God's grace, which is afforded us by the atoning blood of Christ. Furthermore, Paul understands that this graciousness is not in competition with God's righteousness, but rather proves that righteousness.

Romans 3:27-28. Whatever a person accomplishes by his or her own ability or effort might be a cause for personal pride or boasting. And a righteousness that was achieved by "works prescribed by the law" might prompt such boasting. The righteousness that comes by faith, however, leaves no room for boasting, for it is not the accomplishment of the individual. Rather, inasmuch as it is a gift from God, it should not provoke pride, but only humble gratitude.

Romans 3:29-30. Jews rightly cherished and celebrated their covenant relationship with God. The risk, however, was that they would make God too small—as though their God were the exclusive property of Israel. Deep inside, they knew better than that, and their Scriptures affirmed that the Lord was the creator of all things and sovereign over all peoples. Paul uses that truth here to prove that God would also, therefore, provide salvation for all peoples, both Jews and Gentiles.

Romans 3:31. Now we return to the theological problem introduced at the very beginning, namely, does justification by faith nullify the law? If I do not need to comply with the law in order to be right with God, then does the law become irrelevant? Not at all, according to Paul. On the contrary, just as justification by faith proves rather than preempts the righteousness of God, so it fulfills rather than overthrows God's law.

INTERPRETING THE SCRIPTURE

Where There's God's Will, There's God's Way

The Old Testament law often suffers from a bad reputation among Christians. When we read it, we conclude that some parts are tedious, some irrelevant, and some even primitive. We typically regard the law as outdated, no longer applicable to us as Christians. And the accumulated traditions, the legalism, and even the perversions of the Pharisees in the New Testament further undermine the law in our eyes.

Yet much of the longest chapter in the entire Bible (Psalm 119 with 176 verses) is devoted to thanking and praising God for the law. The psalmist also regarded that law as "perfect," and he declared that it revives the soul (Psalm 19:7). That suggests to me that there is more to be found there than perhaps we have appreciated. Jesus himself insisted on the lasting importance of every bit of God's law (Matthew 5:17-19).

When we read Paul, we are sometimes unsure what our attitude toward the law ought to be. Do we celebrate it as a gift from God? Or do we set it aside as the vestige of an expired covenant?

Perhaps our best starting point for understanding the Old Testament law is in a relational context. Indeed,

I might suggest that that is the best way to understand all the things of God, who ceaselessly reveals the divine person and nature in relational terms. And so we might think about the law in terms of the everyday world of parents and children.

Parents routinely make and enforce rules for their children. At every age during a child's growing-up years, the loving parent does a certain amount of insisting. Here are the good things that I insist my children will do, and here are the bad things that I insist they not do.

My rules as a parent do not rival the wisdom of God, of course, but I believe that God's rules do begin with the love of a parent. Such rules are in our best interest. They are designed to protect us and to lead us in the way that God knows is best for us.

When the children are old enough to understand, the parents begin to talk to them about right and wrong. And for the people of faith, God's rules become the ultimate standard for right and wrong. To stray from the guidance of God's law is to take the wrong path. To obey the law, on the other hand, is to do right and, therefore, to be righteous.

The problem, however, is that we do not obey the law. Perhaps, in our fallen nature, we cannot. And if, therefore, we are hopelessly unrighteous, what are we to do?

Remember the Typewriter

Those of us who grew up using typewriters will recall how much more challenging it used to be to format text. Changing fonts was unheard of on the old manual machines, centering text on the page was an ordeal of calculating and backspacing,

underlining was a two-step process, and erasing was difficult and sloppy. Now all of that—and so much more— is easily achieved by the click of a few icons.

As I write on my computer just now, I see four icons that are of particular interest to me. They control how the lines of text relate to the left and right margins. The one icon aligns the text to the left margin. The next one centers the text between the left and right margins. The third one aligns the text to the right margin. And the final icon in that series makes the text of each paragraph align to both the left and the right margins.

That fourth type of formatting is called "justified" text. It was unavailable to the average person with a typewriter. Back then, that neat look was uniquely the province of books and magazines.

The term we use for that text formatting is fascinating to me, for it is deeply theological. What we are saying is that a great many lines of text do not, by themselves, reach the right margin. They fall short. When we click the icon that justifies the text, however, then those lines are brought into alignment with that right margin. They are made right, even though by themselves they fall short.

Paul bore witness to the fact that we human beings have fallen short of righteousness. And if we doubt it, the law of Moses proves to us our shortcoming. Indeed, Martin Luther argued that this was the most useful purpose of the law: "The particular and only office of the law is, as St. Paul teaches, that transgressions thereby should be acknowledged . . . it gives us to know what evil is in the world, outwardly and inwardly." The law, therefore, is diagnostic: It shows us what's wrong. The writer of Hebrews might also say that it is prescriptive, inasmuch as it foreshadows Christ. But it is not curative; it cannot save us.

So the Old Testament law sets the right-hand margin, and by it we see that we fall short. We cannot, by ourselves, attain to that margin, the righteousness of God. And so we need to be made right. Someone must do whatever it takes to justify our text.

The Good News We May Not See

When Paul wrote to the Romans, he wrote in Greek—specifically, a dialect prevalent in the first-century Mediterranean world known as *koine* Greek. That is the language of the New Testament. What we read in our English Bibles, therefore, is a translation from that original Greek. And, as the saying goes, some things are lost in translation.

In English, no obvious relationship exists between our words "righteousness" (3:21, 22, 25) and "justified" (3:24, 26, 28, 30). Yet in Paul's Greek, they are cognates, that is, two words that have a common origin or root. The verb that Paul uses for "justify" is *dikaioo* and the noun he uses for "righteousness" is *dikaiosune*. What is unseen in English, therefore, was

unmistakable to Paul's original readers, namely, that justification and righteousness are natural companions.

As we observed from the familiar world of formatted text, to justify is to make right. So it is, therefore, that the act of God justifying us is closely tied to righteousness. Not just righteousness in general, mind you, and certainly not our righteousness, which is inadequate. Rather, justification is tied to God's righteousness. As Gerhard Kittel and Gerhard Friedrich succinctly put it, "God's righteousness means justification."

We make a mistake when we split the character of God, as though the divine attributes are in conflict with each other—as though God's righteousness and mercy were at odds with each other. On the contrary, they are in perfect harmony, for they seek the same goal, namely, our righteousness. This was the recognition that set Martin Luther free. For as long as he understood God's righteousness as "that righteousness whereby God . . . deals righteously in punishing the unrighteous," it "filled me with hate." But when he realized it was the "righteousness whereby, through grace and sheer mercy, he justifies us by faith, (then) . . . it became to me inexpressibly sweet in greater love."

SHARING THE SCRIPTURE

PREPARING TO TEACH

Preparing Our Hearts

Ponder this week's devotional reading from Ephesians 2:1-7. How does the writer tell us that we have moved from death due to our sins

to life? What does it mean to you to know that you have been saved by grace? What do you learn about God in this passage?

Pray that you and the students will give thanks that you have been set right with God through Jesus Christ.

Preparing Our Minds

Study the background Scripture from Psalm 148; Romans 3:21-31. The lesson Scripture is from Romans 3:21-31.

Consider this question as you prepare the lesson: *Where can people who have no hope find hope?*

Write on newsprint:

❏ affirmation for Goal 3 in Sharing the Scripture.

❏ information for next week's lesson, found under Continue the Journey.

❏ activities for further spiritual growth in Continue the Journey.

Review the Introduction, The Big Picture, Close-up, and Faith in Action, which all precede the first lesson of this quarter. Consider how you might use any of this material in today's lesson.

Option for Goal 1: Bring enough string to class so that each person will have a piece that has been precut to about 8 to 10 inches in length.

LEADING THE CLASS

(1) Gather to Learn

❖ Welcome the class members and guests.

❖ Pray that those who have come today will find hope in their Savior, Jesus Christ.

❖ Post a sheet of newsprint and encourage the adults to brainstorm answers to this question: **What groups of people in our community may feel hopeless?**

❖ Review the list and ask:

1. **What are the underlying causes of such hopelessness?**

2. **What can we as the people of God do to help these people find hope?**

❖ Read aloud today's focus statement: **Some people give thanks for all that is good in life, while others seem to have no hope. Where can they find hope? While the psalmist sings praises for all that God has done in creation, Paul holds out hope that those who continue in sin can be saved through faith in Jesus Christ.**

(2) Goal 1: Recall Paul's Good News that God Provided Jesus Christ as a Way for Humankind to Reestablish Its Loving, Obedient Relationship with God

❖ Read or retell "Remember the Typewriter" in Interpreting the Scripture to help participants understand the theological concept of justification. Explain that through Jesus, humanity was justified with God. The relationship that was out of kilter because of sin was set right as the result of God's grace.

❖ Choose a volunteer to read Romans 3:21-31 and then discuss these questions:

1. **What is the connection between righteousness and justification?** (See "The Good News We May Not See" in Interpreting the Scripture.)

2. **What does Paul say about the source of righteousness and justification?** (See Romans 3:21, Romans 3:22-23, Romans 3:24-26 in Understanding the Scripture.)

3. **What have Christians often been taught, or assumed, about the law?** (See "Where There's God's Will, There's God's Way" in Interpreting the Scripture.)

4. **How do Paul's teachings about the law differ from what many Christians have been taught?**

(See especially Romans 3:31 in Understanding the Scripture.)

❖ **Option:** Demonstrate the brokenness of humanity's relationship with God by giving each participant a piece of string, about 8 to 10 inches long. Ask the students to hold up their strings, showing that the original ball of cord has been severed such that the pieces are no longer connected. Now ask the adults to work with other people to tie their pieces together so that they may be rejoined. Invite two class members to each hold one end of the string to show that it is now united. Suggest that the adults keep this picture in mind as they think about how the "scissors of sin" have destroyed the relationship of the pieces, understood to be the relationship between humanity and God. Further suggest that the students might use this object lesson to explain to a young person how sin breaks humanity's relationship with God and how through Jesus that relationship can be fixed.

(3) Goal 2: Feel Hope Because of One's Belief in Jesus Christ

❖ Form small groups and distribute hymnals, paper, and pencils. Invite the adults to search individually for songs that speak to them about the hope that they have because they are believers. Jot down page numbers. After a few minutes, ask the groups to discuss the hymns that they have identified. What does each hymn have to say about hope? Has the same hymn been chosen by several people? What drew the adults to the hymns they chose? Ask each group to agree on one hymn to present to the rest of the class as an example of hope.

❖ Call everyone together and invite one person from each group to name the group's favorite hymn of hope and explain why this hymn speaks to the group.

❖ **Option:** If time permits, sing one verse from the top choice of each group.

(4) Goal 3: Affirm Belief in Jesus Christ as Savior and Pledge Anew to Follow Him

❖ Post this excerpt from "A Modern Affirmation," found on page 885 of *The United Methodist Hymnal,* concerning what many Christians believe about Jesus. Lead the class in a unison reading.

We believe in Jesus Christ,
    Son of God and Son of man,
    the gift of the Father's unfailing grace,
    the ground of our hope,
    and the promise of our deliverance from sin and death.

❖ Ask these questions:
1. **What connections can you draw between this affirmation and Paul's teaching in Romans 3:21-31?**
2. **Are you able to say "amen" to each of the points made here? If not, which one(s) give you pause? Why?**
3. **What other beliefs, if any, would you want to add, based on today's lesson from Romans?** (Write those ideas on the sheet of newsprint.)

❖ Invite all who wish to affirm their belief in Jesus Christ and pledge anew to follow him to raise their hands.

(5) Continue the Journey

❖ Pray that as the learners depart, they will continue to give thanks for all that God has done to set things right through Jesus.

❖ Post information for next week's session on newsprint for the students to copy:

- **Title: Not Without Hope**
- **Background Scripture: Romans 5:1-11**
- **Lesson Scripture: Romans 5:1-11**
- **Focus of the Lesson: People are weak, endure suffering of different kinds, do wrong, and face various enemies all around them. What sustains Christians in the midst of these difficulties? Paul tells the Romans that through faith in Christ and with the presence of the Holy Spirit, God has given them reconciliation and hope.**

❖ Post the following information on newsprint and provide paper and pencils for the students to copy it. Challenge the adults to grow spiritually by completing one or more of these activities related to this week's session.

(1) **Research the terms "grace" and "justification" as these words are used in a theological sense. How does an understanding of these terms help you to deepen your relationship with God through Jesus?**

(2) **Recall that in the Gather to Learn segment of the lesson you identified groups of people who may feel hopeless. What can you as just one believer do to give an individual or group hope? What first steps will you take this week?**

(3) **Pray for those whose actions suggest that they do not know Jesus. Look for opportunities to share the good news that God has set things right through him. Invite people to seek Jesus.**

❖ Sing or read aloud "My Hope Is Built."

❖ Conclude today's session by leading the class in this benediction, which is adapted from Romans 8:31b, the key verse for August 7: **Let us go forth rejoicing in the knowledge that since God is for us, nothing in all creation can be against us. Amen.**

UNIT 2: A WORLD GONE WRONG
NOT WITHOUT HOPE

PREVIEWING THE LESSON

Lesson Scripture: Romans 5:1-11
Background Scripture: Romans 5:1-11
Key Verse: Romans 5:5

Focus of the Lesson:

People are weak, endure suffering of different kinds, do wrong, and face various enemies all around them. What sustains Christians in the midst of these difficulties? Paul tells the Romans that through faith in Christ and with the presence of the Holy Spirit, God has given them reconciliation and hope.

Goals for the Learners:

(1) to hear Paul's encouraging words about peace, endurance, character, hope, and love as gifts given by God through the death of Jesus.
(2) to appreciate the reality that God's provision of the Savior is God's continuing commitment to God's creation.
(3) to take hope through Jesus Christ into the difficult times in life.

Supplies:

Bibles, newsprint and marker, paper and pencils, hymnals

READING THE SCRIPTURE

NRSV

Lesson Scripture: Romans 5:1-11

¹Therefore, since we are justified by faith, we have peace with God through our Lord Jesus Christ, ²through whom we have obtained access to this grace in which we stand; and we boast in our hope of sharing the glory of God. ³And not only that, but we also boast in our sufferings, knowing that suffering produces endurance, ⁴and endurance produces

CEB

Lesson Scripture: Romans 5:1-11

¹Therefore, since we have been made righteous through his faithfulness combined with our faith, we have peace with God through our Lord Jesus Christ. ²We have access by faith into this grace in which we stand through him, and we boast in the hope of God's glory. ³But not only that! We even take pride in our problems, because we know that trouble

character, and character produces hope, [5]and **hope does not disappoint us, because God's love has been poured into our hearts through the Holy Spirit that has been given to us.** [6]For while we were still weak, at the right time Christ died for the ungodly. [7]Indeed, rarely will anyone die for a righteous person—though perhaps for a good person someone might actually dare to die. [8]But God proves his love for us in that while we still were sinners Christ died for us. [9]Much more surely then, now that we have been justified by his blood, will we be saved through him from the wrath of God. [10]For if while we were enemies, we were reconciled to God through the death of his Son, much more surely, having been reconciled, will we be saved by his life. [11]But more than that, we even boast in God through our Lord Jesus Christ, through whom we have now received reconciliation.

produces endurance, [4]endurance produces character, and character produces hope. [5]**This hope doesn't put us to shame, because the love of God has been poured out in our hearts through the Holy Spirit, who has been given to us.**

[6]While we were still weak, at the right moment, Christ died for ungodly people. [7]It isn't often that someone will die for a righteous person, though maybe someone might dare to die for a good person. [8]But God shows his love for us, because while we were still sinners Christ died for us. [9]So, now that we have been made righteous by his blood, we can be even more certain that we will be saved from God's wrath through him. [10]If we were reconciled to God through the death of his Son while we were still enemies, now that we have been reconciled, how much more certain is it that we will be saved by his life? [11]And not only that: we even take pride in God through our Lord Jesus Christ, the one through whom we now have a restored relationship with God.

UNDERSTANDING THE SCRIPTURE

Romans 5:1-2. During the past several weeks, we have explored the meaning of justification and how it happens. It begins, not with our works, but with the grace of God. That grace is made available to us in Jesus Christ, and we receive it by faith. Thus we are made right with God "by grace . . . through faith" (Ephesians 2:8).

Now Paul begins to elaborate on what comes in the wake of that justification. Specifically, he says that we have peace and hope of sharing God's glory. The goodness of this message is unspeakably rich.

Peace with God is a profound human need, though our innate longing for it is not always rightly diagnosed. We see the first evidence of humanity not being at peace with God when we observe Adam and Eve's reaction to the sound of the Lord walking in the garden after they had eaten of the forbidden tree of the knowledge of good and evil. As a result of sin, their reaction was to hide from God (Genesis 3:8). It makes perfect sense, therefore, that being justified—put right—would restore our peace with God.

Meanwhile, the other byproduct of our justification is this "hope of sharing the glory of God" (Romans 5:2). Even a cursory study of the theme of God's glory in Scripture will make our jaws drop at the prospect of sharing that glory. It was indescribable and overwhelming for Ezekiel (Ezekiel 1:28). It was awesome and frightening for the people of Moses' day (Exodus 24:17). And it will be the source of light in the New Jerusalem (Revelation 21:23). It is against that spectacular backdrop, then, that we begin to understand the mind-boggling prospect of "sharing the glory of God."

Romans 5:3-5. As we saw in last week's lesson, Paul said boasting was excluded (Romans 3:27). Not all boasting, however. In that earlier passage, Paul was denying any room for human pride in our salvation, for the righteousness accorded us in Christ is not self-righteousness.

Within this grace-driven salvation, however, there is so much for us to celebrate. That's why Paul wrote in verse 2 that we may "boast in our hope of sharing the glory of God." Now in verse 3 he also insists that we may "boast in our sufferings." This boasting is not braggadocio. Instead, we "glory" (King James Version), "rejoice" (New International Version), and "exult" (New American Standard Bible) in our sufferings.

Whatever the translation, it seems to us a strange response to suffering. We are more apt to respond with complaint, impatience, and indignation. Rejoicing and exulting are not part of our natural reflex in the face of suffering. But if, in fact, suffering leads where the apostle says that it does—namely, to endurance, character, and hope—then his proposed response makes a great deal of sense.

Romans 5:6-8. Twice in these verses, Paul uses the phrase "while we were still." That suggests that he believes "weak" and "sinners" to be former conditions—part of our past, to be sure, but not necessarily characteristic of our condition in the present. That is a provocative notion, and it may challenge us to expand our understanding of the gospel. Perhaps the good news is not merely that God loves us and accepts us in those conditions but also that he delivers us out of those conditions.

Meanwhile, Paul's real focus in these verses is on the death of Christ and its graciousness. He makes the point that rarely will one person willingly die for another person, even for one who is deserving because of righteousness. How much more remarkable is it, then, to offer one's life for an undeserving person? Yet this is the essence of the gracious, saving act of God in Christ, namely, that he came to us and died for us "while we were still sinners" (5:8).

Romans 5:9-10. "Wrath" and "enemies" are two words that may not have made it into our gospel vocabularies. In a careless splitting of the Bible, we may associate such hostile language with the Old Testament, while thinking that the New Testament does not feature "the wrath of God" or any notion of "enemies." Yet the apostle Paul sets us straight here, for we can only see how profoundly good the good news is if we grasp the larger context.

God's wrath must not be mistaken for lesser things, like capriciousness or a bad temper. No, divine wrath is a natural extension of God's holiness, and we would have it no other way. Would we prefer a God who is indifferent to wickedness? A God who shrugs off evil? And so we welcome the truth of this wrath, and we rejoice in the truth that we are saved from it by God's grace.

The concept of "enemies," meanwhile, gives greater understanding to the truth of "having been reconciled" (5:10). We don't think of ourselves as God's enemies. God's creatures and children, yes, but not enemies. But between the time that God created us and later adopted us, humanity was God's enemy, according to verse 10. Once we were estranged, but now we have been reconciled to God at God's own initiative and expense.

Romans 5:11. Now Paul's escalating song hits the highest note. As we observed earlier, Paul excludes any boasting in ourselves. In this passage, however, he provides this marvelous list of things in which we may boast. First, there is "our hope of sharing the glory of God" (5:2). Later, surprisingly, "we also boast in our sufferings" (5:3). And now, finally, "we even boast in God" (5:10).

Six centuries before Paul, the Lord spoke this same truth through the prophet Jeremiah: "Do not let the wise boast in their wisdom, do not let the mighty boast in their might, do not let the wealthy boast in their wealth; but let those who boast boast in this, that they understand and know me" (Jeremiah 9:23-24a). For all the things that we human beings are apt to boast about, none is as great as our God. Surely the One who is worthy of all glory and honor (Revelation 4:11) is also worthy of boasting!

INTERPRETING THE SCRIPTURE

The Old Beater

When my daughter got her driver's license, she set out immediately in search of a car. It had to be in her price range, though, which is to say that it had to be cheap. The whole experience was new to her, and she soon discovered why some vehicles cost a lot and some don't.

With both cars and houses, we are acquainted with the idea of "a fixer-upper." It is the automobile that needs repairs and new parts. It is the property that has become dilapidated. You can get a good bargain on something that needs a lot of work.

Of course, there is a level below the fixer-upper. The car that has been in a terrible accident is said to have been "totaled," which suggests that it is beyond repair. Or imagine a house that has been ruined by fire, a tornado, or some such catastrophe. Some things don't even qualify as fixer-uppers; they are simply disasters.

Whatever the case, we assume that value and price will go together. We expect to pay a high price for something that is of great value. The lesser the value, however, the lower the price. And only a fool would pay top dollar for something with little or no value.

But then there is the case of God and salvation.

"God proves his love for us," Paul writes, "in that while we were still sinners, Christ died for us" (5:8). It is an astonishing statement, and I think Paul means for his readers to be properly astonished by God's love. For if it is not love, it is unfathomable folly.

The issue, you see, is the condition of the property and the price paid for it. You and I are the property, and we have been purchased by God (see 1 Corinthians 6:20; 7:23). And what condition was the property in when God bought us? "We were still sinners," Paul says. That is to say, we were fixer-uppers, at best. The poet calls us "lost and ruined by the fall." We were wrecks, totaled, slaves to sin (Romans 6:20), and dead in our trespasses (Ephesians 2:1).

Yet it was while we were still in that condition that Christ died for us. The highest possible price was paid. It is an unthinkable transaction, for the value and the price were so incalculably disparate. If any human purchase approached this, we would say that it proves the buyer is a fool. Paul says, however, that it proves God's love for us.

Good News in a Bad Place

I remember hearing a discussion on sports talk radio about a certain NFL quarterback. The host of the radio show was extolling this quarterback's virtues—his arm strength, accuracy, mobility, and such. The caller, however, took issue with the host. The caller's point was that the quarterback in question had not been needed yet to win a game for his team in the fourth quarter. "I want to see him lead a come-from-behind drive in the last two minutes of the game," the caller said. "I want to see him play well in the clutch: then I'll believe in him."

Every sports fan knows what that looks like. We have all seen how certain players elevate their game in pressure situations and come through

with improbable victories. And, conversely, most of us have also watched our favorite teams victimized somewhere along the way by such a player on the opposing team. On either side of the outcome, though, we know what a come-from-behind victory looks like. And if we have a player on our team who has proven himself in the clutch, we feel more hopeful in those high-pressure, must-win situations.

Of course, as a man or woman of God you may always feel hopeful knowing God is on your side and can deliver even in the most impossible situations. And so, if you are in a bad place right now, you may be encouraged by the Lord's past performance in bad places.

Our salvation and our sufferings are closely connected in this regard, for both begin with us in a bad place. In the case of our salvation, that bad place is sin, and that is the worst of all human conditions. It separates us from God, contaminates every area of our lives, damages every relationship, and is eternally fatal. And yet, God stepped in on our behalf and at unimaginable expense saved us from our hopeless situation. "Emptied himself of all but love," Charles Wesley sang of this improbable victory, "and bled for Adam's helpless race."

In any subsequent experience of suffering, you and I may rightly remind ourselves that Jesus has already saved us from a worse condition. We have been in a direr situation than the one we are in now, and he came through on our behalf. We may be confident, therefore, even in the midst of our sufferings. Indeed, the apostle Paul said in Romans 5:3 that we could boast in them: almost like a team that is behind on the scoreboard yet knows they're going to win in the end.

Paul's Calculation of Hope

The idea that we may boast in our sufferings seems counterintuitive to us. We lament suffering; we do not rejoice in it. And so we may be tempted to dismiss Paul as either terribly naive or hopelessly stoic.

If we know Paul's biography, however, we know better than to dismiss him as naive about suffering. In his Second Letter to the Corinthians (4:8-12; 6:4-10; 7:5; 11:24-28), the apostle offers a kind of résumé of suffering. His experiences included being scourged, beaten, and stoned. He had been imprisoned and shipwrecked. He experienced hunger, cold, opposition, and abandonment. When Paul talks about suffering, therefore, he knows whereof he speaks.

We cannot discount Paul as one unfamiliar with suffering, but perhaps he has the opposite problem. Perhaps he experienced so much suffering that he was calloused to it: tougher than we are or would want to be. Perhaps that is why he could write so boldly about boasting in suffering.

Upon closer inspection, however, we discover that it is not just Paul's credentials that are unimpeachable; his logic is too. Specifically, he makes a calculation about what suffering produces, and he concludes that it produces very good things. If he is right in his calculation, then he is right to exult in his sufferings.

We willingly endure pain and difficulty in smaller matters because of the good that they produce. Such is the nature of most diet and exercise. So, too, with various dental procedures. And the point is obvious with almost any surgery we have had as well. We willingly endure pain in these ways because of the promised end result.

We may take it from this expert in suffering, then, that the final product is worthy of our boasting. We are not sadists who enjoy the suffering, mind you. But we reasonably rejoice in the endurance, the character, and the hope it produces. And the hope does not disappoint, for it is rooted in the abundant love of God.

SHARING THE SCRIPTURE

PREPARING TO TEACH

Preparing Our Hearts

Ponder this week's devotional reading from Psalm 42. Some scholars see instructions for enduring exile in this psalm. Where might you see such instructions? What role does memory seem to play in this psalm? What does the psalmist say about his relationship with God?

Pray that you and the students will have hope in God, even as you endure difficult situations.

Preparing Our Minds

Study the background Scripture and the lesson Scripture, both of which are from Romans 5:1-11.

Consider this question as you prepare the lesson: *What sustains Christians in the midst of life's difficulties?*

Write on newsprint:

❏ quotations for Goal 2 in Sharing the Scripture.

❏ information for next week's lesson, found under Continue the Journey.

❏ activities for further spiritual growth in Continue the Journey.

Review the Introduction, The Big Picture, Close-up, and Faith in Action, which all precede the first lesson of this quarter. Consider how you might use any of this material in today's lesson.

LEADING THE CLASS

(1) Gather to Learn

❖ Welcome the class members and guests.

❖ Pray that those who have come today will cherish the hope that is theirs through Christ.

❖ Read: **CBS reporter Debora Patta reported on the ebola outbreak in 2014 from Liberia's capital of Monrovia. Observing the burial of one man who had died from this deadly disease, Patta commented on how dehumanizing ebola is. Katie Meyler, a charity worker from the United States, told Patta and her team, "They are dying of hopelessness, of loneliness, of despair." In fact, those who succumb are treated with little dignity, since it is imperative that people keep their distance and wear protective gear. Although the government has ordered that the deceased be cremated, that order is not well received in a culture where touching the dead as they are lovingly prepared for burial is the norm. Yet amid this horror, there are stories of people risking themselves to care for others and provide them with hope.**

❖ Read aloud today's focus statement: **People are weak, endure suffering of different kinds, do wrong, and face various enemies all around them. What sustains Christians in the midst of these difficulties? Paul tells the Romans that through faith in Christ and with the presence of the Holy Spirit, God has given them reconciliation and hope.**

(2) Goal 1: Hear Paul's Encouraging Words About Peace, Endurance, Character, Hope, and Love as Gifts Given by God Through the Death of Jesus

❖ Read or retell Romans 5:1-2 in Understanding the Scripture.

❖ Select a volunteer to read Romans 5:1-11. Suggest that the students listen for Paul's description of the results of justification.

❖ Read the first four paragraphs of "The Old Beater" in Interpreting the Scripture. Form several small groups to discuss this question: **What connections can you draw between "a fixer-upper" and God's offer of salvation in Jesus Christ?** Call the groups together and get their ideas. You may want to add comments from "The Old Beater."

❖ Discuss these questions as a class:

1. **On what basis can Paul claim that he boasts (or glories or rejoices) in suffering?** (See Romans 5:3-5 in Understanding the Scripture and "Paul's Calculation of Hope" in Interpreting the Scripture.)

2. **Look at the sequence in verses 3-5: suffering, endurance, character, hope. What instances can you think of in your own life where you were able to move from suffering to hope?**

3. **Look again at verses 9-10. If you had been writing to the Romans, would you have chosen to describe humanity's relationship with God as "enemies" who need to be reconciled through Jesus to avoid the "wrath of God"? Explain your answer.** (See Romans 5:9-10 in Understanding the Scripture.)

❖ Conclude this portion of the lesson by reading in unison today's key verse, Romans 5:5.

(3) Goal 2: Appreciate the Reality that God's Provision of the Savior Is God's Continuing Commitment to God's Creation

❖ Post one or both of these quotations and the discussion questions that accompany them. You may wish to form two groups and ask one to work on the Chambers quotation and the other to work on the Newman quotation.

1. The cross of Jesus Christ and his baptism express the same thing. Our Lord was not a martyr; he was not merely a good man; he was God Incarnate. He came down to the lowest reach of creation in order to bring back the whole human race to God, and in order to do this he must take upon him, as representative man, the whole massed sin of the race. (Oswald Chambers, 1874–1917)

Ask: **How does Jesus fulfill God the Father's role for him as of the Savior of creation?**

2. We are not our own, anymore than what we possess is our own. We did not make ourselves; we cannot be supreme over ourselves. We cannot be our own masters. We are God's property by creation, by redemption, by regeneration. (Cardinal John Henry Newman, 1801–1890)

Ask: **How do people who recognize that they belong to God live differently from those who believe they are their own?**

❖ Bring everyone together and ask: **What connections can you draw between God's sending Jesus as Savior and God's commitment to restoring creation to what God intended it to be?**

(4) Goal 3: Take Hope Through Jesus Christ Into the Difficult Times in Life

❖ Read: **The Greek word translated as "hope" in Romans 5:2-5 means "to anticipate" or "welcome." Unlike the tentative way we often use the word "hope" in English, the Greek word *elpis* embodied an expectation of that which is certain. More specifically, "hope" expressed a joyful and confident expectation of salvation.**

❖ Distribute paper and pencils. Tell students to title the paper "Hope" and then write the words "anticipate," "welcome," and "joyful and confident expectation of salvation." They are to think of a difficult situation they are facing and write one sentence using any of these words to express their hope that Jesus will bring them through this.

❖ Encourage volunteers to read their sentences.

(5) Continue the Journey

❖ Pray that as the learners depart, they will go with a new attitude and hope, even in the face of suffering.

❖ Post information for next week's

session on newsprint for the students to copy:

- Title: Death Becomes Life
- Background Scripture: Romans 6
- Lesson Scripture: Romans 6:1-4, 12-14, 17-23
- Focus of the Lesson: People often give in to the temptation to do wrong. How can they overcome this temptation and avoid it altogether? Paul tells the Romans that through Christ they can be freed from sin and become slaves of righteousness, thus receiving sanctification and eternal life.

❖ Post the following information on newsprint and provide paper and pencils for the students to copy it. Challenge the adults to grow spiritually by completing one or more of these activities related to this week's session.

(1) Talk with someone about the reconciliation that is available to all through Jesus. Let your listener(s) know that God is eagerly pursuing them. Encourage them to seek God.

(2) Research the word "hope" as it is used in the New Testament. How is its usage there different from the way many people use "hope" as a synonym for "wish"?

(3) Identify someone who is suffering. Determine what you can do to help relieve the suffering and offer this person hope.

❖ Sing or read aloud "Great Is Thy Faithfulness."

❖ Conclude today's session by leading the class in this benediction, which is adapted from Romans 8:31b, the key verse for August 7: Let us go forth rejoicing in the knowledge that since God is for us, nothing in all creation can be against us. Amen.

UNIT 3: LIFE ON GOD'S TERMS
DEATH BECOMES LIFE

PREVIEWING THE LESSON

Lesson Scripture: Romans 6:1-4, 12-14, 17-23
Background Scripture: Romans 6
Key Verse: Romans 6:4

Focus of the Lesson:
People often give in to the temptation to do wrong. How can they overcome this temptation and avoid it altogether? Paul tells the Romans that through Christ they can be freed from sin and become slaves of righteousness, thus receiving sanctification and eternal life.

Goals for the Learners:
(1) to recall Paul's explanation that accepting Jesus frees one from sin while it enslaves one to righteousness and gains one eternity.
(2) to make the connection between being baptized into Christ, giving up sin, and the renewing of creation.
(3) to renew one's baptismal commitment.

Supplies:
Bibles, newsprint and marker, paper and pencils, hymnals, water pitcher, basin, paper or cloth hand towels

---

READING THE SCRIPTURE

NRSV
Lesson Scripture: Romans 6:1-4, 12-14, 17-23
¹What then are we to say? Should we continue in sin in order that grace may abound? ²By no means! How can we who died to sin go on living in it? ³Do you not know that all of us who have been baptized into Christ Jesus were baptized into his death? **⁴Therefore we have been buried with him**

CEB
Lesson Scripture: Romans 6:1-4, 12-14, 17-23
¹So what are we going to say? Should we continue sinning so grace will multiply? ²Absolutely not! All of us died to sin. How can we still live in it? ³Or don't you know that all who were baptized into Christ Jesus were baptized into his death? **⁴Therefore, we were buried together with him**

by baptism into death, so that, just as Christ was raised from the dead by the glory of the Father, so we too might walk in newness of life.

¹²Therefore, do not let sin exercise dominion in your mortal bodies, to make you obey their passions. ¹³No longer present your members to sin as instruments of wickedness, but present yourselves to God as those who have been brought from death to life, and present your members to God as instruments of righteousness. ¹⁴For sin will have no dominion over you, since you are not under law but under grace.

¹⁷But thanks be to God that you, having once been slaves of sin, have become obedient from the heart to the form of teaching to which you were entrusted, ¹⁸and that you, having been set free from sin, have become slaves of righteousness. ¹⁹I am speaking in human terms because of your natural limitations. For just as you once presented your members as slaves to impurity and to greater and greater iniquity, so now present your members as slaves to righteousness for sanctification.

²⁰When you were slaves of sin, you were free in regard to righteousness. ²¹So what advantage did you then get from the things of which you now are ashamed? The end of those things is death. ²²But now that you have been freed from sin and enslaved to God, the advantage you get is sanctification. The end is eternal life. ²³For the wages of sin is death, but the free gift of God is eternal life in Christ Jesus our Lord.

through baptism into his death, so that just as Christ was raised from the dead through the glory of the Father, we too can walk in newness of life.

¹²So then, don't let sin rule your body, so that you do what it wants. ¹³Don't offer parts of your body to sin, to be used as weapons to do wrong. Instead, present yourselves to God as people who have been brought back to life from the dead, and offer all the parts of your body to God to be used as weapons to do right. ¹⁴Sin will have no power over you, because you aren't under Law but under grace.

¹⁷But thank God that although you used to be slaves of sin, you gave wholehearted obedience to the teaching that was handed down to you, which provides a pattern. ¹⁸Now that you have been set free from sin, you have become slaves of righteousness. ¹⁹(I'm speaking with ordinary metaphors because of your limitations.) Once, you offered the parts of your body to be used as slaves to impurity and to lawless behavior that leads to still more lawless behavior. Now, you should present the parts of your body as slaves to righteousness, which makes your lives holy. ²⁰When you were slaves of sin, you were free from the control of righteousness. ²¹What consequences did you get from doing things that you are now ashamed of? The outcome of those things is death. ²²But now that you have been set free from sin and become slaves to God, you have the consequence of a holy life, and the outcome is eternal life. ²³The wages that sin pays are death, but God's gift is eternal life in Christ Jesus our Lord.

UNDERSTANDING THE SCRIPTURE

Introduction. Today's lesson starts a new chapter but continues a previous thought. At the end of chapter 5, the apostle Paul declared that "where sin increased, grace abounded all the more" (5:20). It is a testament to the magnitude of God's grace that runs contrary to most of our own experience and behavior. Such is the marvel of the abounding grace of God!

Romans 6:1. In the wake of that affirmation in 5:20, Paul anticipates a terrible question among his readers. If, the perverse reasoning goes, more sin yields more grace, then doesn't that make more sin a good thing? Should we not sin more specifically for the purpose of increasing the flow of God's grace?

Romans 6:2. Paul's answer is unequivocal: "By no means," he exclaims. The expression is characteristically Pauline. The underlying Greek phrase occurs fifteen times in the New Testament, and all but one of those (Luke 20:16) are found in the letters of Paul. Furthermore, ten of Paul's fourteen uses of the phrase are found right here in the Letter to the Romans. Such is the emphatic tone of this epistle!

Yet Paul is not being merely emphatic; he is being logical. He answers the question with a question, and the second shows the illogic of the first. "How can we who died to sin go on living in it?" If you grant his premise that we have died to sin, then his point is inarguable. And it is precisely that premise that he will continue to explore in the succeeding verses.

Romans 6:3-11. "Baptism into his death" (6:4) is not the language or imagery most young parents have in mind as they bring their white-clad infants to the baptismal font. Yet this is the strong language and potent image that Paul presents in an effort to help readers rethink their relationship to sin and their relationship to Christ.

Baptism is understood as a uniting with Christ. That uniting is comprehensive, for it includes both his death and his resurrection. Those are not detached episodes from history, but rather saving events in which we participate even two thousand years later.

The Christian's participation in Christ's death and resurrection changes his or her relationship to sin. Our endeavor is not merely to struggle with sin as with a bad habit. Rather, we understand ourselves as altogether freed from its power by virtue of the fact that we have died. Literally died? No, but our participation in the death and new life of Christ is the compelling meaning of our baptism. And so we may rightly think of ourselves as "dead to sin" but "alive to God" (6:11).

Romans 6:12-14. In English, the word "dominion" suggests ownership and lordship, and that is an appropriate concept for the Christian to consider. Who is my de facto lord? If sin exercises dominion in my body, then I misspeak when I call Jesus "my Lord." And so Paul exhorts those who claim Jesus as Lord to a very practical pattern of behavior. You and I come equipped with bodies, and those bodies have numerous parts—"members," in Paul's thinking. They are at our disposal, and we may offer them, like soldiers reporting for duty, either to wickedness or righteousness. The cause my members serve, then, proves the lordship in my life.

Romans 6:15-16. Paul had enough

experience with false teaching to be able to anticipate it. He guesses what monstrosity might come from a misapplication of the gospel of grace, and so he kills it before it gets started. Grace is not license to sin, for sin enslaves us. Grace sets us free *from* sin, not *to* sin.

Romans 6:17-19. Dominion, lordship, and ownership have a flip side. All of the relational terms we use for God have counterparts that apply to us. For example, as soon as we call to our Shepherd, we identify ourselves as sheep. When we call to our Father, we affirm that we are children of God. But when we invoke the language of lordship and ownership, then we are faced with somewhat less appealing counterpart terms for ourselves, namely, servants and slaves.

The concept of being "slaves of sin" is prominent in this chapter, but it does not originate with Paul. Earlier, Jesus noted the universality of the condition, saying, "Everyone who commits a sin is a slave to sin" (John 8:34). Paul rejoices, though, that the brothers and sisters to whom he writes have been set free from that slavery by their obedient response to the teaching they had received. And so now, echoing the exhortation of the previous section, Paul urges his audience to reorient what they offer themselves to, understanding that they have become slaves of righteousness instead of sin.

Romans 6:20-22. What is the gospel message for sinners? More, it turns out, than just forgiveness. For as beautiful, essential, and powerful as forgiveness is in our lives, its influence is somehow relegated to the past and the present. It covers yesterday's sin, but it does not conquer tomorrow's. Yet the good news for sinners is that the salvation offered in Christ is more comprehensive than just forgiveness. The will of God is to set us free from sin.

The theme of freedom continues to be illustrated in terms of slavery. Interestingly, the apostle does not present a choice between either freedom or slavery. Rather, he understands the choice at a more sophisticated level, namely, a choice between whose slaves we will be and from what we are free. No matter what, though, Paul reckons that we are slaves to something or someone, and we are correspondingly free from something else. With that paradigm in place, then, the apostle briefly weighs the relative merits of the two choices. In the end, he regards the choice as simple and obvious, inasmuch as one leads to death and the other to eternal life. In this regard, Paul is reiterating a choice introduced earlier by Moses (Deuteronomy 30:19) and elaborated by Jesus (Matthew 7:13-14).

Romans 6:23. The symmetry of the sentence and the contrast of its parts are reminiscent of a line we might find in Proverbs. The truth Paul proclaims is immediately accessible to everyone, for we all understand the difference between wages and gifts. Simply put: We have earned death, yet God freely offers us life.

INTERPRETING THE SCRIPTURE

The Service Rendered by Slaves

Slavery is far removed from our day-to-day life and experience. Consequently, we may dismiss Paul's slavery language as a kind of hyperbolic metaphor. The world of slaves may be no more real to us than that of cowboys or of knights. In fact, however, Paul was writing from within a context in which slavery was a very real part of daily life. He and his audience knew what it was for a human being to be purchased, and henceforth to belong to someone else. In Paul's letter to the first-century Christians in Rome, therefore, the image of slavery was not empty rhetoric; it was a flesh-and-blood reality.

Although you and I are not personally familiar with the literal kind of slavery Paul's original readers knew, we do have a different advantage. Perhaps more than any other generation, we are equipped to think metaphorically about slavery. Specifically, with our understanding of all sorts of physical addictions and psychological dysfunctions, we may be well positioned to comprehend a kind of bondage that goes beyond ordinary slavery. And this is surely the sort of thing that Paul has in mind.

Paul understood that even a human being who seems "free" by the world's standards might still be living in slavery. He or she is a slave to sin. It may not come with visible chains or whips, but it is involuntary and inescapable bondage, nonetheless. Furthermore, we discover that sin is a cruel taskmaster, for it makes us toil for a reward that is so empty, so disappointing. And, in the end, so damning.

The condition is not hopeless, however. We may be set free. Or, more accurately, we may become slaves of a different, better master. And so the apostle instructs and encourages those first-century Christians about what has dominion in their lives and to what they offer themselves in service.

The good option made available to us is that we may become slaves of righteousness. Now we may resist the notion of having to be slaves at all, yet the reality is that something or someone is going to have dominion in every life. We're going to serve something. We could live for our appetites or for our ambitions. We could live for our families or for our careers, for others or for ourselves. We might devote our lives to serving some cause or meeting some need. Whatever the case, though, the practical reality is that you and I get up every morning and offer ourselves in service to something, or perhaps to a variety of things. Paul's counsel is that we present ourselves to God and offer ourselves as instruments of righteousness.

The Importance of Being Dead

In the 1949 World War II classic movie *Twelve O'Clock High*, Gregory Peck plays a general who takes over command of a squadron of American pilots stationed in England. As the brand-new commander, the general introduces himself to his men with a tough, hard-nosed speech. Lamenting a certain "what are we fighting for?" attitude, the general declares, "We're in a war, a shooting war. We've got to fight. And some of us have got to die. I'm not trying to tell you not to be afraid. Fear is normal. But stop worrying about it and about yourselves. Stop making plans. Forget about going home. Consider yourselves already dead. Once you accept that idea, it won't be so tough."

"Consider yourselves already dead." Perhaps it is easier to go into combat if you've already chalked yourself up as a casualty. Perhaps there is less fear and reluctance if preserving your own life ceases to be a priority. That attitude should certainly be understood by every disciple (Matthew 16:25).

The apostle Paul addressed the Christians in Rome with a similar sort of message. They, too, should consider themselves already dead. Specifically, Paul wrote, "consider yourselves dead to sin" (6:11).

When I was a teenage boy, I was a notoriously sound sleeper. When my parents had the unhappy task of trying to awaken me in the morning, my mom would sometimes complain about how difficult it was. "You were dead to the world," she would tell me later. By "dead," of course, she meant that I was completely unresponsive. There was no rousing me. She could call, poke, and shake me, but all without effect.

That must have been a great nuisance for her, and it was certainly no virtue on my part. Yet at some level I believe that I was exemplary back then. For my "dead-to-the-world" sleepiness provides me with a model of what Paul says I should be like with respect to sin. Let me be dead to it—completely unresponsive. No matter how it pokes and prods, no matter how loudly, how urgently, or how persistently it calls, sin should find it impossible to rouse me.

By contrast, the apostle says that, while considering ourselves dead to sin, we should at the same time consider ourselves "alive to God in Christ Jesus" (6:11). May it be that when he calls, I answer. When he prods, I move. When he speaks, I respond. Dead to sin, yes; but thoroughly alive to him.

Going Down?

Today, Christians around the world use a wide variety of means to baptize people, and there are varying understandings about who ought to be baptized. In my tradition as an ordained United Methodist minister, I will baptize people of any age using virtually any means. More than any other situation, though, I find myself holding relatively young babies in my arms, putting the tiniest drops of water on their small foreheads.

In New Testament, of course, the look and feel of baptism was quite different. It was adults, not infants, coming forward to be baptized. And it was probably not just a little bit of water involved. Rather, the traditional understanding is that the people who came to be baptized were immersed—completely submerged in the body of water. The act was an experience, therefore, and ripe with symbolism.

William Barclay connects the dots for us between that style of baptism with which Paul and his audience were familiar and the words of the apostle in Romans 6. "When a man descended into the water and the water closed over his head, it was like being buried. When he emerged from the water, it was like rising from the grave. Baptism was symbolically like dying and rising again."

So it is, then, that we Christians are both dead and alive.

On the one hand, we may embrace the truth that, by our baptism, we have died with Christ and have been buried with him. Henceforth, then, we are dead to sin. It was our old master, but we are no longer its slaves.

On the other hand, God does not leave us dead and buried. Rather, we are raised to new life in Christ. We are more alive than ever before, and especially alive to him.

SHARING THE SCRIPTURE

PREPARING TO TEACH

Preparing Our Hearts

Ponder this week's devotional reading from 2 Corinthians 5:17-21. What happened that enabled humans to be reconciled to God? What does it mean in your life to know that you are a new creation in Christ? How do you serve as an ambassador for Christ?

Pray that you and the students will celebrate the newness of life that is yours in Christ and live as if you are new creatures.

Preparing Our Minds

Study the background Scripture from Romans 6 and the lesson Scripture from Romans 6:1-4, 12-14, 17-23.

Consider this question as you prepare the lesson: *How can people overcome the temptation to do wrong?*

Write on newsprint:

❑ information for next week's lesson, found under Continue the Journey.

❑ activities for further spiritual growth in Continue the Journey.

Review the Introduction, The Big Picture, Close-up, and Faith in Action, which all precede the first lesson of this quarter. Consider how you might use any of this material in today's lesson.

Talk with your pastor prior to the session about how the class members might renew their baptisms in a way consistent with your denomination's beliefs. Perhaps the pastor would be available to lead a renewal service. The liturgy for such a service is likely found in your denominational hymnal. A main point to remember is that baptism is an unrepeatable act. Baptized believers may, however, choose to *remember* their baptism. Gather whatever supplies you may need, including a basin, water pitcher (preferably clear glass), and paper or cloth hand towels.

LEADING THE CLASS

(1) Gather to Learn

❖ Welcome the class members and guests.

❖ Pray that those who have come today will give thanks for the new life they have in Jesus Christ.

❖ Read: **A survey conducted by** ***Discipleship Journal*** **revealed nine areas of spiritual challenge among its readers: (1) materialism, (2) pride, (3) self-centeredness, (4) laziness, (5) (tie) anger/bitterness, (5) (tie) sexual lust, (7) envy, (8) gluttony, (9) lying.**

Eighty-one percent of those surveyed reported that temptations were stronger when they had neglected their time with God, while 57 percent said temptations were stronger when they were physically tired. Respondents found the best strategies for resisting temptation were prayer (84 percent), avoidance of compromising situations (76 percent), Bible study (66 percent), and being accountable to someone (52 percent).

❖ Ask: **This survey was published in December 1992. If the survey were conducted again today, what differences would you expect to see? Or do you think people would still name the same temptations? Explain your answer.**

❖ Read aloud today's focus statement: **People often give in to the temptation to do wrong. How can they overcome this temptation and avoid it altogether? Paul tells the Romans that through Christ they can be freed from sin and become slaves of righteousness, thus receiving sanctification and eternal life.**

(2) Goal 1: Recall Paul's Explanation that Accepting Jesus Frees One from Sin While It Enslaves One to Righteousness and Gains One Eternity

❖ Choose three volunteers to read Romans 6:1-4, 12-14, 17-23.

❖ Discuss these questions:

1. **What issues does Paul raise in Romans 6:1-2?** (See Introduction, Romans 6:1, and Romans 6:2 in Understanding the Scripture.)

2. **In a way, Paul's comments that believers have been set free from sin and have become "slaves of righteousness" seem** paradoxical. **How does this change in "ownership" affect the lives of believers?** (See Romans 6:17-19 in Understanding the Scripture and "The Service Rendered by Slaves" in Interpreting the Scripture.)

3. **What determines who or what is lord of one's life?** (See Romans 6:12-14 in Understanding the Scripture.)

4. **What good news do you hear in this passage?** (See Romans 6:20-22, Romans 6:23 in Understanding the Scripture.)

5. **What does the symbolism of baptism teach us about our relationship with Jesus?** (See "Going Down?" in Interpreting the Scripture.)

(3) Goal 2: Make the Connection Between Being Baptized into Christ, Giving Up Sin, and the Renewing of Creation

❖ Read the first three paragraphs of "The Importance of Being Dead" in Interpreting the Scripture. Discuss how the illustration from *Twelve O'Clock High* helps believers understand the symbolic death of baptism.

❖ Post a sheet of newsprint and draw a line down the center. On the left write "Before Baptism" and on the right write "After Baptism." Encourage participants to describe as much as possible about life before and after baptism. (See Romans 6:3-11 in Understanding the Scripture.)

❖ Invite the learners to comment on any connections they see between baptism and the renewal of creation. Suggest they think about how their lives have been re-created as a result of their baptism.

(4) Goal 3: Renew One's Baptismal Commitment

❖ Set out on a table that all can see whatever supplies you will need to do a renewal of baptism. At minimum you will need a basin, paper or hand towels, water, and a pitcher, preferably one that is made of clear glass. Begin by pouring the water into the basin in such a way that the students can both hear and see the clear water. If the pastor will lead this service, now is the time that he or she should be invited to come forward. If you will use your denomination's baptismal renewal service liturgy, distribute hymnals. Otherwise, you may wish to have participants form a line and come to the table where they may dip their hands in the water as others say, "Remember your baptism and be thankful."

❖ Ask participants to return to their seats and spend a few moments in quiet prayer thanking God for all that they have been given through their baptism.

❖ Conclude this quiet time by reading in unison Romans 6:4, today's key verse.

(5) Continue the Journey

❖ Pray that as the learners depart, they will continue to choose the life they have been given in Christ through their baptism.

❖ Post information for next week's session on newsprint for the students to copy:

- **Title: Safe in God's Love**
- **Background Scripture: Romans 8:28-39**
- **Lesson Scripture: Romans 8:28-39**
- **Focus of the Lesson: People are constantly tossed about by the trials and tribulations**

of life. Where can they find safe haven? Paul tells the Romans that through the love of God in Christ Jesus they will find a Savior from whose love they can never be separated and by whom they will be loved, protected, glorified, and delivered from all trials and tribulations.

❖ Post the following information on newsprint and provide paper and pencils for the students to copy it. Challenge the adults to grow spiritually by completing one or more of these activities related to this week's session.

(1) **Ponder the importance of your own baptism, even if you were too young to remember it. What difference does it make in your life to know that as one who is baptized, you have been raised with Christ "by the glory of the Father" (6:4)?**

(2) **Be aware this week of your actions. Do they demonstrate that you have been raised to new life in Jesus—or that you are still dead in your sins? Seek repentance as that seems fitting.**

(3) **Recall that Paul taught that believers are to be slaves to God. As free independent people, the notion of slavery is beyond the boundaries of our frame of reference. How, though, is being enslaved to God a positive thing?**

❖ Sing or read aloud "This Is the Spirit's Entry Now."

❖ Conclude today's session by leading the class in this benediction, which is adapted from Romans 8:31b, the key verse for August 7: **Let us go forth rejoicing in the knowledge that since God is for us, nothing in all creation can be against us. Amen.**

UNIT 3: LIFE ON GOD'S TERMS
SAFE IN GOD'S LOVE

PREVIEWING THE LESSON

Lesson Scripture: Romans 8:28-39
Background Scripture: Romans 8:28-39
Key Verse: Romans 8:31b

Focus of the Lesson:
People are constantly tossed about by the trials and tribulations of life. Where can they find safe haven? Paul tells the Romans that through the love of God in Christ Jesus they will find a Savior from whose love they can never be separated and by whom they will be loved, protected, glorified, and delivered from all trials and tribulations.

Goals for the Learners:
(1) to study the principal points of Paul's teaching on Jesus from whose love believers can never be separated by any turmoil or hardship.
(2) to believe that Christ Jesus was God's plan for humankind from the beginning of creation.
(3) to share the joy and love of Christ with others.

Supplies:
Bibles, newsprint and marker, paper and pencils, hymnals

READING THE SCRIPTURE

NRSV

Lesson Scripture: Romans 8:28-39

28We know that all things work together for good for those who love God, who are called according to his purpose. 29For those whom he foreknew he also predestined to be conformed to the image of his Son, in order that he might be the firstborn within a large family. 30And those whom he predestined he also called; and those whom he called, he also

CEB

Lesson Scripture: Romans 8:28-39

28We know that God works all things together for good for the ones who love God, for those who are called according to his purpose. 29We know this because God knew them in advance, and he decided in advance that they would be conformed to the image of his Son. That way his Son would be the first of many brothers and sisters. 30Those who God decided

---
492

justified; and those whom he justified he also glorified.

³¹What then are we to say about these things? **If God is for us, who is against us?** ³²He who did not withhold his own Son, but gave him up for all of us, will he not with him also give us everything else? ³³Who will bring any charge against God's elect? It is God who justifies. ³⁴Who is to condemn? It is Christ Jesus, who died, yes, who was raised, who is at the right hand of God, who indeed intercedes for us. ³⁵Who will separate us from the love of Christ? Will hardship, or distress, or persecution, or famine, or nakedness, or peril, or sword? ³⁶As it is written,

"For your sake we are being
    killed all day long;
    we are accounted as sheep to be
    slaughtered."

³⁷No, in all these things we are more than conquerors through him who loved us. ³⁸For I am convinced that neither death, nor life, nor angels, nor rulers, nor things present, nor things to come, nor powers, ³⁹nor height, nor depth, nor anything else in all creation, will be able to separate us from the love of God in Christ Jesus our Lord.

in advance would be conformed to his Son, he also called. Those whom he called, he also made righteous. Those whom he made righteous, he also glorified.

³¹So what are we going to say about these things? **If God is for us, who is against us?** ³²He didn't spare his own Son but gave him up for us all. Won't he also freely give us all things with him?

³³Who will bring a charge against God's elect people? It is God who acquits them. ³⁴Who is going to convict them? It is Christ Jesus who died, even more, who was raised, and who also is at God's right side. It is Christ Jesus who also pleads our case for us. ³⁵Who will separate us from Christ's love? Will we be separated by trouble, or distress, or harassment, or famine, or nakedness, or danger, or sword? ³⁶As it is written,

We are being put to death all day
    long for your sake.
    We are treated like sheep for
    slaughter.

³⁷But in all these things we win a sweeping victory through the one who loved us. ³⁸I'm convinced that nothing can separate us from God's love in Christ Jesus our Lord: not death or life, not angels or rulers, not present things or future things, not powers ³⁹or height or depth, or any other thing that is created.

UNDERSTANDING THE SCRIPTURE

Romans 8:28. If the number of chapters devoted to the story is any indication, then Joseph was one of ancient Israel's favorite characters. More chapters are given to his story than to other such Genesis notables as Adam, Noah, Abraham, and Jacob. And this verse from two thousand years after the time of Joseph captures the reason why his story was so cherished: because we need to be assured that all things do work together for good. Joseph's experience was full of misfortune and mistreatment, and yet

493

God's grand purpose was achieved for him and through him in the end. And those seeming misfortunes were instrumental in God's providential process. So, here, Paul affirms the same kind of providential process for all who are "called according to his purpose."

Romans 8:29-30. Having referred to those who are called, the apostle offers a fuller explanation about them. Specifically, he presents us with what I call a "theo-chronology"—that is, a theological understanding of God's purpose and activity over time. Being called by God is one part of a larger series of events. In order: God foreknew, then predestined, then called, then justified, and then glorified.

These are all the gracious acts of a sovereign God. And, in keeping with the theme introduced in the first verse of this passage, they are all instruments of God's purpose. In this particular case, the expressed purpose is twofold: first, that people would be "conformed to the image of his Son," and, second, that that Son would be the first in a very large family. Both elements are marvelous to contemplate. The One who created us in God's image has not abandoned that original purpose. And though we began as creatures, God's loving endeavor is to make us sons and daughters!

Romans 8:31-32. Now Paul begins to ponder a series of questions, and in each case the answer is full of gospel. In this respect, these verses may be emblematic of a larger truth. You and I have had many questions that we have wrestled with over the years. I wouldn't be surprised if we discover, in the end, that the answer to every question is full of gospel!

The question in verse 31, "who is against us," is a fascinating one in the context of Paul's own biography. For most of his days, Paul had people against him. He was hounded, opposed, misrepresented, and persecuted. He was chased out of towns, imprisoned, and eventually (according to tradition) executed. So there were plenty of answers to the question of who can be against us. And yet, when God is for us, suddenly all of that other opposition is dwarfed to insignificance.

Romans 8:33-34. Paul is using the language of the legal system when he talks about bringing a charge against someone. Many of us struggle from time to time with guilty consciences, and not without cause. We are guilty—guilty of sin—and we deserve to brought up on charges. Yet in what court and before what magistrate would such a charge be brought? Only before God. Paul's right and beautiful point is that God is the very one who justifies us. And while "the accuser of our brothers and sisters" (Revelation 12:10, CEB) may try to bring a charge against us, Christ himself intercedes on our behalf. The picture recalls the apostle's strong point about who can be against us when God is for us, for if the Son intercedes on our behalf and the Father makes us right, then any case brought against us will be thrown out of court.

Romans 8:35-36. That intercession and justification, of course, are products of God's love for us. And so the practical question is what things or persons might impede, limit, or cut off that love. Paul generates a list of possible impediments in our lives— experiences that could cut us off from many other things that we love. It is a list of experiences with which

Paul is personally familiar, and he finds that the words of Psalm 44:22 resonate with his experience. The question is whether those troubles in life, which can cost us so much, can cut us off from the love of God. The answer, coming in the next verse, is an emphatic no.

Romans 8:37. I wonder if Paul would object to some of our common terminology. I think, for example, of the phrase "cancer survivor" or "recovering alcoholic." On the one hand, both expressions bear witness to a good thing. They both reflect people who are coming out the other side of something that could have ruined their lives. And yet, I wonder if those expressions would be too tepid for Paul. I suspect he wouldn't want us to think of ourselves as mere survivors. And I wonder if he wouldn't want us to claim something stronger than just recovering.

You and I don't live in a world where the term "conqueror" is used much anymore. It may still be employed to describe certain characters from history, but it is not a word that enjoys contemporary application. Yet Paul and his audience—especially that audience in the capital of the Roman Empire—had an appreciation for the concept of a conqueror.

The conqueror is not one who simply struggles to hold on to his own turf; rather, he is the one who marches boldly out and takes new territory. He overcomes all opposition. He emerges from battle stronger rather than weaker. And within the context of the kinds of struggles and trials cited by Paul in the preceding verses, he says that we are even more than that—even more than conquerors.

Romans 8:38-39. How many dimensions are there to life and reality? How many factors, elements, and influences? Paul tries to anticipate them all, putting forth a comprehensive list of all the things that cannot separate us from the love of God. In short, no matter our circumstances or experiences, the great, good news is that nothing can separate us from the love of God that is ours through Jesus Christ.

INTERPRETING THE SCRIPTURE

The Great Mistrial

If I were the prosecuting attorney, I would demand that this Judge recuse himself from the case. For if I were the prosecuting attorney, these proceedings would seem to me patently unfair. I will not object, however, since I am not the prosecutor. On the contrary, I am the defendant. And when I say that the proceedings are unfair, I don't mean that they are less than fair. On the contrary, they are more than fair.

See the magnificent scandal in heaven's courtroom. A case has been brought before God the Judge. Charges are made against the defendant, and you and I know that the charges are factually correct. In some jurisdictions, this would be an open-and-shut case.

When all of the parties to the trial take their places, however, we note that the defendant has two great advantages. First, we see that the defense attorney is the Judge's only begotten Son, whom the Judge personally assigned to the case. That hardly seems fair to the prosecution.

Then, as if it weren't enough to

have the Son pleading the defendant's case, it turns out that the Judge has a relationship with the defendant, as well. For the defendant is among the Judge's adopted children. It is easy to see, therefore, why the prosecutor cries foul!

Surely one of the marvels of grace is even when we have not been on God's side, God remains on ours. God is the one whom we have offended, and yet is the very One who defends us, who pays our penalty, and who declares us not guilty. We would call it unbelievable were it not the gospel truth.

We must remember that there is no obligation, for a sovereign and eternal God to be on anyone's side but God's own. We puny, finite, human rebels could be left behind. But even if that happened, to whom would God have to give answer or explanation? The train of the Holy One could leave the station without us, and we would have no one to blame but ourselves for not getting on board.

Yet in infinite love, God not only waits for us but also beckons, urges, woos, and, yes, even comes back to get us. And though the accuser is right to say that I have not been faithfully on God's side, still God is by my side. The Son pleads my case, and the Father declares me not guilty.

Hyper Nike Christians

The well-known athletic shoemaker from Oregon took a page out of Greek mythology. Among the ancient Greeks, Nike was known as the goddess of victory. And related to her name was the Greek verb *nikao*, meaning to be a victor, to prevail, or to conquer.

Meanwhile, we have a term in common English usage that serves as intensifying prefix. "Hyper" serves as a kind of verbal exclamation point to enlarge the words to which it is attached, as in hyperactive or hypersensitive. We might also associate it with something that is excessive, as in hyperbole or hypercritical. "Hyper" could often be replaced by "super."

We may put these two pieces together—hyper and Nike—in order to understand the dramatic point that the apostle Paul makes to the Romans. "In all these things," he writes, "we are more than conquerors through him who loved us" (8:37). *Hupernikao* is a combination of the Greek preposition from which we get our word "hyper" and the Greek verb for being a victor, prevailing, and conquering. What we use five English words to express in that verse, Paul captures in a single Greek word. "We are more than conquerors" is how we translate the first-person plural form of the verb *hupernikao*. We are, Paul says, hyper-conquerors. We super-prevail.

Observe in what context we experience such above-and-beyond victory. The antecedents for Paul's "all these things" are found in verse 35: hardship, distress, persecution, famine, nakedness, peril, and sword. It is a litany of adversity, and yet it is precisely in the midst of those threats and troubles that Paul proclaims that we are "more than conquerors."

In George Duffield Jr.'s familiar hymn, "Stand Up, Stand Up for Jesus," the poet includes this triumphant declaration: "from victory unto victory his army shall he lead." To go from victory to victory, of course, implies that we are also going from battle to battle. And Paul does not blush to admit the struggles that we face. Yet the apostle and the poet alike affirm the certain and complete victory of the people of God.

Is it that we are so much stronger than our foes? No, not at all. From the days of Joshua and Caleb to the era of Gideon, from David against Goliath to Hezekiah against Sennacherib, superior size and strength have never been the methods of operation for the people of God. Rather, our key is always the superiority of God. We are hyper-conquerors through God, the One who loved us.

Testimony from the Grip

Following the tsunami that devastated Indonesia in December 2004, the rest of the world began to hear terrible stories of destruction, carnage, and heartbreak. Among the tragic reports were some stories of parents who literally had their children ripped from their arms by sudden and violent waves. It is an unthinkable personal tragedy.

For as strong as our love might be as parents, we still are not stronger than many of the forces around us. And we wouldn't have to think for long before we could generate a sad and lengthy list of circumstances that can tear loved ones from each other, no matter how tightly they try to hang on. Something deep within us yearns, therefore, for a love that is greater. Nineteenth-century Scottish preacher George Matheson wrote about such a love. He called it the love "that wilt not let me go." Interestingly, that lovely affirmation was not born out of a moment of bliss and rejoicing, but rather "the most severe mental suffering." That hymn, Matheson later recalled, "was the fruit of that suffering."

Truly it is in the midst of our greatest suffering that we discover the greatness of God's love. It's when the most terrible forces in life tear at us that we come to realize the strength of God's grip on us—the grip of a love that will not let us go.

And that was Paul's discovery and testimony as well. He is not in the midst of counting his blessings, after all, when he declares that "we are more than conquerors through him who loved us" (8:37). Rather, his affirmation comes after a list of trials. And his experience of many trials brings him ultimately to his grand conclusion: that nothing "will be able to separate us from the love of God in Christ Jesus our Lord" (8:39).

Such is the love that defends us and declares us not guilty. Such is the love that makes us more than conquerors. And such is the love that will not let us go.

SHARING THE SCRIPTURE

PREPARING TO TEACH

Preparing Our Hearts

Ponder this week's devotional reading from 1 John 4:7-16. How do you experience God's love in your life? How do you share God's love with other people? What enables you to know that God loves you and abides with you?

Pray that you and the students will have a deep, personal experience of the love of God.

Preparing Our Minds

Study the background Scripture and the lesson Scripture, both of which are from Romans 8:28-39.

Consider this question as you prepare the lesson: *Where can people who are tossed about by the trials and tribulations of life find a safe haven?*

Write on newsprint:

❏ information for next week's lesson, found under Continue the Journey.

❏ activities for further spiritual growth in Continue the Journey.

Review the Introduction, The Big Picture, Close-up, and Faith in Action, which all precede the first lesson of this quarter. Consider how you might use any of this material in today's lesson.

Check to see that the hymnals you have access to include both The Apostles' Creed and The Nicene Creed. If the hymnal is missing one or both of these creeds, download what you need from the Internet and make photocopies of the historic creed(s).

LEADING THE CLASS

(1) Gather to Learn

❖ Welcome the class members and guests.

❖ Pray that those who have come today will rejoice that they can never be separated from God's love.

❖ Read: **Very possibly you live in an area of the United States where certain types of weather phenomena or natural disasters are likely to strike. Depending on your location, you may be all too familiar with wildfires, earthquakes, floods, lava flows, tornadoes, hurricanes, heavy snowfall, or extreme high or low temperatures. You "know the drill" and have emergency supplies at the ready. Some disasters, like tornadoes, occur with little warning. Wailing sirens immediately send**

residents to safe shelters. Others, like hurricanes, can usually be predicted, but those in their path still need to be familiar with evacuation routes and have plans made, just in case. Like the literal storms of life, we can be buffeted about by figurative upheavals. Some will hit with little or no warning, whereas others we may be able to predict are coming. Where can we turn to find shelter amid such storms?

❖ Read aloud today's focus statement: **People are constantly tossed about by the trials and tribulations of life. Where can they find safe haven? Paul tells the Romans that through the love of God in Christ Jesus they will find a Savior from whose love they can never be separated and by whom they will be loved, protected, glorified, and delivered from all trials and tribulations.**

(2) Goal 1: Study the Principal Points of Paul's Teaching on Jesus from Whose Love Believers Can Never Be Separated by Any Turmoil or Hardship

❖ Recruit a volunteer to read Romans 8:28-39.

❖ Discuss these questions:

1. **How are we to understand verse 28, which is frequently quoted? Specifically, what is God's role in bringing about good?** (Notice that it does not say that God *wills* all things to happen, but rather that our Sovereign God will work out for good all that does happen in the lives of believers.)

2. **What do verses 31-34 reveal about how God intended Jesus to relate to those who believe?** (See Romans 8:33-34 in Understanding the Scripture and "The

Great Mistrial" in Interpreting the Scripture.)

3. **In verse 35 Paul asks "who will separate us from the love of Christ" and then proceeds to list problems that have the potential to do just that. Yet he insists that nothing can separate us from Christ's love. How can he be so sure?** (Refer the class to 2 Corinthians 11:23-29 where Paul lists hardships he has endured for the sake of Christ. He is a credible witness because of his own experiences.)

4. **How would you categorize the dangers that Paul lists in verses 37-39?** (Notice that these dangers encompass physical, spiritual, and cosmic forces that have the power to greatly harm or kill a person.)

5. **What does Paul mean when he writes in verse 37 that "we are more than conquerors"?** (See Romans 8:37 in Understanding the Scripture and "Hyper Nike Christians" in Interpreting the Scripture.)

(3) Goal 2: Believe that Christ Jesus Was God's Plan for Humankind from the Beginning of Creation

❖ Select a volunteer to read Colossians 1:15-20 and another to read again Romans 8:29-30.

❖ Ask: **What do these two descriptions of Jesus as the "firstborn" suggest about God's plan for Jesus from the beginning of creation?** (See Romans 8:29-30 in Understanding the Scripture.)

❖ Form groups of three or four people. Distribute hymnals or photocopies of the creeds. Assign half of the groups to The Apostles' Creed

and the other half to The Nicene Creed. The groups are to read their assigned creed in order to answer this question: **What evidence do you find in this creed that God's intention from the creation was to send Jesus to humanity?**

❖ Bring the groups together to discuss their findings.

❖ Read: **Believing that Jesus was part of God's plan from the beginning, we ask again the question of our key verse: "If God is for us, who is against us?" And let us once again affirm that absolutely nothing can "separate us from the love of God in Christ Jesus our Lord."**

(4) Goal 3: Share the Joy and Love of Christ with Others

❖ Read "Testimony from the Grip" in Interpreting the Scripture.

❖ Invite participants to tell brief stories of times when they aware that God was holding them close with a love that would not let them go.

❖ Challenge participants to share their stories of Christ's love with others this week.

(5) Continue the Journey

❖ Pray that as the learners depart, they will go forth as conquerors who share the love and security that God offers with others.

❖ Post information for next week's session on newsprint for the students to copy:

- **Title: Living Under God's Mercy**
- **Background Scripture: Romans 9:6-29**
- **Lesson Scripture: Romans 9:6-18**
- **Focus of the Lesson: People's**

need for healthy feelings of self-worth and self-esteem creates a longing to know who they are and where they come from. Besides ancestry, what other connections with the past and people determine who they are? Paul said all those who trust in God and what Jesus Christ has done for them, by God's mercy, will become God's covenant people and new creatures in Jesus Christ.

❖ Post the following information on newsprint and provide paper and pencils for the students to copy it. Challenge the adults to grow spiritually by completing one or more of these activities related to this week's session.

(1) **Pray for those who are being buffeted about by literal or figurative storms of life. Offer whatever tangible assistance you can.**

(2) **Memorize today's key verse** from Romans 8:31b: "If God is for us, who is against us?" Call this verse to mind whenever you feel that some person, experience, or unseen power is trying to separate you from God. Affirm that you are safe and secure in God's loving care.

(3) **Recall how God has cared for you in the midst of life's challenges. Give thanks for what God has already done and rest assured that God will continue to care for you.**

❖ Sing or read aloud "O Love That Wilt Not Let Me Go."

❖ Conclude today's session by leading the class in this benediction, which is adapted from Romans 8:31b, today's key verse: **Let us go forth rejoicing in the knowledge that if God is for us, nothing in all creation can be against us. Amen.**

UNIT 3: LIFE ON GOD'S TERMS
LIVING UNDER GOD'S MERCY

PREVIEWING THE LESSON

Lesson Scripture: Romans 9:6-18
Background Scripture: Romans 9:6-29
Key Verse: Romans 9:18

Focus of the Lesson:
People's need for healthy feelings of self-worth and self-esteem create a longing to know who they are and where they come from. Besides ancestry, what other connections with the past and people determine who they are? Paul said all those who trust in God and what Jesus Christ has done for them, by God's mercy, will become God's covenant people and new creatures in Jesus Christ.

Goals for the Learners:
(1) to discover the details of Paul's teaching about the true descendants and inheritors of God's promise.
(2) to feel a strong familial connection to the people of God and believe themselves inheritors of the promise intended by God from the time of creation.
(3) to ask Jesus to teach the learners more about themselves.

Supplies:
Bibles, newsprint and marker, paper and pencils, hymnals

READING THE SCRIPTURE

NRSV

Lesson Scripture: Romans 9:6-18

⁶It is not as though the word of God had failed. For not all Israelites truly belong to Israel, ⁷and not all of Abraham's children are his true descendants; but "It is through Isaac that

CEB

Lesson Scripture: Romans 9:6-18

⁶But it's not as though God's word has failed. Not all who are descended from Israel are part of Israel. ⁷Not all of Abraham's children are called Abraham's descendants, but instead

descendants shall be named for you." [8]This means that it is not the children of the flesh who are the children of God, but the children of the promise are counted as descendants. [9]For this is what the promise said, "About this time I will return and Sarah shall have a son." [10]Nor is that all; something similar happened to Rebecca when she had conceived children by one husband, our ancestor Isaac. [11]Even before they had been born or had done anything good or bad (so that God's purpose of election might continue, [12]not by works but by his call) she was told, "The elder shall serve the younger." [13]As it is written,

"I have loved Jacob,
    but I have hated Esau."

[14]What then are we to say? Is there injustice on God's part? By no means! [15]For he says to Moses,

"I will have mercy on whom I
    have mercy,
    and I will have compassion on
    whom I have compassion."

[16]So it depends not on human will or exertion, but on God who shows mercy. [17]For the scripture says to Pharaoh, "I have raised you up for the very purpose of showing my power in you, so that my name may be proclaimed in all the earth." **[18]So then he has mercy on whomever he chooses, and he hardens the heart of whomever he chooses.**

your descendants will be named through Isaac. [8]That means it isn't the natural children who are God's children, but it is the children from the promise who are counted as descendants. [9]The words in the promise were: *A year from now I will return, and Sarah will have a son.*

[10]Not only that, but also Rebecca conceived children with one man, our ancestor Isaac. [11]When they hadn't been born yet and when they hadn't yet done anything good or bad, it was shown that God's purpose would continue because it was based on his choice. [12]It wasn't because of what was done but because of God's call. This was said to her: *The older child will be a slave to the younger one.* [13]As it is written, *I loved Jacob, but I hated Esau.*

[14]So what are we going to say? Isn't this unfair on God's part? Absolutely not! [15]He says to Moses, *I'll have mercy on whomever I choose to have mercy, and I'll show compassion to whomever I choose to show compassion.* [16]So then, it doesn't depend on a person's desire or effort. It depends entirely on God, who shows mercy. [17]Scripture says to Pharaoh, *I have put you in this position for this very thing: so I can show my power in you and so that my name can be spread through the entire earth.* **[18]So then, God has mercy on whomever he wants to, but he makes resistant whomever he wants to.**

UNDERSTANDING THE SCRIPTURE

Introduction. The Lord is occasionally identified as "the God of Abraham, Isaac, and Jacob" (for example, Exodus 3:6; 1 Chronicles 29:18). Those three men, representing three generations, are recognized as the patriarchs of the nation of Israel. Although our text is from the New Testament Letter to the Romans, our real focus is on these characters from the Old Testament Book of Genesis and their stories.

For our purposes in exploring this passage in Romans, however, it is important to note that, while Isaac was Abraham's son, he was not Abraham's only son. Likewise, while Jacob was Isaac's son, he was not Isaac's only son. How is it, then, that Isaac and Jacob enjoy such prominent billing, while their older siblings, Ishmael and Esau, respectively, are left off to the side? That question is surprisingly central to the apostle Paul's understanding of our salvation.

Romans 9:6-7. At first, Paul's statements seem nonsensical to us. How can it be that some Israelites do not belong to Israel? And how can some of Abraham's children not be his descendants? Just being among the biological offspring of Abraham is not the same as being a "true" descendant or Israelite. There is another layer of qualification in Paul's understanding. It is a point reminiscent of his earlier argument about circumcision and uncircumcision (see Romans 2:25-29). We are reminded, too, of how unimpressed John the Baptist was with the genealogy of the Pharisees and Sadducees (Matthew 3:9), as well as Jesus' reinterpretation of who their real father was (John 8:39-44).

Romans 9:8-9. Abraham has two sons who both figure prominently in the Genesis story: Ishmael and Isaac. Ishmael was the result of the union of Abraham and Hagar, who was the slave girl of Abraham's wife, Sarah. Ishmael's conception was the result of Abraham and Sarah's failure to believe God's promise that the two of them would have a son of their own. Because of their advanced age, however, any child born to Sarah would be a miracle. Isaac was that miracle child: the fulfillment of God's promise.

Paul has this background in mind when he makes a distinction between "children of the flesh" and "children of the promise." The former are represented by Ishmael; the latter by Isaac. Likewise, when thinking in terms of salvation, we might distinguish between that which is achieved by human effort and the accomplishments of the flesh, and that which is received by believing the promise of God.

Romans 9:10-13. Paul moves down one more generation in the story, and there finds a new layer of understanding. Having touched on the distinction between Isaac and Ishmael, he turns next to the case of Jacob and Esau. Unlike the previous generation, whose births corresponded to the distinction between spirit and flesh or between faith and works, there was no such distinction here. Jacob and Esau were the twin sons of Isaac and Rebecca. Yet the one, Jacob, emerged as central to God's plan, while the other, Esau, did not. Why the difference?

Here we are introduced to the sovereign choices of God. Paul notes that it was not a performance-based choice. The choice resonates with the larger theme that God does not invite people into a covenant relationship because of their merit.

Romans 9:14-16. Paul recognizes the seeming unfairness of this approach, but he denies any injustice on God's part. The apostle emphasizes God's gracious and sovereign choice to show mercy and compassion to whomever God will. Paul supports his argument with a quotation in verse 15 from Exodus 33:19. The context of this quotation is Moses interceding for the people, asking God to go with them as they depart from Sinai. Moses also asks to see the glory of God.

Romans 9:17-18. In verse 17 Paul cites the example of Pharaoh in Exodus, whose heart God had hardened. Although verse 16 focused on God's compassion, in verse 18, Paul argues that the sovereign God not only can have mercy but can also harden the hearts of whomever God chooses. Yet this hardening of hearts is not an arbitrary action. Pharaoh, for example, had enslaved God's people and refused calls from Moses to release them. God would use Pharaoh's hardened heart to liberate the Hebrew slaves and to proclaim God's power to the world. In other words, God intended good for many people to come out of what otherwise may seem to us to be an injustice against Pharaoh.

Romans 9:19-21. Paul is not afraid to tackle the tough questions, though we may not always like his answers. In the one-way communication of a letter, as opposed to a conversation or a classroom setting, the apostle could have sidestepped the question in verse 19 of why God still finds fault. But then his answer is as tough as his question, as he insists on the sovereignty of God. Still, God does not act capriciously. Rather, echoing the potter imagery of the Old Testament (see Isaiah 29:16; 45:9; 64:8; Jeremiah 18:1-11), Paul affirms the grand purposefulness of all that God does. Just as the potter has the right to "make one object for special use and another for ordinary use" out of the same lump of clay (9:21), God can exercise sovereign control. Humanity is no more able to understand the purposes of God than a lump of clay can understand the purposes of the potter.

Romans 9:22-24. God has patiently endured, put up with, those "pots . . . designed for destruction" (9:22 CEB) because, in the end, God's larger purposes will be served. God's glory will be made known "toward pots made for mercy" (9:23 CEB). Verse 24 makes clear that God has called both Jews and Gentiles to receive this glory.

Romans 9:25-29. Paul quotes Hosea 2:23 and 1:10 in verses 25 and 26. He adds quotations from Isaiah 10:22-23 and 1:9 in verses 27-28 and 29. God will judge, but a remnant of the descendants of Abraham will be saved (9:27) by God's mercy.

INTERPRETING THE SCRIPTURE

Uncommon Genealogy

With the help of Internet resources, it has become increasingly popular for folks to explore their genealogies. We capitalize on the legwork of others and the research we do ourselves to trace back the lines of our family tree to other countries and other centuries. It is a fascinating adventure.

But what if we changed the credentials by which family trees were traced? Instead of the conventional definition of a genealogy, imagine that we applied some other standards. For example, because I played the trombone in junior high, might I claim Glenn Miller as my ancestor?

The suggestion sounds absurd, of course, and yet it is worth our consideration. We remember, for example, the strange reference in Genesis to the brothers Jabal and Jubal. The former, we read, "was the ancestor of those who live in tents and have livestock" (4:20), while his brother was "the ancestor of all those who play the lyre and pipe" (4:21).

Now we know how certain life-styles and abilities do seem to run within a family line. Football fans think immediately, for example, of former National Football League quarterback Archie Manning raising two sons, Peyton and Eli, who grew up to play quarterback in the NFL themselves. Perhaps this sort of natural inheritance is what the ancient author had in mind with Jabal and Jubal.

On the other hand, it may be that the writer of Genesis had a still more poetic meaning in view. Perhaps he thought of Jabal's and Jubal's legacies in the same broad terms as the folks who call Louis Armstrong "the father of Jazz" or Sigmund Freud "the father of modern psychology." Perhaps there is another, less biological way to identify one's ancestors and descendants.

Paul certainly has a different way of reckoning Abraham's descendants. Not all of Abraham's children, Paul insists, are "his true descendants" (Romans 9:7). The matter goes deeper than just genetics. While we typically reckon family trees by biology, Paul does it by theology. And with that new paradigm in place, the apostle redefines Abraham's line.

Some of the folks who traced their genealogy back to Abraham did not, in Paul's view, "truly belong to Israel" (9:6). They were his own coun-trymen, yet he felt that they did not qualify. Meanwhile, there were oth-ers who did not have a drop of Abra-ham's blood in their veins, yet Paul embraced them as brothers and sis-ters, true descendants of Abraham.

From Which We Were Hewn

The Old Testament prophet Isaiah exhorted his audience, saying, "Look to the rock from which you were hewn, and to the quarry from which you were dug. Look to Abraham your father and to Sarah who bore you" (Isaiah 51:1-2). Even though you or I may not be among Abraham's biolog-ical descendants, we may hear that same exhortation addressed to us.

According to the apostle Paul, Abraham's descendants may be divided into two groups. Those groups are represented by the two sons of Abraham to whom the bib-lical text devotes the most attention: Ishmael and Isaac. Interestingly, though, Paul is not drawing the line between those two bloodlines, but rather between those two types of births.

Ishmael, as we have noted, was born in an entirely human way. He was not the offspring that God had promised to Abraham and Sarah. And there was nothing particularly miraculous about his birth. The whole experiment was human cause-and-effect from first to last.

Isaac, on the other hand, was a miracle baby. The writer of Hebrews notes that Sarah was barren and Abraham was too old—"as good as dead," as he bluntly puts it (Hebrews 11:11-12). So Isaac's was, in human terms, an improbable birth. Yet Isaac was the fulfillment of God's promise, and the faithfulness and power of God should turn every improbability into an expectation for us.

This difference between the births of Ishmael and Isaac, then, becomes the basis for Paul's understanding of who is and is not a true descendant of Abraham. It is not about lineage or genetics. Rather, the central issue is the promise of God. Therefore, "the children of the promise are counted as descendants" (9:8). The promise is an extension of God's perfect will, the election is the act of God's sovereign grace, and the salvation is received by us through faith.

You and I, therefore, are invited to count ourselves as among the promised descendants of Abraham. They were, you recall, to be as numerous as the stars (Genesis 15:5), and perhaps just as far-flung. We may not have his blood in our veins, but just as Jubal was "the ancestor of all those who play the lyre and pipe" (4:21), so Abraham is the father of all who receive the promise of God by faith.

Serving the Sovereign

John Wesley famously promoted among the early Methodists a service for covenant renewal. Included in the service was a prayer, which helped the individual believer articulate wholehearted devotion to God. A prayer included in the service asks God to "put me to what thou wilt, rank me with whom thou wilt. Put me to doing, put me to suffering. Let me be employed by thee or laid aside for thee, exalted for thee or brought low for thee. . . . Let me have all things, let me have nothing. I freely and heartily yield all things to thy pleasure and disposal."

Wesley's prayer is one of complete and unconditional surrender. Not a coerced surrender, mind you, like an enemy who has been defeated. Rather, it is the happy and voluntary surrender of a captive being liberated.

At first blush, the prayer seems incomprehensible. Why would one offer to suffer, or to be laid aside, or to be brought low? These actions have no natural appeal for us as human beings, nor should they. But the key to the attitude of the prayer is found in the phrase "for thee."

"For thee," you see, is relational. "For thee" is the stuff of love and devotion. And we all know how willingly true love surrenders to discomfort, inconvenience, and pain for some "thee" or another. Spouses, parents, and friends live out such self-sacrificing love every day. And so do the willing servants of the sovereign God.

Paul cites the work of the sovereign God in the lives of Isaac and Ishmael, of Jacob and Esau, and of the pharaoh of Moses' day. At first, we may be put off by the seeming unfairness of God's choices in some of these stories. Yet the language of Wesley's prayer can help us to see it all differently.

Consider God's statement concerning Pharaoh: "I have raised you up for the very purpose of showing my power in you, so that my name may be proclaimed in all the earth" (9:17). Now if we read those words from God in connection with Abraham, David, Isaiah, or Paul, we would celebrate them. What a privilege, after all, to have his power shown in one's life and to help proclaim his name in all the earth!

But the privilege must not be found only in exalted service. The privilege is in doing and being whatever God calls us to do and to be. The privilege is in living "for thee." We do that willingly because we know ourselves to be spiritual descendants of Abraham who live under the mercy of God.

SHARING THE SCRIPTURE

PREPARING TO TEACH

Preparing Our Hearts

Ponder this week's devotional reading from James 5:7-12. What is James, who may have been the brother of Jesus, calling his readers to do? What evidence does James provide to show that God is faithful to the covenant? How might the prophets serve as examples for you of patient suffering?

Pray that you and the students will wait patiently for the coming again of the Lord.

Preparing Our Minds

Study the background Scripture from Romans 9:6-29 and the lesson Scripture from Romans 9:6-18.

Consider this question as you prepare the lesson: *What connections with the past and other people determine who we are?*

Write on newsprint:
❏ information for next week's lesson, found under Continue the Journey.
❏ activities for further spiritual growth in Continue the Journey.

Review the Introduction, The Big Picture, Close-up, and Faith in Action, which all precede the first lesson of this quarter. Consider how you might use any of this material in today's lesson.

LEADING THE CLASS

(1) Gather to Learn

❖ Welcome the class members and guests.

❖ Pray that those who have come today will give thanks for their connections with Jesus and the entire family of God.

❖ Invite volunteers familiar with several generations of their families to talk about how knowing where they came from helps them to know who they are. In some cases the students will be able to draw comparisons between themselves and an ancestor, perhaps in terms of physical features, talents, or interests. In other cases, the students may note that they are quite different from certain ancestors.

❖ Read aloud today's focus statement: **People's need for healthy feelings of self-worth and self-esteem create a longing to know who they are and where they come from. Besides ancestry, what other connections with the past and people determine who they are? Paul said all those who trust in God and what Jesus Christ has done for them, by God's mercy, will become God's covenant people and new creatures in Jesus Christ.**

(2) Goal 1: Discover the Details of Paul's Teaching About the True Descendants and Inheritors of God's Promise

❖ Read Introduction in Understanding the Scripture.

❖ Call on a volunteer to read Romans 9:6-18.

❖ Discuss these questions:
1. **What point is Paul making in verses 6-9 concerning Abraham's children?** (See Romans 9:6-7 and Romans 9:8-9 in Understanding the Scripture.)
2. **What does Paul teach about how and why God makes**

choices? (See Romans 9:10-13 in Understanding the Scripture.)

3. **To us, God's criteria for making choices may seem unfair. What argument does Paul set forth to show that God's way is just?** (See Romans 9:14-16 in Understanding the Scripture.)

4. **What is Paul's explanation as to why God has hardened Pharaoh's heart?** (See Romans 9:17-18 in Understanding the Scripture.)

5. **How would you summarize Paul's teaching about God's mercy?**

(3) Goal 2: Feel a Strong Familial Connection to the People of God and Believe Themselves Inheritors of the Promise Intended by God from the Time of Creation

❖ Read or retell "Uncommon Genealogy" in Interpreting the Scripture.

❖ Distribute paper and pencils and ask the students to sketch a tree, including roots and branches. (Note that artistic ability is not important.) They are to write the names of people they consider spiritual ancestors on the tree, one per branch. If there is some specific reason why this person is important, students may wish to draw a limb from the branch and write several words of explanation, such as "Sunday school teacher," "children's choir director," "neighbor who took me to church." Similarly, they may want to record information about a specific event, such as "youth counselor who took me on retreat where I made a commitment to Jesus." Suggest that in the area of the roots, they write the names of family members (or other people) who throughout the

years gave them a strong foundation in the Christian faith.

❖ Encourage the adults to show their trees to a partner or small group and talk about one or two of the people with whom they have a strong spiritual connection.

(4) Goal 3: Ask Jesus to Teach the Learners More About Themselves

❖ Lead the students in reading together the excerpt from Wesley's covenant prayer, found under "Serving the Sovereign" in Interpreting the Scripture. Read one phrase at a time and ask the students to echo your words. If you prefer to use the entire prayer and have access to *The United Methodist Hymnal*, turn to page 607 and have the class read in unison.

❖ Look together at the following phrases and ask: **What might you (or any believer) learn about yourself if you are willing:**

1. **to do whatever God asks** ("Put me to what thou wilt")?

2. **to relate to whomever the sovereign God puts in your pathway** ("rank me with whom thou wilt")?

3. **to be actively engaged for God** ("Put me to doing")?

4. **to suffer for the name of Christ** ("put me to suffering")?

5. **to recognize that God has gifted you with many things of this world** ("Let me have all things")?

6. **to live on the margins of poverty if that is what God wills** ("let me have nothing")?

❖ Provide a few moments of quiet time so that the students may open their hearts and minds to the leading of Jesus and in doing so recognize

God's sovereignty and mercy in their lives.

❖ Challenge the learners to share with others what they have learned today about how God's mercy may be experienced in one's life.

(5) Continue the Journey

❖ Pray that as the learners depart, they will rejoice in the privilege of living under the mercy of God.

❖ Post information for next week's session on newsprint for the students to copy:

- **Title: God Prunes and Grafts**
- **Background Scripture: Romans 11:11-36**
- **Lesson Scripture: Romans 11:11-24**
- **Focus of the Lesson: Sometimes, people find themselves living, relating, or working with others with whom they feel no common connection, from whom they feel separated, and toward whom they feel antagonistic. What or who can unite all people in a new community with common values? Paul writes that belief in Jesus Christ is a core belief around which both Jews and Gentiles can be united.**

❖ Post the following information on newsprint and provide paper and pencils for the students to copy it.

Challenge the adults to grow spiritually by completing one or more of these activities related to this week's session.

(1) **Contact a family member who has traced your family tree. Talk with this person about the characteristics of the family, where they came from and why they left their homeland, and what they did to create a new life for themselves in their adopted homeland.**

(2) **Contact one of the spiritual ancestors you identified in class to let this person know how much his or her relationship with you means. If possible, do something special for this person, such as treating him or her to a meal, buying a small gift, or sending a special card of thanks.**

(3) **Give thanks for God's mercy, especially with respect to how that mercy has enabled you to grow closer to Jesus.**

❖ Sing or read aloud "'Tis So Sweet to Trust in Jesus."

❖ Conclude today's session by leading the class in this benediction, which is adapted from Romans 8:31b, the key verse for August 7: **Let us go forth rejoicing in the knowledge that since God is for us, nothing in all creation can be against us. Amen.**

UNIT 3: LIFE ON GOD'S TERMS
GOD PRUNES AND GRAFTS

PREVIEWING THE LESSON

Lesson Scripture: Romans 11:11-24
Background Scripture: Romans 11:11-36
Key Verse: Romans 11:22

Focus of the Lesson:
Sometimes, people find themselves living, relating, or working with others with whom they feel no common connection, from whom they feel separated, and toward whom they feel antagonistic. What or who can unite all people in a new community with common values? Paul writes that belief in Jesus Christ is a core belief around which both Jews and Gentiles can be united.

Goals for the Learners:
(1) to know what Paul said about Jews who have not become Christ's followers and Gentiles who have become believers.
(2) to affirm that God has not rejected the Jews and that Gentile believers have not superseded the Jews, but that believing in Jesus is the fulfillment of creation.
(3) to develop some ecumenical ministry, possibly with Jewish or Muslim communities of faith.

Supplies:
Bibles, newsprint and marker, paper and pencils, hymnals

READING THE SCRIPTURE

NRSV

Lesson Scripture: Romans 11:11-24

¹¹So I ask, have they [the Jews] stumbled so as to fall? By no means! But through their stumbling salvation has come to the Gentiles, so as to make Israel jealous. ¹²Now if their stumbling means riches for the world,

CEB

Lesson Scripture: Romans 11:11-24

¹¹So I'm asking you: They [the Jews] haven't stumbled so that they've fallen permanently, have they? Absolutely not! But salvation has come to the Gentiles by their failure, in order to make Israel jealous. ¹²But if their

and if their defeat means riches for Gentiles, how much more will their full inclusion mean!

[13]Now I am speaking to you Gentiles. Inasmuch then as I am an apostle to the Gentiles, I glorify my ministry [14]in order to make my own people jealous, and thus save some of them. [15]For if their rejection is the reconciliation of the world, what will their acceptance be but life from the dead! [16]If the part of the dough offered as first fruits is holy, then the whole batch is holy; and if the root is holy, then the branches also are holy.

[17]But if some of the branches were broken off, and you, a wild olive shoot, were grafted in their place to share the rich root of the olive tree, [18]do not boast over the branches. If you do boast, remember that it is not you that support the root, but the root that supports you. [19]You will say, "Branches were broken off so that I might be grafted in." [20]That is true. They were broken off because of their unbelief, but you stand only through faith. So do not become proud, but stand in awe. [21]For if God did not spare the natural branches, perhaps he will not spare you. [22]**Note then the kindness and the severity of God: severity toward those who have fallen, but God's kindness toward you, provided you continue in his kindness; otherwise you also will be cut off.** [23]And even those of Israel, if they do not persist in unbelief, will be grafted in, for God has the power to graft them in again. [24]For if you have been cut from what is by nature a wild olive tree and grafted, contrary to nature, into a cultivated olive tree, how much more will these natural branches be grafted back into their own olive tree.

failure brings riches to the world, and their defeat brings riches to the Gentiles, how much more will come from the completion of their number! [13]I'm speaking to you Gentiles. Considering that I'm an apostle to the Gentiles, I publicize my own ministry [14]in the hope that somehow I might make my own people jealous and save some of them. [15]If their rejection has brought about a close relationship between God and the world, how can their acceptance mean anything less than life from the dead?

[16]But if part of a batch of dough is offered to God as holy, the whole batch of dough is holy too. If a root is holy, the branches will be holy too. [17]If some of the branches were broken off, and you were a wild olive branch, and you were grafted in among the other branches and shared the root that produces the rich oil of the olive tree, [18]then don't brag like you're better than the other branches. If you do brag, be careful: it's not you that sustains the root, but it's the root that sustains you. [19]You will say then, "Branches were broken off so that I could be grafted in." [20]Fine. They were broken off because they weren't faithful, but you stand only by your faithfulness. So don't think in a proud way; instead be afraid. [21]If God didn't spare the natural branches, he won't spare you either. [22]**So look at God's kindness and harshness. It's harshness toward those who fell, but it's God's kindness for you, provided you continue in his kindness; otherwise, you could be cut off too.** [23]And even those who were cut off will be grafted back in if they don't continue to be unfaithful, because God is able to graft them in again. [24]If you were naturally part of a wild olive tree and you were cut off from it, and then,

contrary to nature, you were grafted into the cultivated olive tree, won't these natural branches stand an even better chance of being grafted back onto their own olive tree?

UNDERSTANDING THE SCRIPTURE

Introduction. The question at stake is the response of the Jews to the gospel. It is a matter near to Paul's heart, for they are his people. Moreover, we see in his ministry the pattern of going first to the synagogue in each town to preach there. Yet his experience has been bittersweet: The Gentiles have responded to the gospel of Christ, while the Jews have largely rejected and opposed it. And so Paul wrestles here with the reality, the meaning, and the implications of that Jewish rejection of Christ.

Romans 11:11-12. The fact that Paul makes a distinction between stumbling and falling offers insight into his thinking and understanding. The image suggests disappointment, but not despair. Yes, the Jews have stumbled, but they have not fallen such that they are permanently cut off from God. There is still hope, and that hope is woven throughout this passage. A profound aspect of Paul's hope is that even the "stumbling" is not an altogether bad thing. Rather, Paul understands that the Jewish rejection of the gospel has had the effect of opening a wider door for the Gentiles. Thus it serves a good purpose. Even in the midst of that affirmation, though, he recognizes how much better still it would be with the Jews' "full inclusion."

Romans 11:13-15. Paul suggests that there is a cycle involved here. Just as the Jewish rejection of the gospel has opened the way for the Gentiles,

perhaps the Gentiles' response to Christ will serve a good purpose among the Jews. Both the salvation of the Gentiles and Paul's ministry among the Gentiles are expected to have the effect of making Israel (or the Jews) "jealous" (11:11, 14). Note that this word is used not once but twice. For us, "jealous" is an almost entirely negative term. It is not exclusively so in Scripture, however. The Greek word here is formed from two words that together mean to apply heavy pressure in order to provoke change, particularly in an "up close and personal" way. Hence, Paul is hoping that the fact that the Gentiles are receiving salvation will provoke a change that will bring his Jewish brothers and sisters to belief in Jesus.

Romans 11:16. Now Paul uses two word pictures to capture the truths with which he wrestles. The first picture is afforded just a half a verse. The second picture, meanwhile, is so pregnant with possibilities for him that it becomes the basis for the entire next section of the passage.

The reference to the dough hearkens back to a custom with which the Jews in Paul's audience would have been familiar. William Barclay points to the Old Testament law involved (Numbers 15:19-20) and observes: "It was not necessary, as it were, to offer every separate mouthful to God. The offering of the first part sanctified the whole."

Romans 11:17-24. After so briefly presenting the image of the dough, Paul introduces the image of a tree with branches and roots. This becomes an extended metaphor. He uses it both to describe the sovereign choices of God and to illustrate the relationship between the Jews and the Gentiles.

With respect to the sovereign choices of God, the issue is captured in branches being cut off from and grafted onto a tree. The Jews represent the natural branch for the tree, yet "God did not spare the natural branches" (11:21). Meanwhile, the Gentiles represent the branch, which though "contrary to nature" (11:24), was grafted into the tree by God. Being part of the tree is not a permanent condition, therefore, but a function of the kindness of God. Yet for those who fall away, Paul warns of God's severity.

With respect to the relationship between the Jews and Gentiles, Paul's encouragement for the Jews is the prospect that "these natural branches [will] be grafted back into their own olive tree" (11:24). For the Gentiles, Paul offers the perspective that "it is not you that support the root" (11:18), as well as the caution that "if God did not spare the natural branches, perhaps he will not spare you" (11:21).

Romans 11:25. Paul's concern that his audience will "not claim to be wiser than [they] are" still rings true so many centuries later. This is a problem native to human beings in every generation, it seems. And it is part of a larger theme that he addresses elsewhere in various ways (for example, Romans 12:3; 1 Corinthians 1:26-29; Philippians 2:3).

The specific point on which Paul is giving his audience some perspective involves the relationship of Jews and Gentiles. Or, more accurately, he sees a connection between the Jews and the salvation of the Gentiles. This has tremendous significance, for it reverses what might have been the natural judgment of a Gentile Christian. Rather than being condescending toward the Jews who were rejecting the gospel message, the Gentiles had reason to feel grateful, for Paul saw a providential timing in it all. It is not merely, as it might seem on the surface, that the Gentiles were more obediently responsive. Rather, the "hardening has come upon part of Israel" for the time necessary "until the full number of the Gentiles has come in." Paul's understanding is that the Jewish rejection actually serves a purpose in the Gentiles' salvation.

Romans 11:26-32. In verse 12, Paul alluded to the Jews' "full inclusion," and now in verse 26 he is more explicit about his confidence: "all Israel will be saved." He reiterates his point that the Jews' present rejection of the gospel is "for your sake" (11:28) and explains that disobedience qualifies people for the mercy of God. At the same time, Paul affirms the election of the Jews and the irrevocable call of God. These few verses, then, summarize the apostle's understanding of the complex matrix of issues dealt with throughout the larger passage.

Romans 11:33-36. The apostle has been contemplating profound and significant matters. He has explored the salvation, sovereignty, and providence of God. And with all of that on his mind, he breaks into irresistible praise.

INTERPRETING THE SCRIPTURE

God with a Saw

Jesus tells a brief parable about a man who had planted a fig tree in his vineyard, "and he came looking for fruit on it and found none" (Luke 13:6). The parable goes on to describe both the man's disappointment and his intent to cut down the fruitless tree. A servant in the parable prevails upon his master, however, to invest another year of care in the tree, seeing if it might then provide fruit. "But if not," the gardener explained, "you can cut it down" (13:9).

The parable echoes a larger theme that pulses throughout Scripture. It has three parts: the will and design of God, the meaning of fruitfulness and unfruitfulness, and the fate of that which is unfruitful. That larger theme informs Paul's understanding of the issue of Jews, Gentiles, and the gospel message, as well as our understanding of what Paul writes about it all.

In terms of God's will and design, we note that the production of fruit was a deliberate part of creation (Genesis 1:11) and that "be fruitful" was God's first command to human beings (1:28). Jesus told his followers that he had "appointed them to go and bear fruit" (John 15:16). And the apostle Paul enumerated the influence of the Spirit in a Christian's life in terms of fruit (Galatians 5:22-23).

Fruitfulness, then, symbolizes a thing—especially a human life—that is functioning according to God's design for it. If it is not bearing fruit, then it is not doing what it was created to do. The psalmist, therefore, characterizes the righteous person as being like a tree that bears fruit in its season (Psalm 1:3).

Meanwhile, what becomes of a fruitless tree—or of a branch that does not bear fruit? The consistent message is that such failure to function properly is judged. The branch that does not abide in the vine and produce fruit is cut off and thrown away (John 15:1-6). The tree that does not bear fruit is cut down and thrown into the fire (Luke 3:9). And the tree that does not bear fruit when Jesus comes looking is cursed (Matthew 21:18-19).

In exploring the relationship between the Jews, the Gentiles, and the gospel of salvation in Christ, therefore, the apostle Paul turns to that sober image of branches being cut off. The original or natural branch represents the Jews, and Paul says that they "were broken off because of their unbelief" (Romans 11:20). That judgment image is a familiar one. Yet in the midst, there is also the good news of God's mercy. For the Gentiles, the mercy is in God's willingness to graft in the wild branch. And for the Jews, the mercy is God's eagerness to have those "natural branches grafted back" (11:24).

Right of Way

Imagine a police officer directing traffic at an intersection. There are cars coming from every direction, and obviously they cannot all proceed at the same time. Accordingly, the officer makes choices about who will go and who will stop.

You and I are on one road, and there is another road full of traffic perpendicular to ours entering the intersection. We see the officer hold up his hand to stop the traffic on that other road in order to allow the traffic on our road to pass. He beckons to us, and we are able to proceed.

It's a good feeling to get that go-ahead. It's a good feeling not to be stuck, but to be moving forward. It's a good feeling to make progress toward our destination. But as we pass through that intersection, and we see those other lanes of traffic stopped on our behalf, how do we feel about them?

There's no reason to gloat, says Paul. We are not superior to that other line of traffic; we are just fortunate. The attitudes that should characterize us as we proceed, therefore, are gratitude and humility. We are grateful to the officer for stopping the other line of traffic in order that we may pass. And we are humble, knowing that the officer could hold up his hand to stop us too.

Paul grieved the fact that the Jews—his own people and the most natural audience for the gospel and heirs of the new covenant in Christ—were rejecting the good news of Christ. As Paul preached that gospel throughout the Mediterranean world, however, he saw the Gentiles responding to the message and being saved. And as he wrestled with what was taking place around him, he concluded that the opposition of the Jews served a purpose for those Gentiles. Their stoppage, if you will, provided a kind of right-of-way for the Gentiles to come to Christ.

But the Gentiles should not be proud as they drive past the resistant Jews. Paul was confident that Israel's time would come. The officer, it seems, will only hold up his hand "until the full number of the Gentiles has come in" (11:25).

The Last Word

The last word is the one that prevails. The writer of Proverbs noted that "the one who first states a case seems right, until the other comes and cross-examines" (Proverbs 18:17). And so, from a very young age, we show our instinct for wanting to have the last word in an argument.

There are a lot of words involved in our present discussion. We have, in a few verses, been prompted to consider significant words and concepts such as "sovereignty" and "election," "jealousy" and "judgment," "hardening" and "disobedience." But in the end, we want to know what prevails. We hate to think that the last word will be hardness, disobedience, or judgment.

Paul is no-nonsense about these matters. He does not sugarcoat caution or minimize unbelief. Rather, we sense the pain in his eyes as he laments the Jews, and we hear the seriousness in his tone as he warns the Gentiles. Yet, through it all, we recognize that the central issue is the gospel of Christ, and gospel means good news.

The good news, of course, is not about us. It is *for* us, to be sure, but it is not *about* us. We are too inconsistent, too faithless, and too disobedient to be the subject of the good news.

Rather, the good news comes from and reflects the heart of God. The good news features God's mercy, kindness, and salvation. And we see that it is God's good news that gets the last word in this discussion by Paul.

Throughout this passage—even in the most sobering parts—Paul perceives the kindness in God's providence and purpose. He is confident that, in spite of their present resistance, "all Israel will be saved" (11:26). He affirms God's good endeavor to banish ungodliness and take away sins, which is sometimes painful, but essential to our salvation.

He rejoices in God's wisdom, knowledge, and judgments. And he proves to us that the last word is a good one. For the grand problem, after all, is human disobedience. Yet, even in that, Paul declares God's will to "be merciful to all" (11:32).

SHARING THE SCRIPTURE

PREPARING TO TEACH

Preparing Our Hearts

Ponder this week's devotional reading from John 15:1-8, a familiar "I am" passage in which Jesus says that he is the "true vine." What evidence demonstrates that you are abiding in Jesus? What would Jesus say about the quality and quantity of your fruitfulness?

Pray that you and the students will stay closely connected to Jesus so that you can produce the kind of fruit that he expects.

Preparing Our Minds

Study the background Scripture from Romans 11:11-36 and the lesson Scripture from Romans 11:11-24.

Consider this question as you prepare the lesson: *What or who can unite all people in a new community with common values?*

Write on newsprint:

❏ Bible passages for Goal 2 in Sharing the Scripture.
❏ information for next week's lesson, found under Continue the Journey.
❏ activities for further spiritual growth in Continue the Journey.

Review the Introduction, The Big Picture, Close-up, and Faith in Action, which all precede the first lesson of this quarter. Consider how you might use any of this material in today's lesson.

LEADING THE CLASS

(1) Gather to Learn

❖ Welcome the class members and guests.

❖ Pray that those who have come today will feel united with the people and world that God has created.

❖ Read: **We live in a world that is increasingly interdependent, economically and politically. Religious communities that were once separated now find themselves rubbing shoulders with people whose beliefs and religious practices are quite different from their own. Interfaith dialogue is a helpful tool as a means of engaging people of other faiths and getting to know them. In the process of dialogue we can be good, respectful neighbors as we listen to others and share our own witness. While agreement on all points is not the goal, dialogue does enable participants to find common ground and seek greater understanding.**

❖ Read aloud today's focus statement: **Sometimes, people find themselves living, relating, or working with others with whom they feel no** common connection, from whom they feel separated, and toward whom they feel antagonistic. What or who can unite all people in a new community with common values? Paul writes that belief in Jesus Christ is a core belief around which both Jews and Gentiles can be united.

(2) Goal 1: Explore What Paul Said About Jews Who Have Not Become Christ's Followers and Gentiles Who Have Become Believers

❖ Introduce the theme of fruitfulness by reading or retelling "God with a Saw" in Interpreting the Scripture. Ask the class to listen to how Paul uses this theme in Romans 11.

❖ Choose a volunteer to read Romans 11:11-24.

❖ Discuss these questions:

1. **How does Paul use the theme of fruitfulness here?** (Note his discussion on pruning and grafting tree branches, as well as "God With a Saw" in Interpreting the Scripture. See Romans 11:17-24 in Understanding the Scripture.)

2. **What other image does Paul use in relation to fruits?** (See Romans 11:16 in Understanding the Scripture. Point out the source of the image of the dough by looking at Numbers 15:19-20.)

3. **What distinction does Paul make between "stumbling" and "falling" in verses 11-12?** (See Romans 11:11-12 in Understanding the Scripture.)

4. **Now that Gentiles are receiving salvation, what does Paul expect will happen with his Jewish brother and sisters?**

(See Romans 11:13-15 in Understanding the Scripture and "Right of Way" in Interpreting the Scripture.)

(3) Goal 2: Affirm that God Has Not Rejected the Jews and that Gentile Believers Have Not Superseded the Jews, but that Believing in Jesus Is the Fulfillment of Creation

❖ Read: **Although much anti-Semitism, negative stereotypes of the Jews, and teachings insisting that the Christian church has replaced Israel seem rooted in the notion that God has cut off or abandoned the Jews, Paul clearly refutes this idea.**

❖ Call on volunteers to read aloud the following examples in Romans 11 and elsewhere to find support for God's continuing relationship with the Jews.

- Paul himself is an example: Romans 11:1-2
- Elijah as an example: Romans 11:2-4
- Romans 11:24-27
- Psalm 94:14-15

❖ Note that we know from Paul's ministry individual Jews decided not to turn to Jesus. Their actions, however, do not cause God to reject Israel as a whole. Ask: **As you think about what you have been taught regarding the standing of the Jews before God, and the comments of Paul and other biblical writers, what can you now affirm about God's relationship with the Jews?**

(4) Goal 3: Develop Some Ecumenical Ministry, Possibly with Jewish or Muslim Communities of Faith

❖ Brainstorm answers to this question and write responses on newsprint: **What needs exist in our community that we could work together with another faith community to fill?** Review the list and determine which need seems most pressing.

❖ Brainstorm ideas as to what the class could realistically do to meet these needs and list ideas on newsprint. Determine whether you could set up an ongoing project or a one-time event. For example, hunger may be an issue in your community. According to statistics compiled by Feeding America in 2013, 49.1 million Americans, including 15.8 million children, lived in households that were food insecure, meaning that they lack consistent access to adequate food. Perhaps you could establish a soup kitchen to feed people on a regular basis. Or perhaps you collect food to be given to people in need even once a year at the holidays.

❖ Consider which other religious groups in your area you could partner with to fulfill this need. If possible, try to work with a Jewish or Muslim group. If that is not possible, perhaps you could work with a church of a different denomination from your own. Decide who will spearhead this effort and contact potential partners to begin to develop a plan.

5) Continue the Journey

❖ Pray that as the learners depart, they will seek common ground with others who believe in God.

❖ Post information for next week's session on newsprint for the students to copy:

■ **Title: Love Fulfills the Law**
■ **Background Scripture: Romans 12:1-2; 13:8-14**

■ **Lesson Scripture: Romans 12:1-2; 13:8-10**
■ **Focus of the Lesson: People want to know how to live in a manner that transcends the selfish and corrupt ways of the world. How can they live to fulfill the law of love? Paul urges Jesus' followers to allow the love of Christ to transform their minds into Christlike minds, so they will be able to love one another and themselves as Christ has loved and continues to love them.**

❖ Post the following information on newsprint and provide paper and pencils for the students to copy it. Challenge the adults to grow spiritually by completing one or more of these activities related to this week's session.

(1) **Search the Internet for information on Jewish-Christian relationships. What can you learn by reading articles on interfaith dialogue?**

(2) **Visit an orchard to see how grafts enable cultivars of fruit to grow that cannot be grown from seed. Talk with the orchardist about this process. What connections do you see between the grafting of fruit trees and Paul's analogy of Christians being grafted onto an olive tree that symbolizes the Jews?**

(3) **Reach out to Jewish friends or colleagues to learn more about their faith and share your own. Approach these conversations in the spirit of interfaith dialogue that listens respectfully, learns from the other, and seeks common ground.**

❖ Sing or read aloud "Jesus, United by Thy Grace."

❖ Conclude today's session by leading the class in this benediction, which is adapted from Romans 8:31b, the key verse for August 7: **Let us go forth rejoicing in the knowledge that since God is for us, nothing in all creation can be against us. Amen.**

UNIT 3: LIFE ON GOD'S TERMS
LOVE FULFILLS THE LAW

PREVIEWING THE LESSON

Lesson Scripture: Romans 12:1-2; 13:8-10
Background Scripture: Romans 12:1-2; 13:8-14
Key Verse: Romans 13:8

Focus of the Lesson:
People want to know how to live in a manner that transcends the selfish and corrupt ways of the world. How can they live to fulfill the law of love? Paul urges Jesus' followers to allow the love of Christ to transform their minds into Christlike minds, so they will be able to love one another and themselves as Christ has loved and continues to love them.

Goals for the Learners:
(1) to overhear Paul's exhortation to be transformed in order to discern the will of God and to fulfill God's law by loving ourselves and others.
(2) to accept God's will to love one another unconditionally.
(3) to commit to actively carry God's love into the world.

Supplies:
Bibles, newsprint and marker, paper and pencils, hymnals

READING THE SCRIPTURE

NRSV

Lesson Scripture: Romans 12:1-2

¹I appeal to you therefore, brothers and sisters, by the mercies of God, to present your bodies as a living sacrifice, holy and acceptable to God, which is your spiritual worship. ²Do not be conformed to this world, but be transformed by the renewing of your minds, so that you may discern what is the will of God—what is good and acceptable and perfect.

CEB

Lesson Scripture: Romans 12:1-2

¹So, brothers and sisters, because of God's mercies, I encourage you to present your bodies as a living sacrifice that is holy and pleasing to God. This is your appropriate priestly service. ²Don't be conformed to the patterns of this world, but be transformed by the renewing of your minds so that you can figure out what God's will is—what is good and pleasing and mature.

Lesson Scripture: Romans 13:8-10

[8]Owe no one anything, except to love one another; for **the one who loves another has fulfilled the law.** [9]The commandments, "You shall not commit adultery; You shall not murder; You shall not steal; You shall not covet"; and any other commandment, are summed up in this word, "Love your neighbor as yourself." [10]Love does no wrong to a neighbor; therefore, love is the fulfilling of the law.

Lesson Scripture: Romans 13:8-10

[8]Don't be in debt to anyone, except for the obligation to love each other. **Whoever loves another person has fulfilled the Law.** [9]The commandments, Don't commit adultery, don't murder, don't steal, don't desire what others have, and any other commandments, are all summed up in one word: You must love your neighbor as yourself. [10]Love doesn't do anything wrong to a neighbor; therefore, love is what fulfills the Law.

UNDERSTANDING THE SCRIPTURE

Romans 12:1. You and I no longer live in a setting where worship features animal sacrifices. We still have altars in our churches, but they are clean and lovely—a far cry from the blood, smoke, and strong smell that would have characterized the altars of the biblical world. Yet it is against that ancient backdrop that Paul makes his plea to the Christians in Rome to present their bodies as "living sacrifices."

The underlying Greek word that Paul uses, which we translate "present," is one that the Romans had heard Paul use before. In Romans 6, the apostle urged his audience not to offer the members of their bodies as instruments of wickedness (6:13) or impurity (6:19), but rather as "instruments" and "slaves of righteousness," respectively. The verb he uses in chapter 6 for offering the members of our bodies is used again chapter 12 for presenting our bodies as sacrifices.

In some respects, of course, a dead sacrifice is an easier offering to make than a living sacrifice. If I present a lamb from my flock, it is a one-time transaction for that sacrifice. If I present my body as a living sacrifice, on the other hand, then that becomes a constant, daily offering. And that is "your spiritual worship."

Romans 12:2. Paul recognized that the world will try to manipulate and squeeze us in order to make us fit in. We must not be conformed to the world around us, however, and take on its shape or its will for us. We must be firm and sturdy enough to resist being packed in.

Conversely, Paul challenges us to be "transformed by the renewing of your minds." The original Greek word used by Paul for "transformed" is the source of our English word "metamorphosis." It's a beautiful term that suggests something bigger and better than simply curbing our behavior or tweaking our habits. Rather, it is the same word used twice in the Gospels (Matthew 17:2; Mark 9:2) to describe the radiant change in Jesus' appearance at the Transfiguration. In these two verses the Greek word is translated in the NRSV as "transfigured." The gospel does not challenge us to minor adjustments but to total transformation.

Romans 13:8. On the one hand, the instruction to "owe no one anything" was a standard bit of prudence and wisdom. Certainly every Jew familiar with the counsel of Proverbs would be acquainted with the importance of staying free from personal indebtedness (for example, Proverbs 6:1-5). Yet ordinary debt is a small matter when compared to Paul's exception—"except to love one another." There is nothing pricier, more costly, than love. Moreover, in contrast to monetary debt, the debt of love can never be repaid.

Romans 13:9-10. Now the apostle sets out to prove his earlier point that "the one who loves another has fulfilled the law" (13:8), and he turns to the Ten Commandments to make his case. The arrangement of the commandments has sometimes been described as both "vertical" and "horizontal." That is to say, the first four commandments involve our relationship with God and the final six involve our relationships with other people. Paul cites four of those commandments pertaining to other people in order to illustrate that they all fall under the broad umbrella of love. Keeping these commandments, therefore, fulfills the law.

The Ten Commandments are found in two places in the Old Testament: Exodus 20 and Deuteronomy 5. Interestingly, though, Paul turns to a line from Leviticus in order to summarize the whole law. Just as Jesus cited "love your neighbor as yourself" (Leviticus 19:18) as the second-greatest commandment (Matthew 22:39), so Paul claims in verse 9 that that single instruction captures all that is needed to guide our treatment of other people.

Romans 13:11. Paul counsels his readers to recognize what time it is. The Greek word that he uses in verse 11 that is translated as "time" is *kairos*. In contrast to *chronos*, which refers to "clock time" or chronological time, *kairos* refers to a special moment when the time is right or opportune. The day of the Lord, according to Paul, is closer now than when people came to believe. In other words, the kingdom of God is drawing near. Consequently, people need to wake from sleep and live as faithful followers of Christ in this world.

Romans 13:12-13. Paul transitions seamlessly from one metaphor to another. He spoke of knowing the time, urging his readers to "wake from sleep" (13:11), for "the night is far gone" (13:12). That characterization of "what time it is," then, prompts imagery of darkness and light. "Works of darkness," a phrase found both here and in the Letter to the Ephesians (5:11), aptly characterizes behavior of which a person should be ashamed (see John 3:19-20). Since "the day is near" (13:12), however, it is time to live and behave differently. In verse 13, Paul lists behaviors that mark the life of darkness. These behaviors are not acceptable among those who are trying to live "honorably" for Christ.

Romans 13:14. Living differently as Paul calls believers to do—at its essence and at its best—is living like Christ. Specifically, Paul exhorts his readers to "put on the Lord Jesus Christ." His verb is used routinely elsewhere as a word for simply putting on clothing (for example, Matthew 27:31; Mark 6:9; Luke 15:22). Paul uses the word nearly a dozen times in his letters, yet always in a more metaphorical sense—for example, putting on imperishability (1 Corinthians 15:53), "the new self" (Ephesians 4:24), and assorted virtues (Colossians 3:12). Above all, though, Paul encourages us to clothe ourselves with Christ (here and Galatians 3:27). If we put on Christ, after all, then all the attributes Paul has listed are included.

Finally, the instruction to "make no provision for the flesh, to gratify its desires" is a startling one to twenty-first-century Americans. We devote immense amounts of time and money to making provisions for the flesh and gratifying its desires. Yet if we rightly presented our bodies as living sacrifices (12:1), then our flesh will have been put in its proper place.

INTERPRETING THE SCRIPTURE

Our Living Sacrifice

The apostle Paul's original audience would have understood the requirements that a sacrifice be "holy and acceptable" (12:1) for they recognized that there were strict standards for appropriate sacrifices (see, for example, Leviticus 22:17-25). Since we have changed "offerings" from animal sacrifices into monetary donations, we don't think much in terms of what we place on the altar being unacceptable. Yet it is a sobering theme that is as old as the first recorded act of worship (Genesis 4:3-5).

Paul called upon his audience of Christians in Rome to present their bodies, holy and acceptable, as part of their spiritual worship. They were to be living sacrifices. Thus Paul took the familiar language and imagery of ancient worship practices and reinterpreted them for that first generation of Christian believers. And we find that his language remains rich for us today.

The image of a living sacrifice is genius. One of the common Old Testament Hebrew words that we frequently translate as "worship," abodah, also means "work" or "serve." Hence we are accustomed to hearing Psalm 100:2 read as both "worship the LORD with gladness" (for example, NRSV, NIV) and "serve the LORD with gladness" (for example, KJV, NASB).

A traditional animal sacrifice was killed at the altar, and part or all of it was burned there. But a dead sacrifice is a very limited form of worship. A living sacrifice, on the other hand, is a magnificent offering of worship, for that person can continue to serve the Lord with gladness all day, every day.

Meanwhile, Paul's insistence on our physical bodies being part of our spiritual worship is profound. Contrary to the Gnostics, who typically rejected or underestimated the physical body, Paul recognized its value and holy potential.

We see a connection between the physical and the spiritual in God's design at the creation of humanity. Genesis reports that "the LORD God formed man from the dust of the ground, and breathed into his nostrils the breath of life; and the man became a living being" (Genesis 2:7). The account suggests that we are a two-part composition: dust from the ground and breath from God. It reminds us of the spirit-and-flesh dichotomy seen in the New Testament (see, for example, Matthew 26:41; John 3:6). It brings to mind, too, the nature of a sacrament.

Our Total Makeover

Our culture knows all about makeovers. On television shows and in magazines, we see the stories of both individuals and houses undergoing the makeover process. We have examined the before-and-after pictures of the woman with the new hair and wardrobe, the man who lost seventy pounds, and the house that was expertly remodeled.

Part of the popularity of makeovers, of course, is that they appeal to the part of us that wants to hope. We sometimes fear that how things are is the way they always have to be, but we don't want to believe it. And so we like to see the kinds of complete turn-arounds that makeovers represent. We want to know that the out-of-shape guy can become fit, or that the dismal house can be made beautiful.

The gospel, then, is our ultimate hope. We all long for the hope that it brings, even though many don't recognize or acknowledge that fact. And the hope that it brings is that the way things are—indeed, the way we are—is not a permanent and hopeless condition. The total makeover is possible. And Paul recommends it to the Romans.

"Do not be conformed to this world," he writes, "but be transformed by the renewing of your minds" (12:2). Paul's word for that transformation is used only three other times in the New Testament. As we noted above, two Gospel writers employ the potent term to describe what happened to Jesus' appearance at the Transfiguration. And Paul himself uses the word again in order to try to capture for the Corinthians what is taking place within us: "all of us, with unveiled faces, seeing the glory of the Lord as though reflected in a mirror, are being transformed into the same image from one degree of glory to another; for this comes from the Lord, the Spirit" (2 Corinthians 3:18). Inasmuch as the other three occurrences of the word all point to the glory of Christ, we have a sense for its weight and significance.

The popular New Testament commentator William Barclay noted that the underlying Greek of Paul's terminology insists that "we must undergo a change, not of our outward form, but of our inward personality." While the makeovers of which our culture is so fond are typically superficial, the gospel makeover is not merely skin-deep. This is an inner transformation, which of course is where it really counts (see 1 Samuel 16:7; Matthew 23:25-26).

Specifically, the holy makeover that Paul commends happens by a renewing of our minds that enables us to discern the perfect will of God. Apollinaris of Laodicea associated that transformation with the Lord's word in Jeremiah about writing his law upon his people's hearts (see Jeremiah 32:37-44). Apart from such a saving reorientation, we are doomed to live in a fog that makes the will of God unclear to us: either because we do not know it, or, knowing it, we do not understand it. And, consequently, we cannot possibly do it or live by it.

Our Love Life

Ultimately, of course, the will of God is most perfectly summarized and embodied in love. This is the truth that Jesus taught (Matthew

22:37-40), that James echoed (James 2:8), and that Paul wrote about to the Christians in Rome. For all of the complexity and all of the details found in the Old Testament law, the apostle understands that it all distills down to a single principle: love. It is the only debt that we should owe to anyone, and it is the way of living that fulfills God's law.

John Chrysostom explains the comprehensive effectiveness of love simply. "Note that love has two excellent qualities: it abstains from evil and does good deeds." All of the particulars that we find in the law, then, might be categorized in terms of either good to be done or evil not to be done. And, as such, the law becomes a prism through which we see the beautiful array of colors that are found in love.

It should come as no surprise to us that love is so vital and so complete. Paul famously lifts it up to the Corinthians as "the greatest of these" (1 Corinthians 13:13), surpassing all other gifts and virtues. And according to John, love is the quintessential attribute of God (1 John 4:8). To love, therefore, is to be like God, and thus fulfill God's perfect will.

This, then, is our high calling. In a fallen world characterized by self-interest and self-indulgence, you and I are not to be "conformed to this world" (Romans 12:2). Rather, the Lord transforms us more and more into the likeness of Christ. And, as Jesus taught the disciples when he gave them a new commandment, there is no greater way to show oneself as a disciple of Jesus than to love (see John 13:34-35).

SHARING THE SCRIPTURE

PREPARING TO TEACH

Preparing Our Hearts

Ponder this week's devotional reading from Deuteronomy 13:15-20. What do you learn from these verses that explains what will happen to a town that turns to idolatry? What does the writer say will happen if people obey God? Why do you think obedience is so important to the Lord?

Pray that you and the students will obey God by keeping the commandments, especially the command to love.

Preparing Our Minds

Study the background Scripture from Romans 12:1-2; 13:8-14. The lesson Scripture is from Romans 12:1-2; 13:8-10.

Consider this question as you prepare the lesson: *How can we live so as to fulfill God's law of love?*

Write on newsprint:
❏ information for next week's lesson, found under Continue the Journey.
❏ activities for further spiritual growth in Continue the Journey.

Review the Introduction, The Big Picture, Close-up, and Faith in Action, which all precede the first lesson of this quarter. Consider how you might use any of this material in today's lesson.

LEADING THE CLASS

(1) Gather to Learn

❖ Welcome the class members and guests.

❖ Pray that those who have come today will fulfill God's law of love.

❖ Distribute paper and pencils. Read: **Please number your paper from 1 to 11. Listen as I read this short quiz, titled "Which Disturbs You More," that appears in numerous places on the Internet. If the first part of the sentence disturbs you more, write A; if the second part disturbs you more, write B.**

1. **A soul lost in hell . . . or a scratch on your new car?**
2. **Missing the worship service . . . or missing a day's work?**
3. **A sermon ten minutes too long . . . or lunch half an hour late?**
4. **A church not growing . . . or your garden not growing?**
5. **Your Bible unopened . . . or your newspaper unread?**
6. **The church work being neglected . . . or housework neglected?**
7. **Missing a Bible study . . . or your favorite TV program?**
8. **The millions who do not know Christ . . . or your inability to keep up with your neighbors?**
9. **The cry of multitudes for bread . . . or your desire for another piece of chocolate cake?**
10. **Your tithes decreasing . . . or your income taking a drop?**
11. **Your children late for Sunday school and church . . . or late for a game?**

❖ Ask the students to tally the number of A's and B's, though they will not announce their scores. The A's suggest someone whose life is being transformed by the love of Jesus.

❖ Read aloud today's focus statement: **People want to know how to live in a manner that transcends the selfish and corrupt ways of the world. How can they live to fulfill the law of love? Paul urges Jesus' followers to allow the love of Christ to transform their minds into Christ-like minds, so they will be able to love one another and themselves as Christ has loved and continues to love them.**

(2) Goal 1: Overhear Paul's Exhortation to Be Transformed in Order to Discern the Will of God and Fulfill God's Law by Loving Others and Ourselves

❖ Choose a volunteer to read Romans 12:1-2 and then explore these words and concepts:

1. **present** (See Romans 12:1 in Understanding the Scripture.)
2. **living sacrifice** (See Our Living Sacrifice in Interpreting the Scripture.)
3. **holy and acceptable** (See Romans 12:1 in Understanding the Scripture.)
4. **spiritual worship** (See Romans 12:1 in Understanding the Scripture.)
5. **transformed** (See Romans 12:2 in Understanding the Scripture and "Our Total Makeover" in Interpreting the Scripture.)
6. **renewing of your minds** (See Romans 12:2 in Understanding the Scripture and "Our Total Makeover" in Interpreting the Scripture, especially the final paragraph.)

❖ Select a volunteer to read Romans 13:8-10 and state: **Although we might not associate the words "love" and "law," Paul claims that those who love fulfill the law. Let's see how "love" relates to "law" by turning to the Ten Commandments in Exodus 20:1-17, especially the six commandments that concern how we are to relate to one another.**

❖ Form six groups and assign one commandment to each group: Exodus 20:12, 13, 14, 15, 16, 17. Ask each group to consider how their assigned commandment helps them to fulfill the law of love and how breaking this commandment shows a lack of love.

❖ Bring the groups together to report their findings. Again point out the close relationship between love and the commandments.

(3) Goal 2: Accept God's Will to Love One Another Unconditionally

❖ Recruit a volunteer to read 1 Corinthians 13. Create a chart on newsprint that shows what love is—and what it is not. Tell the students to look especially at verses 4-7. Their chart may look something like this:

Love is. . .	Love is not. . .
Patient	Envious
Kind	Boastful
Able to bear all things	Arrogant
Able to believe all things	Rude
	Insistent on its own way
Able to hope all things	Irritable
Able to endure all things	Resentful

❖ Invite the students to offer silent prayers asking God to help them love others unconditionally as Paul has taught us.

(4) Goal 3: Commit to Actively Carry God's Love into the World

❖ Point out that "love," understood as Paul understood it and as Jesus practiced it, is very active and concerned with the other person.

❖ Form small groups and distribute newsprint and markers. Encourage each group to write a brief example to show one way that they can demonstrate God's love to the world.

❖ Call the groups together and invite each one to report on their example.

❖ Conclude by challenging the students to commit themselves to actively demonstrating God's love each day, especially to someone who is difficult to love.

(5) Continue the Journey

❖ Pray that as the learners depart, they will show love to everyone whose path they cross.

❖ Post information for next week's session on newsprint for the students to copy:
- **Title: The Peaceful Kingdom**
- **Background Scripture: Isaiah 11:1-9**
- **Lesson Scripture: Isaiah 11:1-9**
- **Focus of the Lesson: We live in a world full of divisions, hatred, trouble, and chaos. Will we ever experience harmony? Isaiah's prophecy reveals that the sovereign God will bring about a world of peace.**

❖ Post the following information on newsprint and provide paper and pencils for the students to copy it. Challenge the adults to grow spiritually by completing one or more of these activities related to this week's session.

(1) Recall that Jesus not only taught that loving one's neighbor is the second great commandment (Matthew 22:39) but also that we are to love

our enemies (Matthew 5:43-48). Take action this week to show love for someone with whom you have had conflict.

(2) Make a list of ways that you feel Jesus has transformed you. What other positive changes would you like to see him make in your life? Tell him in prayer that you are open, available, and awaiting his leading.

(3) Practice sharing God's love with family members or other persons you regularly see who are difficult to get along with. Be especially mindful so that your "walk matches your talk." People are unlikely to accept what they hear if they cannot see it enacted.

❖ Sing or read aloud "The Gift of Love."

❖ Conclude today's session by leading the class in this benediction, which is adapted from Romans 8:31b, the key verse for August 7: **Let us go forth rejoicing in the knowledge that since God is for us, nothing in all creation can be against us. Amen.**